A Tempest
in a Small Town

The Myth and Reality of Country Life
Granby, Connecticut, 1680-1940

by Mark Williams

1996
Salmon Brook Historical Society
Granby, Connecticut

*for Adam, Amy, Lonnie, Ben, Taegan, Kaily
and Myck*

Contents

Illustrations

Maps

Acknowledgments

In this work I have relied upon many people to help me see the project through. First and foremost was Seth Holcombe of North Granby, who set this work in motion, and whose enthusiastic encouragement, as I shared early drafts, has meant the world to me. Seth cares a great deal for the preservation of Granby's past, and I have been sincerely honored by his support.

I am also deeply indebted to Carol Laun and Bill Vibert, who agreed from the start to read and correct all my feeble early efforts, and responded with suggestions which have saved me from permanent expulsion from the ranks of historians. Carol is an accomplished journalist, historian and archivist, and her work in those capacities to date has made my research job, as well as the revision of the manuscript, a lot easier. Bill has been through all this before with his own book on Simsbury, and along with his many insights and suggestions, he provided valuable moral support, and has guided the final product through to publication. Furthermore, both Carol and Bill were adept at giving me the reaction the lay reader would have to my manuscript - an invaluable service considering I was writing principally for the people of Granby.

I would also like to thank Barbara Askew for a close editorial reading, the other members of Carol Reid's book committee for contracting with me, all of the patrons and sponsors listed at the end of the book for helping to finance the publication, Richard Caley for his expert touch with important illustrations, and Put and Nannie Brown, local history enthusiasts, who provided me support and critiques far beyond the call of duty or even friendship. Because of Put and Nannie's attachment to the project, Andrew Ward and Christopher Bickford were kind enough to read a good part of the manuscript and offer much appreciated suggestions. I must add, too, dipping back into ancient history, that my own love of local history would not have come into existence without the early encouragement of Jane and Bob Endter, Gene and Gemma Baker and Richard Brown.

Finally, I want to express my gratitude to John Ratté, Alice Baxter, Bob Andrian, and all of my students for all the times they said, "Well, we'll let that go - he's working on his book;" to Lou Ratté for inspiring me to think of the story in an even broader context; to my father-in-law, who always enjoys hearing about Connecticut's past; to my sister, who first collaborated with me on major theatrical works; to my parents, who taught me that no matter where you are there is always something interesting to be learned; and to Adam, Amy (my research assistant), Lonnie, Ben, Taegan, Kaily, and my wife Myck - my patient family, who will be delighted to know this project is finally finished, and whose high standards and good sense of fun were always on my mind as I strove to make every sentence the best I could possibly write.

MW
West Granby
June, 1996

A Tempest
in a Small Town

The Myth and Reality of Country Life
Granby, Connecticut, 1680-1940

Introduction:
Of Landscape and Curiosity

A few steps north from my front door on Simsbury Road in West Granby there is a place where the west branch of Salmon Brook runs close by the street (or "highway," as the old land records call this country way). There, between the road and the brook, hidden from the passing motorist by weeds and bushes, is the foundation of Trumbull Wilcox's blacksmith shop, which was later Matthew Fancher's wheel shop, and still later, the Simplex Manufacturing Company. In old photographs, this shop, in its later, fully developed years, appears to tower a good three stories above the brook; but the shell it had become by 1955 was swept away in that summer's famous flood. Its mill dam is completely gone, and the smokestack for its steam engine is reduced to a square of cement and a pile of rubble. The periodic torrents that have raged down out of Huggins Gorge have not yet claimed the massive blocks of quarry stone seemingly placed there by the Greek gods to whom these early "mechanics" paid homage with the architecture of their houses. It may yet happen that these stones will one day come tumbling down as well and spread out across the brook like so much glacial debris.

For now, though, the straight walls, expertly shimmed and laid in place without a drop of mortar, sit solidly beside a picturesque brook that runs zigzag through woodlands, then fields, then hills, and eventually down to the Farmington River. These walls are curiosity itself. Who put these stones here before anyone could imagine today's bucket-loaders and cranes? Who had a vision that this place could be the seat of a manufacturing establishment? How

1

Mark Williams

Old mill seat in West Granby

could anyone hope to make a living with a brook of this size? Were there other shops along this brook? Did they thrive? What happened here to people's families, to workers, to fortunes, to dreams? Could they have imagined an automobile, with an engine as powerful as the steam engine that once chugged and clanked outside the shop, flying by this place as though it did not even exist?

Across the street is a small cemetery, an ancient ruin from a civilization of which we know so little. Many of the stones say "Hayes," "Wilcox," and "Holcomb;" and a few have names that don't seem to fit, like "Gutierrez." Some of the monuments are artfully carved with mournful poetry, death's heads, weeping willows, urns and sobbing widows. Others are unadorned, others still crumbling, leaning or face down. Are these memorials to the owners and workers of brook side shops, or to farmers who lived simpler, unmechanized lives, tilling the soil according to Thomas Jefferson's model

2

of peace and harmony in a nation of honest yeoman? What was the world of West Granby like when these people lived in it? How did the farmers relate to a noisy, smoky steam engine in their midst? Or was it actually some farmer, disgusted with the annual crop of glacial stone that littered his tillage, who decided that, in such an environment, it would be more sensible to make plows than watch them break?

I had lived in West Granby only a few weeks before these curiosities got the better of me, and for the next two decades I devoted a good share of my spare time to indulging that nagging desire to find out about the lives of those who had preceded me at this place. From my initial purchase of *The Heritage of Granby* at John Avery's general store, through a tangled trail of land records at the Town Hall, and on to interviews with the likes of John Fancher and the venerable Tudor Holcomb, I struggled to know the farmers,

Salmon Brook Historical Society

Mill Seat with its Mill, circa 1900

mechanics, housewives, widows, orphans, merchants, and laborers who had made this town their home. Around 1977, Bill Vibert, anxious to set the Salmon Brook Historical Society (of which he was president) onto a scholarly course, introduced me to some of his work and the material in our archives. Yet through all this, as all historians discover, the more I learned, the more questions I had.

In spite of years of research, I was not prepared for the question that Carol Laun and Seth Holcombe, board members of the Salmon Brook Historical Society, put to me in the fall of 1989. Carol, the Society Curator, had reached the point where she felt the Society's bulging collection of artifacts and documents was finally under control, and Seth, a devoted Director, was of the opinion that something substantial should be made of that collection - namely a narrative history of the town of Granby, Connecticut. Would I write it? Seth was eager to arrange for any aid or assistance that might be required. If direction were needed through the collections, Carol, who had

Mark Williams

West Granby Cemetery

already written extensively on the subject as she culled through the papers, books, ledgers and brittle pieces of the past, would point the way.

Just like that. The task I had envisioned as something to occupy years of retirement, when I would be otherwise useless, was now presented to me as a current need. I was to stop fiddling around with piecemeal research on rickety houses and obscure individuals, disregard inner voices about the need to transcribe more town meeting and ecclesiastical society records, and get down to serious business. Yes, it would be nice to have a lifetime of this sort of activity behind me and so write authoritatively and with all the data that could possibly be found; but, Carol pointed out, we Granby historians were already behind schedule.

When the Society had published *The Heritage of Granby* over two decades before, it had not intended that collection of thematic essays to be the sourcebook on Granby history for the next half century. Carol related that, in fact, Eva Dewey, her predecessor as Curator, had harbored the hope that a new history of the town would have been completed for the Bicentennial in 1986, when the Granby Bicentennial Committee printed Carol's *Granby, Connecticut: A Brief History*, and when the Society published my edited and transcribed version of the first two volumes of the town meeting records. Seth was even more insistent. Were there not things that would be lost in the waiting? What if no history were attempted for another twenty-five years - would we have the same capability to write one at that point?

This was a good question. On the surface, it seemed almost to question Carol's ability to hang on to all that she and Eva Dewey had labored so long and hard to collect and put in order. It also suggested that there were, scattered about town in various attics, treasure troves of documents and memorabilia that might soon find their way to trash barrels! Actually, Seth did not have these concerns in mind at all. He was well aware of Carol and Eva's vigorous and long-standing efforts to educate Granby's well-rooted families about the importance of even the most trivial piece of paper. Furthermore, there can be no question that the trend toward a more professional and scholarly approach to the Society's archival work was irreversible, given the number and variety of individuals now committed to the success of the Society's goals. Our collections were secure, descendents of the old families were conscious of our preservation concerns, and we would continue

5

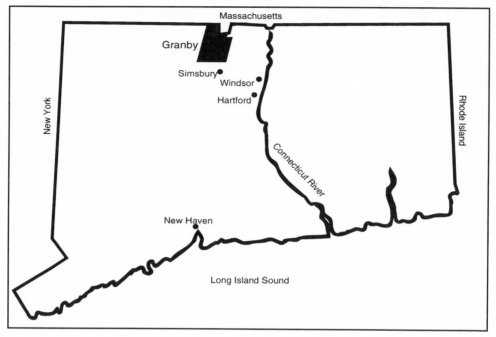

Granby in Connecticut

to discover more and more about Granby's history in the years to come.

What concerned Seth Holcombe the most, I think, was not the potential loss of the documents, artifacts, and human resources upon which a historian must depend for the substance of his work. There was, in fact, a growing number of these items even as his worry intensified. What concerned him was that we were losing something far more subtle but just as valuable to the historical inquiry process: *landscape.*

In the latter half of this century, Granby has been changing rapidly from a small rural farming town to a modern suburb. Pasture, woodlots, croplands, and even rocky hills have been transformed into building lots and housing developments. Where there was a grocery store and a hardware and feed store, there is now a busy intersection with gas stations, restaurants, convenience stores, and banks. Stone walls, decaying buildings, and even brooks have been subjected to the bulldozer. Low maintenance siding, modern additions and garages disguise 18th and early 19th century dwellings. While the farmer's tractor still can be found chewing up rows of corn into silage or plowing furrows, their numbers have dwindled to single digits, and their owners are frequently petitioners for subdivision at regular meetings of the Planning and Zoning Commission.[1]

For some, this transformation has been a tragedy - Granby is no longer a "country town" where one can find tranquility, fresh air and pastoral scenery. For others, the changes of the past decades have represented the realization of the American Dream: a house in the country, a good place for children to grow up, peace and quiet, fresh air and pastoral scenery. Indeed, it is interesting that some mourn the loss of the very qualities that continue to attract the thousands of "newcomers." And yet, whatever the perspective from which one views the situation, no one can deny that as the twentieth century draws to a close, there is less and less visual evidence of the "old" Granby.

What does this all this mean for the historian? We still have old maps, photographs, documents, pieces of furniture, houses undergoing restoration or fully restored (for example, the complex at the Salmon Brook Historical Society, including two 18th century houses, a 19th century schoolhouse, and a tobacco barn, all furnished and filled with remnants of the rural past). Some of the main roads in town even follow ancient Algonkian trails. Why be concerned about suburban development that provides so much for so many, when there will always be a wealth of information about the town's past? The answer to that question has a lot to do with the very purpose of having a town history.

In spite of our preoccupation in this age with national and world events, the local scene is still important to us. Annually we pay a hefty share of our income to support schools, libraries, roads, bridges, and all sorts of other services we provide for ourselves through town government. Certainly people demonstrate their greatest concern about the quality of the environment, when the soil, air or water of their own neighborhood is threatened. The number of public offices set aside for planning and regulatory commissions, as well as the number of lawn-care services and nursery businesses in this area, is fair testimony to the concern people feel for the way their own property and their surrounding properties look. In fact, it would not be unreasonable to suggest that television, satellite communications, and a world economy have not really made us any less local in our outlook - just more worldly at the

7

same time.

We are schooled in national and world history, and there is certainly an abundance of literature, both popular and scholarly, on the market, all to provide us with perspective on our current situation and to satisfy our curiosity about how the human race arrived at the present. At the local level, however, history is not always so readily available either in the schools and libraries or in the book stores; and even if it were, of what use would it be?

Satisfying curiosity is obviously the first purpose local history can serve. Every day we are in direct contact with remnants of the past, and it is difficult, even for those who most despised their high school history courses, not to feel some degree of wonder when looking at an old house, a cemetery, an old foundation concealed in the underbrush, or a clutter of stones lined in a row that stretches back into a hillside. We know immediately that there were people here before us, who lived lives that were obviously different from ours today. What we have left of their time are pieces of a puzzle, clues to a mystery - and puzzles and mysteries have a way of attracting the human imagination. A local history is a natural object of imagination; in fact, local history, because it is so conveniently illustrated in our own "back yard," may stimulate greater wondering about the past than national or world history.

A second purpose of local history is the providing of perspective for a free people who are accustomed to making a lot of decisions for themselves. By "perspective," I mean the centuries of experience we gain vicariously from learning about the lives and activities of those who have gone before us, as well as the way in which that experience broadens our vision, sharpens our critical faculties, heightens our appreciation of human nature, and generally enriches our thinking about the challenges of today's world. Of course, any history provides perspective, and should we lose track of our local past, we can always gain wisdom from learning about our broader heritage. It's just that, as suggested in the preceding paragraph, we are not as often inclined to do that as we are to be curious about our more immediate surroundings. Thus, we are more likely to gain perspective - and be able to share that perspective with our neighbors - when local history is available for our consideration.

Landscape, defined broadly as the way in which human beings have shaped their environment, plays an important role in making local history available. It provides us with the objects that stimulate our curiosity. Without the old walls and foundations, without the quaint architecture, the twisted roadways, the cleared fields, and the old mill seats, we won't have that stimulation. Furthermore, landscape gives us a three-dimensional illustration of the patterns that have emerged from the past - the way space has been organized, the ingenious devices people have created to make their living in that space, and the way in which that space reflects the values, goals and aspirations of those who have gone before us. In other words, landscape is a living signature of the past, begging us to ask the questions that will give us answers to the very puzzle of who we are.

This is the historical resource that is quickly vanishing in Granby as the once rural town gives way to suburbanization. Landscape, for the most part, is privately owned, and its preservation, when measured against the financial and housing needs of people of Connecticut today, often seems to be merely an act of sentimentalism or "taste." Yet, as we see more and more of the landscape of the past transformed or obliterated by the landscape of the present, we are fast losing touch with the path that Granby, and many other communities like it, have taken to get to the present. This means we are losing touch with a good sense of who we are. We are relegating that understanding to a few avid historians and antiquarians, or to the realm of popular mythology.

The myth is that Granby was, since its beginning, a small, peaceful farming community, where the pace of life and the pace of change was pretty slow. Everyone knew everyone else, and everyone got along as one big communal family. As William Scoville Case wrote at the end of the last century, "Farming is the prevailing occupation of the people, the distance from good water power, as well as from railroad connections, rendering the place undesirable for manufacturing purposes."[2] James Lee Loomis recalled nostalgically that Granby "was a typical agricultural town with a few craftsmen and professional men. It was a quiet village then [in the late 1800s] with well-kept sidewalks near the fence line....Stately elms bordered the highway. Neighbors walked to the store and the Post Office and to visit each other."[3] This way of life had marched (or strolled, it would seem) to the beat of tranquil rhythms of the seasons for centuries until shortly after World War II when a new American Dream came bustling forth from the cities with all of its aerials, paving, two-car garages, water and sewer lines, and schools and playing fields. The independent-farmstead dream gave way to the single-family-home-on-two-acres-plus-a-Buick dream. Almost overnight Granby changed from a town that never changed to one that was an integral part of a "mass society" that was mainly characterized by change. The old saying that one was not considered to be a true resident of Granby until one had lived here twenty-five years seemed ridiculous by the early 1970s - most residents would not have been considered residents.[4]

This is a dangerous myth. It pits "old-timers" against "newcomers." It implies that "newcomers" should feel guilty about destroying some pastoral paradise that will never return again. It suggests that we have somehow lost control of a world our ancestors managed much better, and that old small-town values, such as the maintenance of strong family and church ties, support for neighbors in hard times, and modesty in ambition and self-indulgence, are going by the wayside in a society that has become overly competitive and materialistic. This is not a healthy perspective by which to live our lives or to make the decisions for our futures.

The reason why it is not a healthy perspective is that it isn't based on the truth! If there is a "message" at all to the narrative history to be related between the covers of this book it is just that - the myth of a tranquil and harmonious past is simply not true. It may be of some comfort to think of the past in this light when we are faced with the challenges of the present, but, in fact, Granby has always been a community of change, and what pieces of old landscape we have left to us today should be allowed to continue to reflect not so much the tranquility of an agricultural past, but more the turmoil of a people facing, over three centuries, the stresses of modernization and a continual barrage of new circumstances.

The place that has become Granby, Connecticut has experienced a tempest of turmoil and transition from the beginnings of its known history. First an Algonkian community of some size simply disappeared in a period of fifty years. Then a small outpost of a few adventurous families grew rapidly into a contentious, complex "ecclesiastical society" that would rebel against the status quo to conduct its church services in its own way.[5] As the Revolution approached, this independent-minded "society," still growing rapidly in numbers and changing in character, joined the patriot cause and then adapted it to its own desire to be independent of Simsbury. The

10

incorporation of the town in 1786 only led to more disputes, more tensions, and more change as the people debated the status of the established church, the evils of alcohol, the exodus of their young to the West, and the need to have a more humane system of dealing with their poor. Efforts to create "manufactories" changed the face of the town before the Civil War, but the manufacturers themselves had to change or face doom as the national economy continually created new circumstances for the local entrepreneurs. Throughout the nineteenth century and early twentieth century, Granby people struggled with these changing circumstances, only to be rewarded for their labor with the discouraging impact of a worldwide depression in the 1930s. Thus, there were many transitions and continual tension, breeding dramatic changes in what may appear on the surface (apparently even to those who lived in these times) to have been simply a farming town.

Unfortunately, the truth that is under the surface becomes more and more difficult to perceive. Very often the well-meaning efforts of today's owners of older houses to reconstitute old landscape have been selective in the direction of the simple and the agricultural. The result is that what is saved supports the myth, and what is thrown out are the messy, rusted remains of a more complex and temptestuous world.

Knowledge of the turmoil and stress of the past, in fact, would better equip us to face the challenges of our own world than would a nostalgic longing for a tranquility and harmony that never existed. Therefore, this history is written from the vantage point that Seth Holcombe feared we were losing. We are still surrounded, when we look carefully, by landscape - three-dimensional illustration - of our community's past, a past that is far more complex than popular mythology gives it credit. This landscape still makes us ask the right questions, and still offers clues to the puzzle of how our predecessors lived their lives and faced the challenges of changing circumstances. A history written years from now and based on what will certainly be a greater body of collected documents and artifacts will be better informed, but may, if current trends continue, lack that vantage point - that of "being there" - that is, being surrounded by the clues of the landscape. We will not be able to stand amidst the building blocks of a former world and look around us at pieces of change and complexity. And not "being there," we will be less inclined, in the first place, to do the wondering that leads eventually to useful perspective.

      I wrote this story of tension, change and dislocation primarily for one audience, the people of Granby. Some who have read early drafts have suggested it has broader meaning. I would not go so far as to say this town's history was "typical" of communities everywhere in America. In fact, if it shows anything, it is the multiplicity of ways in which Americans have responded to the forces acting on their nation. Historians themselves may find the narrative useful to the extent that it provides additional detail from the history of one community, to add to the growing accumulation of material we have to understand the history of ordinary people - the so-called "new social history," which, since the 1960s, has provided us with an entirely new outlook on national and world history. Likewise, students, scholars and other persons interested in Connecticut and New England history may find additional data here on a small town in north-central Connecticut that could help shape or reshape our understanding of the region's past. Even for the primary audience, though, I have taken pains to write the history with a good deal of reference to the regional and national context in which that local history developed. This may be somewhat cumbersome to wade through for those who already are well-schooled in American and New England history, but it is the understanding of that "broader context," often missing from local histories, that is so essential to the appreciation of the forces of change that were acting upon this community. As much as its residents from time to time may have wished their town to be a little "world within itself," isolated from the corrupting influences of the rest of the world, Granby was a part of Connecticut, New England, the United States (or formerly the British Empire) and the rest of the world, and involved in all the significant trends of those larger contexts.

      As the people of Granby approach the twenty-first century, they are watching their landscape being altered at an unprecedented rate. Yet pieces of landscape from all of the "ages" of Granby's history are still with us, provoking curiosity, illustrating the turmoil of the past, and, thus, allowing us to develop historical perspective that will shape our lives for the future. With these readers in mind, I write this narrative, placing events of Granby's past in the context of regional and national history to relate a story of change in a small town on Connecticut's northern border.

Prologue
1786

The sunny day that had greeted Rosanna Hays when she had gone to feed the barnyard animals earlier was now turning raw and windy, more typical of December. The year was 1786, and Rosanna, age 54, mother of 10, wife of the town's first elected selectman and herself a respected member of the Church (there was only one, regardless of what the Baptists claimed), was taking time for a reflective moment while waiting for the oven bricks to heat up. Most women her age seemed to have more of those moments as their children grew and daughters took on their share of the household chores, but Rosanna's daughters had all married and moved away. With her four youngest sons still living with her - one just ten years old this year - she had as much work as she had ever had. Well, there was the one summer of '76 when half the family was off at Long Island thinking they could stand up to trained British and Hessian soldiers - she had more than she could handle then, what with a new baby, three wild young boys and only Temperance and Theodotia to help with all the chores while she herself brought in the hay, sheared the sheep, repaired the barn roof, drove the team at the cider mill, and did all manner of things she had since been told women were not put upon earth to do. She doubted thirteen-year-old boys were put upon earth to parry bayonets while playing a drum, but had not found anyone she could convince of that in these times.

They had become a haughty lot, these Salmon Brook men, quickly forgetting what a bedraggled mess they had been in the fall of '76 or how bitterly they had protested meeting quotas for the Continental Army. Now they claimed to have won the War single-handedly, and threatened to do the same to Simsbury First Society and the state assembly and tax collectors if they could not have their own town, or if the Congress should pay bonuses to Continental officers. They cry for their "Liberty," she thought indignantly. And yet how they laugh when their women seek a proper place in the new order of things! (Would that they would try to do woman's work for one day.)

She thought about how, like the weather itself, people's ways change. In her mother's day, women had their work, but they had their place, too - or so it seemed when she was young. Even in her early years of marriage, she had heard Reverend Strong preach about the equality of souls before God. It was he who had admitted her and her husband together as equal members of the Congregation, and had convinced the elders at last to allow the women to sit together with the men at meeting.

In those days, too, families had stayed together. A society like Salmon Brook was one big family. Young people married, their parents found them a good farm nearby, and everyone helped each other. Just like her Theodotia and young Samuel - marrying Chauncey and Anna Pettibone. But now Levi had married the Parsons girl, whose family she knew nothing about, and Pliny wouldn't let a day pass without begging his father for his release so he could go off with some girl from Lyme, of all places. Her husband had bought the old Higley farm, but with all this talk about the children going off to Vermont and what not, he had finally decided to sell it to the parish for the new minister to have. Ah well - these things happen as God wills them. Good things come too. Except for young Rosanna who had died in the epidemic in '79, all of her children were healthy, strong, God fearing, and, thanks to her, literate; the crops had been good these past two years; and the Society, some seven years since Reverend Strong had left in a huff, had finally settled a new minister. She reached her arm into the bake oven and winced as she counted.

On the hillside behind the house a short, stout man, Samuel Hays Jr., age 56, the new town of Granby's most prominent citizen, took a moment from his fence repairs to put his coat on. Turning to gaze south at Barn Door Hills, he too took note of the sudden turn in the weather, and of its resemblance to human affairs. He too worried some about the young people and their lack of attachment to family and community. Many young men and women had already left for Vermont lands - they could be had cheaply, and the Salmon Brook commons had all been granted before the War. Fortunately (and as a

14

result of hard work and healthy sons), he had become prosperous enough to set his children up with their own farms - but even so, some of his sons seemed eager to move away.

There were new people coming to town too - some who could not even afford to be there, as though it was their "right" to be just anywhere they wished to be. One of the first things he would do as selectman for this new town would be to see that the vagabonds, like the Davis family and the widow Butler, were warned out. Otherwise they would drain the town treasury, and, more important, threaten the harmony and unity he and his friends had worked so long to establish. He remembered back to his father's day when there had been much squabbling about what kind of preacher the society should have,

Salmon Brook Historical Society

Samuel Hays II House (c.1769) at 67 Barn Door Hills Road

15

and later in his years as selectman of Simsbury how they had fought about building roads and bridges way down near Farmington bounds. Reverend Strong, God bless him, had brought the Congregation (there was only one, regardless of what the Baptists claimed) together, and the folly of Parliament, the Devil take it, had kept the First Society men from unfairly taxing Salmon Brook.

He had seen a lot of bad times - the argument over the new meeting-house, Reverend Strong's disgust at not being paid, the controversy over officer bonuses, the horror of war itself, the calamity it had caused in town with epidemics and food shortages, the depression now just coming to an end, and the general growth of downright insolence among the lower ranks of people, to say nothing of ridiculous notions of women being part of the government. But much good had come in the end. The boycott of tea had done wonders for his cider business (and his dispensing of cider brandy had done wonders for his militia career - he had been elected Captain in '73), the independence movement had spilled over into local affairs to bring about separation from Simsbury, and his efforts to keep Reverend Strong and to bring in Reverend Haley had convinced the brothers to elect him Deacon this past spring when his father-in-law had resigned. In spite of the troubles, there was such a spirit of independence and confidence in this new town! And he was certain the real power to shape the community in a godly, moderate and cooperative fashion would remain in the right hands. Perhaps at last the dreams of the forefathers of God's "city upon a hill" would be realized. He bent over the cedar post lying on the ground, and with the powerful wrists for which he was so well-known in his new town, Captain Deacon Selectman Hays slowly turned his augur.

*   *   *

It must have been an exciting moment in October, 1786, when the Connecticut General Assembly declared that "the Northern Part of the sd Town of Simsbury...Shall be and are here by Incorperated into and Consti-tuted a Town by the Name of the Town of Granby & Shall Ever Here after have and Injoy all the Rights Privilidges & Immunities That other Towns in this State are Legally Intitled to.'"[1] Just three years earlier Great Britain had recognized its former Atlantic seaboard colonies as "free and independent states" and now the parishes of Salmon Brook and Turkey Hills seemed to have won an even more important recognition. They were no longer a backwater of Simsbury, but their own community, controlling their own affairs in their own town meeting and electing their own men to run their government.

It was in this context that Asahel Holcomb thumped the gavel at the first "town meting of the Inhabitens of Granby Legally Held at the meting House in Salmon Brook Society on the first monday of December 1786."[2] Their first act was to elect Judah Holcomb Jr. the town clerk, at which time Judah took up the quill and dutifully recorded the subsequent election of his brother-in-law, Captain Samuel Hays, as the town's first selectman. Granby, however, was not just beginning. If there is anything to be learned from the thoughts of Rosanna and Samuel Hays, it is that the story of this new town begins long before 1786.

Chapter I
Crossing Talcott Ridge

Chronology

Europe	America	Granby
	1497 John Cabot claims North America for England	
1533 Henry VIII divorces Catherine of Aragon		
1558 Elizabeth I crowned		
	1584 Raleigh attempts to set up Roanoke colony	
1603 James I crowned	1607 Jamestown, Va. founded	
	1616 Epidemic among New England tribes	
1618-1648 Thirty Years War	1620 Plimoth Plantation founded	
1625 Charles I crowned		
1628 William Laud made Bishop of London	1630 Mass. Bay Colony founded	
	1633 First English settlement in Ct. at Windsor, Smallpox epidemic among native tribes	
	1637 Pequot War in Ct.	
	1639 Fundamental Orders of Ct.	
1642 English Civil War begins		
1649 Charles I executed		1648 John Griffin gets Massaco land
1653 Cromwell made Lord Protector	1653 Ct. General Court begins to grant land at Massaco	
1660 Charles II restored as King		
1662 Charles II grants charter to Connecticut	1662 Halfway Covenant	
	1670 Massaco becomes town of Simsbury	
	1676 Simsbury burned	
	1677 Simsbury settlers return	
		1680 Algonkians agree to give up land including Salmon Brook, settlers begin to move there

The community we know today as the Town of Granby is the direct descendant of a British settlement by the name of "Salmon Brook" which had its beginning in 1680. Originally a descriptive name for one part of the vast one hundred square mile domain west of Talcott Ridge called colonial Simsbury, Salmon Brook soon became associated with a group of people who were, from the start, shaping a distinct community north of Simsbury's main village. In the years to come they would chart an independent course for themselves, first by establishing a separate church parish, and second, by incorporating, along with families to their east, the town of Granby in 1786. In their manner of settling, living, and relating with each other and with the rest of the world during those years, it is apparent they were as destined to be a separate town as Americans of the thirteen Atlantic colonies were destined to be a separate nation.

The emergence of an independent spirit in Salmon Brook between 1680 and 1786, then, is the pre-eminent theme of the story of early Granby. However, it is impossible to understand that story completely without understanding the roots of colonial Salmon Brook's culture deep in European heritage and in the European conquest and settlement of the region we call New England. Salmon Brook, the community, was founded by people of British descent, who crossed Talcott Ridge from their former homes in Windsor to make new homes for themselves in what they called "the wilderness." Their parents, or they themselves, had crossed the Atlantic as part of two great waves of emigration from a troubled and turbulent Old World. These migrants of the 1630s and the 1660s had brought few earthly possessions with them, but they did bring all they had known, both that which they hoped to change and that which they would try to reproduce or make use of in the New World. They passed on to their children values, ideals, ambitions and hundreds of notions which had evolved over the centuries in Britain and on the European continent, as well as in the dreams of religious reformers, aspiring farmers, traders and adventurers who were shaping the new American civilization. As they interacted with Europeans of different backgrounds, with the new American environment and with the natives of America, the immigrants to New England changed, even when they tried not to; and in changing themselves, they also changed America, prodding, hammering, pushing, and squeezing it into a shape never imagined by its original inhabitants, nor even by its newcomers. The complex process of change that was occurring in New England as the first settlers were crossing Talcott Ridge and arriving in Simsbury and Salmon Brook would have lasting impact on the future of Granby, Connecticut.

19

"The Land Grows Weary"

People who came voluntarily to America in the 17th Century based their decision to come on their present situation and on their expectations of what they would be able to do or find in the New World. The journey was difficult and dangerous - that many would not survive it was well known by the 1630s; and yet, since so many attempted the crossing, the assessment many made must have been one that produced some stark contrasts between the New and the Old World. In general, people were motivated by a combination of two almost contradictory impulses. The first was a concern over unsettling and sweeping changes that were taking place in England and on the European continent during the 16th and 17th centuries. Many of those who came to America were actually fairly conservative folk who wanted to escape these changes and live a more tranquil existence, playing by the old rules, so to speak. On the other hand, many others, including some of those motivated by the "conservative" impulse, had specific ideas that were altogether revolutionary. To them, America represented an "unspoiled" place where ideals could be realized, and these contradictory impulses of restoration and revolution would be expressed in the settlement and development of the Salmon Brook community.

As for unsettling changes, two great developments shook all of Europe during the 16th and 17th centuries. One was the emergence of powerful nation states, complete with international rivalries and all the trampling of the rights of weaker groups of people that usually accompany such rivalries. France, England and Spain, and to some extent Holland and Portugal, were the "superpowers" of the era, and exploration, conquest and settlement of the Western Hemisphere was largely a result of efforts by these nations to out-maneuver one another. They raced to establish trading posts, garrisons, ports and alliances with (or conquests of) native groups, and as their outposts became domains, they fought each other for supremacy. Probably the event most symbolic of these growing rivalries was the Battle of the Spanish Armada in 1588. By that time Spain had grown rich on her conquests in the Western Hemisphere, while England had only just begun to consider the advantages of outposts that did not immediately yield precious metals or control trade routes to the Orient. In spite of Spain's vast expenditures on military might, though, the attempted invasion of England ended in failure and a protracted war with Elizabeth I's infamous "Sea Dogs." All this had the effect of heightening political instability in Europe, and delaying, even while it made more imperative, England's efforts to stake a claim in the New World.

A second development that changed the face of European civilization was a relative respite from the plagues of the 14th and 15th centuries. Without this form of "population control," Europe's population exploded in the 16th century. In England alone the population doubled between 1530 and 1680. The rapidly growing population all over Europe required food and clothing, and that put increasing pressure on the continent's grain supplies and heightened the demand for wool and woolen goods.

The rich of European port towns may have been excited by the prospects of new trading partners in the East shipping silk and spices to Europe, but most people looked to traditional domestic agricultural products to fulfill their needs. For the landholding class of Elizabethan England the increase in demand for grain and wool was a real incentive to dispense with age-old tenancy arrangements and to develop more efficient ways of cultivating land with hired labor. Thus products could be mass-produced with fewer workers and profits would soar. This movement to evict tenants and take over their common fields, known as enclosure, had dramatic effects.

In the 17th century, more than ever before, it did seem that the world was not following the usual plan. Some people whose families had never owned land were somehow wealthy, - wealthy enough to buy land. Some of those who owned land already had decided that they would use it for a new purpose. Some great landlords now raised grain for export and sheep for wool instead of renting their lands to farmers. Sheep farming required fewer workers and drew a better profit. Those people who used to farm the land were out of work, and they wandered around the country aimlessly, receiving no sympathy from the government. Parliament, England's traditional law-making body, now dominated by the wealthy gentry, made vagrancy a crime and unemployment a man's own fault. Nevertheless, the number of vagrants grew by leaps and bounds and, as more workers competed for fewer available jobs, wages plummeted. The result was poverty for vast numbers of people who crowded into unhealthy and rapidly growing cities like London. Here emerged the beginnings of a more modern class structure with a large,

21

unpropertied working class at the bottom and an increasingly wealthy class of merchants and capitalists at the helm. The various strata of artisans, tenants and small property owners in between were fast becoming a memory in this urban world.[1]

As far as the English government was concerned the early years of the 1600s were not "happy days." James Stuart opened his reign in 1603 by depriving a thief of his right to a jury trial and proclaiming himself the final arbiter in all legal matters, whether the lawyers and judges agreed with him or not. Unfortunately, many of these lawyers and judges were just the sort of increasingly wealthy landowners he needed both to help pay off the enormous debt that had piled up during his predecessor's war with Spain, as well as to support the continuing costs of a modern government beset with the tumult of economic dislocation. In Parliament's House of Commons the landed gentry sputtered and protested as James became more entrenched in his notion of the Divine Right of Kings. The King himself, of course, was not without supporters, and for nearly fifty years he, and then his son Charles I (crowned 1625), fought with Parliamentarians over privileges and prerogatives.

When the House of Commons defied Charles in 1629, he sent them home and tried to rule England without them. He did rule for ten years alone, but he learned too late that the only way to get enough money to run the English government the way he wanted was to have Parliament give it through their ancient practice of granting "subsidies" to the King. By the time he called Parliament back into session in 1640, even the more conservative members were angry with him. Henry VIII once said "I am the King of England! When I pray, God answers!" but by 1649, Charles I would have been happy if he could have said "I am the King of England." He fought a long and bloody civil war against Parliament's army, led by Oliver Cromwell, from 1642 until 1648. When it was over he was tried as a tyrant and traitor and beheaded, as the House of Commons declared Parliament the new supreme authority.

All this is not to say that fate was smiling on the landed gentry in the early 17th century. When war broke out in Europe in 1618, the market for wool disappeared almost instantly. In counties such as Somerset where the cloth industry was very important to the economy (and from which would come a number of the original Windsor, Connecticut settlers), the result was

22

disastrous. Changing tastes on the continent had already directed wool buyers away from these farmers toward East Anglia, and now there was not even much demand for East Anglian wool.[2] Everyone on the continent was spending too much time and money fighting each other to buy wool. To farm laborers, artisans, and younger sons of landowners, England was hardly a land of opportunity. Farm laborers were out of work; blacksmiths, coopers, sawyers, millers, and metalsmiths had fewer and fewer customers; and since, by laws of primogeniture, only a man's oldest son could inherit his property, younger sons had to look outside of England for employment. The only place left was America, it seemed. Even John Winthrop, a wealthy Suffolk gentleman who would later become the first Governor of the Massachusetts Bay Colony, felt the pinch in England. "The land grows weary of her inhabitants," he wrote. "My means here are so shortened [now that my three eldest sons have come of age] as I shall not be able to continue in this place....Why then should we stand striving here for places of habitations...and in the meantime suffer a whole continent as fruitful and convenient for the use of man to be wasted without any improvement." If a prosperous man like Winthrop felt this way, you can imagine the hopes and expectations of the hundreds of thousands in England who had no land, no work, and no likelihood of getting either. As one man put it, "The world's in a heap of troubles and confusions, and while they are in the midst of the changes and amazes, the best way to give them the bag is to go out of the world and leave them."[3]

At the same time Winthrop was lamenting his situation, a minister named John White was recruiting passengers for a colony in the New World from the West Country (Dorset and Somerset), where the wool crisis had hit the hardest. In his pamphlet *The Planter's Plea,* he complained "we have more men than we can employ to any profitable or useful labor." He felt many were drawn into serving in "luxury and wantonness to the impoverishing and corrupting of the most," and artisans who had no work were "reduced to such low condition as is little better than beggary."[4] Richard Eburne, another pamphleteer from the West Country, put it even more poignantly: "Our land...swarmeth with multitude and plenty of people, it is time and high time that, like stalls that are overfull of bees or orchards overgrown with young sets, no small number of them should be transplanted into some other soil and removed hence into new hives and homes...The true and sure remedy is the diminution of the people."[5] This was the sort of thinking being circulated around the region from which would come families like Thomas Holcombe's, whose children would one day move from Windsor across Talcott Ridge to Simsbury and Salmon Brook.

Against John White and Richard Eburne's praise for the abundant natural resources of the new world, including the fisheries off Cape Cod, an already thriving fur trade, and products for shipbuilding ("planks, masts, oars, pitch, tar and iron"), English people looked about them and saw the crop failures of 1622, 1629 and 1630, the recent outbreaks of plague, and the dried-up export market. The risks of the crossing seemed more and more acceptable. Add to the economic frustrations of the times the rapidly changing social structure, vagrancy, crime, deteriorating conditions in the cities, the disturbing conflicts between King and Parliament and the threat to ancient privileges, and the recipe for mass emigration of people from the gentry, artisan, and yeoman farmer classes was nearly complete.

These were not wildly revolutionary people who gave up on Britain and shipped their families and belongings to Massachusetts Bay and eventually Connecticut. Most ordinary folk, in fact, cared little about national affairs, but they did know that their daily lives had changed for the worse in recent decades. The people from the West Country, ancestors of many of the settlers of Salmon Brook, had grown up in an area that was once prosperous and productive, producing not only wool for export, but also hemp, flax, oats, barley, wheat, corn, cattle and sheep, beef and dairy products, and, most significant for the future of Granby, Connecticut, apples and cider. They fully intended that in the New World they would reinstate the old way of life and engage in the production of these agricultural products (as well as other opportunities New England offered in lumber, fur and fish). The promoters, such as John White and John Winthrop, worked hard to solicit those who had the most potential and desire to recreate the prosperity England had once known.[6] These emigrants would also carry their deep respect for the English Common Law, which guaranteed such ancient privileges as trial by jury and was generally thought to exempt English people from arbitrary rule. They would reassert their belief in representative government in their colonial legislatures, and simply call by different names the multitude of town, county and vestry officers they had been accustomed to choosing or having chosen

Map 1-1: 17th Century England, Scotland and Wales

from the various strata of society to order their affairs at the local level. They would manifest a desire to maintain a class system with all the customs of intermarriage, privilege and deference of the old country.[7] They may not have liked the present circumstances in England, but they certainly weren't about to create a wholly new order. What revolutionary ideals they had were fairly well confined to the sphere of religion.

"Liberty and Purity"

As though it were not enough to have an age characterized by political, social and economic turmoil, the 16th and 17th centuries were also times of great religious upheaval in European civilization. In fact, so central were Judeo-Christian traditions and beliefs to the overall world view of Europeans that the religious conflicts of the time invariably found their way into politics and the dynamics of the changing social structure. With religion acting as such a strong force on the course of events in the Old World, it is not difficult to imagine that it would play an important role in shaping the development of the New. In New England in particular, the impact of the Protestant Reformation would be great, not only in the original settlements of emigrants from England and other countries, but successively in the communities that their offspring would create, such as those across Talcott Ridge.

John White, the promoter of the "planting" effort that would eventually lead to the establishment of Windsor, Connecticut, saw religion as the ultimate motive for emigration to the New World. He wrote, "the most eminent and desirable end of planting colonies is the propagation of Religion." To underscore his position, he continued, "This nation is in a sort singled out unto this work, being of all the States that enjoy the liberties of the Religion Reformed, and are able to spare people for such an employment, the most Orthodox in our profession." White used a network of parish clergymen throughout southwestern England as his agents to recruit pious prospects for his ideal colony; and of those who would respond to his call to emigrate he wrote, "Necessity may press some; novelty draw on others; hopes of gain in time to come may prevail with a third sort; but that the most sincere and godly part have the advancement of the Gospel for their main scope I am confident. That of them some may entertain hope and expectation of enjoying greater liberty there than here in the use of some orders and ceremonies of our Church it seems very probable."[8]   This was the sort of visionary thinking that propelled whatever sentiments of reform would travel to New England, and particularly to Windsor, the town from which Salmon Brook's founders would originate.

Martin Luther had ignited the Protestant Reformation in 1517 by challenging the authority and doctrines of the Roman Catholic Church. As the movement to break apart what was once the only church in western Europe grew, many powerful rulers as well as religious thinkers declared their independence from the Church. Henry VIII of England was originally a strong opponent of Luther, but in 1533, when the Pope refused to grant him a dispensation to divorce his wife Catherine of Aragon (daughter of King Ferdinand and Queen Isabella of Spain), Henry established the Church of England with himself as its head. Mary I, Henry's daughter by Catherine, came to the throne in 1554, and earned herself the ugly nickname "Bloody Mary" as she tried zealously to reestablish the Catholic Church. Following her death in 1558, however, Elizabeth I, Henry's daughter by Anne Boleyn, his second wife, adopted the policy of her father - that she, as Queen, and not the Pope, would be head of the English (Anglican) Church. She also proclaimed that she would not persecute those who disagreed with her Church (as long as they kept their thoughts to themselves and attended her Church!). Thus, the Protestant Reformation found a home in one of Europe's most powerful nations.

Encouraged by what sounded like a fairly tolerant religious policy, followers of John Calvin, a protestant theologian residing in Geneva, began to return to England, hoping that Elizabeth would allow them to "purify" the Church of England. Called Puritans for this reform effort, they believed that a person's chief responsibility was to glorify and honor God by performing his life's work (his "calling") as best he could. Calvin had preached the doctrine of "predestination," based on the famous passage from Ecclesiastes that only God's grace, not human "works," could save souls from death and damnation. The Puritans proclaimed all the ceremony, decorations and many of the doctrines of the English Church to be "idolatry and superstition," or, at least, passed them off as an effort to achieve salvation through good works, rather than relying on God's mercy (which was reserved for a select few from the start). Although Elizabeth's church was changing, it was not going far enough for the Puritans. They wanted to cleanse the Church of all but those who showed that they were God's chosen few (the "elect"). In place of doctrines regarding the role of the priests and church ceremonies in an individual's salvation, they wrote about the notion of the "covenant." Individuals who were "elect" had entered into a covenant with God, and, similarly were expected to covenant with each other to work together as a "congregation" to help each other to maintain their covenant with God.[9]

Some Puritans had long since given up on the Church of England. It could never be purified, said Robert Browne, and continued association with it would only lead to corruption and a fall from grace for those who may have been predestined for salvation. Eventually, many of Browne's followers, called Separatists, left the country. In 1620, after spending twelve years in Holland, a group of these exiles (the so-called "Pilgrims") founded the colony of Plimoth in New England. As Separatists they maintained a colony distinct from the other mostly non-separatist Puritan colonies that would settle in New England.

Most English Puritans felt that the Church of England could be saved. They did not give up their membership in that church, but tried to change it in their own parishes or in Parliament. However, even though they were gaining in numbers and political power during the reigns of Elizabeth I (1558-1603) and James I (1603-1625), the road to "purity" was steep and full of obstacles. One obstacle was William Laud, who became Bishop of London in 1628. This post gave him power over parishes in eastern England where many Puritans lived.

Laud would hear nothing of purifying his churches. He insisted that all of the clergy follow strictly the Anglican way of worship, and, in 1633, when his devotion earned him the position of Archbishop of Canterbury, the highest office in the Church of England, English Puritans everywhere began to think there was no more point in trying. People like John Winthrop still claimed to be part of the Church of England, but felt that the only solution was to set up God's true church in America. Staying in England, thought the future New Englanders, would be no way to glorify God. In America there was no Archbishop Laud. There they could worship the way people ought to. Doubtless this was the sort of sentiment John White had in mind when he recruited passengers for the *Mary and John* which would sail to Massachusetts Bay, delivering many of the parents of the settlers of Simsbury.

Do not be mistaken about these Puritans, though. They did not bring the idea of religious *freedom* to America - at least not intentionally. The non-separatists, including John White as well as his colleague John Warham, who would actually lead the congregation White recruited to Windsor, Connecticut, still felt that they were part of the Church of England and that that Church ought to change its ways. To the Puritan leaders of New England there was only one way of worshipping, and as much as anyone, they persecuted people for not conforming. In New England they turned out to be quite intolerant of the beliefs of extreme Calvinists such as Roger Williams and Anne Hutchinson, both of whom they banished. Later, Massachusetts Puritans would proffer similar treatment to the Quakers, or the Society of Friends, as they called themselves. Quakers actually did accept the idea of religious freedom, and believed that ministers and priests were unnecessary. Like Anne Hutchinson, they believed that those who would be "saved" would know of their state of grace through an "inner light," and this applied to women as well as men. At Quaker meetings all were considered equal, and anyone, male or female, could speak at any time. To the Puritans, this represented chaos, and they, along with leaders of the Established Church in England, often treated Quaker women as though they were witches. By "Liberty of the Gospel" Puritans did not mean freedom of religion.

Winthrop, not a clergyman himself, but certainly a pious political leader by all accounts, was clear in his notion of what he and his fellow Puritans should be doing in New England. "Wee shall finde that the God of Israell is among us," he said to his flock on the *Arbella* before they landed in Massachusetts Bay, "...when he shall make us a prayse and glory, that men shall say of succeeding plantacions: the lord make it like that of New England: for wee must Consider that wee shall be as a Citty upon a Hill, the eies of all people are uppon us." New England, in his view, was a Holy Experiment that would reform the Church of England by example. More importantly, Puritan preachers said, New Englanders should create a Godly nation to prepare for the coming of the Kingdom of God. "The Lord looks for more from thee, than from other people," warned Reverend Peter Bulkeley of Concord. "...Take heed...lest God remove thy candlestick out of the midst of thee." The radicals were quick to point out the contradictions in using the government to enforce "the New England Way," but Bay Colony leaders stood by their Holy Experiment.[10]

The founders of Connecticut, who differed with the Bay Colony leaders in some aspects of the relationship between Church and State, still echoed the belief that God's law was not a matter of individual interpretation when they agreed upon *The Fundamental Orders of Connecticut* in 1639. In the preamble to what some have called the world's first written constitution they put forth this statement of purpose:

> Forasmuch as it hath pleased the Allmighty God by the wise disposition of his divyne p'vidence so to Order and dispose of things that we the Inhabitants and Residents of Windsor Harteford and Wethersfield are now cohabiting and dwelling in and uppon the River of Connectecotte and the Lands thereunto adioyneing; And well knowing where a people are gathered togather the word of God requires that to mayntayne the peace and union of such a people there should be an Orderly and decent Government established according to God, to order and dispose of the affayres of the people at all seasons as occation shall requir; doe therefore associate and conioyne our selves to be as one Publike State or Comonwealth; and doe for our selves and our Successors and such as shall be adioyned to us att any tyme hereafter, enter into Combination and Confederation togather, to mayntayne and p'searve the liberty and purity of the gospell of our Lord Jesus wch we now p'fess, as also the disciplyne of the Churches, wch according to the truth of the said gospell is now practised amongst us....[11]

The "liberty and purity of the gospell...which we now profess" - it may not have been the only purpose European settlers had in coming to New England, but it was certainly going to play a leading role.

The Coastal Peoples

Grand dreams of religious purity and the reclamation of prosperity and stability aside, the European immigrants were not, by an altogether different perspective, "founders" of a "New World" hitherto untouched by human hand and thought. There were people already in New England, and had been for over 10,000 years. To the Native Americans (known to the Europeans variously as "Indians," "heathens" or "savages"), the immigrants would be more appropriately classed as "invaders" of their domain, bringing with them all sorts of unwelcome changes, including ultimately, the almost complete displacement of the original peoples of the region and their way of life. Between 1630 and 1790, Connecticut was transformed from a land of approximately 6000 Native Americans to an English colony with a mostly white population of over 200,000.[12] Yet, even though the newcomers were obviously politically dominant at the end of the colonial period, they had been influenced deeply by the Natives of the region, and the new communities would continue to bear the stamp of those societies encountered when the first settlers (or "invaders") arrived.

Granby's soil is full of evidence of people who lived here prior to the arrival of Europeans. A large amount of material - arrowheads, charcoal, pieces of pottery, and stone tools - has been sifted out by inhabitants over the years as they have cultivated their fields and dug foundations. In the early 20th century, a few local collectors gathered various samples of these fragments of the past, and deposited them with local historical groups.[13]

Three sites have been excavated by archaeologists, the so-called "West Point Site," a site in the Mechanicsville area and a collection of survey sites in the McLean Game Refuge. The first two were identified as dating to the so-called Archaic Period (9000-3000 years ago) and have yielded flint projectile points in large numbers. The flint apparently came from upstate New York in the Hudson River Valley, and as collector Benton Holcomb surmised in the 1920s in regard to the arrowheads he was finding, this imported flint is strong evidence of widespread trade networks in North America thousands of years ago. According to Nicholas Bellantoni, Connecticut State Archaeologist, the flint points found at the West Point Site render the site "of great importance as representative of a little known period of occupation in southern New England." More recently, at various places in the McLean Game Refuge, Kenneth Feder of Central Connecticut State University has found evidence of seasonal hunting and fishing camps of around 1000 years ago.[14] Aside from these findings, though, and what we can discern from the material in the Griffin and Holcomb collections, we do not have too much to go on that will tell us about the first 10 millennia of Granby's human experience. Documents from the days of Salmon Brook's first settlement by Europeans in the 1680s help to shed some light on the situation

31

at that time, but mostly we are left with a few pieces of stone and the impact they may have on our imaginations, as well as what archaeologists and historians can tell us generally about Native American life over the centuries in the immediate region.

As the last ice age was coming to an end approximately 10,000 years ago, small groups of nomadic peoples began moving into Connecticut. These "Paleo-Indians" hunted, fished and gathered wild plants for food, moving from place to place among the largely evergreen forests and along the banks of rivers and shores of glacial lakes. Though such a lake covered a large portion of the southeast quarter of Granby, with its water lapping against the edge of Bushy Hill, no evidence of Paleo-Indian life has been found in Granby.

As the environment changed around 8 or 9000 years ago, more people moved into Connecticut to take advantage of more diverse plant and animal supplies. During the Archaic period, people lived in larger groups, and developed more sophisticated technology for hunting and gathering, but still tended to migrate from place to place with the seasons.[15]

About 2500 years ago, life began to change in this region so that eventually the inhabitants of New England were relying significantly on domesticated plants for food, lived in more permanent villages near the seashore or on river banks and had created some ingenious means of adapting to the world around them. It was these so-called "Woodland" people who met the Europeans in the 16th and 17th centuries. Unfortunately, because Europeans often settled on the sites of former Woodland villages, we have fewer remains of these more recent people to analyze than we do of the Archaic people who lived thousands of years earlier. Until recently, in order to know what these people were like before European contact, historians and archaeologists had to rely heavily on reports of European explorers and settlers. Many of these tended to be pretty biased and sketchy, since few Europeans were interested in a culture they considered inferior at best, and thus have led to an extensive mythology about Native Americans that can produce all sorts of misunderstandings about what happened when the settlers began to inter-relate with the Natives.

One of the most persistent myths actually has to do with the environment in which the Europeans found the Native Americans. Because of their fears of being "cut off" from civilization as they knew it, their exhaustion from a long ocean voyage and their lack of training in surviving in a land without roads, road signs, cultivated fields, villages and cities, Europeans often tended to describe America in terms of a "dark, desolate stretch of howling wilderness" where there were "trees everywhere they looked," and these forests were "filled with wild animals and wild men." Even today a form of this myth still distorts the picture. In the modern version, the natives are viewed as the "original environmentalists" who lived with nature rather than changing it to suit their needs. Thus the image of pristine wilderness which frightened early modern Western Civilization has become inspirational for us, but, nevertheless, remains a continuous perception of a "wild" environment.

Actually, the Algonkian-speaking peoples of New England had altered nature considerably. When the European settlers arrived, they found a lot of open, cultivated fields that the Natives were either using or had abandoned in the not too distant past. Furthermore, the Natives had burned underbrush extensively in the forests in order to make hunting easier, and the woodlands were more like parks than the jungles they may have appeared to be on first glance to tired and apprehensive Europeans. The overall treatment of the land by the Algonkians was certainly far gentler than that which would be dealt out in the future by the Europeans and their descendants, but the place was hardly a "howling wilderness."[16]

As for the "wild men," that too is far from the truth. The Algonkian people had a complex culture and had developed sophisticated ways of making a living in their world. They did practice mobility to some extent in order to best exploit the food resources available in the region. However, they were hardly roaming, disorganized bands, even though exasperated English settlers felt they were as they tried to find some authority who could quickly convey them title to the land. The main unit of political and economic organization was the village. This institution was not the settled collection of "homesteads" that Europeans were used to, but rather a group of people who might just pick up and move to another location more favorable to growing or hunting, and still call their village by the same name. Loose confederations of villages might owe allegiance to a chief "sachem," and thus be viewed as a tribe, but these alliances among villages or confederations of tribes again bore no similarity to the nationalism of the Europeans. And rather than build a system of law and courts, the Natives relied upon custom and public opinion for the maintenance of order. Positions of power and influence were held by the elderly, including women, and only vague territorial boundaries marked out land assumed to be held in common by the members of a village.[17] All this was extremely foreign to the hierarchical and property-loving newcomers whose object was to get control of the New World as soon as possible. Villages that moved - land without owners - people without a nation - all of this was very suspicious indeed.

The importance of women in Native society was also a phenomenon that amazed Europeans. The English immigrants of the 17th century, recalling nostalgically the reign of Queen Elizabeth, were certainly not intolerant of an occasional female political leader. But the status of Native American women of the Eastern Woodland peoples went well beyond that. The basic social unit, the clan, was actually a collection of descendants of a common female ancestor, and society generally had a matriarchal organizational pattern to it. Lines of descent ran from mother to mother; the earth itself was considered the mother of everyone; and women ran the households, responsible not only for the cooking, preparation and storing of food, and raising of children, but also for planting, tanning of hides, weaving of textiles and baskets, and cultivating and harvesting of crops. They were considered the owners of the wigwams (small dome-shaped dwellings made from saplings and bark or hides) and all household goods. These attitudes toward women not only amazed most Europeans, but disgusted quite a few, who saw the Algonkian men's role as hunters and fishermen as evidence that the Indian squaws were treated as slaves while the men lived a life of sport.[18]

Even though we call the period 1000 B.C. to A.D. 1600 the "Woodland Period" in New England, it would be inaccurate to refer to the New England natives as "Woodland" Indians. More appropriately they should be called "Coastal" peoples, even those who lived in what later became the town of Granby. They relied heavily on fish and shellfish for food, and seem to have chosen river and stream banks as the sites for their villages, when not actually living near the seashore. Their principal crops, maize, squash, and beans, required a growing season of decent length, and that could be assured closer to the water. The women burned off thousands of acres across Connecticut

Richard Caley

Native American artifacts found in Granby. The grinder and stone are part of the Salmon Brook Historical Society collections and the arrowheads are from a private collection.

35

for cultivation of these crops, and indications from early land records are that there were a number of these open but abandoned "meadows" available for early European settlers along the banks of Salmon Brook in the late 17th century.[19]

What life there was in the actual woodlands consisted of lengthy hunts well away from the villages, for the Algonkians did all they could to discourage wild animals from living near their gardens, fishing places and clam banks. Sometimes a whole village would head for the sea shore for the summer months, leaving their field corn to mature, and thus it was imperative that woodland creatures be taught to stay far away. Widespread travel was common throughout New England, not only by birchbark canoe, a major technological achievement by itself, but also on a network of trails. Some of them, such as the one that once followed the path of today's Connecticut Route 10 through Granby center, were as wide as a single lane dirt road.[20]

Europeans were also not very impressed with the general health of Native Americans or the cleanliness of their living habits. The literature is full of references to wigwams being "smoky holes," and to the tendency of the natives to live much like animals, seldom washing or wearing decent clothing. In actuality, the natives, prior to the onset of European diseases, were pretty healthy, and had a longer lifespan, on average, than the Europeans. The "smoky holes" in which they lived were tight, comfortable dwellings, and probably warmer in winter than most houses the settlers built. They were a hospitable, religious people who had a deep sense of the sacredness of nature, and saw themselves, along with every bird, rock, plant or animal, as an integral part of a great plan that was to be respected. They realized there would be conflict within nature, but they did not expect to conquer nature in the manner instructed to the European immigrants in the book of Genesis ("Subdue the earth and have dominion over every living thing...").[21]

Such was the life of the people who were here before the so-called "first settlers." There is no doubt that Granby was inhabited by significant numbers of coastal natives from time to time in the centuries before the arrival of Europeans, and probably even within a half century of "settlement." The settlers found extensive cleared ground along Salmon Brook and other streams, and today there are places, including Manatuck Lake and Mountain, and Poppetunuck Mountain, still bearing their Algonkian names. But when the Europeans arrived they found only the abandoned fields, and few, if any, of their former inhabitants. By 1700 there were no Algonkians living anywhere near Salmon Brook. What happened to all of Granby's original inhabitants?

In the end, we can only make a well-educated guess, from what we know of the history of the region immediately prior to the 1670s. It is probable that during the 16th and 17th centuries Granby was the destination of hunting parties from at least four groups whose villages ringed the area. To the south the Massaco, possibly a branch of the Tunxis, lived along the Farmington River, especially in the Hopmeadow and Weatogue sections of Simsbury. To the north the Waranoakes lived around the Southwick ponds. Beyond them the Agawams made their home on the Connecticut River and its tributaries around Springfield; and to the east, the Poquonocks lived in what is still called the Poquonock section of Windsor. It was from people of these three groups between 1640 and 1690, that Europeans managed to extract grants of land for present-day Granby. Because of the previously cleared "meadows" that early settlers found in such places as today's Salmon Brook Park and west and south of Manatuck Lake, we can assume that people from these groups did more than hunt for deer, bear, porcupine and beaver, and fish for the salmon so abundant in the brook that bears its name. They probably came for lengthy or even permanent stays. The foothills of the Berkshires rise in the western third of Granby, and these demarcated a boundary, or "no-man's land" of sorts, between the so-called "River Tribes" such as the Poquonocks and Agawams, and the powerful Mohawks of the upper Hudson River valley.[22]

For nearly three centuries after European settlement historians believed that there had been a long history of feuding between the River Tribes and the Mohawks, and, further, that the River Tribes also were quite fearful of the Pequots, their neighbors to the southeast. Governor William Bradford of the Plimoth Colony reported that representatives from a Connecticut River confederacy had come to both Massachusetts Bay and Plimoth in 1631 to invite English traders to their region in hopes of securing a powerful alliance against their traditional enemies. He claimed that, at the time, the Mohawks were collecting tribute from the River Tribes.[23]

More recently, however, both historians and archaeologists have made discoveries that have raised questions about this old assumption that the conflict observed by the early settlers was rooted in ancient animosities. In a 1978 excavation of a Woodland Period site at the junction of the Farmington and Connecticut Rivers, for example, archaeologists found a great deal of evidence of a "very successful trading system" between the Algonkians of Connecticut and both the Mohawks and people as far away as Eastern Pennsylvania. On the heels of these findings, historians have begun to think that what hostility the early settlers observed among native groups was, perhaps, more a result of the European's themselves, who, by the 1630s, had destroyed the traditional trading system of the Northeast.[24]

This "European presence" actually predated the traditional years we associate with the settlement of New England by at least a century. European fishermen and explorers had been trading with Native Americans on the coast of New England for some time when the Pilgrims first arrived at Plimoth. French explorers reported trading metal goods and articles of clothing for animal furs and skins as early as the 1520s, and by the beginning of the 17th century this sort of trade had become a complete economic system all of its own. Dutch, English, French, and Swedish traders competed with each other to secure trading relationships with coastal villagers who were happy to supply furs for the metal that was far superior to the flint they had been acquiring from inland peoples such as the Mohawks. But as the beaver population rapidly declined in New England, the inland tribes became important again, and could be persuaded to provide furs for "wampumpeag," or "wampum," which consisted of strings of shell beads manufactured by the coastal natives and used as adornment and status symbols, and in the rituals of the inland peoples. Thus, an entirely new trading system emerged, but the eventual winners in the battle for profit were the Europeans, a phenomenon that led to a good deal of frustration and bickering among the Native American groups of the St. Lawrence, Hudson and Connecticut Valleys and along Long Island Sound.[25]

Another disruption for the Algonkians of New England occurred immediately as Europeans first began to establish permanent trading posts and settlements on the mainland. In 1616 and 1617, and again in 1633 and 1634, the region was ravaged by epidemics of age-old European diseases, such as chicken-pox, bubonic plague and smallpox, to which the natives had absolutely no immunity. Mortality rates were dreadful across the region.

Estimates have varied from 60% to 80%, and in many cases entire villages were wiped out. One can imagine not only the devastating effect on morale, but also the massive social, economic, and political impact, as some powerful confederacies suddenly lost most of their warriors; others lost all their sachems and others could no longer fulfill their role in the new trading system upon which they had come to depend.[26]

Thus, the European immigrants arrived at a time of great dislocation and confusion, and found villages without leaders, alliances in disarray, acres and acres of vacant fields with no one to sell them (not that any one person ever had any authority to sell land in the first place), and native peoples bitter about changes in their lives that had made making a living difficult and life itself precarious: a region seething with anxiety. While struggling to maintain their traditional culture, the people of Massaco, Poquonock, Waranoake and Agawam were many fewer in numbers, disorganized politically and in social disarray. The world they and their ancestors had known for two thousand years had fallen apart even before the English newcomers began to eye their lands across Talcott Ridge. A whole way of life was on the verge of disappearing before any European could see it and describe it to his or her descendants. When the "invaders" arrived, the conquest was already well underway.

"A More Excellent Way"

The story of the European settlement of New England is actually a number of seemingly contradictory and incongruous stories all at once, and these contradictions and incongruities will help to explain the dynamics of early Salmon Brook society as it was fashioned by the second and third generations of European immigrants in the late 17th century. The first story is one of an ethnocentric and acquisitive group of traders and "planters" conquering and subduing the land and its native people. A second is that of Puritans, led by devoted preachers, striving to create a religious utopia to continue the Protestant Reformation. Finally, there is the story of conservative English people trying to restore the "civilization" - the political, social and economic order - they perceived to be disappearing in the old country. On the one hand we could paint a picture of the newcomers as a frightened people

39

seeking security in a wilderness, and on the other, a seemingly fearless people striding boldly into a strange new world to tap its potential. They would not succeed in any of these quests completely, but their pursuit of all of them at once resulted in tremendous change in the ecology of their new home land, a lot of upheaval, for better or for worse, in their own ideals and traditions; and, in fact, the creation of a culture of change itself as mobility and adaptation to new people and circumstances became a common experience in the lives of all Americans.

As we have seen, and as was true of all the early English ventures to North America, the initial impetus was interest in trade. The first trading partners were to be the Native Americans themselves as the newcomers adjusted to "the wilderness," but the ultimate goal, the promoters stated, was to create an imperial mercantilist system where colonists, emigrants from Britain, would exploit the natural resources of the New World and trade them for the manufactured goods of the Old, thus supporting English national strength by creating a favorable balance of trade. Joint stock operations, supported financially only to a small extent by Queen Elizabeth and later only with charters by Kings James and Charles, had funded the efforts to set up trading posts at Roanoak, Jamestown and Sagadahoc (on the Maine coast). The Puritan dissenters who set forth for the Plimoth and Massachusetts Bay colonies also presented themselves to the crown under the guise of trading companies whose activities would be beneficial to the national good. The Dutch too were in New England in the early 1600s, establishing bases for trade at New Amsterdam (New York) and at the House of Hope on the "Quinnetucket" (Hartford). To the north, the French probed far into the interior, exploring the St. Lawrence basin and the Great Lakes region in search of trading opportunities. All this activity wreaked havoc on traditional native trading systems and economies, and the European presence soon led to demographic disaster as diseases spread across the region.

During the 1620s a settlement of English Puritan separatists struggled into existence at Plimoth Plantation on Cape Cod Bay, to be followed by a much larger Puritan non-Separatist colony on Massachusetts Bay with its headquarters, eventually, at Boston. As these colonies grew, and other independent communities branched off in southern New England (Connecticut 1633-36, Providence Plantation in 1636, and New Haven in 1638), it was

40

clear that commerce was not the only purpose to which the immigrants were directing their attention. Most people had come to live as farmers and tradesmen, some communally and some independently, and to practice "the religion reformed." If Charles I had not been so busy arguing with parliamentarians and religious dissenters at home, he might have begun to wonder how some of his courtiers were defining "trading venture" and where his fifth of the gold was. But with the Crown preoccupied, New England's European population grew by the thousands: as rapidly as the Algonkian population declined.

The first European settlers to come to the Connecticut River Valley were traders, but communities of "planters" soon followed. Emissaries from the River Tribes traveled to Boston and Plimoth in 1631 to try to get the English to come to Connecticut. Offering good fur trading opportunities as inducement, the Podunks and Poquonocks hoped the English presence would discourage more powerful peoples to the east and west from collecting tribute from them. When the Plimoth traders arrived in 1633 the Dutch had also set up a fort at Hartford, and in the following year John Oldham established connections at "Pyquag" (Wethersfield). In 1635 groups of land-hungry settlers began streaming down from Massachusetts Bay, not even waiting for sticky questions of who had authority over the Connecticut River to be worked out between the Bay Colony and the so-called "Lords and Gentlemen" who held a patent for Connecticut from the Earl of Warwick.[27] The people of the new river towns of Windsor, Hartford and Wethersfield simply dealt directly with the Algonkians for the land they wanted to occupy. In Windsor the Bay Colony settlers even ignored the fact that the traders from the Plimoth Colony had preceded them by two years, and calmly went about granting land all around the Plimoth trading house as though they were simply waiting for the earlier commercial venture to disappear.[28]

Most of the natives watched nervously and continued to trade for metal goods, textiles, and influence as the newcomers spread about the region. The Pequots, however, were less easily cowed. Dutch traders, who seemed no different to them than English traders, had already killed their Chief Sachem before the English began to take an interest in the Connecticut River, and they were thoroughly disenchanted with the way the new economic system was shaping up. They were the most powerful people in the

41

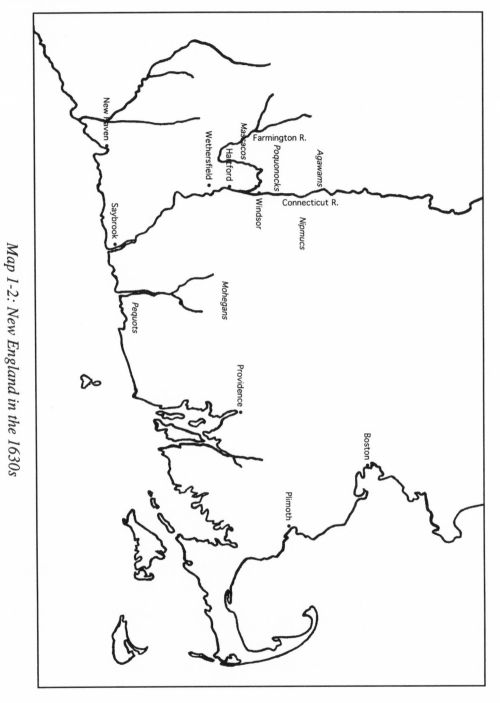

Map 1-2: New England in the 1630s

region in the 1630s, having been less affected by the smallpox epidemic; but wampum, which had become the medium of exchange in southern New England, was losing value and they were not about to join other Algonkians in giving up land in exchange for wealth and power. After abortive attempts both to negotiate and to frighten the English, the Pequots gathered in the Mystic area to discuss what was to be done. The climate throughout New England was pure fear. Misunderstanding followed misunderstanding. Soon the killing of John Oldham, a talented negotiator (if only because he liked to do business better than he liked to fight), and the perfectly correct perception on the part of the Pequots that the English meant to get rid of the region's natives as soon as they could, led to war in 1637. In two "battles" all the English settlements in New England, as well as a group of Mohegans and Narragansetts, joined to effect the near destruction of the Pequot people. Miantonomo, the Narragansett Sachem, made a similar effort to stave off the "invasion" in 1643, and was captured and turned over for execution to the ambitious Mohegan Uncas, who through some crafty politicking emerged with his warriors as about the only Algonkian to have much influence with the English after the 1640s. The fur and wampum trade continued, but the English traders and their supporting militias had clearly eliminated anyone who had any questions about who would profit the most and who would make the rules of the game.[29]

By 1660 the European demand for beaver pelts had dropped so much that wampum was no longer used for payment of debts, of which the Native Americans had accumulated quite a few. Many of the English planters had turned to raising livestock for the West Indies trade, or exploiting the pine forests for turpentine, tar, and lumber for shipbuilding. The fur trade had not been the principal interest of most of the migrants. They wanted the land, which was, of course, the only thing of value the Algonkians had left to exchange for the English goods on which they had become so dependent. Thus they sold the land, in many cases, for pathetically small quantities of trade goods. It is doubtful that they understood the English concept of private property, and probably were under the impression they were merely granting an economic right to the use of the land, which right would end when the particular use ceased.[30] The English authorities who bought the land had a different perception of the transaction. Their sense of the transaction as a permanent dispossession of a bounded parcel of land was doubtless influenced by their understanding of the need for vast amounts of land for the livestock and lumber business, and also for expected new waves of immigration. After a decade of discordant rule by Parliament and Lord Protector Oliver Cromwell, the political situation in England had stabilized with the restoration of Charles II to the throne in 1660. Some Anglicans and loyalists, particularly from Wales, had already come to New England in the 1650s, but colony leaders expected many more to follow.

The settlers were quick to rationalize the apparent injustice of the land deals being executed throughout New England by suggesting that the natives did not really own the land anyway. "As for the Natives," wrote Governor Winthrop, "they inclose noe Land, neither have any setled habytation, nor any tame Cattle to improve the Land by, and soe have noe other but a Naturall Right to those Countries."[31] In Winthrop's view the Natives simply did not take advantage of their natural right and thus surrendered it for a few knives and kettles. The English claimed the land by discovery and sat comfortably behind their liberal royal charters (Connecticut got its own in 1662), which gave the colonies rights "as of our manor of East Greenwich, in the County of Kent, in free and common Socage, and not in Capite, nor by knightes service." No "Socage" or "Capite" meant there would be no feudal quitrents (except the one-fifth of the gold found that was to go to the King), and the colonies' own governments, which from the beginning consisted of elected governors and representative assemblies, would decide how the land would be parceled out. When the land was parceled out, the new tenants held it as a free possession, to be totally under their control, or the control of their "heirs and assigns forever." In other words, the Algonkians, whose way of life ironically required ten to twelve times the space per family as that required by Europeans, were quickly dealt out of the Europeans' concept of ownership in New England. By the 1660s the traders and planters had taken charge.[32]

Of course, these were not ordinary traders and planters - these people had a mission, and believing that made their conquest all the easier to justify. Until 1660 the vast majority of the immigrants were English Puritans whose leaders looked upon the new land as did John Winthrop - as a site for "a city upon a hill." The charters may have been penned with trading companies in mind, but the pattern of settlement clearly reflected the religious ideals of these reformers. Groups of people set off more often as congregations than as trading ventures to establish new towns. In Massachusetts, only accepted members of a congregation could vote for representatives to the colony government, and in Connecticut, the governor had to be a member of an approved congregation. As people began building, they clustered their houses around a "meetinghouse" which was used primarily for religious services and only occasionally for the political business of the congregation. Some congregations, such as John Warham and John Maverick's group that sailed on the *Mary and John* to Dorchester, Massachusetts, and then traveled on to Windsor, Connecticut, were gathered even before the colonists left England. When, in 1639, the Windsor church's new teacher Ephraim Huitt preached his inaugural sermon on the Corinthians text, "And yet show I unto you a more excellent way," he was intoning the accepted view of the reason they had come to Connecticut - to establish a Bible Commonwealth, blessed by God as a model for all the world to follow.[33]

These efforts to produce a Bible utopia did not result in perfect harmony among the planters of New England on the subject of religion. Roger Williams, the founder of Rhode Island, was actually banished to those parts for calling the Massachusetts Bay charter a lie and refuting the authority of the colony's leaders to tell people what religion to practice. He was a radical Separatist, even more so than the leaders of Plimoth Colony who had also asked him to leave. In addition, Massachusetts Bay had to contend with the "Antinomian heresy" (the idea that preachers had no more authority than the ordinary person to interpret scripture), propounded by Anne Hutchinson, who was banished not only for preaching instead of listening, but also for "being a husband rather than a wife"!

These were the extreme cases, but minor doctrinal disputes kept church authorities busy and strained their ability to create peaceful and exemplary Bible commonwealths in both Massachusetts Bay and Connecticut. After all, the religious leaders were some of England's most troublesome dissenters, and it is not surprising that each would arrive in New England with his own self-righteous confidence in his particular views. Probably Hartford's Thomas Hooker, once considered by Archbishop William Laud to be the most dangerous man in England, left Massachusetts Bay for Connecticut in part because he had some differences with other strong-minded ministers there.

In Windsor the Rev. John Warham was not a particularly radical reformer, but disruption eventually came to his congregation as well. In the late 1650s the second generation of English settlers and some new immigrants were demanding that the churches of New England baptize their children, even though they themselves had not yet "owned the covenant" (a Puritan term for declaring one's faith before the congregation, being judged, and, if found sincere, being accepted as a member of the church). Many of these young people had not endured the hardships of persecution in England or of a long ocean voyage, and others, more recent immigrants in particular, were more Anglican than Puritan. The idea of professing some profound spiritual experience before a large group of people did not have the same appeal as it had for the zealots who had come in the 1630s, and so they had simply not bothered. A Council of Ministers and Elders met in Boston in 1657 and proposed a "Halfway Covenant" whereby children of church members could be admitted without profession of faith in order to have their children baptized. Warham, who had always believed in a church that embraced both "saints" and "sinners" (both the elect and otherwise), began admitting people under this doctrine, which was confirmed by a synod in 1662.

However, in 1664 he changed his mind, perhaps out of self-doubt, or perhaps because he was offended by a paper circulated the previous year by Windsor residents Michael Humphrey, James Eno and others, members of the Church of England, demanding privileges of church membership.[34] With Charles II returned to the throne in England, these "troublemakers" were clearly worrying the Puritan establishment that had managed to keep Connecticut's church independent for three decades while England was in a state of turmoil. The upshot of all the controversy that followed was the creation of a second church in Windsor under Rev. Benjamin Woodbridge in the spring of 1670, a gradual weakening of the influence of religious leaders in the colony generally and a long residue of bitter feelings in the Town of Windsor. Judging from the large proportion of dissenters in this matter who eventually ended up moving to Simsbury, including Humphrey and Eno, we might suppose that these bad feelings had a lot to do with the founding of the new community across Talcott Ridge.[35]

As traders, promoters, and preachers strove for various goals, so too did the ordinary settlers as individuals and as groups, and the sum total of all of these individual pursuits also had a dramatic effect on the shaping of society in the region. These ordinary folk certainly did not intend to live their lives much differently from the way they had in the Old World, but it is here perhaps, in the everyday order, that the immigrants experienced the most profound revolutions.

One would think that they would have expected as much as soon as they got a look at the New World they had arrived in and took cognizance of their situation. Things would have to be different if they were to survive. The soil was different, the landscape was different, and instead of living in a land teaming with excess population, they were entering a land in which a sparse population, by their standards, had become considerably more sparse of late, and their own numbers were miniscule. If all this did not occur to them just by looking around, surely it did when they first began to build their houses. There was timber everywhere (which meant the half-timbered houses with thatched roofs of the Old World would be replaced by all wood houses with wooden shingles), but processed iron and even blacksmiths were few in number. From the beginning, they would change the way they lived by living in different dwellings.[36]

Farming became the principal occupation for everyone, even the many immigrant artisans who had relied almost strictly on their trade in the Old World. For the farmers themselves, the New World offered volumes of change. In Windsor there is a good deal of evidence that the early settlers put in orchards almost immediately and that cider became a staple drink as it had been in the West Country from which a large number of Windsor's founders had emigrated. English grasses also found a new home in New England, but English grains did not work very well and soon gave way largely to the hardy maize, or "Indian corn." Without plows, they had to learn to cultivate the new grain by drilling holes for the seed, as the Algonkians did.

Whole systems of farming to which settlers were accustomed had to change as well. In England, there had been a variety of approaches to farming to begin with. Some of the immigrants to the New World had been used to an "open field" system where groups of tenants or freeholders divided large common fields into long narrow strips, and grazed their livestock in common grazing areas. In other parts of England, for example in the West Country, there was little of this communal culture and "husbandmen" enclosed their

47

farms and worked independently.[37] Some areas of England had elaborate commercial systems and numerous market towns, and other economies were more provincial and villages maintained a great degree of self-sufficiency. When people from different backgrounds met in the New World and tried to reestablish that to which they had been accustomed, adjustments were inevitable, even if one group managed to hold on to its precious habits for some time.[38] The passengers of the *Mary and John* were West Country people accustomed to individual farms. When they first settled in Dorchester, Massachusetts in 1630, they found that they had to adopt a communal culture just to survive, and their town took on the appearance of an English open field village. Worrying over land allotment policies that were too stingy for their rapidly growing livestock population and neighbors who seemed too radically Puritan for their tastes, the bulk of them moved on to Windsor, Connecticut in 1635 and 1636 where they again created a communal village system foreign to what they had known in England.

The social fabric in the New World had to be rewoven. In the New World there was no nobility, and there were few from the lowest classes of English society as well. In fact, the community instituted by those first immigrants of the *Mary and John* voyage in Dorchester, and soon in Windsor, was remarkably homogeneous. Most of the men were yeoman farmers with a sprinkling of artisans and only moderately wealthy gentry, most were carefully selected from one region in England and practically all were, or soon were to become, family men. They seem to have made a serious attempt to stay together, as people with a region of common origin in England, but any attempt they may have made to reproduce their customary social structure dissolved for the lack of distinctions. When they began doling out land in Windsor they planned, as did most communities, to give more land to those who had a "greater estate;" that is, those who had been more wealthy in England (and had thus been able to contribute more to the enterprise). But it turned out that, except for a few who received larger lots, the parcels distributed were roughly equal. Furthermore, everyone, whether they had been a tenant or freeholder in England, became a landowner in the New World. These people were hardly egalitarian democrats - their leaders believed each person should know and stay in his or her place. After all, the disruptions in the social order in England had sent many of them to the New

World where some order and "harmony" might be reestablished. In England the deferential world of gentlemen, yeomen, tenants, artisans and laborers was changing to a world of owners and workers. In America, the newcomers made the most of what vestiges of the old distinctions there were, but even their "great men," whom they allowed to rule in small tight-knit oligarchies, were farmers and family men just like everybody else. Furthermore, they were only "great" by the authority of the "town meeting," New England's primary political institution, and there every town "inhabitant" could speak his mind.[39]

The new face of New England by 1670, as Russell Bourne has said, "was like a figure by Picasso, wracked by change and disruption."[40] The very ecology of the region had changed tremendously since the first European contacts of the previous century. The Native Americans, responding to new trading opportunities, had begun the change themselves, depleting the environment of beaver and altering their own lifeways and relationship with their surroundings. As thousands of Europeans moved in, farmer and logger alike produced devastating effects as they cleared forests by vast burnings, consumed 30 to 40 cords of firewood per family per year, and exploited pine and cedar stands for commercial products. The rivers ran fuller with greater runoff, and soils at higher elevations dried more quickly and eroded; and because of their practice of allowing animals to graze at large, they had no manure and used up the fish supply rapidly to fertilize their fields.

As they threw the ecology into a tailspin to force it to conform to their goals and customs, they also created a new set of customs for themselves. To some extent they devised new ways to establish a religious utopia, a covenanted "city upon a hill." But ironically, the efforts to create a communal paradise characterized by "unity, concord, and harmony," fell upon the rough waters of individual aspirations. As the second and third generations took charge of the region people began to move about more regularly, old tight-knit communities among people from the same region in England became less identifiable, parent-child relationships became increasingly strained, religion was less of a central concern as the great ministers of the first generation died one by one, farmers began to participate more and more in the overseas trading system and fewer and fewer people seemed to "know their place."[42]

Indeed, it was a New World. What had begun as a trading venture, and had grown large as a religious reform movement, was now a new society, complex and rumbling with dislocation. Both the Puritanism and the commercialism of the founders remained important elements in this new society, and the Algonkians of the region were hardly out of the picture, but new dynamics had arisen from the clashing of old ways with new ideals and from the adaptation processes occurring everywhere. In Windsor restless people were looking for new lands for their growing families, idealizing new community structures in their minds, and dreaming of new ventures for profit. To their west loomed an ancient volcanic ridge that would not long be a barrier to their aspirations.

Massaco becomes Simsbury

The forces behind the beginnings of the town of Simsbury were as complex as those behind the founding of all New England. This was not a simple case of a gathered congregation pulling up its stakes and moving in a covenanted mass to a new location. Nor was Simsbury purely the result of a capitalist scheme or a trickle of pioneers to a newly discovered river valley. All of these familiar elements of colonization were present, but there was more to it as well.[43] 1642 seems to be the first date associated with the settling of Simsbury. To understand the European interest in the area it is important to look closely at what Simsbury had to offer and what was going on with the Connecticut Colony at the time.

By 1639 the first great wave of immigration into New England had come to an end. Over twenty thousand immigrants had come to live in New England during the previous decade, but the political situation in England had become so tense that colonial enterprises and interest in emigration were at a standstill. This meant considerable adjustment for those already in New England who had become accustomed to a pattern of settling an area and then making a large share of their living selling land and farm produce to the new arrivals streaming in. Land values dropped, surplus livestock had no market, and morale declined. Windsor lost some of its leading citizens, such as Roger Ludlow, to shore communities that offered better access to the West Indies trade.[45] Furthermore, although the Pequots had been soundly defeated, the authorities were still nervous about relations with the region's remaining tribes who were becoming increasingly fearful of the English and increasingly aware of the land they were losing to English livestock if not to the settlers themselves.

Ten miles up the Tunxis (Farmington) River from Windsor lay a great meadow, the home of the Massaco people, named after either the *massa sawk* (great outlet) of Hop Brook into the river or the *massa agu* (great meadow) itself.[37] The waters in this area and to the north along the Salmon Brook ran thick with salmon and shad. Great pine stands, ideal for harvesting pitch for tar and turpentine and for making candlewood, stretched back into the hills. There were marshes frequented by game and waterfowl, and offering the possibility of bog iron, or, when drained, grassland or rich farm soil. And besides Hopmeadow, there were numerous other meadows and small cleared areas only recently abandoned by the natives and not yet overgrown. Thousands of acres of hardwood would provide wood for barrel staves and planks, or, if burned, millions of barrels of potash. The Massaco do not seem to have been a numerous people, and so the usual cheap sale would once again be easy to justify.[46] While only about ten percent of the Massaco country was as rich for cultivation as the meadows along the Connecticut River, and the rest a combination of light, sandy soil and glacial gravel, that did not stop farmers with growing families from urging their representatives to the General Court, Connecticut's legislature, to open the region across Talcott Ridge for settlement.[47]

Thus, in 1642, the General Court, ignoring any right of the Massacos to the land, but still using their name, attached "Massaco" to Windsor, resolving that "the Governor and Mr. Heynes shall have liberty to dispose of the ground Uppon that parte of the Tunxis River cauled Mossocowe, to Wyndsor inhabitants as they shall see cause."[48] The General Court was the supreme government and closely regulated settlement in order to best further "the purity of the gospel." Even so, little came of the 1642 resolution regarding Massaco, nor of a subsequent one in 1647 when a committee was established to dispose of the land.[49] We can only speculate on the reason for this inaction. The drop in immigration and concern about the civil war in England may have put a damper on the fire under the land speculators. More likely, though, the problem may have been the natives who had been so blithely ignored in the official record. 1643 was the year Miantonomo's

Narragansett conspiracy was uncovered, which would naturally contribute to general nervousness about the Algonkians throughout the region. More locally there is good evidence that both the Massacos and the Waranoakes were behaving in a most unwelcoming manner during the 1640s.

Consider, for example, one Manahannoose, a man who had lived at Massaco and Waranoake for a long time before the white men had come to his country. He had seen his friends and relatives die horrible deaths; he had seen the last of the beaver in his country; he had heard the terrible story of 600 Pequots burned alive at Mystic; he had argued with the English about how a knife that cost 10 fathom of wampum one year would cost 50 the next; and he had listened to the Poquonocks complain about the damage to hunting grounds caused by the English animals. He was sorry that the villagers on the Quinnetucket had ever asked the English to come to the river. He knew the English were very powerful, but he also knew the evil ways by which they got that power. He saw them working in his own forests. They made the trees bleed and carted off the sap to their smoldering fires that billowed smoke for weeks and oozed foul smelling liquid. They cut down great pines where spirits once whispered and took only the heart, leaving the rest to rot. They had no respect for the land and its creatures, or for the spirit world, and what was more, they had less and less interest in trading with his people.

It was possibly with these thoughts in mind that Manahannoose set fire one night in 1645 or 1646 to the tar kilns of a Welsh immigrant to Windsor named John Griffin. Griffin was one of those colonists trying to adjust to the new economic conditions now that the immigration rate had declined, and had been exploiting the pine forests of Massaco and Salmon Brook to manufacture tar and turpentine in the vicinity of the Tariffville falls. He was in business with Michael Humphrey, a West Country merchant from Lyme Regis, Dorset, and the tar trade promised fortunes for them both. Their ambition, however, did not impress the Algonkians.[50]

Other Waranoakes had done the same to tar works around the Southwick ponds. These were acts of anger - the Algonkians living near Windsor had seen the future and many were not content to sit by and let it happen. But somehow Griffin found out who ruined his manufacturing operation, and somehow he managed to catch him. How this happened is unclear, but in 1646 we find him taking advantage of a newly passed law that required Native Americans who committed "Wilfull and Hostile Practices" to be given over to the plaintiffs and ordered to be their servant or be shipped off in return for enslaved Africans. The miscreant's village, according to the law, could pay damages in order to prevent this from happening. Griffin estimated the damage at £100, or 500 fathom of wampum, and in 1648 received a favorable judgment from the General Court. At that point, Manahannoose's relatives came forth and secured his release by signing over to Griffin all but two acres of Massaco.[51] This was hardly legal, since individuals were forbidden from buying land from the natives. Griffin himself probably considered the deal an economic one at any rate, and thirteen years later turned over his deed to the colony in return for their recognition that he was the first to make pitch and tar in the colony and for 200 acres of his choice north of the falls.[52] By that time, presumably, he had slashed and cut all he had wanted among the great pines Manahannoose had seen bleeding on his land.

Meanwhile, feeling more confident once the Algonkians had been taught their lesson and as a Puritan regime was established in England, the General Court again pushed for settlement at Massaco. In 1653, the Court itself made grants to Thomas Ford, Lt. Aaron Cook, and John Bissell. Ford was Cook's father-in-law, and Cook and Bissell were members of the elite "Troop of Horse," and connected to Connecticut's more wealthy class and ruling oligarchy. All three seem to have had a West Country origin in common. The Court then ordered Simon Wolcott and Daniel Clarke, also of West Country families, to "dispose of the remainder of Ground at Massaco to the inhabitants of Wyndsor, as they judge convenient." Evidently Cook had already begun working his and his father-in-law's plot on the north end of what is now called Terry's Plain, and he soon moved there to become Simsbury's first permanent resident.[53]

From all accounts, though, all of these men - and those others who received grants in 1660, such as Benjamin Newberry, Joseph Parsons and John Moses, - were more interested in profits than in settling. They were an ambitious lot, probably looking forward to the next wave of immigration. Cook was the first actually to settle, but sold his farm in 1661 to Simon Wolcott, who seems to have stayed just long enough to have the new town named after his and Thomas Ford's ancestral village of Symondsbury

53

(pronounced Simsbury) in Dorset.[54]

New immigrants did arrive, but during the 1650s the settlement of Massaco remained stalled. Again, it would appear that prospective settlers were nervous about the intentions of the Algonkians, whose claims to the land continued into 1661. This time, the problems came from three men named Mamanto, Keepoquam and Metapage, who seem to have felt that they were not part of the deal for Manahanoose's freedom. Exasperated at their inability to find a chief who could, once and for all, give clear title, the Court bought off Metapage for a coat, Keepoquam for 40 shillings (paid in worthless wampum), and Mamanto for a two-acre plot. This was the point at which Griffin turned over his deed from Manahanoose's relatives.[55] The Court then set up a new committee in 1663, consisting of Benjamin Newberry, Edward Griswold, Deacon John Moore, and Simon Wolcott, to try again to get the settlement effort going by making new grants.[56]

There was quite a bit of moving about in Windsor in the early 1660s, and it appeared that people were serious about Massaco. John Griffin moved in 1663 to take up his 200 acre grant, Thomas Maskell built at Terry's Plain, and John Moses and a few others took up residence at Weatogue.[57] When the Halfway Covenant controversy hit in 1664 some had even more reason for leaving, as the emigration of Anglicans Jonas Westover and James Eno indicates.[58] Still, the committee felt obliged, in 1666, to issue residency terms by which further grants would be made: lot holders would have to improve their land by building houses and fences within two years, and take up residence within three years, or they would not be able to hold or sell their lots.[59]

That was all that was needed. By 1669 at least half of those who had received grants - some thirteen families - were in Massaco building their houses and creating a "plantation" with every intent to end their status as "an appendix to the towne of Windsor," and become a town of their own. The settlers included disaffected Anglicans, sons of prominent men of Windsor, a now bankrupt Michael Humphrey and a remarkably large representation from Windsor's Welsh community, for whom the Welsh identity was still fairly important. Where people came from in the Old World still had a strong influence upon whom they settled with in the New.[60] Some probably planned to stay long enough to establish ownership, and then profit by a sale; others probably looked forward to a new independence in their fledgling community. Whatever the case, both groups had succeeded by 1669, and the General Court ordered the appointment of John Case as Constable in preparation for the petitioning for town privileges.

By the following May, when the court declared Massaco to be the Town of Simsbury, twenty families had taken up their grants. The bounds of the new town were to run ten miles north from Farmington and ten miles west from Windsor.[61] How the settlers fared in the first few years is not altogether clear, since their early records were lost in a fire in 1680 and had to be reconstructed from memory a few years after that.[62] We know they looked to John Griffin, Simon Wolcott, and Joshua Holcomb for leadership in those years, and organized their town government pretty much on the same model as most New England towns. There were three "townsmen" chosen annually by the town meeting to "order the affairs" of the town. As in most early communities, the "open field" plan seemed to prevail at first, with a large fenced-in field for crops, each inhabitant responsible for a section of fence, and animals roaming "at large" throughout "the commons." (The "commons" was the name for the bulk of the town grant which was still undivided.) The houses in this community, however, seem to have been spread out in at least four different groups: one at Weatogue at the south end of town, one at Hopmeadow along the present main street of Simsbury, one East of the Farmington River nestled along the west side of Talcott Ridge at what is now Terry's Plain, and a fourth at "Scotland" around the bend on the east side of the ridge. John Griffin's "Lordship" was north of the Falls, and Simon Wolcott was clearing considerable land north of what is now the Hoskins Station area. Land distribution was egalitarian at first, and this produced the usual squabbles between conservatives and ambitious young men. Seemingly inconsistent with Puritan preachers' views of the great mission of the colony, the town was lukewarm about establishing a church. From what little record we have, it would appear they asked Samuel Stone of Hartford to preach to them only because they had to.[63]

Relations with the Algonkians continued to be uneasy at best. Townsmen Griffin, Peter Buell and Samuel Wilcoxson managed, in 1671, to get a sachem named Youngcowet, one of those who had bailed out old Manahannoose, to identify what he would consider to be the north bounds of

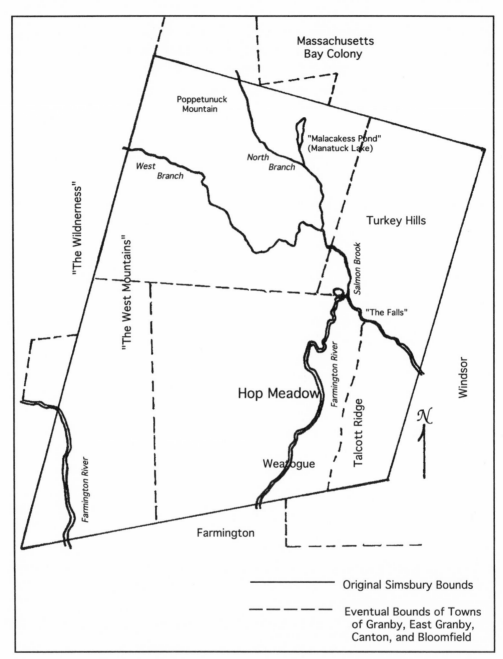

Map 1-3: Colonial Simsbury, as described in Patent of 1686

the town at the upper end of a pond called "Mallakakess," but Youngcowet still insisted that he and six others retained the right to hunt deer anywhere in Massaco for the rest of their lives.[64] Whatever worries the new settlers had about the local natives were soon dwarfed, however, when, in 1675, New England exploded in a war for regional dominance which nearly put an end to the Massaco enterprise altogether.

Metacom, chief of the Wampanoags and known to the English as "King Philip," began leading attacks against English settlements in the summer of that year in an effort to drive the acquisitive and self-centered newcomers from the region forever. His war cry inspired bitter Algonkians all across New England to follow his example, and by August Nipmucks and Agawams were attacking outlying settlements on the western end of the Bay Colony. In October they raided Springfield and burned it to the ground. In response the General Court of Connecticut looked to its newest and outermost settlement and ordered Simsbury settlers to abandon their homes and move to Windsor. Thousands were being killed all across New England as the Algonkians made their last effort to stem the tide that had ruined their world.

When it appeared that Muttawump, the Nipmuck sachem, was headed north, some of the Simsbury settlers began returning to keep up their new homes. Metacom himself suffered a disastrous defeat at the hands of the Mohawks during the winter.[65] Yet as spring of 1676 approached the English realized this war was not a one-man show, and that the Nipmucks and the Narragansetts were determined to wipe out every settlement. Once again the Simsbury settlers left their homes, and this time they were glad they did. In a few weeks' time forty dwelling houses lay in ashes, as well as barns, outbuildings, fences and fields. Simsbury's April town meeting would be held in Windsor that year.[66]

During the summer, the tide of the war turned, first with a victory for the English at Turner's Falls, and then with the death of Metacom in August. The fighting sputtered on until 1678, when a campaign at Casco Bay destroyed the last resistance and New England was finally the domain of the English. The economy, particularly in Massachusetts, lay in ruins, however, and it would be years before it would recover to pre-war levels of prosperity. Not only was there enormous loss of property, wealth and lives on all sides, but the English were henceforth very hesitant about venturing into "the wilderness" to invest time and money that might, at a moment's notice, go up in smoke.[67] The Simsbury settlers were the exception to the rule.

In the spring of 1677 ten families returned even before the war had ended. At least fifty more families expressed interest, and a firm of Thomas Barber, John Moses, John Terry and Ephraim Howard agreed to erect a grist mill. Certainly this indicates a fair degree of courage. Even though Connecticut's natives had not, on the surface, been hostile to the English during the war, the settlement had been burned to the ground and no one knew who did it. The other explanation for this eagerness to return to Simsbury is purely economic. Cleared meadow land was running thin in Connecticut and Windsor's population had more than doubled between 1650 and 1677. In 1680 the General Court was writing to the Committee for Trade and Foreign Plantations in England that "Most land that is fit for planting is taken up. What remains must be subdued, and gained out of the fire as it were by hard blows and for small recompense."[68] Thus, Simsbury's meadows may have been the only easy land in sight for those not interested in dealing out a lot of "hard blows," although as things turned out, living there was hardly an easy matter. The town begged the legislature for tax relief, and for special orders to require those who had been given grants to move and to keep up their part of the common fence and build their "mansion house" immediately.[69] Probably this terminology was to distinguish a permanent dwelling in which settlers would invest considerable effort from a "cellar house" which could be quickly dug out of a bank by a settler intending to make a show of improvement, but in actuality planning an abode for his livestock in winter months while he sat comfortably before his parents' fire in Windsor. Most of the early "mansion houses" turned out to be crude huts at most.[70]

The settlers began to trickle in, but it was apparent that there was still concern about the "savages." Many of the Massaco had left the area, but a few remained, and it was clear quite a few Poquonocks still simply did not understand the permanence of the sale that had been made supposedly on their behalf back in 1661 (100 square miles for two acres, a coat and some old beads). Enter Major John Talcott of Hartford, who, as Treasurer and leader of the war effort, had become one of the most prominent men of the colony. In 1680 Talcott invited Aups, Massacup, Cogunosset, Totoe, Nesechegan, Seakets, Mamantoes, the wives of the last three and two other women (finally the Europeans were beginning to understand), and half a dozen unnamed others for a parlay lasting several days. He fed them "meet and bread, beer and sider" and proceeded "to drive on the bargain" on behalf of the nervous proprietors of Simsbury. Several coats and bushels of corn later (and obviously after a fair amount of liquid refreshment), Talcott managed to make it clear that old Massaco was now English (except, of course for Mamantoes' two acres), and, while Native hunting and fishing would be permitted, the "Indians" would make no more noise about how long the English were staying or how many were coming.[71] Two years later, in a masterful stroke of municipal finance, the town awarded Major Talcott 300 acres and immediately went back to work trying to populate the rest of the 64,000 he had paid for with his own supply of corn and coats. Furthermore, they bestowed upon Talcott the dubious honor of being the final arbiter in any future disputes they themselves might have.[72]

Whether he had enough "beer and sider" for that was questionable. The bickering about building fences, paying taxes, dividing lands, and holding on to unimproved and unsettled grants continued throughout the 1680s. Slowly and haltingly, the settlement took shape. And actually it was not one settlement, but several, one being boldly planted in meadows five miles to the north of the first Massaco farms. There, at "Sammon Brooke," the vanguard of the culture of change, summoned by their own inner pursuit of prosperity and independence, had begun a new community. Leaving behind them the quarrels over infant baptism, the crowded lots of Windsor and petty animosities between groups from different parts of England and Wales, and yet carrying with them the echoes of all of that past and more, seven families agreed in March, 1679/80, to be a buffer against "the wilderness" and carve out farms in the middle of ground the Poquonocks still thought was free for hunting. They were Puritans, and yet not thoroughly pious ones, they were traders, and yet not worldly businessmen, and they were farmers, and yet they had already learned they would not make their living by farming alone. They had crossed Talcott Ridge as part of the planting of Massaco, now Simsbury, but they were already going well beyond that as they took up their bit of ground in "the outlands."

59

Chapter II
At a place commonly called
Sammon Brooke

Chronology

Europe	America	Granby
		c.1667 "Salmon Brook" first explored
	1675-6 King Philip's War	
	1677 Settlers return to Simsbury from Windsor and Hartford	
		1679 General Court Committee says 13 will live at Salmon Brook
		1680 Settlers begin moving to Salmon Brook
		1683 House lots granted near Salmon Brook meadows
1684 James II crowned King of England		
	1687 Charter Oak incident	1686 Common field system ordered for Salmon Brook
1688 Glorious Revolution - James II abdicates. William and Mary crowned		1688 Town meeting orders a pound set up in Salmon Brook
1689 War of the League of Augsburg begins	1689 "King William's War" begins	1688/9 Exchange of lots as Salmon Brook settlers return to Hopmeadow
	1690 French attack northern N.Y. and New England, English seize Port Royal, failed expedition against Canada	1691 Settlers begin to return to Salmon Brook
	1692 Salem Witch trials	
1697 Treaty of Ryswick ends war	1697 Haverhill, Mass. attacked	
1700 Charles II of Spain dies, Grand Alliance formed		1700/01 Minister's House fortified in Hopmeadow, Fencing Agreements in Salmon Brook
1702 War of the Spanish Succession		
	1703 "Queen Anne'sWar" begins	1703/4 School Dame ordered for Salmon Brook
	1704 Deerfield, Mass. attacked	
		1707 Daniel Hayes kidnapped
	1708 Saybrook Platform	1709 Eleven families living at Salmon Brook
1713 Treaty of Utrecht ends war		1713 Daniel Hayes returns

No sooner had the second effort to establish a permanent town of Simsbury begun in 1677 after King Philip's War, than the seeds of a separate community at Salmon Brook were also planted. Over the next three decades, between the arrival of the first two families in the spring of 1680 and the Peace of Utrecht that ended Queen Anne's War in 1713, the new residents of Salmon Brook struggled to build their farms, forming a common bond as together they faced the challenges of wartime in a country exposed to all sorts of danger on the edge of the Connecticut colony's domain. By the end of this initial period of "wilderness" living, Salmon Brook had its own pound for stray animals, its own school teacher and some officers appointed specifically for that section of town. All this was institutional confirmation that the "place commonly called Sammon brooke," as the land records so often read, was far more than just a place.

Old World traditions and conflicts as well as recent developments in the New World continued to exercise their influence as the new community came into being on the edge of New England. While the individualistic forces of the new American civilization were at the root of the establishment of this little enclave, other factors helped to promote a kind of community spirit like that which New England's founders had hoped for when they first arrived in the 1630s. They were an adventurous and rugged group of people from the start, willing to accept exposure to the dangers of wilderness living and the possibility of attacks on the English frontier for the privilege of owning land and of being out on their own. But they were united in these characteristics, and the hardships they faced bonded them together. They also shared some ethnic and economic backgrounds, as well as some institutional needs as a somewhat isolated settlement. All of this began to shape their identity as a group apart from the mainstream of Simsbury society and as a group that pulled together. Salmon Brook was far from being a town of its own in 1713, but its destiny as an independent community was clear.

Probing the Wilderness

The records we have left to us do not clearly indicate when it was that Connecticut colony explorers first set foot on Granby soil. John Griffin probably did his share of wandering around to investigate the pines as he worked his business in the 1640s and 1650s. But until 1667, there is no mention at all of any particular region north of those meadows at the bend of the Farmington River where Thomas Ford, John Cook and Simon Wolcott first staked out their claims. As Wolcott, Matthew Allyn, Daniel Clarke,

61

Benjamin Newberry and others, in the name of the General Court, were parceling out land to ambitious young Windsor men in the 1660s, Salmon Brook remained the domain of Algonkian hunters and fishermen, who assuredly were not interested in showing off their world to land-hungry Europeans.[1]

In the spring of 1667, though, the area that was to become Granby was officially recognized as fit for settlement. Along with a list of men who were granted land at Weatogue and Hopmeadow, the General Court's committee, then led by Benjamin Newberry of Windsor, recorded this announcement: "Also y^t the proprietors Below Joshua Holcombs Lot wer to have a suitable alowance as an addition at a place called Sammon Brooke which was deemed to be as good Meadow as that which was Called Hazell meadow."[2] Hazel Meadow is located between Weatogue and Hopmeadow, but apparently the committee thought it was a good idea to encourage at least some settlers to take up lands on the northern edge of Massaco. Whom they meant by "the proprietors below Joshua Holcomb" is not clear; nor is it clear how far north on Salmon Brook the settlers would find these attractive meadow lands.

It is difficult to picture what Granby looked like to those first explorers searching for spots of cleared land to farm among the forests. Houses, offices and places of business cover the landscape today. In constructing roads and highways, hills have been graded, streams bridged and gullies filled. In the late 18th and early 19th centuries, lumbermen took nearly all of the original timber, so that today almost all of our woodland is second-growth. After the hills were clear-cut, erosion significantly altered the topography, and flash floods changed the course of brooks. Further complicating our attempts to visualize the original Granby, the Simsbury town records burned around 1680, and had to be pieced together from personal records and memory during the next decade.[3]

Nevertheless, there are enough hints scattered through the town meeting minutes and surveys of early land grants to give us some sense of the Granby that the Algonkians knew.[4] The first European explorers of the 1660s probably approached the future Granby trudging north along Salmon Brook from where it emptied into the Farmington River. Another possibility was to follow an Indian trail north along what is now Route 10-202. By either route, the explorer found himself first in some open land, either natural meadow or ground previously cleared by the Algonkians. Later records would refer to this area, just south of the Simsbury Airport, as "the Lower Meadows," not because it was at the low end of the Salmon Brook settlement, but because it was farther "down" the Farmington from Hop Meadow. It may have been these meadows that the Newberry committee had in mind when they were comparing land to Hazel Meadow, although subsequent records suggest that the term "Salmon Brook" referred to a region farther north, and probably originally focused on the junction of the brook's two branches.

North of the Lower Meadows, an expansive pine forest stretched from the area of today's Simsbury Airport north and west toward Barn Door Hills. Here, no doubt, John Griffin, and others following his lead, had done considerable work "boxing" the trees and collecting sap, or taking down the yellow pines to make candlewood. ("Boxing" a tree meant to chop a notch in the trunk so that sap would run out into a bucket.) Even though the tar makers had been at it for two decades, there were probably many towering trees still growing quite contentedly as they had for hundreds of years in the sandy soil above the brook land to the east.

To the east across the brook from this pine plain, lay the one-and-one-half-square-mile parcel that would become "Griffin's Lordship" granted to John Griffin in recognition of his work in wresting all of Massaco from the natives and in beginning a profitable manufacturing operation in those parts. At the north end of the plain, where Floydville Road currently crosses Salmon Brook, the brook is more shallow and the ground around it more swampy. The best path would be to the west, through the pines and around a small hill just north of the intersection of Canton Road and Route 10. By going that route, the explorer avoided "Raven's Swamp" near the brook, and came down to the West Branch of the Salmon Brook, where it passed through about 75 acres of open land. Today the managers of McLean's Game Refuge keep the land south of the brook open, and Salmon Brook Park, a town recreation area, occupies the area north of the Brook. It must have been a very tempting sight to land-hungry farmers, who did not relish clearing the huge pines and hardwoods that surrounded the meadows. No doubt Algonkians had, in the not-to-distant past, used these meadows, or cleared them themselves for crop land.

Following the West Branch, the explorer then came to a large expanse

63

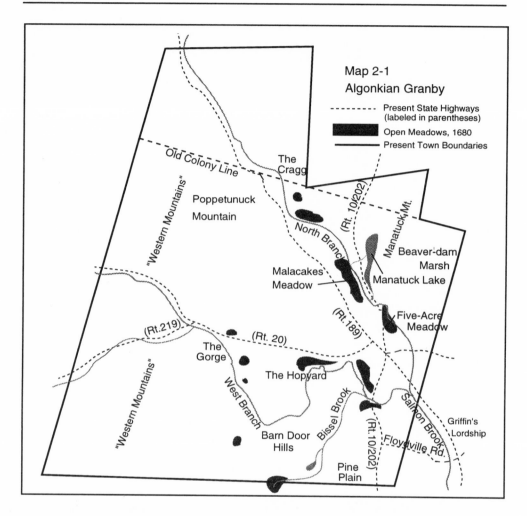

Map 2-1
Algonkian Granby

- - - - - Present State Highways (labeled in parentheses)
▰ Open Meadows, 1680
── Present Town Boundaries

of grassland they called the "hopyard," where the brook makes a sharp turn as it flows north from Barn Door Hills. Here the ambitious settler, temporarily setting aside his thoughts of how far he was from "civilization," could envision his livestock grazing happily, separated from his crops by a good strong fence. The more ambitious and bold explorer might travel farther up the West Branch and find numerous other smaller patches of open land among the marshes and former Indian campsites beyond Bushy Hill on the edge of the "Western Mountains." There is not much evidence they explored beyond the gorge in West Granby in the 17th century - the thought of exploiting timber resources or rounding up livestock in this rough terrain was probably then well beyond the vision of even the most rugged frontiersmen. The hills stretched west into what must have seemed an endless forest. Even officials from the colony government would not bother to venture into them to mark something so fundamental as the town's boundary until the next century. Simsbury was simply bounded on the west by "the wilderness."

Back at the "Salmon Brook Meadows," where the West Branch crosses under Route 10, our explorer could also wander north along the Indian trail that headed toward Agawam country and beyond. To the east were "Salmon Brook Woods," where the North Branch flowed through hardwood stands of maple, hickory, beech, and oak, many of whose girths were doubtless well beyond that of our prized "Granby Oak" on Day Street. After proceeding north about a mile, the trail dipped and crossed the North Branch. There to the east was another forty acres of meadow, and to the northwest yet another sixty, just west of Manatuck Mountain. The natives called the meadow to the northwest Mallacakes, and the pond between them and the mountain, now Manatuck Lake, Mallacakes Pond.

Manatuck (from the Algonkian, meaning "to see a long way off") was probably the best spot for the explorer to see how far he had come, so he would scramble up to one of its lookout points to see what else the area had to offer. To the east he could see a huge marsh created by a deteriorating but still magnificent beaver dam at its southern end. To the north stretched another pine forest, and to the west rolling hills soon became the imposing mountain the natives called Poppetunuck, beyond which lay "the wilderness." He may have caught a glimpse of a few more meadows below Poppetunuck where the North Branch wandered up to the "Cragg" in North Granby.

It was an attractive land in many respects. For the Algonkians it was a pleasant country brimming with fish and game. Deer were abundant, and the river and brooks were full of salmon and shad. But the English and Welsh settlers from Windsor had other uses in mind for this land. They did not much like salmon and shad, although they seem to have restricted dams that got in the way of these fish, and large numbers of them were taken throughout the early 18th century (perhaps for trade or fertilizer).[5] There were already patches of cleared land that could be converted to crop land without too much trouble. In fact, some 160 acres of this meadow land lay in three sizable and closely related chunks that could be divided among a small number of farmers who could work closely together and create a common fence to keep livestock and wildlife out. What ground did not get plowed right away would provide grass for winter feed, as would the open marshes. Marshes also offered the possibility of bog iron. There were large stands of pine, for those wishing to emulate John Griffin's successful enterprise. Brooks and ponds offered plenty of fresh water and numerous sites for future mills, if adventurous men with the proper skills could be found to take up residence.[6]

From the perspective of the colony's magistrates viewing these lands in the late 1660s, and from the perspective of the leading proprietors of the new town, these attractions were important, for they were eager for people to live at Salmon Brook. This may seem surprising, since the Puritan model for town development stressed communal living and discouraged towns from allowing settlers to spread out all over the countryside. However, the experience of King Philip's War would soon prove the necessity for a strategic buffer settlement north of Simsbury's main village. Perhaps this area could be populated by young people whose estates might not insure them large grants in Hop Meadow, but who could be induced to serve as an "early warning system" for the rest of the town with sizable grants on the northern frontier. Perhaps some veterans of the recent war would be among them.

Even before these strategic concerns would be felt, the powers that be were always interested in extending the colony's *actual* domain and making clear to the local Indians that the English were the *owners* of the territory. Furthermore, it made good sense to ensure that everyone prospered. Young people who had no land on which to build a farmstead could produce little, and it was well known that there were vast resources just going to waste as settlements clung to the river. At the very least, the magistrates knew that poor farmers paid few taxes. Thus, at the risk of fragmenting a town that was barely begun, Benjamin Newberry and his committee recommended that meadows at Salmon Brook be taken up as well. It is not clear, though, whether they actually intended people to build houses there, or simply to work the fields.

Nathaniel Bissell seems to have been the first to make claims on lands within the bounds of present-day Granby. On October 11, 1669, the Newberry committee noted, "Also we being certified y[t] goodman Bissel [meaning John Bissel of Windsor] had formerly expended money about Masaco and that he hath given it to his son Nathaniell we granted the sd Nathanell Twenty Accres of Land where it may not be exceeding prejuditiall to the plantation - as namely by the river or at Samon Brooke." On May 25 of the following spring, the committee designated Bissell's 20 acres to be a marshy field along the present Granby town line at the junctions of Simsbury and Barn Door Hills Roads.[7] The brook that flowed through this land would later be called Bissell's Brook. Apparently, he also received another grant, at some point, at the "hopyard," which is south of Route 20 just west of the end of Salmon Brook Park.[8] However, Bissell was not among those listed as residents of Massaco in 1669, and although he maintained his proprietary interest in the town until his death, it is doubtful he ever seriously considered moving across Talcott Ridge, let alone into Simsbury's outer lands.[9]

A few other men received grants at Salmon Brook in this early period before King Philip's War, and the records suggest that there were, indeed, considerable efforts being made to exploit the lands beyond the Hop Meadow settlements for winter feed for livestock. There may have been a general division of outlands in April, 1672, but apparently that was rescinded in 1681.[10] At a Town Meeting on January 16, 1673, a Thomas Rowell was granted 12 acres near Bissell's grant and John Slater, the town's clerk and surveyor, who was probably one of the few to have viewed the lands at Salmon Brook, received a choice 14 acres of meadow south of the West Branch where Route 10 presently crosses the brook.[10] John Drake also received 20 acres on Bissell Brook, but farther up the brook from Slater's Meadow.[12] An agreement among eight men, including Slater and Drake, to drain Great Pond in Simsbury the following year "for the land thereon," helps to clarify what was happening. These were ambitious husbandmen searching throughout the vast lands of Simsbury to lay claim to parcels that would produce immediate sustenance for the livestock they hoped to raise for profit.[13] Even John Griffin took up the quest for grass land, asking for a grant of 20-30 acres on the west branch north of Barn Door Hills.[14]

Grass, however, not house sites, was all these men sought, for King Philip's War came and went, and the settlers of Simsbury went and came, but by 1677 no one had yet come to live at Salmon Brook. John Griffin had his house north of present-day Tariffville, and Slater and Drake lived at Hop Meadow (although Drake returned to Windsor before moving to Hop Meadow permanently). Nathaniel Bissell, in fact, moved to East Windsor. In November of 1677, John Griffin joined a Nicholas Gossard, originally from Windsor, to take up 60 acres in partnership along Salmon Brook north of Barn Door Hills, but Gossard first lived at Weatogue when he moved across Talcott Ridge, and seems to have built nothing but a "cellar" on this lot at Salmon Brook. One wonders, actually, how much mowing they did in those years when Simsbury inhabitants were complaining that poor harvests and lack of commitment on the part of some land grantees made life so difficult they could not be expected to pay colony taxes.[15]

Getting people to come to live even in Hop Meadow was a serious problem in the late 1670s. The plan had always been to farm the huge Hop Meadow in one large plot, divided into strips, but surrounded by a single fence, of which each husbandman would build his portion. But if many of those who were to have parcels of the meadow did not soon come to Simsbury, the fence would not get built, nor would there be enough people to combat the "garden pests" that would not be deterred by fences. Thus, all the plowing and planting would come to nothing, as livestock and various rodents grazed freely among the crops. A petition in the fall of 1679, asking the General Court to take action against the proprietors who had not yet taken up their grants, reflected the desperation the present inhabitants were feeling. The fact that some of the members of the General Court's own distribution committee, including Benjamin Newberry himself, were among those summoned to answer for their lack of commitment to the new settlement shows just how difficult it was going to be to entice people to move.[16]

The response of the Court to the petition represented a realization that, if the Connecticut Colony was going to widen its domain through the securing of new settlements, it would have to loosen its adherence to communal settlement patterns. Outside the Connecticut valley attractive meadows were simply not expansive enough to accommodate a large number of families clustered in one place.[17] The lots would be too small to attract people to an exposed region. Even Hop Meadow, the largest known meadow available, would serve for no more than twenty families. This would not do, as a town meeting the following summer noted. A greater "peopleing of the Towne" was necessary "so that the towne might be strengthened the better to with stand the assault of an enemy in time of danger [and] so that those lands might be made improvement of for helping to bear publique charges."[18] Thus, a committee led by Major John Talcott, and including Newberry, recommended, in October, 1679, that seventy families be recruited for the populating of Simsbury, and that eleven be settled in the Lower Meadows, fifteen at Hop Meadow, seventeen at Weatogue, five at Terry's Plain, nine east of the ridge, and thirteen at Salmon Brook.[19] They even went so far as to declare that the grantees must be living on their allotments and must have built a "mansion house" within six months, or face a fine of 40 shillings and loss of their grant.

At a town meeting in January, 1679/80, the inhabitants themselves placed further conditions on the settlers at Salmon Brook:

> The Articles or obligations upon ye Towne of Simsbury which do dispose of lands upon Salmon Brooke which were formerly agreed to be Divided among the Inhabitants are as followeth: (viz) they have agreed to dispose of it which is about 160 acres into lots: and those that are to setle upon them (excepting a lot for the minister and a lot for Michall Humphrey) they be to setle upon their lots: by their personal living upon their lands with their Familyes: by the last of may come twelve moneth. the time thus granted will be expired in ye year of our Lord one thousand six hundred and eighty. They be to continue in possession there off by living on them Seven yeares and they are obliged to make improvement by Fenceing and breaking up of ye lands and personally live in them seven yeares before they shall have liberty to make alienation of any of ye Said lands: unless they may be taken off by some remarkable providence of God:

The town also agreed to levy a fine of £5 on any who left their lots earlier than the seven years and ordered that they shall "run their ranges of Fence together where it is most Feizable so that they may not damnify one another: and those two sequestered lotts do their proportion where they lye in common with the rest:" The new residents at Salmon Brook would also be free from paying the town rate for a year.[20]

In March, Talcott's Committee named the men who were to bring their families to Salmon Brook: Richard Segar, Nathaniel Holcomb, Michael Humphrey, Samuel Wilson, Daniel Addams, Josiah Owen, Andrew More, Nicholas Gossard, Elizur Hill, George Sanders, and Nathaniel Bissell.[21] Some of these, Gossard and Humphrey, for example, and possibly Nathaniel Holcomb, were already living in Simsbury, but most were Windsor residents, and some had just recently expressed interest in Simsbury lands.

When it came time to sort out the lots at the end of March, 1680, Richard Segar, Nicholas Gossard, Elizur Hill, George Sanders, and Nathaniel Bissell had apparently declined the offer of land at Salmon Brook. Replacing them were only Nathan Gillet and Josiah Ellsworth, both of Windsor. Each family was to get twenty acres of Salmon Brook meadow land.[22] What was causing the shifting of interest is not clear. Perhaps the assignments to different sections of Simsbury had been done by lot, and many of those chosen for Salmon Brook had been hoping either for a more southerly and less exposed houselot, or for a different group of neighbors. Perhaps the three days between Major Talcott's "bargain" with the Algonkians (see Chapter I) and the surveying of lots was not enough time to convince the prospective settlers that the Algonkians would respect English property rights. Whatever the case, it is clear that adjustments had to be made if a settlement at Salmon Brook was to become a reality.

Moving In - and Out

Beginning a settlement at Salmon Brook in the 1680s amounted to moving into an invasion route on the eve of a war. King Philip's War discouraged settlement efforts throughout New England. The need for renegotiating with the Algonkians over Massaco lands, and a general lack of confidence in the future among a war-weary population, would mean the farmers had to be of the bold sort. Although Metacom's allies had been defeated, there were other enemies threatening from the North. Still, children in the old settlements along the Connecticut River were becoming adults and beginning their own families, and meadow land was virtually unavailable.

Yet, while there may have been some enthusiasm in March of 1680 for settling at Salmon Brook, that did not translate into an actual settlement for some time. In the summer, the town recalled how seven men had agreed to bring their families to Salmon Brook, but

> these failing except two persons the Towne being met Ano one thousand six Hundred & eighty y[t] summer and not being willing to take advantage of their neglect hath granted three months further liberty they yet failing the Towne being

mett in ye year 1680'y: to agitate Concerning the breach of those articles have granted further liberty till the middle of April 1681 in case they accept and by Subscribing hereunto in case they do not fulfill their articles they that so neglect Shall forfeit and pay to the Towne for their use teen pounds...[23]

This was a pretty stiff fine, and indicates a fair amount of impatience. In fairness to the timid grantees, however, we should note that it was at this same time that the town enacted a bounty of eight shillings per head on wolves.[24] If the predator population was becoming an overwhelming problem and relations with the Algonkians remained uneasy, it is not surprising that there would be some hesitancy about building abodes in the outlands.

Who those first two intrepid families were is not altogether clear, but there can be little doubt that Nathaniel and Mary Holcomb was one. In fact, Holcomb family tradition has it that they first settled at Salmon Brook in 1677.[25] Unfortunately, there are no other records that can either confirm or deny that. Nathaniel was born in the Poquonock section of Windsor in 1648 to Thomas and Elizabeth Holcomb, a fairly prosperous farming couple, Thomas having been among those who had come to New England on *The Mary and John* with John Warham in 1630. Thomas died in 1657, and Elizabeth remarried to James Eno the next year. Nathaniel's wife Mary, originally Mary Bliss, was born in 1651, and, although her father's family was among the first group to come to Hartford, she was living in Springfield when she married Nathaniel in 1670. It is not clear if the couple lived in Springfield for long, but by 1675 they were back in Windsor with their two children, Nathaniel (b.1673) and Mary (b. 1675). Nathaniel Sr. is not listed among those who moved to Simsbury immediately following the war, but his older brother Joshua is, and his mother and step-father did move to "Scotland," the section of Simsbury east of the ridge, in 1679. It is possible they did live with the Enos briefly, while renting land at Salmon Brook from someone such as John Slater. Or it may have been that they even began building a homestead at Salmon Brook and that the record of Nathaniel's 1677, '78 or '79 grant was among those burned; no one bothered to record it again since he received new grants, possibly for the same land, as a result of the land divisions in 1680. He continued to pay taxes in Windsor through 1686, but only because he owned three acres of upland there, not because he was a resident.[26] Certainly the

71

couple was well established with their four children in Simsbury by 1681, for Nathaniel was elected town constable in December of that year.[27]

The other family that actually fulfilled its mission of settling on its lands at Salmon Brook in 1680 was either Josiah and Mary Owen, or Daniel and Mary Addams. These two families, along with Michael Humphrey (who continued to live in Weatogue) and Nathaniel Holcomb, were the only two of the original seven to hold onto their meadow grants at Salmon Brook past 1683, and so it is reasonable to assume that one of them must have been the other family that joined Nathaniel and Mary Holcomb in 1680. The Owens, both children of Welsh immigrants to Windsor, had been married in 1674, and had brought three children with them to Simsbury in 1679. Like Nathaniel Holcomb, Josiah Owen was elected to a minor town office in late 1681, indicating he had firmly established his residency by that time. His father, John, had been one of the earliest grantees of lands in 1660, but had not returned after King Philip's War. Mary Owen's father, John Osborn, had not been involved in the settlement of Simsbury, and continued to live in Windsor.[28]

Daniel Addams, son of a glover who had come, possibly, from East Anglia, migrated from Watertown, Massachusetts, having moved to Windsor before King Philip's War, although he served in a Massachusetts unit with his brother Samuel during the war. He married Mary Phelps, of West Country parentage and Windsor birth, in 1675, and moved to Simsbury with his brother Samuel sometime before 1682. Probably he settled in the lower meadows, even though he received grants of meadow land at Salmon Brook.[29] In all likelihood, Daniel and Mary continued to live at the Lower Meadows.

It may be unnecessary to determine the first European settlers, however, since they hardly built a permanent community. 19th Century historian Noah Phelps, who may have had access to sources long since disappeared, says that, owing to "Indian difficulties," the 1680 grantees were ordered to build their houses at Westover's plain, just above the Lower Meadows. In fact, he claims that none of the first grantees occupied their property continuously for the conditional seven years, that there were frequent alarms given when "strange Indians" were sighted, and that, exposed as Salmon Brook was to "Indian depredations," the "settlement was often deserted."[30] The Owens, the Holcombs and the Addamses all had houselot grants in the Lower Meadows, and may have lived there between 1680 and 1683, going to Salmon Brook only to take hay from their meadow allotments.[31] Daniel Addams, in fact, seems to have stayed on in the Lower Meadows.[32]

The records indicate that lots continued to change hands as the town struggled to find settlers willing to risk their lives on the northern edge of Simsbury. In April, 1682, shoemaker George Sanders, who had, in March of 1680, declined land at Salmon Brook and settled instead in the Lower Meadows, was given Nathan Gillet's 20 acre allotment that the town had reclaimed. Also Thomas Griffin received the allotments "that was Brother Williams" on Salmon Brook, as well as land that once had been set out to Samuel Wilson, who had given up his grants in 1680.[33] There is no record of "Brother Williams" receiving a grant in the first place; the town seems to have given up on him before anyone had a chance to record it.

It was certainly the exposed location, and not the quality of the land, which accounted for the problems getting people to live at Salmon Brook. The meadows were limited everywhere in Simsbury, and the town made sure some name was attached at all times to every little parcel of them. That those at Salmon Brook are named in the record books shows they were considered good land. Major Talcott himself confirmed how precious good meadow was in Simsbury. When the selectmen showed him around in the spring of 1682, hoping he would be content selecting a small piece of property in exchange for his services in bargaining with the Algonkians, it became clear just how rare a good piece of meadow had become. After his tour he remarked that he could

find no one place, where anything considerable can be taken up: the most of that which some call meadow, is full of small Brush and Vines through which y^r is no passing; or full of Trees, small and great, which will be very cheargeable subduing: and ye place where the best land of that sort is, there is no accommodation of upland to it saveing onely mighty Tall mountayens and Rockes, and the way bade to it, and a great way to all of it, and will be dismally obscure and solatary to any that shall live upon it and very hard comeing at the Market, not onely because of ye remoteness, but badness of the passage and the Society or Neighborhood will be very thin, all which be discoraging.[34]

Talcott, of course, had already established himself as a talented negotiator, and so we may take his bleak picture to be somewhat overdrawn. Nevertheless, aside from what had been already granted, nothing was available that appeared to him to be convenient. The Salmon Brook meadows had been granted, but not yet settled. If grantees were slow to move to lands at Salmon Brook that had been already set aside, it was most likely because of the frighteningly "solatary" existence offered there.

By May, 1683, though, the momentum for establishing a group at Salmon Brook was picking up. The town meeting declared that there would be a row of house and pasture lots granted to those who would build and live on them within a year, and that this row would extend north from the brook (where the West Branch presently crosses under Salmon Brook Street), to the "spruce swamp" (which was across from the present entrance to Salmon Brook Park) on the east side of the road (See Map 2-2). The northernmost lot is presently the site of the Salmon Brook Historical Society.[35] The southernmost lot was reserved as one of many lots of land in town used to attract a qualified minister, and the others were given to Nathaniel Holcomb, John Slater, Nicholas Gossard, Daniel Addams, Samuel Addams, Josiah Owen, Richard Segar and Michael Humphrey's son Samuel.[36] All of these men were already living in Simsbury, and Holcomb and Owen may have already built houses on these lots. Across the road was the first group of meadow lots carved out in the 1680 division. All but Segar were already working those meadows, and now were looking for a home base closer to their new land.

It is puzzling, though, that Gossard, Slater and Daniel Addams would ask for a house lot at Salmon Brook. Gossard and Slater already had homesteads and other lots of land in Weatogue and Hop Meadow which they did not give up at this time, and their children were hardly old enough to want house lots of their own.[37] Addams, as already mentioned, had a house in the Lower Meadows. Furthermore, there were actually other families interested in Salmon Brook. At the same town meeting, Josiah Owen's brother Joseph, John Pettibone Jr. and Samuel Willcockson Jr. all received 20 acre grants at Salmon Brook "where they could find it," John and Samuel to "take up said land or their fathers for them."[38] All this suggests that some Simsbury families were actually considering having two houses even though the need for homes for their children was not immediate. The conditions for keeping Salmon

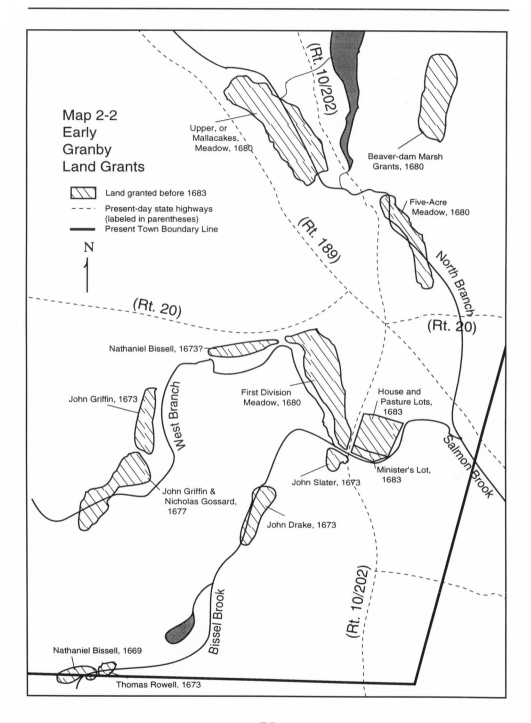

Map 2-2
Early
Granby
Land Grants

Land granted before 1683
Present-day state highways (labeled in parentheses)
Present Town Boundary Line

N

(Rt. 20)

(Rt. 189)

(Rt. 10/202)

Upper, or Mallacakes, Meadow, 1680

Beaver-dam Marsh Grants, 1680

Five-Acre Meadow, 1680

North Branch

(Rt. 20)

Nathaniel Bissell, 1673?

John Griffin, 1673

West Branch

First Division Meadow, 1680

House and Pasture Lots, 1683

Salmon Brook

John Griffin & Nicholas Gossard, 1677

John Slater, 1673

Minister's Lot, 1683

John Drake, 1673

Bissel Brook

(Rt. 10/202)

Nathaniel Bissell, 1669

Thomas Rowell, 1673

Brook allotments did not stipulate how much of each of the seven years the grantee and his family needed to be in residence. Therefore, if they could build a domicile at Salmon Brook, and keep one up elsewhere as well, the extra labor could be considered a worthwhile investment in good land upon which their or their children's prosperity would one day depend.[39]

Of course, we need to realize that these were people for whom "home" had a somewhat different meaning than it does for us today, or, for that matter, than it had once had for their European ancestors. If Lucius Barber's description of the houses of this period as rough dwellings, a single story with a thatched roof, no floor or windows and daubed with clay, is accurate, then it becomes a bit clearer how they might not see two houses as a significant commitment.[40] Cellar houses were also common in colonial America, and may have been built at Salmon Brook. These were essentially square pits six or seven feet deep, lined with timber, and covered with bark or green sod.[41] It might be said that their "homes" should be called "shelters," and were closer to Algonkian wigwams than English "mansion houses."

Thus, in 1683, the town was making every effort to get a group settled and working the meadows in its northwest quadrant. Still, however, actual settlement proceeded haltingly. It is difficult to tell exactly when each family moved in to secure its grant, for the actual surveys of both the meadows first parceled out in 1680 and the more recent tier of houselots of 1683 were not recorded until 1687. Town meeting minutes are helpful, though. First, they show that the town was strict about adherence to deadlines and time commitments. At a meeting on December 31, 1685, the town declared that all grants had to be taken up within six months of the grant, or be lost. They then took up the issue of whether to give allotments to those who had already lost a grant because of failure to move in or improve the land. John Slater, himself, was forced to "resign up" his house lot at Salmon Brook, and it was summarily given to Joseph Owen. Two months later, Daniel Addams lost his site for a second home to Richard Segar, who already must have had to give up the grant he received in 1683; and John Griffin's son Thomas was given the lot originally set out to Samuel Humphrey. The next fall Samuel Willcockson Jr. picked up the lot Joseph Owen had taken over from John Slater.[42]

An entry in the records of the colony's General Court for the May session of 1686 helps to firm up our understanding of who was living at

Salmon Brook. The record lists a number of Simsbury men "propowned for freemen," indicating that, having title to at least £10 of real estate and the recommendation of their selectmen, they were now eligible to vote in colony elections. The list read, "Daniel Addams, John Moses, John Saxton, John Humphrey, Arthur Henbury, John Case jr., Samll Adams, Nath. Holcomb, Nicho. Gossard, Josia Owen, Joseph Owen, John Griffin, Thomas Griffin, Richard Segar."[43] Interestingly, Daniel Addams through John Case Jr. were all "Lower Meadow" occupants, and the remaining names, with the exception of John Griffin, were Salmon Brook occupants.

Sorting out the comings and goings is further complicated, however, by the fact that some farmers were able to make acceptable improvements on their Salmon Brook meadow lands, but did not live among the house lots. Furthermore, the town had to find other house lots for additional families, who, by 1686, were ready to move to Salmon Brook. John Matson, a single man of 28, for example, received a grant in 1686. Nathaniel Holcomb, Nicholas Gossard, Josiah Owen and John Slater wanted to reserve land for their oldest sons, who were not yet of age.[44] The following table shows, as best as can be determined, when individuals moved permanently to Salmon Brook.

Table 2-1: Family Heads Building at Salmon Brook, 1680-1688	
1683 or earlier	Nathaniel Holcomb, Josiah Owen, Samuel Addams, Nicholas Gossard (note: all had houses or house lots elsewhere as well)
1685	Richard Segar, Thomas Griffin, Joseph Owen
1686	John Matson
1688	Samuel Willcockson Jr.

Others may have made brief attempts to settle, but they gave up and went elsewhere. For example, a Samuel Brookes received a 3-acre houselot in 1687, and some meadow to go with it, but had to give it up the next spring.[45]

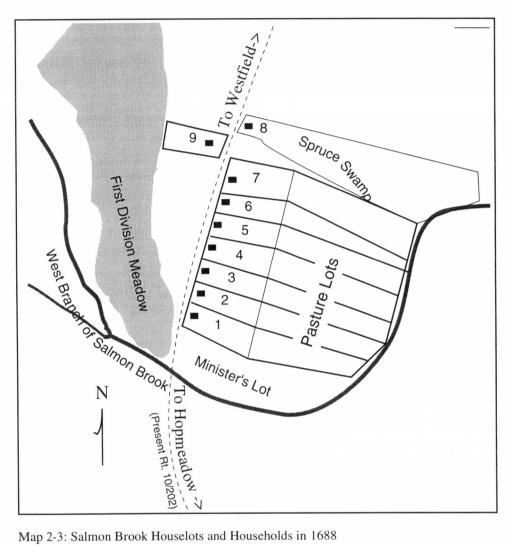

Map 2-3: Salmon Brook Houselots and Households in 1688
(ages shown in parentheses)

1.Nathaniel (40) and Mary Bliss (37) Holcomb and 7 children (ages 15, 13, 10, 8, 6, 4, 1)
2.Samuel Willcockson Jr. (22) bachelor
3.Samuel (33) and Elizabeth Hill Addams (?) and one daughter (1)
4.Nicholas (52) and Elizabeth Gillet (49) Gossard and 3 children (15, 11, 6)
5.Richard (36) and Abigail Griffin (28) Segar and 2 children (4, 2)
6.Thomas Griffin (30) bachelor
7.Josiah (37) and Mary Osborn (33) Owen and 7 children (13, 10, 8, 7, 6, 4, 2)
8.Joseph (28) and Elizabeth Osborn (?) Owen and 3 children (5, 3, 0)
9.John Matson (24) bachelor

Map 2-3 shows the probable location of the homesteads of those families living at Salmon Brook by 1688.[46]

The origins of these people were varied. Some, like the Gossards, Samuel Willcockson Jr., Elizabeth Hill, Abigail Griffin and Thomas Griffin, were already living in Simsbury when settlement at Salmon Brook began. Others moved into town to stay with family or on the land of others, such as the Owens and the Holcombs. Samuel Addams and John Matson came from the Boston area, and Richard Segar, prior to a brief residence in Windsor, had come from Hartford.

We should take note of the significant variety of households: 3 bachelors, 3 young couples with small children, and 3 not-quite-so-young couples with teenagers as well as young children. Tax records for the 1690s indicate that they were a varied group economically as well, with men of relatively little property, like Samuel Addams and John Matson, mixed in with Nathaniel Holcomb and Josiah Owen, whose estate was three or four times as great.[47]

On the other hand, all the shifting around of grantees in the early 1680s did produce a group that had some things in common. For one thing, very few of them were of families with roots in England's West Country, unlike the predominantly West Country establishment of 17th century Windsor. Of the fifteen adults, only Richard Segar, Nathaniel Holcomb, Elizabeth Gillet Gossard and Elizabeth Hill Addams had parents of that stock; but Elizabeth Hill was third generation American, and Nathaniel Holcomb had, in fact, been raised by his step-father James Eno since he was ten. Eno's roots were Huguenot, as were Nicholas Gossard's; and the six other adults of the fledgling community whose ethnicity is known were Welsh.[48] This means that this group was decidedly on the fringe of a society dominated by an English Puritan elite, for the Welsh and Huguenot immigrants to England, while staunch Protestants, had tended to side with royalty and the Church of England in the disputes over prerogative and religion that had torn England apart in the early part of the century. That these inclinations were carried to America had been born out by the role played by James Eno and Michael Humphrey in the dispute with the Puritan authorities over the Half-Way Covenant in the 1660s. Humphrey's later business partnership with John Griffin and Nicholas Gossard also reveals how relationships developed as a result of people's special place in society. Even Richard Segar, whose father came from the West Country, could be tossed into the "fringe of society" category, for his mother had been, until Governor Winthrop reversed the court's decision, a convicted witch, and had later drowned under mysterious circumstances, an event which probably prompted the father's subsequent move to Rhode Island in 1678.

Kinship connections were also apparent. Thomas Griffin lived next door to his sister Abigail, and his other sister, Mindwell, would soon take up residence two doors down when she married Samuel Willcockson Jr. in 1692. Elizabeth Gillet Gossard's brother would marry Josiah Owen's sister in the same year. Similarly, Mary Addams, who would soon marry John Matson, was possibly the sister of Samuel Addams. Finally, some of the men were probably associated with each other as veterans of King Philip's War. Of course, it is hardly surprising to find that interest in settling outlands might be limited to experienced soldiers, or that Simsbury and Connecticut leaders would be offering land in the outlands to tested Indian fighters.[49]

By 1688, this group of bachelors and families had become well-established at Salmon Brook. This was a time when Simsbury in general was feeling confident enough to grant lots as far off as Turkey Hills, and to agree, at last, that the inhabitants of the whole town were well off enough to pay their colony taxes.[50] In the spring of 1687, there had apparently been enough householders at Salmon Brook for the town to declare that the first meadow, just west of the houses, should be a common field with each lot owner taking care of his share of fencing. In August, 1687, Nathaniel Holcomb was designated to be a lister (tax assessor) particularly "for Samon Brooke," and the following March the town meeting set Salmon Brook up as a separate district to have its own pound for keeping stray animals.[51] The proprietors of the meadow met in January, 1687/8 and drew up this agreement:

> that we will Fence the first Division in our low[e] Meadow in a generall way: from the uper side of Sam[l] Adams lot to the low[e] side of Richard Segars Lot: that is to Say each Man concerned to make and maintaine a good sufficient fence of Polls and Five Railes or other fence Equivolent: Every one to Fence the Breadth of his Lot at the front and Rear of it: and the common Fence at Each end to be equaly Divided among all: that fence at each side to runne with as straight a lyne as may be where it may be judged most convenient. Which fence do and by

those presence Bind our selves heirs and successors & Assigned to make and
finish well and Substantially at or before the first of April next Ensuing the date
hereof.[52]

As the little band of householders planted itself more firmly, changing
shelters into dwellings, bushy meadow into corn field, and trees into fences,
Simsbury town leaders, including Nathaniel Holcomb himself, grew more
confident about granting small parcels of marshland and grassland to the
north and west to town residents from lower Simsbury as well as from Salmon
Brook, on condition they take up the land and "improve" it.[53] Even town clerk
John Slater asked for a houselot grant, probably for his son, at the May 21,
1688 town meeting.[54] Salmon Brook had definitely begun.

Meanwhile, however, there were serious troubles for all of Connecticut which would once again delay progress for the tiny settlement. In 1684,
James II, the Catholic brother of Charles II, ascended the throne of England,
and immediately decided to bring Puritan New England under tighter control
by sending Edmond Andros to demand the return of colonial charters and to
establish the Dominion of New England. When Andros reached Boston he
collected the Massachusetts charter and declared it revoked. Then he moved
on to Connecticut. Worried that acts of incorporation of towns would be
disallowed and that the keystone of self-government, the town meeting,
would lose its authority, Connecticut's General Court began issuing patents
to groups of proprietors for lands of towns that had already been incorporated.
Simsbury's was voted on in May, 1685, and issued the following March to
"the proprietors inhabitants" of Simsbury, led, oddly, by John Talcott, who,
as we know, was not an inhabitant.[55] The patent was far more than simply a
confirmation of the 1670 act establishing Simsbury as a town of its own. It
was a defensive measure against what was viewed as an impending attack
upon the right of towns to control their land, and, for that matter, to organize
themselves to secure their future prosperity.[56]

When Andros came to Hartford, Connecticut's General Court was less
than cooperative, and someone even had the gall to spirit off the Charter to an
oaken hiding place until he left. Fortunately, the crisis dissolved when the
Parliament forced James to abdicate in the Glorious (but bloodless) Revolution of 1688, and a rebellion in New York resulted in the jailing and

deportation of Andros. But until 1689, there was no knowing when Andros would return, or with how many troops, to put the upstart province in its proper place.

As though a stagnant economy and worries about the power of their own imperial government were not enough, the people of Connecticut, and particularly those living on the colony's outskirts, faced even greater concerns as a result of the unfolding of imperial designs of another growing superpower. Louis XIV's France, managed by his determined finance minister Colbert, was turning mercantilism into an art form. In the St. Lawrence valley, far from Salmon Brook, French emissaries had been busy since mid-century courting numerous Algonkian groups who were opposed to the Iroquois of New York, forming tight fur-trading alliances and expanding their influence into the Great Lakes and Ohio Valley regions. Thomas Dongan, English governor of the New York colony in the 1680s, correctly understanding French intentions, began to encourage his Iroquois allies to raid their various rivals to the north and west, hoping to send a message to Algonkians that the British did not look kindly on their alliance with the French. These raids, of course, sparked a cycle of retaliations, and, as the warfare proliferated, word spread throughout the British dominions that outlying settlements could expect to be attacked.

In Simsbury, distant as it was from the New York frontier, the concern was very real. Once before this town had experienced what could happen when word got around among the Algonkians that one group was attacking English settlements - others with festering resentments quickly joined in, and Simsbury, among other places, had become ashes. And if their own imperial government was ready to take away their charter and all the liberties that went with it, who would protect them now that they would have to fight not just the weakened and disunited natives of New England, but powerful alliances of inland peoples, and, perhaps, French soldiers as well?

On February 4, 1688/89, Edward Thompson, then the resident minister in Simsbury, called together a group of his neighbors in Hop Meadow, and got them to issue a collective invitation to their fellow townspeople to the north, in the Lower Meadows and at Salmon Brook, saying that the Hop Meadow residents would be willing to exchange allotments with them if they would move their families back to Hop Meadow and join in a general fortification effort. Within a few days the matter was settled, and Rev. Thompson busied himself negotiating the land trades necessary to draw the outlanders back to the main village. Seven of the nine families were involved in this exchange. Nicholas Gossard already had a house at Weatogue and was not interested, and John Matson probably went to live with his business partner, James Miles, in "Scotland" on the east side of the ridge.[57] The rest presumably picked up and moved, giving up between 3 and 8 acres of their Salmon Brook land for enough Hop Meadow land to plant on that spring.

How long this arrangement continued is not clear, although subsequent land records indicate that it turned out to be only a temporary exchange.[58] Nevertheless, as England's new monarchs William and Mary joined the League of Augsburg to fight Louis XIV's expansionism in Europe, as rebels in New York packed off Edmond Andros on an eastbound ship and as gathering Algonkian forces threatened Albany, the little settlement at Salmon Brook sat empty once again. A decade had passed since the Holcombs and the Owens had first made their homes on the edge of the Connecticut Colony. A small community had gathered around them beginning to do things for itself; but now all that would have to begin again. Its bold but never foolish pioneers prepared for the worst in Hop Meadow, where the Salmon Brook men joined with the rest of Simsbury to form a "train band," or militia unit, to prepare for attack.[59]

Moving Back

King William's War, as the War of the League of Augsburg was known in America, raged on in the colonies into the 1690s. In early 1690, the French commander Frontenac ordered raids along the English frontier. Schenectady, New York was attacked in February, Salmon Falls, New Hampshire in March, and Falmouth (Portland, Maine) in July. But in May, a Massachusetts force under Sir William Phips had captured Port Royal, and New England's leaders began planning an invasion of Canada that summer. Connecticut sent only a few men into action during this war, and these were involved principally in scouting expeditions defending Massachusetts' western frontier. While the settlements that had been nervously rebuilt in the decade after King Philip's War were still considered at risk, it seemed that the situation was not so dangerous this time.[60] Salmon Brook proprietors began to rethink their retreat to Hop Meadow, as they worked their fields in the outlands without incident.

Just the same, it was some time before a community was reestablished at Salmon Brook. In April, 1692, a town meeting granted John Matson 10 acres on "Crooked Brook" (now Kendall Brook, flowing east from Bushy Hill Road toward North Granby Road), on the condition that he come to live at Salmon Brook within two years and improve two acres. Apparently the town thought it safe to make such a condition, and, in fact, must have been eager to have Matson living there, since he was a veteran of King Philip's War. Although Matson must have planned to abide by the condition (or he would not have asked for the land), he did not move back until 1697, when his grant was "renewed."[61] The previous year he was still living in "Scotland" where he served as the local fenceviewer. Joseph Owen could not even be persuaded to remain in Simsbury, and pleaded to be given "liberty" to sell his allotments to some other Simsbury inhabitant before he left town.[62]

Meanwhile, the train band, which had chosen Nathaniel Holcomb as one of its Sergeants in 1691, prepared for the worst. These militia units were traditional in British communities, rooted deep in Anglo-Saxon times. Now, however, they had become a necessity in America. The Simsbury unit probably trained more seriously than most, and had some experienced Indian fighters, like Daniel Addams and probably Nathaniel Holcomb, to educate them in effective tactics.[63] By the end of the decade the train band had expanded to a full company of 77 men, commanded by John Higley, Thomas Barber and Samuel Humphrey. In 1700, even though the Treaty of Ryswick had ended the war in Europe three years earlier, the town added timber to the minister's house for extra fortification. Frequent alarms from the colony government and scouts along the frontier had encouraged general caution, including hesitancy in returning to Salmon Brook.[64]

All this did not stop the ambitious farmers from continuing to broaden their land-holdings as they sought more and more mowing land to support more and more livestock during the winter months.[65] During the 1690s, nearly all of the householders of Salmon Brook, and occasionally some who dwelt elsewhere in Simsbury, went before the town meeting promising to "make improvement" on various patches of open, or semi-open land on the outer edge of Salmon Brook. Nathaniel Holcomb and Samuel Addams each picked up 10 more acres at Raven Swamp; John Pettibone and his son John Jr., Samuel Willcockson, William Willcockson, Nathaniel Holcomb and John Griffin Jr. all began working land north and west of Barn Door Hills; up Crooked Brook, east of today's Bushy Hill Road, Samuel Addams, John Barber and Nathaniel Holcomb Jr. staked out claims to marshy grassland; around Manatuck, Jonathan Holcomb, Samuel Slater and Luke Hill found various pieces of workable land; a newcomer named Humphrey Prior bought John Slater's first meadow lots and his land at Raven's Swamp; and John Slater took over Daniel Addams's upper meadow lot.[66] Even as early as 1691 the town meeting thought there was enough work going on at Salmon Brook to justify ordering, once again, a "common field [for the first division meadows] and every man to fence the Breadth of his Lott: and Each End to be fenct in a common way according to the number of acres inclosed within Said field."[67] There were nine lot holders at the time.

Of course, the threat of attack was not the only cause for a less-than-adventurous approach to Salmon Brook among Simsbury inhabitants. The plain fact was that the people of Simsbury had limited resources with which to do much of anything, and it is not surprising that few of them would risk what little they had to set up housekeeping on the front lines of a war zone. The town records are full of references to the economic troubles of the town during the 1680s. In a petition to the General Court in 1687, inhabitants blamed much of their poverty and inability to pay colony taxes on destruction of their crops by wandering livestock, some even belonging to people of Farmington. The Court replied that they had better build a common fence quickly, but it still took a number of years before the town meeting could confidently set a date in the spring when the common meadows would be cleared of "all swine and cattle" and fences would be repaired or fines imposed.[68]

Another clear indicator of Simsbury's economic woes is the saga of the settling of the first permanent minister. From its earliest years, the town had been served by itinerant preachers, usually Samuel Stone of Hartford. Stone had traveled across the ridge once a week during the 1670s, when there was a group of inhabitants present, to lecture the fledgling town on standard Puritan themes, such as their destiny as a people of the Word, the imminent disaster New England would face if the people did not walk with God, and the need for a "gospel order" in all aspects of community life. He had not "settled" (the New England term for permanently hiring a minister) with the Simsbury congregation, however. He pleaded ill health, probably avoiding mention of his correct perception that a residence in this town would be far less comfortable than in Hartford. Nevertheless, the town continued to seek a minister who would be brave (or foolish) enough to make Simsbury his permanent abode. After all, New England clergymen had shown a remarkable ability to predict the advent of the wrath of God by speaking constantly of imminent doom on the eve of King Philip's War. Simsbury, like most New England communities of the late 1670s, was feeling needful of spiritual leadership.

In 1681, the town sent out "the call" to Rev. Samuel Stow of Middletown, and petitioned the General Court the following year to be allowed "to settle ourselves in gospel order, with the approbation and helpe of approved Elders of Churches among us; That as we might, according to ye obligation y^t God hath layd upon us, through ye application of ye representative blood of his Son, walk mour orderly to his prase, and the Salvation of our Soules, in observance of whatsoever he hath commanded us in his Holy worde, having ye means and helps that he hath appointed thereunto."[69] According to Noah Phelps, a church was formed during Stow's ministry.

However, Stow never got his "settlement," because the town could not figure out a way to pay for his services. A proprietors' meeting held in the spring of 1681/2 "in paquanick" (that is, Poquonock, the northern section of Windsor - probably to be more convenient for the more prosperous proprietors who had not moved to Simsbury) struggled with the issue, but could only come up with a formula based on taxation of lands only, and not improvements, including land grants not taken up by absentee owners. The "gentlemen proprietors," including many like Nathaniel Bissell and Benjamin Newberry who had not moved to Simsbury, agreed; but apparently it was too difficult to raise taxes in this manner, and Stow finally left in 1685.[70]

Another reason for his leaving may have been the prolonged squabble over the site of the meetinghouse. Since the town had a number of centers of residence, it was difficult to reach an agreement, and the argument had been going on since the beginning of town meetings in Simsbury. In 1683, the location was determined by lot, but, no doubt, many uncharitable words had been uttered by that time, and Stow must have wondered what he was getting himself into.[71]

In 1687 the town gave the call to Edward Thompson of Newbury, Massachusetts, and managed to attract him with various grants of prime meadow land, £50 per year in "wheat, pease or rye, corn or pork" and firewood, and a signed agreement of support by nearly fifty of the family heads in town.[72] Thompson had graduated from Harvard in 1684, and was a mere twenty-two when he arrived. Nevertheless, he distinguished himself by working out the land exchanges during the crisis of 1689. With his salary in arrears, however, and dim prospects for a comfortable future, Thompson moved on in the summer of 1691 and refused to return when called again four years later.[73]

Next the town called on Rev. Seth Shove, who was even younger than Thompson. While at Simsbury, Shove got word of certain developments in the small community of Salem Village, Massachusetts, not far from where he had been teaching school before moving to Simsbury. "Am very glad," he wrote Judge Samuel Sewall, his former mentor who was presiding over the witch trials, "y[t] any more of those wicked Instruments of Satan are found out. Hope y[r] will a spirit of Judgment be given to such as sit in judgment; further Discovery made and Deliverance appear for y[e] miserably afflicted...."[74] Perhaps, he was a bit too zealous for the struggling community of Simsbury. At any rate, he too resigned, and left for Danbury.

At this point Simsbury had developed a pretty poor reputation among the local clergy. The congregation resolved that "they are willing to be examined, and tried, as to their knowledge, and fitness, for such fellowship and ordinances [that is, having a church], by the elders of other churches," but nothing would satisfy the neighboring elders except that which Simsbury was apparently unable to do: provide suitable compensation for a minister. Finally, in 1695, Dudley Woodbridge, the twenty-year-old son of Reverend John Woodbridge of Wethersfield, received the call, and, after the usual hemming and hawing, agreed to come in return for substantial land grants, a finished parsonage, and a salary of £60 per annum, 20 of which was to be paid in silver. As young and inexperienced as they come, Woodbridge was hardly one of Harvard's "best and brightest." Wrote one biographer, "After a

87

blameless freshman year, he began to offend against the college laws regularly and frequently, but not seriously. Neither he nor his brother John, of the same class [1694], took an [advanced degree]."

In actuality, he seemed to be exactly the person Simsbury was looking for, and on November 10, 1697, after the standard trial period, he was installed as Simsbury's first ordained minister, and their first to stay a full tenure.[75] While he badgered the congregation about his unfinished parsonage, he managed to bring half the town to the communion table in the first year, a fair accomplishment in a community of dissidents, closet Anglicans and Indian fighters. Before the turn of the century many more, some from Suffield, Windsor and Westfield, came forward to be baptized for the first time, or to "own the covenant," having been inspired by the power of his words. As his activities during the next decade would prove, he was a pragmatist, and could turn a profit as well as a soul, a talent that probably endeared him more to this particular congregation than his willingness to live in a frontier town or his ability to preach the word of God. When he died after a long illness in 1710, he was deeply mourned - another major achievement for a man of 35.[76]

While the neighboring clergy were convinced in the 1690s that Simsbury's piety was negligible, the interpretation which seems closer to the truth is that they simply could not afford a minister. For these people there were no alternative public messages. They did not read pamphlets, newspapers or books espousing different philosophies. There were no dissenting preachers traveling the countryside despite a colony Act of Toleration of 1689 tailored to please a suspicious, newly crowned royalty across the ocean. Probate inventories of estates generally included but one book - the Book from which Puritan preachers took the main point of each sermon every week for an hour or two Sunday morning, and again in the afternoon, and often once again midweek. On average a New England resident, whether an admitted church member or not, listened to approximately 150,000 hours of sermons in his or her lifetime. Even though second and third generation New Englanders, who had not known persecution in England, complained about the control their parents and clergymen had over their lives, there just wasn't any other show in town. And when the preachers' predictions of impending doom all came true with King Philip's War and with Andros's threats to their charter liberties, New Englanders knew they had to hold tightly to the covenant with God their ministers seemed to understand better than anyone else - even if some of those ministers were younger than most men were when they got their first freehold.[77] The people of Simsbury may have been more concerned about mundane survival issues than people in the more established towns along the river, but that does not mean they were any less concerned about the salvation of their souls. They simply had little surplus in those years with which to pay a minister. A report of "Persons behind of their towne Rate" for 1696, tucked away in the town records, is practically a census of the town, and shows person owing half or more of his tax bill.[78] This was not a thriving community.

The answer to their problems was, of course, the end of the war. That would mean better markets for their surplus, and more interest in settlement in Simsbury, thus enlarging the tax base. On the other hand, the inhabitants of the early 1690s were ambivalent about the extent to which they wanted their numbers to increase and business to grow. While they gave out land to just about any inhabitant who could show that he could make some use of it, they maintained strictly the town meeting's control over land allocation and residency. For example, when John Roberts and John Saxton simply wanted to exchange land, they had to get special permission from the town.[79] Poor Nathan Messenger applied twice to be allowed to live in Simsbury, and was rejected each time.[80] As immigration picked up during the 1690s, the town created the office of "Sizer" to take account of everyone's estate and to make sure land was being distributed fairly. Even John Higley, the town's richest inhabitant, had to get permission to erect something so necessary as a saw mill.[81]

In spite of these tight controls, however, the number of "admitted" families in Simsbury nearly doubled between 1689 and the end of the century.[82] Then there were all the others that came anyway, as an ordinance of 1701 suggests:

> Town Act against leting in of Strangers etc.
> Whereas this Town of Simsbury being greatly damnified by persons thrusting themselves into our towne wch proves greatly to the Damage of the Towne, for ye prevention thereof, this towne do order therefore for the Future no Persons shall croud and thrust in themselves into our Towne to reside there above one moneth without liberty first obtained from the said Towne or Townsmen upon

the forfeitur of Twenty Shillings to the Towne. the one haf to the complayner that prosecuts it to Effect and the other to the Town treasury.[83]

Perhaps it was best to allow only those who could pay taxes to thrust themselves into the town.

Benjamin Dibol, whose Wethersfield creditors chased him to Salmon Brook, was probably one of those the town fathers might have preferred not to have been "thrust" upon them. He arrived in 1698 and purchased, probably on credit, Samuel Addams's meadow lots at Salmon Brook. Two years later, though, the town clerk recorded "Whereas Benjamin dible of Simsbury hath deserted his wife and children his wife being in a distracted condition and his said wife and children a Town charge: we whose names are under writen do give our advice and Fre consent to the binding out of the children of sd dible mentioned in the Indentur written on the other sd of this paper as the law directs." Who the undersigned were was not recorded, but Dibol was, indeed, a problem. His creditors issued "cautions," and, in 1702, one of them attached some of Dibol's land at Salmon Brook. Anxious not to have such land in the hands of absentee landowners, the town declared in January, 1702/3 "that Benjamin Dibble and John Adams who also now lives at Samon Brook are not inhabitants of the town."[84] Still, he did reside in town, at least until he got himself arrested in Suffield for trespassing on land then contested between Simsbury and Suffield and for trying to cart off some barrels of tar.[85] Somewhere along the way he must have reformed his ways to the extent that he was admitted to the church, allowed a share of the copper mine in 1707 and lived out his life in Simsbury. But he died penniless in 1712, his property mortgaged to creditors from Hartford to Westfield.[86]

Regardless of Simsbury inhabitant's ambivalence toward new residents, they surely did all they could to get their outlands settled, and the end of the war did usher in some prosperity, if not security. Even before the Treaty of Ryswick was signed in 1697, people were moving back into Salmon Brook houses. Some, like Thomas Griffin and Josiah and Joseph Owen, did not return, having inherited land elsewhere that was a little closer to civilization. In their place came even more families than there had been before the settlement was abandoned in 1689. New houselot grants went to John Slater's son Thomas, Thomas Barber's son John, and Nathaniel Holcomb's son Nathaniel Jr. Nicholas Gossard died in 1694, leaving his house at Salmon

Brook to his wife Elizabeth (although she probably lived in Weatogue with her new husband, allowing her son Nathan to occupy the Salmon Brook house when he came of age). In 1698 both Richard and Abigail Segar died within two weeks of each other and their children were sent to different families to live. Elizabeth Addams died and Samuel remarried to the widow Deborah Gillet. John Matson and Samuel Willcockson Jr. both married and brought their brides to Salmon Brook. Young Luke Hill bought Josiah Owen's lands in 1697, and the following year Thomas Griffin sold his house and land to George Hayes from Windsor. Samuel Addams, while not moving out, sold land to Benjamin Dibol in March 1698/9, and at that time the town gave a grant to a new inhabitant, Peter Rice, from Concord, Massachusetts, provided he live in Town four years, build a house, and pay "Scot and Lot [assume taxes and other obligations] with Town Inhabitants."[87] Jonathan Holcomb came of age in 1699, and probably occupied his father Nathaniel's original house (see Map 2-4).[88]

We should note once again the frequency of Welsh and Huguenot background, although by 1701 it was mixing with East Anglian and West Country origins as well. Of the eighteen adults whose ancestry is known, only seven are of Welsh or Huguenot background, including Jonathan Holcomb and Nathaniel Holcomb Jr. It would appear that, for these people, ethnic identity was no longer of great importance in determining where they would settle in the New World. In fact, almost half of the adults had American-born parents.

Of greater importance was their common bond as "outlivers," that is, people willing to endure the hazards of having "the wilderness" just up the road. In addition, kinship relationships were even more abundant in this community than its 1688 predecessor. The nuclear family household continued to be the norm, the Addams household being the only extended family in one household. But the community itself approached an extended family. Jonathan Holcomb was Nathaniel Jr.'s younger brother. Luke Hill Jr. was Samuel Addams's brother-in-law before his sister died and Samuel remarried. Peter Rice was the brother of Samuel Willcockson Jr.'s mother; Mary Addams Matson was possibly Samuel Addams's sister; before the Segars died Abigail's sister Mindwell Griffin Willcockson was living next door; and Benjamin Dibol was a cousin of Abigail Dibol Hayes.

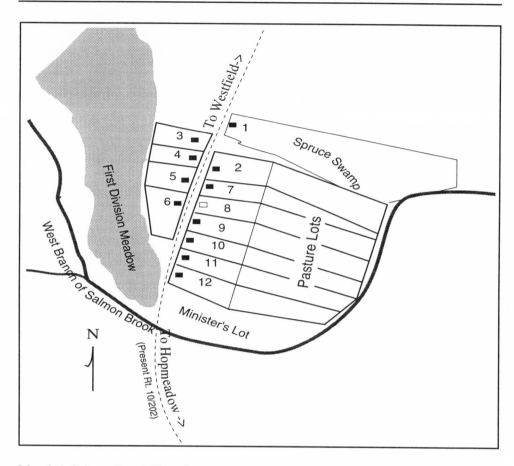

Map 2-4: Salmon Brook Houselots and Households, 1701
(ages shown in parentheses)

1.Peter(?) and Mary Ford(?) Rice and at least two children (?, 0)
2 Luke(40) and [?] Hill and 1 child (2)
3.John(37) and Mary Addams(c.40) Matson and 4 children (9,6,3,1)
4.Samuel Slater (27) bachelor - brother Thomas died 1700.
5.John Barber (37) bachelor
6.Nathaniel(28) and Martha Buell(26) Holcomb Jr. and 3 children (5,2,0)
7.George(46) and Abigail Dibble(35) Hayes and 9 children (17,15,13,11,9,6,4,2,0)
8.Estate of Richard and Abigail Segar, deceased 1698, possibly rented to Benjamin(?) and Mary Benjamin(30) Dibol
    and 2 children(4,2), although Benjamin may have been in jail in Suffield
9.Nathan Gossard (24) bachelor
10.Samuel(46) and Deborah Bartlett Gillet Addams(?) and 6 children (14,11,11,6,2,0) and Samuel's brother John
    (56) and Abigail Pinney(47) Addams and at least one child (?)
11.Samuel(25) and Mindwell Griffin(29) Willcockson Jr. and 4 children (9,6,3,0)
12.Jonathan Holcomb (23) bachelor

Salmon Brook was still not a place for town leaders to live. Samuel Willcockson might send his son to live there, and Nathaniel Holcomb's sons, Peter Buell's daughter, Luke Hill's son and daughter, Thomas Barber's son, Daniel Addams's younger siblings and John Griffin's daughters might all go there, but these older men would live nearer the Hop Meadow meetinghouse where they were occupied with the business of running the town. Griffin, of course, had died in 1681, but the others were the core of Simsbury's leadership. Samuel Willcockson Sr., Peter Buell, Nathaniel Holcomb Sr. and Daniel Addams were all frequently elected drill sergeants for the train band, now a full company led by Captain John Higley and Lieutenant Thomas Barber, the only men in town who could qualify as "gentry;" and Willcockson, Buell and Holcomb were elected together in 1693 as selectmen for the following year.[89] Holcomb was elected almost regularly during the 90s to serve on high level town committees and to serve as selectman. He lived, apparently, in the Lower Meadows, and from there kept in touch with his family (and lands) at Salmon Brook, with his finger on the pulse of the rest of the town as well.[90]

Access to meadow land and independent living were important forces propelling these people to the outlands, but commercial ambitions also continued to be important, as they were throughout Simsbury. An agreement between John Matson and a James Miles in early 1694, as Matson was considering moving back to Salmon Brook, reveals some of these ambitions. Miles and Matson had come "as partners" to Simsbury, the agreement said, but, wishing to go their separate ways, were now dividing their "livestock and commodities." Among the goods were "cattle, swine, horses, corn, flax," and, interestingly for this region, tobacco.[91] Some of the commodities used in exchanges also reveal interests beyond subsistence farming. In a land purchase in February, 1700/01, John Saxton, who had various parcels in the Salmon Brook outlands, paid Nathaniel Bissell £20 in silver and ten barrels of tar.[92]

The naval stores industry was, apparently, a substantial one in Simsbury, for the town meeting, which had originally allowed unlimited use of timber on common lands, began placing restrictions on the tar-men and lumber-men around the turn of the century.[93] They voted "a stop put to the cuting any turpentine tree within the Town comon...until they can agree upon

93

some way of equality...every man shall have his proportion of pin trees according to his lyst," paying twelve shillings *per hundred*. The trees on common lands were a prized asset, as the Slater family well knew. When young Thomas of Salmon Brook died in 1700, the family petitioned the town meeting:

> In as much as my Son Thomas Slater being latly dead who in his lifetime as I am informd did cut in the town commons sundry boxes in pin Trees for the gathering of Turpintin: and faced sum of them. he having expended Labor on sd Trees for the gathering of Turpintin, but he being dead. So that his work ceases. Therefore it is myn and my Sons earnest desire and Request that you would be pleased to grant and conferre upon us. the use and Improvemt of sd Trees for the gathering of Turpintin for our use and Improvmt we paying for his labores: for the use of his creditors as is or firstly ought to be in his the sd Thomas Slaters Inventories.
> -John Slater, John Slater Jr., Samuel Slater[94]

As ambitious men considered various ways of exploiting the local resources for profit, the families of Salmon Brook had also been active making the land around them more and more suitable for profit. Meadow land was not extensive, nor convenient (see Map 2-2), but with time, farmers could move the forest back little by little. A few roaming hogs could, in a short time, clear out a lot of underbrush, and even strip the bark from large trees, making them easier to deal with once they had died.[95] This, no doubt, describes the fate of the upland just north of the Salmon Brook houses. On this plain, Thomas Griffin, John Matson, Richard Segar, Samuel Addams, John Barber, Nathaniel Holcomb Jr., Jonathan Holcomb, Thomas Slater and Nathan Gossard all staked out six-acre claims in March, 1696/7, accepting the condition that the parcels would all lie in a single common field and be fenced in within two years. This land had once been woodland, but the only reason to fence it in would have been that it was cleared, the wood having been used for housing, fences and fires. They had put the axe to the trees, hewed timbers, sunk fence posts, split rails and carted off logs to exchange at the Hopmeadow mill for boards. Now they would put oxen and powder to work pulling stumps and rocks, preparing the land for permanent homes and barnyards. Nathaniel Holcomb Jr. and Samuel Slater also picked up what might have been new house lots there in 1698, further confirming the temporary nature of many of the earlier dwellings.[96]

Apparently, however, only four of these men actually did any work on the common fence within the time allowed, and we find them, in 1701, forming this agreement, the other five having forfeited their rights to the new lots:

> There being four of us of the s^d Company (viz) Nathan^ll Holcomb John Barbur Jonathan Holcomb & Nathan Gozard so we could fence our proportions being six accres appertaining to each of us somewhat conveniently this by verball agreement we did bring twenty-four accres into our Intire field. but the fire burning down to the ground considerable part of said fences this last Spring for want of a written agreement Some of us had [?] to sustained great damage to the loss of our winter corne. Therefore, for our selves our heirs successors & assigns have thus agreed and concluded this year of our Lord 1701= & do bind our Selves to each other, by those presents in a Bond of ten pounds of good merchantable currant provision pay of the country to be payd by each deliquent, to the rest of the abovsd company - a five rail fence or other fence equivalent by the middle of next march 1701/2.

They also agreed to set a date when "creatures" would be allowed in the field.[97]

The town took note, at this time, that there was once a similar agreement for the first division meadow across the road from the houses, but "by reason of troubles it has lyen to the Commons a while and now comes to be peopled again," and, therefore, ordered it to be fenced again, with a five-rail fence.[98] The following winter, John Matson and Nathaniel Holcomb Jr. were appointed fenceviewers for Salmon Brook to enforce these orders and agreements. Pounds were ordered set up for various districts in town, Salmon Brook being put under the charge of John Matson. Newcomer George "Hayz" was appointed the Hayward for Salmon Brook to collect stray animals and bring them to the pound. Indeed, while there were not enough school children to justify schoolmaster John Slater making a special trip to Salmon Brook for part of the year, Salmon Brook had come "to be peopled again" by 1701, and to require its own band of administrators of order.[99]

This did not mean life in the outlands had become comfortable - or even safe. Predators continued to be a problem throughout the town, and as people raised more livestock in hope of pulling in some extra cash for essentials they could not produce on their own; and as they grew more corn to keep those animals fattened during the winter months, they produced more attractions for wildlife the Algonkians had once kept at an arm's length. In 1681, the town had placed a bounty of eight shillings a head on wolves. That bounty was doubled in the February, 1692/3 town meeting, when blackbirds (two pence) and crows (four pence) were added to the list of condemned species. "Wolfe Pits" began appearing in the woodlands around the Salmon Brook pasture lots. "Pantors" also brought a reward, for the town clerk began recording them when Jonathan and Nathaniel Holcomb Jr. brought in the skin of one in 1694. So many wolves were killed in 1701 that the bounty was lowered a shilling, probably to balance the budget (£5 of bounties that year - for a town that was hard pressed to come up with £20 of silver to pay its minister). Blackbirds had similarly lost value the previous spring, bringing only six pence per dozen "'till the next Indian corn harvist." John Case, of Lower Meadows, was to be the accountant to collect heads from Salmon Brook.[100]

Predators were not the only hazard of outland living. Of course, all of Simsbury was isolated, to some extent, from the more populous and better supplied river towns, but town records paint a stark picture for the people of Salmon Brook in the 1690s. For one thing, family life appears to be a necessity. Bachelors did not stay bachelors for long once they moved to Salmon Brook, and families grew to substantial numbers. There was good reason for this - no one could survive alone for long in the outlands. Everyone played his or her part.

The sad references to the plight of widows bears testimony to this. When Samuel Brooks, who had come briefly to Salmon Brook, died, the town had to pay for the upkeep of his widow, bartering with Humphry Prior, and later Peter Buell, for her "keeping" at two shillings six pence per week. Humphry and Peter were not going to feed her much on that, but probably hoped she could do enough work to make it worth their while. Elizabeth Gossard, daughter of Nicholas Gossard who died in 1694, married Samuel Neal, who died the day their daughter was born, July 14, 1700. Soon after Elizabeth penned her own will, complaining in it that Neal had left her "with a poor waistable estate and I having been forced to pay sundry of his debts and the child being a young infant, I was hard put to it, to bring said Child ere yet I have reserved for her his bible - six shillings, skillet and iron Kettle - forteen shillings six pence, his gun - one pound ten shillings."[101]

Widows Brooks and Neal, however, were lucky. Their husbands had managed to establish residency in town, so that the town viewed them as a community responsibility. Another entry in the records from 1696 sounds a less compassionate note: "Elizabeth Miles the wife of James Miles you being now resident at your sons John Matsons these presents are to warrant you and admonish you, to depart out of These Bounds and Limits of the Township of Simsbury forth with...and you may not any longer reside here." The records do not detail why the selectmen felt she should not be allowed to stay with Matson. Was she so much of a drain on his resources that he could not attend to community responsibilities (like fixing his portion of the fence)? Was she a widow, or had Matson's old partner, James, abandoned her? It is a puzzle, particularly since the Matson genealogy does not give Elizabeth as his mother's name, nor Miles as his wife's parents' name.[102]

The Segar family (with three children ages 12, 10, and 2), seemed to be having a hard enough time even as a full family in 1696 when Richard Segar had to beg off from appointment as collector of the Minister's Rate because of some hardship - perhaps long-term illness. Then disaster struck. Richard died March 19, 1697/8, with Abigail eight-months pregnant. She died in childbirth on April 28, leaving four children without parents. The inventory of their estate reveals a stark lifestyle for the inhabitants of Salmon Brook. Household items included some tallow and bees wax for making candles, earthen dishes and bowls, a pewter cup and two pewter spoons, two glass bottles, a meal sieve, an "old iron pot," an iron kettle and a frying pan. Together the ironware alone was valued more than Richard's clothing.

For furniture, there was but one bed, a chest and a box, and one blanket and a "civerlend" (coverlet) - no chairs or table. Richard must have had to borrow a plow, for he had none. He had no axe, no hoe, nor a saw. He did have four "old barrels," a pail, two tubs, two "old siths and sith tackling," "arms and ammunition" and a hammer. Their livestock was limited to an ox, "one old horse," a three-year-old heifer, "one swin" and one calf with its mother, the last having been Abigail's total inheritance from her father "Lord John" Griffin's estate. For real estate, their children would inherit their six-

97

Town of Simsbury

Inventory of Nicholas Gossard's Estate

acre house and pasture lot, their twenty acres of meadow, spread out around Salmon Brook, and ten acres of marsh and swamp land east of Manatuck. The house and barn did not even rate a line in the inventory. In terms of capital, the Segars owned two pairs of "Lumes" with pertinent equipment, and associated with that were some "sheeps wools" (worth four shillings - not as much as a wolf's head), some "swinged flax," "two skeins of twine[, and] one skein of woolen yearn." In exchange for rental of tools they did not have, and purchase of what little they did, the Segars must have woven cloth and linen. Lest one think they were among the poorer of the settlement, the tax rate they were charged for 1696 is exactly average for those living in Salmon Brook.[103] What they used to pay their taxes is not clear, although deeds in the town land records indicating payment in "wheat pease and Indian corn att Equall proportion at Current prices" suggest that the use of commodities for money was more common than the use of hard currency.[104]

An example of someone living a higher life would be Nicholas Gossard who died a few years earlier than the Segars, leaving a widow and three children not yet of age. The inventory of his estate shows that, like the Segars, his principal assets were his land, of which he had 92 acres spread out from Weatogue to the great swamp. He had two houses, a fair number of tools (including a shovel, three hoes, two axes, a trammel, a saw, a hatchet and a badger) a cumbersome firelock musket, considerably more livestock than the Segars, a goodly amount of produce, both on the ground and in storage, and home furnishings amounting to two beds, two chairs and a chest.[105] It was, indeed, a rugged existence for the outlanders.

Edward Eggleston's description of Salem Village, Massachusetts in the 1690s is probably not far from a good description of Salmon Brook: "Men still wore buckskin breeches and hats with a brim narrow in front and long behind. Wolves, bears, and catamounts were trapped. Some of the settlers had participated in the desperate battle at the Narragansett's town sixteen years before. The sword and the rapier were still worn at the side, the fowling piece six and seven feet in length was in use."[106]

Nevertheless, by 1701, Salmon Brook had become "peopled again." With a hayward, a poundkeeper, a fenceviewer, fence agreements in place, new land cleared and twelve families at least under some form of shelter, the little community had rebuilt itself and built itself anew. Some of the original settlers had gone elsewhere, to be replaced by others attracted by free land and the independence of living away from the more "ordered" communities of New England, or even of Hop Meadow. But there was a heavy price to pay for land and independence. Livestock and crops were more subject to predators, and young families more exposed to the uncertainties of "wilderness" life and to the possibility of attack. As the town fortified the minister's house as a place of refuge, they spoke as one in their belief that the antagonisms of 17th century Europe would soon erupt again in the 18th and find their way to Simsbury's borders.

Life in Fort Simsbury, 1702-1713

The death of the heirless King Charles of Spain in 1700 was the spark which touched off the next war in Europe, as the Grand Alliance of Austria, England and Holland sat squarely behind Leopold I's claim that a Hapsburg should occupy the throne. Louis XIV of France had different ideas, and the Alliance declared war on him in May, 1702. England's King William had died in that year, and the crown of England went to his daughter, the last Stuart, Queen Anne, after whom the ensuing struggle for empire in America was named. In New England, settlements in Maine were hit again by Abenaki raids in 1703. Then, for Simsbury, the situation they had been fearing in the years of quiet since 1697 was upon them as Algonkians attacked Deerfield, Massachusetts in the winter of 1704, killing most of its inhabitants and burning the village to the ground.

At this point the Connecticut General Court took strong action. In case anyone had thoughts of repeating the retreat of 1676, the Court declared that anyone deserting any of the "frontier towns," such as Simsbury, would forfeit his land grants. They further authorized a permanent garrison of ten men to protect Simsbury, and called for 400 volunteers, including local Algonkians, to fight a campaign against the French and their own Algonkian allies.[107] In the winter of 1707, the government further ordered "a sufficient number" of houses to be fortified, and a group of scouts to ride into the northern territories and look for enemy raiding parties. Yet, while John Higley drilled his company and men oiled their rusty firelocks, there was no further word of enemy activity for three years. Far off on the Canadian frontier, bands of French and English militiamen battled inconclusively for strategic locations.

In the fall of 1707, Simsbury was attacked for the second and last time. In actuality, it was not an attack in any way comparable to those levied on outlying villages in Maine and Massachusetts, but the response to it was just as strong as though it had been. George Hayes's son Daniel, just recently come of age and about ready to set up his own farmstead at Salmon Brook, was captured by a band of Algonkians in the meadows just west of his home. The alarm was sent out to neighboring towns, but before a force could be gathered, Hayes and his captors were long gone. There had already been rumors in Connecticut of a French and Indian expedition being fitted out to attack New England earlier in the year, and this incident seemed to confirm the reports.[108]

With funds appropriated by the General Court, the town built two forts, one on the plain below Salmon Brook houses, and one about a mile north of the settlement. More funding for permanent garrisons in Simsbury came the next year from the General Court, where John Higley and Nathaniel Holcomb were serving as Simsbury's representatives. Meanwhile, the colony sent a scouting expedition toward Lake George, New York, offering a £10 bounty for Indian scalps. In 1709, it issued its first lot of paper currency to pay for attacks on Canada. Six Simsbury men, three of them from Salmon Brook, joined the 1711 invasion, which met with disaster (nearly half the troops died in the preparation stages of the expedition). Lt. Samuel Humphrey also led a group of men joining in the hunt for hostile forces in Hampshire County, Massachusetts.[109]

In spite of all this activity, Daniel Hayes was given up for dead. Simsbury had become a fortified town, and while men spent time preparing for war and scouting the edge of the wilderness, predators raged out of control at home. Crows and blackbirds caused "great damages in our corn," and wolves hunted the livestock. The farmers conserved their ammunition for the greater danger.[110] With all these troubles, it is not surprising that there was little in-migration to Salmon Brook.

In fact, the only change in the population resulted either from people moving out, or continued growth of the families already there. Luke Hill sold his property, where the Salmon Brook Historical Society now stands, to

101

Samuel Slater, and moved to Branford. Other pieces he sold to Nathaniel Holcomb Jr. Samuel and Deborah Addams may have stayed until the 1720s, when they moved to Windsor, but there are indications he had financial troubles during this time, and had to sell a large share of his property. The Segar family slowly came into its inheritance, and disposed of their parents' estate, and Nicholas Gossard's children gradually sold most of their inheritance to brother Nathan, although John Gossard seems to have moved to Salmon Brook at a later date. John Barber also sold his lot - to Peter Rice's son William. Jonathan Holcomb married Mary Hillyer in 1701, and they raised a family of five over the next two decades. Presumably Nathan Gossard married as well, but there is no record. The only newcomer was a Joseph Messenger, who arrived toward the end of the war.[111]

Thus, a majority of the people at Salmon Brook in 1709 were original settlers or offspring of the original settlers of the 1680s. The Holcomb brothers, Nathaniel and Jonathan, and Nathan Gossard were sons of two of the first couples to come to the area. Samuel Addams, John Matson and Samuel Willcockson Jr. had come then as bachelors. Now all of these men had married and begun families, joined by the Hayeses, the Rices and possibly the Dibols, who already had families.

Salmon Brook in 1709 was much more of a permanent community than the one that had been there in 1688. Unlike King William's War, which had sent Salmon Brook residents scurrying for houselots at Hop Meadow, Queen Anne's War did not disrupt the stability of the community that had been put in place. The establishment of a local school in addition to the continued election of a fenceviewer, a hayward and a poundkeeper specifically for Salmon Brook, is a clear indication that this group of Salmon Brook families was not going to give up on what it had built, and that they looked upon their local garrisons as adequate security. In December, 1701, the town meeting had established Simsbury's first school board, which had appointed John Slater to teach school six months of the year. Two years later, recognizing that Simsbury was really several individual communities, and that those communities were fairly permanent, each "squadron" was allowed one representative on the committee - Nathaniel Holcomb Jr. represented Salmon Brook. When the committee met January 20, 1703/4 it declared that, in addition to Slater's teaching, there would be four "school Dames" to teach at East Weatogue, West Weatogue, Scotland and Salmon Brook. Salaries were paid out of town and colony funds, and by a special charge to the parents as well. A note in the town records for 1712 indicates that "goodwif Rice," probably Mary Ford Rice, wife of Peter, was the school teacher at Salmon Brook, and was paid forty shillings for the year (enough to get her 13 bushels of corn at current rates).[112]

Another indication of the permanence of this settlement came in the winter of 1709. Though there were few people moving to Salmon Brook at that time, a number of men already living there asked for grants of three-acre homelots. These were made on the plain north of the first row of houses. The town also recognized the growth and stabilization of the settlement by opening a new road, complete with ox-cart bridge, along the present route of Hartford Ave. (Route 189).[113]

The people of Salmon Brook probably had the same ambivalent notions in regard to their ideals of community as did many people in New England at that time. Puritan theology, as well as traditions carried forth from centuries of English village life, stressed the need for a close-knit, harmonious and orderly community, in which everyone knew his or her place, agreed on basic beliefs and morals, and worked together for mutual well-being. There were, however, strong forces at work throughout the 17th century and early 18th century that caused people to behave with a more individualistic and independent spirit, disrupting old habits and bringing about a good deal of turmoil. Among these forces were the rise of the commercial opportunities in the Atlantic trading community that fed individual ambition for wealth, conflicts between Puritan ministers and their congregations over the power of the clergy in church and everyday affairs, the influence of Enlightenment ideas coming out of Europe, and the spreading out of a rapidly growing population searching for the remaining good land widely scattered in the outlands.[114]

Salmon Brook's communal ideal now contended with individualism. The pattern of settlement that evolved in Simsbury may not have been strictly according to the ideal "ordering of towns," since scattered meadows required scattered housing, but the people of Salmon Brook themselves grouped their houses closely together.[115] The extent to which this was a response to the need for protection and mutual assistance (how many plows *did* they have among them?), or to a desire by leaders to maintain close supervision and moral control is unclear from the records. We do know that Simsbury, like most New England towns, did maintain considerable control over its people. They tried desperately to regulate who came to live in the town, continuing into the early 17th century to vote on who would be admitted and who would be rejected.[116] While neighboring Puritan elders may not have thought too highly of Simsbury, the town did allot major expenditures toward their ministry, set aside funds for schooling, even during war time, and, when they built the meeting house, appointed a committee "for the seating of the peopl of Simsbury according to their estat offices age and dignity."[117] These were not revolutionary people.

As a group, however, the people of Salmon Brook seem to have been on the leading edge of the growing independence and the unbridling of ambition which Connecticut's conservative leaders were so concerned about in the late 17th and early 18th centuries. Simsbury, itself, was growing slowly. In 1689 there were 70 men between the ages of 16 and 70 with estates totaling £3606; twenty years later there were 85 with estates totaling £4093.[118] Yet in Salmon Brook, people were expanding their families and land holdings at a more rapid rate.

Farming was the foundation of Salmon Brook's economy, to be sure, but no farmer in colonial America was totally self-sufficient. Few farmers had the skills required to build a saw mill or a grist mill, or to tan hides. Not many farm wives could spin thread, and the Segars were exceptional in having looms for weaving. They all needed a musket, iron cooking ware and salt, all of which had to be imported, and for those seeking a bit of prestige, pewter, linen and a suit of clothes made from English fabric also became necessities.[119] Thus, even in a frontier settlement like Salmon Brook, people were trying to find products that could be bartered for these goods they could not produce themselves.

The land records indicate that many tried to take advantage of the markets for livestock. The continued acquisition of grass land confirms this. For those who had mastered the routine of running a farm while opening up new land for use at the same time, the war was actually an economic boon. Troops needed provisions, and the colony had begun, as of 1709, to print money with which to pay for them.[120] Thus, while settlers may have been reluctant to "thrust" themselves into Salmon Brook in the early years of the 18th century, those who were there happily added to their holdings, fencing in marshland and other parcels that could be easily converted to fields of corn and hay to fatten profit-bearing livestock.

The town was eager to help the growing prosperity of these outlanders, for their well-being meant increased revenues for town coffers as well. When John Matson, Nathan Gossard, Daniel Hayes and William Rice went before the town meeting in 1706 to ask for land north of today's Creamery Hill Road, the town readily granted them eight acres each as long as they agreed, in turn, to "break up said land within the space of one year after this their grant and to pay rates for the land according to the Town Vote."[121] The following winter, the town passed an act "that any Inhabitant of s^d towne shall have liberty to make use of any of the out lands not Intrenching on any other grants Either by plowing or mowing and at the end of two years he or they shall have confirmation of s^d Land."[124] This act, amounting to an early Homesteading Act, had the desired effect, but residents of Salmon Brook seemed to stay out of the fray, perhaps having enough to do with the land they already had.

Residents of other parts of Simsbury, and even some men who had proprietary rights for Simsbury but did not live in town, began working lands at Salmon Brook. So popular was the land rush for Simsbury outlands in general, that by 1713 the town had to push the occupancy requirement to eight years and limit new grants to homelots designed to encourage new residents. It was during these years that the first settlers began moving to Turkey Hills, east of the ridge and north of the falls. Meanwhile, Salmon Brook inhabitants began trading land with each other, consolidating larger parcels in one place for more convenient access.[123]

The livestock industry in Salmon Brook was only struggling into existence in the early years of the 18th century however, and as we have noted, subject to predator problems while inhabitants stood guard against a more terrifying enemy. The more profitable industry at this time, at least for some, was timber products. Aside from their own substantial needs for wood (a typical household consumed twenty to thirty cords of wood for fuel each year), there was good demand for lumber, tar and turpentine for ships, and staves for barrels. In 1685 Parliament passed a law reserving all pine trees over two feet in diameter, unless privately owned in a township before 1690, for use of the British navy. Although the law was frequently ignored, as we can see by the width of some of the planks in floors of our oldest houses, it is testimony to how valuable American lumber was to the British Empire at the end of the 17th century.[124] The attempt by the town to control the cutting of timber and boxing of trees, even before war broke out, shows that many people in Simsbury, including some at Salmon Brook, had been eager to take advantage of this trade. Clearly the squabbling that took place between Simsbury and Suffield (then part of Massachusetts) over the boundary between the two towns was related to much coveted pine resources. The argument came to a head in 1703 and 1704, when Suffield confiscated over twenty barrels of turpentine belonging to Simsbury men, and did not end until Connecticut surveyed its boundary in 1711 and reached agreement with Massachusetts two years later.[125]

Other "merchantable commodities" included tobacco, grown in Connecticut as early as 1660 and among John Matson's interests; cider (once orchards were established and someone with the skill to build a mill moved to town); and grains such as wheat, rye and corn, which the town declared could be used to pay taxes at set rates.[126] However, trade in all of these items depended upon the ability of the town to provide facilities and assistance to the aspiring traders. The town needed to regulate the use of timber on the commons, but not restrict its use to such an extent that the tar manufacturers and lumberers were discouraged. The town had to enforce strong measures regarding the upkeep of fences and bounties on predators. It had to respond to requests for additional acreage from those who were ready to make good use of the land. Finally, the town had to build good roads.[127]

As we have seen, Simsbury was slow to respond to all of these needs, and individual inhabitants were generally not well equipped with skills, material, capital or even time necessary to build prosperous trading enterprises. It is reasonable to assume, then, that endowed as Salmon Brook was with the natural resources needed for a thriving livestock and timber products industry, it would be some time before the families there would be able to make much of those resources. That did not stop them from exerting considerable effort, even in these early years, in attempting to get such enterprises off the ground. The difficulty they had doing that may explain the enthusiasm with which they greeted the news in the fall of 1705 "of either sillvar or copor mine or Mines all found within the Lymetts of the township of Simsbury Eastwardly."[128]

The story of the copper mine at Newgate is really one for the history of the town of East Granby, but its discovery and the pursuit of its possibilities during Queen Anne's War is a good example of the eagerness of people in Simsbury, including those at Salmon Brook, to take advantage of commercial opportunities and not be content with a life of subsistence farming.[129] From the start, the town meeting assumed that since the mine was on town commons, it belonged collectively to the inhabitants of the town, as did all land in practice (even though, according to the 1685 patent, the ungranted land belonged to "the proprietors inhabitants"). The town meeting had been granting parcels of land all these years, and so it presumed to grant shares of the mine to all the inhabitants who wanted them. John Matson, Benjamin Dibol, William Rice and George Hayes, while not patent proprietors, nor even sons of patent proprietors, subscribed to the shareholding agreement in this way. This created a good deal of discontent, as proprietors and their heirs claimed the more recent inhabitants had no right to the mine, or, for that matter, grants of common land! It did not help that Rev. Dudley Woodbridge was on his death bed while this debate was raging. Regardless of rights, however, it was apparent that no one had the skills to create a profitable mining and refining operation anyway. Actual operation did not begin until 1714 after a number of attempts at leasing agreements and speculators from New York, Boston and London (as well as Timothy Woodbridge, Dudley's cousin and successor in the pulpit) had become involved.[130] It is significant, just the same, that Salmon Brook men were willing to sacrifice some of their claim on common lands to get a share of the mine.

In spite of wars, wolves, crows, bad roads and inextractable minerals, the quality of life did improve for the people of Salmon Brook in the early years of the 18th century. For nearly a century, New England farmers had been making important adjustments in generations-old practices that had been better suited to the mild climate of southern Britain, and for nearly three decades, two generations of settlers had been working at making sufficient alterations in their new environment to accommodate their need to be more English than Algonkian. They could now mandate the mending of fences by a spring deadline so that, without putting the crops at risk, swine could forage freely in nearby woods without "yokes or rings." They could live comfortably with the few remaining Massaco and Poquonock families without always looking over their shoulders. They could send their children to school, take up new parcels of marsh or even woodland and "improve" them, and pay a minister who was not fresh out of college.[131]

Even poor Benjamin Dibol's estate inventory of 1712 reveals this improved life. Though deep in debt, in arrears on his taxes, and embarrassed by one episode after another, Dibol could, at least, boast of a broad ax, a saw, a hoe, a sickle, a horse, a gun, a bible, "one of Mr. Williams books," a decent cloth coat, two blankets and an inkhorn and pen.[132] If someone was putting a roof over his head he was living a little better than Richard Segar, the average farmer of 1698.

Samuel Willcockson Jr., who died the next year, is more representative of the lifestyle of the more established residents of Salmon Brook. He and his family had actually moved back to Weatogue next to his father's house, but still worked his lands at Salmon Brook with rakes, chains, pitchforks, axes, an ox sled and, astonishingly, a plow. Among his livestock were two cows, an ox, three yearling steers, 3 horses, three swine and two pigs. He had stored quantities of tobacco, "sider," flax, pease, deerskins, Indian corn, 20 pounds of wool and 28 "runn of lining yarn," although the appraisers would not put the wool and yarn in the inventory "because the family hath very great and presant nesesity for cloathing and probably would bin made use of on that account if siknis had not prevented the family having bin much exersised for the space of a whole year or more."

Samuel Jr. was also a literate man, holding a library of five books, including a Bible, a sermon book, a psalm book, "another book" and a "phisickbook." To protect himself, he owned three guns and two pistols. He apparently owed at least some of his wealth to his skill with his "gunstocking tools," and to Mindwell's use of her wool cards and spinning wheel. Their house was relatively well furnished: five "old chairs," four beds, four chests, trays, "knot dishes," tubs, fourteen "trenchers" and assorted pots, basins, and kettles. Richard Segar's brother-in-law had done well for himself, leaving an estate of £326, including over 150 acres of choice pieces of land, to his wife and six children.[133]

Yet he had died at the age of 47 after a year of sickness that had afflicted his entire household. How well-off was this? This was not an age of advanced health-care either. A few years earlier there had been a physician fifteen miles off in Windsor, specializing, it appears from his account book, in bleeding and purging.[134] Actually, Samuel Willcockson Jr. was somewhat exceptional. While Puritan ministers warned their congregations to be prepared for death at any minute, the general rule in New England, even on the frontier, was good health, longevity and low infant mortality. Occasionally, smallpox epidemics appeared in the port towns, but outlying areas often missed them.[135] Of the nine adults living at Salmon Brook in 1709 whose birth and death dates are known, the average life span was 70; and of the 66 children in all of those families, only four are known to have died in childhood.

All this is remarkable considering their diet and living conditions. Their houses were small and crowded, usually filled with smoke. While they generally ate well, adding American foods such as beans, pumpkins, corn and succotash to formerly dull English stews and pottage, they distrusted water, relying instead on a lot of hard cider. Even though their rivers teemed with fish, they disliked salmon and shad, favoring pigs as their source of protein.[136]

Furthermore, their lives were filled with dreary toil. Women not only worked at the traditional tasks their grandmothers had in England, preparing meals, milking cows, washing clothes and tending the kitchen garden, but, in a frontier community like Salmon Brook, also helped their husbands in the fields at planting and harvesting times and tended livestock, especially if their husbands were off on a scouting mission. Children, too, were expected to work hard around the house, and, in spite of New Englanders' high respect for education, spent little time in school. Social activities all revolved around work, such as husking bees, or house raisings, and even the folk rites and seasonal celebrations of the Old World were replaced by tedious and somber Sunday gatherings led by long-winded Puritan divines.[137] Men had a little more variety in their work and spent more time outdoors, and that, as well as not having to bear 7 to 12 children in a lifetime, probably accounted for their living longer on average. Yet, the harsh life seemed to be what they sought.

In the first decade of the 18th century the leaders of the determined little settlement continued to be George Hayes, John Matson and the Holcomb brothers, Nathaniel Jr. and Jonathan. Others who were not residents of Salmon Brook were asked to serve as fenceviewers from time to time, since some of the meadow lots were still in the hands of Lower Meadow and Weatogue inhabitants, but these four men generally took charge of enforcing the agreements on "common field and particular field" fencing, and collecting and keeping those stray animals who had broken through fences and destroyed crops.[138] As long as the fence was well kept, the guilty animal's owner was responsible for paying for damages if he wanted his animal back.

Of those four, John Matson presents the most interesting success story, and a good illustration of the opportunities Salmon Brook offered to enterprising individuals. Born in Boston to a family of gunsmiths in 1664, he had come to Simsbury as a relatively young bachelor with his partner James Miles, settling first in Scotland, and then venturing, in 1686, to Salmon Brook where he was offered better meadow land. Sometime before 1692 he married Mary Addams (probably the sister of other migrants from Massachusetts, Samuel and Daniel Addams) with whom he raised a family of six. Even as late as 1696, however, he was still near the bottom of the economic scale in Simsbury, according to the tax list that year, but he was higher up than he had been in 1693. He was not even allowed to take in his partner's widow (or abandoned wife) while he and Mary were building their lives at Salmon Brook. Yet over the years, he gradually added to his land holdings, picking up land at Crooked Brook, in the East Woods and, eventually, some 200 acres "under Manatuck" and "at the sawmill." He received grants, upon asking, in recognition of his value to the community (apparently Simsbury was anxious to have him as an "outliver"), as well as his obvious ability to make use of the land. Raising an extra steer or hog here and there, spinning yarn for the neighbors and assisted by their children as they grew in the early 1700s, the couple gradually added to their estate, so that by 1728, when John died, his inventory amounted to £382. In a society that still tried to pay attention to "estate and dignity," the Matsons are an example of the reality of opportunity, even for the poorest, on the frontier.[139]

Led by people like the Matsons, the community of Salmon Brook had survived the worst of times by 1713 when diplomats in Europe signed the Peace of Utrecht. Scouting patrols would continue in Connecticut, for few trusted that peace would last, and there would be an occasional alarm during the next decade. But in 1713, the people at Salmon Brook celebrated what was, for them, a true sign of good times to come. One day in the autumn of that year, Daniel Hayes walked into the settlement, alive and well, full of tales of running the Indian gauntlet, being sold to a French trader and working for his freedom. The colony legislature granted him £7 for his troubles in October.[140] At the December town meeting there were surely smiles all around as he requested a renewal of a homelot grant on the brow of the hill just north of today's Salmon Brook Historical Society - "Voted affirmative," wrote the town clerk.[141]

They had stood firm this time, and their settlement had survived the war. In the process, they had formed a special bond with each other as outlivers, yeomen struggling against the challenges of converting an Algonkian hunting ground into a home for husbandmen and traders. Their homes were still small, crowded and sparsely furnished, and their lands still had plenty of stumps and rocks to be cleared, but they were there to stay, and they knew that it was so because they had worked together. They had kept up their common fence, hunted down the wolves and "pantors," helped each other through childbirth, cared for orphans, put up barns, spun wool and flax and begun to teach the children to read and write so that they could do more than put their "mark" to deeds as most of their fathers had. Salmon Brook had become far more than just a place by 1713. With high ambitions and hopes for the future, a group of "rugged individuals" had built a new community.

Chapter III
Of Meetings and Meetinghouses

Chronology

Europe	America	Granby
1713 Peace of Utrecht ends War of the Spanish Succession	1713 Queen Anne's War supposedly ends; New England colonists begin trading with West Indies	1713 Daniel Hayes returns from 6 years of captivity in Canada
1714 Queen Anne dies, George I crowned		
1715 Louis XIV of France dies		
1718 England declares war on Spain		
1720 Robert Walpole becomes Prime Minister in England, argues for "salutary neglect" of colonies	1723 Rumors of attacks from Canada reach Connecticut; scouts sent to Litchfield Cty.	1722/3 Three-day town meeting over distirbution of the "common lands" of Simsbury
1727 England and Spain end fighting		1725 Beginning of movement to divide Simsbury into separate ecclesiastical societies; George Hayes dies.
	1734 Jonathan Edwards begins revivalist preaching in Northampton, Mass.	1733 First Church services held at Salmon Brook
		1736 Salmon Brook set off as a separate Ecclesiastical Society
1739 England and Spain at war again	1739 George Whitefield arrives in America	
1740 War of the Austrian Succession begins		1740 First Meetinghouse built at Salmon Brook

---

In retrospect, the narrative so far hardly presents a proud heritage. First the land that became the town of Granby was wrangled from Algonkians unfairly. Then colony leaders and town proprietors moved rapidly to "people" the "place commonly called Sammon brooke," in order to exploit what little meadow land was available and to solidify the English claim to some one hundred square miles of new territory. They created a forward line of settlement, occupied by former soldiers and other venturesome people (no doubt regarded by the colony's leaders as "low life"), as a buffer against

112

attacks by both Native American and European enemies. And when these bold and rough-hewn souls settled in, they leapt vigorously to the work of emptying the trees of their sap, destroying predators and birds, and clearing timber with abandon. In three decades a woodland once ideal for hunting and fishing had been dramatically altered and was now the domain of English goodwives, husbandmen, sheep, pigs, cattle and those who preyed on all of them.

While all this may sound like a less than glorious beginning, the voracious hunger of these particular Europeans for land they could possess and do with as they pleased is understandable. In the places from which they had come, whether it was the Connecticut River towns, the Bay Colony, London, the West Country or Scotland, they would have been on the bottom of the list when it came to parceling out land. Considered even in the colonies, outsiders and newcomers (or, in the parlance of the times, "strangers"), born into large families, or branded as the "meaner sort," their only chance for a sizable estate lay in the "outlands," which was where the colony's conservative elite was happy to have them living. Let them live face to face with "the wilderness" (a term describing not only the plant and animal life, but also the human inhabitants the colonists feared). Let them clear the land - and let us be the market through which their produce must pass, thought the Talcotts, the Allyns, the Newberrys, the Saltonstalls and the rest of Connecticut's established leadership. If they survive, we can worry about establishing some control over this rough breed later.

It was an interesting relationship. The leadership was giving power and independence to people from whom they would normally withhold it, but in return they saw their own position become more secure. As the colony expanded and prospered, so did the status of the leaders. Who could complain if these "outlanders" balked a little in paying a minister who was not exactly the pride of Harvard anyway? What difference did it make if they took in a few of the black sheep who hadn't fit in in other towns? What if it did cost a few pounds to help them build solid fortifications and to pay some of them to serve in the garrisons? The fact was that, aside from the Hayes kidnapping, the colony had not been attacked in either King William's War or Queen Anne's War, and the Algonkians who remained within the domain had been friendly and had led quiet lives at increasing distances from the settlements.

113

The policy of encouraging the development of frontier towns such as Danbury, Waterbury and Simsbury, with its little collection of houses at Salmon Brook, had been a wise one.

All of this wise policy, however, revolved around one crucial element: land. The men and women of the "fringe" of Connecticut society had been willing to take on the rigors of "wilderness" living on the condition that they could have, without payment, a "freehold." In addition, the possibility of sharing in the ready market for raw materials such as pine products and copper, was an attraction not lost on any of them. But, in the early years of the 18th century, the town had begun to restrict the exploitation of its valuable natural resources. Furthermore, the majority at town meetings had begun to grant parcels of land in Salmon Brook to people who were not going to live at Salmon Brook, yet had the resources to "improve," and thus lay claim to, large parcels of land far from their homesteads.

By 1713, Salmon Brook was only a tiny community, but institutionally it encompassed nearly every dimension of a recognized township except the town meeting and a gathered congregation. Having people who were not living within this little community, but who were working lands near the settlement, was surely a matter of some concern for the people of Salmon Brook, even if some of those people were inhabitants of Hop Meadow and Weatogue. In the years after the Peace of Utrecht, the ambitious people of Salmon Brook struggled to hold on to their and their offspring's perceived rights to free grants of the commons of Simsbury; and to their independence as a community of freeholders, a community which grew significantly as the threat of attack from the northwest waned. In this struggle, they were decidedly victorious.

Nathaniel and Thankful, 1720

On October 9, 1717, Nathaniel Holcomb III, eldest son of Nathaniel Holcomb Jr. and Martha Buell, married Thankful Hayes, fifth daughter of George Hayes and Abigail Dibble. He was twenty, she was seventeen. The second generation of the Euro-Americans at Salmon Brook was marrying earlier in life than the first had, and this may explain the tendency for the young couples to continue to live a few years in their parents' households before moving on to their own homesteads. It was not until the fall of 1719, a year after the birth of their first child, Hannah, that they had a house of their own next to "Crooked Brook" at the foot of Bushy Hill (now 45 Bushy Hill Road). There, in the winter of 1720, Thankful would give birth to Nathaniel IV.[1]

It was a large house for a family of four - probably a good deal more roomy than they had been used to. (In their parents' households, Nathaniel had been one of ten children, and Thankful one of twelve!) Today, aside from the relatively steep pitch of its roof, the house has the appearance of any of a vast number of white center-chimney colonials that provide our New England landscape with domestic charm. A closer look, however, reveals a unique and very old structure, offering what we do not have for the first generation of Salmon Brook residents. Recognized in 1986 as the oldest house in Granby, it provides us with a wealth of information on how the second generation lived. Exposed members of the frame on the ceiling of the second story show where a later owner tied in additional lengths of beam to change what had been a long sloping shed roof, typical in the evolution of domestic structures of the early 1700s, into a standard 2 1/2 story house, more typical of the latter half of the century (See Figures 3-1 and 3-2).[2]

When repairing the roof a few years ago, carpenters discovered clear evidence that there had been only three, relatively small, windows across the upper front elevation, where there are five today. Hand-wrought nails with large, irregular heads dot the old clapboards, on which, underneath layers of white paint, are hidden traces of a very early crimson paint, belying the mythical aversion of Puritans to colors. Inside as well, Thankful and Nathaniel rejoiced in color, if not daylight, painting their woodwork in the entrance hall and north front room a rich blue-green (called "Prussian Blue"). While most of the interior handiwork is fairly plain, there are subtle gestures toward decoration in delicate variations of molding on wall and door panels, beam casings, mantels, chair rails, handles on the door latches, and balusters and treads on the narrow, steep stairway that rises against the chimney in the entrance hall. There are three fireplaces in the older part of the house, including a large keeping-room fireplace four feet in height, supported by huge fieldstones, where Thankful did her cooking, using a deep domed bake-oven at its rear. Fieldstone, cut in some cases, and very little brick, served for

115

Elizabeth Mowell

Figure 3-1: Artist's rendition of Nathaniel Holcomb III and Thankful Hayes Holcomb's house when first constructed in 1719.

Richard Caley

Figure 3-2: Nathaniel Holcomb III House (45 Bushy Hill Road) in 1996.

the masonry. Wide pine floors speak loudly of Nathaniel's disrespect for Parliamentary restrictions on use of pines of diameter greater than two feet. One room, panelled with raised wood panelling on the outside walls as well as on the fireplace walls, must have resembled, in an elegant way, the officers' quarters of a fort with the smaller windows, and may well have been built to some extent with that purpose in mind. Rumors of new hostilities were still common for Salmon Brook residents (See Figures 3-3 and 3-4).

In fact, this was not simply another house squeezed in on the main street among the first-generation houselots or on the "plain" just to the north, where some of their brothers and sisters were building. Nathaniel and Thankful had chosen to repeat their parents' experience and establish their homestead on the outer edge of Simsbury, fully a mile to the northwest of the Salmon Brook settlement. In that, they represent the coming of age of a second generation, equally as ambitious and bold as the first, and equally hungry for the land and access to timber and foraging space for their livestock. Wolves still carried a heavy bounty in Simsbury, and this homestead was on the very edge of the hills where wolves, panthers and bears were the only undisputed title-holders, and where a large force of attackers could easily conceal themselves until they were practically on English doorsteps.[3] It is not surprising that they reinforced one room and were content with limited outside light, striking out, as they did, further into the outlands.

Simsbury was becoming more developed. Nathaniel's grandfather now managed a large gristmill on Hop Brook, funded by outside investors. New immigrant laborers were entering the community to work there, or in the copper mines, which, now operated and largely owned by outside investors, were beginning to turn a profit. And, while the town was regulating turpentine extraction, Nathaniel's father and others had secured their rights, five years earlier, to "box" a share of trees on the common lands, in order to market the turpentine for cash.[4]

Yet, regardless of all this, Nathaniel and Thankful were not content to live in the safer and more populated sections of town. On his new six-acre parcel, Nathaniel would clear the stumps of huge trees, begin his orchard, and build a barn for the animals he hoped to raise. Thankful would keep her garden, process and prepare foods, probably with only a few utensils, and share in the care of the animals. Over the next twelve years she would give

117

Richard Caley

Figure 3-3: Interior of Nathaniel Holcomb III House (45 Bushy Hill Road), Panelled Room.

Richard Caley

Figure 3-4: Interior of Nathaniel Holcomb III House, Keeping Room Fireplace.

birth to five more children in the little borning room in the back south corner of the house (Ephraim, 1721; Ruth, 1724; Thankful, 1726; Joseph, 1728; and Amos, 1732). In their next house she would have six more, for a total of thirteen.

Life was spare and, surely, harsh at times - but they were out on their own. According to Connecticut's Code of Laws, town "Select Men...in the several precincts and quarters where they dwell, shall have a vigilant eye on their brethren and neighbours," and, armed with that statute, these selectmen did not hesitate to walk into people's houses at will to see that rules of order were followed strictly.[5] But few town officials would venture out to keep an eye on the Holcombs.

In addition to the advantages of isolation, they counted others. Their homestead was surrounded by common land, and, although they did not own that land yet, their livestock used it freely, and probably Nathaniel took plenty of wood and turpentine from it in spite of regulations. If they did not appear at Rev. Timothy Woodbridge's mid-week lecture, or occasionally were absent from service on the Sabbath, few of the town fathers were inclined to run right out and march them to Hop Meadow. And finally, their parents would not be demanding their continued assistance in the family household or meadows, now that they had their own place to manage.

Within a year, they would have a few neighbors - all young people they had grown up with at Salmon Brook. Thankful's brother Samuel had married her friend Elizabeth Willcockson in 1719 and her brother George would marry another friend, Jane Matson, in 1722. Both of these couples received lots just south of the Holcombs. Farther down the path toward Barn Door Hills her sister Sarah and husband John Gossard would soon build a house, and just to her north, her friend Mary Matson and husband Ebenezer Lamson had a new houselot.[6]

Unlike their parents' generation, however, these young and ambitious settlers did not cluster their houses tightly together in a traditional European village. They were spread out along the path that is now Bushy Hill Road almost in a deliberate plan to keep a distance from each other, as if to say that not even their neighbors, not even their childhood playmates, would interfere with the living of their lives (See Map 3-1).

This was the independent life they sought, but it had not been easy to

119

come by. While Nathaniel had certainly enjoyed the support of his grandfather, the senior Nathaniel Holcomb, a church Deacon, town clerk, mill operative and former selectman and representative to the colony government, the little land grants on the edge of Bushy Hill had not been passed out as a matter of course.[7] For Nathaniel and Thankful Holcomb, their six acres were a ticket to independence, and, they hoped, prosperity. For Simsbury, they

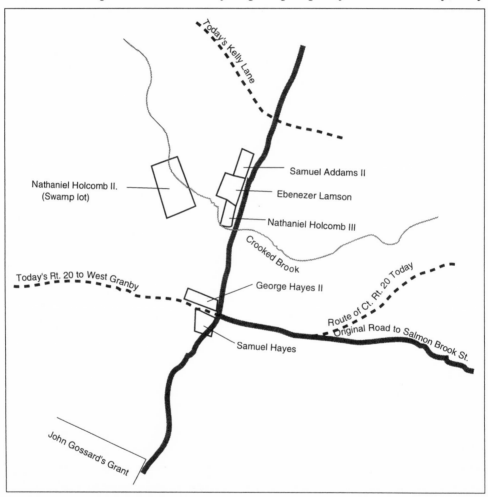

Map 3-1: Land Grants, 1719-1720, to second-generation Salmon Brook Residents along what are now Bushy Hill and Barn Door Hills Road. Source: Simsbury Land Records, Vol. 4, p. R10.

were the first prizes won in a long and bitter fight between the haves and the have-nots.

"In a Town Way"

Every narrative of Simsbury's history in the early 18th century has included some discussion of the famous town meeting of December 31 through January 2, 1722/23.[8] For three entire days, the people of Simsbury filled their meetinghouse from dawn until dusk with arguments, harsh words, and, no doubt, threats, fulminations, and protests. And in the evening of January 2, they adjourned to Andrew Robe's house to carry on until an hour before daybreak (actually into a *fourth* day), trying to reach a settlement about the division of the common lands, still the vast majority of the town's total area. Chroniclers have correctly identified the conflict as one between those who claimed "proprietary rights" and all the other inhabitants of the town, who thought they also had a right to share in the distribution of the town's most valuable resource. Indeed, this was a legal issue, and lawyers had been active in the disagreement for many years before the famous three-day-and-a-night meeting, but legalities were only the surface turbulence. Underneath it all ran the dangerous cross-currents of vast regional economic and social changes and all the resentments and alienations usually washed along with such changes. Against these cross-currents, the lawyer's argument carried little weight.

The first indication of disagreement over the future of the town's common lands is an undated list of grantees of land at Turkey Hills which is stuck into the town records near the minutes of the annual town meeting of 1713. What is interesting about this list is that it includes people, like Nicholas Gossard, Ephraim Howard and Edward Thompson, who not only were not living in Simsbury in 1713, or, in some cases, not living at all, but also were not around when land grants were made for Turkey Hills in the early 1700s. In fact, this must have been a list of original grantees going as far back as the 1680s. This list had been annulled in the 1690s when there was so much difficulty getting people to work their outland grants. Near this list in the records is another dated 1715, which has several important changes.[9] Why the old list was included is a mystery, although it would be fair to conclude that someone wanted to document a series of grants the town meeting had annulled. Who that someone was begins to become apparent in succeeding records.

For August 31, 1716, we find this entry: "This may Certifie to all Concerned that I Samuel Higley being a proper proprietor and inhabitant of Simsbury Do by These presents utterly forbid disalow and protest against any act or Acts Votes or Vote that shall be made Taken or Recorded in any Town Meeting in Simsbury concerning or Relating to Rights or Title of land or Lands."[10] It appears this protest was made in response to such town meeting actions as a series of ten-acre grants to John Matson, Daniel Hayes, and others, on the North Branch of Salmon Brook in the brook land below the Cragg the year before. Also, in that year, several men, mostly from Salmon Brook, had badgered the town meeting into letting them have one last run at the turpentine trees on the commons, and then "forever after this be prohibited from cutting any boxes for Turpintine...anywhere...in the Town comons."[11]

Samuel Higley, son of the wealthy gentleman-farmer and town militia captain John Higley, was concerned about setting the inhabitants of the town straight before they had made too many precedents establishing the control by the town meeting over the common lands. As a lawyer (among other professions), he knew the history of land grants in the colony, and had decided that it was in his interest to work for the acceptance of the concept of "proprietary rights" to land that had not been granted. Thus, he reminded the town leaders of who the original proprietors were (a list which included his father), and noted his objection to new inhabitants of the town having anything to say about, or deriving any free benefit from, the undivided land of Simsbury. No doubt he was not alone in expressing his concern.

He did have a reasonable case in legal terms. The land patents granted by the colony's legislature in 1686 were superficially an effort to make a distinction between economic, political and social status of individuals in the towns. Royal official Andros had made it clear the provincial assemblies had presumed too much in establishing towns as corporations, saying that only the crown had such power and exercised it through the granting of colonial charters. Grants of land, therefore, could only be made to individuals by the chartered colony governments. As a defensive measure, before Andros arrived to lay claim to the old charter, Connecticut's government issued patents to "proprietors inhabitants."[12] These proprietors were, in effect, the collective owners of all the lands of the town, and, at the time, all present inhabitants were considered proprietors. In Simsbury's case, as we have seen, some proprietors, like Major John Talcott, were *not* inhabitants. Regardless of where they lived, the proprietors, after 1686, legally had control over the town land which had not been granted out to individual property holders. A new resident of town might achieve the status of "inhabitant," but that did not mean he would become a "proprietor," a legal status passed on in English common law by inheritance to "heirs and assigns." Higley, by this tradition, was correct in saying that the town meeting, where all inhabitants had a right to participate in decision making, had no authority to distribute grants from the common lands. Only those who had inherited proprietary rights could do that.

English law does indeed rely heavily upon precedent. However, in many cases disputing parties are able to find conflicting precedents. Back in the 1640s, as people began to move into new areas outside of the three river towns, the General Court had given selectmen the power to decide how common lands were used, divided and "improved."[13] And, although, the *Fundamental Orders of Connecticut*, and subsequently the Royal Charter of 1662, had recognized a distinct status of "freeman," to discern who had the right to vote for the colony's government, all town inhabitants could vote for town officers, including selectmen. In fact, it was the selectmen who played the most influential role in determining who would be freemen.[14] What all this amounted to was a deep tradition, which had evolved before the 1686 patents, of the town meeting being the ultimate source of both political and proprietary, or economic, status.

Higley might still have argued that the 1686 patents changed all that, but everyone in Connecticut knew they were intended to change nothing. The term "proprietors inhabitants" was carefully chosen terminology to insure that the *practice* of corporate government within the towns would continue. These patents named some names, but the accepted interpretation continued, from then on, to include all the accepted town inhabitants of 1686 among the town's proprietors.

By 1686, Simsbury had already had some disagreements about the permanence of proprietary rights granted in 1672,[15] but these arguments had also had their roots in the resettlement troubles after King Philip's War. Throughout the 1680s and 90s the town meeting clearly assumed the power to grant lands. Of course, the number of new inhabitants who could not claim connection to the "proprietors inhabitants" of 1686 were few in number, and like John Matson and George Hayes, men willing to raise their large families on the front lines of the war zone, were accepted by most as rightful heirs to the common lands. When copper was discovered during the war, the "lawful" proprietors were hardly disposed to disqualify these few individuals from sharing in the mine's profits, and it was decided to include all taxpayers of 1706 among the proprietors of the mine.[16]

As in-migration picked up after the Peace of Utrecht, however, those who claimed proprietary rights from the patent began to feel differently. There were disputes in town about who could be considered an "admitted" inhabitant. George Hayes, in fact, was admitted all over again, just to make sure; but at other meetings, some residents were denied inhabitant status, lest they begin to act as proprietors.[17] Samuel Higley, who may have already secretly discovered another vein of copper on common land, was determined to put a stop to the trend of acquisition of economic status through the town meeting. Still, he was up against serious precedent, including the granting of proprietary rights to the mine, which weakened his argument.

It is not difficult to understand the root of the confusion. Not only had the whole issuance of patents been a defensive measure to protect a practice already in place, and thus confuse royal officials while colonials acted with discretion; more fundamentally, leaders of the colony and of individual towns, particularly where frontier towns like Simsbury were concerned, began to understand the need to be generous to the bolder, albeit "meaner," sort who would be happy to live "at risk," as long as their status improved measurably, first as freeholders, and secondly, as active participants in decisions which would insure the freeholding status of their children. Thus, while threat of attack was very real, upward mobility was equally real for former outsiders. Surely this is one of the great constants of American history. And just as surely, the formerly generous established class has always continued to remember who the outsiders were well after they have been let in.

The intensity of this conflict was even greater in Simsbury's case because of significant regional economic changes which were being felt there in the early 1700s. The forest products industry had always been important to the town, but this trade became increasingly significant all over New England at this time. As the population grew, vast quantities of wood were needed for fuel for home use, as well as for forges, kilns, tools, carts, fences, barns and houses. The demand came from outside the region as well, for lumber, barrel staves, tar, pitch and turpentine for the Royal Navy and merchant ships, and for trading with the European colonies in the West Indies. By 1728, Rev. Timothy Woodbridge could collect five tons of turpentine from his neighbors in a year and find a buyer for it in New York City.[18] After the war, potash, or pearlash, demand picked up. (Potash was produced by burning wood to ash and running water through the ash to create a lye which, when boiled to a concentrate, was used for soap, glass making, gunpowder and some medicines.)[19]

In addition to forest products, New Englanders took advantage of the market for all kinds of agricultural products stimulated by the wars between 1690 and 1713. This market extended to the West Indies as well, where merchants carried cattle, horses, and flour from colonial farmers, as well as lumber. By 1717, they had opened up trade with French colonies in the Caribbean. All of this meant much needed cash income for farmers, such as those in Simsbury, who had access to foraging ground for livestock and timber to cut, extract from, or burn. With the cash, they could purchase imported salt and spices, ironware and textile goods.[20]

The expansion of trade in agricultural and forest products had an immediate impact on Connecticut's social and economic structure. For one thing, land became more valuable, and as towns began to restrict burning, lumbering and turpentine extraction on their commons, people became more and more interested in owning large quantities of land where they could do as they pleased. The legislature, in turn, was more and more inclined to sell proprietary rights to individuals, particularly in eastern Connecticut, rather than grant land without cost to groups of settlers. People who had extra money began to invest in land, and their investments yielded profits quickly.

Along with a class of land speculators, there emerged a class which specialized in trading. As these local merchants became more adept at moving products around, they accumulated a good deal of cash, with which they became the region's first banks, lending money at 10% interest. Timothy Thrall of Windsor, who died in 1724 with an estate that included £411 in store goods, £1145 worth of land, and £2923 in mortgages, bonds and notes, is a good example of the era's *nouveau riche*, growing increasingly wealthy as farmers in the outlands borrowed against their expectations for future surplus to buy themselves a bit of productivity and comfort in the present.[21] While times were good, helped along by the legislature's paper money issues and trade expanding as rapidly as was farmers' production, everyone did well; the gap between the prosperous and the ordinary grew wider nonetheless. It would not be long before ordinary people would become aware that their hopes for the future did not necessarily lie in the well-being of the already prosperous.

In the meantime, the leadership class insisted that government, at both local and provincial levels, in both church and state, should respond to the new needs of a more complex society and economy. Conservatives, who longed for the old days when individual ambitions supposedly took a back seat to communal harmony, also joined the call for more control over their towns and congregations.[22] A good example of this tightening-up in Simsbury is a carefully ordered agreement between the town's selectmen and the owners of a reconstructed grist mill on Hop Brook on January 20, 1714/15, in which the owners agreed to hire outside expertise to build the mill (a list of acceptable millwrights was agreed to), and to give Nathaniel Holcomb Sr., apparently one of the most trusted men in town, sole management power, in return for the right to run the mill. A few years later, a heavy fine was ordered against anyone who transported millstones out of the town without its permission.[23] Entrepreneurs would be allowed to seek their fortunes, but the government would strictly control their activities, particularly where public utilities, like a grist mill, were concerned.

While Connecticut society was becoming more diverse and more stratified, and government more complicated and coercive, all shared in the lust for land; and, for the moment, most were able to satisfy their acquisitive tendencies. The Simsbury land records from the period between 1713 and 1721 are a good indication that outlanders, such as those at Salmon Brook, had high hopes for the future, and were doing all they could to exploit the resources in their immediate surroundings. Meadow land was relatively expensive at £1-£2 per acre, but land that needed work could be had for free under the current regulation that granted land to any inhabitant who cleared and fenced it (which might amount to no more than a fast burning, and surrounding the charred area with a tangle of rubble). Brewster Higley was among the new grantees of Salmon Brook land. John Matson and George Hayes began buying up land that river-town creditors were eager to unload, assembling considerable estate to divide among their heirs by the late 1720s, and newcomers Ebenezer Lampson, Josiah Alvord, Thomas Morton and Barnard Bartlett also purchased property at Salmon Brook. Hayes seems to have built a saw mill at this time on the North Branch in the vicinity of the current Route 20 bridge. William Rice, Joseph Messenger, Jonathan Holcomb, Daniel Holcomb and Daniel Hayes all began purchasing parcels here and there, even as far north as the Cragg on what was, until 1713, the colony line. And as these ambitious farmers cleared more land and raised more livestock, with the help of a town stock of bulls provided at public expense, the town kept on paying hefty bounties on wolves. The town even obliged these farmers by surveying a road north of the original houselots to the upper meadows and on to the Massachusetts line (today's Route 10).[24]

By 1719, the appetite for land was getting out of hand. At a town meeting on February 28,

> it was considered that where as it is found by Experanc that maney men who have had Lands Granted to them in our out Lands and do by their Exesive Surveys or falce bound claim mutch more Land then was Granted them contreary to the Intent of the Town and their being mutch UnEquality in Such Exesive Surveys and the Town having consedird the Sam and to prevent futer Trouble and to Regulat the Sam do now conclud and at this their meting February the 28 1719 have by an affirmative vott chosen a comitte to Inspect and also to Demaund a Regulatin of all sutch Exesive Surveys of aney parson or parsons So incrotching Town Lands into his or their hands.

This resolution may have been in response to concerns of men like Samuel Higley who saw ambitious outlanders grazing, lumbering and extracting unbridled, and feared for the future of the social and economic order; or it may simply have arisen from a general perception that, unless the town stepped in, everyone would be at each other's throats. At any rate, there was, apparently,

127

"mutch dispute" about the use of the common lands, and a committee consisting of Rev. Timothy Woodbridge, Thomas Holcomb, and John Pettibone was appointed to draw up a plan that would "make us Sitt Easie in respect of our comon and undevided lands." It was also at this time that various men came forward to secure their status as inhabitants, in order to be included in future land distributions. Among these were George Hayes, Joseph Segar, Josiah Alvord, Josiah :Alvord Jr. and William Rice of Salmon Brook.[25]

The committee came back on April 28 with a predictably middle-of-the-road position, making four recommendations, the first of which suggested that the solution to the whole uneasiness was for the town to have access to thousands more acres of forest land. That is, they announced the town should request the colony government grant an appendage to the town of land on the western boundary. Second, the committee equivocated on the inhabitant vs. proprietor dispute, saying that the right to dispose of common lands should be vested in *both* present and future inhabitants or their heirs *and* proprietors or the proprietors' heirs. Third, it recommended that land "sutable and sufficent for comonage convenant as may be for the several squadrons of the Town for said use may be sequestred for Ever." And finally, they declared that land should be divided "as a major part shall alow of said major part to be acounted not by number of parsons but by a Trew List of their Ratable Estate."[26]

The committee report must be understood in the context not only of a local conflict between the Samuel Higleys on the one hand and the John Matsons and George Hayeses on the other, but of a frontier town attempting to avoid interference by provincial leaders in their local affairs. Woodbridge, Holcomb and Pettibone did want to see if they could appease outlander, newcomer, proprietor heir, the first generation, and the second and third generations all at once. They raised the possibility of the town having so much land that everyone would get all they could ever want "for Ever." They held on to the idea of a perpetual commons. They gave respect to the inhabitants who could not claim proprietary rights, and, at the same time, reached out to non-resident proprietors, subtly reminding them that they were getting a break having something to say in a town they did not even live in. They also restricted participants to being *admitted* inhabitants. But, in the last recommendation, they hinted at their underlying concern. By insisting that more weight be given to the preferences of those who have a larger "estate," they were appealing to the conservative instincts of the provincial leadership, hoping that this concession to a more traditional notion of decision-making would dissuade the lawyers in the colony's government from declaring flatly for the proprietors, and, in the process, igniting a rebellion in Simsbury. They were clearly close to chaos, - land was everything.

Apparently persons from the proprietor class, possibly even those of Simsbury's proprietors (other towns were also having these sorts of disputes), had already approached the General Court at the October, 1718 session about the problem. At that time the government had asked the towns to show their "state and condition" as relating to the common lands. Probably members of the General Assembly knew very well that they were going to have to tread carefully to avoid alienating frontier farmers, while responding to demands of some very influential people whose continued loyalty was needed if the colony itself was to maintain its independence from royal authority. But Samuel Higley was not letting them off the hook. Not satisfied with the Woodbridge committee report, he and others petitioned the General Court on May 14, 1719, demanding they take action on the issue. In fact, he complained, the town had not yet laid its report before the assembly, and he and the other proprietors had already prepared an answer to those who had no rights to the common lands. And here it was three weeks since the committee had reported to the town meeting![27]

Meanwhile, on the west of Talcott Ridge, town meetings were getting hotter and hotter. A growing majority was bent on spiting the proprietors and demonstrating openly the rebelliousness Timothy Woodbridge wanted to keep hidden from the legislature. At a town meeting on January 5, 1719/20, the town voted to ask the General Court to confirm all past grants and actions taken regarding land by the town. Furthermore, in an intermediate victory for outlanders, it made new grants to young men who had been already hard at work building houses and fencing land on the commons. George Hayes's sons William, George Jr. and Samuel were among these, as was Nathaniel Holcomb III, Ebenezer Lampson and Jonathan Holcomb. Jonathan had been working a field in what is now West Granby for over two years.[28] As their deputy to the May session of the General Assembly, and as their new town clerk, this confrontational majority selected the senior Nathaniel Holcomb, a respected elder statesman who could well understand the concerns of outlanders.[29]

They were clearly in no mood to be discreet, and in May, Holcomb arrived in Hartford with a portfolio of papers, including copies of town acts of the 1680s reversing the original proprietor grants of the 1670s and setting conditions for land-holding in the outlands. He also brought the report of the Woodbridge committee, and was ready to answer back to Samuel Higley's arguments with a litany of anecdotes about the risks of living on the front lines of Connecticut's domain, and the expectations such risk-takers had a right to hold their government to.[30] In the face of this now very open dispute, the legislature, unconvinced that a grant of additional land would be a solution, stalled, perhaps hoping the whole thing would simply dissolve. Indeed, they preferred to stay uninvolved if there was any chance of these contentious farmers dealing with the matter themselves.

Neither side would give an inch. By December, the battle was so intense a town meeting adjourned without action, only to meet again in January, and adjourn again. In April, 1721 another committee, composed of one man from each section of town, was appointed to draw up a new plan for dividing the common lands, but when January arrived, there was no solution acceptable to all parties.[31] The town meeting did continue to make small grants, and David Holcomb (Nathaniel Jr. and Martha's son) received four acres on the plain above the original Salmon Brook settlement. Young men of this sort, however, were not going to be content for long with four-acre grants, when thousands of acres of hardwoods, turpentine trees and grazing lands were lying unused and under "Regulatin."

Time was, as a matter of fact, running out. While the outlanders could claim victory in dispensing the 1720 grants, they were under a lot of pressure from another direction. The economic expansion of the early 18th century was coming to an end, leaving those who had overextended themselves in a desperate situation. Becoming accustomed to the inflationary forces unleashed by the wartime paper money issues, and borrowing heavily to build houses and buy land, tools and breeding stock, outland farmers throughout Connecticut were beginning to feel the pinch of interest payments, growing families and declining produce prices (not only from increased production, but also as a result of a constricted money supply and war between England

and Spain which made the Caribbean a treacherous marketplace).[32] Barnard Bartlett, for example, had borrowed to buy land at Salmon Brook in 1715, and was forced to sell some of it in 1719 to keep the rest.[33] Others, such as Abigail Segar and Samuel Slater, were selling out to land speculators from Westfield, Massachusetts.[34] As Jonah Westover, a friend of Samuel Higley's from the Lower Meadows, bought land at Salmon Brook, and two merchants from New York City bought Captain Thomas Holcomb's share of the grist mill at Hop Brook, it appeared to Simsbury's debtor class that the vultures were circling.[35] The larger grants of land the outlanders sought were becoming more important for yesterday's expenses than for tomorrow's prosperity.

As they became more desperate, and as the conflict dragged on without resolution, inter-class resentments began to surface. A petition in 1723 for an addition to the town noted that, not only had Simsbury taken the lead in promoting copper works and in developing tar and turpentine operations important for the empire's navy, but also, in being a frontier town for forty years, they had suffered "a double part in the expense and fatigues of war, being fastened down by an act of this assembly [the 1704 law outlawing desertion of homesteads in frontier towns] on penalty of loosing our Freeholds, which however just it might be for the present, yet challenges a consideration when the Assembly have wherewith and leizure to do it."[36] In other words, the outlanders had given a great deal to people who lay claim to a considerable amount of power over them.

County Court records continue to reveal the sorry state of the debtors at Salmon Brook. In 1725 Alexander Allyn, a Windsor merchant, summoned Barnard Bartlett to pay a £3 debt. Bartlett assaulted him before Justice of the Peace Samuel Mather, only to incur a jail sentence with a £20 bail set. He couldn't post the bond, but escaped from jail, piling up more fines and court costs. He tried to sue John Howard of Simsbury for £1 without result, and then seems to have disappeared for a few years until the Court gave up on him. Other pitiable debtors included Jonathan Holcomb, John Rice, Nathaniel Holcomb Jr., George, Benjamin, Samuel, and William Hayes, John Holcomb and Nathaniel Holcomb III, all leaders of the Salmon Brook settlement.[37]

A principal plaintiff in many actions against these men was William Thrall of Windsor, who had inherited his father Timothy's merchant trade in 1724. In the late 1720s he was snatching up deeds to land grants as fast as

131

Salmon Brook farmers could be granted land.[38] Nathaniel Holcomb Jr. owed him as much as £41 at one point. Thrall had him confined to the county jail when he couldn't pay, but Holcomb "from thence breaking the gaol made his escape, and has since gone at large;" requiring Thrall to petition the legislature to order the sheriff to pursue Holcomb "with horse and foot, and to remand said prisoner back again to the gaol, there to remain until he satisfy said execution and be by law released."[39]

All of this litigation points to increasing problems with the distribution of wealth, and to what historian Richard Bushman has referred to as a general breakdown of homogeneity in communities.[40] As the colony was beset by factionalism brought about by land disputes and resentment over greater and greater concentration of wealth in the hands of a few, the struggles between proprietors and inhabitants took on an emotional edge that went well beyond arguments about legal precedent and an appreciation for a need for discretion. The proprietor class in Simsbury was generally free from debt and well connected with the merchant class elsewhere in the region, and, in town meetings where the common lands were discussed, increasingly faced the deep-seated frustrations of the other inhabitants of town. Those in the middle, like Rev. Woodbridge, who hoped to maintain order and some degree of harmony, if only for the sake of allowing all (including himself) to prosper, found themselves unable to get everyone to "sitt Easy," and were pushed aside in the growing confrontation.

Town leaders certainly made every effort to appease the outlanders. John Matson Sr. was finally allowed 40 shillings out of public money "towards keeping his mother Miles," the same woman who had been expelled for her poverty from his house and the town in the 1690s. A surplus in revenue for the year 1724 was put to use paying Jonathan Holcomb to give instruction "in reading and in wrighting" to the children of Salmon Brook.[41] Daniel Hayes, in an ironic action, was paid to take up loose stallions in the woods west of town (he had been captured in 1707 while on his way to find a horse).[42] Yet nothing would do. Nothing would satisfy the majority of residents yearning for release from the town's stranglehold on thousands of acres of land.

Besides, the town was still trying to attract new settlers who had special skills: millers, merchants, miners, carpenters, and blacksmiths. A good example was Rene Cossitt. Cossitt had come to Simsbury not long after his marriage to Ruth Elizabeth Porter of Farmington in 1719. Born into the French nobility in 1690, he had been educated at the University of Paris, and then at Oxford. Family traditions differ on how he got to America, but somehow, in spite of his noble blood and Roman Catholicism, he ended up in Middletown, Connecticut after Queen Anne's war, where he taught school prior to his marriage. Supposedly, Ruth would marry him only if he would agree never to return to France. She, herself, was, apparently, a "well educated and refined lady." Such a couple had obvious attractions as schoolteachers in a frontier town like Simsbury, whose clerk could barely write legible or intelligible English. He may have had a hard time getting land in other towns, but Simsbury was willing to offer the residency status that would get him a freehold if he were to come and live there. Attracting such people was clearly on the mind of town leaders as well as outlanders as they tried to work out a settlement on the common lands in the early 1720s.[43]

Then came the meeting of all meetings. It convened on December 31, 1722, carried on all day, adjourned, and reconvened the next day. Finally, the resolution passed: "voted by the maior part of the inhabitants in s^d town that they would dispose of the undevided Lands in a Town way by granting out the same." After another day of bickering, the majority agreed to follow the original recommendations of the Woodbridge committee, granting out land in proportion to estate, and creating a committee for that purpose consisting of one man from each "squadron," or settlement area. Jonathan Holcomb served for Salmon Brook. They also stipulated that grants would be "sized" for quality of land; that wood, stone and clay in each squadron's remaining undivided land would be for the common use of those in that squadron; and that every effort would be made to lay out an individual's lots in close proximity. Then on into the evening and toward daybreak it went, arguing and disputing over each person's proportion. 172 individuals, including some widowed women, received grants ranging from Thomas Gleason's nine acres to Captain Thomas Holcomb's three hundred.[44]

In the midst of all this a number of proprietors leveled their objection in writing and had it entered in the town records. Led by John Pettibone Jr., John Drake and John Saxton, twenty men, some of whom were not proprietors, but may have been objecting to how little they would end up with, signed their names and planned to launch further protests with the legislature.[45] But the majority ignored them, declaring that the assigned acreage was just the beginning, and that future grants would continue to be made in the same proportions. This was the meaning, apparently of "in a town way." The whole town commons would be divided up, eventually, not by the proprietors, but by the authority of the town meeting itself where all admitted inhabitants had a voice. Furthermore, it was solely a town action, - without even a glimmer of a request of permission from the General Court.

Finally, the town followed through with the Woodbridge committee's initial recommendation and sent forth a petition to the General Court's May session, asking for a large grant of land to the west of Simsbury to be added to the town. According to the petition some had already purchased rights of the natives there and had laid out lands. Everyone in town, except Samuel Higley, signed, and once again, it was noted how, for forty years Simsbury had been a frontier town, its inhabitants "fastened down" to their exposed location on pain of "loosing our Freehold," that which they held so dear.[46]

Higley responded at the same session, on behalf of a substantial group of proprietors, detailing the long history of land grants up to the patent, and arguing that the inhabitants had never had any right to grant to "strangers" lands belonging to proprietors. Now after "much Disturbance," he went on, the General Assembly should "disanull" all of those grants. He then brought forth witnesses, Jonathan Westover, John Saxton and John Perry, who described the great meeting in detail, revealing that Benjamin Hayes, John Rice, Nicholas Erwin and Samuel Willcockson, apparently not even admitted inhabitants, had "acted and voted" at the meeting, as had Nathaniel North, who lived in Farmington. How could this be anything but a mockery of legality?[47]

The House of Representatives declined to get involved, and so Higley took his case to the Council, who ordered the House to make a reply. A similar situation in New London combined with the Simsbury case to produce, eventually, a resolution from the legislature that former town grants would stand, but that proprietors would be in charge of land distribution thereafter.[48] Even then, in the face of what seemed to be a reasonable compromise, the inhabitants of Simsbury continued to ignore the proprietors, saying they could not say who the original proprietors were or how many votes each should have, and went about granting land by town committee well into the 1740s.

Immediately after the meeting, lots were drawn and land distributed in the various "squadrons." Salmon Brook men who lived near the "First Division Meadows" were granted land in a long tier east of Manatuck and running south to Hayes's sawmill. Residents of the plain south of the settlement received sections of the so-called "Long Lots," which ran in long thin strips over three miles west from today's Route 10. Other Salmon Brook men who already had grants west of the village received greatly expanded lots around their homesteads on Bushy Hill and Barn Door Hills Road. The surveying continued throughout the decade and into the early 1730s, when the committee had huge tiers of lots marked out on the west end of town (See Map 3-2). Even as late as 1747 miscellaneous lots in prime spots were being chosen by the grantees to "make up their proportion."[49] To all of this, Samuel Higley, Jonathan Westover, Daniel Holcomb, John Hill, John Enno, David Enos and John Hill Jr. protested in vain.[50]

The lawyer had made his case before the provincial government, a forum where he might well have expected the sympathetic support of prosperous conservatives alarmed at the growing individualism and disrespect for authority throughout Connecticut. But in Simsbury all this had accomplished was the igniting of smoldering resentments among an increasingly debt-ridden group of people who saw themselves as defenders of the commonwealth.[51] There was so much land - filled with timber, grass for livestock, and minerals, - and they felt they deserved it by their residency in this forbidding wilderness. They had been wanting in material needs for too long, and they were beginning to look upon proprietors, creditors (whom they would pay off with their land grants), and colony magistrates with the same affection they had once reserved for Algonkians, wolves and "panters." The legislature was not about to tangle with this powder keg, no matter what their devotion to the rule of law. Samuel Higley and his allies would have to accept their grants "in a town way" along with everyone else.

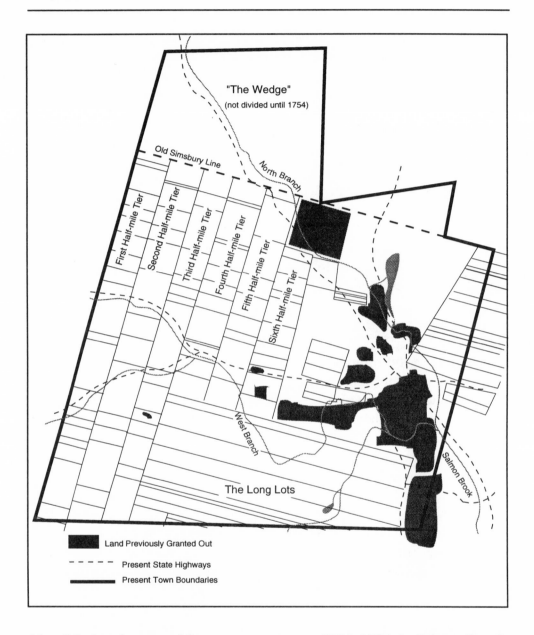

Map 3-2: Lands granted from town commons, 1723-1734, in Salmon Brook, in accordance with a vote at the town meeting of January 2, 1722/23.

Nathaniel and Thankful, 1733

It had been nearly fourteen years since Nathaniel and Thankful Holcomb had built their house on the little hill above Crooked Brook. Their family had grown considerably in that time. When they had first moved in they had had one child. Now Hannah was fifteen years old, and she had four younger brothers, Nathaniel 13, Ephraim 11, Joseph 5, and Amos not yet a year, and two sisters, Ruth 9 and Thankful 7. As their family had grown, the world around them had changed dramatically.

Every year more and more of the land had been cleared. There had been arguing about taking turpentine, wood and stone from the common land at first, but after the long town meeting of 1722/23, all the Salmon Brook families had received grants to as much land as they could deal with for the time being. Most had grants north of the Hayes saw mill, to which they hauled timber in large quantities. The families on the path that ran along Bushy Hill got their grants around the houselots they had picked out in 1720. Nathaniel had received 103 acres stretching almost a mile back from their house up the side of Bushy Hill. In 1726, he had added twenty more to that - a piece of marsh his father had been taking hay from since 1698.[52] During their fourteen-year tenure at Crooked Brook, their wooded property had become pastures and orchards, surrounded by sturdy stone and rail fences. They had raised extra livestock for market, and, with the help of their neighbors, had carted timber off to the saw mill.

It had not been an easy life. Livestock and lumber prices were not what they once had been, and merchants in Windsor and Hartford were less eager than they once had been to lend money to young people just starting out. The land grants had come at the right time, and they had worked hard to make the most of the resources on their lot. Others at Salmon Brook had not been so fortunate. Some, including Nathaniel's father, had piled up huge debts and had had to hide from creditors like William Thrall of Windsor. And there was always the problem of wolves. Nathaniel had shot quite a few, saving his livestock and gathering in bounties at the same time.[53]

In addition, in spite of the so-called treaties between England and France, there was the ever-present possibility of war breaking out again. By 1716 Simsbury had grown large enough to have two companies of militia, the

137

northern one commanded by Captain Thomas Holcomb, with Nathaniel's father elected lieutenant and second in command.[54] But this was not altogether reassuring military might for the people of Salmon Brook who were still living on the edge of English territory in New England. On August 19, 1723, the General Court was advised by authorities in Albany of the breakdown of treaty arrangements with Canadian Algonkians and the possibility of attack. They resolved that "Symsbury and Litchfield are the frontier towns of this Colony, westward of Connecticut River, which are most exposed to danger by those parties of Indians."[55]

In response to the danger, the court ordered scouting parties of Englishmen and friendly Algonkians be organized and sent to the Housatonic valley to search for possible enemy forces. Nathaniel's uncle, Sgt. Jonathan Holcomb, headed up one of these scouting parties, and Nathaniel went with him, as did eight other Simsbury men. The next summer they were ordered out again, and again, nothing came of it. In the fall, however, there were rumors of 200 of the "enemy" headed toward Connecticut, and the colony sent out more sizable forces to reinforce the scouts and to create garrisons in Salmon Brook and Turkey Hills.[56] Once again in the summer of 1725 the Council ordered the scouts out, this time to go to "Housatunnack" to warn even the "Scatacooks" and other friendly Algonkians there that they had better stop hunting for a while, for it was hard to distinguish them from attacking forces. Along with making life difficult for the Algonkians of the Housatonic valley, all of this time away from work at home did not make it easy for Nathaniel and Thankful to keep their farm in good order. The legislature did pay Nathaniel three to four shillings a day, but a 1725 petition arguing that they had not been paid on the Sabbath when they were out risking their lives as much as on any other day, suggests they were in need of every penny of their pay.[57]

After 1726, however, all that had subsided. There were no new rumors of attack, the French seemed more interested in trade than conquest (as did the English Parliament), and it seemed as though peace was permanent this time. The Salmon Brook farmers had more time for their work at home, and everyone felt more secure about the future. Property values had begun to show some improvement, especially now that more and more land was cleared, and that helped a few of the indebted farmers find buyers for their newly awarded grants. Nathaniel and Thankful did not become wealthy, but they did manage to pay off their debts and build a substantial farm. Now, in September, 1733, Isaac Dewey of Westfield had already paid them for some of it, and Nathaniel Higley of "the plain" was willing to pay them £202 for the rest of it.[58] They were resourceful people, they had other land, and their children were now good helpers - it seemed like a good idea to take the cash and start a new farm, well equipped with tools that would make life easier.

While they had been living at Crooked Brook, they had acquired land elsewhere: 10 acres in a spruce swamp farther north along Bushy Hill, and 23 acres of prime crop-land in the upper meadows which Nathaniel had purchased from his father, Nathaniel North and Abraham Dibol, all of whom were happy to have the cash.[59] In 1732, he had been granted an 80-acre lot in the western hills, where he could take timber (or, more likely, ashes) and wait for the lot's value to grow.[60] They had also asked the selectmen in 1732 to survey an 11-acre upland lot just west of their new meadow lands, as part of Thankful's inheritance from her father's estate. George Hayes had died in 1725, but his heirs made sure that every time land surveys were made in accordance with the 1722/23 town meeting resolutions, a grant was made in his name to them. On this upland lot they would build their new homestead, overlooking the fertile meadows others had been too poor, too frightened, or too lacking in tools to farm for so long.[61]

As Thankful's father's death had announced, however, those days were passing - the first generation was reaching old age, and Salmon Brook was changing considerably. The same pursuit of independence and opportunity characterized this generation as it had the previous one, but the environment in which these people pursued their dreams was different. Besides there being fewer trees, other obstacles were changing. They feared outside attack less, and they were succeeding in discouraging wolves and panthers. Yet new enemies replaced the old. Creditors wanted their money, economic forces beyond their control drove prices of their products down, proprietors tried to stand in the way of their need for land, and now there was a new problem: the town was in complete disarray over something so simple as where to build a new meetinghouse.

This was the world in which Nathaniel and Thankful lived. They had raised the first half of their family in a homestead on marginal farm land on

139

the edge of Bushy Hill, and now they were moving to better land and better prepared to make the most of it. It was a time of transition for all of Salmon Brook, as a second generation came into its own and went about the work of building farms and exploiting the resources their parents had come for. They rode the region's economic currents and stood firm for their own visions, gradually shaping a new, more populous, more secure and more complex community - one that could be more independent and more prosperous than the one in which they had grown up.

Pleas and Allegations, Orders and Disorders

The controversy regarding Simsbury's meetinghouse first surfaced in the town records on February 20, 1715/16, when the clerk noted "the great affair of providing a comfortable and decent house for the publick worship of God and differances arising amongst us which we desire may be healed."[62] Obviously, the "great affair" had been a matter of conflict for some time. The selectmen put the following questions before the town meeting: Should the town repair the old meetinghouse, and to what extent? Or should a new one be built, and, if so, in what form, and, more perplexing, where?

In the good times after the war many inhabitants could conceive of paying higher taxes, and so public expenditures, even for a new meetinghouse which could accommodate a growing population, were not out of the question. There may have been a number of people who habitually balked at taxes, but the really big issue in all of this was location. Simsbury had a central village, at Hop Meadow, but as was the case with many towns founded in the late 17th century, the great majority of the population did not live in that central village. In fact, by 1736, only 8% of Simsbury's population lived at Hop Meadow.[63] Thus, with centers of population in Weatogue, at "The Falls" (now Tariffville), along the east side of the river between Terry's Plain and East Weatogue, on the east side of the ridge (areas then called Scotland and Duncaster), at Salmon Brook, and at Turkey Hills, there was bound to be a lot of argument over where to place a new meetinghouse (see Map 3-3).

It was not just the convenience of getting to town meetings which was at issue. Town meetinghouses were, since the earliest days of English colonization in New England, used by the Puritan congregations once or twice a week - all day on Sundays, for lectures and services. Even though there were some Baptist and Anglican churches in Connecticut by 1720, there were none in Simsbury. In 1708, the colony legislature made into law a number of resolutions agreed to by a group of Puritan ministers. Collectively these resolutions were called the Saybrook Platform, and among them was the provision that "sober dissenters" would be allowed to worship in their own churches. However, they had done this only because they feared royal interference with the colony's charter and established church. In many other ways they had centralized control over religious matters in the hands of the Puritan elite. The principal method of control was the establishment of "consociations" (or "associations") composed of ministers and lay leaders at the county level, who would oversee the activities of churches, the settling of ministers, and the general support of religion. Everyone, dissenter or not, was required to pay taxes to support the local Puritan minister and to attend some church on the Sabbath. Each consociation would organize its county into "ecclesiastical societies," delineating, as did English parishes, the boundaries of each church's jurisdiction, the church being the admitted members. Not only would the society be responsible for seeing that the church was supported financially, but it also became responsible for providing schooling for children within its bounds.[64] In most cases, town bounds and society bounds were identical. Thus, with one society and one meetinghouse for all of Simsbury, the location of that meetinghouse was very important to everyone, young and old.

Aside from house and barn raisings, these gatherings for church and town meetings were the only community activities in the colonial period. Even the militia trained on Sundays when the whole town assembled for church anyway. In the summer, when the roads were in repair and dry, most families did not mind what was for many a five-mile trek to meeting. But as days turned cold, and in the winter when roads were impassable and few had sleighs, or in the spring before the surveyors of highways had turned out their districts to make repairs on what had become pot-hole-strewn muddy gutters, everyone thought about the advantages of a meetinghouse closer to home. Salmon Brook inhabitants surely found the trip to Hop Meadow, where the meetinghouse had been located since the 1670s, an arduous journey. Those who had to cross the Farmington River were even more unhappy.

In view of the great importance of this issue, then, the town meeting of February 20, 1715/16 sent a committee, Benjamin Addams, Samuel Pettibone and Nathaniel Holcomb Jr. (from east of the river, Weatogue and Salmon Brook, respectively), to meet with colony magistrates Matthew Allyn, Joseph Talcott and John Hooker to get their advice on what ought to

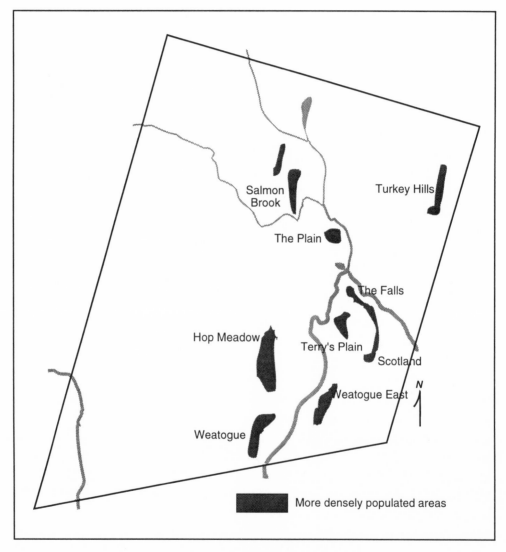

Map 3-3: Population Centers in Colonial Simsbury.

be done. In March they returned with the recommendation that the present meetinghouse should be repaired and enlarged.[65] Over the next two years the town put £50 into alterations and repairs, and created a new seating arrangement.[66] From then until 1725, the town was beset with the controversy over dividing the common land. However, when that calmed down, it became apparent that simple additions were not going to accommodate the rapidly growing population and that the town would have to face the meetinghouse problem again. The people at Turkey Hills had already secured permission to have their own burying ground, and probably all of the outlanders were wondering why they should travel five to seven miles every week to be crowded into a tiny old meetinghouse.[67]

A town meeting of October 7, 1725 seemed to be moving toward building a new meetinghouse, but could not agree on a location. After "several town meetings" they turned to the legislature for some impartial arbitration, but the General Court committee's choice of a location on the west side of the river near Bissel's Landing (presently Simsbury's north bridge is located there) was not satisfactory to a majority of the town. In spite of the committee's stern declaration that the people should "proceed...in a Christian and peacable manner becoming such a work," inhabitants continued to argue through the summer of 1726. Finally, at a meeting on August 17, the town voted to divide into two ecclesiastical societies divided north and south by Hop Brook and the river.[68] This prompted petitions to the General Court arguing this way and that, and even more debate. Again they voted, and again the division people won. And again they asked the General Court to send a committee to determine how the town should be divided, this time asking for a different group of magistrates. Yet another "meeting about y[e] meeting house" in December was adjourned until February, when it was adjourned again until April's freeman's meeting.[69]

After the February, 1727 meeting the people of Salmon Brook met and began to sort out where they stood on the matter. What resulted was an interesting petition to the legislature providing insight into some of the dynamics of the controversy. The petition was signed by the following persons, whom we may take to be nearly all of the male family heads of Salmon Brook at that time (although John and Brewster Higley lived in the area where the Simsbury airport is currently located):

143

John Higley	Bernard Bartlet	Abram Dibol
Daniel Hayes	Nathaniel Holcomb Jr.	Samuel Hayes
John Matson Jr.	George Hayes	Brewster Higley
Benjamin Hayes	Samuel Smith	Ebenezer Lamson
Jonathan Holcomb	James Smith	Joseph Willcockson
John Howard	William Rice	John Rice
Nathan Gozard	William Hayes	Nemiah Lee
John Gozard	Joseph Lamson	

Note that few of these men were newcomers and that whatever population increase there was at Salmon Brook by 1728 was largely natural increase, which was, of course, substantial.[70]

The petition argued that there should be only one ecclesiastical society because (1) the assessment of the north section of town (£2533) was too small to support a minister all on its own; (2) "Wee Being so far different one from the other and a Rocky wods where sd Stake is set that it is easer for us to Joyne with the whole Town then Come their the Land being so infertile;" and (3) the people of Salmon Brook never desired to be set off into a separate society and always wanted to have the meetinghouse in its present location at Hop Brook. A large number of men from the plain and the southern part of town sent a supporting petition.[71]

It can be inferred from this petition that at least some of the pressure for two societies was coming largely from Turkey Hills residents. The population of that section of town was growing rapidly, up from two families in 1709 to 35 - 24 of which were east of the ridge, by 1728. In fact, Turkey Hills was the section of town which was growing the fastest, benefiting not only from the natural increase of typically large families, but also from migration from Windsor on the part of men like Samuel Clarke, who could claim proprietary rights in Simsbury and asked for lots at Turkey Hills.[72] The petition also confirms what we have already discovered about the mindset of the Salmon Brook people: that they saw themselves as "so far different one from the other" when they envisioned being in a society with the people of Turkey Hills - people they had fought bitterly (and continued to fight) in the common land conflict. The only puzzle remaining is how a majority kept emerging arguing for a division into two societies, as they did at the freemen's meeting on April 25, 1727.[73]

Finally in May, the legislature, upon hearing advice from its committee that had gone to sit in on a town meeting, voted to divide the town into two societies.[74] More town meetings, memorials and petitions followed, and the legislature sent another committee in October, 1728, to investigate all of the "pleas and allegations," to "finally determine" whether there should be two societies or the town should "continue undivided," and to make an "Utter End of Controversy" in the matter.[75] In the meantime the south society, as set off the previous year, had begun to have meetings to organize itself. Furthermore, feelings were becoming so intense, tax collectors were beginning to have trouble collecting the old society's rate which was supposed to fund Timothy Woodbridge's salary, and the building committee was becoming weary of carting the timber for the new meetinghouse from one "finally determined" location to another.[76]

When the legislature's committee arrived at the town meeting in November, it heard from representatives of each section, Barnard Bartlett and James Smith representing Salmon Brook. With its help, the town decided to remain a single society. The committee then pitched a stake on the west side of the river, and hurried back to Hartford as objections were being filed. In fact, a majority of the town objected, since the committee had placed the stake on a flood plain, the exact location of which all parties seemed to have been too embarrassed, in the long run, to record.[77]

At that point the town leaders made an effort to settle things at the local level, and, perhaps, salvage the town's reputation. At the annual meeting on December 26, 1728, they came forth with "orders and Constitutions to prevent disorders in Town Meetings for y[e] future." According to these, (1) the selectmen, the town clerk and a Justice of the Peace would nominate the moderator from now on; (2) if five inhabitants asked for it, the moderator would put a matter to a vote; (3) no one could "argue or dispute" unless recognized by the moderator; (4) the moderator could dismiss or adjourn a meeting only by majority vote; and (5) there would be a 5 shilling fine for violations of these "orders," half of which fine would go to the prosecutor, half to the town poor.[78] In April, 1729, in accordance with these, we must assume a very orderly town meeting voted to divide the town into two societies, north and south.[79] And the next month, too, things seemed to be settling down, as Salmon Brook people joined to petition the legislature to free Turkey Hills people from paying the rate to the old society and to allow them to hire their own preacher.[80]

Now, however, it was the legislature's turn to be difficult. Apparently they were not happy with the idea of Turkey Hills hiring its own minister, nor with the division line set by the town meeting. Perhaps Timothy Woodbridge was beginning to exert his own influence, getting a bit impatient about money he should have been paid by the Turkey Hills inhabitants, and wondering about the future security of his position. The House of Representatives, generally sympathetic to whatever a respected minister might say, continued the Turkey Hills petition until the next session, and considered, as well, a petition from Salmon Brook people *against* a single society, since the decision on location had been to place the meetinghouse further *south* than it was at the present.[81]

At the October session a petition arrived from inhabitants of Weatogue accusing Samuel Higley and his Turkey Hills neighbors of developing a "design... to weaken [the southern part of town] and so to obtain the meetinghouse on the East side and to be so set as to be attended with much greater difficulties than ever." They went on, saying, prophetically, that "by adding the plain and Higleys northward [to the north society], a foundation is laid for a perpetual Contest between Salmon brook and Turkie Hills."[82]

The following year, an impatient legislature assessed the town for costs in sending committees to fix society boundary lines, and, interestingly, sent yet one more committee to "persuade the people of said town to surcease their contentions" and decide what they wanted done.[83] But, alas, even though the Hartford County Association of ministers was also becoming involved, rushing, no doubt to Woodbridge's aid, nothing seemed to work. At a July town meeting, with Governor Talcott in attendance, majorities voted against dividing the town, voted against building a new meetinghouse at the same place as the old one, voted against building a meetinghouse on the east side of the river, and voted in favor of remaining united and building a meeting-house at Bissel's landing, a place that had provoked the first onslaught of petitions five years earlier.[84] The legislature quickly approved this at their October session, but it almost seemed that was reason enough for inhabitants to change their minds.[85] The December town meeting was the scene of great arguing, two adjournments, and finally a decision to divide the town by the river, east and west, and allow Salmon Brook, Turkey Hills, and the Falls to be excused from the minister's rate as long as they "maintain ye gospel amongst themselves either whole or separate."[86]

At this point Rev. Woodbridge complained to the Association, concerned, no doubt, that he'd be traveling all over the countryside all day and all night doing services, and getting paid no more than before. The Association agreed with him, saying the church at Simsbury was so destitute "of a good and christian frame of spirit, as to be unfit for communion at the Lord's table," and said he ought not to feel obligated to continue his ministry in Simsbury.[87] To this, the next year's town meeting answered that they would not pay him for 1731 "for sundry Reasons which to us seems sufficient," principally because "he not being obliged to us we cannot be obliged to him." Only the "West Society" would pay him that year. This embarrassment continued into the following year, when a town meeting attempted without success to raise money to cover his salary since 1729, and have some to pay Revs. Butler and Collins, who had been preaching to Turkey Hills and Falls residents. However, some collectors refused to do their jobs.[88] Again the legislature stepped in, noting that no measures had "had the desired success of quieting the minds of the people and settling them in peace," and that the colonial government itself would have to enforce the collection of the minister's rate. They further decided not to appoint any Justices of the Peace for that year because of "the excited state of feeling among the people." Finally, they insisted (of course, that would mean nothing) that the town use the old meetinghouse for three years, with Turkey Hills having "winter privileges" (worshipping in their own village during the winter).[89]

While all this may sound like a silly argument among some severely stubborn and petulant farmers, closer examination reveals that the issue was impossibly complex, and riddled with strains of other tangentially related factors. Historian Lucius Barber says the complexity of Simsbury's settlement patterns, resulting in the lack of a clear town center, were at the root of it all, and to a great extent that was so.[90] The dispute between the east and west sides of the river in Simsbury, settled a half century earlier by lot, had never gone away (since there were not yet any bridges over the river). However,

147

there was even more to the controversy than geography. Obviously the Turkey Hills people were one strong interest group who felt their rapidly growing numbers and estates should exempt them from arduous travel every meeting day. Generally more wealthy than the average Simsbury resident, they carried more influence in the legislature, which, in turn, was afraid of alienating outlanders, or of stirring up a hornets' nest which could invite stricter control from England. The increasing numbers of people living in the outlands was also a complicating matter, as were their feelings of alienation toward anyone of higher economic or social standing, including not only proprietors and creditors, in this case, but also elite collectives of ministers who seemed to give no good reason for supporting Woodbridge over ministers they might have preferred. As each solution was proposed, over the years, a different combination of people would join to voice their objections. Also, as time passed, the composition of each section of town was changing significantly. Finally, the most contentious became more practiced at the art of obstructing solutions that were in the least bit inconvenient to them. With all these factors at work, some having little to do with distance (in miles), it is not surprising the "contentions" lasted so long.

Until 1733, the Salmon Brook people seem to have been "swing voters," on the one hand, eager to have a meetinghouse a little closer for the sake of their aging parents and more and more numerous children, and on the other hand, suspicious of uniting with the inhabitants of Turkey Hills, who were "so far different" from them. By March, 1733, their position was hardening, as Barnard Bartlett, Jonathan Holcomb and Nathan Gossard submitted a petition to the town meeting on their behalf asking that "the place Called Salmon brok with the adjacent neighbors shall have Liberty to be a distinct ministeriall Society by themselves."[91] In May, they wrote to the legislature indicating that they were giving up on the town's finding a place for the meetinghouse with which everyone would be happy. 36 men signed this petition, one more than the number of families reported as living at Salmon Brook in a petition later that year, when the area's population was given at 196.[92] The town meeting voted that Turkey Hills and Salmon Brook be set off as a separate society, but the Assembly rejected this in May.[93]

The next year Salmon Brook people repeated their request, arguing that the whole town supported their desire to be a separate society, that for fifteen months they had been paying their own minister, "a young candidate" whom they liked and hoped to settle, that the present meetinghouse was a long way from them (five to seven miles) and that there was a "great uncertainty of enjoying the word and ordinances when we come thence," that their estates (now a total of £2167) were growing considerably and they could support a minister (even though they had argued seven years earlier that the combined £2500 of estates of Salmon Brook and Turkey Hills would not be enough!), that with the Falls and "Higleys" they numbered 50 families, or 276 souls, and that there was no disadvantage to the rest of the town in their breaking off. Apparently, they had been meeting at Daniel Hayes's house for services. In spite of all these arguments, the House of Representatives responded negatively again, not giving a reason.[94]

Petitions, complaints and memorials continued to roll in from each section of town and from Woodbridge, who, after taking his family and leaving town, took his case to the County Court as well (a litigation not settled until after his death in 1742).[95] In May, 1735, the legislature sent yet another committee, "considering the divided state of said Symsbury, and how often the inhabitants of that place have in their town meetings changed their votes," but again no solution could be found. Meanwhile, the Salmon Brook population continued to grow and to hear the word via a Mr. Roberts, their "young candidate," increasingly confident they would win their independence in the end.[96]

Samuel Higley of Turkey Hills submitted a masterful map to the legislature, exaggerating the distance between the north half of Simsbury and the meetinghouse, and showing great mountain ranges and other natural barriers sealing people off from each other (See Figure 3-5).[97] Yet his plan was to include some people who considered themselves Salmon Brook residents in the Turkey Hills society, or at least their land, which could be taxed by the society it was in, according to a 1735 law.[98] The Salmon Brook people fought off this "design" as well, and, at the October session, 1736, the legislature's committee came forth with a plan for division of the town which was very close to what Salmon Brook had wanted all along. According to this plan, there would be four societies: a "Northwest Society" (to include Salmon Brook, and some of the Falls, but not Higleys), Turkey Hills (which also included some of the Falls), Wintonbury (an inter-town society created by

149

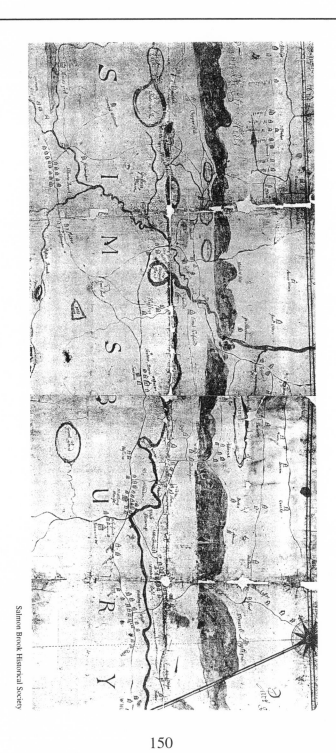

Figure 3-5: Samuel Higley's elongated map of Simsbury, created circa 1735, to support division of the town into separate ecclesiastical societies.

Salmon Brook Historical Society

joining those east of the ridge and south of the river with people living in the west end of Windsor and in the northeast part of Farmington), and the rest of Simsbury south of Saxton's Brook and east of the ridge (See Map 3-4).[99]

It was a sacrifice for people at Salmon Brook to give up the tax revenue which could have been derived from some of the residents at the Falls and from John and Brewster Higley, but all the while the controversy was going on, more and more people were moving to Salmon Brook, including Philip Loomis, whose estate ranked the highest on their 1736 list, and Nathaniel Higley, who had moved into young Nathaniel Holcomb's house at Bushy Hill.[100] These two men, in particular, had holdings in the other societies, but would, no doubt, sell them to increase their holdings at Salmon Brook, which they would improve. The future looked bright. They would have their own meetinghouse, select their own minister, both of which they were increasingly able to afford, and, in turn, more and more people would be interested in moving to Salmon Brook, thus driving up the value of their division land.[101] Taking on their own "minister's rate" now would be more of an investment than a sacrifice.

In less than three years they voted to build a meetinghouse for themselves, and a weary legislative committee arrived in the summer of 1739 to pitch a stake "upon a piece of undivided land; near the North End of a Broad Street or highway, on the Brow of a Hill near the place where two highways meet which lead into S[d] Street." This was at the east end of today's Granby Cemetery at the north end of the village, now that it had extended up from the original settlement onto "the plain." In December, a building committee was appointed, and a frame was up and other building material purchased before May, 1740. It measured 30 feet by 45 feet, was 20 feet high, had no steeple and no fireplaces (people were to bring footwarmers on cold days). As for their "young candidate," however, he appears to have moved elsewhere, for in 1739 the society paid Timothy Woodbridge, of all people, to preach to them.[102]

As of 1736, however, they had come closer to complete independence. As they had grown from a tiny village of eleven families in 1713 to a parish of over 200 souls and 40 families, they had won battles against proprietors, creditors, wolves and panthers, and had held their own against colonial magistrates and clerical elite who hoped to centralize authority in

151

Connecticut and stem the tide of individualism. Their community was now spreading north along the Westfield Road and other north-leading paths toward the colony line, and west toward the "wilderness." It was equipped with a sawmill, and possibly a storekeeper (Philip Loomis) and a grist mill (James Hillyer Jr., who had married George Hayes's daughter Joanna, moved

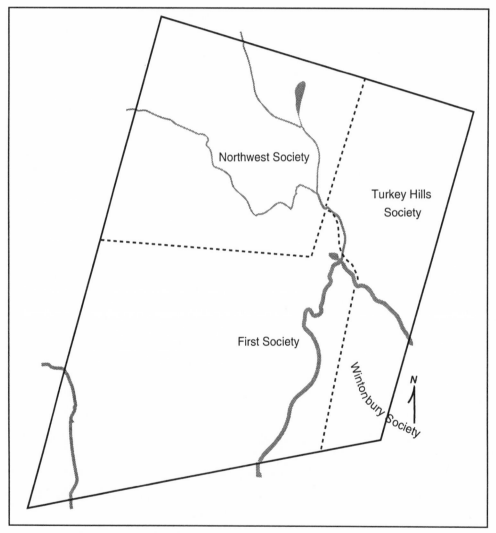

Map 3-4: Division of Simsbury into separate ecclesiastical societies.

to Salmon Brook in the 1730s and may have built the grist mill on Manatuck Lake at that time);[103] and as of 1740, it had a meetinghouse.

All of this coincided with the rise to prominence of the second generation. Nathaniel Holcomb III was chosen a selectman in 1736, in a new, more complex town order which called for five selectmen, one from each of the major "squadrons" of the town. Joseph Willcockson Jr. succeeded him in 1738, as Nathaniel became more involved in militia leadership, first as an Ensign, then as Captain in 1739, with his brother David soon to be chosen Lieutenant, and Willcockson, Ensign.[104] It was a new era for a more independent Salmon Brook, with a new generation in charge.

In their minds they could feel the independence too, as they shaped a common identity. While there were some differences in rank among them, they looked upon each other as relative equals who had common interests driven by the way they chose to make their livings: farmers hoping to prosper from the vast wealth of resources which had been placed under their control, or, if not prosper, at least to pass on a sizable freehold to their sons. Few of the second generation had moved away from Salmon Brook, but, instead, had done a lot of intermarrying creating kinship, as well as social and economic bonds. They considered themselves God-fearing farmers too, only lacking a suitable "young candidate" for the ministry who would settle among them and bring them the Word of the Gospel. Little did they know what a great challenge it would be to find one who was truly suitable for such a rough-hewn, independent-minded collection of outlanders.

153

Chapter IV
'Tis the brittle thread of life that sustains you

Chronology

Europe	America	Granby
1740 War of Austrian Succession	1740 George Whitefield tours Connecticut bringing the Great Awakening 1742 Connecticut enacts law banning itinerant preachers	1740 Northwest Society builds first meetinghouse
1744 England and France at war	1744 King George's War begins	1744 William Gibbs installed at St. Andrews
1748 Peace of Aix-la-Chapelle	1748 War ends	1745-9 Ministry of David Sherman Rowland
1756 Seven Years War begins	1754 French and Indian War begins	1752 Joseph Strong settled as minister, Congregational Church adopts covenant
1763 Peace of Paris	1762 War ends 1763 Canada ceded to Great Britain	1761 First public library at Salmon Brook
		1764 Baptists begin meeting in Bushy Hill Road neighborhood

In the earliest days of European settlement in New England, the Puritan leaders had dreamed of such a community as Salmon Brook. It would consist of a tight-knit group of families, bravely facing the wilderness with the knowledge that they were the chosen children of God, destined, if they could keep their end of the covenant, to demonstrate for all the world how to form a community and how to live and work together according to "the Word." They would be one congregation of pilgrims in the New Land, given to them, "my people Israel," to use for the creation of "a city upon a hill." They would watch out for each other, help each other through hard times, share in each other's joys and troubles alike, and do all that was needed to be "a praise and glory" to God. They had to think alike, of course; and they had to know each other well. They had to sacrifice and remain ever committed to the public welfare over their own private interests.

As they dug their meetinghouse foundation in the spring of 1740, surely it occurred to the people of Salmon Brook, people who had heard these visions of covenanted communal harmony preached week in and week out all their lives, that they were on the verge of achieving these great New England ideals. Their little village had grown considerably with every family large and healthy and joined together in a web of marriage as one great extended family. They had the means, through ownership of large quantities of land, of sustaining themselves and their children and grandchildren. They were about to find a permanent minister and enter into a covenant as an independent congregation. And there had been no threat of attack for well over a decade.

Yet even as their little community became more secure and more independent in the second quarter of the 18th century, winning battles against creditors, proprietors and wolves, and setting itself up as a separate ecclesiastical society, the side effects of growth were becoming apparent. First of all, the second generation itself had sought good land and independence as had their parents, which had led to a dispersal of households over a broad area. Second, newcomers, most of whom were happily admitted as inhabitants and brought a measure of wealth with them, did not always share the same values and attitudes as those who had been born and raised at Salmon Brook. Finally, trade in surplus goods with an increasingly complex outside world continued to involve more and more people in the community. These factors tugged and pulled at Salmon Brook society and as its new complexities began to manifest themselves in various ways, particularly in arguments over religion, it became obvious that the old vision of a covenanted community would not work for the future.

An Awakening

Turmoil over religion at Salmon Brook came about as a result of regional upheaval which eventually found its way to the newly established ecclesiastical society in the northwest corner of Simsbury. While Salmon

155

Brook was growing and changing in the early 1700s, great changes were also taking place across New England. Large families expanded into more and more land, trading opportunities continued to open, particularly after the Peace of Utrecht in 1713, and more and more people were producing surpluses to meet that increased demand. As the economy hummed, Connecticut River valley merchants became wealthy, and the whole structure of society changed dramatically.

The region's religious leaders reacted with characteristic ambivalence to these developments. On the one hand, they saw economic growth as a sign of God's blessings upon His chosen people. On the other, they worried that worldly ambitions would divert attention from "the holy experiment." They were concerned also about both the declining respect they themselves were accorded by their congregations and the increasing number of "dissenters" in their midst.

They might have expected the declining respect. After all, their audience was hardly the zealous and persecuted lot of a century past who had crossed an angry ocean to set up a pure church. The purpose of the Halfway Covenant of 1662 and generally relaxed standards of church admission in the late 17th century had been to extend the influence of the church and maintain community order, but an unforeseen result was that there were now many communicants whose loyalty to the minister and the doctrine he preached was less than enthusiastic. In 1675, Massachusetts had to pass a law requiring meetinghouse doors to be locked during sermons because so many people were leaving church early. A less coercive approach to securing devotion was an Act of the Connecticut Assembly in 1699 which allowed every inhabitant of a town to have a voice in choosing the minister, church member or not.

The Saybrook Platform, made into law in 1708, was supposed to shore up the perceived loss of status of the Puritan ministry and to bring some order to the expanding network of established churches in the colony. Consociations on the county level would oversee the licensing of ministers in the various "ecclesiastical societies" (their term for parishes), and, by organizing the churches in this "presbyterian" manner, oversee generally the preaching of the Word. But these provisions faced stiff resistance from parishioners who often continued to stand by the autonomy guaranteed them in the old Cambridge Platform of 1649. Similarly the new law did not round up the strays.

    In Connecticut "sober dissenters" were theoretically free to worship as they pleased under the law that put the Saybrook Platform into practice. Pressure from the crown had seen to their protection. This category included Baptists, Quakers and Anglicans (but not Catholics). Each of these denominations had a few churches in Connecticut by 1708, when the Assembly declared "that nothing...shall...prevent any society or church that is or shall be allowed by the laws of this government, who soberly differ or dissent from the united churches [established under the Saybrook Platform] from exercising worship and discipline in their own way according to their consciences."[1] It was hardly a giant step forward toward toleration, though. Members of these other churches were still required to pay taxes to support the minister of the established church, and to appear before the county court to get permission to attend their own church.

    After the Peace of Utrecht both Baptists and Anglicans argued forcefully that they should be extended even greater toleration. The Baptists criticized the establishment for not being pure enough and for being dependent upon a secular authority, and the Anglicans faulted congregationalism for being ineffective in promoting social order and respect for authority. The latter charge had a particular sting to it at the time, since the Congregational ministers did feel they were losing respect. Finally, in 1727 and 1729 the government relented and passed laws freeing Baptists and Quakers from paying the establishment minister's rate and allowing Anglicans a proportion of that local rate equal to their proportion of the society's population.[2] This arrangement, of course, only encouraged the growth of dissenting churches.

    Third and fourth generation Puritan ministers fought back ably against these threats to their hegemony. They invoked traditional notions of deference to authority figures rooted deeply in the souls of New Englanders. They kept up with all the latest discoveries, not only in religious studies, but also in science and agriculture, in order to be the primary source of knowledge and wisdom in their communities. They "modernized" their speeches by incorporating into sermons libertarian ideals which seemed complementary to Congregational ideology. And if that didn't work they cited recent calamities such as the frequent small pox epidemics, some particularly severe fires in the port towns, Queen Anne's War, and the great earthquake of 1727, as continued documentation of God's controversy with His people and their need to walk the straight and narrow path. Following closely the themes of individual salvation, human sinfulness, and divine grace preached since the beginning of English settlement in New England, they made good use of their dominance of the only show in town to train their flock in habits of respect for the ministers of the gospel.[3]

As Simsbury's first settled minister Edward Thompson had once preached, conversion was a "soul satisfying Enjoyment" of heavenly things in which "our heads will be so full of knowledge and our hearts with joy, that we shall say Lord we have enough!"[4] Surely both Dudley and Timothy Woodbridge harped on these notions over and over again, as well as being down-to-earth businessmen ready to lead their frontier community into the thriving worlds of commerce and mining. All this they did to secure a principal place for the gospel and to inspire the conversion of their rough-hewn followers. But it wasn't enough.

The well-honed rational rhetoric these ministers learned at Harvard and Yale in the early 1700s was missing something, and the result was obvious. Certainly Timothy Woodbridge could tell he was not connecting when he went three years without his salary! The town had always been somewhat deficient in regard to compensation for the minister, but things were clearly getting worse. Little good it did him to have the Hartford Consociation on his side - he would have been better off if they had stayed out of the mess in the first place.

Not too far north of Salmon Brook, in Hampshire County, Massachusetts, Rev. Solomon Stoddard was forging a path by which, he believed, New England could yet be redeemed for God's work. His answer in the 1720s was to deliver his sermons with more emotion, more "fire-and-brimstone," and to make use of special events, such as the great earthquake, to inspire revivals which would snowball into numerous conversions. His grandson, Jonathan Edwards of Northampton, reacting to the ordination of Robert Breck as an Anglican minister in Springfield, took up the same approach in the 1730s (Breck, incidentally, would later speculate in land in "the wedge" between Salmon Brook and Granville, Massachusetts). However, even these revivals ran out of steam after a year or two.[5]

The more popular and emotional tone of the sermons continued to develop into the norm for successful preaching for many ministers, though. Unfortunately, the result was a further weakening of clerical authority, as the public watched their shepherds argue over the means to conversion, with Anglicans and Baptists criticizing from the extremes. In the midst of this, in the fall of 1740, the twenty-four-year-old English Evangelist George Whitefield made his triumphal tour of Connecticut, unleashing fiery "New Light" rhetoric about the wrath of God, the utter sinfulness of the human condition, and the need for immediate repentance. He traveled all over the colony, and by the end of October of that year most inhabitants had heard him preach one or more times, and had at least watched as he had galvanized people into convulsions and emotional conversions. In areas where there had been the greatest changes in the lives of his listeners, regardless of their economic and social class, he made the most impact (particularly in eastern Connecticut where the economic expansion of the early 1700s had been the most pronounced). But many church leaders ("Old Lights") began to grow nervous about the nature of this impact, particularly when he began to criticize the clergy for being unconverted themselves. "The reason why congregations have been dead," he wrote in his journal, "is because they have dead men preaching to them...." Obviously this attitude was destined to offend some.[6]

All this was occurring while Simsbury was dividing into four societies and the people of Salmon Brook were in the midst of building their first meetinghouse. The "contentions" that had resulted in the birth of the Northwest Society, however, were not related to the religious controversy of the day. Instead, as we have seen, they centered around the issue of having a meeting house closer to their home village, a village separated naturally from Hop Meadow. Timothy Woodbridge of Simsbury was not an evangelical minister to be sure, and it was he, not some Edwards or Whitefield disciple, whom the Salmon Brook people asked to preach to them when they began to hold their separate meetings in 1739. And when Nathaniel Holcomb Jr., Philip Loomis and James Smith went looking for a permanent minister in 1740, they came up with Eli Colton, also a fairly conservative preacher.[7]

When the Great Awakening came to Salmon Brook, however, it exerted tremendous influence on the community, both in the near term and in the long run. Although it may be difficult for us today to appreciate how significant religious issues were for these people, we should keep in mind that

159

these were, to be sure, God-fearing people, who were required to attend meetings twice a week and hear sermons and lectures sometimes lasting two hours. On Sundays, there were always two services with a 1 to 1 1/2 hour intermission, during which people would remain at the meeting house socializing. Sometimes a prayer could last an hour by itself, with the congregation standing![8] The average weekly churchgoer in New England listened to approximately 7000 sermons (150,000 hours) in a lifetime.[9] The church was all they had for salvation from what had always been described, either in rational or emotional terms, as a dismal fate should they fall into Satan's clutches. And it was the only institution they knew that would bring people together in harmony and peace. It was their social life, the overseer of their public school system, the hope of their political life, the rationale for their economic life, and the stable bulwark of their morality. These were facts of colonial New England life throughout the region. Religion made a big difference; and, as we shall see, the impact of religious turmoil would not only become a matter of great community concern, but also would shape the attachment people had to various political ideas later on during the Revolution. The Great Awakening may not have brought about the division of Simsbury into different ecclesiastical societies, but when it did hit Salmon Brook, a tight-knit Puritan frontier community much like many of the frontier communities of the region, it would, indeed, shape values and ideals for generations to come.

Young Samuel Hays Jr. and Rosanna Holcomb, the subjects of our Prologue, were teenagers in the 1740s, and certainly the eventual prominence of this couple dictates a close look at events that would make a great impression on them in their formative years. We need to remember that to be a teenager in colonial times was, even more than today, to make final preparations for adulthood. This was their time to learn the work of adults, to find a spouse, to consider "owning the covenant" (becoming church members), and generally to acquire (verbatim almost) the values of their parents. All the sage pronouncements of the day and all the advice pamphlets to parents dictated that childhood was simply the kindergarten of adulthood. Their parents were good Puritans and would be signers of the original Salmon Brook covenant, members five and six and twelve and thirteen, along with fifty-three other souls who promised faithfulness to God, to each other and to their collective sense of right and wrong.[10] This group was composed heavily of families of the earliest settlers: for example, there were eighteen Holcombs and nine Hayeses, almost half the congregation from two families. Surely one can imagine Samuel and Rosanna being indoctrinated by a strong Puritan emphasis on "working together for the glory of God," watching out for each others' salvation, keeping peace, harmony and order, holding respect for one's superiors on earth (even though all men and women, rich and poor, were equal before God), knowing that the outside world (particularly Europe and the Catholic Church) was brimming with corruption and decadence, understanding the need for the civil government to uphold the status of the church and to enforce fair and godly laws, and seeing the work of God (as well as the temptations of Satan) in every part of life.

Young Samuel and Rosanna surely were taught as well to value independence and to see their community in terms of Salmon Brook. Doubtless, if their parents had been among the agitators complaining of the distance to Hop Meadow, their children would hardly see much of the world south of "the barren Pine Plain." When the Great Awakening hit Salmon Brook it contributed more building blocks to that already existing spirit of independence. Here too, we will see how intensely independent Salmon Brook people could be as individuals, as well as a covenanted community.

O Sinners!

The Awakening arrived at Salmon Brook in 1741. At the time Rev. Eli Colton, an "Old Light," was preaching, and some of the leaders of the congregation and society were hoping to "settle" him as their permanent minister. They even sent a committee to the Hartford North Consociation to ask its advice on what to arrange with Colton, and in June the Consociation had agreed that settling Colton was the right thing for the Northwest Society.[11] Then the trouble began, although the records do not say how. Perhaps the consociation thought the society should pay Colton more than already planned; perhaps some of the society had heard "New Light" preaching elsewhere; perhaps one of these soul-wrenching preachers had wandered into Salmon Brook. We don't know. In July, Jonathan Edwards had preached his famous sermon "Sinners in the Hands of an Angry God" in Enfield, and itinerant revivalist preachers were becoming more and more a part of the landscape.[12] Sometime during the fall of 1741 a movement to reverse the decision to settle Colton developed. A meeting on October 19, 1741 was recorded only as "opened and dissolved" - and that always meant trouble. Farmers have better things to do in the fall than to go to meetings to adjourn. The explanation for what happened then can be read between the lines in the Society meetings held the next year:

> Att a Meting of the Northwest Society in Simsbury at the Meting house on the first friday of May=AD=1742: to Conclude whether Wee should setel Mr. Colton on our former Trety with him or on the advice of the association or conclude anything Else concerning him as should then and there be thought fit = and att sd. meeting Capt. Holcomb was Chosen moderator for sd metting and first voted whether wee should setel on our former Trety and past in the negetive. Secondly voted Whether wee would proceed to Setel on the advise of the asociation and paste in the negetive. and Lastly voted that the Meting should be dissolved.[13]

Quite simply they could not agree on anything except ending the meeting.

After what seems to have been a month of "cooling off" the leaders managed to pull people together and extract a vote to send a committee to the Association to seek advice "under our presente Difocoltys with Respect to Seteling a Minister." In the meantime, the Association, which had been in support of the Awakening a year before, had declared against itinerant preaching, and its Old Light members had convinced the legislature to pass a law against revivals conducted by ministers who were not licensed by an association. "Besides Reading, hearing, meditation and Prayer," the Association prescribed, "[the people] should seek to their own stated pastors as their Local guides, and to neglect them and ordinarily betake themselves to Lay persons is irregular and unsafe."[14] In Salmon Brook, this inspired a renewal of efforts by the Old Lights to keep Colton, but also a vote "to open a doer for preaching agreeable to our Late Law."[15] Colton responded guardedly to the new developments, but the movement to send him packing was growing stronger.

The squabbling continued through September with desperate efforts at a compromise attempted. On Sept. 13, the Society voted to invite "some neighboring <u>ordained</u> ministers of the North association and also Mr. Timothy Edwards of Northhampton, Mr. Timothy Woodbridge of Hatfield, Mr. Balantine of Westfield and Mr. Gays of Suffield First Parish." The New Lights of Salmon Brook apparently would not hear of such a compromise and created such an uproar at a meeting the next week that the moderator had to "divide the Meeting House" (stand the yeas on one side and the nays of the other) in order to get an accurate vote count. And even then there was contention over who was qualified to vote.[16] Colton gave up and left without having been paid more than a quarter of his past salary due. The Association ordered that the society accept a committee of area ministers as arbitrators in regard to what they owed Colton, but no one in Salmon Brook seemed to pay attention.[17]

On and on the bickering went. The Old Light leaders, such as Captain Nathaniel Holcomb (Nathaniel III) and Daniel Hayes, barely holding their seats on the Prudential Committee, tried to install an "orthodox" or "regularly ordained" minister, while obviously a large contingent of the society wished to bring the Awakening permanently to Salmon Brook, even against the wishes of the colony's ecclesiastical hierarchy. In December another angry meeting squeaked through a vote to give "the call" to a "regularly ordained" minister whose character must be known to a major part of the society, "nor to any that are not free from any Censor of being Disorderly in there Ministry or Eronous in there Doctrine or Scandelous in their lives."[18] During 1743 the Association proposed four different ministers, but none of them met with the approval of the majority.[19] Some in the society, like James Hillyer and Paul Tomkins, grew disgusted with an assembly obviously becoming too demo-cratic for their tastes and joined the new Anglican congregation in "Scotland" (now North Bloomfield).

The emergence of an Anglican church as an alternative for Simsbury residents adds another element to the story of Salmon Brook as a case study in the changes unleashed by the Great Awakening. The earliest settlers of the Scotland area, principally persons of Welsh and Huguenot extraction, had expressed their preference for the Church of England when Simsbury was first trying to settle a minister. If that had come to anything permanent they, like other early Connecticut Anglican congregations would have represented fringe elements of the colony's society. During the Awakening, however, it was more common to see fairly prominent and wealthy members of society

163

joining the Anglican churches as an expression of their dissatisfaction with the lack of respect for authority which seemed to be infecting the Congregational churches. To an extent this was what happened in Simsbury, for James Hillyer, owner of Salmon Brook's grist mill, and Paul Tomkins, an occasional member of the society's prudential committee, were certainly prominent individuals. Residents of Scotland had gathered an informal society during the 1730s when there was so much turmoil over the dividing of Simsbury into separate ecclesiastical societies. Membership began to pick up quickly, though, when London's Society for the Propagation of the Gospel dispatched William Gibbs, an ordained minister, to establish St. Andrews in 1744. Eventually Gibbs's activities and those of his assistant and successor Roger Viets (who had once, incidentally, been a member of the Congregational Church) would result in 'St. Ann's church at Salmon Brook in 1762, but for the moment, disaffected conservatives bundled up their families and trudged off to the Falls to worship in an atmosphere where people apparently knew how to behave! This attitude and the gradual loss of parishioners (depleting the amount of tax revenues available for the congregational minister) obviously fueled some resentment.[20]

Thus we see that the Awakening divided the community - hardly what its advocates had intended. It had begun with disputes among ministers over how best to reach people. The Old Lights maintained that education was more important than an emotional experience with the Holy Spirit.[21] Ironically, the New Light ministers did support the same old values of community, harmony and congregational unity, they just did it with such disturbing vigor they tore communities apart! They touched on nerves that had been frayed by growing resentments over economic change; and the result was guilt over covetousness or wealth, depending on who was listening. They also appealed to the more democratic and egalitarian inclinations of frontier people who had long felt discriminated against. As people like the second generation of Salmon Brook's farmers learned from itinerant preachers that established authorities may not necessarily be worthy of respect, the issue became less one of doctrine and more one of community autonomy and individual choice.[22]

In the winter of 1744/45 the New Lights of Salmon Brook, probably including the entire Bushy Hill neighborhood (Isaac Dewey, Nathaniel Higley, Samuel Hayes Sr., and John Gossard), tried themselves to offer a compromise.[23] They had actually found an ordained minister they liked, one young David Sherman Rowland, a Yale graduate (class of '43) who had been ordained by the Fairfield Association in August of 1744. Perhaps, the Prudential Committee did not really want to know that the Fairfield Association was dominated by closet New Lights[24] - perhaps it is significant that there were new names on the Northwest Society Prudential Committee later that year (David Holcomb, Abraham Dibol and James Smith Jr.)! At any rate, it did not take Rowland long to make clear to all where he stood on issues of the day. First of all he invited George Whitefield to preach at Salmon Brook. On top of that, he himself had his own special speaking style. Here is a sample of his preaching:

> Your state and condition, O sinners! is infinitely hazardous, however insensible you may be of it; there is but a step between you and the world of spirits, where they have no rest day nor night. ‖ — 'Tis the brittle thread of life that sustains you, and prevents you from immediately sinking into endless despair and misery. Should God's patience be worn out, should he cut short the thread of life, into what a hopeless and miserable condition must you immediately plunge? What raging despair would you be fill'd with, to find yourself surrounded with insulting devils, those ghastly, those horrid fiends, whose rage and malice will add to your torment?[25]

One can imagine the reaction of the conservative Hartford North Association to this! In October, 1745, they wrote the society "that under the present circumstances of things, they do not advise to [Rowland's] settlement in the work of the ministry there."[26] When it became apparent that the majority was not listening, they called forth Rowland, demanded to know if he would repudiate Whitefield's teaching and be loyal to the Saybrook Platform. "The sd Rowland will not countenance and Encourage Mr. Whitefield," they declared," by inviting him to preach or attending his administrations or any other Itinerant preachers or any other of the errors, Separations or disorders prevailing in the country." Rowland refused to accept this order, and consequently the association proceeded to advise once again against his settlement in Salmon Brook.[27]

The parish was in an uproar. Truly a new group of leaders had come to the forefront: Samuel Hayes Sr. and Nathaniel Higley now joined the

165

regular corps of leaders and were guiding the collective actions of the society; and now that collective action turned to open defiance of the centralized power structure of Connecticut's churches. Rowland continued to preach and be paid for preaching until early 1749; and the society voted, at the beginning of this illicit ministry, the following almost seditious declaration:

> 1. y^t we chuse y^t ye church in this Society Shall be Setlod a Congregational Church [as opposed to Presbyterian, which would have been under centralized control - "Congregational" here means independent]
> 2. voted y^t ye Scriptures of ye old and New testament as they are ye only Rule of faith and practis to Christian So they are ye only unering Rule of Church Government and Disapline.
> 3. voted y^t as we know of now human Compoasiour y^t come nearour to ye Scriptuor than Cambrig platform [as opposed to Saybrook Platform] in ye Substance of it so we chuse y^t ye Church in this Society Shall take it in ye Substance of it....[28]

Then followed a clause providing that membership could be obtained upon application to the pastor as long as there was no objection after a three week probation (hardly consistent with the owning of the covenant practiced by Old Lights). Finally, they offered a tolerant welcome to members of neighboring, even Presbyterian, congregations to come to communion in Salmon Brook "as the opportunity may present."

Here we have one of the plainest statements of New Light ideology issued from any congregation during this period. In the sphere of existence that mattered most to them, the people of Salmon Brook declared their independence, said that they were as good as anybody at making the law (that is interpreting God's word), ignored a civil law of the commonwealth, democratized the process of acquiring citizenship in their "body theotic," and constructed a verbal Statue of religious Liberty (as in "give me your tired, your poor" - and your bored too!). Keep in mind young Samuel Hays Jr. growing up through all this, a virtual apprentice to the revolution his father had joined in leading.

Actually it is surprising there was such confrontation between the Association and its parish in the northwest of Simsbury. For Connecticut in general, these years were years of compromise. Revival activity had waned in 1743, and when Whitefield had returned to the colony in 1744 he found most pulpits closed to him. On the other hand, even Old Light ministers were trying to find ways to reconcile differences as more and more new ministers were coming forth from Yale inclined toward New Light ideas. Particularly after 1744, when news of a new war between England and France arrived, the ministry was bent on emphasizing old themes, such as the supremacy of the Bible and New England's holy mission, which had always held the region together in hard times.[29]

Of course, revolutions often have their aftermaths in which the moderates take hold before things get too turned upside down. This happened in Salmon Brook as well. Captain Nathaniel Holcomb, Joseph Willcockson, Lt. David Holcomb, Azariah Holcomb and James Smith Sr. never did give up trying to talk sense into the rebels. They watched and waited until a meeting when it was too cold, or too rainy, or perhaps too sunny for many to attend, and quietly voted to "invite some proper person who is a candidate for the ministry...," who presumably would calm down the stern God of John Calvin. More maneuvering followed - Old Lights brought in old Isaac Burr from Windsor. New Lights brought in Evander Morison from who knows where (perhaps Pennsylvania). Burr left, probably horrified, and Old Lights tried to get the association to throw its weight against Morison. New Lights threatened again to be openly defiant and keep Morison no matter what; Old Lights publicly protested; the whole society fasted and asked God's direction; Morison left for the new parish beginning in West Simsbury (now Canton - he lasted eleven months there despite the legislature's dropping of the law against itinerant preachers and despite the generally declining power of the consociations); New Lights tried to bring in Ebenezer Booge, a recent Yale graduate, to assuage the Old Lights; Old Lights countered by inviting Aaron Brown (Yale 1749), whom the Association had licensed;[30] and finally - they found him.

His name was fitting: Joseph Strong. He must have been a remarkable man to pull together this contentious, painfully independent, determined group of farmers in Connecticut's northern hills. And he was so young too - 23 years old - a classmate of Aaron Brown. Yet he came, spoke, formed a church, laid down doctrine, and converted the lambs in droves (among them Samuel Hays Jr. and his new wife Rosanna Holcomb, by profession of faith). How? Not with fire and brimstone. Not with tomes on obedience and

167

accepted truth. Although he did devote some attention to "church discipline," he worked primarily through simple, straightforward plain talk that brought joy to a people weary of quarreling. "That wisdom which is from above, or true religion, is first pure, then peaceable, gentle, and easy to be intreated,"[31] he told them; and they all breathed a collective, harmonious, peaceful and loving sigh of relief.

He walked the middle road. He allowed them to object to certain parts of the Saybrook Platform (actually practically all of its most important features), as long as they declared acceptance of it in principle.[32]   He introduced singing, a practice independent-minded congregations had often rejected when Old Light ministers had tried to introduce it in the early part of the century. He argued quietly, yet firmly and logically that individual ministers (not congregations) could legitimately differ with Association doctrine. And while he called forth professing communicants with one hand, he baptized infants and admitted people under the Halfway Covenant with the other.[33] In December of 1752 his smiling congregation gave him house, land, salary and a covenant of his own dictation; they brought in ministers from half of Connecticut to ordain him, and they celebrated at a banquet for which the society footed the bill for fifty-three meals, six quarts of wine and three quarts of rum, an appropriately moderate celebration.[34]

Ecclesiastical peace at last reigned in the Northwest Society of Simsbury in 1753. Most of the conservatives, who were bulwarks of the community, had been reunited with the radicals. After a dozen years of searching, a fiercely independent and contentious group of farmers had entered into a covenant to love and watch out for each other in the name of God. Some might see in this the necessity of able leadership and the inevitable triumph of the "middle way," but that would be missing a lot that had happened in those twelve years of bickering and division.

First of all, the whole experience must have been a wrenching one. Most of the parishioners were children of the first settlers, born and raised in Salmon Brook, and united by a bond of frontier living. Then they had intermarried - New Light Samuel Hays's sister Abigail was married to Anglican Paul Tomkins, his sister Joanna was Anglican James Hillyer's wife, and his sister Thankful was Old Light Captain Holcomb's wife. New Light John Gossard had also married into the Hayes family. Timothy Cossitt, son of Anglican Rene Cossitt, married Old Light Joseph Willcockson's daughter Mary and the couple joined Strong's church in 1753. As for newcomer and religious radical Isaac Dewey, whose brother was a Baptist minister, he came from Westfield as had the wives of William and George Hayes.[35] Yet Tomkins and the senior James Hillyer did not return to the society from the Anglican church, and John Gossard and Isaac Dewey would not profess their faith and become members, even though they continued to pay taxes to the society.

Treatment of the Anglicans demonstrates the lingering resentments. Rev. Gibbs, in 1754, was beaten and thrown over a horse to be transported to the Hartford jail for not paying taxes to the Hop Meadow society. He never did recover from the experience.[36] Apparently, so desperate was the Northwest Society for funds to make up for years of unsettled ministers and the expense of building a meeting house without the financial support of some of the society's most prosperous residents, that they asked the legislature special permission to tax absentee landholders on unimproved lands in the society.[37] All this suggests there was an economic basis for a lot of the bad feeling which family ties could not overcome, for many of the absentee landowners by then were rich merchants from the river towns, just as many of the Anglican converts were more prosperous than most of the locals.

Eventually the radicals who would not compromise their New Light views, like John Gossard and Isaac Dewey, did separate and hold Baptist meetings in the 1760s, although an aging and cancer-ridden Nathaniel Higley relented and rejoined the Congregational church shortly before his death in 1773. Unlike the Anglicans, who enjoyed (supposedly) the privilege of receiving their proportion of the society taxes to support their own minister, Connecticut Baptists, or "Separates," did not win exemption from paying taxes to support the society's established minister.[38] And since they were hardly the more prosperous individuals in the society, they faced the discouraging prospect of having to pay for two ministers when they considered exercising their legal right to worship as they pleased. Thus, the divisions which exploded in the 1740s festered away throughout the 1750s.

Even more important than these lingering bad feelings was the heritage of independence and rebellion passed on to the next generation as a result of the struggles between the rank-and-file of the society, who obviously

169

preferred the emotional style of the evangelical preachers, and the ecclesiastical hierarchy of Hartford County.[39] Local leaders like Captain Nathaniel Holcomb, Daniel Hayes, and Joseph Willcockson appear to have been unable to do much to mitigate the hostility being expressed by either side, and, probably they, themselves, sympathized with their neighbors, if only on the issue of the right of the society to choose whatever minister and abide by whichever platform it wanted. After all, they were veterans of the conflicts of the 1720s and 30s where the issue of autonomy was a bread-and-butter issue. The society did, technically, "knuckle under" in the end and settle a minister acceptable to the Consociation; but it was only Strong's deft and firm parrying of a deep-seated impulse to be an island unto themselves that quieted, for a time, expressions of anger and disrespect for anyone who made claims to authority over a community and a congregation which had always wanted to rule itself. In time, the lessons they had learned about resistance to interfering authorities would assist in the dissolution of an empire, and the founding of a town, but for the moment, they had simply learned to live uneasily together.

Unsettlements

Beneath all of the arguments over preaching and autonomy and the unruly behavior so disparaged by the conservatives, was a sea of change in Salmon Brook. Even though the majority of the settlement was composed of the second generation of the original inhabitants and their numerous offspring, there was a steady trickle of newcomers who were making their presence felt. They came for a variety of reasons, and this in-migration, coupled with a backdrop of renewed war for empire between France and England, added all sorts of new dimensions to the community.

Simsbury as a whole was becoming a far more complex community during the early 1700s. As was true of most towns in Connecticut during this period, the powers and responsibilities of the local government and its officials were growing significantly.[40] We have already seen how the discovery of the copper mine called for a good deal of government activity prior to 1713. Also a continuing problem from that time, with which selectmen and town agents were required to grapple for an entire century, was the issue of the town's boundaries. Surveys were made by colonial admin- istrators in 1711, 1713 and 1750, and yet it was still a matter of contention whether land in the "Wedge" (between a mistaken colony line and the present Massachusetts line) was part of Connecticut, and, if so, part of Simsbury. Arguing the town's case in these and other disputes with Suffield, Windsor, Massachusetts, and the Connecticut colony itself, occupied a good deal of town leaders' attention as settlement spread northward after 1730.[41]

As though these issues were not enough, the town's growing popula- tion during the period between 1720 and 1760 called for all sorts of additional agencies of regulation.[42] In 1731, Nathaniel Higley was appointed to a new office, "brander of horses." In 1735, the town acquired its own set of weights and measures. In 1738, the town clerk began registering earmarks to distinguish one farmer's sheep from another. The following year, substantial improvements were voted for the town's stock of ammunition as war loomed once again on the horizon, and the meeting also voted to look a lot more carefully at the situation with town roads than they had up to the present. As travel and commerce picked up, the issue of bridges and ferries was found more and more on the town agenda. Private enterprise provided the early ones, for toll privileges, but by 1760 it was apparent getting people across the river would have to be a function of local government - not that government's assuming of that responsibility would necessarily mean it was done.[43] All of these activities suggest Simsbury was changing from a small frontier town, where everyone knew everyone, to a larger, more diverse community that required a "referee" to help manage the increasingly complicated affairs of its people.

The most striking evidence of the extension of this complexity into Salmon Brook itself is found in series of petitions of 1753 to the town meeting. While James Hillyer was the first to establish a grist mill at Salmon Brook, others soon became involved in the business as the population grew. Joseph Willcockson, Brewster Higley and Hosea Willcockson formed a partnership to build one, and Abraham Dibol built another. In 1753 Dibol complained that someone was pulling down his dam, and the others responded saying that, of course, they did not know who was doing that, but that Dibol was holding up everybody else's water power. Hillyer claimed he was the only rightful mill operator since he had been on the North Branch first, but the town had actually not given its customary damming rights to anyone.[44]

As town government raced to keep up with the needs of a growing population, Salmon Brook had also changed as a community. While much of Salmon Brook's population growth was a result of natural increase, there were significant numbers of newcomers who added new elements of diversity to the community. Tax lists of 1736 and 1742 include a lot of people, who, like Nehemiah Lee, Isaac Dewey and Philip Loomis, had recently migrated to the parish: Gideon, Othenial, Nathan, Zabod and Joseph Gillet; Solomon, John and Jacob Halladay; George Granger; Ebenezer Caudwill (sic.); Edmond Edmonds; John MacDaniel; and Jonathan Read; not to mention people like Rene Cossitt, Nathaniel Higley and James Hillyer who had recently moved into the society from the southern part of Simsbury.[45]

Among these family heads were obviously some renters and very temporary inhabitants, for there are few records of land grants or purchases for any of them. They came from a variety of places and backgrounds, and the tax lists indicate a wide range of individual wealth. James Smith and Philip Loomis seemed to be the richest men in the society in 1742, paying £7 - 8 in taxes, while Consider Holcomb paid only 7 shillings. Those on the lower end of the economic scale tended to be newcomers and young men just starting out for themselves, while those on the upper end were both newcomers and longtime residents.

We met Rene Cossitt in the last chapter, a highly educated Frenchman, brought to Connecticut in captivity around 1711, a resident for a time at Middletown, and then after marriage to Ruth Porter, attracted with a land grant to Simsbury in 1723 where Ruth's grandparents, Joshua and Ruth Holcomb, lived.[46] He bought a farm in the old Griffin's Lordship from John Gaspar Huffman, a mine operative, in 1725, and lived there for at least eleven years, struggling along with other debtors in the town to keep up with the changing economy of that era.[47] As a former Catholic, he preferred the Church of England to the pope-bashing Puritans, and took part in the Anglican congregation then organizing below the Falls.[48] Although he was not yet an inhabitant of Simsbury in January, 1723, when the town meeting decided to divide the commons, he did receive a grant of land among the lots of the Sixth Half-mile tier laid out on April 9, 1734. This lot was located at the present junction of Day St. and North Granby Rd., and, as a matter of fact, Day St. is its original east boundary line.[49]

It is not clear when Rene moved to this forty-eight acre lot, for only his son, Rene Jr., is listed in the 1742 tax list of the Northwest Society, and since the family was Anglican, we do not see much of them in the society records, Salmon Brook's principal public record prior to 1786. Certainly he was there by the late 1740s, for he referred to the parcel in a deed of 1749 as "my homestead...with my dwelling house."[50] At that point he was setting up his sons Rene Jr. and Franceway (an Anglicized version of Francois, no doubt) with farms in the North Granby area. His eldest daughter Margaret had already married Nathaniel Holcomb IV, and they lived on a farm just south of the Cragg on the North Branch of Salmon Brook. Here in the brook land and hilly upland near the Cragg, Rene and Ruth completed the raising of their family of nine children, and, apparently prospered. Although he had deeded a good deal of his land holdings to his children before his death in 1752, the estate of Rene Cossitt (or Raney, Ranna or Ranney, as his English neighbors called him) amounted to over £3500. The Cossitts expanded into the brook land and tier lots to their north and, along with Nathaniel Holcomb IV, were largely responsible for the settlement of North Granby, where a library bearing the family name stills serves the public. It did pay, in the long run, to risk living on the outskirts. The land produced well, and if his daughter Mary's marriage to Thomas Welton of Waterbury is any indication of the breadth of Rene's trading contacts, it would appear he had mastered the regional network by the 1740s.[51]

The Halladay brothers of Suffield were another family willing to take on the risks of outland living in search of opportunity. In 1738, John and his new wife Elizabeth Walworth, Solomon, Samuel, Ebenezer and Jacob Halladay joined together to purchase a 200 acre lot in present West Granby from Captain Jonathan Westover of "Westover Plain" near present Floydville Rd. At the time no one lived in this part of town, although as early as 1717 and 1720 Thomas Holcomb, John Saxton and Jonathan Holcomb had staked claims to patches of grassland probably cleared by former Algonkian inhabitants. The attraction of the Westover lot, for which they paid £120, was the gorge where the West Branch flowed "out of the mountain," and into the flatter land northwest of Barn Door Hills (See Map 4-1). The Halladays saw "grist mill" written all over this beautiful piece of rock and waterfall, and

173

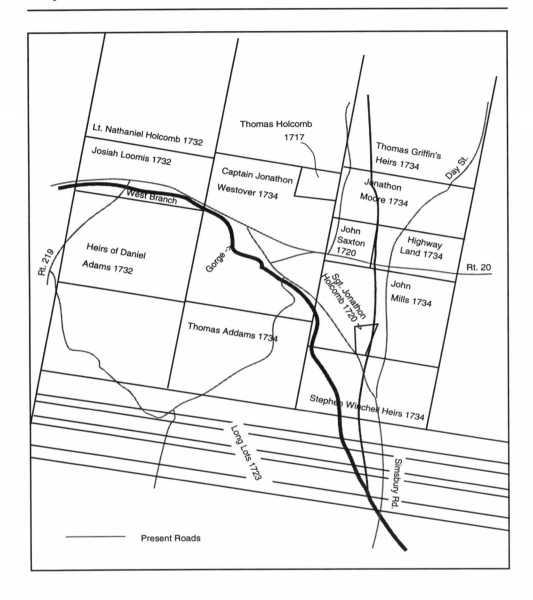

Map 4-1: Original Land Grants in West Granby area, 1717-1734. The "Long Lots," surveyed in 1723, reached into the hilly land from almost four miles away where they bordered on what is now Route 10 below Granby center. The other large lots are from the 4th, 5th and 6th half-mile tiers laid out in 1732 and 1734.

174

when their father died in 1741 they packed up their families and widowed mother and headed for a neighborhood they thought would soon be filled with farmers needing a convenient place to bring their grain. Unfortunately, the farmers did not arrive for another decade, and the Halladays themselves even had to build a road to the houses along Bushy Hill and Barn Door Hills Roads to encourage business. In the meantime, they sunk deeper into debt.[52]

Their experience, however, did not stop another Suffield couple from following in their footsteps. Serajah and Eunice Stratton had lived in Simsbury with Eunice's parents Samuel and Elizabeth Case when they first married in 1728. At the death of Samuel, however, the couple had reassessed their position and decided to move to Suffield, then part of Massachusetts, where Serajah's brother William lived. Serajah was trained to be a blacksmith, and apparently there was work in Suffield - not in Simsbury. Before long, though, the Strattons and their family of three, Martin (b. 1730), Eunice (b. 1733), and Serajah Jr. (b. 1740) were back in Simsbury. In April, 1742, Serajah bought a house, barn, and orchard on a three-acre lot west from Hop Meadow, and the following year he took the freeman's oath as a full-fledged member of the town and colony.

The reason for this moving back and forth is unknown. Perhaps Simsbury suddenly needed a blacksmith after 1740 - perhaps Serajah thought he had a better chance of competing against other craftsmen with the new technology he brought from Suffield. In March, 1745, he purchased from the Pettibone family the "Liberty of setting up a blacksmith shop on the Bank of the Brook adjoyning [the Pettibone's] gristmill [Hop Brook], and for setting up a wheel at the foot of the mill for carrying a hammer called a Tripp Hammer...as long as he is a blacksmith." The trip hammer was a water powered blacksmith's hammer, far more powerful than even the strongest of smith's arms.

It may be that things did not go well on the south branch of Hop Brook (later called Stratton's Brook). In 1747, the couple was able to purchase a ten acre lot at the head of the brook (Slater's Marsh) from Elias Slater, but Eunice was the grantee of the deed. Placing property in a wife's name was often a strategy employed by men in debt to safeguard the property from their creditors. Whatever their circumstances at Hop Brook, for some reason Serajah and Eunice got the urge to move on - to find a better place. Such a

175

place was in the northwest corner of Simsbury, in a forest that would, they thought, soon be settled by Simsbury's next generation, who would not be able to get enough land in the settled areas and who were still uneasy enough about the French and their Indian allies not to move too far from home. The Strattons didn't care that the land was not the best farming land - Serajah was a craftsman, and getting there first was what counted for craftsmen.

So in 1749 the Strattons sold their home lot near Hop Brook for £300, and in 1753, for £262, they persuaded Jacob Loomis to part with a rocky, forested seventy-five acres he had inherited. This lot bordered on the Westover lot the Halladays had bought, but, even though Serajah was a blacksmith, he and his son Martin decided to build a saw mill and a corn mill to compete with John Halladay. They dug a canal from Salmon Brook, where it presently crosses under Route 219, to a mill pond on Higley Brook just before it empties into the West Branch, and finding that they had an easier time than Halladay keeping ice flows from ruining their dams and mill, built both a grist mill and a trip hammer shop. Perhaps this competition explains why John Halladay had such difficulty getting out of debt.[53]

Similarly from Suffield came Peter and Abijah Rowe, also blacksmiths, and their brother Joseph. In 1748, Joseph had married Elinor Rice, daughter of William and Mary Hayes Rice, who lived at the north end of the old row of original house lots (opposite the present entrance to Salmon Brook Park). Probably they lived with her parents after moving to Salmon Brook, and in 1757 they "owned the covenant" (became church members under the Halfway Covenant). Peter married Elizabeth Lee, the daughter of Nehemiah and Marcy Frost Lee, and bought Nehemiah's house from him in 1750. He built a substantial blacksmith shop there, and then sold it to his brother Abijah, who had just become twenty-one in 1753. Abijah married Deborah Forward of Turkey Hills and continued as a blacksmith at Salmon Brook, opening a larger shop across the street and living in the house until his death in 1812. (See Figure 4-1. The house was given in 1966 by Mildred Colton Allison and Carolyn Colton Avery to the Salmon Brook Historical Society for its headquarters.) His daughter Mary married Joseph Gillet Jr., son of Joseph Gillet. Joseph had come to Salmon Brook from Windsor in 1739 to marry Samuel Hayes Sr.'s daughter Elizabeth and built a house next to her father on Barn Door Hills Road.[54]

176

Salmon Brook Historical Society

Figure 4-1: Abijah Rowe House (front), since 1966 the headquarters of the Salmon Brook Historical Society. The house may, actually, have been built by Nehemiah Lee as early as 1732. Abijah purchased the property in 1753.

These new inhabitants of the Northwest Society added depth and breadth to the parish. Attracted by cheap land on the outskirts of the settled area and by the possibility of making a good living on it, they risked the still present dangers of predators, attack, and isolation, as well as the uncertainty that others would join them, and moved to a town torn by religious dissent and contention. They brought new skills in trades like blacksmithing and mill construction, new ideas and new energy. In general they were welcomed by a group of people who may have differed with them in habits and church doctrine, but who were equally committed to living independently in every sense of the word. They all still believed in the ideals of community and harmony, hearing them from New Light and Old Light preachers alike, but their lifestyles expressed an individualism which often worried their ministers in all sorts of ways. Whatever the case, the new people, and Simsbury's

177

generally expanding population brought change, and the people of Salmon Brook at once welcomed it and remained anxious about it.

Hill Farmers, Speculators and Soldiers

As a third generation began coming of age in the 1750s and more families moved into the society from Suffield, Westfield, Windsor and other parts of Simsbury, interest in the outer lands began to pick up. By 1740, most of the good land along the two branches of Salmon Brook or scattered grasslands in the foothills was taken up. The choice in that year for the new meetinghouse site considerably north of the original settlement shows that a good number of people had moved north and west into the lands that needed clearing and that the settlement was much more spread out than a decade earlier. The only land left to expand into was the hilly six tiers of lots west of Bushy Hill. There was also land to the north of the Cragg in the "Wedge," the old Bedford tract above the pre-1713 colony line. Although this piece of Connecticut was not yet placed under Simsbury's jurisdiction (it would be in 1774), Salmon Brook inhabitants still looked to it for cheap land.

During the 1730s many Simsbury inhabitants had used the tier lots to extract themselves from debt or to raise cash to buy more attractive and convenient land near their homesteads. Others had managed to hold out and use the land to provide their sons with a start in life. Where there were inhabitants who needed the money immediately, land speculators from Windsor, Hartford, Simsbury itself, and even as far away as Boston, had leapt in to provide the cash, and by 1750, many of the lots in these tiers were in the hands of absentee owners poised to take profits. So intense had been the land speculation frenzy regionally, that it was at this time that the legislature began organizing towns like Hartland and Barkhamsted and auctioning proprietorships off to raise revenue.[55] Similarly to the north of Salmon Brook wealthy Massachusetts investors John Hunt, Robert Breck and Charles Apthorp divided up their holdings in the "Wedge" in preparation for sale.[56]

The efforts by Samuel Hayes Sr. and David Holcomb to find homesteads for their third generation children, illustrate the new land settlement patterns of the 1750s. In 1751, David Holcomb, who lived on Salmon Brook St. north of what is now the South Congregational Church, traded some lots

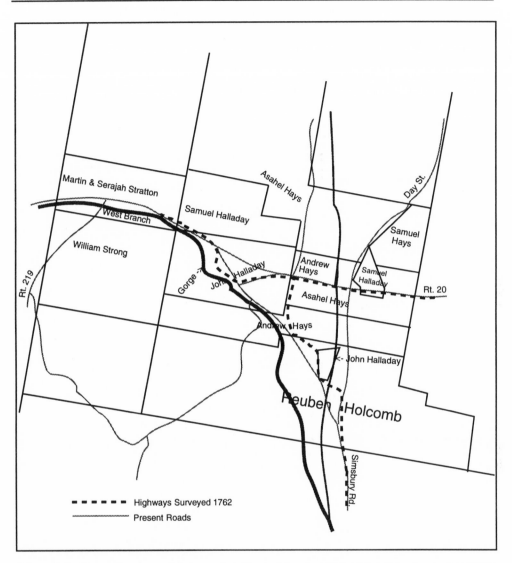

Map 4-2: Boundaries of farms developed in the West Granby area by 1762 when the town of Simsbury surveyed a "highway" to accommodate the growing settlement. Note the path of Simsbury Road then, when the surveyors were circumventing tillage. Later, when inhabitants built houses near their shops along the brook, the road was moved to its present course. None of the dwellings from the earlier period has survived.

179

with Thomas Adams of Simsbury and ended up with the last lot of the 6th Half-mile tier which Adams had bought from its original grantee. Holcomb held on to this until 1757 when he gave it to his son Reuben as his share of David's estate. Reuben had already purchased the 5th tier lot to the west of this land to make a total of 180 acres (See Map 4-2). By 1762, he had bought even more land contiguous to his new farm and moved into a house on the west side of Bushy Hill. (This farm, incidentally, was passed from father to son to son to son to son. The last Holcombs to live and work on the farm were siblings Tudor and Laura Holcomb.)[57]

Samuel Hayes Sr., whose daughter Susanna was Reuben Holcomb's wife, had four sons in need of farms between 1750 and 1765. He began by purchasing a relatively new farm from Return Holcomb in 1750 for his eighteen-year-old son Asahel (who had just married Reuben Holcomb's sister Martha). In 1753, he helped his son Samuel Jr. buy land east of Bushy Hill Road and north of what is now Rt. 20. Three years later he bought land from Solomon Halladay, who was in the process of giving up on Salmon Brook and returning to Suffield, and saved it three years for his son Andrew. He also took care of nineteen-year-old Silas in that year, giving him land north of Samuel Jr.'s (which made sense since these two brothers had married daughters of Judah Holcomb). When Asahel, Andrew and their brother-in-law Reuben Holcomb used £135 of the late Samuel Hayes Sr.'s estate in 1762 to pay speculator John Roberts of Windsor for a large lot straddling present Rt. 20 in West Granby, this collection of brothers and sisters had pretty much laid claim to that little valley at the foot of the West Granby Gorge.[58]

At this point town officials decided the area was indeed "settled," and surveyed a road south from "the road to Halladay's" toward Hop Meadow. The survey is interesting in that it mentions houses and confirms what the Strattons and the Halladays were relieved to know: that the farmers had come at last.[59] It is interesting too that there are revealing differences between the route this road followed and the present route of Simsbury Road. The 1762 survey brought the road down through fields that are essentially the back yards of today's Simsbury Road houses. These houses we now see were built later on the present course of Simsbury Road along the brook west of the original road. In 1762, this was a settlement of farmers whose business was in the fields. The next generation would take more interest in the potential of

180

the water power to make machines work, and they would move the road toward the shops on the brook. But in the 1750s, Parliament had all sorts of regulations forbidding manufacturing in America and it is probable that even Serajah Stratton's trip hammer had to bang away discretely.[60]

Other young couples were also venturing across Bushy Hill at this time, beginning the long, slow process of carving farms out of the heavily wooded hillsides near Stratton's and Halladay's mills. In 1755, George Hayes Jr.'s son Elisha, who had just married Mercy Lamson the previous year, paid £365 for a fifty-six acre lot straddling what is now the junction of Silkey and Higley Roads in West Granby. This lot had already been through three speculators in the preceding five years and had nearly doubled in price (there was considerable inflation at that time, however). Elisha planned to build a farm, and there he stayed until his death in 1787. By that time his younger brother Benjamin, who had married his cousin Rosanna Hays, daughter of Samuel Jr., had also moved to this neighborhood, buying Samuel Halladay's farm.[61]

Timothy Cossitt, son Rene and Ruth, moved from his North Granby home to the western hills in 1757. He and his wife Mary Willcockson had first lived near the Cragg, along with other young Cossitts, but he sold his property there, retaining only an interest in the mill site. He moved to what was then a deep forest on the western boundary line between Simsbury and Barkhamsted. The property, which is now returning to its wooded state as part of Enders State Forest, was a lot his father-in-law had received in the first half-mile tier. It was not until well after the Revolution that other people began to move into that area, both on the Granby side and on the Barkhamsted side of the line, but Timothy and Mary seemed to have found the independence, and solitude they wanted at that time.[62]

Young farmers, some from other parts of Simsbury, were also beginning to move into the hills at the north end of town in the 1750s. Among the first were Hezekiah and Hannah Phelps of Turkey Hills. Hezekiah's grandfather, Joseph Phelps, had received a 240-acre grant of land on the top of "Popatunuck" in 1732 when the second half-mile tier had been surveyed. He had held this lot, located around the junction of Mountain and Silkey Roads, and passed it on to his son Joseph Jr. in 1744. Joseph Jr. had all the land he needed in Turkey Hills, but still held the lot until his sons Hezekiah,

Abel and Ezekiel needed farms in the mid-1750s. At that point, he divided the lot among them, and they began to move to the mountain. Hezekiah and his new wife Hannah Hayden began to clear their land in 1757 - he was 25 and she was 19 - but may not have taken up permanent residence until 1764. Surely they exploited the timber resources, not only to build their own house, but also to feed the continually growing world-wide demand for lumber. According to Rev. Roger Viets, the successor to William Gibbs at St. Andrews and the new parish of St. Ann's in Salmon Brook (which had just been created in 1762) Hezekiah and Hannah attended his church, rather than Joseph Strong's Congregational church.[63]

Also moving into this neighborhood were Silas Holcomb and his wife Mary Post, Ozias Holcomb and his wife Rachel Cornish, and Benajah Holcomb. Silas, Ozias and Benajah were all sons of Judah and Hannah Buttolph Holcomb, who had, themselves, moved north from Salmon Brook Street in the 1740s to build a house on North Granby Road in the same neighborhood as Judah's brother Nathaniel Holcomb III and Hannah's brother Jonathan. Now, in the late 1750s, Judah was buying lots on the mountain for his sons, one just inside the Wedge, from the Hunt family; one just south of that; and another in the fourth half-mile tier on Mountain Road which had been through three land speculators before Judah acquired it and deeded it to his son (See Map 4-3).[64]

Thus the third generation of Simsbury settlers consisted of a group of pioneers who took advantage of the lands won from the commons by their parents in the "contentions" of the 1720s. When they moved, they moved as groups of "in-laws," forming new little settlements which amounted to a few extended families. Even more so than their parents they spread out among the hills, building their houses in the center of their land holdings, often several hundred yards from their nearest neighbor. Yet it is clear they still clung to communal values supported by kinship networks even as they became more individualistic. They still settled the land as families.

Anyone wandering in the woods in the hills of West Granby or North Granby today cannot fail to see the testimony to the energy and ambition of these young families in the form of mile after mile of stone walls thrown up in the latter half of the 18th century for the triple purpose of clearing out fields and pastures, containing livestock and marking boundaries. These walls,

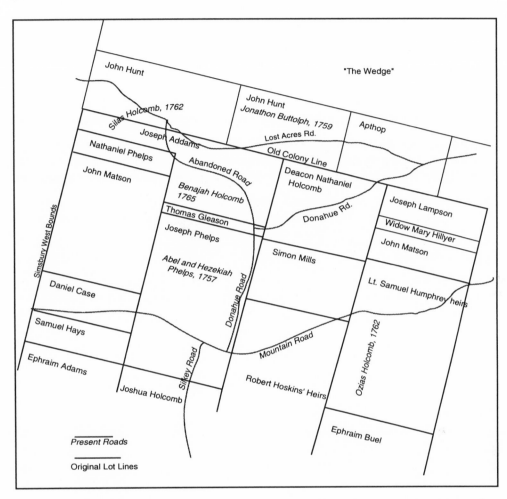

Map 4-3: Original grantees and some eventual settlers on "Popatunuck," now the Mountain Road and Lost Acres Road sections of North Granby. A number of the lots were purchased by Judah Holcomb for his sons Ozias, Silas and Benajah in the late 1750s. Judah and Hannah Buttolph Holcomb lived in a house on North Granby Road. Hannah's brother Jonathan, who once lived near her on North Granby Road also moved to Popatunuck at that time. Hezekiah and Abel Phelps were sons of Joseph Phelps of Turkey Hills Society. All of these people who lived on Popatunuck were members of Roger Viets's church at one time or another.

183

Paul Bazyk

Figure 4-2: Early 20th-century photograph of a field in West Granby looking east off Broad Hill. The area under the tobacco tent was the same field granted to John Saxton in 1720. The larger rectangle created by old fence lines trace ancient lot lines that are reflected still in today's property lines.

some still up to four feet in height, have survived the earthquakes of the colonial period and annual frost heaves to help us to plot out the original land grants of the 1720s and 30s and to understand the settlement patterns of the 1750s and 60s. What is truly remarkable is how closely these lines of stone follow the lines which can be drawn on a modern survey map based on the written descriptions of the original tiers in the land records. In spite of rugged hills, rocky outcroppings, heavy forest growth, crude surveying equipment and limited training for the surveyors themselves, the rectangles formed by the stone walls in the western hills are as sharp and precise as though they had been done by an aerial survey in the 20th century (See Figure 4-2). Undoubtedly the fact that dozens of young families moved into these tier lots in the space of ten years, each making every effort to secure the full extent of every square inch of land they had been given or paid for, had a great deal to do with the precision by which they marked their domains.

At any rate, by 1763, Salmon Brook was a far more developed community of farmers than it had been in 1730 when the land grants were first made. The families of the first generation had been large, but the grants of the early 1720s had provided the second generation with plenty of good land not far from the original meadows of their parents. But the families of the second generation had also been large, and new people needing land had moved in to the community. Prices, even for acreage in the western hills, had gone up; yet, many young people had been able to acquire farms of one hundred acres or more.

They worked hard to clear that land, plant apple trees, build fences for sheep, cattle and hogs, and trade around their lots until they had a good balance of land for vegetables, orchards, pasture, grass and grain. Since they did not burn their fields regularly as the Algonkians had, they fought with garden and fruit tree pests without the benefit of sprays. To buy tools, hardware, glass, paint and other imported products on which they relied, they exported lumber, cider brandy (the only way it would keep), beeswax, candles, honey, wool and some woolen clothing (mittens, stocking, caps) they could make at home. To do all this required a lot of work, and laborers were not plentiful. Nor could they afford to buy slaves even if they had wanted to. Instead they involved their children in the everyday work as soon as they could walk, or bound them out to a neighbor who might be able to teach them more efficient ways of producing from the land. There was little time for recreation, and most of that involved work of some sort or other: quilting, husking, fishing, haying, house raising. Furthermore, they had little time for, nor desire to travel long distances to the local school (although their parents saw to it that they learned to write their name and read the Bible and an almanac). There was a library formed by subscription in Salmon Brook in 1761, "to promote useful knowledge, piety and virtue," and one wonders if this was not Rev. Strong's effort to try to reach out to his more and more numerous hill farming families by loaning them the books they could not buy or send their children to read in school.[65]

Even though they attacked this work of settling the hills with as great a zeal as their ministers would have liked to see them attend to religious affairs, Salmon Brook in 1763 was still a frontier community. Compared to other communities in Hartford County, its population density was relatively

185

light, and in spite of the mass migration of young people to its hilly sections, large areas remained uncleared. The commons had been almost completely divided up by 1734, and so one might reasonably ask, even taking into account the extent to which settlement had spread, why it was still a frontier community three decades later.

One reason was that it took some time for the impact of the third generation at Salmon Brook to be felt. But even when they did begin building farms in the hills in the late 1750s, they seemed hesitant, almost as though they were afraid of the independence their parents and grandparents had so eagerly embraced. Lots which were acquired in 1757 were not occupied on a permanent basis until 1762 or 1763. What slowed them down? Why did the Strattons and the Halladays have to wait so long for a clientele?

The answer lies in the escalating imperial conflicts which were renewed in the 1740s. The peace that most people did not expect to last began to fall apart in 1739 as England went to war with Spain and was consequently drawn into the War of Austrian Succession. Finally, in 1744, France and England declared war on each other. Called King George's War in British America, it posed particular danger to New England, for France knew that if it was to win control of North America it would have to take New England first. For New Englanders, ridding themselves of the French menace meant taking Canadian strongholds at Louisbourg on Cape Breton and at Quebec and Montreal on the St. Lawrence. This conflict, which lasted, for all practical purposes, until 1763, was clearly a decisive factor in shaping the settlement of lands in Salmon Brook.

In early 1745, the governor of Massachusetts issued a call for troops to attack Louisbourg at the mouth of the St. Lawrence, and thus isolate the rest of Canada. Ministers everywhere, including George Whitefield himself, were also called upon to stir up enthusiasm against the agents of the pope in the New World. The Connecticut Assembly responded by commissioning dozens of officers and sending them into their communities to recruit volunteers for the assault. Samuel Pettibone of Simsbury was commissioned an Ensign and instructed to draw a body of men from his locale.[66]

We do not know who from Salmon Brook accompanied him to Louisbourg - he ended up as a second officer in a company from Hartford, so there may not have been too many from Simsbury. The expedition, composed entirely of New Englanders with no help from British regulars, did succeed in the capture of the fort, but this did not bring the expected end to New England's problems with the French in Canada. As the war dragged on there were attacks on Massachusetts towns, enlistments fell off and Connecticut resorted to offering large bounties for Indian captives and scalps.[67] In 1748 peace was declared and Louisbourg returned to the French, an insult for which New Englanders never forgave the British government. Furthermore, their clergy informed them that the peace would not last, that this was merely a time of testing and chastisement, and that they should realize that the "season of war" with the pope and his French mercenaries had only just begun.[68] With this sort of rhetoric, it is not surprising that young couples delayed taking up lands in the northwest of the Northwest Society of Simsbury.

Indeed, frontier skirmishes in the Ohio Valley in 1754 ignited the final round of the conflict between France and England, called the Seven Years War (in British America, the French and Indian War). This was an immense fight to the finish for North America in which one out of three men able to bear arms in New England enlisted at some point. By the time the war in America had ended in 1762, virtually every family in the region had at least one soldier.[69]

Salmon Brook men enlisted immediately, first in a Suffield Company run by regimental commander Phineas Lyman, and then in greater numbers in a company formed by Jonathan Pettibone of Simsbury. Men such as Return Holcomb, Hezekiah Phelps (who had not yet moved to his mountain home), Moses Dibol, Abraham Dibol, Dudley Hays and James Halladay fought in the Lake George area in the fall of 1755. That November, the largest earthquake in three decades struck New England, which, with the renewed war, gave ministers plenty to talk about. In New York, Fort Oswego fell to the French in 1756. Connecticut dispatched soldiers to Crown Point and Lake Champlain to block what seemed to be imminent invasion, but not many Salmon Brook men participated in this campaign.[70]

Then in August, 1757, came the news that Fort William Henry, at the south end of Lake George, had surrendered to a besieging force of French regulars and Hurons; and as the British soldiers, militiamen and their families were leaving the fort, the Hurons massacred them. To people living on the outskirts of Connecticut and Massachusetts the implications were clear: only

187

Fort Edward just east of Lake George protected them from a cruel fate. Jonathan Pettibone raised a large company from Simsbury to reinforce Fort Edward, including fourteen men listed separately as "Samon Brook Companey," but their service was required for only a few weeks.

Again the next spring, alarms went out and more troops were raised. This time Captain Nathaniel Holcomb put together a whole company of Salmon Brook men, among them young Serajah Stratton, age 17, as well as his father, age 51, who served as company clerk. Why he went to war at age 51 (although his company commander was 60!), and why he was appointed company clerk, when a few years earlier he could not put more than a "mark" to a land deed, are two great mysteries. One explanation might be that when he was only two, his father was killed by the French during Queen Anne's War and he hoped to get even. Another might be that he seriously thought he was protecting his home. At any rate, one can imagine the impact the loss of two of the three men of the Stratton household for the entire summer had on the mill business. To top it off, Serajah Sr. died that summer as the company marched toward Quebec. Also in that company were Alexander Cossitt, Rene's son, and Ebenezer Halladay.[71]

The 1758 and 1759 campaigns marked the turning point of the war. Louisbourg and Quebec fell, and in 1760, so did Montreal. Casualties were light for Salmon Brook and enlistments continued strong, as it became apparent that the war to defend God's people and religion against popish tyranny (and to protect Salmon Brook from attack) was coming to a successful conclusion.[72] In between campaigns, with cash in their pockets from soldiers wages or payment for provisions, and with new deeds to land in their hands, young people began to build their farms in the western hills. Then the powers that were, reached too far.

With Canada won, the leaders of the war turned their attention to the Caribbean and launched an invasion of Cuba in the spring of 1762. Noah Humphrey led the 47-man company from Simsbury which included fourteen men from Salmon Brook. The expedition was a disaster. The enemy was not the Spanish, but malaria. Of the fourteen from Salmon Brook twelve died, including Elinor Rice's husband Joseph Rowe, William Hayes's sons Ozias and Aaron and their cousin Zadock Hayes, son of Benjamin. Only Dudley Hays and Andrew Hillyer were alive when Col. Lyman's regiment returned to Connecticut.[73] After that experience it was a good thing the Peace of Paris ended the fighting the next year.

This time England did not give Canada back to the French. The war represented a decisive defeat for France and the end of the French empire in all but a few islands in the western hemisphere. Never again would the Algonkians of northeastern America be encouraged to attack English settlements and outposts, although, everyone knew they still lived in a world inhabited by people who did not want them there. Even in Simsbury there were still a few native inhabitants, and certainly there were plenty in western Connecticut and Massachusetts. The Iroquois of New York, although allies of the British in the war, continued to be a force to be reckoned with, and none of these peoples was ready to disappear just because the French had.

Surely there was great rejoicing, though, and even if some areas of the parish were just beginning to appear somewhat tame, there was a lot of hope for the future. The soil in the hills, fortified by centuries of leaf mold, was not as bad as some had thought it might be, even if the clearing process was painfully slow. A wrenching and divisive struggle within the church had been settled, and people were learning to live with the idea of more than one denomination. As for the Congregational Church (Presbyterian "in principle"), its membership was increasing every year. There was plenty of money in circulation and prices for farm surplus were good. And best of all, they had secured their independence as a community.

Things like that, which mattered most to them, and had mattered most to the parents and grandparents of the third generation of inhabitants, had remained constants. The religious piety they had been brought up with as the defining characteristic of their region, the ambition that had been the underpinning of their survival, if not exactly their prosperity, their spirit of adventure and enthusiasm for a rugged life - all this had been passed along from the first settlers at Salmon Brook to the young people now building in the hills.

The changes had been great as well. They had required adaptation and struggle. The society was not the close-knit closed corporate community of 1730, so consistent with Puritan ideals. It was part of a larger, more complicated town whose government had had to get involved in all kinds of regulation and refereeing. Their little community in the northwest corner had seen a substantial population increase itself, including families from other communities who had brought some degree of disruption with them when they arrived. They were much more spread out than ever, and more laced into the world economic system than those who feared the corruption of the outside world (or of individual ambition) might want. They had a history now of resistance to authority figures, including the colony's church hierarchy, as well as proprietors and civil magistrates who tried to collect on behalf of creditors. In addition, they had a heritage as soldiers defending their country against tyranny and terror, and a culture far more contentious and democratic than early New England leaders had ever intended. As an outgrowth of the manifestations of all of this in the dynamics of their central social institution, they had an Anglican church, a group of Baptists holding meetings, and lingering sour feelings within the Congregational Church itself. But just the same, in 1763, most people, war widows and frustrated millers aside, must have felt that even in a world of individualism, dislocation and disruption, their community was on the right track. Meanwhile, three thousand miles across the Atlantic Ocean, leaders of the world's greatest empire were fashioning policy which implied even greater changes for Salmon Brook.

Chapter V
Patriots

Europe	America	Granby
1763 Peace of Paris ends Seven Years War	1763 Canada ceded to England by France in Peace of Paris	1763 Roger Viets becomes Rector at St. Andrew's, preaches at St. Ann's in Salmon Brook
1764 Parliament passes Sugar Act, first revenue tax on American colonies		1764 Baptist Church begins meeting at Isaac Dewey's house on Bushy Hill Road
1765 Stamp Act	1765 Stamp Act riots, Congress, boycotts	
1766 Stamp Act repealed		
1767 Townshend Duties		
	1768 Massachusetts Circular Letter, more boycotts	1768 Petition from people in "the Wedge" to be a town
1770 Townshend Duties repealed (except tea)	1770 Boston "Massacre"	1770 First petition to legislature to separate Salmon Brook from Simsbury
	1773 Boston Tea Party	1774 Protests against the Boston Port Bill, aid sent to Boston, Committee of Correspondence
1774 Coercive or "Intolerable" Acts	1774 First Continental Congress, Continental Association	
	1775 Lexington and Concord, Seige of Boston	
	1776 *Common Sense*, Declaration of Independence, Battle of New York	1776 Smallpox epidemic, Town meeting called to divide town postpones decision
	1777 Articles of Confederation, Battle of Saratoga	
1778 France agrees to aid American colonists		1781 Simsbury Town Meeting votes to divide Simsbury
	1781 Battle of Yorktown, Cornwallis surrenders	1782 Commutation protest, another vote to divide town
		1783 Repeal of 1782 vote
1783 Treaty of Paris ends Revolutionary War		1786 Incorporation of Granby
	1786 Daniel Shays Rebellion	
	1787 Constitutional Convention	
	1788 Connecticut Ratifies new Constitution	1788 Hezekiah Holcomb votes no at Ratification Convention

The quarter century which followed the end of the French and Indian War was one of the most cataclysmic periods of all American history. Conflicts over new Parliamentary policies found expression in protests, riots, boycotts, and finally, war. A new nation, based on republican ideals, was formed out of thirteen Atlantic seaboard colonies and successfully secured its already declared independence through the Treaty of Paris in 1783. Four years later its nationalist-minded leaders wrote The Constitution of the United States of America, which, after two hundred years, is still the framework of our central government, as well as a model for the governments of fifty states and many other nations around the world.

As was true of the previous seventy years of the community's existence, the Revolutionary Period was a time of important changes for the people of Salmon Brook. But was there a relationship between the American Revolution and the developments in the little farming town in the northwest corner of Hartford County? The big local event of the period was the incorporation of the Salmon Brook and Turkey Hills Societies as the town of Granby in 1786. Was this related to the American Revolution? Since the two parishes were virtually independent communities anyway, does it even represent much of a change?[1]

These times were, indeed, revolutionary and Revolutionary times for Salmon Brook. As a third generation of inhabitants assumed positions of leadership, they faced a world of change. Their responses, among them a concerted effort to break off from the town of Simsbury, not only produced more change, but were intimately tied up in the spirit of the American Revolution. We need to be careful, though, in defining what that Revolutionary spirit was.

Today our images of the American Revolution include Patrick Henry crying for "Liberty or Death," "Indians" throwing tea into Boston harbor, Ethan Allen treating the Ticonderoga garrison to some New England vernacular, an historic signing of a Declaration at the statehouse in Philadelphia, a cold encampment at Valley Forge, and Washington and Lafayette outfoxing British regulars. These images define our sense of patriotism. American History textbooks recount how a great republic was created, great principles of law and politics articulated, great leaders tested, and great movements toward equality and freedom generated. The voices of the whig leaders were dramatic, their pens vibrant, and their deeds were fiery. All this is *national* history, however. By the "spirit of the American Revolution," do we mean a nationalist spirit? Is a "patriot" someone who shared in the creation of the new national republic?

If so, Salmon Brook fails miserably as a patriot community. In fact, when the Constitution was drafted in 1787, Hezekiah Holcomb, representing the new town of Granby, voted against it at the Connecticut ratification convention.[2] The best Granby has been able to do to connect itself to the creation of a new nation seems to be to display Newgate, once the copper mine in Turkey Hills, as a revolutionary depository for loyalists - and not a very secure depository at that.[3] Certain individuals have been noted for their active participation in the fighting of the Revolutionary War - Richard Case and Asahel Holcomb, for example - and Salmon Brook residents did attend a Simsbury town meeting on August 11, 1774 where radical resolutions protesting the Boston Port Bill were passed.[4]

From a different perspective, though, Granby can be viewed as a patriot town, caught up in the spirit of the American Revolution, and, in fact, sharing as much as any community, in the shaping of that spirit. Its people had a different brand of patriotism from what we might expect to find, and were hardly united in their sentiments about the British Empire, or anything else going on at the time. In the final analysis, looking at the American Revolution through their eyes, and understanding how they fit in as patriots at this time, actually sheds light on the larger national picture and the forces behind it.

Rosanna Holcomb Hays and her husband Samuel Hays Jr. were small children when the Northwest Society became a separate parish, and teenagers as that parish struggled with the upheaval of the Great Awakening, defying central authority and defining itself as a complex and independent community. In the midst of the great wars for empire, they had married and joined the church newly reconciled under Rev. Joseph Strong. Now we can witness their generation taking its place as the heirs of Salmon Brook in the 1760s and 1770s. In those decades, Samuel became a leader in Salmon Brook and in 1786, the first selectman elected in the new town of Granby. Throughout those years all that the new leaders of Salmon Brook had learned as children, teenagers and young adults exercised its influence to bring forth a multi-dimensional revolution. Samuel and Rosanna's experience during this time provides us a window into their patriotism. Marching to battle and separating as a town were all one - and there was even more to this revolution.

Dancing Around the Liberty Tree

The career of one of Granby's principal founding fathers in the two decades preceding the outbreak of hostilities in 1775 could not paint a clearer picture of some very basic elements often associated with the Revolution. For one thing, Samuel Hays Jr. presents a classic case of middle class upward mobility. Not only did he gradually acquire more wealth as time passed, but he also rose as a leader in his church, in local government and in the local militia. As a political leader, he emerged as one of the chief spokesmen for the independence of Salmon Brook from the town of Simsbury; and in religious affairs he played an important role in the continuing popularization of the church in Salmon Brook. Self-improvement, independence, popular participation - it is almost too coincidental that the rise of this independent yeoman should parallel the development of the rebellious feelings against England's government - in fact, it is no coincidence at all. It was people like Hays and his followers in Salmon Brook who made the Revolution throughout America what it was.

In the 1760s, once again, as in the 1730s, the Salmon Brook area was experiencing some significant undercurrents of change. The French and Indian War had ended with the French permanently expelled from the North American continent; and that fact of French absence made for a feeling of renewed security everywhere in the colonies. Surely Salmon Brook residents, and prospective inhabitants, no longer feared French aggression as they had early in the century, and more recently in the last "Great War for Empire." That did not mean a mass exodus for western lands, however, and, as the population of the town grew rapidly, there was again, as in the 1720s and 30s, renewed pressure for land.[5] The town responded by granting the last of its commons scattered about the town, but these grants were made only to heirs of inhabitants of the 1720s.[6] Newcomers, who in former times might have relied upon extensive commons to establish themselves within the economy, felt cut out. Apparently they were making incursions on what little common land was left, for a committee had to be formed to deal with the problem. Rosanna's father served on this committee.[7]

Young Samuel had, by this time, secured a solid position of social status for himself. With the help of some generous grants from his father, a

194

moderately prosperous farmer, he had acquired holdings of over 150 acres of good crop and grazing land before 1763. He had been a freeman and church member since 1753, and had held some minor offices in the town government, including the position of Tythingman, a sort of "morality supervisor" in a community. Also he and Rosanna had begun raising a large family (five out of a final ten, already born), the first born of which were, in 1763, arriving at an age when they would contribute to the family's prosperity.[8]

During the next ten years, as his family and landholdings continued to expand, we can observe the steady growth of his involvement and influence in all aspects of community affairs. In 1764, as the English Parliament was considering enacting the Stamp Act and had already passed the Sugar Act, resulting in a slew of protests from colonial leaders, he took a position on the Grand Jury, which he assumed again the following year. Then, in December of 1765, he was elected to the Prudential Committee of the Northwest Ecclesiastical Society, the post his father had held once in the 1740s when Samuel Sr. was trying to install a New Light preacher in the Salmon Brook pulpit. He sat on this committee, which made vital decisions for his own section of Simsbury, until December, 1768 when he was elected to the post of selectman for the town of Simsbury.[9]

Salmon Brook had always had spokesmen among the town select-men; it was not as though they were the unrepresented "back country" farmers. Generally someone from Salmon Brook, like Captain Nathaniel Holcomb, was elected to a high position in town and saw to it that the concerns of the people of Salmon Brook were met. For some time though, this had seemed hardly important. After the turmoil of the 1720s and 1730s, which had been resolved by land grants and division into separate ecclesiastical societies, there were few issues dividing Simsbury's different settlements. The bulk of the taxes paid were collected by each ecclesiastical society for schooling, the minister's salary and upkeep of the meetinghouse. The town rate was relatively modest and most men worked off their highway tax on the roads each spring.

Yet, by 1768, it was important that Samuel Hays was among the selectmen, for there were hints in that decade that civil relationships were beginning to deteriorate between the southern end of Simsbury and its independent northern appendage. The first hint was in December, 1761, when a vote was taken that all town meetings would be held in "first society" (Hop Meadow).[10] This vote may seem innocuous enough, that is, until one begins to ask why they had to take the vote in the first place. Somebody must have wanted to have the town meetings held somewhere else.

Growth was catching up with the inhabitants. They were finding that a large number of people were living in what used to be frontier regions of communities. Town government continued to become more complex. To the usual list of offices (listers, surveyors of highways, fenceviewers, and howards) were added leathersealers, packers of beef, packers of pork, packers of "tabacca" and branders of horses, creating a bureaucracy which must have taken hours to elect on an annual basis.[11] More people were calling on the government for improvements in roads and bridges, although the demand generally did not come from the newly settled areas. A growing government and a need for better roads meant that there would be more taxes. In turn, more taxes meant that there was now more reason for "outlanders" to attend town meetings (to vote against them). In the late 1760s, the hints of conflict turned to solid evidence that tension was developing.

In 1767, it took two adjournments before the townsmen could even settle on a group of selectmen, and then another curious vote passed to keep all annual town meetings in "first society."[12] During the final three years of the decade, when other colonists were supposedly concerned with boycotting items tagged for the detested Townshend duties, the people of Simsbury were concerned about preventing the General Assembly from ordering the town to build bridges, one in the southwest corner of town at "Sufferage" (now Collinsville in Canton), and others across the Farmington River. Captain Jonathan Pettibone of Weatogue was sent to the Assembly to argue that the town should not be expected to pay for a bridge at Suffrage but then when he, Hezekiah Holcomb and Josiah Phelps tried to get bridges built across the Farmington in Hop Meadow, the town meeting sent Joseph Forward to fight that.[13] All these petitioners for bridges were prosperous men, trying to outflank the town meeting by having the colony legislature order the town to build bridges so they could more easily engage in the regional trade in the goods they purchased from their neighbors. The town meeting, however, would have none of it.

There are indications that many of the town's rank-and-file, particularly at Salmon Brook, may have been experiencing some financial duress at the time. Settlement of the western hills still continued apace, but surely that was stretching the budgets of the young people who had little to their name but the rocks and trees and the lots they marked off with same. Extra taxes for bridges a good ten miles from their ambitious building projects were not exactly what they were eager to stretch and pay for. Families like the Strattons who had invested too much too early struggled to extricate themselves from debt. Young Eunice Stratton had married Dudley Higley. A record in 1766 shows Dudley had been ill for some time and had to ask the town for help making ends meet. Serajah Stratton Jr. never turned in the money he was supposed to have collected as tax collector in 1766 and 1767.[14] He disappeared and was not heard from again in Simsbury. It was also at this time that John Halladay gave up on carrying the financial burden of his mill place just below the Strattons and sold a majority of the interest to Simeon Baxter, a wealthy land speculator then living in the new town of Barkhamsted, who could afford to wait a bit for profit to materialize.[15]

Probably everyone was affected by the tremendous hail storm in the summer of 1768, which ruined fruit trees, gardens, animals and whole fields of grain.[16] To top it off, the damage to the glass in the houses could not be easily remedied, since glass was one of the products port-town merchants had been boycotting. In general, the Townshend Duty boycotts must have driven prices of manufactured goods sky-high before the repeal by Parliament in 1770.

While the colonial leaders in the legislatures were busily rejecting efforts by the Parliament to increase their tax bill, so too were people of Simsbury trying to avoid increased taxes. And what is more significant, there seems to be a connection between the bridge issue and the debate over where to hold town meetings. Whenever one issue was hotly debated, as can be inferred by the number of adjournments it took to get a proposal passed, the other issue was also very much on the agenda. In the thick of it were the Salmon Brook men, apparently pushing for more control over the town meeting and for fewer taxes for bridges at the opposite end of town. These were the concerns of Samuel Hays, one of their leaders. They were the same sort of concerns held by better known patriots like Samuel Adams and Patrick Henry - only the principles of home-rule, representation and freedom from government control were applied to issues that mattered more to the farmers of Salmon Brook. Salmon Brook men certainly were infected with the rebellious spirit of the times, but they were less concerned with the implications of an import tax on tea than they were with a tax on their land. That did not make them any less revolutionary.

In 1769, Hays's vision turned even more to local and individual matters. He gave up his seat among the selectmen and took a year to build himself a new house - one more suitable for an up-and-coming community leader. It was a stately house, and unique even for the time it was built. Instead of building the traditional rectangular two-and-a-half-story, five-bay center-chimney house with gables on the short sides, as was typical in the mid-18th century, Hays chose to construct a square house with a hip-roof. In each of the four lower rooms there was a fireplace on the inside corner set at 45° facing out toward the outside corner of the house. Its squat appearance was fully offset by the steep pitch of the hip-roof, producing a combination of Georgian and center-chimney architecture which actually seems quite regal (See Figures 5-1 and 5-2).[17]

Hays was truly making a statement with this house, and when it was finished he returned to what he believed to be his calling: community leadership. He worked his way up in the local militia - a lieutenant in 1770, and a captain in 1773. In church affairs, he continued to be a leading figure, serving regularly on the Prudential Committee, and, after 1770, on the committee to deal with the issue of whether to repair the society's meeting-house or rebuild it at a new location.[18]

It was not an easy time to be a church leader in Salmon Brook. As comfortable as he and some of the sons of early families were, he was not rich. As for the rest of the community, they continued to struggle through hard times in the early 1770s, still fighting renewed efforts to build bridges in the south end of town, and worrying whether the funds, which they had balked at voting to support the increasing numbers of "indigents and debtors," might one day be denied them as well.[19] A serious cankerworm infestation in 1771 and 1772 ruined their orchards and further complicated their problems.[20] Building a new meetinghouse would be an expensive proposition, especially since the population of the society had grown so large - a large house would be needed. Then there was the question of where to put it, since the center of

Richard Caley

Figure 5-1: Samuel Hays II House (1769), now 67 Barndoor Hills Road, as seen from the road.

Richard Caley

Figure 5-2: Interior of the Samuel Hays II House

199

the population had inevitably shifted north and west with the settlement of the western hills. And finally, would the meetinghouse be "seated?" That is, would they sell pews at different prices as a fund-raising technique, relying on the sense of social distinction they had little affection for, to solve their financial problems?

These issues were touchy subjects for Salmon Brook farmers, and yet, through all the arguing and bickering for the next five years, Samuel held on to his seat on the Prudential Committee. What is more, this was a *good* time for the *congregation*. Between 1759 and 1769 there were but nine souls newly admitted to the church. In the next six years there were that many admitted each year. Former radicals, like old Nathaniel Higley, who, when Joseph Strong had first started preaching, had not joined because Strong was not inspiring enough for them, now came in enthusiastically, along with the children of the generation who had fought so hard over those issues in the 1740s.[21] Changes were made in the traditional sexually segregated seating arrangement: men and women were now allowed to sit together; and Strong continued to argue in favor of the need to sing in church. All this time in the First Society in Hop Meadow, dissension over doctrine and class conflict brought on the dismissal of the Rev. Roots in 1772, followed by five years of no settled minister. "I think we've had preaching a pretty good spell," one resident is purported to have said, "and now I think we'd better have a little respite."[22]

Essentially what was happening in Salmon Brook was that the church was becoming a truly popular institution, even at a most stressful moment. Surely Samuel had something to do with at least holding the people together, if not bringing what was often an elite institution in other communities, closer to the people. Perhaps it should not surprise us that it was he who brought members of the County Court to Salmon Brook in the spring of 1775 and kept them at his house until they, at last, pitched a stake for the new meetinghouse at a spot the majority could accept (actually it was the old meetinghouse taken down and moved to this spot at the junction of Creamery Hill Road and Kelly Lane).[23] Clearly he was devoted to those ideals his parents and grandparents had believed in before him. The regularity of his election to the Prudential Committee attests to his desire to build strong community spirit, to his belief that this could be done through the church if the church reached out to the

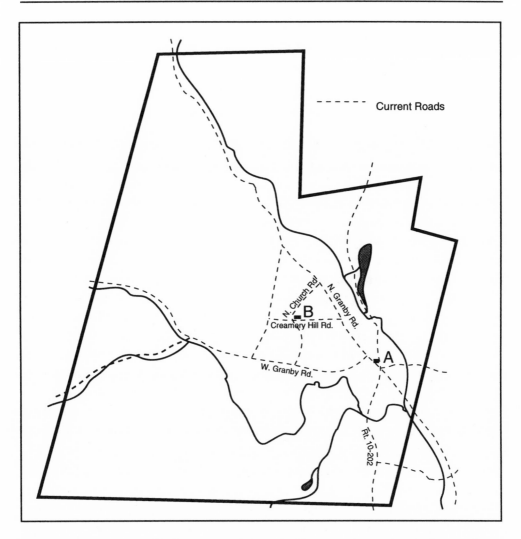

Map 5-1: Location of Salmon Brook Meetinghouses. Location A shows where the first meetinghouse was built in 1740 at the junction of today's Routes 20 and 10-202. Location B is the site of the second meetinghouse, built in 1775, showing that the center of population had shifted north and west. In 1989, the First Congregational Church placed a marker at the northeast corner of Creamery Hill and North Church Roads, but it is not known for sure if that was the exact location.

201

people, and to his understanding of his duty as a man of status to work toward these ends. His regular election to this committee, as well as to the militia leadership, also attests to his community's support of those ideals for which he stood.

It was in these early years of the 1770s, too, that Hays and his neighbors began to address more directly the issue of paying taxes for far-away bridges. The legislature held Simsbury responsible for rebuilding the bridge at "Suffrage," which kept getting carried away by ice and floods. Increasingly the hard-pressed people of Salmon Brook began to ask, what if they were not a part of the town of Simsbury? In that case, too, they would not they need to worry about ensuring large turn-outs at town meetings held five to seven miles away, if the town meeting were at their own meeting house (and excluded First Society voters).

The inspiration for the movement for a separate town came from the north in 1768. A group of people who lived in "the Wedge," the area north of the 1711 Simsbury town line (but since 1713, considered part of the Connecticut colony), petitioned the legislature to become a town. This group included people in the hilly region along the Hartland boundary like Jonathan Buttolph, as well as people who lived along the Westfield Road (now Route 10-202) like Joseph and Shadrack Moor - people who had purchased lots from investors Hunt, Apthorp and Breck, and those who had bought lands which were once under Westfield's jurisdiction, but now south of the colony line and not really under anyone's jurisdiction. They said they were 41 families who had worked their land for some time and "find by experience that the said Tracts of land when cleared from the heavy timber &c are good and profitable Tillage and pasture &c and may well answer the Expectation of the Farmers and Husbandmen" who would come to populate the area. They went on to say that their families were large, but that they had no schools for their children, and no "Blessings of the Gospel." Further, their region was rough country, and creating and maintaining good roads would require hard communal work. Therefore, they asked to organize for these ends - that is, to become a town.[24]

The legislature stalled on the matter, and in the meantime the south part of Westfield broke away and became the town of Southwick, much to the consternation of those people along the road to Salmon Brook below the 1713 colony line, who now seemed to fall under the jurisdiction of Massachusetts.[25]

The concerns of these people came to the attention of leaders in Salmon Brook. On March 29, 1770, Captain Nathaniel Holcomb and his son Nathaniel Holcomb IV, Judah Holcomb, Franceway and Ranna Cossitt, Nathaniel Hillyer, Hezekiah and Abel Phelps, Benajah Holcomb and Joel Loomis, among others, principally residents of the northern part of Salmon Brook, joined in a petition with the people of the Wedge and asked that the Wedge and the Northwest Society together be considered for a separate town. They stated,

> the Wedge of Land aforesaid (not being incorporated with nor included with the Limits of any Township whatsoever) is presently in great measure without Law and order where (there being no Town nor civil Officers) anyone may avoid distbusting [sic] anything for the defraying of publick Charges and with impunity do what is right in his own Eyes; and the public worship is quite utterly neglected and the Place is become infamous as a Nest for spurious Births.

And since many people of the Northwest Society could not "without great labor and Difficulty attend the public meetings of the Town and Freemen in said Simsbury," it made sense to create a new town of about 160 households, which number included at least those in the old Bedford tract (the western section of the Wedge), if not those who were now included in the town of Southwick.[26] The description of the householders to the north of the Simsbury boundary was certainly not very flattering. It is hard to say how close it was to the truth, since the arguments were obviously put forth to convince the legislature of the need for a town government.

After summoning the selectmen of Simsbury to answer, the legislature ignored the matter again. Three years passed and the same group put forth basically the same argument, but asking that the Wedge be annexed to the town of Simsbury, adding that the children of the families in the Wedge were growing up without an education. However, this time the petitioners ran into trouble when one of their number, Nathan Gillet, broke ranks and joined a group from lower Simsbury, claiming he had been "drawn into the petition by trick." It was all "only a scheme," they said, "of Judah Holcomb Esq. and some of his neighbors at Salmon Brook who live Northward of the center of s^d Society in order to bring the meeting house which they are about to build nearer to them." The families in the Wedge, they continued, did live under the jurisdiction of Hartford County, the people were as well educated and attended public worship as regularly as most of those at Salmon Brook, and 23 of the 25 families did not want to be annexed to Simsbury, but wanted to be their own town.[27]

In fact, in 1774, after the legislature annexed the Wedge (including most of those in the "Southwick Jog") to Simsbury and to the Northwest Society, now called Salmon Brook Society, Judah Holcomb did get the meetinghouse moved a lot closer to his house on North Granby Road (and in 1832 it moved even closer!).[28] But that was clearly not the primary motivation of the Salmon Brook men in seeming to take up the cause of the people of the Wedge. As the 1770 petition implies, they hoped to enlarge the ecclesiastical society to the point where it could be considered of sufficient numbers and wealth to qualify as a town. In Connecticut, the freemen of every town were allowed two representatives in the Assembly and the legislature was a little hesitant to allow these additional votes unless the area represented was roughly equivalent to other constituencies in the colony.

The next step after annexation of the Wedge to Salmon Brook would have been to petition for separation, but matters of larger scope became distracting. In December, 1773, citizens of Boston, protesting the continued tax on tea and the new monopoly of the British East India Tea Company of the tea trade in America, emptied a fresh cargo of tea into the harbor. The following spring, newspapers pushed aside stories of local controversies in the legislature and began reporting a depressing decline in support for the American colonies in Parliament. Finally, the news arrived that Lord North's ministry had pushed through a series of measures devoted to punishing Boston and bringing it to its knees, among them the formal closing of the port until the destroyed tea was paid for. This brought cries of indignation from all over the Atlantic seaboard. An act that had once been condemned for its destruction of private property was suddenly elevated to an act of Liberty-loving patriotism.[29]

Until this point, Simsbury had largely ignored, officially at least, the conflict with Parliament while worrying about its own problems building bridges and roads, taking care of its debtors and paupers, and maintaining its churches. But in the summer of 1774, a special town meeting responded forcefully:

> This meeting taking into consideration the unhappy Difference and Contention arisen Between the British Ministry and the Province of Massachusetts Bay especially the Arbitrary Proceedings against the Town of Boston by the Act called the Boston Port Bill and an [?] Force blocking up their Harbour Stopping their trade etc and consedering our near connections with said Province and how much our Trade and interest is affected thereby Do Judge ourselves loudly called upon to make the following Declarations and Resolves.

They noted the implied violations of their charter privileges, their loyalty and willingness to contribute constitutionally to the welfare of the empire, the illegality of taxes passed without the consent of those being taxed, the suffering of the people of Boston "under the cruel hand of oppression and arbitrary government," their desire to contribute to the relief of Boston, and their approval of the Continental Association established by the Continental Congress to boycott British goods. They then set up a Committee of Correspondence (on which Judah Holcomb served) to keep the flames of rebellion burning bright and to collect donations to be sent to Boston.[30]

Salmon Brook people, of course, were right at home bucking authority and claiming independence. "We hear from Simsbury," read a report in *The Connecticut Courant,*

> that a number of the most respectable inhabitants of Salmon-Brook society, being deeply affected with the present melancholy state of affairs, on account of the unconstitutional proceedings of the British Parliament with regard to American Liberty — Met together, as well to display their loyalty to the King, as their united zeal for the Support of the darling Liberty, which is the birth right of every American, as well as Englishman; and after having erected a stately pole as an ensign of Liberty; they formed themselves into a circle round the tree, and having a table well furnish'd with liquors of various kinds, a number of loyal toasts were drank; — after which everyone repair'd to his usual employ, the whole was conducted with the greatest decency and good order.[31]

They had put off, for a bit, their quest for independence as a town, but these gatherings could only serve to reinforce their belief that they rightfully ought to have independent status, and that once all Americans agreed on the fundamental principles of constitutional government, no legislature could deny them their right to independence.

By the end of the year they had returned to the business of protecting their community's interests. In December, the annual town meeting was the scene of considerable bickering over representation on the board of selectmen. The meeting opened with the regular selection of the moderator and town clerk. Then the town debts were read and "discoursed upon." The characteristic adjournment followed what must have been an angry "discourse." Then the election of town officers followed with a vote "to choose 5 selectmen and no more Cpt. Noah Phelps, Captain Samuel Hays, Lt. Joseph Cornish, Capt. Ezekiel Humphrey, Isaac Gillet." More minor officers were chosen, then another indicative adjournment, and then a vote to choose two more selectmen, Zacheus Gillet and Elisha Graham, making an unprecedented total of seven men on the board.[32] While it is unclear which area of town ended up with more weight on the board of selectmen, all this does indicate a considerable amount of argument over representation and concern about who would be spending the money the town voted to collect in taxes.

This was the community in which Samuel Hays had become a leader. His leadership in the church, in the militia, and among the Salmon Brook men at the town meetings on the eve of the Revolutionary War, tells us a good deal about him and about his community. He was a strong supporter of the ideal of the closed "covenanted" community, bound more by the covenant of the early Puritans than by the "social contract" of the whig philosophers of the Enlightenment. At the same time, as a yeoman farmer who had built his own prosperity, and as a church member who had "seen the light" at a time of great turmoil in Puritan Connecticut, he was determined that the institutions of the community, both political and religious, should not lose touch with the people they served. These attitudes together are very supportive of the spirit that would make it easy for this man to identify with the goals of the war that was fast approaching. Since he emerged as such a clear leader in Salmon Brook it is quite understandable that the spirit of the Revolution would receive a hardy welcome when it spread to these hill farmers in northern Connecticut - the fact was, that spirit had been there all along.

Summertime Soldiers

The "unhappy Difference and Contention" only got worse as more news of "intolerable acts" filled the papers, and as protests and pamphlets became more incendiary. That Salmon Brook inhabitants read these reports and arguments is a certainty, for the print media was becoming thoroughly established in Connecticut. People from Salmon Brook advertised in both the *Connecticut Courant* and the *American Mercury*, and one advertisement in the *Courant* showed Jonathan Humphrey, Simsbury's representative to the General Assembly in 1774, offering political pamphlets for sale.[33]   In addition, if Joseph Strong was anything like the vast majority of Congregational ministers across New England, they heard on a weekly or twice-weekly basis about the direct relationship between the British ministry and the Anti-Christ who was planning the destruction of God's people of the Word. Shortly after the struggle over representation among the selectmen at the 1774 annual election meeting, the town meeting set up a Committee of Inspection to enforce the boycotts rigidly.[34] But in April, 1775, before spring planting, and before the Continental Congress had reconvened to assess the situation, war had erupted in Massachusetts. In a matter of days towns all over New England, Simsbury not excepted, had dispatched militia units to the aid of the farmers in the Boston area who were soon laying siege to the city.

The records of the town of Simsbury and of the Salmon Brook Ecclesiastical Society, as well as the records of the military units involved in the war with the British authorities, continue, between 1775 and 1781, to document the distinctive patriotism of the people of the future town of Granby. These were times of great stress for all of Simsbury, and some of the response to that stress may not, on the surface, appear to be particularly patriotic or "revolutionary." Nevertheless, when viewed in a certain light, the issues that occupied the minds of these people do form a pattern that is consistent with the great ideals of the time.

In spite of the growing conflict with Parliament (or, for that matter, inspired by it), there continued to be agitation for division of the town. At the December, 1775 annual town meeting, the town returned to five selectmen, Samuel Hays among them, but then voted that the "selectmen shall warn a town meeting before the 1st of May to consider dividing the town." War or no war, the people of Salmon Brook wanted to deal with their own financial problems (such as paying for the relocation and construction of their society meetinghouse), have their own leaders, and have town meetings close to home. Before the appointed day, however, it was clear that these concerns would simply have to wait. In April, 1776, considering "the present situation of Public Affairs," referring both to the war and to a smallpox epidemic then raging in Connecticut, the town voted to defer doing anything about separation, and the matter was not taken up again until after the war. In place of debating this issue, they petitioned the legislature to help with the building of roads in the recently annexed north part of Salmon Brook.[35]

The war, itself, did not come to Simsbury in the form of marching redcoats as it did to Concord, and later to Danbury and Groton in Connecticut. It came, as it did for most rural New England towns, in the form of shortages, requisitions for supplies, calls for soldiers to fill the ranks of the Continental Army, a smallpox epidemic, rampant inflation and downright chaos in the currency system, and constant interruptions in the ability of the workforce to make a decent living. Simsbury town records are filled with references to these problems.

The smallpox epidemic in Simsbury was reported in the *Courant* in April, 1776, but had apparently run its course by the next spring when the town voted to stop giving inoculations. So serious was the drain on the town treasury though, that the town voted the next winter not to pay for the inoculations that had been given, except for the town poor.[36]

The *Courant* also reported civil strife related to lingering loyalties to Great Britain and unwillingness to support the common cause. On September 4, 1775 the paper ran this advertisement on behalf of Simsbury's Committee of Inspection:

> The Committee of Observation for the Town of Simsbury, having had due process against Joshua Holcomb of said town, according to the association of the Continental Congress, and finding him obstinately fixed in full opposition to the spirit and meaning of said association — Hereby give notice therof to the public, that he may be treated with that neglect and contempt which is so justly due for his incorrigible enmity to the rights of British America.[37]

Other suspected loyalists were deprived even more of those precious

Figure 5-3: Reverend Roger Viets

rights for which the patriots were fighting. Rev. Roger Viets, by this time quite a popular individual (the 1774 census reported over 900 Anglicans living in Simsbury), was watched very carefully during the war and harassed on numerous occasions. Once he was arrested for performing a marriage (supposedly the province of Congregational ministers), and another time fined, sentenced to a year in jail and subsequently confined to the bounds of Simsbury, for allegedly feeding some loyalists who had escaped from Newgate.[38] Young Ranna Cossitt (grandson of René), who had also become an Anglican minister, incurred the wrath of a mob when he asked town clerk John Owen to write Governor Trumbull for permission to go into New York in April, 1779, under a white flag, to get some belongings of Brewster Higley. Not surprisingly, he fled to Nova Scotia to resume his ministry.[39]

As many towns in "the provision state," Simsbury suffered shortages in order to procure supplies for the army. Town committees sought beef cattle, grain and clothing and paid precious little for them. The most acute shortage was in salt, a necessity in a world without refrigerators. The School Committee was responsible for doling out what little was alloted the town by the new State of Connecticut (same old government, new name). At first it was proportioned equally per person, but a quantity was kept in reserve and used in 1778 to give extra to widows and the families of soldiers in the Continental service.[40] In a town that was *still* paying bounties on dead wolves, conditions were deteriorating fast.[41]

"It is a mellancole Time," wrote Ensign Jonathan Pettibone's young wife Hannah, after both her husband and hired hand went off to New York in the summer of 1776 leaving her to care for their three children (including a new-born) and Jonathan's seriously ill father, Jonathan Pettibone Sr. (of bridge petition fame). "I feel very much troubled about you but I hope God will preserve you in all your dagers. I shall send you a pare of Stockings as quick as I can....I can Hire Tom Tary but his prise is three pound a month and I cannot hire anybody els. Martha and Hannah send there love to their dady." "Father Pettibone" soon recovered and, before departing himself for New York to take command of a regiment, wrote additional testimony of the stress and worry on the homefront to his son:

> I take this oppertunity to Let you know your biseness goes on your Harves is got in all but your first crop of hay your hilling dun flax pulled your plowing som lys behind we do as well as we can but...what to do I know not....and I would Have you take cair with Ensign Sadoca Willcocks [a neighbor in Weatogue who later built a house in West Granby south of Reuben Holcomb] and see that he is as Comfortable as the Rest of the Solgars and not to spend his money neadelasly and take cair of him in all biseness.[42]

Jonathan Sr. later became sick again while in New York and died in Rye, New York, when Jonathan Jr. was trying to bring him home.

At times, the pressure grew so intense it seems that the town was about ready to declare itself independent of Connecticut in order to get away from the demands being placed upon it. In 1779 they pleaded,

> That it is the opinion of this meeting. That a Late Act of the General Assembly of this State Raising the Courts Fees &c. Is:Prejudicial & Injurious to y[e] Public. and has a great tendency to hurt and Depreciate the Continental Bills &c. and therefore this meeting prays that some speedy measures may be taken that the Said Act may be repealed.[43]

On the military side, raising troops for the Continental Army presented a very serious problem. There were three classifications of soldiers in this war after 1776: those in the Continental Army under General Washington and engaged in full-time service; "state troops," raised for specific regional campaigns by inducements from the state government; and local militia units, which had always been in existence. The militia units were based upon the towns from which they came, were designed strictly for local protection and

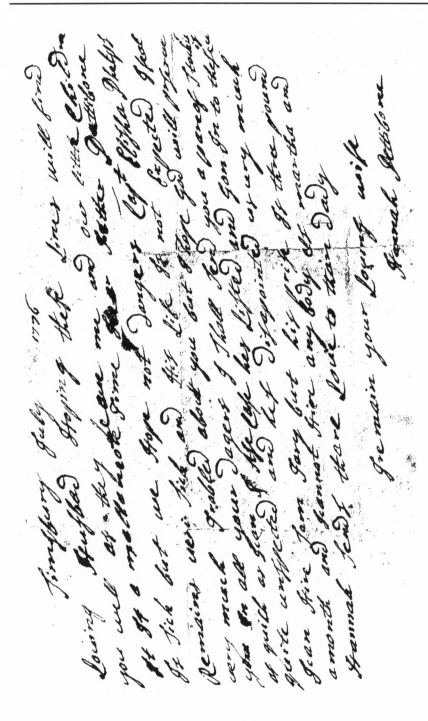

Figure 5-4: Letter from Hannah Pettibone to her husband Jonathan, July, 1776, illustrating the difficulties faced even by prosperous Simsbury families while men were off at war.

elected their own officers. Before 1776, however, the Continental Army had been composed largely of militia units. This was fine for bottling up a few regiments of British regulars in Boston and forcing them to evacuate by the summer of 1776, but when it came to pitched battle in an open field, the farmers and their elected officers were no match for trained troops disciplined to heed the orders of officers who never had to ask twice.

In September of 1776, the militiamen of Simsbury learned about war. The 18th Regiment of Connecticut Militia, commanded by the temporarily-healthy Col. Jonathan Pettibone, and composed mostly of men from Simsbury, had marched to New York with Washington to defend the city against the expected attack. The British landed on the American left flank on Long Island, and with the help of Hessian mercenaries, made quick work of poorly trained colonial troops on August 27. The Simsbury men, including Captain Samuel Hays's company of 25 Salmon Brook men, were stationed at Kip's Bay on Manhatten on September 15, three weeks after their arrival, when its brigade was attacked and put to flight. Washington arrived on the scene and tried to rally "the disgraceful and dastardly" troops, but nearly got captured himself. Needless to say, this event was not a morale booster, and most of those who were not captured, killed or confined to a hospital bed with wounds or sickness, deserted, or were quickly discharged before the month was out. Among those captured were Franceway Cossitt's sons Jesse and Roger, both of whom died in a British prison ship in New York harbor. This was definitely not a moment to be proud of - but then, how well could they be expected to do with three weeks of "training?"[44]

It is also understandable after this experience, that the town had considerable difficulty filling its quota of recruits for the Continental line. The military records do not, in fact, show a lot of recruits from Simsbury in the Continental Army, although the militia companies did respond on occasion to action in relatively nearby locales. The 18th Regiment was called out in the spring of 1777 when Danbury was raided and burned.[45] Simsbury men furnished a few troops at Saratoga, and on the Hudson in 1778, but as the war dragged on, it appeared that the 18th Regiment was behaving strictly as what Thomas Paine called "the summertime soldier - the sunshine patriot." When the crops were planted and before the harvest, they could go to war. Otherwise, they spent their time dealing with the shortages and finding ways to pay unwilling farmers to join the Continental Line. This is the way Connecticut men had always fought. In March, 1777, the town meeting resolved to inform the Governor and Committee of Safety of the State

> that under the present Circumstances of the Inhabitants of this town that it appears very difficult to Raise ye soldiers in this Town to furnish our Quota for so long a term as 3 years or during the continuance of the present war. Therefor sd. comitee, to pray to his Honor & Comitee aforesaid to have Liberty for the soldiers in this town to Inlist themselves to the number aforementioned for our Quota and to be formed into suitable Captains, Companies and they to have Liberty to chuse their own officers in a Regiment they shall chuse and to be holden in said service only for the term of Nine months.[46]

The Governor and Committee of Safety apparently responded negatively, for in September the town meeting was busily figuring out ways to entice individuals to serve in the Army. It offered £4 per month salary in addition to whatever Congress decided to pay them (an additional £4 they hoped, or they would make up the difference - but then they voted that down the next year).[47] The town was divided into a number of "classes," and each "class" was supposed to provide a soldier. How each came up with its soldier was up to the members of each class. Ranna Cossitt and Ezra Holcomb's solution was to go to Litchfield and purchase Phillip, "a Negro...from Andrew Adams...and freed him for his agreeing to serve as a soldier in the Continental Army." This seemed to be an innovation at the time, since the selectmen had to ponder a bit before deciding "he may answer for Continental Service." Phillip, it should be noted, had the presence of mind to have the agreement registered in the Simsbury record books so that there would be no question when the war was over about his status.[48] The recruiting of African-Americans with promises of freedom from slavery, actually initiated by the British governor of Virginia, became a regular practice on both sides as the war progressed and soldiers were harder to get.

These "times that try men's souls," as pamphleteer Paine called them, had an effect upon the affairs of the Salmon Brook Society too. Apparently Joseph Strong, who had gone with the militia to New York and who continued to pull converts in dozens to the church, was not being paid, or was being paid in worthless currency. Inflation between 1776 and 1779 was as much as

2400% on some commodities.[49] In February, 1779, the society voted to set up "a committy to treat with the Revd Joseph Strong Respecting the unesiness that subsits between him and his people."[50] Samuel Hays was on this committee, and served as moderator of the meetings that followed to try to devise some way to keep Strong - he knew how important it was to keep the man who had inspired the congregation for so long, and the people of the community knew that he, Hays, understood the difficulties that they faced. Strong did leave, even though the Congregation offered to increase his salary - an increase apparently as worthless as the paper it was printed on. He went to Williamsburg, Massachusetts where he lived until his death in 1803.

All this, the resistance to filling the recruit quota, the temporary service, the unwillingness to pay a preacher of twenty-five successful years, the denial of civil rights to Anglicans, and the fussing about local representation, roads and separation in the midst of the siege of Boston, may suggest a rather harsh indictment of the Simsbury people, particularly those of Salmon Brook, for not looking beyond local interests and accepting the sacrifices that broader consideration entailed. On the other hand, we have to remember where the loyalties of these people lay. They believed strongly in the independent, corporate, "covenanted" community. To be a patriot was to work for one's "own people," to share in the problems of one's immediate neighbors, to protect each other from the evils, corruption or "ungodliness" of the outside world, to insure the survival of one's usually large family, and to fight for the independence of one's community.

Samuel Hays is a prime example of this sort of patriotism. These are the pursuits he engaged in during the revolutionary period. He served as a selectman throughout the war, and on a committee to assist the families of soldiers. When the newspapers and pamphlets called for sacrifice in the name of life, liberty and pursuit of happiness, when the war became a war for independence and freedom from tyrannical rule from afar, this rhetoric only reaffirmed to Samuel that he was living up to the highest ideals of his day. He served Salmon Brook - he led their militia, led their religious society, and represented their interests in town affairs, probably to the point of arguing forcefully at town meetings for independence of his "covenanted community" from the town. The people in Hop Meadow may have had a more nationalistic outlook, since a number of them actually volunteered to enter the

Continental Army; but Samuel and his militiamen and churchmen from Salmon Brook were no less patriotic - only less interested in communicating with a world they could not see beyond their surrounding hills.

A Patriot Town

By 1781 the war was virtually over, but the Peace of Paris had yet to be negotiated when the Salmon Brook patriots launched again their own drive for independence. The economic problems of the day, along with differing perspectives on the war itself, exacerbated tensions. The final outcome was inevitable, though, for the leaders of Salmon Brook were determined to be free to rule themselves, not only religiously, but politically as well, now that civil decisions were becoming so significant - and so costly. Simsbury in general was determined not to be subject to the goings on of the outside world, but Salmon Brook was even more so. In 1786, led by their own brand of patriots such as Samuel Hays, the community finally completed the independence movement begun a half century earlier, thus maintaining the dream of their parents' generation to live independently and to rule themselves.

A serious depression had set in in America by 1780. During the war production had fallen off, trade had suffered, and there were currency problems everywhere. When farmers returned to their homes and communities returned to normal production patterns, the currency problem lingered on. Many of the soldiers were not paid, and those that were paid were paid in worthless money or worthless land.[51] Creditors, furthermore, would not accept paper money, no matter how much farmers complained in the state legislatures. According to historian Barber, alcohol abuse raged.[52] Finally, the resolution of the war opened up land in western New York, Vermont and even across the Appalachians for settlement by young ambitious people declaring their own independence from their families. Productivity on the New England farms correspondingly fell off as farm families lost their prime labor force. Nathaniel Higley's children were among the earliest to set out for these new lands.[53] Samuel Hays moved to encourage his two oldest sons to stay in Salmon Brook in these years by giving them each good farms - he gave his own to Seth, and bought a part of his friend Alexander Cossitt's for Samuel III.[54]

215

Taxes for roads and bridges were again an issue in the town meetings, and the farmers of Salmon Brook were not in any position to pay them.[55] Another issue was the question of a special privilege for officers who had served in the Continental Army. The United States Congress passed a bill in 1783 to give the officers five years full pay in place of a pension. People in every state were in an uproar about this special bonus. In Simsbury where most of the soldiers had served in the militia and thus, would not be eligible for this benefit, the town meeting resolved on a number of occasions to oppose the plan and to send delegates to a statewide protest convention in Middletown.[56] It would appear that the Salmon Brook people were even more united in their opposition to the bonus than were the other people of lower Simsbury. In fact, there were some former Continental officers from lower Simsbury who would have benefited from the measure, and it was probably they who kept bringing the matter up before the town. No doubt the persistence of these people of lower Simsbury encouraged the Salmon Brook patriots, who probably viewed the officers as being elitist, to think harder about separation. There is, as we shall see, a relationship between the specific issue of the bonus payments and Salmon Brook's separation from Simsbury.

Regardless of how much that specific issue upset them, the Salmon Brook men were already on their way to winning independence before the matter of pensions arose. In July of 1781, they got the town to vote to petition the legislature to divide the town. There was considerable debate, for an exact vote (119 to 52) had to be taken to settle the matter - and even then it was *not* settled. The following year a few of the people who were appointed to serve the petition to the legislature asked to be excused from the task, and the town meeting excused them, rescinding the previous vote for division at the same time.[57] At that point the Salmon Brook people took matters into their own hands. On May 2, 1782, a Simsbury town meeting was held at the meetinghouse in Salmon Brook Society "by order," as the clerk muttered into his record book, "of Three Selectmen of Said Town" (no doubt Samuel Hays, Timothy Cossitt and Elisha Graham, all of whom favored separation).

> Asahel Holcomb Esqr. was chosen Moderator of Said Meeting (55 votes in the affirmative. 44 negative) Voted to proceed accordin to said warning, affirmative 87 negative 54 [The meeting house was filling up.] Asahel Holcomb Esqr

and Mr. Pliny Hillyer were Chosen agents of Said Town to Join with Capt Elisha Graham to prefer a memorial to the General Assembly of this State at their next Sessions at Hartford in May instant Praying that this Town be Divided....Proposed to vote whether this meeting will proceed to Doom those Military Classes who have been Negligent in procurring a Continental Soldier yᵉ year past in the affirmative 87, Negative 95 [By now quite a crowd had drifted in.] Voted to vacate and disanul the former Vote of this Town Respecting holding the anual Town Meetings in this Town [to be held only in Hop Meadow], which Vote was passed on the 3rd Monday of December 1767: which vote is now made Void. - Then Said meeting Voted to hold the next annual Town Meeting at the Meeting House in Turkey Hills Society (the moderator says) on the first Monday of December next at 10 Clock in the morning. Said meeting was Dissolved by Vote.[58]

One can almost imagine the Town Clerk being held in his chair and forced to write down what he was told. It must have been a wild night - vote counts were seldom recorded in other meetings. Certainly service in the Continental Army received a slap in the face, since they reversed former fines against those who had not put up their soldier (which had been primarily people of the Wedge).

At the following meeting, the First Society people must have pulled together a majority, for they managed to repeal all of the above and to disempower the selectmen from warning a town meeting anywhere but at First Society. The officers' bonus, or "commutation," issue dragged on into 1784 when the town even considered refusing to pay state taxes (Samuel Hays got himself elected collector of state taxes for the town that year - no doubt to keep anyone else from collecting the taxes).[59] Still, that was not enough for the Salmon Brook men - they wanted assurance that they would be well represented in this or any other issue that threatened their concept of who ought to pay, or be paid, for what.

Again in January,1785, they brought the separation issue before the town and lost a close, but well-attended vote (172-149). In March of the following year, they tried again, this time with a majority of their own (one would assume, since Asahel Holcomb was elected moderator), and won. The petition reached the legislature, and the town was divided north and south with the parishes of Turkey Hills and Salmon Brook joined as the town of Granby. In an effort to alleviate the concern of conservatives in the state's upper house about the number of towns recently "hived off" from older towns, the legislature allowed each half of the former Simsbury only one representative instead of the traditional two. Simsbury itself, quickly won back its second seat in the Assembly, but it took a few years before the more democratic northern villages were granted their fair share of legislative power.[60]

Where the new town's name came from is still a mystery. The contention in Hughes and Allen's *Connecticut Place Names* that the town was settled by residents of Granby, Massachusetts has no basis.[61] Granby, England, on the other hand, a little hamlet 12 miles east of Nottingham, is nowhere near any of the ancestral homes of any of the 1786 leaders or first settlers of either Turkey Hills, or Salmon Brook. Traditionally, the Dukes of Rutland have lived in this hamlet, and the son who will inherit the duchy holds the title of Marquis of Granby. During the late 18th century, one Marquis of Granby was quite a hero in the English-speaking world. The governor of Massachusetts named Granby, Massachusetts after him in 1768. Similarly Granby, Vermont had been named for him in 1761, as were towns in Quebec and Newfoundland and pubs and inns in both England and America. The gentleman in question was A. John Manners who had served in the cavalry in Germany during the Seven Years War and had achieved notoriety by courageous, if insubordinate, actions during a battle at Minden.

After the Seven Years War, he was honored in court and countryside and became the central legendary figure of that war. The crown appointed him Commander-in-Chief of Ordnance, but he was probably held in higher regard by commoners than nobility. After all, his fame had come at the expense of his commander, Lord Sackville, who had by contrast appeared cowardly at Minden. Furthermore, the Marquis's succeeding lifestyle of hard drinking and big spending was an embarrassment to his peers and family.[62] In 1784, fourteen years after his understandably early death, the *Connecticut Courant* reported that his son had "settled all his father's...debts, amounting to fifty thousand pounds; a phenomenon infinitely more surprising and uncommon than the ball of fire that appeared last Monday."[63]

While it would not be unusual that Salmon Brook and Turkey Hills people might find someone who had annoyed the British nobility worth applauding, it is hard to imagine, after all they had been through, that they

218

would want to name a town after a British soldier. *Connecticut Place Names* also suggests the possibility of the Marquis's son, Charles Manners, who held the title of Marquis of Granby from 1770 until 1779, when he became Duke of Rutland upon his grandfather's death. Apparently, as a member of Lord Shelburne's party in Parliament, he had "hotly opposed the policy that led to the war with the American colonies."[64] Indeed, Salmon Brook, and most of Simsbury, had officially declared their opposition to that policy as well, and initial efforts by Salmon Brook patriots to declare independence from Simsbury had begun at the time the Marquis was making his stand in defense of the rights of the colonies. Whether or not people in Salmon Brook were aware of his stance is a good question, though, for Connecticut papers did not report his actions in Parliament in the 1770s.

The *Courant* and the *American Mercury* both reported Manners's career in the 1780s as Lord Lieutenant of Ireland, however. He received this appointment in 1784, and proceeded to develop a reputation which would sour the stomach of any lover of Liberty and Independence. "I am determined that the execution of the law not be wantonly resisted, as far as my power have influence," he wrote to officials who were concerned about mob violence.[65] The American papers seemed very sympathetic to the Irish rebels, apparently convinced by the recent French alliance that Catholics were not so bad after all. They printed Irish press releases characterizing Rutland as a "corrupt tool of a tyrannical ministry, profligate in his private character, and the base executor of a system of oppressive laws." Another editor fumed that "The Court of his Grace the Duke of Rutland will shortly vie in splendor with that of our beloved sovereign at St. James's." With relief, the *American Mercury* reported in September of 1784 the recall of Rutland, and his replacement by Lord Temple. As Irish riots, bloodshed and fighting continued through 1784 and 1785, the papers likened Ireland to the American colonies ten years earlier.[66]

Whether or not Charles Manners was, in fact, the tyrant these reports pictured is beside the point. This was the story Connecticut residents were getting, and makes very suspect any contention that any of these residents would consider naming a town after his former title. His son, furthermore, the Marquis of Granby when Granby, Connecticut was actually incorporated, was then but eight years old, and had done nothing, we assume, to distinguish or darken his reputation. All-in-all, the choice of the name Granby is baffling.

Creating this town of Granby, whatever the origin of its name, was not, by the way, the preference of the Turkey Hills Society which also became part of the town. Just prior to the last town meeting vote before division of the town, the society voted 30 to 7 "to remain with the south part of Simsbury and not to be separated therfrom in case the town should be divided."[67] The old differences still remained, even if some of their children had moved to the western section of the town. They were "so far different," and loath to become the prosperous minority in a town controlled by the "middling" farmers of Salmon Brook. To add insult to injury, in December, 1786, the first Granby town meeting elected as their leaders Judah Holcomb (Rosanna Hays's brother), clerk, Captain Samuel Hays, Lieutenant Pliny Hillyer, a lawyer and storekeeper, and Asahel Holcomb Esq., selectmen, all but the last inhabitants of Salmon Brook Society.[68]

These were the men who had secured their independence - the men whom they respected most. Samuel, in fact, had also just been elected Deacon of the Church - a post he well deserved, having spent the last five years not only arguing for independence, but also looking for a new minister and perhaps personally paying for and remodeling the new minister's house.[69] Thus did Granby become a town - the independent community that had existed for a century was finally recognized as a distinct political entity. But to make clear just how separate they really felt they were, in January, 1788, they sent a delegate to the convention in Hartford, which was supposed to ratify the Constitution of the United States, with instructions to vote "no."

A great deal has been written about the American Revolution and the meaning of that whole period (1763-1789) in American history. Historians have analyzed the writings, speeches and resolutions of political leaders at the national and state level as well as the twists and turns of events as tensions escalated into first a war for "the rights of Englishmen," and eventually a war for independence and republicanism. The struggle has been portrayed alternately as a conflict between tyranny and liberty, as an effort to protect the status quo, as a violent upheaval and overturning of an entrenched and corrupt order, and as a great lie on the part of slave holders and wealthy merchants to protect their assets.

In an attempt to bring to these debates concrete evidence, scholars have often turned their attention away from the leaders of the town of Boston, various colonial assemblies, the Continental Congress and the Continental Army and have investigated material on ordinary people whose names never made the history textbooks. They have asked if Americans slowly changed their minds, as John Adams claimed, during the years preceding the Revolutionary War, and decided that a monarchy was not the government for them. Or did they already live in a society which was egalitarian and remarkable for its democratic institutions? Was the conflict a question of home-rule, or one of who should rule at home? How did the circumstances of Americans' daily lives and local concerns play into the creation of a new nation founded on ideals hitherto considered radical by most leaders of the western world?

What has emerged from the studies on New England communities is a complex picture, and not at all what anyone expected to find when historians first began to look at history through the experience of ordinary people. Amidst all the complexity of the subject, though, it has become clear to scholars that it is important to recognize that colonial New Englanders walked the earth with their own assumptions about what a community was, and where an individual fit in, in the grand scheme of things. Those assumptions, furthermore, were fluid, and not just during the Revolutionary Period, but throughout the entire colonial period as immigrants from Europe and their descendants adapted to rapidly changing conditions in their New World - and in adapting, created new sets of conditions requiring more adapting.

Yes, they were a deferential and consensual lot, only now and then resorting to disrespect and internal conflict as change got the better of them. But the "nows and thens" were so momentous, so wrenching, and the outcome so lasting. Yes, their society was becoming increasingly marked by differences in wealth and status. But they still lived together, rich and poor, and treated each other as though all were one. Yes, congregational piety was responsible for a strict social order which never fully gave way to the individualism against which ministers preached. But those ministers also had their own differences among themselves, which confused their parishioners; and then these same ministers' sense of New England's destiny led them to preach revolution when the Parliament threatened, apparently unwittingly, the precious "Liberty" the Winthrops, Hookers, and Warhams had first

221

installed in this "city upon a hill."[70] How did the ordinary person respond to all of this contradiction?

The answer was, the same way they had always responded to turmoil and upheaval in their lives - by first ensuring that the local community they identified as their own, had as much control as possible over its own affairs (and, in turn, that there were very few affairs which were not theirs alone). And those who led them successfully to these ends - they were, of course, the patriots.

Captain Samuel Hays was such a patriot. As the conflict with England escalated in the 1770s, Captain Hays could easily identify with the principles of the rebels. He was for independence, home rule, and representation. His devotion to the Puritan ideal of a godly community led by hard-working and thrifty farmers, predisposed him with sufficient distaste for distant governments of the "mother" country so that he could eagerly protest the "Intolerable Acts," fight in various campaigns with his militia company, and sustain shortages, in order to provide for the Continental Army and the families of its soldiers.

This participation in the whig cause of the 1770s was an integral part of a lifelong independence struggle on behalf of the people of Salmon Brook. Captain Hays was brought up a patriot in the convulsions of the Great Awakening, by people who had, in turn, been brought up on picket duty in "Fort Simsbury." Throughout his life he lived and led in the tradition of home rule and communalism that was the very backbone of New England's existence and of its response to the changes of the 1760s and 70s. In choosing Captain Hays as their leader in civil and ecclesiastical affairs, the majority of citizens of Salmon Brook were making a statement of their principles. They believed in self-rule, representation, and popular sovereignty. They were suspicious of distant government, whether five miles or three thousand miles away, and they were not going to pay taxes for other people's benefits. No doubt this ethic characterized many New England towns of this era. These attitudes and values were what drove the people of Salmon Brook to separate as an independent town in 1786, which separation must be understood as an event very much a part of the era of the American Revolution. That they were unwilling to trek off to a winter campout in none-too-cozy Pennsylvania, or to stand their ground at Kip's Bay in the face of British bayonets, or to vote in favor of the Federal Constitution, makes them no less patriotic - they were not nationalists nor even disciplined soldiers. Nevertheless, for nearly a century the people of Salmon Brook had been true to the confusing and contradictory ethic of independence that was a cornerstone of the new nation and of their new town.

Chapter VI
In Our Corporate Capacity

Chronology

Europe	America	Granby
		1787 Roger Viets moves to Nova Scotia
1789 French Revolution begins	1789 George Washington inaugurated first President of the U.S.	
	1791 Bill of Rights ratified	
1792 France attacks neighboring countries - war begins	1792 Democratic-Republican Societies founded	
1793 "The Terror" - radical phase of the French Revolution, King and Queen guillotined, England and France go to war	1793 Washington elected for second term, 1794 "Whisky Rebellion" in Pennsylvania; U.S. Navy established	1794 Isaac Porter ordained Congregational Minister
	1797 John Adams' Presidency begins	1797 Commons closed to livestock
	1798 Alien and Sedition Acts, Quasi-War with France begins	1798 St. Peter's Church founded
1799 Russia begins colonizing Alaska	1799 Death of Washington	1799 Methodist meetings begin in West Granby; petition for Granby Turnpike Company
	1800 U.S.Capital moved to Washington, D.C.; Second Great Awakening begins	
	1801 Thomas Jefferson becomes President, Federalists lose control of Congress	1801 Samuel Hays dies
	1803 *Marbury vs. Madison;* Louisiana Purchase	1802 James Kilbourn leaves for Ohio
1804 Napoleon becomes Emperor of France		1804 Southwick "Jog" ceded to Massachusetts by Ct. legislature
	1805 Jefferson's second term begins	1805 Hezekiah Goodrich appointed Granby's first postmaster
	1806 Aaron Burr plot; Lewis and Clark return	

In spite of the conservative inclinations of its Revolutionary era leaders, the new town of Granby changed rapidly in the years after the Revolution. While leaders clung to communal ideals rooted in the early days of Puritan New England, strong forces were at work reshaping the town and its citizens' lives. As the children of the Revolution came of age and new people moved into the community, the local economy and government became increasingly complex and the "common good" more difficult to

224

define. In the sphere of religion as well, the ideal of a single church providing the glue of the community became more and more a dream of past generations. And when the community did not answer the needs of all those young people entering adulthood, old bonds of family and tradition seemed insufficient to keep them within, or even close to the town's bounds. There was great energy in those first years of the town's incorporation - too much, in fact, for nervous elders to contain.

Ambition's Rough Edges

In the 1770s, the patriots of Salmon Brook had told the legislature that their proposed town, if it included the families in the Wedge, would have 160 families. That would probably amount to around 900 people. When the new town was incorporated in 1786, it included the Turkey Hills parish as well, which may have accounted for an additional 70 to 80 families in 1770. By 1790 when the first Federal Census was taken, the town's population had doubled to 2595 in 489 families. As a town, it was as large as almost every other in Hartford County, even more populated than Simsbury itself, and not all that far behind Hartford, which weighed in at 4090 souls in 1790. Natural increase accounted for a good deal of Granby's growth, since the war had not taken a significant toll on the "sunshine patriots," and farm families continued to be characteristically large. There was as well, a significant number of newcomers to the town - people of all walks of life, looking to take advantage of the resources still plentiful in the area.

Since the census takers of the early years of the republic listed the name of every family head in the town, we can understand even more clearly how the town's population was changing. Among the more familiar Salmon Brook names on the 1790 Heads of Family schedule, many new family names are listed: Alderman, Ates, Burr, Brewer, Clemmons, Colton, Day, Edgerton, Huggins, Jewett, Miller, Moore, Spencer, Stephens and many others. In fact, a close look at the lists of family heads in 1790 and 1800 indicates that there was an astonishing level of movement both in and out of the town which the slight increase of 140 people by 1800 disguises. Over one half of the heads of family in the 1800 census were not listed in the 1790 census, and similarly more than half of those listed in 1790 were no longer listed in 1800. While some of this was surely due to mortality and coming of age, together the new names and the statistics on family head turnover go a long way to undo any notion we might have that this was a community untouched by change.[1]

As Granby's population grew and changed in the years after the Revolution and separation from Simsbury, its economy boomed. While it is impossible to develop the sort of statistics we have today on overall production of goods and services and business income and profits, surviving town records and business accounts contain considerable testimony on the extent and nature of the economic growth of the time.[2] The town was alive with enterprise and prosperity. Craftsmen opened new businesses, lumbermen were busier than ever, farmers trooped into the county court to acquire tavern keepers' licenses, people began clustering together in small village centers of trade and manufacturing, and those who made early profits began to look for even larger and more ambitious investment opportunities.

The part of town which experienced the most dramatic development at this time was West Granby. Here, both newcomers and children of the first farmers to cross Bushy Hill joined to create a thriving village where there had once been only scattered farmsteads. No entrepreneur stands out more than the brash and charismatic James Huggins, who moved from Southwick first to the east side of Bushy Hill in 1780, and then to West Granby in 1783. Raised in a prosperous New Haven family, he had served in the Revolutionary War, married Nancy Smith in Wallingford, and afterward joined with Roger Moor of Granby (the part that was later annexed to Massachusetts) in a business partnership in Southwick, a one-time frontier community now growing as rapidly as Granby. Thus, he came to West Granby a man of regional contacts and great ambition. In 1781, he and Moor bought controlling interest in the Strattons' mill business at the junction of Higley Brook and Salmon Brook, and he himself purchased the Stratton house and farm in 1783.[3] The Strattons, as we recall, had been struggling to make a living above the West Granby Gorge since the French and Indian War, and by this time, Martin Stratton had given up and decided to join his brother-in-law Joab Griffin in rebuilding the Halladay mill at the foot of the Gorge.[4]

It may be difficult for us to figure why such an obviously well connected young man would stake his luck (and inheritance) on West Granby, but obviously Huggins saw a bright future for the place. He moved in and began operating the grist mill and at least three different shops - a distillery, a trip hammer shop, and a wire shop (for carding machine wire). All these he built above the gorge around a pond the Strattons had created by damming up Higley Brook as it emptied into the West Branch of Salmon Brook. Since Higley Brook was small, they had also fed their pond with a canal they had dug from Salmon Brook above the present intersection of Routes 20 and 219.[5] There in the 1780s, while the turmoil of Simsbury's division into two towns, the anger of Shays' rebellion in Massachusetts, and the debate in the state over the highly suspicious workings of a certain convention in Philadelphia whirled about him, James and Nancy calmly went about the business of launching their family into prosperity - no easy task in what was then a thinly settled rock strewn world of hills and forest. By 1790, they were a success - enough to hire three laborers for the mills and to build a new house.[6] The house still stands today at 70 Hartland Road, above the "great rock" on which the grist mill leaned, its elegant woodwork speaking of the enterprise of the age in which it was built (See Figure 6-1).

In the 1790s, Huggins' road to success became a little bumpier as he weathered events that were clearly not part of his plan. To begin with, his wife Nancy died in childbirth in March of 1792.[7] A man of high emotion, he might at another age, have been able to present his two children with only a depressed and broken father. But this was the 1790s and there was still an institution ready to prevent such a catastrophe. Three weeks after Nancy died James Huggins shared his grief - now a religious experience - with the congregation of the Salmon Brook Ecclesiastical Society and was admitted as a church member on "profession of faith."[8] Instead of lapsing into depression, he was soon ready to begin a new life - at the age of forty, he was a man "reborn."

Not only was the congregation impressed and inspired, but so was the rest of the town when he agreed to take on the duties of both lister (of taxable property) and hayward (poundkeeper) for the year 1793. For the church he was willing to do the undesirable task of telling the minister, Mr. Holly, that he was to be dismissed. The next year, he headed the church committee to make improvements on the meetinghouse, and then, in April, he went to call on a prospective minister, young Isaac Porter, to invite him to preach for the people of Salmon Brook.[9] During the next decade his new-found prominence

227

would bring him into the center of town politics with its battles over which roads to build and how much to charge the taxpayers. Here he represented the western section of Granby that was eager to see better roads built along the Hartford-Albany path of commerce. The people of Turkey Hills preferred to build up the north-south byways and ignore everything to the west of the ridge.[10]

Apparently Huggins was a galvanizing leader, for in 1795 he was elected Moderator of the Town Meeting, an honor usually reserved for a town's "first citizen;" and the meeting also gave him the title of Agent for the Town, showing they trusted his ability as an advocate as well as a business-man.[11] As time passed, he continued to rise in stature among his neighbors in the Salmon Brook parish. The records provide us with a picture of a vivacious and zealous public servant, buoyed by a second marriage to Chloe Pratt, daughter of a prominent Granville couple. There were three new children; honorable positions on the Ecclesiastical Society Prudential Committee, the state legislature, and the militia; and slowly growing profits from his mills and from the tavern he had opened on one end of his house to accommodate new stage traffic that went by his house. With an older son and daughter who could be of real economic assistance, he was so confident of his future that in 1805, he mortgaged all he owned for $3,000 (a large sum at that time) to build a new distillery and a carding machine and a shop to house it.[12]

Quite a few other people from outside of Granby were also attracted to the possibilities offered by West Granby. Land and census records suggest that families were literally crowding into the area in the 1780s and 90s. As of 1790, in addition to the Hayes, Stratton, Holcomb and Halladay families, who had been building their farms in West Granby since before the Revolu-tion, there were now Joab Griffin originally of Turkey Hills, Giles Hickock, Lemuel Kilbourn, Philo Kilbourn, Sadoce Wilcox, Elnathan Strong and Asher Frank, an African-American Revolutionary War veteran. Lemuel Kilbourn had been in the clothier business with his brother James, in Simsbury (Tariffville area), but both had given up the trade to become farmers in Granby.[13] In 1787, young Sadoce Wilcox of Weatogue bought land near the Simsbury Road bridge over Salmon Brook and built a blacksmith shop and a large house that is occupied by his descendants today (See Figure 6-2).

During the next fifteen years, others arrived. Noahdiah Kendall

228

Mark Williams

Figure 6-1: James Huggins House (c. 1790) in West Granby, now 70 Hartland Road. Originally this structure had a gambrel roof, but was altered in the mid-19th century by owner Byron Goddard. Huggins lived on this property from 1784 until his death in 1819.

Mark Williams

Figure 6-2: Sadoce Wilcox House (c. 1787) in West Granby, now 147 Simsbury Road. The house is still occupied by the descendants of this early blacksmith. Note that both this and the Huggins house represent a subtle advance in decorative detail.

229

brought his family and set up a new farm on the west side of Bushy Hill. Isaac Phelps Jr. of Granby Center moved into a house Reuben Holcomb's son Phinehas had built on Salmon Brook. Phineas Kingsbury bought Asahel Hays's farm near the center of West Granby in 1796, but then moved away before the decade was out. Josiah Tovils gave a try at operating a shoe shop on what is now the corner of West Granby and Simsbury Roads. Austin Cadwell set up a hatter's shop near today's Broad Hill Road bridge shortly after 1800. Oliver Kellogg and David Lee were also newcomers to the area.[14]

From Weatogue came Jacob and Rosetta Barber Pettibone. Jacob had been a builder there since before the Revolution. At age 40, he and Rosetta (she was 33) moved with their children, to open a sawmill just below the grist mill at the foot of the Gorge. He built a small house, of which the chimney stack still remains within the present house at 15 Simsbury Road, and had high hopes of cashing in on the lumber business that was continuing to grow rapidly in the hills on the west side of Granby. He also contracted with the town selectmen to care for one of the town's paupers. Unfortunately, both his and his wife's poor health prevented them from prospering as others had. From 1801, when his cousin and partner Jonathan bailed out of the business, until his death in 1807, Jacob could not extract himself from debt. His widow found herself penniless and was forced to move in with her brother, Calvin Barber of Simsbury. She died three years later.[15]

Of course, the grist mill at the foot of the gorge, near Jacob Pettibone's sawmill, was the earliest business operation in the vicinity. We noted in Chapter IV that in the 1740s, the Halladay family of Suffield had been the first white settlers in West Granby, and that they had come to establish a grist mill in an area they thought would soon be populated. Farmers only trickled into the area, however, as relationships between France and England continued to be hostile until after the Peace of Paris in 1763. In 1767, John and Samuel Halladay took in their neighbors Serajah Stratton and Asahel Hays as partners in building a new mill. Stratton actually may not have paid for his share, but claimed it for being the only person in the area (along with his brother Martin) to have received permission from the town meeting to establish a grist mill on the brook. At any rate, the Halladays soon sold all of their share of the venture to Simeon Baxter, a land speculator of Barkhamsted (and earlier of Hartland), and Asahel Hays sold out as well. By 1776, the mill was in the hands of

Benoni Griffin, who lived at "the Lordship" five miles to the east and was himself a land speculator. Griffin's son Joab seems to have been designated to live on and oversee this and other property his father had purchased in West Granby. Joab, however, probably did little grinding of grain, since his sister Hannah was Martin Stratton's wife. During all that time the mill, or its supposed site, was on the southwest side of the brook, probably off the end of today's Granby Tennis Club pavilion.[16]

As John Halladay slowly sank into poverty, and the Strattons struggled to stay afloat during the Revolution, the populating of West Granby had only just begun. It was in the 1780s that James Huggins took over the Stratton mills, including their grist mill above the gorge, and other new people set up house in what was becoming a village center. Martin Stratton may have contemplated opening a mill on his brother-in-law's land, but his family seemed more interested in going west, and did so in 1790, leaving their father behind in a Granby cemetery.[17]

During the 1790s, though, the population of West Granby was growing so rapidly that new investors felt the area could, at last, sustain even two grist mills. A partnership consisting of Col. Ozias Pettibone and his son Ozias Jr., who lived in Granby Center, David Goodrich of Bushy Hill Road and Simon Clark of Hartford, bought eight acres around the old mill site and sank $1500 into the construction of a new mill, this time on the northeast side of the brook. Instead of damming up the basin at the foot of the gorge, as the Halladays had (which probably accounted for a ruined mill wheel and dam every spring as ice rattled through the gorge), "Pettibone, Clark & Goodrich" built their dam at the top of the gorge and ran a sluice across the boulders to an overshot wheel on a building well out of the way of winter ice jams.[18]

This firm was something new for this area, for none of its proprietors were in residence in West Granby. After 1804, Pettibone had two new partners, Elizur Hayes, whose parents Benjamin and Rosanna Hayes had been living just north of the mill on the Hartland Road since before the Revolution, and Nathaniel Pratt, who had bought a farm on what is now Fox Road around 1790. The firm also acquired Jacob Pettibone's sawmill when he was forced to sell out. After Col. Pettibone's death in 1812, his right passed to his sons Ozias, Jr. and Chauncey. Chauncey was a true absentee capitalist, eventually collecting his share of the mill proceeds from his new home in Natchez,

Mississippi. The grist mill must have been a success in this period of growth in West Granby, for the value of the property grew by 67% in the first four years of its operation.[19] Venture capital had come to West Granby, and the influx of farmers made it profitable.

Along with new farmers, millers and craftsmen, the village also housed a new industry: manufacturing of clothing. While our surviving land records do not include the deed by which clothier Alpheus Hayes acquired an advantageous location on the bank of Salmon Brook, the Granby town records provide a valuable clue to the dramatic change that was taking place in West Granby in the 1790s. In 1794, the town meeting approved "the Doings of the Select men in Laying out a Road from Joab Griffens to Mr. Nahum Holcombs."[20] Joab Griffin had recently built a stately federal dwelling on a hill at what is now the northeast corner of West Granby and Simsbury Roads, and Nahum Holcomb had likewise built a similarly appointed house at what is now the junction of Day Street South and Simsbury Road (the house which his great grandchildren Tudor and Laura Holcomb would one day give to the University of Connecticut).[21] The significance of this road is related to the fact that there already was a north-south road from Joab Griffin's land to Nahum Holcomb's. However, that road, surveyed back in 1769, ran among farmers' fields. The new road ran along the brook. From land records of the early 1800s, we learn the reason for this change.

Alpheus Hayes had erected a new dam just below the sawmill dam, and was using water power to drive a fulling mill (for making felt), a dressing shop and dye works, and a clothing shop.[22] He probably purchased wool carded in Huggins' or some other shop and spun and woven by neighboring farm families, dressed and dyed it, softened some of it into felt, and created clothing from the finished cloth. The surveying of a new route for the road along the brook and between his shops and his new house signifies that this was a major operation, at least as ambitious in scope as the new grist mill had been.

Alpheus Hayes was born in West Granby in 1773. His parents were Benjamin and Rosanna Hayes, and he had been raised on their farm up the hill from Joab Griffin.[23] He married Betsy Higley, the daughter of Ozias Higley, who lived just northwest of the Hayes family farm, but that was clearly not until he had established himself as a clothier, for their first child was not born until 1805. At some point he was joined in the business by his older brother Thaddeus who lived a little north of him on the new road between Griffin and Nahum Holcomb.[24] They may have learned some of the clothing trade from their father, who seems to have done some tailoring as a sideline, but their dream was to have it be their principal business, leaving farming for someone else.[25]

As the area around the old "Halladay Mill Place" changed from a collection of farms into a recognizable village (See Maps 6-1 and 6-2), more families set up homesteads among the surrounding hills. Surely they profited initially from the timber they struggled to remove from their lands, as had the generation before them when people first began living in this part of town before the Revolution. With more building than ever going on throughout the town, they had a ready market for lumber without even dealing with river-town merchants. Moreover, as they cleared land, they found, as had others before them, that centuries of leaf mold had left them a workable and productive layer of top soil for doing what they knew how to do best. Where the hills proved too rugged, craggy or rock strewn for the plow, farmers learned to specialize: the carding and the clothing shops down on the brook were as eager for their wool as the grist mills were for their grain, and so they raised sheep in abundance. Without fail, probate inventories from the period generally list a small collection of anywhere from 5 to 25 sheep in every farmer's holdings.[26] The introduction into Connecticut after 1800 of merino sheep, whose yield was three to four times as great as earlier types, encouraged even further specialization in wool production.[27]

In addition, they found that boulders held heat well, and although late spring frosts might ruin a potential crop of apples for their lowland-dwelling neighbors, their hill-top blossoms often survived unscathed.[28] Those with the knowledge and skills built cider mills and distilleries, and made a good living participating in the growing market for cider brandy. One of these was Thomas Buckland Gillet, who, around the time of the Revolution, had bought some craggy parcels of land between Broad Hill and "Pine Cone," just west of the village. After the war, he and his wife Rhoda Gozzard Gillet moved up onto this land, planted their orchard, fenced off their sheep pasture, harvested lumber, erected a cider mill, and raised ten children in a small dwelling. They were so busy building this collection of enterprises that Buckland, as he was

233

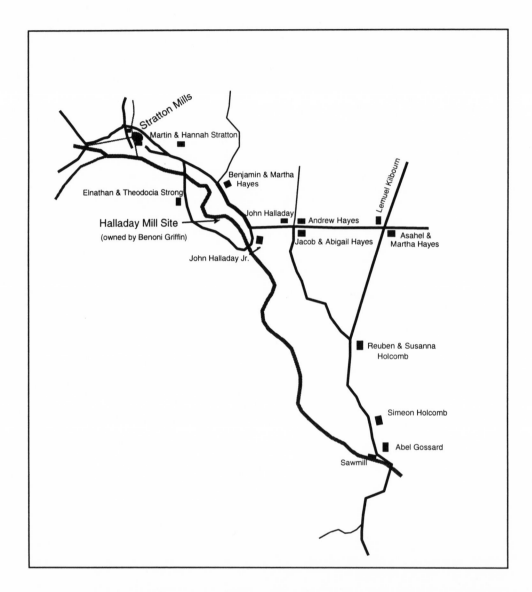

Map 6-1: West Granby, circa 1781. These locations of houses, roads and mills along the west branch of Salmon Brook are based upon references in the Simsbury Land Records, Simsbury Town Records and some account books from that period. There is no map from this time, but the records do allow us reasonable grounds for assumption.

234

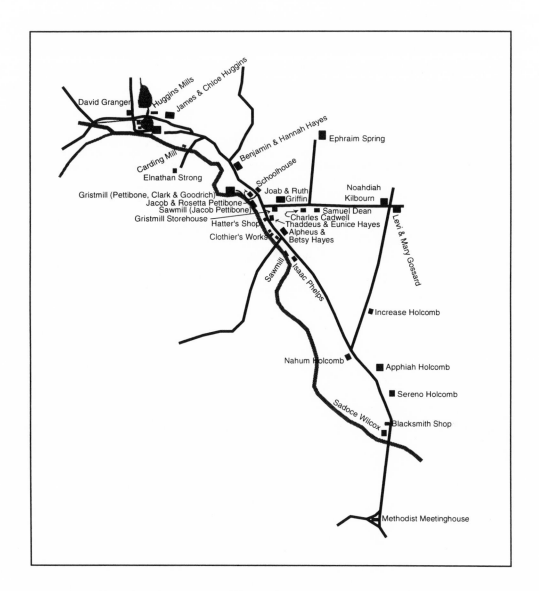

Map 6-2: West Granby, circa 1805. Again many of the estimates of locations are not certain. However, the records are clear enough to allow us to show that in the two decades after the Revolutionary War, the area had changed from a few scattered farms to a village with manufacturing establishments.

235

called, did not even take time to register to vote until 1792.[29]

So good were times for people in West Granby that even those young farmers who had had to settle in these hills before the Revolution because it was the only land available, had no inclination to leave for better land. Benjamin Hayes's older brother Elisha, and his wife Marcy Lamson, had set up a farm on the steep southern slope of Popatunuck (at what is now the foot of Silkey Road) even before the French and Indian War was over, and when Elisha died in 1787, their eight children carefully carved up the farm into long thin strips, everyone getting fair proportion of the valued hillside property.[30] Asa and Ozias Higley, who had been living on the same hillside between the Elisha Hayeses and the Strattons since before the Revolutionary War (along what was then the best route to Hartland - now Higley Road), refused their father's pleas to move to Becket, Massachusetts to develop land he had acquired there. Instead, they continued to live among the hills of West Granby. Ozias's son, Ozias, Jr. was engaged in a tanning business by 1804.[31]

In the hills west of the Gillets, Timothy and Mary Willcockson Cossitt had built a homestead before the Revolution on a hilly lot on the Barkhamsted town line (the old "Kimberly Line," before there was a Barkhamsted, when Salmon Brook was simply bounded on the west by "the wilderness"). Cossitt was a millwright who had had an interest in a mill at the Cragg in North Granby, and here in West Granby, he built a saw mill. By the 1790s, he and his two sons, Timothy Jr. and Martin, had created quite a farming and milling establishment in the hills on the western edge of town. His estate record in 1795 is testimony to considerable prosperity. His furniture included feather beds, a drop-leaf table and several chairs; among the rest of the inventory were listed pewterware, silver shoe and knee buckles, linen table cloths and curtains, a sizable herd of cattle, 17 sheep, a large stock of cider, an array of tools, some silk clothing, spinning wheels and looms, horses, pigs and over a hundred acres of land to himself, not to mention similarly sized farmsteads owned by his sons.[32]

His neighbor Moses Weed also set up his homestead around 1790, building the house that would later be moved from Enders Road to Salmon Brook Street and become part of the Salmon Brook Historical Society complex (See Figure 6-3). On a hill to their east, Nathaniel and Sarah Perkins Pratt, originally of East Hartford, and since moved to Hartland, bought a farm

Salmon Brook Historical Society

Figure 6-3: Weed-Enders House (c. 1790). This dwelling, built by Moses Weed, once stood on Enders Road near the west bounds of the town. It was moved to the Salmon Brook Historical Society and restored in 1974.

Richard Caley

Figure 6-4: Giddings-Pratt House (c. 1783) in West Granby, located at the top of Fox Road. Built by Thomas Giddings for his son Jabez, the house was sold to Nathaniel Pratt a few years later.

237

from Thomas Giddings, one of Hartland's first settlers, and settled in with their family (See Figure 6-4). Both the Weeds and the Pratts, while living in small one-story houses with sleeping lofts, enjoyed success similar to the Cossitts and the Gillets.[33] The topography that had once presented so many obstacles now seemed to contain only opportunities as ambitious farmers turned profits from cash crops.

Other sections of town also experienced growth around the turn of the century. In North Granby, Silas Cossitt, grandson of the French immigrant René, built a cider mill and distillery at the junction of what is now Mountain Road and Granville Road, and he and his father, Ranna Cossitt, opened a tavern together. When Silas left town in 1804, Eber Banning Clark moved down the hill from Hartland to take over the "sider mill" and tavern. In twenty years, the intersection property had grown in value from a few hundred dollars to $5700.[34] In the 1790s and early 1800s, it was becoming clear that this crossroads would see a good deal of traffic. Near the intersection, James Kilbourn, who had once owned a cloth and dye shop in Simsbury near the Falls, opened a general store. Up Mountain Road, both Aaron Post and Benajah Holcomb expanded their apple orchards, paid out the $67 bond for tavern licenses, and fired up their distilleries, anticipating new traffic, improved roads, and thirsty travelers.[35] Probably they hoped to engage in other retail business as well, since taverning in those days was often the way a person worked himself into a larger merchant operation.[36]

Ever since the tea boycott, apple cider and cider brandy had become one of Granby's principal industries. Samuel Hays, and his son Seth, continued to run their mill on Barn Door Hills Road, and in North Granby nearly every farmer had a distillery - whether he had a tavern or not.[37] Even farmers who did not run stills grew plenty of surplus apples to sell to those who did. As a result, areas of town which might look today as though they could never support more than a few hill farmers, hummed with activity. Aaron Post and Benajah Holcomb's taverns on the top of Popatunuck were nestled among a bustling neighborhood. Benajah Hills, an African-American blacksmith, moved in, financing a shop with Aaron Post.[38] Job Case, a farmer from Terry's Plain, purchased Captain Jonathan Buttolph's farm, and, after Case moved on to Ohio, a distinguished blacksmith from Berlin, Oren Lee, moved in, set up his shop, and of course, built a cider mill.[39]

As they prospered, these hillside entrepreneurs reconstructed or refashioned their houses, inside and out, in new architectural styles of the Federal Period. Entranceway surrounds became more elaborate, windows became more numerous and had larger panes, Adam-style woodworking appeared under the eves, and molded cornices triangulated the gables. Inside their dwellings, some, like Enoch Buttolph and James Holcomb, both Popatunuck Mountain dwellers, removed the old center chimney, replacing it with a more spacious entrance hall, and built two chimney stacks for the rooms on either side of it (See Figure 6-5).[40] Those who later inherited these structures often had little use for elegance, and the improvements gradually languished until only a trained eye could discern these expressions in wood by farmers proud of their new world of enterprise.

A short distance south of the North Granby crossroads where Silas Cossitt built his "sider mill" one businessman created one of these enterprising neighborhoods single-handedly. When Hezekiah Goodrich moved from Portland, Connecticut to Granby in 1800, he set up his tanning shop on what is now North Granby Road, just north of today's First Congregational Church meetinghouse (the meetinghouse was then on Creamery Hill Road). At that time the surrounding area was much like West Granby had been before 1790 - scattered farms, mostly owned by one or two extended families. Hezekiah, in fact, had married into one of these families in 1798, and it was probably his new father-in-law, town clerk Judah Holcomb, who set him up with land for his house and a shop in which to practice his trade of tanning.

A tanner was one of the more respected craftsmen of early New England. The trade, like that of blacksmith or millwright, required years of special training. Furthermore, virtually everyone used the tanner's products in virtually every way: saddles, harnesses, reins, whips, shoes, boots, clothing, straps of all sorts - in a farming world, leather was the binding of survival. Tanning hides required knowledge of a detailed process, patience, strength, tolerance of stench and grime, willingness to experiment, and an eye for quality. Hides first had to be salted down and drained to get the major fat off. Then they would be soaked in boiling water for a short time to loosen the grease and soften the hair so that the tanner, using a scraping knife, could remove everything that would interfere with the deep tanning of the hide. Finally, they were soaked six months or more in large vats or a pond of water

239

with layers of pulverized oak bark between. Even with ingenious machinery, the crushing of the bark was not for the weak.[41]

Goodrich was possibly Granby's first tanner, and, with considerable energy, skill and business acumen, turned a good profit in his early years. He and his wife Millicent also took in hired hands and kept a few paupers, and in 1805, he managed to win himself appointment as Granby's first postmaster. At that time, Granby was one of only a thousand post offices in the new nation. Eventually, shoemakers moved in nearby to ply their trade with his leather, and as Hezekiah's sons took up both tanning and shoemaking, Hezekiah's neighborhood became "Goodrichville."[42]

In the old Salmon Brook village, now Granby Center, two men accumulated veritable fortunes engaging in a variety of businesses. Col. Ozias Pettibone, who had moved to the village from Weatogue before the Revolution, not only owned a major share of the West Granby grist mill, but also several dwelling houses and nearly 1000 acres of land spread out around Granby (and a farm in Norfolk as well). In 1805, he built himself an elegant domicile at the head of Salmon Brook Street, with all sorts of decorative woodwork, including facsimile stonework (quoins - a technique also known as "rustication") on the corners (See Figure 6-6). His personal inventory in 1813 filled nine pages of the probate record book and was valued at $22,373.70. He also had the distinction of being one of Granby's two slave owners at the turn of the century. His wealth was a result of years of careful attention to real estate investment, lawyer's work, storekeeping, cash-crop farming and cider production (when he died, he had over 150 barrels of cider in stock). A reference in his estate to "money in the loan office in Hartford," suggests the scope and type of his investment activities.[43]

His neighbor, Pliny Hillyer, while not quite as rich, was, nevertheless, as enterprising. Born in 1748, the son of Captain James and Mary Humphrey Hillyer, Pliny studied law and rose to prominence in post-Revolutionary Salmon Brook as one of the leaders of the separation movement. He was also Ozias Pettibone's partner in a general merchandise business in the 1770s. After Granby's incorporation, he served often as selectman, town meeting moderator and representative to the General Assembly. Near his house at the head of Granby's main street he kept a general store, conducted his law business, busied himself with town and state politics, and, of course, manu-

Richard Caley

Figure 6-5: Enoch Buttolph House (c. 1810) on Popatunuck, now 151 Silkey Road at the junction of Mountain Road. The house seems to have been constructed from materials of an older structure. Note the "center hall" design with the two chimney stacks.

Salmon Brook Historical Society

Figure 6-6: Ozias Pettibone House (c. 1805) in Granby Center, now 4 East Granby Road. Pettibone was Granby's wealthiest citizen.

factured cider and cider brandy.

In the 1790s, he had Jeptha Curtiss as his partner in running the store, and they together did an astonishing volume of business in a wide range of goods. As well as being licensed "spirits" dealers, they sold glass, wool cards, silverware, hats, gloves, cloth, buttons, kitchen utensils and gadgets, sheet lead, china tea sets, chamber pots, wine glasses, "Irish linen," tools, hardware, coffee, tea, spices, tobacco and, to service Granby's building boom, nails by the cask. To acquire these items, they sent agents to Hartford, Boston and New York, carrying wagon loads of rye, corn, wool, cider brandy, beef, pork and cheese, which local farmers brought to them in exchange for their new standard of living.

From Hillyer's papers it is also apparent he acted as a pawn broker, loaning out money and holding as collateral such things as Thompson Kimberly's saddle (worth, it would appear, $9.86). Furthermore, his store seems to have served as a local clearing house for IOUs farmers passed among each other in place of currency.[44] Regardless of how much this local economy expanded, it was still, and would continue to be, plagued by a shortage of hard currency. Farmers, artisans and merchants operated through an elaborate bookkeeping system in which debts would be kept on account books for years at a time, sometimes not settled with cash until after a person's death. Every so often among their papers or accounts would appear the notation "Reckoned and Setteled all our privet book akounts from the Beginning of the world to this Day and Ballanced Even by us," as brothers Increase and Nahum Holcomb declared on "october 31, AD 1794."[45] Such a "reckoning" might involve the exchange of a few pennies after years of exchange of goods and services, or, more commonly, a passing on of IOUs from other cash-poor, commodity rich farmers. In such an economy, a Pliny Hillyer was essential to help move accounts and IOUs around in a more orderly and efficient manner. Of course, Hillyer was not the only storekeeper in town. We know that James Kilbourn kept store in North Granby, and a man named John Ashley, and another local merchant known to us only by his initials ("WBC"), also operated general stores in Granby in the 1790s.[46]

In every corner of the new town, in the late 1700s and early 1800s, mill wheels turned, grindstones spit out corn and rye flour, saws turned out planks, clapboards and shingles, hammers banged against anvils, barnyards and pastures teemed with animals, men and women labored over clattering looms, oxen slogged through fields, grinders chewed up apples to be pressed for cider, stills and tanning pots gurgled and wagons lumbered across rough roads known as "the traveled roads" even before selectmen had a chance to survey them for town upkeep. It must have been quite a scene, and one can easily imagine the looks of satisfaction and determination with which these ambitious people greeted each other as they welcomed the enterprising spirit of the post-Revolutionary age. There were, to be sure, a sizable number of men and women on whom fortune did not smile, or who had expended their entrepreneurial energy before the good times set in; but their plight would not characterize this era. Rough ambition ruled the day. Granby was on the cutting edge of a new world of commercial prosperity.

Defining the Common Good

One would think that a blooming economy such as this would mandate an era of prosperity, peace and contentment for all the people of Granby. This was hardly the case. Even though townspeople of all classes, origins and backgrounds seemed to live side by side sharing in the opportunities of the new age, the changes in the economic climate were disruptive and their benefits enjoyed unevenly. In turn, these changes fostered a society with greater complexity and more sophisticated needs. This meant that the government's task of sorting out the common good, an already habitually clumsy process in a community ruled by the town meeting, would be more difficult than ever.

A clear indicator of the increasing complications of living together is the greater number of residents engaged in the legal profession. There seemed to be plenty of business for lawyers and justices of the peace as the 18th century came to a close. Pliny Hillyer's brother Andrew's account book details busy days serving writs, writing letters, drawing up deeds, and certifying marriage licenses. He represented the town selectmen, heard cases on his own docket and argued cases before other justices of the peace.[47] In a community where litigation was increasing, the town clearly had to adapt its policies to new conditions.

An early sign that the town, in its corporate capacity, recognized the

243

need for change in its domestic policy appeared in 1797. At a special town meeting in March of that year, the town passed "Some Regulations Relating to Restraining Horses & Cattel Swine Sheep & Geese from Going at Large on the Commons or High Way in sd Town." For one thing, the highways were about all that remained of the common land once considered obscenely abundant by covetous outlanders in the 1720s. Even so, many farmers apparently still followed the old "open field" practice of allowing livestock to roam freely, fencing in their private lands for crops and orchards. One can imagine the impediment to travel and transportation of goods that resulted when a growing population funnelled its livestock to the town grazing land, alias "highways." Geese must have been the most offensive miscreants, for their retrieval after removal from a highway would cost an owner 8¢ a goose - a hefty expense for the cash-poor owners of these renowned escape artists.[48] At any rate, the townspeople, or at least the ones who had pastures of their own, clearly recognized that the era of open field grazing should be laid to rest. No doubt those farmers with small holdings resented having to build pens for their "swine" on land that might have produced more apples; and yet, they did not seem to control the majority at the town meeting.

The most expensive responsibility of local government in a developing town like Granby was the construction and maintenance of roads and bridges. A 1791 petition authored by Selectmen Pliny Hillyer and Silas Holcomb spelled out the various dimensions of this burden. The people of Granby, they said, had endured heavy taxes ever since the Revolutionary War. In addition, it didn't help that the town was on the Massachusetts border, across which citizens from that state annually brought their households "doubtless with a view of screening themselves from being taxed in that State," only to flee back when the Granby listers set out on their rounds. The town was responsible, the petition continued, for two long bridges across the Farmington River at either end of the Falls, and nine additional "framed Bridges," all of which needed rebuilding every decade, plus a great number of smaller plank bridges. The petitioners humbly requested permission to conduct a lottery to rebuild the bridge from Turkey Hills to Scotland, but the none-too-veiled implication was that there was a great deal of traffic between Westfield, Suffield and the communities to the south of the river, and here was poor, beleaguered Granby single-handedly supporting all this beneficial commerce.[49] At that point, the town "rate," or tax, had been fluctuating between two and four pence on the pound,[50] which is the equivalent of 8 to 16 mills - a fair amount considering the ecclesiastical society assessed a second rate for the upkeep of the Congregational meetinghouse, the minister's salary, and whatever schooling the society could provide (then the State would come in with its own rate on top of that).

The following year, the town meeting took further action on the problem of funding bridge and road upkeep by voting to request the legislature allow them the liberty of enacting a "highway tax." Prior to this vote, the town had elected "surveyors of highways," and each had been responsible for calling out his neighbors and requiring highway work of each in proportion to his "list," the assessed value of his property. No doubt farmers in poorer neighborhoods complained that they did not have enough time to devote to highway work, that farmers in wealthier neighborhoods (such as Turkey Hills east of the ridge, with its six little bridges) paid laborers to do their work for them, and that roads in the poorer sections of town (such as the hills west of Salmon Brook village with their forty bridges and a "labyrinth of roads") suffered as a result. It would appear that the new proposal for a town-wide highway tax was put forth with these concerns in mind and with the intent of using the total wealth of the town to pay equal attention to all of its roads and bridges.

Certainly the Turkey Hills citizens saw it that way, for they proffered a petition at a special town meeting in April, 1793 to divide the town in two.[51] From their viewpoint, it was unfair to take their money and use it for road repair in Salmon Brook Society. They were more interested in the north-south path of commerce from Massachusetts and Suffield down through Turkey Hills to Windsor and Hartford, and did not see much to be gained by improving transportation routes to their west. Since their share of the grand list was twice Salmon Brook's, even though they had only half the population, they feared a "tyranny of the majority" would annually carry off their money to mend roads they would never use.[52]

The town meeting resolved the issue with a typical Puritan compromise: the town would not be divided, but the petition to the legislature for town wide highway taxation was pulled for the time being.[53] This was only the beginning of the wrangling over roads at town meeting, however. As time passed, Turkey Hills residents had even more reason than ever to continue their efforts to form a separate town.

In 1794, the selectmen surveyed two new roads in Salmon Brook Society, and in 1795, the dreaded townwide highway tax became a reality. Not only was the town rate that year 3¢ on the dollar (30 mills), but on top of that was a highway rate of 4¢. Furthermore, the town appointed the dynamic James Huggins, outspoken advocate of the interests of West Granby, its agent "to act & transact for & in Behalf of said Town & to make Defence in any Suit or Matter in behalf of sd Town."[54] That was the year in which the state legislature was mightily enriched by a windfall from the states' sale of lands in its "Western Reserve." This was an area in northeast Ohio that Connecticut had been allowed to sell as part of a settlement of western land claims which states were making after the Revolution. The legislature decided to use the revenue to establish a fund for the support of local "school societies" in each town to replace the generally ineffective schooling efforts on the part of the ecclesiastical societies.[55] Therefore, the ecclesiastical society rates declined that year to reflect the change, and the town meeting thought it could get away with increasing its own taxation, even though it was not taking on the cost of schooling.

This must have met with an irate response from Turkey Hills Society, for in the 1796 town meeting, held to their good fortune at their own meetinghouse, they managed to get the town and highway rates both set at 1.5¢ and the selectmen were ordered to oversee both the assessing of tax liabilities and the fixing of prices for labor and use of teams for road work.[56] The struggle continued between the eastern part of town with its relatively wealthy farms and few brook crossings, and the western part with its many bridges, steeper grades, more abundant ground water, more serious problems with spring run-off and equally large aspirations toward becoming a player in the regional economy. It seemed that no settlement would be satisfactory for long, and the discord dragged on for over a decade.[57]

Meanwhile, Pliny Hillyer settled on a scheme by which his part of town might get the good roads that would encourage the commerce it coveted, and he might make a little money for himself as well. In the spring of 1799, he and seventeen other men and one woman, with James Huggins as their agent, petitioned the legislature to be allowed to pool their funds and be incorporated as the Granby Turnpike Company, a private enterprise which would create a good road from the Massachusetts line through Granby and on to Hartford (approximately the route of today's state Route 189). The genesis of this action had been Granby's dispute with Simsbury that year over the need to rebuild the bridge to the west of the Falls. Granby, of course, did not need another highway expense, but according to the settlement which divided Simsbury in 1786, Granby was required to keep up the bridge near Pickerel Cove. Simsbury had had the legislature order Granby to rebuild the bridge to accommodate a new road surveyed by the county court.[58]

Hillyer and company claimed the new county road was unsatisfactory, and asked that they be allowed to improve a route that went south from Salmon Brook, then cut through Hatchet Hill and used the Scotland Bridge which had been rebuilt eight years earlier with lottery money. Thus, another bridge above the Falls would not be needed. They requested that two gates be permitted, one at each end of the town, for the collection of tolls, and that the legislature set the toll schedule. The turnpike was to be a major undertaking, capitalized at $10,000 through the selling of shares.[59] The petitioners clearly recognized the treble advantages in the plan: their town would be relieved of a troublesome expense, a good road would be built among their farms and businesses (most lived right on the route and probably looked forward to the business greater traffic and accessibility to markets would bring), and as a corporation, they might make some profit on the tolls.

The legislature seemed to be favorably disposed and the company was created. The following rate schedule was set:

4-wheel pleasure Carriage	12¢	5 mills
Chaise, Chair or Sulky	8	5
Loaded cart or sled	12	5
Pleasure or travailing Sleigh	6	2.5
empty cart, wagon or sled	4	2.5
Single horse cart or sleigh	4	6
man & horse	4	
Horses, Cattle and Mules in droves	1	4
Sheep and hogs	0	5

Persons traveling to public meetings, meetings on the "Lord's Day," grist mill and military training were exempt from payment. By 1802, not only was the company up and running, but its shares were trading.[60]

247

Inspired by this venture, another group of investors, including some of the Granby Turnpike shareholders, put forth a petition for another company to develop a route from the Granby Turnpike, west across Granby toward Hartland (along today's Route 20). Unsuccessful on their first try in 1800, they petitioned again in 1803 after the county court had prescribed a similar route and asked the town to improve the road. The petitioners tactfully noted that turnpikes were being created in Massachusetts and that one would connect with this route, making a major artery both to Albany and to a nearby turnpike that ran east to Boston from the Hudson River. The proposed road, they said, "runs through a rich & fertile Country & is a road of great travel or which a great quantity of produce is conveyed from Granville & other adjacent towns in Massachusetts & the adjacent towns in this state to Hartford it being the only market town to which their produce can be sent." They argued there was a need for a better road than one kept up by the towns of Hartford County, and that their company would make such a road. A number of the signers were of West Granby, and, not surprisingly, the petition suggested one gate be set up near the house (and tavern) of James Huggins.[61]

To their great frustration, the legislature did not act on this request. The next year, another group suggested a turnpike company be incorporated for a route from the Turkey Hills meetinghouse across today's Route 20, then up today's Route 219 to Barkhamsted and the "Greenwoods Turnpike." At present, they argued, this route ran over a rough and stony road and heavy wagons loaded with iron and nail rods, bound from Canaan for Newgate, now a state prison that manufactured nails, and the U.S. Gun Factory at Springfield, had to detour through Simsbury. In the spring of 1805, these petitioners, mostly Turkey Hills residents, were joined by Pliny Hillyer and his neighbors in Granby Center, along with what appears to be the entire population of West Granby, creating an unusual alliance that was not to be duplicated very often in coming years. Prospects for passage looked so good, James Huggins borrowed heavily to stock up on tavern supplies in anticipation of the coming traffic.

Still the legislature did not respond, but listened to a competing petition from a group of men of North Granby and the Copper Hill section of Turkey Hills Society who said that actually a more direct route from the forges of Canaan to Newgate lay through Hartland, across Popatunuck, through

North Granby and across today's East Street and Notch Road. The legislature sent a committee to investigate. Upon their determination that, indeed, the northern route was the most direct, the Barkhamsted Turnpike Company was incorporated without Pliny Hillyer, without James Huggins, without West Granby, and without Granby Center.[62] To add further to the bad luck of the original petitioners, a flood in early 1807 carried off the Farmington River bridge used by the Granby Turnpike Company, and there was controversy over whether or not to collect tolls at the North Granby gate since the bridge was lost.[63] Furthermore, the Massachusetts legislature seemed to lose interest in chartering the proposed turnpike that would connect Granby's turnpike to the Boston-Albany path of commerce.[64]

Undaunted, Hillyer and his followers led two special town meetings during 1807, one to double the highway tax in order to rebuild the bridge, and a second to raise the highway tax to a phenomenal 14¢ on the dollar to repair bridges and roads throughout the town.[65] Clearly, they were desperate for good roads, toll booth profits or no. They could hardly do the kind of business they wanted to, or attract the volume of traffic and commerce they thought healthy, by continuing to rely on rocky, rutted mudwashes which barely qualified as field roads, let alone town "highways." If the town did not act fast, the world would pass them by. And yet, the town had grown to the point where it was not all of one mind about how best to proceed with development of transportation facilities. What was good for some never seemed to be good enough for all.

This absence of homogeneity of interests was also increasingly apparent in the evolving social structure of the new town. While wealthy and poverty stricken, farmer and manufacturer, merchant and artisan, and black and white lived and worked side by side, and, in fact, depended upon one another, there were signs of more clearly differentiated social classes, continued racial distinctions and growing consciousness of individual status. These trends were most obvious in the case of Granby's tiny African American population.

In response to Revolutionary ideology, Connecticut had banned the slave trade in 1774 and enacted a gradual emancipation law in 1783. However, it would be decades before slavery was finally declared illegal in Connecticut, and even those African Americans who were "free" were far

249

from equal participants in the new democratic order. For one thing, "free person" did not mean "freeman," as black males discovered when they were not allowed to vote upon reaching the age of 21. But the course of racial discrimination ran even deeper.

Many of Granby's African Americans of the 1790s were either former slaves of colonial families who had lived in Simsbury and Granby, or veterans and the families of veterans of the Revolutionary War - soldiers who had enlisted on condition of being freed after the war. Most of these men were newcomers to Granby, like Philip Negro who had been purchased from his former master in Litchfield in order to serve in place of the two Granby men who had paid for his freedom.[66] In the years after the war, they and other free African Americans joined in the "pursuit of happiness" that was in full gear in Granby. Some worked trades, like blacksmith Benajah Hills, others worked family farms, and some were laborers who boarded with white families.

Where these men and women ran into difficulty, however, was in becoming independent, a condition tied directly, in Granby, to the ownership of property. As we have seen, financial survival in this economy was tenuous. Those who invested in land or shops and tools in the 1790s - James Huggins of West Granby, for example - often did quite well, in spite of the slow development of roads in this town. Those who had to borrow their way into a mill business, farm or store were in a more precarious position, for creditors themselves were not always securely established and notes and mortgages could easily find their way into the hands of strangers or otherwise unsympathetic people. Where African Americans were concerned, the additional obstacles of generally being new to town, and of racial prejudice as well, made credit nearly impossible to obtain in the first place. While the land records show a good deal of lending and mortgaging to finance property holding for white farmers and artisans, it appears that few were willing to loan money to former slaves, regardless of how much they had contributed to the founding of the nation. Continental Army service just did not convert to capital in a town run by militiamen, and where two of the most prominent office holders in that militia were Colonels Ozias Pettibone and Hezekiah Holcomb, both slave owners.

Benajah Hills was one of the lucky ones to be able to get a shop and a mortgage from neighbor Aaron Post (who, as a newcomer to town himself, probably was more sympathetic to Benajah's struggle for acceptance). Others, like Asher Frank of West Granby and Philip Negro, had to be content with renting small pieces of less-than-desirable land, and supporting their families on that. Thus, it is not surprising that a great many of African Americans found themselves barely able to eke out a living, and certainly unable to make payments for rents or mortgages. Philip Negro found himself on the pauper's roles by the time of his death in 1795. Asher Frank received that classification in 1799.

This is not to say that the only paupers in Granby were black. In fact, one of the first acts of the new town government in 1787 was to "warn out" eight people who had no "legal settlement" in Granby and could not care for themselves. What this meant was that Micah Miller and wife, the Widow Butler, and Davis Williams, his wife and three children ("Tranchant Persons") had not been born in Granby, had no relatives living in Granby, had no employment in Granby, and owned no property in Granby. Therefore, the selectmen instructed Constable Thomas Spring to escort them to the town line and order them not to return, a practice dating to Elizabethan times when England was becoming besieged by wandering poor. At the same time, Benoni Viets was declared "by Reason of age mismanagement and bad husbandry...Likely to Come to want and be Chargable to Sd Town," and told to follow the orders of his new overseer Asahel Holcomb.[67] Many records from that era contain references to poor white residents.

For the African Americans though, the rituals of poverty must have been doubly discouraging. Paupers who did have a legal settlement, and many of Granby's African Americans of the 1790s did, were placed under the watchful eye and strict orders of an "overseer," who kept track of them from dawn until dusk. Alternatively, they were "bid out" in the notorious "vendue" system. This was a rather cruel process in which poverty-stricken individuals were put on display before a crowd, probably on a meeting day, and "bid out" to someone who would agree to care for them for a period of time. Sometimes families were split up and divided among people who shared the common belief that poverty was the fault of the pauper. African Americans could not have missed the irony as they labored in their fields under a white man's eye, or as they stood on an auction block - although this time people were bidding

251

down instead of up as the selectmen tried to find the person who would charge the town the least for the care of the paupers. Some bidders, like Jacob Pettibone, who took in Asher Frank, could scarcely support their own families, and may have hoped to make a little profit by paying less for their boarder's care than the town gave them.[68]

Nevertheless, some black families managed to avoid this fate. John and Phoebe Freeman, for example, married in 1792, and raised a family of six children over the next twenty years. James Fuller married Eleanor Freebody sometime around 1780 and raised their family in Granby. She died young of consumption, but he lived on in town until 1810, apparently well enough off to take in pauper Asher Frank at one point. Unfortunately, the solvency of these families for the time they continued to live in Granby was not the rule, particularly as time passed.

Thus, around 1800 the initial period in which African Americans attempted to become full-fledged members of Granby society came to an end. After that this small segment of the population drifted into poverty or out of Granby, only to reinforce the prejudices that had pushed them to these ends in the first place. Probably the more youthful of them left Granby for greener pastures, one would hope, for those who were still among the 48 in the 1810 census were old and infirm people who, instead of being "bid out" were often transported to or buried at town expense in "Shacktown" - location uncertain, living conditions imaginable. Not only did Granby have an underclass that was not much better off than the slaves of an earlier time, but there was also a ghetto for those assigned to that class. Table 6-1 shows trends indicative of the struggles and eventual disillusionment among Granby's black population in the town's early years.

Among whites, social distinctions were emerging as well. This is surprising, since Granby was a community first settled by outsiders, developed by outlanders, and incorporated by Antifederalists. One would think that the town that had opposed bonus payments to the Continental elite would avoid social classes altogether. Furthermore, as the town grew in the 1790s and early 1800s, it became clear that it was one of those exceptional New England communities whose sympathies were decidedly Republican. That is, they identified with the Democratic-Republicans, the national political party that opposed the Federalists, whose merchant-nationalist coalition so

Table 6-1
African-Americans in Granby, 1790-1810[69]

Census	Total #	Slaves	Free In Black Families	Free In White Families
1790	31	5	0	26
1800	55	3	43	9
1810	48	3 (?)	28	17

dominated New England politics. Evidence of this can be found in a letter from Pliny Hillyer to Jonathan Humphrey of Simsbury in February, 1803, in which Hillyer urged Humphrey and Jonathan Pettibone to avoid controversy, for "it might give a fatal blow to Democracy in Simsbury, and bring about once more the arbitrary reign of Federalism, and restore things to their ancient rigid order."[70]

Additional evidence of Granby's Democratic political leanings at that time is found on the roles of the St. Mark's Lodge #36 of Free and Accepted Masons. In the 1790s, Masons were often politically sympathetic toward the Jeffersonian Republicans, even though the organization itself expressly denied any political commitments. St. Mark's Lodge began in that decade, meeting in various places along Salmon Brook Street. By 1802, it had 80 members, including nearly all of the town's political leaders and gentlemen farmers and businessmen. They thought of themselves as rationalists and heirs of the Enlightenment, who resisted "rigid orders" as much as they disapproved of disorderliness and disrespect for propriety. But above all, they saw themselves as their self-exiled mentor Roger Viets described them in an address in 1800: "men of enlightened understanding, the strictest integrity, and conspicuous rank in society."[71] In other words, in spite of their disdain for Connecticut's "Standing Order," they were not above designing their own distinguished order to mark themselves from the common folk of their own community.

Men of this "conspicuous rank" were behind the development of certain secular cultural institutions that were coming into existence in Granby. There had been a subscription library at Salmon Brook since 1761, in which residents purchased shares in return for the right to borrow books from wherever the repository was located. Mason James Kilbourn, who was also active in the Episcopalian church, took charge of reviving this institution in the 1790s. Five decades later he wrote,

> Invited the young Gentlemen in the town Married, and unmarried, to form a Literary Society, which was affected by those of the best characters, and proved useful, and reputable; took an Interest in an Old Circulating Library, of about 200 volumes, of Old Books which had been established many years before by 40 or 50 Associates. The management of this institution was soon devolved upon me. By imposing sufficient fines for damages done to the Books, by bidding on Books at two quarterly drawings, for early chances of reading New Books, by selling off the Old Books from time to time at auction on a year's credit, and by selling new rights, I succeeded in renovating the concern, so that without taxing the existing shares, at all, the Library so increased that when I left the place [in 1802] it contained about 600 Volumes, almost as good as new, - adapted to the advancing state, tastes of the people; the shares meantime increased in value 400 per cent. Was often called on to deliver addresses, on the 4th of July, to Literary Associations, and Masonic Lodges....

The Salmon Brook Historical Society has books from that period which were part of the library.[72] Historian Phelps also takes note of an Academy that existed at Salmon Brook in 1790. This was also a private operation, since secondary schooling was not yet compulsory.[73] Generally, the Academy movement in rural areas was a secular educational movement designed to create secondary schooling for students who were not interested in becoming clergymen. At any rate, these cultural institutions and the newly created school societies, which had resulted from the legislature's use of proceeds from western land sales, were indications that Granby's leadership joined with much of post-Revolutionary America's educated elite in putting a high premium on learning that was not necessarily tied to recitation of the catechism (although the Academy seems to have disappeared after 1800).

The trend toward isolating the poor, recognizing respectability and developing some high culture in Granby may seem discordant with the town's ancient egalitarian, rough-hewn, rebellious character, as well as with its Republican political leanings, but there is a certain light by which those contradictory tendencies may be understood. Those who led Granby in the 1790s felt the presence of great changes in their lives, and their proclivity for social distinction probably followed from a felt need to preserve or restore some order before things got out of control. It is true that this society had not advanced far beyond its colonial antecedents, judging by the fate of Judah Benjamin who, after his conviction for polygamy in 1785, was condemned "to receive 10 stripes, be branded with the letter A, and wear a halter about his neck during his continuance in this State."[74] On the other hand, in the past two decades the world's greatest empire had been tossed off, formerly well respected individuals had left for places like Nova Scotia, and all sorts of radical notions had been hotly debated. All of this turmoil had reached deep into the marrow of everyday life.

Young Hezekiah Goodrich had grown up in Portland in a family committed to the Revolutionary cause. His uncle, David Goodrich, who had been a baptist preacher in Granby before the war, had died with his entire militia company in a winter storm, and his widow Penelope Holcomb Goodrich, and their two sons, had lived with Hezekiah's family during the war. Hezekiah, born in 1771, was a child of the Revolution. Conceived out of wedlock to begin with, he had been brought up on devotion to the "life, liberty and pursuit of happiness" for which those close to him had paid so dearly. But in the late 1790s, when his father, now a well-respected community leader, had expected Hezekiah to take up the family tanning business in Portland, Hezekiah turned away from the man who had trained him and moved with his new wife, Penelope's niece, to Granby to enjoy the freedom and independence he had learned to cherish as a child.[75]

The story of Hannah Phelps of Popatunuck is another illustration of a world coming unhinged. Daughter of a man who had, himself, had to "make his peace" with his church for committing adultery, she married Joel Buttolph at the tender age of fifteen, in July, 1773, and gave birth to their first child in December. Apparently she was not alone in this predicament, however, since the neighborhood to her north was known as "a nest for spurious births." After Joel died prematurely in 1786, she and her *new* husband, Aaron Post, marched

255

into probate court and refused to accept the terms of Joel's will by which she would not inherit any of his estate if she remarried. Instead, she demanded the traditional "widow's thirds," to be added to the land she would soon inherit as the only (legitimate) child of Hezekiah Phelps. When Aaron died in 1810, she held clear title to her own land, as well her widow's thirds of his, and maintained control of it until her death four decades later. Even her son had to be content building his new tavern on her land.[76] Sanctions against premarital sex, obedience to her husband's last wishes, deference to the norm of men being the property owners - Hannah had little use for these shackles of a former order. She made it clear that the social upheaval and challenges to traditional mores actually *feared* by many Revolutionary leaders was a real force in the new America. As Granby filled rapidly with new faces, new ambition and new enterprises, surely there was not a little nervousness among its elite about what greater changes the future would hold in store.

Dramatic and rapid change in Granby in its first two decades as an incorporated town had resulted in a new complexity in both the political and social order. The town government responded to a new economic environment by addressing issues ranging from the containment of livestock to the building of roads and the provision for a growing number of paupers. Economic growth was uneven, and amidst its shifting currents, tempers flared at town meeting. A general perception of upheaval fostered entrenchment in more stratified social structures and conscious efforts to define distinctions among people on the basis of race, wealth and "conspicuous rank." The outcome was a town filled with competing interests - divided economically, socially and geographically, even as its people sought to define the common good. In that respect, their task seemed increasingly out of reach.

Going Their Own Way

As new enterprises, separate villages, thorny issues and social distinctions emerged in the 1790s and early 1800s, Granby also experienced other types of strains on its sense of collective purpose. Within the town and its two ecclesiastical societies religious dissent continued strong, even as Connecticut clung to its established church. And as parishioners drifted to various denominations, so too did young people begin to drift out of town, beginning a trend that would eventually be of great concern to those who stayed behind.

As if pre-Revolutionary Salmon Brook had not had enough discord over religion, divisions continued through the turn of the century. The Congregationalists found what they thought would be the answer to their chronic problems in a new minister. However, the former Anglicans, now called Episcopalians, were not moved to return to the church of the Puritan founders, and, in spite of the loss of their popular leader to Nova Scotia, were more resolute than ever in remaining independent. Baptist organizations, as informal as ever, sputtered along; and to make things more incomprehensible to those who thought "the church" was the glue of a community, Methodist circuit riders began collecting converts. In the background of all this was a state-wide movement of gathering momentum, to disestablish the Congregationalist Church and perhaps with it, the old political order that had seen Connecticut through the Revolution. Granby responded to these developments with ambivalence.

After the Revolution, the Salmon Brook Ecclesiastical Society had a difficult time replacing their first settled minister, Rev. Joseph Strong. Strong had left in a huff in 1779, disenchanted with his flock's unwillingness to support the preaching of the gospel with anything but devalued currency. His eventual replacement, in 1784, was Israel Holly, who struggled for a decade with a Congregation riven by petty squabbles and personal animosities among farmers fighting the forces of recession. In 1794, things changed, however. A fresh burst of enthusiasm for religion resulted in decisions to enlarge and paint the interior of the meetinghouse, to "dignify the pews," and to settle a new minister, the Rev. Isaac Porter.[77]

Porter had been raised in Farmington during the Revolution, educated at Yale (class of 1788), and trained in theology by Rev. Dr. Smalley of New Britain. In 1790, he received his license to preach from the Hartford South Association of Ministers, and spent the next four years trying out and being tried out by various Churches in the vicinity of Hartford, one of these being Granby.[78] At a special meeting of the Salmon Brook Ecclesiastical Society in February of 1794, it was voted "to Give Mr. Porter a Call to Settel with us in the work of the minister," and thus began one of the longest ministries at any church in Granby (38 years).[79]

If they needed someone to be a leader like Joseph Strong, it seemed Porter was their man. He quickly established himself as a decisive and firm advocate of "church disciplyne," calling forth miscreants to make their peace

257

with the church. No doubt he had been deeply influenced, while at Yale, by the popular tutor Timothy Dwight, who would become the College's new president shortly after Porter settled in Granby. Dwight believed that religion was the basis of morality, peace and order in a society. He greatly feared the influence of the followers of Thomas Jefferson, who called for an end to state-supported churches. To Dwight, the movement for disestablishment was a veiled and misguided effort on the part of atheists to distract men from their duty and upset the order God had determined for society. The current "Terror" in France, which beheaded the King and Queen, was a startling example of what would happen when the uneducated mob got hold of the ideas of the "philosophes" and the "illuminati," Enlightenment pundits who had so vigorously opposed organized religion in 18th century Europe. Even though France's church had been Catholic, at least it was Christian and at least it ascribed to a clear set of morals.[80] Dwight even linked Masonry to this worldwide campaign against piety and decency, a charge that must have gone over well with many of Granby's men of "conspicuous rank!"

Whether or not Porter made the same mistake of alienating the local Masons is not known, but every description of him, by those who knew him confirms that he lived up to Dwight's constant charge to his students that they stand up to the threat of atheism perpetrated by those who advocated religious toleration. Ann Eliza Edwards remembered his conservative garb of knee breeches with buckles, buff stockings and a three-cornered hat, and the rather unflattering name, particularly for a Puritan minister, of "Priest Porter" by which some of his parishioners knew him.[81] Noah Phelps of Simsbury noted that he was a strict disciplinarian who ruled the Congregation with an iron hand, censoring and fining members for absence from services, even after the law no longer required attendance.[82] Even Porter's own carefully kept records of Church meetings from 1794 to 1832 show a man consistently concerned with proper behavior, temperance and the revival of religion at a time of increasing secularism.[83]

He came to Granby at the very moment that the Hartford North Association of ministers began calling for "a concert of prayer for the revival of religion." While it is ironic that this was the very enclave whose predecessors had once been so unwilling to accept evangelical ministers in their midst, fifty years and a Revolution had created even more threatening circumstances for the survival of the Bible Commonwealth. Now the local

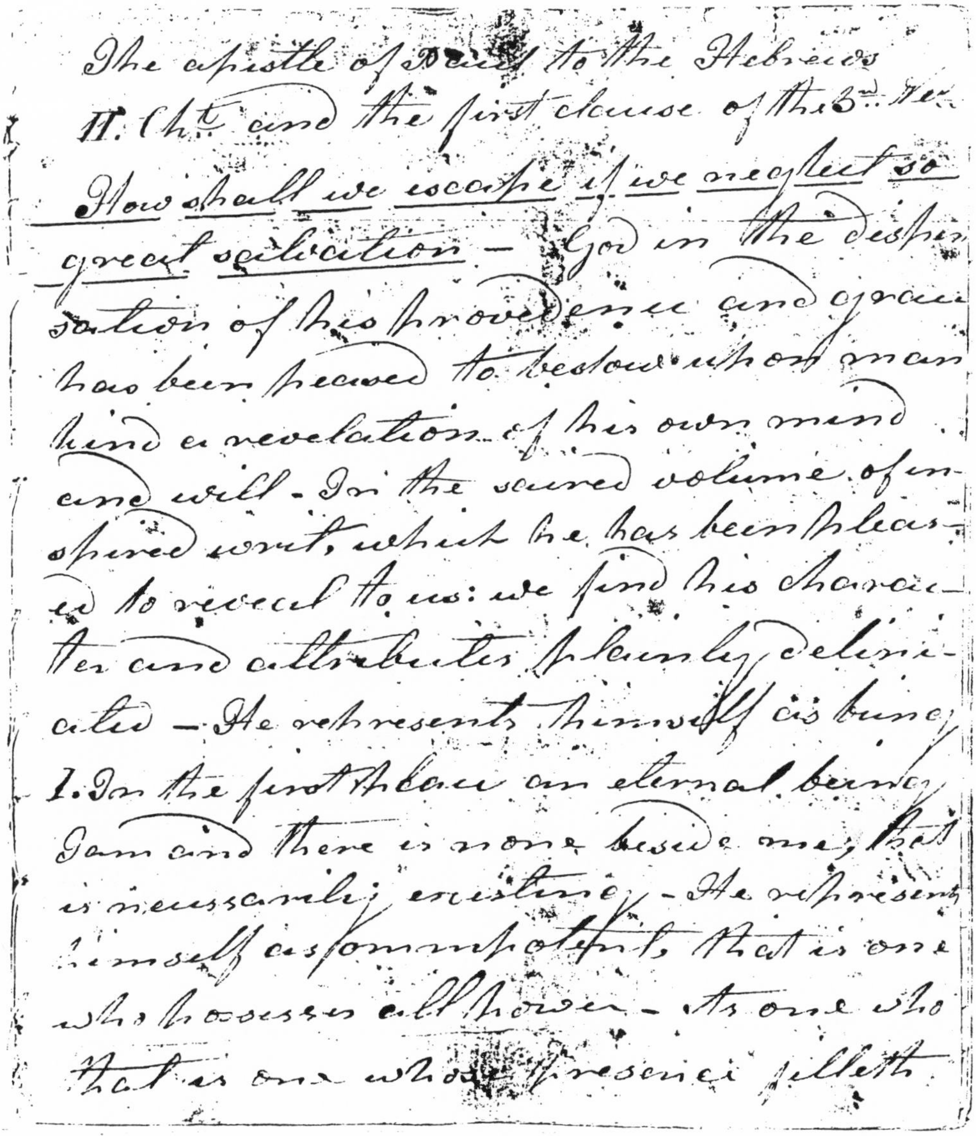
The epistle of Paul to the Hebrews
II. Chap. and the first clause of the 3rd Ver.
How shall we escape if we neglect so
great salvation — God in the dispensation of his providence and grace
has been pleased to bestow upon mankind a revelation of his own mind
and will - In the sacred volume of inspired writ, which he has been pleased to reveal to us: we find his character and attributes plainly delini-
ated — He represents himself as being
1. In the first place an eternal being
I am and there is none beside me; that
is necessarily existing - He represents
himself as omnipotent, that is one
who possesses all power - As one who
that is one whose presence filleth

Salmon Brook Historical Society

Figure 6-7: A page from Isaac Porter's sermon notes. The date of this manuscript is unknown and it is unsigned. The handwriting is the same as Porter's in the church records.

ministers welcomed revival meetings and even established themselves as a missionary society, sending forth Rev. Perkins of West Hartford to preach among the Connecticut migrants to Vermont.[84]

It is clear from what little we have of his sermon notes, that Porter did his level best to respond to the moral decay he saw all around him in Granby, preaching regularly about the depravity of man and bringing in revivalist ministers. As the Second Great Awakening spread throughout the nation from roots like the Hartford North Association, he was obviously trying to do his share. "There is no possible way," he intoned,

> for those to escape everlasting punishment who neglect this gospel salvation....Those who neglect this salvation which Christ has by his suffering and death purchased for them are guilty of the blackest ingratitude towards him....It proves to a demonstration the moral deprivation of the human heart — Mankind are in a great measure insensible of their situation: they are insensible of the importance of closing in with the offers of salvation they have not the least vestage of holiness remaining in them: they are spiritually dead: as the scriptures inform us they are dead in trespasses and sins — Eyes have they but they see not ears have they but they hear not and their foolish hearts are darkened — If mankind were once to see the awful situation in which they are by nature; were they to be sensible of the perishing need in which they stand of a saviour they would cease to be guilty of that stupidity and negligence towards religion that they now are.[85]

One wonders how such speeches as these could be very effective in reviving religion among Granby's Congregationalists. But new members came forth to profess their faith and Porter's longevity in the job is certainly a fair indication that the congregation's elders approved of his stern approach.

Although the Congregationalists probably hoped their own church would be reborn and grow at the expense of both atheism and all other denominations, there were people of different faiths in Granby who claimed as great a dedication to religion's revival. By 1800, Granby also had a thriving Episcopalian church. It had been a nearly fatal blow to the Anglicans of old St. Andrew's parish, called Episcopalians since the end of the Revolution, when Roger Viets had left for Digby, Nova Scotia in 1787. During the Revolution, Viets endured a great deal for being a cleric in England's established church, but when a wave of accusations were directed towards ministers after the Revolution for being too interested in temporal gain, he had

had enough. "What influence the difference of constitution between Connecticut and Nova Scotia may have on me, is not proper for me to mention," he added in his farewell sermon, swiping one last time at the intolerance of the established church and its friends in the legislature.

With Christian charity he expressed his gratitude toward his parishioners, and even those of "other sects," who had been so hospitable toward him since he began his work in 1759. Even without a minister, he urged them, they should continue to meet together three hours every Sabbath, read the common prayer and published sermons, and otherwise preserve "an understanding of Christianity and a spirit of rational devotion amongst the episcopal people of Connecticut." He further admonished them "never to admit of any material alterations in your form of public devotion...When a spirit of idle innovation is let loose, none can foretell when or where it will cease."[86] Thus the man who had baptized 122 adults and 1749 infants, married 176 couples, and become the shepherd of over 280 families in Simsbury, Granby, Windsor and Suffield, took his leave.

The record of the next few years is somewhat murky. St. Andrew's seems to have struggled along, but it would appear that Viets's St. Ann's mission at Salmon Brook did not survive its Rector's departure.[87] After a few years, though, Granby Episcopalians began to meet at Salmon Brook under the ministry of Ambrose Todd. In 1794, a committee formed "to build a new Church house in Granby near Pliny Hillyer's Esq." This project took a few years, but by 1798 it was completed, except for the steeple, and the St. Andrew's parish voted to divide in two, the Granby-based group to become St. Peter's Church. The steeple went up in 1799.[88]

Apparently, the St. Peter's meetinghouse was a magnificent structure for a town of farmers. Its dimensions were 58 by 35 feet, with a ridge pole 30 feet above ground. "The interior," according to Mary Holcomb (Mrs. Franklin) Loomis, "had beautiful box pews. There were two aisles with a double row of pews in the center, pews at ends and in the galleries. The pews on the main floor were high seats all around with panel doors. There were little spindle rails about 6 inches high, around the pews and on the doors. It was very ornate and handsome. There was also a high and handsome pulpit."[89] The Episcopalians, who listed among their membership the families of Ozias Pettibone, Hezekiah Holcomb, Pliny Hillyer and probably of most of the men of St. Mark's Lodge of Masons, do not seem to have felt bound by the traditional New England strictures against ostentation.

It was to this bright new structure that Roger Viets repaired on June 29, 1800, on a visit to Granby, to glorify the revival of the faith among his former parishioners. One would think he would have celebrated the achievement of his flock, and yet his message was filled with foreboding. Beware, he said of "the prevailing infidelity of the present age." Do not be lured away from the faith by deism (a belief held by Thomas Jefferson, among others), for "Deism persisted in, generally leads to Atheism," as it has in France and England. "Let us be cautioned against listening to a set of superficial writers," he continued, "who slander the God, who created them, who redeemed them, the Holy Spirit who admonishes them, and all regular governments, which protect them." Attend church regularly, stay together, support the clergy, be kind and charitable to the poor, be patient with each other, and do unto others....[90]

A few days later he preached before the Masons, where he noted that the Order had lately been "abused most outrageously....Our adversaries have denied us to be either Christians, or peaceable subjects of our respective civil governments. And have accused us of inventing and propagating Atheism, and the execrable plundering, levelling principle commonly called Jacobinism [a reference to the chaos of the French Revolution]." In the face of these charges by Timothy Dwight, Viets insisted that Masons required that their members "believe in the Trinity, but no further religious test is required, and every denomination of Christians is equally countenanced." He said he had been a Mason for 35 years, and that regardless of the Society's habit of maintaining a few ancient secrets, nothing could be found in any of its principles or rituals that might suggest that Freemasons were anti-religious.[91]

Speaking (and subsequently publishing these views) on behalf of both Episcopalians and Freemasons, Viets obviously felt a strong need to counter any perception that either group was interested in the downfall of religion. In fact, he sounded almost like Timothy Dwight himself, or Isaac Porter, for that matter, and seemed to take pains to distinguish his faith not only from atheism, but also from those who were at present arguing for religious toleration in Connecticut.

Of course, Dwight himself maintained that there was religious freedom in Connecticut. In making this seemingly preposterous statement, he was thinking of laws which had been passed since the turmoil of the 1740s.

These allowed persons of different denominations to be excused from both attendance and taxation by the Congregational ecclesiastical societies as long as they could present a certificate from their minister saying they were regularly attending their alternate church and paying for its support. Now that the state had taken over funding of local schools, these laws seemed all the more reasonable. However, they did not accommodate non-Christians, or anyone who did not wish to be affiliated with any church, or, for that matter, anyone who did not want to be branded with the social stigma of being a "certificate man."

The Episcopalians had a special place in all of this, though. While they had suffered by association with the Crown during the Revolution, many of Connecticut's wealthiest patriot leaders were of that faith. In the years after the Revolution, not only had they secured the right to tax themselves locally for their own church, but also, they had persuaded the legislature to turn back to their churches a portion of state taxes which were used to support the established church's county Associations. It was almost as though there were two established churches in Connecticut. Thus, it is not surprising that Roger Viets and his followers would agree with the need for continued public support of Christianity, or that they would join Congregationalists in being suspicious of less established denominations, such as Baptists and Methodists.

In spite of this opposition from the members of St. Peters and from the members of the Salmon Brook congregation, people of a different mind did make an effort to create new churches in Granby. Not only did the Baptists struggle on in their own independent way, but Methodism emerged as a new faith.

Methodism in the 1780s and 90s represented a reaction against the perceived worldliness and lack of vitality in the more established churches.[92] Probably some of those who complained about Joseph Strong's salary during the Revolution, and Roger Viets's after, were future Methodists. By 1800, there were only a small number of converts in Connecticut; but among those was a group of people who lived along the border of Barkhamsted, Granby and what would soon become the town of Canton. Itinerant preachers of the Granville, Massachusetts circuit found these people had an appetite for a more populist brand of religion - they were tired of being talked down to by their more educated Congregational and Episcopalian ministers, and, like the early pioneers to Salmon Brook, felt a mild degree of alienation from the neighborhoods that had been settled longer. One society was organized on the edge of Barkhamsted (Washington Hill), and people who had trudged into the hills to this center of heresy encouraged the ministers to spread their preaching into North Canton (then called West Simsbury) and West Granby. Tradition has it that West Granby had a Methodist Society, which first met in the barn of Ebenezer Gozzard in 1799, but nothing else is known of the group.[93] Only fragmentary and cryptic references to these dissenting groups remains to us today, but they were there, brazenly defying the status quo in their insistence that religion come to them.

Another ominous genesis of independence asserted itself in the 1790s and early 1800s in the form of groups of emigrants departing for lands west of the Appalachians. Granby's population was, indeed, growing steadily, both because of natural increase and in-migration of various people attracted by the community's growing economy. But as these newcomers took their places, a steady trickle of adventurous young souls packed up their worldly possessions and said goodbye to Granby and to New England.

The exodus had begun, actually, on the heels of the Revolutionary War, when quite a few young families from Granby moved to Vermont. The upper Connecticut Valley offered tempting land, and the Treaty of Paris had assured, supposedly, some security to Americans moving to the frontier. In Granby, these children of large families could only look forward to small pieces of the 100-160 acre farms their parents owned. There were only slivers of common land left, held for distribution to land owners who lost a few acres here and there to a new road. There would be no new grants to the heirs of the inhabitants of 1722. With land prices tripled from pre-War levels, even the greater availability of credit in the late 1780s was not encouraging.

When prices of land in Vermont began to climb, emigrants, like the Stratton family of West Granby, looked to backcountry Pennsylvania, or to western New York State, where Iroquois power had been broken during the War. From Canandaigua, New York in 1800, Sylvanus Holcomb wrote to his brother Nahum of West Granby:

> Enjoyed a god stat of helth Sence we Left your hous and Had a good gurney all our way til we Got to the Ginesea and when we arrivd to our brothers was received with goy and Have ate out of one stove sence...

have Sixe hogs that i expect to fat for my family and expect to have one hundred bushel of Corn...

the small debts that you rote to me is a ly the pease and rum we had and the pig i paid...and the gun is at Mr. Benona buttles house...Seth gave us 15 lbs wool & i have 150 weight flax.[94]

One cannot help but note the impact of distance and the finality of separation implicit in Sylvanus's letter. Even siblings had to settle affairs carefully before making the move west.

By the turn of the century, rising prices even in these "frontier" lands were pushing people on into Ohio, where speculators were selling off whole townships in the Western Reserve and other parts of the territory. This part of the country was not nearly as secure as New York and Vermont, for British garrisons had occupied old forts long after the Treaty of Paris, and their old trading partners among the Shawnee and other nations were none too happy to see settlers flooding into the lands the British government had once tried to preserve for them. Nevertheless, at prices like 25¢ an acre, which is what Titus Hayes and Uriel Holmes of Hartland paid for the township of Wayne in Trumbull County, Ohio in 1796, people from Hartford Country, Connecticut, could hardly resist. That settlement drew over forty families from Hartland in just five years between 1799 and 1804.[95]

The most famous exodus from Granby at this time was of similar magnitude. James Kilbourn, the former clothier, who had trained as an Episcopalian minister before turning storekeeper of North Granby, organized the Sciota Land Company, with people from Granby and neighboring towns, to invest $20,000 in a 16,000-acre township they called Worthington, near present-day Columbus. To this "new Eden," Kilbourn led forty families in 1802 and 1803, including those of Dr. Josiah Topping, Levi Hays (son of Samuel Hays II), and Job Case and Levi Buttolph of Popatunuck.[96] Planning their town in great detail before they left, they looked forward to a new community that was "morally unspoiled," and blessed with rich soil, where they could practice their Episcopalian faith without having to answer to the sour looks of "Priest Porter."

While the numbers of people moving to greener pastures out of state must have astounded Granby residents at the times of their departure, the emigrants represented only a small fraction of the town's population before

1810. Although there was little land left for new farm families, enterprising people were turning to other ways of making a living, and welcoming the change. Also, by 1807 relations with Great Britain were turning sour and only the bravest (or most foolish) would think of testing the Shawnee bitterness that British agents fomented. Just the same, the vanguard of the "yankee exodus" in the early 1800s would chart the course for much larger numbers in the years following the War of 1812. Furthermore, their spirit is indicative of the great forces unleashed by the Revolution which were steadily chipping away at the structures and institutions of old New England. Granby was not immune to these forces, and as hard as Isaac Porter and his church deacons struggled against them, as vehemently as Roger Viets, the founders of St. Peters and the members of St. Mark's Lodge denied they were a part of them, one by one small groups went their own way.

Community or Place?

On October 10, 1803, Selectmen James Huggins, Samuel Clark and Chauncey Pettibone convened a special town meeting to consider an act by the state legislature which directly affected the town of Granby. It seems that the century-old issue of the location of the boundary between Massachusetts and Connecticut had finally resulted in a compromise of sorts which entailed the ceding by Connecticut of a piece of land in the northern part of Granby to Massachusetts. This piece of land was to become known as "the notch," because of the new appearance of Connecticut's northern border. The result was that several families in an area called "Mooretown" (along the Westfield Road where families by the name of Moore lived) were placed under the jurisdiction of Southwick, Massachusetts. Since Granby had not been consulted in the matter and the objections of its leaders had been ignored, the town meeting passed the following angry resolutions:

> 1st Resolved as the sence of sd this meeting that it is the Duty of all good citizens to yield a ready and Cherfull support to all wise and wholesome laws and regulations that from time to time are enacted by the legislature to protect private rights and promote the publick welfare.
>
> ———
>
> 2nd Resolved as the sence of this meeting that the act of the General Assembly at the Session of May last respecting the cession of part of this town to the

Commonwealth of Massachusetts do matearally effect the Rights and in the opinion of this meeting is a serious injury to the town in its Corporate Capacity & more especially to the Eclesiastical Society which by the opperation of said act is severd & perhaps broken up.

———

3rd Resolved as the sence of this meeting that as well in our individual as in our corporate capacity we at all times feel and will support a decent respect for the Constituted Authority of our State and that Deeply Impressed as we are with these truths still we hold our Special Right as freemen to inquire wheather the ordinary Legislature of the State are vested with Constitutional powers to ceed a part of the Territory of this State so as to Place the Citizens living within the limits of the Ceded Tract under any Foreign Jurisdiction than by subjecting them to Laws and Customs to them unknown and without their consent depriving them of their inestimable Jurisdiction civil and religious under which they were born and educated & to support which they have ever cherefully contributed their full purportion of the publick Burthens.

———

4th Resolved that in the opinion of this meeting the Publick Emergency of this State was not so urgent as to call on the Inhabitance of this Town as such or as members of the Eclesiastical Society to sacrifice so Great a partition of our substantial comfort and conveneance as the proposed measure of the Legislature if carried into Effect will inevitably Deprive us of.[97]

This set of resolutions is significant, not only because it signals a radical transformation in the shape of Granby (including the loss of some prime property around Congamond Ponds), but also because it implies some important assumptions about what it meant to be a community. Most obvious of these assumptions is that Southwick, Massachusetts was considered a "foreign jurisdiction." Regardless of all the nation-building that had been going on over the past two decades, the community-centered patriotism which had motivated Granby's Revolutionary generation was still embedded in their values and ideals. Nor had improvements in roads or migration both into and out of Granby done much to broaden the provincial perspectives the town meeting would express.

A second assumption implicit in the resolutions is that the people of Granby, in their "corporate capacity," thought of themselves as united not simply by an encompassing political boundary, but bonded as well by ecclesiastical ties. These sentiments echo those of the earliest founders of New England who envisioned a "City Upon a Hill" for God's people, and they

267

seemed as strong in the 19th century as they had been in the 17th. In fact, they were so strongly felt that the town meeting doubted the state had the *authority* to disrupt a perfectly happy ecclesiastical society. Timothy Dwight celebrated these feelings about community in his poem "Greenfield Hill," where he painted this picture of the typical New England town:

> Beneath their eye,
> And forming hand, in every hamlet, rose
> The nurturing school; in every village, smil'd
> The heav'n-inviting church, and every town
> A world within itself, with order, peace,
> And harmony, adjusted all its weal.[98]

These were the ideals which Granby's patriots had fought for, and its town fathers, church elders, Rev. Isaac Porter, and even visiting Rev. Roger Viets, had preached throughout the early years of the town's independence.

Samuel Hays, who had continued as an "elder statesman" in community affairs until his death in 1801, had embodied these ideals of a harmonious society of sturdy and pious yeomen. He moderated town and ecclesiastical society meetings, presided as Deacon over Church meetings, helped to organize the new school society, and brought his sons up to assume these positions of leadership for eight decades after his death. When he died in December, 1801, the administrators of his estate recorded a perfect description of the patriot Captain Hays wished to be. His estate was valued at a comfortable £923, and the inventory included farming implements, a few sturdy sets of clothing, carpentry tools, the cider mill that brought in the hard money, and a "bible and a testament," his only books.[99]

The new town had practiced great deference to this patriot yeoman and to a few others like him. In fact, in the two decades after incorporation only 23 different men held the offices of moderator of the annual town meeting, town clerk, selectman and representative to the legislature. The moderator, town clerk and three selectmen were elected annually, and the freeman's meeting, after 1794, elected two representatives in the spring and two again in the fall. Thus, in two decades, there was the possibility of nearly 150 open positions for those offices held tightly by Samuel Hays and his son Seth, Pliny Hillyer, the Pettibones, Judah, Hezekiah and Asahel Holcomb, James Huggins, Samuel Clark and not too many others.[100]

Even so, in spite of patterns of deference to a small coterie of elected officials, in spite of public expressions of communal ideals bolstered by Christian piety, Granby was not the tightly-knit "world within itself" of Timothy Dwight's vision. In its first two decades as a town, it grew rapidly and changed, marching to the beat of the post-Revolutionary generation's "pursuit of happiness." The people of this era sought opportunities to improve their standard of living through commerce, surplus agricultural production and industry. As the economy changed, they fought for their individual interests in town meetings and in petitions to the state legislature, exposing serious differences between different neighborhoods and different classes of people. As their society became more complex, they took pains to distinguish themselves from each other and, in the process, laid the groundwork for more alienation in the future. When the Congregational Church was not quite right for them, they began new churches, bucking the state's "Standing Order." And, of course, a significant number of families simply left the town, ready to try out altogether new ideas on how to establish a community.

As a matter of fact, the real-world Granby had never been a "world within itself." That may have been the goal when there were so many common enemies: wolves, "panters," Algonkians, French soldiers, creditors, proprietors, state and county officials, conservative clergymen, the British Parliament, the Continental elite, Hopmeadow residents, Federalists and so on. Now however, secure in their "corporate capacity" as a town, they were beginning to see that they had less capacity to be corporate than they had been brought up to believe was essential. Almost as if to say "that's true," the state had lopped off a piece of their township and delivered it up to a "foreign jurisdiction."

That was not the death knell for the communal ideal in Granby, however. As in most New England towns, the two parallel ideals of individual enterprise and corporate harmony would continue to be prime movers, in a confusing and frustrating way, behind the manner in which the people of Granby shaped their community and responded to changes in the new national environment, as well as changes they, themselves, initiated in their own worlds. It was a dynamic environment in which they lived. It required constant adjustment and adaptation. In those tasks, some would succeed and some would fail miserably.

Chapter VII
A World of Changes

Chronology

Europe	America	Granby
1807-1812 Napoleonic Wars continue	1807 Embargo against Britain and France	1807 Town meeting repeals large tax increase to fund road improvements
	1808 U.S. halts importation of slaves	
	1809 James Madison becomes fourth President of the U.S.; A. Lincoln born	
1812 Napoleon's disastrous Russian campaign	1812 W.H. Harrison defeats Tecumseh at Tippecanoe; U.S. declares war against Britain	
1813 Napoleon abdicates, banished to Elba	1814 Treaty of Ghent ends war with Britain	
1814/15 Congress of Vienna, Battle of Waterloo, Napolean abdicates a second time	1815 Battle of New Orleans	1815 Excommunication of James Huggins
	1817 James Monroe President	
	1819 Florida purchased, Financial panic touches off first great depression	1819 First Board of Relief elected
		1820 Granby's population (3012) at highest point in 19th century
	1823 Monroe Doctrine	
1824 Beethoven's 9th Symphony	1825 J.Q. Adams President; Erie Canal finished	1825 Construction on Farmington Canal begins
		1826 Great Flood
	1828 "Tariff of Abominations"- highest protective tariff yet	1828 Post Offices open in West and North Granby
	1829 Andrew Jackson President	1829 Farmington Canal open to New Haven
		1832 Universalist Society Founded; Isaac Porter dismissed as Congregational Minister
	1833 Jackson vetoes Bank of U.S., Whig Party founded	1834 Third Congregational Church Meetinghouse built
	1836 Texas becomes a republic	
1837 Victoria crowned Queen of England	1837 Martin Van Buren President, financial panic - depression follows	
		1840 *The Weekly News* runs six issues
	1841 William Henry Harrison, a Whig, becomes President	

As James Huggins, the West Granby innkeeper, mill owner and politician, took cognizance of his affairs in the spring of 1805, he probably experienced some mixed feelings. He had succeeded in developing profitable business enterprises. Around his mill pond just below his house were clustered a number of small buildings housing a carding mill, two distilleries, an old trip-hammer shop converted to a wire shop (for manufacturing wire for the carding mill), and a small house for one of his workers. His grist mill also turned a fair income, and he held title to considerable property in the hills around his home. Widowed once, Huggins had raised his first two children, remarried and enlarged his family with two more children. In town, he was a respected member of his congregation and had been elected at one point or another to all of the town's major offices, including the command of a militia company.

Nevertheless, the effort to route an east-west turnpike through Granby center and past his house had ended in failure, and the frequent visitors he had expected at his tavern had not materialized. He was currently fighting to get the town to improve its public roads to encourage additional commerce and traffic through West Granby. In anticipation of this new traffic, he had taken on considerable debt in order to invest in the distillery equipment and an addition to his house. His income was not going to be enough to pay off these debts, or even to continue to pay the interest.[1]

Huggins was not alone with these concerns. There were quite a few citizens in Granby who had put themselves at risk in order to capitalize on the new environment of growth and movement during the first two decades of the town's independence. Farmers' sons had taken up "mechanical trades;" others had bought expensive land on newly available credit and directed great energy toward specialized production in wool and apples; partnerships and companies had formed to finance large ventures like turnpikes, mills and stores; professional men had settled into a community that appeared to offer life-long opportunity; and lumbermen had dotted the town's landscape with their sawmills. As a community they had all, albeit reluctantly, invested in roads, bridges, schools, and church meetinghouses. It had been a time of extraordinary change for the new town of Granby. But markets beyond the town's borders had not lived up to expectations, and most businesses continued to rely upon local clientele for their income. Furthermore, newcomers to town were generally not in the best financial situation when they arrived, and, in fact, a significant number of young people, even from the more established families, were leaving.

Over the next four decades the people of Granby would experience

271

severe trials. The failure of the first Barkhamsted Turnpike Company to establish a route through Granby Center and West Granby, the religious dissent of the 1790s, the trickling of families to the west, and the financial failure of a few individuals in the early 1800s, turned out to be dark clouds on the horizon. For the businesses, churches and families of Granby, a series of storms would follow and unsettle the young town for years. As the nation and region experienced the early phases of the transportation revolution, industrialization, urbanization and westward migration, the citizens of Granby struggled to maintain their individual and community spirit.

Disasters

Beginning in 1807, Granby was struck by a series of disasters which caused catastrophic damage to its businesses and farms. Decisions made in far-away governments were the first signs of trouble. Although relations with Great Britain had been on the mend since the end of the Revolution, they took a turn for the worse in the early years of the 19th century. There were numerous factors behind this change, the paramount being the imperial ambitions of both France, under Napoleon Bonaparte, and the United States, under Thomas Jefferson. Federalist and Republican administrations alike had proclaimed neutrality in the European conflicts, but it was difficult for a nation full of aspiring entrepreneurs and land-hungry farmers to remain aloof from these affairs, or to appear a harmless bystander to contests among the principal contenders for wealth and power. The Treaty of Paris of 1783, which had ended the American Revolutionary War, had as usual, settled things only temporarily between France and England. It had not prepared the world for a revolution in France, a Napoleon, or a Louisiana Purchase.

The result of all this was growing tension between the United States and Great Britain over such matters as borders, trade and fishing, blockades of French-controlled Europe, impressment of sailors, and suspected British support of angry American Indians west of the Appalachians. In an effort to force Britain to acquiesce to American interests in all of these matters, the Jefferson administration proposed, and had Congress enact, an Embargo on trade with Great Britain in 1807. Boycotts had been one of the most effective means of forcing Parliament to change its policies before the Revolutionary War, and the Republicans hoped that cutting off American markets and products would bring the British to the bargaining table once again. Unfortunately, New England had become heavily dependent on good relations with Britain for its continued economic development. Cheap British manufactured goods were always in demand and New England merchants profited from sale of their cargoes in the British West Indies. They had also developed lucrative trading relationships with merchants of other countries all over the world now that they were no longer bound by the British trade and navigation restrictions. Even when trading with others, though, it paid to be on good terms with Britain, for the British Navy was still a great power. Just a temporary halt to the growing commercial ventures of New England merchants could mean great hardship for those merchants and all who depended upon them for a living. Certainly this explains the inclination of New England politicians to support Federalist policies, which had favored good relations with Britain.

Granby, and particularly the Salmon Brook parish, was not, of course, a typical New England town dominated by a Federalist "Standing Order." While there were many in Salmon Brook who hoped to thrive on commerce and industry, most of the town's farmers did not see a clear connection between their interests and the interests of the regional and coastal merchants with whom they traded surplus for imports. Probably many of them, who had children looking for cheap land, sympathized with the "War Hawks" of the Ohio valley who suspected British conspiracies with the American Indians. Their Republican sentiments were even more deeply rooted, however, in their community's heritage of political independence, religious dissent and suspicion of Connecticut's upper crust. Yet Granby was not solidly Republican. Certainly Turkey Hills (now East Granby), whose parishioners dismissed their Republican minister Whitfield Cowles from the pulpit on a "heresy" charge, was a Federalist enclave; and, no doubt, there were representatives of that party in Salmon Brook.[2]

The majority at Salmon Brook, while led by men like Republican Pliny Hillyer, was less concerned with national political alignments and more interested in how government policies would affect their own lives. At first, they may not have been worried that the Embargo would hurt them directly. They and their parents had boycotted before and had forced Parliament to relent; and in the war with Great Britain their troops had been victorious - eventually. They forgot the ignominious defeat at New York, the shortages, the epidemics, the months of trying to make ends meet with family members absent and the high state taxes.

Instead of fearing a breakdown of relationships with Britain, many embraced the idea of economic pressure. Tavern owners stocked up on supplies of liquor in anticipation of large-scale movement during a war.[3] Militia leaders, like Captains Isaac Phelps and Ozias Pettibone, trained their troops and schooled them in the virtues of patriotism. After war was declared, one group of twenty men from the Bushy Hill district put their names to a declaration that read, "Whereas great pains have been taken to impress the public mind with the idea that a war in which we are engaged, with Great Britain is extensively unpopular, and that it will not be supported by the people of New England, the undersigned think proper to declare, that while they lament the necessity of a war, they are fixed in the determination to support it, till the attainment of an honorable peace."[4] We know of twelve Granby men who went so far as to enlist in the regular army.[5] At one point in the summer of 1813, Granby's militiamen were called out to march to New London in anticipation of a British attack.[6]

As coastal merchants closed shop though, prices for goods from the interior plummeted. New England port towns were hit hardest, but towns such as Granby could not escape the downturn. For one thing, those in Granby who owed money to the troubled merchants of other towns were now called upon to settle their debts. And how were they expected to do this if no one was buying their goods? The investors in the northern route of the east-west turnpike through Granby, those who had won over Pliny Hillyer, James Huggins and their partners, gave up on their venture and the project languished until well after the war was over. In the town records, the effects of the Embargo are apparent as early as 1808. Taxes were cut drastically, road improvements were put off, incentives were offered to those who would pay cash, and abatements were granted to those who had trouble paying the reduced rates.[7]

The war lasted over two years, but brought little of the traffic innkeepers had hoped for. Some, like Oren Lee, the blacksmith who had moved to North Granby from Berlin in 1806, were able to sell cider brandy to the army, but generally, the war meant unusual shortages and hardships for the people of Granby, including an explosion at a local powder mill which killed three men.[8] By the end of 1814, when negotiations at Ghent resulted in a settlement, Granby's farmers and businessmen had been feeling the pinch for seven years. They were ready for an economic revival, but instead, things got worse.

British manufacturers flooded American markets with their goods, slashing prices in an effort to put nascent American industries out of business from the start.[9] Manufacturers in Granby could not compete and had to settle for low prices themselves, or turn to other enterprises. Some had little credit left and could not invest in anything else. Briefly local banks, and even the second Bank of the United States, chartered in 1816 to deal with the growing crisis, propped up the faltering national economy with large issues of bank notes. This expansion of credit and of the money supply, however, only served to promote unbridled speculation in western lands, rather than the sort of economic stability Granby farmers needed.[10] In addition, many were weakened by the spotted fever epidemic which swept the region in 1815 (the same year that a hurricane leveled grain fields and orchards).[11]

As if pestilence were not enough, the ash from the massive eruption in that year of Mount Tambora on the other side of the globe affected world-wide weather patterns so drastically that there was frost and snow the following summer, making 1816 forever known as "Eighteen-Hundred-and-Froze-to-Death." "The principal injury done by early and late frosts," wrote Daniel Humphreys, president of the Connecticut Society of Agriculture, "fell on our most important crop, Indian corn. Of this, there is not more than half the usual quantity: and in many places in this neighbourhood, not more than a quarter part sufficiently hard and ripe for being manufactured into meal. That which is unripe, mouldy or soft, when given as feed to hogs and cattle, has little tending to fatten them.... Grasses, for pasturage and hay, have been diminished by the drought about 50 per cent." Few farmers harvested much that year, and the winter that followed was full of sickness and death.[12]

As calamity followed upon calamity, bankruptcies became increasingly common throughout the state. Even those who were fairly solvent, found it hard to be optimistic. Wrote Oren Lee in December, 1817, "The failure of Smith Wheeler has unexpectedly thrown a debt on me of four hundred dollars - - - How I shall get along with it I know not but I hope some way will be provided."[13] When one merchant went under, his creditors set out

275

looking for those who owed the man money. The chain reactions set in motion in 1818 eventually led to a nationwide bank panic in 1819, followed by the nation's first major depression since independence was won.

Again, as in the years after the Embargo went into effect, the town records reflect the downturn with tax cuts and discounts for timely payments. 1819 was the first year in which a Board of Relief was chosen to make decisions on abatements for taxes, and the usual tensions over road improvements and who was to pay for them brought on renewed efforts on the part of Turkey Hills residents to divide the town in two.[14] Bankruptcies became even more common than ever. Pliny Hillyer's son Maltby went under in 1823 and Pliny, who had just entered retirement, had to fend off the creditors.[15]

On top of all this, Granby had to deal with more permanent ecological disaster. The town's best cash crop for years had been its lumber, and Granby farmers had cut trees with abandon. The clearing of land after the Revolution had proceeded at a rapid pace - so fast that many of the hills in the western half of Salmon Brook that had been covered with forest in the 1750s were completely clear cut by 1810. This meant more land for grazing sheep and cattle and for orchards, but the soil on these hills had been held in place by the trees that were now gone. Improvements in plow designs around that time had the effect of drying out soil even more. When heavy rains came, it quickly washed away down the steep slopes, leaving poor, sandy soil and gravel behind. The orchards survived, but there was little to grow grain in after the erosion of the top soil.

What was worse, when heavy rains came the water ran off too - causing flash floods, or "freshets" as they were called, raging down the brooks where rickety shops, mills, mill-races and dams proved no match for the forces of nature. Each new spring brought greater rampages of water, and in an age when insurance was not an available service, the floods brought bankruptcy as well. The flood of 1812 destroyed James Huggins's wire mill and trip-hammer shop and the gristmill at the foot of the gorge, and carried off a scythe shop which had been set up farther down the stream.[16] Two summers later, a summer rainy spell brought what Andrew Hayes described as "the Greatest flood known for many years." A year later, he wrote again, "Sept 23, 1815 the greatest Flood I known for many years carrying away Bridges fences and the like and did much damage to the Roads meadows &c."[17] The Granby town records make reference to a flood in the spring of 1818 which damaged bridges and caused considerable expense to the town.[18] Oren Lee noted that the weather had "caused the most destructive freshet perhaps known in this country, many bridges, mill dams, and other propperty to an Emence amount were destroyed."[19]

Again, in 1826, Andrew Hayes wrote of "the Great Flood which swept away Sawmills Gristmills Silas Cones Blacksmith shop tan works Clothiers works Roads fences Bridges did a great deal of damag to the Crops."[20] Oren Lee revoked his previous designation of the 1818 flood as being the most destructive in history and titled the one in 1826 "The most destroying freshet that ever was sent on this town," and recorded the destruction of all the mills at the Cragg, roads and bridges throughout the town, and parts of the newly built Farmington Canal.[21] This flooding was part of a regional phenomenon. In his 1821 description of New England, Timothy Dwight noted that the Connecticut River was "now often fuller than it probably ever was before the country above was cleared of its forests, the snows in open ground melting much more suddenly and forming much greater freshets than in forested ground."[22]

In spite of embargo, war, epidemics, floods and bankruptcies, Granby farmers, tradesmen and businessmen struggled on, and it is remarkable how persistent they were in establishing new enterprises even as their neighbors were going under. The *Gazeteer of Connecticut and Rhode Island* for 1819 listed for Granby:

> 2 card factories (making equipment for cleaning wool)
> 2 wire factories (wire for the cards)
> 1 powder mill
> 6 grain mills
> 2 fulling mills
> 3 carding machines
> 3 tanneries (manufacturing finished leather)
> 4 mercantile stores[23]

To all this should be added the many sawmills that still churned out semi-finished lumber all over the hillsides. In the midst of the Embargo, Obadiah Hayes and Seth Hayes both secured rights to build new mills on their property.[24]

Silas Cone and Harlow Wilcox are examples of ambitious young businessmen who took on the whims of nature and economic fluctuation. After the flood of 1818, Wilcox, the son of a local blacksmith, began purchasing the rights to Salmon Brook in West Granby where Ozias Pettibone, Ozias Pettibone Jr., Collins Griffin and Nathaniel Pratt had operated the gristmill that had been swept away in 1812. His design was to erect a sawmill where Jacob Pettibone had once had his, as well as to operate the grist mill if he could. In 1819, as speculators around the nation were selling bank notes in a major panic, he was spending hundreds of dollars buying land and building a new house for himself at the junction of what is now West Granby Road and Simsbury Road.[25] He sold some of his newly acquired property to Silas Cone, a blacksmith.[26]

Born in Winchester, Cone must have been living in West Granby in 1818, for the record of his marriage to Ezekiel Hayes's daughter Sarah in Barkhamsted in that year, gives West Granby as his residence. Perhaps he had his training at the scythe shop that was carried off in the 1812 flood. Sarah and Silas first moved to Norfolk, but were back in West Granby by 1822, with two young children, preparing to open a trip hammer shop and a scythe factory near the site of the old gristmill at the foot of the gorge. He completely remodeled Jacob Pettibone's small house into an impressive Greek Revival style dwelling.[27] The nation was in the midst of its first great depression, sparked by the bank panic of 1819, but Wilcox and Cone had their eyes on the future.

The 1826 flood destroyed everything they built.[28] Cone was back in business within a year, but Wilcox had difficulties. Lumber prices had declined precipitously, not only because of the depression, but also because New Englanders were heading west at record rates, reducing the demand for building materials in the region. He borrowed heavily from friends and relatives, but was never able to extricate himself from debt and finally lost his property. Nevertheless, he continued to operate the sawmill on what used to be his portion of Salmon Brook.[29]

Luther Pratt was another example of persistence in hard times. His father, Nathaniel Pratt, a prominent Justice of the Peace who had a farm at the top of what is now Fox Road, had died along with many others in the winter after the frostbitten summer of 1816. The farm was put on the auction block

Figure 7-1: Shops on Salmon Brook in West Granby. This photograph, taken in the early 1900s, shows the remains of the waterpowered industry which was built and rebuilt in the early part of the 19th century. The buildings may have once housed the Hayes clothing works.

Figure 7-2: Log dams such as this one at the top of the West Granby Gorge were easier to replace after winter ice and spring floods had taken their toll. This dam served the grist mill, which was located at the top of the gorge and was powered by water which ran through a wooden sluice across the top of the gorge.

279

and not redeemed by the family for many years. Meanwhile, Luther and his brother, Nathaniel Jr., began making improvements on land near the village of West Granby above the gorge. Luther built a carpentry shop and went into business calling himself a joiner. Nathaniel appears to have taken up the blacksmith's trade.[30]

In North Granby, persistent entrepreneurs also worked hard to build stable businesses. Among them were Philander Dibble and Miles Godard, who demonstrated how making adjustments as market conditions changed could keep a business afloat. Dibble began his business in 1799 as a jack-of-all-trades, dressing flax, making bonnets, gowns and trousers, sawing lumber, making cider and cider brandy and even selling powder and shot. He rented property and horses, traded produce in exchange for labor and brandy in exchange for pork. After the War of 1812 he went into business with Godard, becoming more specialized in lumber, but starting a shoe business as well. When Dibble died in 1817 his inventory included a tan house, vats, a bark mill, part of the Cragg grist mill, and part of a saw mill. Godard took over the business, or businesses, and continued to work the sawmill along with the cider mill. In 1818, he distilled 41 gallons, and by 1820 he was selling cider by the barrel to local storekeeper Abner Case.[31]

Case himself had built quite an enterprise. His general store eventually rivaled that of Pliny Hillyer at Salmon Brook Street. He had moved to North Granby in 1805, purchasing the farm that had been James Kilbourn's before Kilbourn left for Ohio. This farm was located on the northeast corner of East Street and Granville Road, then the intersection of the newly chartered Granby Turnpike Company and the road that was supposed to become the Barkhamsted Turnpike. Kilbourn had not seen a future in this location, but Abner Case did. In 1808, Case joined the rush to open taverns and took out a liquor license. He reopened Kilbourn's store and invested in nearby properties, including the shops of a few local artisans and a share of the Cragg grist mill. Across the road, John Willey bought real estate in 1813 which had once belonged to Silas Cossitt (now in Vermont), and went to work as a blacksmith and cider-brandy distiller, marketing his goods through Abner Case's store. At times, Case and Willey were partners as taverners, distillers and investors in the Cragg mill. Both were to become quite prosperous in spite of the depression of the early 1820s. Case seems to have replaced Ozias

Pettibone and Pliny Hillyer as the principal loan agency in Granby, holding thousands of dollars in mortgages in the 1820s. He survived and thrived, actually, because he did not foreclose on his neighbors, but patiently waited out the depression.[32]

Meanwhile, Salmon Brook Street was in a state of decline awaiting a new generation of entrepreneurs. Three years after his son had lost the family store, Pliny Hillyer died in 1826, his estate unable to cover his debts.[33] Even though the town used the Episcopal meetinghouse for town meetings, the business center had clearly shifted northward. In 1823, perhaps as a result of Maltby Hillyer's bankruptcy, postmaster Hezekiah Goodrich moved the post office to his tavern (now 235 North Granby Road, just north of the Congregational Church). Stephen White and some seventy residents of "The Street" sent off a petition to Postmaster General John McLean requesting him to order Goodrich to return. McLean did so, but had to retract his order a few weeks later with an apology, after Goodrich produced a petition with five hundred signatures attesting to the convenience of Hezekiah's tavern. There it stayed until 1828. Salmon Brook Street did get its post office back at that point, but only because North Granby and West Granby got their own.[34]

In a way, the War of 1812 and the difficulties of the years after, were somewhat responsible for the persistence of Granby citizens. With the West in a state of war, there was not much chance that many could move out of town. After the war some did move, but higher land prices in the West, and little opportunity to save money or stock up on necessities in the East, put that option out of reach for most until well into the 1820s. They really had no choice but to do the best they could with the resources available here. Without good farm land, many turned to water-powered industry. The 1820 census-takers found the town's population at the highest point it would reach from its beginnings in the 1690s until 1950. One of every four workers identified his occupation as either "manufactures and trades" or "commerce," as opposed to "agriculture."[35] Furthermore, many of those who saw themselves as farmers were also engaged in some form of manufacturing to supplement their income. These statistics almost present a town on its way to becoming a city. For various reasons, the trend would not continue.

Troubles of the Spirit

While Granby struggled against economic and natural disasters in the early years of the 19th century, its churches faced spiritual challenges of equal magnitude. These difficulties had deep roots, of course, reaching back into the ambiguities of New England Puritanism. They were becoming apparent as early as the 1740s when the turmoil of the Great Awakening kept Salmon Brook's church unsettled for over a decade. After the Revolution, when most states were writing constitutions that prohibited established churches, Connecticut remained committed to supporting its Puritan Congregational, or "Presbyterian" Church, even though the leaders claimed the state's certificate laws allowed freedom of religion. This commitment only served to strengthen the resolve of Baptists and Methodists to overturn the established order and disestablish the ecclesiastical societies. Of course, Granby had its share of these dissenters. The state-wide conflict sputtered on into the early 1800s in a pamphlet war that was intertwined with the partisan politics of the time. The Democratic-Republicans took up the toleration cause, not only as a matter of principle, but also because they saw the potential for drawing certain classes of people away from their traditional loyalty to the "Standing Order," which in Connecticut, was solidly Federalist.

The Baptists and Methodists did not make much progress in the first decade of the nineteenth century in loosening the connection between church and state in Connecticut. Not only was the Congregational establishment against such a change, but, as we have seen in the case of Roger Viets, many Episcopalians were as well. While former Anglicans resented the hostile treatment they had been accorded during the Revolution, there was no denying that many of them occupied high positions in society and government in the state and that their church had received special consideration in receiving a portion of state revenues to fund its work. Finally, in Granby, as elsewhere, Episcopalians were often wealthy enough to keep their names on the rolls of the Congregational Church as well and did not bother seeking tax exemption. Therefore, most of those Anglicans who had remained in Connecticut and determined that they could be Episcopalians without continuing to swear allegiance to Britain, were satisfied with the continuing establishment of religion. In Granby, parishioners of St. Peter's included the wealthiest people in town, and they felt little or no discrimination for their desire to be their own church. This was even more true after 1795 when schooling became a civil government function. The state began funding all public education with the interest from the sale of the lands in the Western Reserve. Thus, even as Baptists and Methodists struggled to create congregations in Granby, they stood little chance of becoming free of social stigma, or even ecclesiastical taxation. The leaders of the two larger churches simply felt the efforts of these dissenters were directed toward the downfall of morality and community ties.

Great undercurrents were at work, however, which would mean trouble for the traditionally central role played by religion in the lives of the people of Granby. While there were four different denominations already in the early years of the 19th century, it was not these divisions that were fundamental to the deterioration of church loyalty after the War of 1812. For a clearer understanding, particularly in the case of the Congregational Church, we need to continue the story of the remarkable life of James Huggins of West Granby.

We will recall that in 1805, Huggins was involved not only in his own enterprises, and heavily in debt on account of his investments, but also in an effort, along with Pliny Hillyer, to create an east-west trade route through Granby Center and West Granby, connecting their burgeoning business centers with northwest Connecticut and the Connecticut River fifteen miles to the east. When they were outmaneuvered by the farmers and tavernkeepers of North Granby and Copper Hill, they sought to induce the town to fund major improvements in roads and bridges with a huge tax increase at a special town meeting in September, 1807. That December, at the annual town meeting, their initiative met with determined resistance, probably from their brief allies in the turnpike venture, the wealthier taxpayers of Turkey Hills. The town meeting repealed the huge tax increase and virtually doomed the future of commerce through West Granby.[36]

This was the beginning of a long downward spiral for James Huggins. At age 55, he had run himself ragged serving the community and his dreams, trying to lead his town in a direction he saw to be the way for communal prosperity. He had turned Godly, impressed the town with his spirit, his eloquence, and his determination; had married a beautiful woman; together with her, had become prosperous and raised a fine family; brought in new technology; and had put everything he owned on the line in the name of progress.[37] How long would he have to fight to turn these soggy, pothole-strewn mudwashes into thoroughfares of commerce and industry?

He began to rein in, dropping his community activities and concentrating on getting out of debt. First, he sold some of his now extensive landholdings, and borrowed some additional money from his friend Alexander Cossitt. With still a relatively young family to support, his financial situation was tenuous at best. The effect of the Embargo on the local economy was obvious as he struggled to raise money.[38] But no sooner was he regaining control than his second wife died in April, 1811. For a while, he would appear to stay strong. His daughter Nancy and her husband Phinehas Holcomb Jr. (married 1805) stood by him loyally, as did his older son, James Jr. But Nancy and Phinehas were beginning their own family, and Huggins was desperately in debt. He had to borrow first from a group of merchants in Hartford, and when bankruptcy of one of them saved him from being foreclosed, from a merchant in New York City.[39] His friends could not risk the funds. As the conflict with England turned to war, everyone was holding on to his reserves. Gradually, he became more and more frustrated and depressed, more embittered over the loss of his wife, and more resentful of the community to which he had given so much of his energy.

He would not join the militia expedition to New London. In fact, he may have been opposed to the War of 1812, seeing it as ridiculously unnecessary. He might have had ideas about increased travel and tavern revenues, but in fact, little profit came from the war - only an interruption of commerce in every way and threats of destruction to property of his relatives in New Haven and his wide-ranging acquaintances elsewhere in New England and New York. Business grew worse and worse, particularly after the nation's capital was burned in 1813, initiating a round of severe currency depreciation.[40] Then in the fall of 1814, his son-in-law Phinehas died suddenly, leaving Nancy with two small children, as well as her struggling father to care for.[41]

In this context of frustrated ambitions, hard times, war and personal tragedy, we can now appreciate the depths of the final conflict into which Huggins and his community had plunged. This was a conflict not with the farmers of Turkey Hills, nor with creditors from Hartford and New York, but with the church, the very institution that had saved him from ruin after his first wife's death and the very minister he himself had hired, Isaac Porter.

Porter, as we recall, had been "settled" in Granby to restore "church disciplyne" and to shore up a congregation disintegrating under Israel Holly's leadership. He had taken his job seriously, and fought bravely against the forces of dissent, disestablishment and secularism.[42] However, he was a man of principle, and although competing faiths of the time offered their communicants a brighter, more optimistic version of Christianity, Porter would not cast off his Puritan views simply to gain the favor of potential converts. Instead, he preferred to revive religion in the spirit of the first Great Awakening. He brought in evangelical preachers, and carried on at great length in his own sermons about the depravity of man, the need for temperance (meaning abstinence from drinking "ardent spirits"), regular attendance at church, and strict attention to the precarious condition of one's soul. He felt he had to stand up to the challenge to the word of God, to the threat to his ministry, and to the forces opposing public morality. In the twenty-first year of his ministry, Porter's compulsion to revive religion and combat heresy collided head-on with the depression of a plummeting James Huggins. Porter must have known intuitively that this conflict, from which no one would emerge victorious, was the climax of his career, for he allotted fully one-fifth of the number of pages of the records he kept for the Church to detailing the progress of the altercation.

On May 5, 1815, Roger Holcomb, Levi Chapman, Thaddeus Hays, and James Huggins's old political ally, Pliny Hillyer, the church deacons, entered a complaint against Huggins in a church meeting. The nature of the complaint, though, leaves no doubt who the true plaintiff was. Huggins was accused of

> An irreverent and profane use of God's name, - of slight, reproachful and contemptuous expressions concerning the Holy Scriptures, - of discouraging extraordinary meetings for religious exercises, - of neglecting the public worship of God, and the ordinances of the Gospel, - And of uncharitable expressions and insinuations against the accredited Ministers of the Gospel, tending to destroy their influence and usefulness.[43]

The Church voted to consider these complaints of "unchristian and immoral conduct and conversation" in a public trial, and ordered the deacons to gather their witnesses by June.

It is easy enough to imagine the circumstances that brought about these charges: Porter had grown desperate over the declining spirit and numbers of his congregation. He had imported revivalist preachers, breathed a bit of fire and brimstone himself, preaching abstinence from "intoxicating drink," and sent deacons and tythingmen out to round up those who were reluctant to endure two-hour sermons. Huggins was moping around in deep depression, perhaps drinking too much, perhaps worried about what a temperance movement would do to his tavern and distilling revenues. He was growing ever more cynical about himself, other people, and life in general, and feeling less than inhibited, in the current secular atmosphere, about venting his hitherto secret feelings about "Priest Porter." Both men, in their late middle age, were watching their causes and livelihoods shrivel up under pressure of forces beyond their control. That they should collide with each other is sad testimony to the limited outlet for tensions in early New England towns.

In June, Huggins, after pleading "not guilty" to all charges, requested and obtained a delay in the "trial." Finally on Friday afternoon, June 16, 1815, the Church met to hear the case. After witnesses were called in support of the complaints, Huggins spoke in his own defense. If Isaac Porter's notes on the "trial" can be considered accurate, the sarcastic and mocking speech given by Huggins is one more indication of a man who had aged quickly and sourly. Wrote Porter, Huggins's speech

> was lengthy and for the most part wholly foreign from the case, consisting in a detailed history of the rise and progress of persecution from the days of Cain and Abel down to the present time, including a minute account of the proceedings of the Court of inquisition - their horrible injustice and cruelty &c - He alleged that our forefathers of this land brought the same persecuting spirit with them which has been handed down from generation to generation to this present time, and that wee (evidently meaning this church) were a branch of the inquisition providing with the same spirit, And concluded by asserting that it was Malice and hatred which had produced the charges against him and brought him to answer to them before the Church - except this, he only objected in excuse for non-attendance on the worship & ordinances of the Gospel, that the

doctrines preached were not the gospel, i.e. good views &c - and the inconveniences of attending & c.[44]

The Church apparently was not impressed. They voted to strike out the charge concerning discouraging attendance at revivals, but on all others they voted "guilty." Further, they voted to admonish Huggins in public, and if "he was not reclaimed," to give a second admonition.

Porter admonished Huggins in church on June 25, and again on August 13, but to little avail; and on September 7, Porter called the congregation together to consider what was to be done. Apparently Huggins had mellowed a bit over the summer, for at this meeting his tone seemed quite mild. He began by saying he was ready to repent for his bad language, but that he could not recall when he had said anything "uncharitable" about the Minister - that he did not allow such talk "in himself or family." As for his neglect of public worship, he offered as excuse "his age, the distance - his having but one horse - and the desire that others of his family might be accommodated in riding to meeting, which if they were, he could not get there by going on foot, which on the above accounts was very inconvenient."[45] But "the Brethren" were not satisfied. They met again on September 26 and voted to excommunicate James Huggins from the Church, and on Sunday, October 22, Porter made the decision public at meeting.

There was a time when such a punishment would have had grave consequences - especially for a man who had ambitions for political and economic status. But those times were apparently behind the people of Granby - Huggins was elected to the legislature in June of 1815, and was chosen in December, two months after the public announcement of his excommunication, to preside as Moderator of the annual town meeting.[46] A number of his friends, like Nathaniel Pratt who lived just west of him, were in fact, asking the Church to "withdraw its watch" from them. It appears that Huggins knew that excommunication would cost him little in terms of respect, and thus we might suppose he was only mildly concerned about the implications of his rejection by the Church.

For Porter, the conflict seems to have had simple dimensions. The man had misbehaved. If God's law was to survive the present crisis, the Church would have to take action. Surely there would be an end to morality and community if the flock were to ignore a miscreant who had gone so far as to flaunt church discipline. The consequences were plain in the communal vision of this pastor, whose notions of prosperity and order were set firmly and directed only toward the service of God. Porter was a stern man. For him there was no compromising with Evil, no deliberating when the survival of the community was at stake. An example must be set. A stand must be taken. If the fallen soul could not be reclaimed from the Devil, the purity of the Church must not be tarnished by continued association. No matter how important Huggins was, no matter who his friends were, in the end only God must be served (which could best be done, of course, with Porter remaining unchallenged in the pulpit of the established Church).

Simple enough - and yet, we cannot fail to detect a certain sympathy between the lines of Porter's records of Huggins's defense. Why was Porter not content to say only that the speech was "lengthy and for the most part wholly foreign from the case?" Why did he carefully outline Huggins's main points (which, indeed, were anything but foreign from the case!), when he recorded nothing the witnesses said? Why did he wait and wait - the month of May - the whole summer - all of October? In truth, Porter respected this man, James Huggins, as much as he feared him. In truth, Porter could identify with what Huggins was feeling - the two did live in the same world.

Perhaps we could rethink James Huggins's sentiments too. Was he simply being bitter and cynical? Was he really unworried about the consequences of excommunication from a Church he no longer cared about? Then why plead a defense at all? Probably, he never had much love for Porter - the "priest's" personality was not one Huggins could admire. But he did love the Church, and his friends and neighbors. It must have been traumatic to be called "uncharitable" by them; and perhaps speaking before them in the manner that he did was the only way he could maintain his sense of dignity.

James Huggins died in 1819, not four years after his excommunication - deep in debt, deep in depression and very lonely.[47] He had spent his last three years losing all his property to creditors, and doubtless in 1819, his creditors were looking for far more than the depressed value of his real estate to cover the debts. His house in West Granby was sold at auction and soon became the residence of a young clock peddler, Abiel Higley. His son, James Jr., continued to live in the village, but did not carry on his father's businesses.

The conclusion of James Huggins's life presents a picture of the wrenching tensions that were pulling the community and its established church apart. It was already a far more fragmented and complex community than it had been before the Revolution, but, battered by economic upheaval, bad weather, floods and religious dissent, it needed more than a stern preacher to heal its wounds and revive its spirit.

Porter continued to fight for his cause. During the 1820s his efforts to convince people to sign "the pledge" (to abstain from the use of "ardent spirits") became even more intense. He was undaunted by the new Connecticut Constitution's guarantee of religious freedom in 1818, and continued to chastise, and even fine parishioners for absence from church meetings. Hiram Pettibone, for example, was put on trial in 1823 for not attending church, even though he insisted he was an Episcopalian.[48] The church claimed he was not an Episcopalian until it had "released" him by letter to that church. Porter was still successful in bringing in converts, but these were mainly young women - not the family heads he needed to secure the church's status in the community. Throughout his career, he admitted 78 men and 147 women to the church.[49] Men seemed to be less inclined to "profess their faith." In fact, after 1828, church members were withdrawing at an alarming rate. Over fifty left the church between October, 1828 and June, 1833.[50] Although he maintained a loyal following, their numbers were dwindling.

His sermons continued to speak of the rarely forgiving, angry God he had always believed in, and as he aged, they were delivered increasingly in a dull monotone that inspired only rebellion and disaffection. As James R. Hayes recalled in 1907, Rev. Porter "was a large man preached the doctrine of election in two written sermons a day of an hours leangth to the disguest of most of his hearers reading them in the same tone of voice never looking up to see wheather his people were awake or asleep no matter what his text was the doctrine of election was the beginning and the end."[51] Indeed, one nineteen-year-old woman of Porter's flock wrote in her diary in 1834 that she attended a funeral at which Charles Spear, a Universalist minister, preached on the text, "Yea though I walk through the valley of the shadow of death I will fear no evil for Thou art with me. Thy rod and thy staff they comfort me." "I never heard [that] one before," she wrote.[52] Probably she was directing some disdainful sarcasm toward a minister of a rival faith, but when one considers Porter's typical texts (an 1810 funeral sermon he preached for Oren Lee's wife was from Job: "Man that is born of woman is of few days and full of trouble."[53]), we could very well believe she was sincere in her ignorance of the 23rd Psalm.

In the late 1820s, there was considerable unhappiness within the Church. Not only was Porter's leadership style turning people away, but the Universalist doctrines were picking up converts. The "universalist heresy" was not new to New England, but had its roots along with other dissenting doctrines in the first Great Awakening of the 1740s. Advocates of Universalism rejected the Calvinist notion of an angry God who chose only a few for salvation and doomed the rest of the corrupt and depraved human race to eternal punishment. Instead, they saw human nature as basically good and the entire human race loved by God. Salvation was open to all (hence it was "universal") as long as people would accept Jesus Christ as their saviour.[54] As dissenting preachers circulated these views, especially in the years after the American Revolution, people in Granby began to take interest. Clearly, Universalism offered an alternative to the doctrine being handed down from Isaac Porter's pulpit.[55]

As Porter rumbled on about the neglect of religion, some of his congregation were paying attention to the writings of Hosea Ballou, a Universalist minister in Hartford. Oren Lee made it clear in his diary as early as 1829 that he found the Universalist doctrines more appealing than those preached at Isaac Porter's revivals. "Great excitment in religious Concerns has taken place here," he wrote at one point, referring to the revivals,

and in many places in New England, and in many parts of the United States. I hope these revivals as their called may result in much good...and that there may be a universal reformation through the land and through the world, but when I reflect on the many Cases of murder and Suicide; and many who are Drove into black Dispair, my hart Trembles for the result. I think I have reason to fear the rong Impressions are made on their (those 'brought out of Darkness into Gods marvelous light' during the revivals) minds, respecting the nature and True Character of God, for the gospel is glad Tidings of great Joy to all people, and when preached in its purity and received into good and honest harts Is productive of Love, Joy peace and every Christian grace, but When God is represented as hateing his Own Ofspring and that he will punish them in hell as long as he exists, unless they have evidence of their being reconciled to God, they will naturally be Drove into Horror and Darkness and Black Dispair.[56]

Lee was a leader of a sizable group of "heretics" within the Congregational Church, and in May, 1832, was sent as their representative to a Convention of Universalists in New Haven. In September, twenty-seven people signed a constitution for The First Universalist Society of Granby. "We the undersigned believe," they wrote, "in the promise made by the Father that in the latter dayes he would bless all men and we doe hereby unite ourselves together as a Society for the advancement and support of the sentiment of Universal Salvation which brings good tidings of great joy to all people...."[57] Wrote Lee in his diary, "may every member of this Society conduct wisely and walk in the paths of vertue and Convince our Enemyes that Our Doctrine is not licentious but that it is best Calculated to incline mankind to Love God and Our neighbour and to promote the best good of Society."[58] The mention of "Enemyes" suggests the split was not without acrimony.[59]

A few months later, Porter was ignominiously dismissed from his position. At that time the congregation, or what was left of it, was also seriously divided over where to build a new meetinghouse.[60] Whether Porter's dismissal was part of some conflict over the new meetinghouse location or part of a campaign to stem the exodus to the Universalist Society, now sharing the Baptist meetinghouse near the junction of Day Street and North Granby Road, is unclear. It may have been that both factors provided an excuse for the remaining congregation to find some much-needed new blood for their pulpit. There is no doubt, though, that 1832 was a year of "Black Dispair" for Isaac Porter and his church. The church, already having suffered financially during the depression of the twenties, lost many communicants who could have helped to build the new meetinghouse; and Porter lost his house and property, doomed to live out the rest of his years pitiably as a virtual pauper in Granby.[61]

He was not without his loyal supporters, though. Even as the church regrouped, there was a sizable contingency who resented his ouster. Alice Hayes Mellen, in her 1855 novel *The Female Skeptic*, based on her childhood in West Granby, makes reference to these times of spiritual trouble in a dialogue about the challenge of Universalism to Puritan doctrine. In this

291

comment made by the heroine's grandfather, Mr. Parker is undoubtedly a none-too-veiled rendition of Isaac Porter:

> "When good men do wrong," grandpa answered, "there surely will come a retribution. God will vindicate his ways with men. I believe our church at this day is suffering for the sins of its people toward our old minister, Mr. Parker. It grieves me to the heart to see the meek, venerable, grey-haired old man, sitting in the sanctuary Sabbath after Sabbath - the shepherd turned off in his old age, penniless, by his unworthy, ungrateful flock. The parish never will prosper; the sins of the father will descend in judgment on the children, till there is expiation for that guilt."[62]

Needless to say, there were still those who revelled in the glory of God's wrath and found no tidings of great joy coming from Universalist writings.

After Porter's dismissal, the congregation remained divided about where to build the new meetinghouse, finally settling, more or less, on its present site on North Granby Road. There was an effort to reconcile the factions to the extent that the Universalists and the Ecclesiastical Society would build the new meetinghouse together, but the attempt failed.[63] A new minister, Charles Bentley, was recruited, and came on condition that he be given a house and that the meetinghouse be built. But with diminished numbers, subscriptions for the pews, the traditional means of raising money, sold slowly.[64] The cornerstone for the meetinghouse was laid March 25, 1834, and the building dedicated November 25. Surprisingly, Isaac Porter, who had received $300 from the financially-strapped church as an inducement to leave, was asked to preach the first Sabbath in the new meetinghouse.[65] Bentley never got his parsonage, however, and resigned five years later.

At that time there were at least four, and possibly five churches in "Salmon Brook Society." The Congregationalists and Universalists were the most numerous. St. Peter's still met in Granby center, and the town meetings shared its meetinghouse. By 1840, they too were experiencing declining membership.[66] Little is known of the Baptist Church, except that its meeting-house, built around 1790, was sold in 1850 after the Universalists built their own meetinghouse. James Hayes recounted in his memoirs that a Baptist meetinghouse was still meeting there when he was a boy in the 1820s and 30s.[67] A group of Methodists held meetings in West Granby. As we recall

Figure 7-3: The Congregational meetinghouse constructed in 1834 on North Granby Road.

from Chapter VI, they had first met in 1799 and, during the 1820s, had a small meetinghouse south of the village. In the 1830s they were holding meetings in the schoolhouse north of the village and had gained some converts from those who resented the Congregationalist meetinghouse being placed farther away from West Granby in 1834. How numerous they were, or how dedicated, is subject to question.[68] "This never should have been," wrote James Hayes seven decades later. "Three or four weak Churches in a town like this cannot suport a popular Minister nor the enthusiasm which a well filled Church produses."[69]

The sad stories of James Huggins, Isaac Porter and Granby's Congregational Church in the early 1800s reveal much about the tensions rising within the fabric of community life in Granby at the time. Certainly people were frustrated with what they perceived to be immense contradictions within Puritan ideology. They had been through some very rough times, and their spiritual leader, until 1832, offered comfort only by telling them that this was their fate as members of the human race. This approach had actually made

293

Salmon Brook Historical Society

Figure 7-4: James R. Hayes (1821-1914), whose memoirs have revealed so much about life in early Granby.

sense to past generations of New Englanders who had patiently struggled with harvests of rocks, wars for empire and independence, and the bitter cold of New England's winter. But when winter came in July and torrents of water ended hopes for profit, when hard work resulted in little gain and simple comforts fell out of reach, "the great salvation" Porter asked the select few to embrace, became far too mysterious. These stories reveal Granby citizens at their worst - but the painful thing is, that in so doing, they unfold the anguish at the very depths of their souls. Regardless, most kept one faith or another. Just as they kept on working their farms and opening new businesses, they kept on forming new churches, seeking salvation in this life, and after, in their community spirit, battered as it was by the turbulence of the times. And when Granby simply could not produce that which they sought, either of this world or the next, they went elsewhere looking for the good and Godly life.

Exodus

One clear manifestation of Granby's economic and spiritual woes of the early 1800s was the renewed emigration of large numbers of people to the West, as the depression of the 1820s dragged on. Granby had already lost hundreds of people to westward migration before the War of 1812. Lands in Vermont, western New York State, Pennsylvania and Ohio had been open to settlement for a generation, and we have seen how groups from Granby and neighboring towns were responsible for the development of whole communities in what were then far-away places. The emigration which occurred between the Revolution and 1812, however, was miniscule compared with

294

that of the 1820s and 1830s.[70]

In 1820, Granby's population stood at 3012, its highest point ever. By 1830, the total had dropped to 2722; and in 1840 the marshalls counted only 2611.[71] During that time, there were still new people coming into the town, including a few who were actually returning from the West to live in New England. For example, Sylvester Parmalee, who had grown up in Pompey, New York, moved back east to Granby in the 1830s to take up work as a wagon painter in West Granby.[72] The birth rate, while falling in the early 1800s, was still high by today's standards. Thus, considering the forces of population increase at work, the fact that Granby's population was dropping during these decades, indicates substantial movement elsewhere.

Some were heading for urban areas in the northeast in search of higher wages, but most Granby people who left town at this time were farmers simply looking for more land and better land on which to make a living. The exodus was a regional trend. All rural towns throughout New England experienced similar losses of population and the old Northwest Territory soon became a new New England. Throughout Connecticut, manufacturers were expressing concern that their labor force was being depleted. During the first half of the 19th century, 23,000 people made their way from the state to Ohio alone.[73]

Land west of the Appalachians was still relatively cheap in the late 1820s and early 30s, and for a number of reasons, this area became increasingly attractive at that time. In the first place, as the depression waned, people began to save more money or climb out of debt, and were more able to finance a move west. Second, a town of Granby's size could not sustain too many more than 3000 as an agricultural town, and new shops and mills were moving only slowly to increase their labor force. There simply wasn't room for the expanding population in Granby - and there was a lot of room in Ohio and westward. Finally, the Erie Canal opened in 1825. This was important to some extent as a transportation facility for families heading to western New York, or the Great Lakes region, but even more important as a guarantee to migrating farmers that the surplus goods they expected to produce would find their way easily not only to local markets, but also to buyers back in eastern cities and mill towns.

Even with plenty to be optimistic about, departures were still troubling events. In her 1834 diary, Eliza Ann Colton gave more of an accounting of her spiritual life than anything else; and yet when a neighboring family decided to leave North Granby, she set aside a full week's entry:

> March the 31 Cousin W. Veits packed up their goods Pa and Ma went down and made a visit Mr. Wilson and Fanny and Charlott and Cornelia and Aunt Viets came up to see them start for the west but they did not go untill April th 2 when Cousin Watson Viets and his Wife and Marshal their son started for New York the town of Hamilton Madison County. Mr. Winchel carried them on They called to our house a few moments as they came along they appeared to be [?] and glad to leave Granby.[74]

In West Granby, young Samuel J. Hayes, son of Amasa Hayes, chose not to follow the route his brother Austin had taken through New England schools and on to the ministry. In 1836, after his father's death and some hard years trying to reap much of value with his mother and sisters from rocky land in the hills along Barkhamsted Road, he set out for Pennsylvania looking for a better farm. By 1836, he had gone as far as Uniontown, in the southwest corner of Pennsylvania, and from there he wrote home reporting he had heard of better land to the west. His mother encouraged him to move on to see what he could find. She could make do at home this year, she said, and the girls were earning some wages working in Hartford for the time being:

> Jeanette is in Hartford, boards with Adeline and is folding books. you would be pleased to see her now. She thinks board is worth, or at least costs, something. She worked four weeks and did not more than half earn her board. The next four she nearly earned it and now I think she will do more. She thinks it rather discouraging to work as she has done but I am encouraged now and think she gets along very well.[75]

By the next summer, some of his family had moved to New York State, while Samuel had pushed on into central Illinois. His letter from Bloomington, Illinois in July, 1837 is an astonishing rendition of his experiences, and speaks well, if anything, for whoever ran the school in West Granby in the 1820s. Inasmuch as it paints such a clear picture of the typical migrant, I have printed a large portion of it here:

> I had company as far as the Western part of Pennsylvania and fine weather with good roads which you know are very desirable when on a journey. From

Wheeling my journey was not altogether of the pleasantest kind owing to cold, rain, snow, high water etc, etc. The people in this Western country make bridges over mud and leave the streams for fording which in a time of high water makes it difficult and not unfrequently highly dangerous for people to attempt to cross. I was under the necessity of tarrying several days from these causes and after I came into this State I actually lay by one day on account of the cold....Language is not capable of giving a description of the dread occasioned by crossing a large Prairie in a severe cold day with the wind blowing in one's face. I have experienced it once to my full satisfaction. In traveling across a twelve or fifteen mile prairie in the winter you are liable to lose your way and in that case you might perhaps go until night found you without your finding woodland or timber as Suckers call it. Imagine yourself in the middle of a large prairie where you might look East, West, North or South and where the eye could rest upon nothing above but clouds curtaining down to the earth on every side and the earth covered with snow with no vestige of even savage habitation,— not a tree or shrub,—nothing to human appearance but a solitary dreary desert. I say imagine yourself in this situation after having been exposed to a bleak winters wind for an hour or two and then a keen piercing wind mixed with flakes of snow blowing from the very direction in which you are bending your course....But change the scene to a spring or summer day when instead of snow the earth is clad in "Verdent robes" and instead of clouds a clear sunshine and gentle breezes of air. You would then say in crossing these Western Prairies that it was the most beautiful country you ever saw.

I arrived in Bloomington, Ill. on the 3rd day of January. After spending a few days without knowing whether to look about the country for a more desirable situation (as the ground was covered with snow) and there was no chance to judge by looking I had an opportunity of enquiring of several individuals who had travelled over this and the adjoining states all who agreed in saying that Bloomington and its vicinity was not surpassed and seldom equalled by any other part of the western country either for beauty of location, health of climate, or fertility of soil. under these circumstances I had the offer of ten acres of timber land at $20 per acre. This I purchased. Since then I have been offered $30 per acre for the same. I also purchased 10 acres more about 2 miles from town at $18 per acre. The first I bought is within 3/4 of a mile of town. I also bought 80 acres of prairie 2 miles north of town at $112 for the whole 80 acres. Since then I have entered 240 acres about 3 1/2 miles south or southwest of town. I have also contracted for the half of an improved farm containing 310 acres. There is a frame house upon it, a small barn, a well of water, 50 acres under cultivation, 25 or thirty more fenced, 30 acres of which 310 are timber. For this I am to pay $5 per acre. People in this vicinity say it is worth at least $10 per acre. So you see I have land enough to make a pretty good farm if it was well husbanded.

I told you I arrived here on the 3rd of January. After having been here 3 or 4 weeks I found my expenses were accumulating a bill rather higher then my circumstances would justify. I therefore concluded as I made up my mind to locate here to get a housekeeper and board myself. As wages were high and my funds rather limited I thought rather than hire a housekeeper it would be better for me to take a partner. Having been as you know quite intimate with Miss J. Cowdery I made known my plans to her. She having reflected upon them for a few days approved them and concluded to become my partner although engaged in school teaching and under contract for 8 or 9 months following. The ceremony of our copartnership was ratified publicly on the evening of the 5th of February 1837. And now to give you a history of our management of matters and things I describe the schoolhouse which answers for a schoolhouse, meeting house and dwelling house. It contains 2 school rooms on the basement story with a hall or space running through between them of 6 feet wide. The upper story is a meeting house. It is built very much like the school house in West Granby excepting the stairs go up inside of the building. Under the stairs is a small room partitioned about 6 by 8 or 9 feet square running back under the stairs. This we make use of for a buttery. I have put up a partition across the space. One end we use for a bedroom. We have an old fashioned cookingstove in the schoolroom where we do our cooking. For furniture we have of Mr. Foster in part pay for J's board a bedstead and bedding. This he furnished together with the privilege of living in the school house and pays me 87 1/2 cents a week for my wife's board. Don't you think he is a very liberal man? Boarding is worth in this town only from $2 to $5 per week. We have bought a set of common winsor chairs second hand not new by a good deal at the moderate price of $10. We have table of my own make. Don't you think it is a nice one? Mrs. Foster has been kind enough to lend us three knives and forks and three teaspoons. We have bought some necessary articles of crockery. Also a dutch oven or bake kettle, and a tea kettle, tea pot, 3 twelve quart pails, 6 six quart pails, 2 tin pans, 11 tin dippers, and a frying pan. Don't you think we are well provided for? For provisions I bought a hog that weighed 155 lbs. when dressed, 250 lbs. of flour, 2 bushel of cornmeal, 2 venison hams, 5 or 6 bushels of potatoes, etc, etc. I made sugar—probably 150 lbs— did not weigh it. Our stock consists of a horse, 1 cow and calf, 6 hogs, 2 hens, and 3 chickens. The hens were a present by one of our neighbors. We have plenty of beans, peas, cucumbers, squashes, and new potatoes. Just come over some afternoon and make us a visit and see how we live in the "Sucker State."

....

Since I wrote the above I have sold my horse on a credit till Christmas for $100. I have been making preparations for building a house in this town. I have my lumber mostly ready and expect to commence framing in two weeks to make it ready to live in this winter. Labor is very high, common labouring hands get one dollar per day. A man and a team from 3 to 4 dollars per day. I have paid 4 dollars a day for a team to draw logs to the saw mill and one dollar per hundred for sawing boards. People here hardly know when they ask enough for doing anything. However, I am tolerably well pleased with the appearance of the people of Bloomington and with Bloomington itself.

You say you looked on the map and away out of the business world near the center of the future state of Illinois you saw the town of Bloomington. Now you are a little behind the time to think that Bloomington is out of the business part of the world or that Illinois is a future state. Illinois has more advantages for comfort and luxury, wealth and distinction, than any other state in the Union and Bloomington is not far behind many of our eastern Villages for business (ie) County seats. Bloomington contains at the present about 500 inhabitants. It has 2 meeting houses, 2 steam sawmills, an elegant brick courthouse, a log jail with one tenant, 7 stores, 2 taverns, 2 grog shops, etc., etc. The houses are mostly painted white which gives the village an air of neatness which I have not seen equalled in any part of the country except New England. There has been about a dozen houses built this summer and there are some more to be built yet and quite a number are making preparations for building next year.

My business is such that I shall not be able to go East until next summer. If I live till next summer and am prospered I intend to go East and then if Mother and the rest of you will come back with me it will be very gratifying to me indeed. Till then believe as ever,

Your affectionate brother,

Samuel[76]

Samuel's mother and sister eventually moved to Bloomington, leaving West Granby behind forever.[77] Just before the move in May, 1838, Adeline wrote her sister Amelia, "I have been home so long I can't bear to think of leaving it but this is a world of changes and friends must be separated."[78]

While Samuel J. Hayes's writing ability was hardly typical of the Connecticut farmer moving west, his experiences were. A series of letters between Goddard relations, points out many of the common elements. As Adeline Hayes was preparing to move west to join her brother in Bloomington, young Henry and Reform Goddard were writing Henry's parents from Troy Grove, Illinois, extolling the wonders of frontier living. The land was good, they wrote, and they had been able to purchase 100 acres for $545. Like

299

Salmon Brook Historical Society, gifts of Louis B. Howard

Figure 7-5: Two of the children of Amasa and Ruth Hayes of West Granby. Amelia Orpha Hayes (left) migrated to Bloomington, Illinois around 1840 to join her brother Samuel. There she married James T. Walton. Her sister, Jeanette Elizabeth Hayes (right), the future wife of Lyman Ferry, also moved to Bloomington prior to 1850.

Samuel Hayes, they planned on buying more land for Henry's parents, Isaac and Abigail Goddard. They were selling timber from their property at a good price, they had been healthy and were living in an area inhabited by a lot of their relatives and friends from back East. "I do not think that you would stay there in old Connecticut a great while," added Henry's sister Abigail, "if you knew what a beautiful Country this is it is such a good place for young people to get a start in the world. I think that the girls would do well at their trade here, for good sewers are sparse in this country."[79]

The main force behind the migration was clear: the availability of good land for farmers who saw nothing but crowding and gravel in "old Connecticut." The presence of friends and relatives in the new communities also provided encouragement, as did prospects for good wages from a trade, or the possibility of finding a spouse, as had Samuel Hayes, who had apparently tracked Jerusha Cowdery, once a teacher at an Academy in

Granby, nearly to the Mississippi River to unveil his "plan" for a partnership.

For the Goddards, though, the good fortune did not continue, and the dangers of frontier living, as well as the inability to leave old troubles behind completely, soon became obvious. Henry's brother Riverus wrote home as winter approached, that everyone had been sick during the summer. The whole family was experiencing hard times and were in desperate need of money to buy housing materials so scarce on the prairie. Later that winter, Reform wrote that Riverus was still sick. Some people they knew were heading further west for "Ioway Territory," and even they themselves were planning on leaving for financial reasons. "The reason we do not stay here is on account of Uncle Warren's conduct concerning this note he is determined to hold the land as security, until it is paid or get the money some other way out of Harry if possible not for Aunt Asenath as he pretended at first but for his own use to pay for his half of this land for he is very hard crowded for money now." She went on to detail more problems with mortgages and notes, problems experienced by people across the nation as the effects of the Panic of 1837 began to spread into the economy as a whole.[80] Throughout the 1840s, money problems continued to plague the family and prevent them from trying their luck in "Ioway." Their parents seemed reluctant to come West to join them, and Riverus moved back to New York State.[81]

Others overstretched the bounds of safety as well. On Creamery Hill Road, a cemetery contains a monument to Richard Pratt "who was killed by Indians from Santa Fee, Mexico on his way to the United States. Jan. 1833. Ae 42." Pratt's body was shipped back to Granby in a barrel of brine.[82] Another Granby man, Gordon Jennings, arrived in similar packaging after being killed at the Alamo in 1836.[83] Samuel Hayes, our eloquent young correspondent, died in 1841 in the fourth year of his marriage. Abiel Higley, a restless clock pedlar who had lived in James Huggins's house after Huggins's death in 1819, moved with his wife Prudence and five children, first to Bloomington in 1841. The next spring, they pushed on to Marion, Iowa, a rough country full of horse thieves and cutthroats. Abiel died there in October, leaving his family penniless to cope with the elements. His son Henry, who lost his wife in childbirth in 1846, tried gold prospecting in California in 1849, but returned to Iowa no richer than when he had left.[84]

In fact, many of these difficult experiences, along with news of the

301

Texas Rebellion in 1836, and ten years later, the war with Mexico, did serve to discourage some prospective emigrants from Connecticut. Most of those who left Granby were young, single or newly married people, traveling with neighbors and relatives and settling together with those they had known, or who had gone before them to act as their land agents. Those in financial difficulties, while probably eager to get away and "get a new start," found the going extremely difficult. While land in Illinois was cheaper than the poorest land in Granby, it was not free, and had gone up considerably from the $1 to $2 per acre it had sold for before 1820.[85] Those who had no land in Granby to sell, or who had land but could find no one to pay cash for it, would have a hard time setting themselves up in the West.

Nevertheless, the migration continued, draining a much of Granby's youth to the namesake Granbys, Hartlands, Cantons and Granvilles of other new states. Like their ancestors who had come to Salmon Brook in the previous century, these adventurers sought the opportunities available to those willing to take tremendous risks in an environment they would have to tame to their tastes and needs. They left behind a community that was still largely agricultural, but increasingly driven by the machinery of a different age.

An Economic Roller Coaster, 1820-1850

In the years before the Civil War, the American economy changed dramatically. A nation, which had been growing as an agricultural and commercial power ever since its days as a string of colonial outposts, quickly developed industrial and financial strength as emerging transportation systems, such as the Erie Canal, spawned regional specialization and interdependence. Although most towns in New England did not see the kinds of changes which occurred in Hartford, New Haven, Boston or Lowell, they were deeply affected by their connections with this new urban and industrial world, and even more so by the forces which were giving rise to that new world everywhere. As the national economy alternately surged and skidded, Granby residents experienced a difficult and bumpy ride. Some succeeded, some failed, and for most, it was sufficient simply to endure.

One type of change which was at the heart of the turmoil of the times was the high turnover within the population. On the surface, there does not appear to be much fluctuation, for the total number of people living in town remained fairly constant after 1820 (See Table 7-1). Under the surface, however, statistics tell a different story. Every ten years, over half of the heads of family in Granby were no longer listed on the census, and each decade that proportion had been replaced by names new to the list (See Table 7-2). Some of this turnover can be accounted for by deaths and coming of age, not by in- or out-migration. However, the evidence already discussed regarding westward migration suggests that there were, perhaps, equally large numbers of young people leaving town before they had a chance to be listed as a family head, and similarly, significant numbers of people coming and going between census years. This was hardly a stable population.

The movement in and out of town is clearly related to patterns of westward migration. Significant emigration affected the figures from 1795 to 1805. That emigration slowed during the War of 1812 and the years of economic trouble which followed. By the mid-1820s, emigration had picked up again, only to fall off by 1840 when the nation slipped into another depression. In the late 1840s people began heading west again in large numbers.

Table 7-1
Granby's Population, 1790-1850[86]

1790	2595
1800	2735
1810	2696
1820	3012
1830	2722
1840	2611
1850	2498

The exodus to the West, however, does not account for all of the moving in and out of Granby which was taking place in the early 1800s. Those leaving the town were replaced almost as rapidly by people who were coming to Granby. Some of these newcomers were buying the farms being sold by the people leaving town. Included among these were Granby's first Irish immigrants for the period in which hundreds of thousands would move from Ireland to America. In 1840, Myles Rogers of Ireland bought a farm on Loomis Street in North Granby, and other Irish Catholics would soon follow, buying farms on nearby Silver Street and trudging all the way to Tariffville, seven miles away, to attend mass on Sundays.[88] For staunch congregational-ists rooted in two centuries of the Bible Commonwealth, this development, miniscule as it was at the time in Granby, represented a radical change in the character of their community. In spite of increasing toleration of Protestant denominations, two centuries of Puritan domination in Connecticut produced a legacy of distrust toward Catholics, regardless of Ireland's long-standing struggle for independence from Great Britain.

Table 7-2 Heads of Family Turnover(%), 1790-1850[87]		
Census from to	% Names on Earlier List Not on Later List	% Names on Later List Not on Earlier List
1790-1800	58.4	59.7
1800-1810	63.6	57.8
1810-1820	49.4	58.3
1820-1830	60.6	52.9
1830-1840	51.8	64.0
1840-1850	58.9	56.5

As we have seen, though, more often than not, it was young people with no prospect of getting much land who left Granby, while their parents and one or two siblings stayed behind at the homestead. A significant proportion of the newcomers, in fact, were not buying farms, but coming to work in the new manufacturing establishments which were building "power dams" at virtually every place where high banks crowded in on the two branches of Salmon Brook. Of those family heads who resided in Granby only long enough to get their names on one of the four censuses between 1820 and 1850, about half gave their occupational category as "manufactures and trades," while only a quarter gave it as "agriculture." The other quarter of this "transient" class could not list an occupation at all, which probably meant they were willing to work wherever there was employment - or that they were simply unemployed. Many of these were foreign born or, at least, from another state. Factory work was clearly drawing New Englanders who were on the move to Granby, as fast as poor prospects for farming were sending them away. Moreover, quite a few of those who moved out of town were not farmers, but tradesmen and shop workers, continuing to look for better opportunity elsewhere in New England.

Of course, there was also a sizable number of young people who left Granby temporarily, or so they hoped, to earn some money in nearby cities. This was particularly true of young women hoping to supplement their family's income, or perhaps to expand their horizons beyond what they sensed was a confined world should they decide to wait for marriage in Granby. A letter from Roxey Wilcox, who traveled to New Britain to work in the 1840s, to her sister Eliza Ann in West Granby, gives us some insight into this type of experience:

> am going to Mr. Judd to work tomorrow I called there last evening he said he was in a great hurry and wanted to have me write to you soon as I could wants you to come to work as soon as you can possibly when James was down he said you talked of going to school but I think you had better come to B this winter and if you go to school next Summer you can pay your own tuition Mrs. Seymour says she will board you if you come it is a first rate place no one but Mrs. S and myself mr. Judd says if our folks cannot bring you down he will meet you in hartford if you will write when you can come I suppose our folks wont know how to spare you but you wont help them much if you go to school; how do the folks get along in G is mary married yet and I expect Fan and Soph every moment to go to meetin have our folks fetch you down if you can and fetch bub if it is not to cold and all the apples and chustnuts you can get and my combs they are in a box some where write me so I can get it Saturday without fail for Mr Judd has got another girl partly engaged and if you can not she will take your place write when you can come and how if you have much sewing to do fetch it and do it evening[89]

Eliza Ann disregarded this urgent advice and attended the West Granby

Academy, from which she graduated valedictorian in 1847. She then married a local shoemaker, Carlton Holcomb, and lived the rest of her years in West Granby - probably not the life Roxey had in mind for her sister.[90] In fact, even in raising the issue of schooling, Roxey must have been thinking about Eliza Ann going away to school, as more and more young people, both male and female, were doing.

The improvements in transportation which made all of this moving about possible, ranged from better roads both within and around the town, to newer facilities, such as canals and railroads. While towns had been held responsible for maintaining good roads since the settlement of Connecticut, it was clear after the Revolution that the prosperity of the state required a more coordinated approach. Even coastal and river merchants were eager to have improved links with their customers and suppliers of agricultural products in the back country and urged the county courts to sponsor road building projects. As we have seen in the case of the Granby Turnpike Company, the legislature was also ready to offer incentives to private investors who would improve and maintain roads on well-used routes of commerce. Although the conflict with Great Britain put a damper on projects requiring substantial capital, the effort to build better roads began to pick up again after the War of 1812. The Granby-Barkhamsted Turnpike Company received a charter in 1818 to build on the route which the Hartland Turnpike Company had failed to improve before the war. Again, they hoped to profit from the transportation of iron to Newgate Prison and Springfield.[91]

Private turnpike companies, however, were not generally profitable, and good roads depended largely on town and county funding even in these early years. The Granby-Barkhamsted Turnpike Company never completed its project, and by 1844, the Granby Turnpike Company was actually trying to go *out* of business, while the town was initiating legal action to continue to hold it responsible for the upkeep of its route from Tariffville through Granby center to Granville.[92] The town did make an effort to improve its roads throughout the 1820s and 1830s, but as it continued to change from a community of independent farms spread out around the hills, to a collection of village centers struggling to develop manufacturing enterprises, selectmen had all they could do to fund the rerouting of roads, let alone make established roads easier for travel.[93] The result was some improvement in roads within the town, but not to the extent hoped for by its businessmen. As the traveler or freight hauler drew closer to the Connecticut River, though, heavier traffic had justified more substantial road construction by both private and public enterprise.

The most dramatic change in transportation facilities resulted from the construction in the 1820s of a canal from New Haven through Granby to Northampton, Massachusetts. The Farmington Canal Company was chartered in 1822, when the Erie Canal itself was still under construction. The plans outlined a tremendous undertaking which would link New Haven and sixteen other Connecticut towns to Westfield and Northampton, where a Massachusetts company would connect the route to the Connecticut River for travel northward into New Hampshire and Vermont, and one day, it was envisioned, all the way to the St. Lawrence River. In an age when digging was done by hand, with some help from horse-drawn scoops, it was truly an ambitious project to build a ditch thirty feet wide, four feet deep and eighty miles long, with sixty locks for lifting the boats (six in Granby for a rise of 37.5 feet) and aqueducts for keeping the canal filled with water. After three years of planning, surveying and struggling to raise money during a depression, construction began on July 4, 1825 with a ceremony in Granby. One observer remembered, "On Monday, at five o'clock this morning I rode with brother Martin Cowles in a chaise to Granby Village where a large concourse of people assembled to celebrate American Independence and to perform and witness the ceremonies of breaking ground for the Farmington Canal —— Gov. Wolcott read an address and performed the ceremony of breaking ground by digging a small hole with a spade. Mr. Lyman of Northampton made an address on horseback, and, after a few other ceremonies, the multitude returned to Granby, and about three hundred dined together on the village green under a bowery." There was a large parade, complete with a canal boat on wheels, all designed to convey a heady sense of optimism about the new world of commerce the canal would open. But the governor had broken the spade slicing into Granby's "topsoil," and that was just the beginning of the company's bad luck.[94]

No profit ever came to the investors, some of whom were from Granby. It was four years before the canal was navigable all the way from New Haven to Granby, and another six before it was open to the Connecticut

307

River at Northampton. The planned branch to New Hartford and Colebrook never materialized, and the cost of construction far exceeded estimates. Floods in 1826 and 1828 undid much of the work, including the washing away, both times, of the large stone viaduct in Granby which carried the canal across Salmon Brook (the site of the viaduct is now in East Granby in Granbrook Park).[95] In addition to natural catastrophes, farmers along the route, angry about leakage that turned their fields into bogs, and unhappy with high, rickety bridges that frightened their cattle and made hauling big loads difficult, were continually knocking holes in the banks and draining the water out. The intervention of the city of New Haven, buying $100,000 of stock in 1829, saved the company from disaster just as the full length in Connecticut was being completed. While tolls paid for upkeep and salaries, the company could not get out of debt, and after another serious flood in 1836, just a few months after the Massachusetts link was opened, the company was forced to reorganize as the New Haven and Northampton Company. More damage from floods, an interruption in service because of drought in 1845, and the growth of railroads, sealed the company's fate as one of the great failures in American corporate history. "After spending a mint of Money," wrote James R. Hayes, "it was an Eliphant on the hands of the Stockholders a ruinous thing to all concerned."[96] In 1846, the charter was annulled. Officially the canal was closed when the Canal Railroad, which used most of the old towpath, was opened from New Haven to Plainville in 1848. By 1850, the railroad had been built as far north as Granby.[97]

All this is not to say that the canal came to nothing just because the stockholders lost their money. For the sixteen years it was open from Granby to New Haven, the canal carried thousands of tons of freight and thousands of passengers. By 1838, there was a daily packet through Granby, taking on passengers on the 24-hour Northampton to New Haven trip for under $4 each, including meals. From New Haven, freight boats brought coal, salt, molasses, oranges, codfish, rum, furniture, oil, oysters and ironware; and Granby consumers paid far less for these items than they used to. From the freight house on Hartford Avenue in Granby, boats carried to New Haven lumber, shingles, hides, potatoes, pork, wool, tar, turpentine, cheese, charcoal and, of course, cider and cider brandy. For small towns like Granby along the route, the ability to get products more cheaply and to expand their markets was surely a benefit in the 1830s before railroads were available.[98]

Some of this canal traffic apparently resulted in the permanent transfer of people. On September 4, 1839, Thomas Newton Taylor of West Granby, married Polly Palmer Alling in her home town of Woodbridge. Taylor's father, William, was a farmer and sawyer who undoubtedly sent his son down the canal with lumber and produce to market in New Haven, or in towns like Woodbridge, along the way. In a few year's time, not only had Thomas and Polly moved to Granby to begin a family, but Polly's younger half-brother, Marcus Alling, a carpenter by trade, had moved to town as well - to marry Thomas's younger sister Eliza Ann.[99] The Taylors and Allings thus became part of the legendary romance of the canal, which was a facility for wedding trips, pleasure cruises, boating and skating, as well as practical transportation needs.

Greater access to the rest of the world, via better roads, canals and, by 1850, railroads, meant a lot more than movement of people. It meant that Granby producers, whether farmers or manufacturers, could get their products to market more easily, and, in turn, had more access to cheaper goods they needed. Thus, the transportation revolution combined with greater availability of capital resources and favorable national tariff policies to be among the key factors responsible for local economic growth, particularly of industry and commercial agriculture. By 1840, Granby was a leading producer of finished leather for shoes in the region. The town boasted three tanneries (four by 1845) to Hartford's one, and also produced more metal goods than any other town in the county (primarily because of a spoon factory at the Falls, in what is now East Granby). Granby's shops and mills manufactured flannel, carpeting, sewing silk, scythes (two factories), ploughs, tinware, brassware, musical instruments, clothing (three factories), saddles, harnesses, trunks, coaches and wagons (four factories), whips, boots, shoes, flour, lumber (seven sawmills) and charcoal.

Even its farms seemed like factories. With over 2000 sheep scattered among them, they held the highest number in the county in 1840, producing over 9000 pounds of wool in one year. Granby farmers also produced 31,180 bushels of potatoes in that year, a high for the county. Of all Granby's products, though, none stood out among other towns in the county so much as cider brandy. In no less than eighteen distilleries in 1840, the town's cider men made 25,800 gallons of brandy. The market was hardly glutted, for in 1845 (the year of the drought), the number of stills had increased to 41! In the 1850 census, town assessors reported a similar array of industrial and agricultural enterprise. Another carriage shop was added to the list, as were two more sawmills, another whip lasher, an eavespout factory, a cigar maker and a twine factory.[100]

To be sure, there was substantial manufacturing going on at the Falls (whose residents on the Simsbury side were so grateful for federal government protection that they named their village "Tariffville" after the 1828 "Tariff of Abominations," as it was called in South Carolina).[101] We do know the locations of many of Granby's manufacturing establishments, and they were spread throughout the town. West Granby had its share with a scythe shop, clothing works, lumber mills aplenty and a major carriage works. North Granby also had a carriage works and its farmers were the source of most of the cider brandy that was so plentiful in 1845 that it might have been used to float boats to New Haven. In the center of town, Hezekiah Goodrich and his sons still turned out leather; not far from him in "Mechanicsville," at the southern end of Manatuck Lake, there was a brass foundry and another clothing works; and in Pegville, just south of Goodrichville, a man named Truman Allen did an interstate shoe business.[102]

It was Hezekiah Goodrich, Granby's first tanner and postmaster, who gave Truman Allen his start. Allen, born in Colebrook in 1792, had come to Granby shortly after the War of 1812, having married Susan Holcomb in 1814 and taken over Daniel Marshall's shoe business in North Granby in 1815.[103] By the 1820s, he and Goodrich had formed a partnership, and with some other investors, had built a shoe factory along the North Branch of Salmon Brook at the junction of Day Street and North Granby Road. Goodrich undoubtedly supplied the leather for this enterprise, as well as the initial capital, but it is clear from subsequent transactions, that Allen was the marketing specialist in the partnership. In 1832, after recovering from the failure of this first venture and his first wife's death, he moved to a new location, south of Goodrichville, buying a large house (now 10 Wells Road) and opening a new shop.[104] By 1840, he was contracting with shoemakers in Connecticut and Massachusetts and selling his shoes and theirs all over the state, and soon, out of state as well. In 1847, he sold 6600 pairs of boots, shoes and slippers, which were either sent

Figure 7-6: Truman Allen's house (after 1834) at 10 Wells Road. Nathaniel Holcomb III originally built at this location a century earlier, but Benjamin Reed reconstructed the house in the 1780s. Allen's shoe shop was located near the road to the right of the dwelling.

Figure 7-7: Truman Allen (1792-1876), c. 1865.

Figure 7-8: Electa Hayes Allen (1800-1889), Truman's second wife.

311

to agents or peddled by Allen's own salesman. At one point or another, he held interests in sawmills, grist mills, cotton mills and a shingle mill. He also played an active role in local politics and reform movements, and was the leading financial supporter of the Universalist Church. Clearly, Allen had benefitted from the new world of trade ushered in by better transportation facilities. And as his business expanded, those who invested with him as partners, sold him leather, or furnished him commodities locally in exchange for shoes, were swept along toward some degree of prosperity themselves.[105]

The carriage works in North Granby began operation in the late 1820s under Ezekiel Alderman, who was a prominent local politician as well. He lived just south of the North Granby Road bridge over Mountain Brook, where he used water power for a smith shop, body and trimming shops, a wheel shop and a paint shop. There he constructed high quality carriages to travel the improved roads of the new age, trained a number of young mechanics and operated an undertaking business as well. The apprentices included the Fancher brothers, who would later open their own carriage works in West Granby, and the Dewey brothers, who would take up Alderman's business after his death.[106]

Mechanicsville got its name when Isaac Porter's son Richard and his brother-in-law, Stephen Cornwell of New Britain, turned an old blacksmith shop into a brass foundry for the manufacture of shovels and tongs for the more elegant parlors of the day. Young Richard had left Yale in his sophomore year to work with Cornwell in this business. In 1829, they moved to Granby, but Porter quit the enterprise in 1831, even though his father, not yet fired from his post in the church, had helped to finance the machinery. At that point, Cornwell took on Calvin Dibble and Daniel Hayes of Salmon Brook Street as partners. To raise more capital they sold some of their property to Orin H. Lee, who proposed to build a satinette factory next to the foundry, and dug a new feeder ditch from the brook to accommodate his own complex of machinery. Dibble and Cornwell spent a lot of time on the road during the winter months drumming up orders in New York, Boston, Philadelphia and even in the South, and slowly, the business expanded.[107]

With the growth of industry and increasing contact with the rest of the world, came the emergence of a more urban outlook. This may seem surprising to those in the twentieth century who have struggled to maintain

Granby's rural ambience, but in the early nineteenth century, Granby was as much involved in the process of urbanization as any other town in New England. This trend is evident not only in the development of industry, but also in the significantly smaller families, the higher turnover of public officeholders, and the decreasing number of families which might be classified as "permanent" residents (See Tables 7-3, 7-4 and 7-5). As time passed, the average size of families dropped from nearly seven people in 1800 to under 5 in 1840, a trend historians have identified as typical of urban areas.[108] Instead of continually reelecting the same people to public office, voters varied their choices. Similarly, as people moved in and out of town, there seemed to be a declining number of families who stayed in town for more than twenty years.

Table 7-3
Average Family Size by Decade in Granby[109]

1790	5.80
1800	6.87
1810	6.83
1820	5.60
1830	6.40
1840	4.92
1850	4.56

Table 7-4
Officeholder Turnover by Decade in Granby

Decade	Different Reps. to Legislature	Different Town Meeting Moderators	Different Selectmen
1786-1797	5	3	9
1797-1806	8	4	12
1807-1816	19	3	18
1817-1826	21	6	14
1827-1836	15	6	15
1837-1846	17	8	19

Beyond statistics, the incursions of urban culture are evident in reports of people's daily lives. In the brief excerpts we have from Eliza Ann Colton's diary, she recorded not only her life as a pious farm girl, but also her entry into the consumer economy with purchases of handkerchiefs and lace for a cape, and on a shopping trip to Hartford, of a bonnet ($3.09), a parasol, a pair of gloves (75¢), some light silk for a dress, and a few other odds and ends. To finance her spending, she learned how to weave chair seats from Ferdinand Clemmons of North Granby. On May 31, she wrote "I seated 11 chairs this week and 7 last week which would make 18 that I have done for myself besides the 14 that I did for Mr. Clemons to pay for learning."[110] She was only one of many young women who experienced fewer demands on their time in the household. As the factory produced more of what housewives and their daughters used to make themselves, young women were taking up paying jobs outside of the household, and as with Roxey Wilcox and Samuel J. Hayes's sisters, often outside of the community.

Table 7-5
Permanent vs. Impermanent Family Heads
(by percentage of total number of family heads)

Census	Listed in That Census Only	Listed in Three or More Censuses
1800	29.9	51.5
1810	33.9	48.8
1820	26.8	48.6
1830	28.7	48.4
1840	34.5	42.1
1850	35.0	43.9

Yet another subtle indication of a farming town acquiring an urban soul can be seen in the manner in which Alpheus Hayes's heirs divided his 1828 estate and shaped their property in the succeeding years. When he died in 1828, he owned clothing works and some other property on the bank of Salmon Brook in West Granby. His house stood across Simsbury Road which ran parallel to the brook. His children divided the homestead property into parcels which had roughly equal frontage on the road. Then, over the next decade, they began building houses. In the case of each parcel, the house was built as close to one edge of the property line as possible, suggesting that they were leaving room for the additional houselots they hoped to sell, as industrial enterprises multiplied and more people moved into the village to work in the shops and mills.[111] In the early 1800s, the shop owners of West Granby hoped their village would become a mill town.

Some factors, such as the lack of hard currency, would retard Granby's entry into the urban world around it. Account books for Granby businessmen paint a picture of a system stubbornly clinging to barter exchange well into the middle of the 19th century. Farmers brought their carts to be repaired and their boots to be mended, and then, sometimes months later, delivered several pounds of butter or beef to pay the bills. A West Granby blacksmith recorded services for sharpening plough shares, shoeing horses, fixing iron tools and carts, and renting his horse and wagon, but nearly every one of his customers lived within a mile of his house. They brought him veal, lamb, pigs, casks, loads of wood, beef and iron. Only occasionally did anyone pay cash.[112] So backward was the system, that Eliza Ann Colton was paying for purchases at Abner Case's North Granby store with shillings and pence as late as 1834.[113] IOU's and mortgage deeds floated about from neighbor to neighbor, only to be rewritten when the probate judge ordered an estate settled. Even though there were state banks and a national bank issuing bank notes, little of this currency found its way into the local economy unless a local manufacturer sold a large order to some urban distributor. Even then, since the balance of trade between Granby and the rest of the world regularly tilted away from the town, neither bank notes, nor hard currency, stayed in town for long.[114]

In the 1830s, the struggle between the Jacksonians and the Bank of the United States was resolved, more or less, with the President's veto of the bill to recharter the Bank. As the Bank closed up its twenty-year business, President Jackson began to insist that all payments to the federal government be made in gold or silver. This, and successor Martin Van Buren's policy of depositing federal funds in a sub-treasury system instead of banks, led inevitably to considerable upheaval, and finally, panic in the national banking system. In settling an estate in December, 1837, the year of the bank panic, Granby's Bildad Kendall wrote to Henry B. Curtis in Ohio, "I presume you are well informed on the bad state of our Banks - not one payes specie for their

315

Bills - In New England - As the prospect appears to offer nothing better in future I concluded to send it you of such Money as we use in our State and shall inclose in this letter a certificate of deposit subject to your order of $116 on Hartford Bank - Said to be the best in the city."[115] The problem of lack of currency had been with Granby for some time, and after 1837, it was even worse. This made doing business beyond the town's borders very difficult, and those who had aspirations to expand often failed in their efforts.

Bankruptcy was again a frequent occurrence in the late 1830s and early 1840s. Even with the advent of fire and flood insurance, there were still uncontrollable forces that could bring ruin to a business in a matter of months. Harlow Wilcox was not the only person who lost his property in West Granby during the volatile 1830s and 1840s. Edward Hayes, son of Alpheus, who had died in 1828, tried to start a wagon-factory in 1837 on his share of his father's estate. A flood in the winter of 1839 may have contributed to some of his problems, but it was simply not a good time to do business. In 1845, suffering "from misfortunes and business losses," his property was assigned to neighbors and relatives to be sold at auction. It was hoped that his shops and tools would bring over $5000 to help pay his debts totalling $5683.77. In the end, though, his creditors only got 32.5¢ on the dollar, and Edward fled west to try to begin a new life.[116]

Joab Griffin Jr., a West Granby Justice of the Peace was another who was hit hard by the convulsions of the late 1830s. Under financial duress in 1838, he borrowed money from a state government agency set up to stem the financial crisis, but he was unable to keep his creditors at bay and was forced to move from the large and elegant house his father had built (286 West Granby Road) to a small abode carpenter Luther Pratt had recently abandoned (7 Simsbury Road). Wrote Adeline Hayes to her sister in 1838, "Esqr Griffin has moved where L. Pratt used to live how their pride must be humbled. I think from what I have heard that they are quite miserable. I really can't help but pity them."[117]

In 1844, as his younger sister was about to be married to Marcus Alling of Woodbridge, young Thomas Taylor, a farmer for barely five years, was forced to declare bankruptcy, dooming his new family to a life of poverty. His neighbor Ovil Wilcox was also in trouble, with Harvey Allen of Simsbury hounding him for repayment of a debt. Ovil escaped Thomas's fate only when

Thomas's wife Polly began a series of real estate transactions that kept Ovil's property title hidden from Allen for a few years.[118] Stephen Cornwell himself was feeling pressed in 1846 when he asked Truman Allen to take care of a debt he had. When Cornwell died in 1849 of "heart disease," the brass foundry had to be closed. These and other stories of people caught in the throes of a seemingly uncontrollable economy abounded in Granby between 1820 and 1850. Truman Allen, Ezekiel Alderman and Hezekiah Goodrich were the lucky ones. In all probability, most of those shops and mills listed in the various surveys of industry and trade were barely clinging to solvency.

As people experienced difficulty, either in adjusting to change or in effecting it in their lives, there grew a sense of frustration. With frustration came the sort of sentiments we imagined James Huggins to have expressed, even before the wild economic gyrations began. There was a sense that the community was "decaying," that the old spirit of enterprise was fading - or heading west. This was troubling even for those who were making ends meet without great difficulty. In 1840, two men in Granby center began publishing a weekly newspaper as part of the national election campaign of that year. At one point in the paper's brief run they wrote, "We are happy to witness the enterprising spirit which is manifested by many young men in Granby. A class is coming on to the stage of action, who feel a deep interest in the welfare of their native place, and are determined to redeem Salmon Brook from its decaying condition....With one or more Manufactories in the place, men of all honourable profession and trade would thrive."[119] One is led to think that this editorial constituted wishful thinking and that, in fact, the "decaying condition" of the town was something many were assuming to be a true description of the state of their community.

Indeed, if we believe the advocates of "abstinence from intoxicating drink," there is substantial evidence of frustration in the widespread indulgence in liquor drinking. This was apparently a problem in rural towns across the region, and some historians have estimated that alcohol consumption by the average citizen in the 1820s (five gallons of 200 proof alcohol per year) was nearly triple what it is today.[120] Isaac Porter was certainly concerned, and brought people up on charges for "excessive use of strong drink."[121] Alcoholism was difficult to prevent, though, since taverns were the principal meeting place and information center for the men of the community. Furthermore,

317

A. Case.

WEEKLY NEWS

Truth in a small compass.
VOL. 1.   GRANBY, CONN. MAR. 18, 1840.   NO. 4.

POETRY.

A Prayer.
(Author unknown.)

Give me one kind, confiding heart
To cheer me on life's pilgrimage,
To soothe me when my hopes de-
    part,
And shield me when misfortunes
    rage,
And then, though Fotune's brow
    be dark,
Or bright before me is Hope's
    form,
Light o'er life's waves my bound-
    ing bark
Shall onward sweep through sun
    and storm.

Surmise is the gossamer that
malice blows on fair reputation;
the corroding dew that destroys
the choice blossom. Surmise is
the squint of suspicion, and suspicion is established before it is
confirmed.—Ladies' Companion.

"Sarah says she's twenty-two.
She said so fifteen years ago.

A little jokeing now and then
Is relished by the wisest men.

A boy held out his hat to a
gentleman and asked for a few
cents: 'money, (said the gentleman,) you had better beg for manners than money.' 'I asked for that
replied the boy, which I thought
you had the most of.'

We heard a man say, some time
ince, that he had lived with a
Barber for years, and could shave;
but could neither shorten a man's
hair nor beard—albeit, he might
his purse!

A man was recently tried in
Philadelphia, for stealing a goose.
He got off in consequence of a
croney swearing that he remembered the goose ever since it was
a gosling.—An Irishman, who
was arested for stealing a gun,
hearing the successful defence,
got a countryman of his to swear
that he had known the gun ever
since it was a pistol, and that it
belonged to the prisoner.

Figure 7-9: Most local newspapers in 19th century Granby were handwritten, but the Centreville Weekly News, which ran for about six months during the 1840 presidential campaign, was printed. The paper actually carried little local news.

318

cider brandy was so readily available in Granby and there was little else to drink that would keep so well. As James R. Hayes noted, "Cider Brandy which was I think the principal drink of the common people...was pretty freely used in almost every family and the Tavern a common resort for bad weather days and evenings."[122] Still, the number of times sextons noted "scirrhuses of the liver" as a cause of death, and the frequency of complaints of drunkenness - even taking into account the propensity of reformers to exaggerate - suggests that the whims of the economy were often overwhelming for the small businessmen and farmers of Granby. The Salmon Brook Historical Society has in its files bills from the 1820s to storekeeper Pliny Hillyer from his supplier in Hartford for wagon-loads of rum, and on one bill alone, he accepted 37 gallons of gin and two barrels of brandy.[123] With cider stills popping up all over the countryside, Granby citizens still felt they had to import more liquor!

Even as people struggled with hard times, however, there was no denying that there was an increasing availability of services making life easier. In addition to the first post office under Hezekiah Goodrich, new offices were added in 1828 in West Granby and North Granby, with Justus D. Wilcox and Abner Case's son Horatio, respectively, as postmasters. Instead of a once-a-week delivery, mail arrived by stage from Hartford twice a week by the 1830s.[124] The post riders and stages, contracting with the government to carry mail, also brought newspapers like the *Hartford Times* and the *Connecticut Courant*, although generally only tavernkeepers had subscriptions. And even though greater contact with the outside world had produced some turmoil and insecurity, insurance companies were coming into existence, providing a measure of security for businesses still threatened by Salmon Brook's flash floods.[125]

Medical care, such as it was, was also more available. Postmaster Justus D. Wilcox was also the village doctor in West Granby, and, although he never finished medical school, was highly regarded by his neighbors for providing the care their parents had never had.[126] Another physician, Consider Morgan, moved his practice to Granby when he bought Isaac Porter's house after Porter lost his position.[127] In North Granby, Daniel Benjamin ministered to the sick, although his reputation as Ezekiel Alderman's drinking partner raises questions about the dependability of that service.[128] At

319

Salmon Brook Street, Jairus Case started up a medical practice in 1833. Probably the most educated and "modern" of his fellow physicians in town, Case toured the town endlessly, giving advice, administering medicine, plugging teeth, setting fractures and soothing burns. His most frequent treatment was to prescribe opium, along with more than occasional bloodletting and plenty of cures with an alcohol base. We presume he returned some to health, and the rest, at least, were relieved of pain.[129]

It may have been that these conveniences, by putting Granby people in closer touch with the rest of the world and making life a little more secure, raised expectations beyond what was realistic in a community characterized by poor soil and only moderate sized watercourses. Granby farmers were not going to be able to increase their production much more, even with specialization in wool or potatoes. Their other major product, cider brandy, apparently brought as much ruin as prosperity. As for industry, it was dependent on Salmon Brook until there was capital enough to invest in steam engines; Salmon Brook dams, while plentiful, would only fill enough each day to run a piece of machinery for an hour or two. That sufficed in the 1790s for farmers supplementing their income in their shops, but would hardly sustain aspiring industrialists. Thus, Granby was as much buffeted by cross currents of regional economic dislocation as it was by competing sentiments of optimism and pessimism among its entrepreneurs.

By mid-century, political and ecological disasters, spiritual dissension, westward migration and a boom-and-bust economy, had taken their toll on Granby. For those living through the hard times of the early 1840s in this small community on the edge of Hartford County, there was much to support their sense that things were decaying. Through our eyes, there is much they should have felt good about, but they did not see the world through our eyes. We can admire their considerable fortitude in the face of serious challenges to body and spirit; yet many of them felt they were visited by the wrath of God. We are aware of some surprisingly successful enterprises; yet many of them perceived only a plague of bankruptcy. We applaud the growing diversity of churches, as established religion disappeared; but they worried about "enemies" of another faith. We welcome the idea that their community was open to newcomers and that, in turn, their times were not so restrictive that people were afraid to move around the country in search of opportunity; but they probably worried over the rapid changes in their population.

In terms of today's ideals, they were doing pretty well, considering the resources with which they were working. In terms of the industrial aspirations of many of them, success was fate's cruel bait. In terms of ideals that stressed community harmony and unity, independence from the corruption of the outside world, stability of family and relationships with one's neighbors, the virtues of sobriety, piety and hard work - the values espoused by the leaders of the generation that had seen Granby prosper during its first two decades as an independent town - things were coming apart all over the place. Of course, we know the town had never really lived up to these Puritan visions any more than it succeeded in becoming an industrial metropolis. But to those who lived through the first years after incorporation, when there was a good deal to celebrate and a sense that the dream was within reach, the ensuing years were extremely frustrating. In typical New England fashion, though, the leaders of this generation, both male and female, faced their adversity with a zeal equal to that of their predecessors in Granby.

Chapter VIII
Redeeming Salmon Brook

Chronology

Europe	America	Granby
		1812 Social Literary Society
		1813 Good Morals Society established
1814-15 Congress of Vienna reshapes Europe after Napoleonic Wars		
		1821 Salmon Brook Library revived
	1825 American Temperance Society founded	
1833 Parliament abolishes slavery in English colonies	1832 American Anti-Slavery Society founded	1832 Universalist Society founded. Youth's Temperance Society
		1834 New Congregationalist meeting-house and associated Academy constructed
1837 Victoria crowned Queen of England		
		1840 Tippecanoe Club supports Harrison for president
	1841 First degrees given to women by an American university (Oberlin)	1841 Granby Lyceum founded
		1842 West Granby Academy
	1845 Texas annexed, Oregon settlement	1845 West Granby Methodist Church builds meetinghouse
	1846 War with Mexico	1847 Universalists build meetinghouse
1848 Urban uprisings throughout Europe, *Communist Manifesto*	1848 Seneca Falls Declaration, Treaty of Guadelupe Hidalgo	1848 Rough and Ready Club supports Taylor for president
		1849 Granby Literary Association
	1850 Compromise over slavery in the territories	
	1854 Kansas-Nebraska Act	1855 Know Nothing Party organizes in Granby
	1856 Republican Party founded	
	1857 Dred Scott decision	
		1858 Turkey Hills separates to become East Granby
	1860 A. Lincoln elected President	
1860 Giuseppe Garibaldi unites Italy under King Victor Emmanuel II.	1861 Civil War begins	1861 Town enacts strict regulations for "moral" education in its schools
	1863 Battles of Gettysburg and Vicksburg	
	1865 War ends, Lincoln Assassinated	

Facing "a world of changes" in the early years of the 19th century, and uncertain of their economic future, Granby citizens involved themselves in numerous activities they hoped would "redeem Salmon Brook" from what many perceived to be a "decaying condition." Of course, what each person did to effect this redemption depended upon what it was about Granby that he or she felt was decaying. Some endeavored to reform the habits of their neighbors. Some concentrated on self-improvement. Some counted themselves among that enterprising "class" of young people who would bring prosperity to the community, while others exerted themselves in local government to find ways to deal with the poverty in their midst. As in the past, when an even smaller and more homogeneous population had responded to change, divisions developed both socially and geographically. The traditional ideal of harmony proved elusive. Only the great tragedy of the Civil War would inspire some unity of purpose, but at a terrible price.

Reviving the Spirit

On December 2, 1814, some unknown Granby chronicler recorded the death of Amasa Moor, aged 42 years. "His death," continued the record, "was Occationed by being in a Habbit of Drinking for many years and at Last by Drinking Cider Brandy by the Pint until it Destroyed his life and he became a lump of Clay."[1] There was no doubt in the mind of the author of this notice that Moor had single-handedly killed himself and that all should take heed of his fate. Over the next few decades, however, many people in Granby would come to believe that a strong will to resist the path of ruin was not easily come by for an individual. One problem they faced was that the traditional guardian of community and individual morality, the Congregational Church, was fragmented and after 1818, no longer supported by the government. Not only were there doctrinal disagreements among the various denominations which led to confusion about acceptable behavior, but piety and attendance at church were generally on the wane, particularly among men, the authority figures both at home and in the town. Some substitute was needed, - revived or new institutions which would continue to provide education, motivation and pressure on individuals to conform to standards of morality and decency.

Between the end of the War of 1812 and the middle of the century,

Granby citizens, old and young, male and female, created numerous organizations which expressed their continued desire for collective action which would renew their spiritual vigor. In "the Wedge" in North Granby, from 1812 until 1820, a group of men pooled their resources as a "Social Literary Society," to purchase books and hold discussion meetings.[2] In 1821, a larger organization of 97 men and women from all over Granby took its place reviving once again the library at Salmon Brook Street which had nearly disappeared in the aftermath of the War of 1812.[3] In West Granby, Hiram Case organized a Drum Corps in the 1820s.[4] At Salmon Brook Street in July, 1841, sixteen men, led by Dr. Jairus Case, Willard Griffin and Edmund Holcomb met at "the High School room" to create the Granby Lyceum, a discussion group dedicated to "the intellectual and moral improvement of its members." Among the topics of their discussions were capital punishment, geology, mineralogy, "intoxicating drink," abolition of slavery, and voting privileges for immigrants.[5] In 1849, this same group established the Granby Literary Association to purchase a library and encourage intellectual discussion.[6] Perhaps the most ambitious of the attempts at reform through collective action was the movement to rid the town of alcohol.

Prior to 1830, organized opposition to alcohol consumption was limited to Isaac Porter's leadership in the Congregational Church. Simsbury was home to the Simsbury Aquatics, one of the first temperance societies in the country, begun by Benjamin Ely in 1805, but aside from Granby's branch of the Connecticut Society for the Promotion of Good Morals, we have no record of any such organization in Granby in the first quarter of the century. The constitution of the Good Morals Society, signed by Porter and 45 other Granby men, declared that the object of the association was to "promote good morals, and to discountenance vice universally; particularly, to discourage profaneness, gross breaches of the Sabbath, idleness and intemperance; and especially to discourage intemperance."[7] Porter worked hard throughout his career to influence those under his tutelage to embrace sobriety, even bringing charges against parishioners for "excessive use of strong drink" in the same way he pursued those who failed to attend services. However, since such charges would result merely in a public admonition from the pulpit, or at worst, excommunication from a disestablished church led by an increasingly unpopular minister, it is unlikely Porter or his allies in the Congregational

Church experienced much success. He may have felt some encouragement when national organizations such as the American Temperance Society, an organization devoted to social order and evangelical piety, began in the mid-1820s. However, there is no record that he received much organized support outside of his own congregation. In the final year of his ministry, Porter appointed a committee to try to bring in those who had not yet pledged "total abstinence from ardent spirits," but he was soon dismissed from his position, and the movement found itself leaderless.[8]

Into the void marched the Youth's Temperance Society in Granby, founded in West Granby in 1832. This group collected and distributed reading material on the evil effects of alcohol, relying less on moral admonition than on supposed scientific data and reports of ruined families and businesses. Within their organization, they debated issues such as "Can legislation aid the cause of Temperance?" (decided in the affirmative), and rallied young people to the cause through pledges similar to Porter's. Dr. Jairus Case of Granby Street had apparently taken a leading role in the movement by 1835, delivering lectures to temperance meetings in town. He was also active in the Granby Lyceum which took a stand against "using, furnishing or vending intoxicating drink" in 1841. In 1842, temperance advocates were encouraged when Truman Allen, by then one of the most prominent men in the community, signed "the Pledge" for his family (including his children's spouses). Momentum was building to bring the matter to discussion in town meeting, as was happening elsewhere in New England. As concerned community leaders began searching for ways to reestablish traditional social bonds worn thin by rapid economic changes, they often settled on temperance thinking as a means to that end. The movement stressed self-discipline and individual perfectibility and salvation, which was consistent with emerging free market thinking and provided a guide for behavior in the unsettled decades of the early 1800s.[9]

Granby, however, was hardly the town to ban alcohol by majority vote. Its forty-one cider brandy stills brought considerable income to a town battered by economic misfortune, and all reports of the popularity of its many taverns suggest the general public would not abide prohibition. "Our hills and valleys are literally covered with brandy bearing apple trees," lamented one reformer.[10] Temperance supporters themselves were divided between those

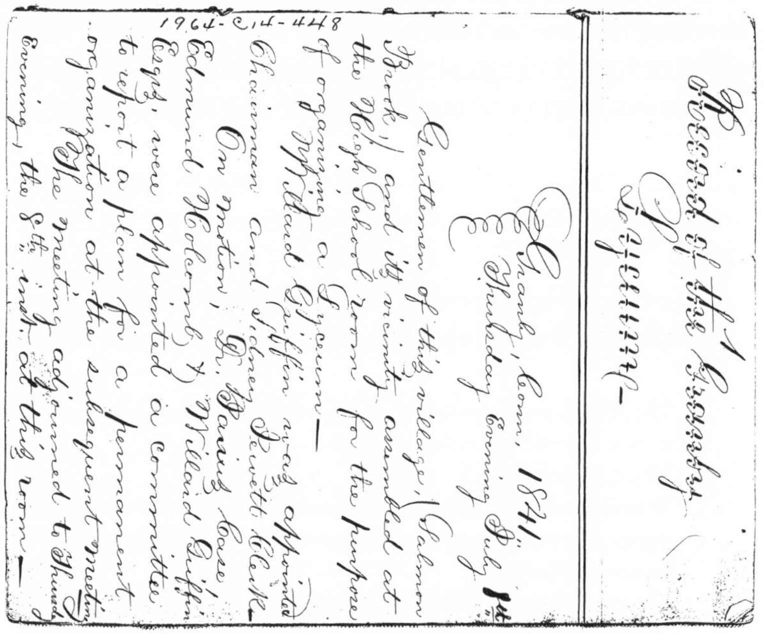
1964-C14-448

Record of the Granby Lyceum

Granby, Conn. 1841.
Thursday Evening July 1st

Gentlemen of this village (Salmon Brook) and its vicinity assembled at the High School room for the purpose of organizing a Lyceum — Willard Griffin was appointed Chairman and Abner Dewett Clerk —

On motion, D. Davis Case, Edmund Holcomb & Willard Griffin Esqs. were appointed a committee to report a plan for a permanent organization at the subsequent meeting.

The meeting adjourned to Thursday Evening, the 8th inst. at this room —

Family Temperance Pledge

We as members of the Family of Truman Allen do pledge our selves to each other to abstain from the use of all intoxicating drinks except as medicine when sick and to use our influence to stop the use of it in other Families by precept and example this pledge is to be preserved by the head of the Family during his lifetime and then to be preserved by the oldest living member of the Family

Granby January 1st 1842

Male members	Female Members
Truman Allen	Chloe Allen
Eustus L. Allen	Alma Allen
Martin Harold	Frances A. Sanders
" A. Allen	
Wm Dibble	Susan M. Allen
Henry L. Allen	
Lewis S. Allen	
Oliver Allen Jr	
John Charles Allen	

Salmon Brook Historical Society

Figure 8-1: Left: Title page of the Records of the Granby Lyceum, an organization begun in 1841 and composed of a number of temperance-minded men. Right: "The Pledge" by which members of the Truman Allen family agreed to abstain from "intoxicating drink."

who favored total abstinence from any alcohol and those who accepted the drinking of wine and hard cider. When, in 1839, the state legislature passed a bill designed to establish closer regulation of the sale of "spirits," a town meeting in Granby responded by refusing to pay attorney fees to Silas Higley and Samuel Woodruff for prosecuting Alonson Edgerton for selling liquor without a license. They further voted not to pay for any complaints on the issue of spirits in the future. Selectmen Ovil Wilcox, Anson Cooley and Oliver Alderman were unseated, and the new selectmen promptly installed seven of the town's tavern owners, including Alonson Edgerton, as grandjurors. A special town meeting early in the next year met to pass the following:

> The following Preamble and vote after considerable discussion was passed by a vote which vote was by ballott
> Nay 11, Yea 133
> Whereas we hold these truths to be self-evident, that all men are born with equal rights and that we have no right to prohibit any person from following any honest avocation
> Therefore Voted - That all persons nominated and all who may be nominated as Taverners by the Selectmen & Civil Authority During the year 1840 and all those who retailed Spirits the Last year and all other persons being inhabitants of this Town be and they are hereby permitted to Sell wines & Spiritous Liquors in Pursuance and according to the statute Law of this State.

Essentially, they invoked the Declaration of Independence and licensed the entire population of the town to sell liquor - applied retroactively to the previous year as well.[11]

In the presidential election campaign of 1840, prohibitionists were similarly frustrated in their efforts to bring an end to alcohol consumption by legislation. Political leaders were actually vying with each other for the cider vote as the Whig party successfully reinvented its image under "Old Tippecanoe" (William Henry Harrison), the "Log Cabin" candidate. At the first meeting of the Tippecanoe Club in Granby, a poetic resolution was unanimously adopted, beginning
"Resolved
That a cabin we'll build, and we will not delay
We'll build it of logs and we'll chink it with clay
A door we will make, with a latch and string

And a jug of hard cider to the work we will bring."[12]
Though limiting their libation to hard cider, a drink tolerated by many temperance supporters, they still managed to convey a rough-hewn spirit. Democrats, once the party of "the common man," and traditionally the defenders of hard cider against campaigns of total abstinence, lost an important issue - and an election. Even so, the cider brandy stills continued to multiply, producing the more potent beverage by the barrel. As each year opened, the town continued to license everyone to sell liquor.[13] None of the clergymen of Granby's churches dared speak out in favor of temperance for fear of losing parishioners. Nevertheless, reformers, although a small minority of the town, pressed on.

Their efforts must have been threatening to a good many people, for they became the object of outright violence during the next few years. Citizens attending the Granby Washington Temperance society meeting emerged to find their carriages vandalized, and in 1845 at a temperance meeting held at the Granby Academy, brass manufacturer Stephen Cornwell's carriage was mutilated by "some person or persons unknown." The following summer, after a regional Temperance Convention was held in Granby, someone put arsenic in the well of Daniel Hayes, a temperance-minded tavern keeper. No doubt the perpetrator wished to make a statement about the relative safety of drinking only water.[14]

The reformers fired back with vituperative messages in local publications, once even accusing Judge Oliver Owen of murder for supplying brandy to a man who later, in a drunken rage, shot his wife. (What made it worse, ranted an anonymous writer, was that Owen, who had sold the "liqued death," had then sat "in judgement of his own work.")[15] In September, 1846, after the well-poisoning incident, supporters of Daniel Hayes dished out their own version of the Spirit of '76 when they had the town meeting accept the following resolutions:

> Whereas we recognize in the political compact that binds us together correct principles of government and that we regard the preservation of life liberty and the pursuit of happiness as the prominent Objects of protection by government and that condign punishment be inflicted upon all violations of our laws is essentially requisite for the promotion of public as well as individual safety Therefore

<u>Resolved</u> That the late outrages committed upon the persons and property of the citizens of this town call Loudly for the aid of every individual in the town to expose and bring to Justice the offenders,

<u>Resolved</u> That we hereby Tender our warmest Sympathies to Mr. D. C. Hayes and others who have suffered by these violations of law and also our willingness to co-operate with them in prosecuting the criminals to conviction.

<u>Resolved</u> That the Selectmen of this Town offer a reward of Two hundred dollars to be paid from our Treasury to any person or persons who will arrest or cause to be arrested & bring within the Jurisdiction of our laws and furnish the requisite evidence that Shall convict the culprit who put arsenic in the well of Mr. D. C. Hayes on the night of the 23d Aug last.[16]

More often than not though, Granby's ancient tradition of political autonomy was the weapon used by the cider faction to guard its right to produce and sell liquor as jealously as a constitutional right, and it used its majority power to protect that right.

In spite of "unparalleled opposition," temperance advocates did make progress during the first half of the 19th century. Nationwide alcohol consumption had declined by over two-thirds by 1840, and intemperance, once ignored as part of a landscape in which everyone drank, had become a social sin. In fact, a great many apple orchards were abandoned by 1840.[17] In Granby, some discrimination was being exercised by 1846 by the "Civil Authority" (Justices of the Peace, Selectmen, Grand Jurors and Constables) in the licensing of retailers (Stephen Cornwell was among those licensed that year); and in 1848, a group of temperance reformers led by Truman Allen, successfully protested the licensing of Clytus Pinney, who for the past year had "kept a disorderly public house, a constant resort for idle, vicious and intemperate persons and has been during said times in constant habit as well on Sabbaths as other days selling ardent spirits." Pinney was forced to give up his business and abandoned the house in which he kept it.[18] At least one temperance advocate was not impressed, however, writing in a local publication, "Nothing of importance is going on in this great metropolis the tavern lately occupied by Mr. Clitus Pinney is now occupied by Ezekiel Alderman who will keep a worse gray hole (if possible) than Mr. Pinney kept we sincerely hope that the time may soon come when this otherwise beautiful village will be freed from the worst of curses a rum tavern if there is a law in the land let it be executed on this merciless destroyer of lives, character and happiness."[19] Other local publications continued to describe the evils of intemperance into the 1850s.[20]

In 1854, the state actually passed a prohibition law, but it was widely ignored and considered unconstitutional even by some temperance advocates.[21] Furthermore, the issue soon became submerged in the controversies arising between North and South, touched off by the issue of the extension of slavery into territories west of the Mississippi. One devotee of sobriety was soon complaining that "the Temperance Car seems to be going the other way than ahead....Granby is still the banner town for brandy making, if not for drunkenness. Our forty stills are not still, it is too profitable to make Cider Brandy."[22] It was, indeed, a lost cause in Granby, but the enduring devotion of its followers to the redemption of their neighbors is as remarkable as their opponents' determination to be free from the moralistic control of the community.

Meanwhile, citizens sought to improve their community in other ways as well. Granby's women, in particular, took the lead in reform. Freed by the industrial and transportation revolutions from many of the production tasks which had occupied so much of their mothers' and grandmothers' time before 1800, they still felt as much need as ever to make worthwhile contributions to their families and neighborhoods. The sense of liberation that had spread to women like Hannah Phelps Buttolph Post in the wake of the democratic spirit of the 1770s was not the principal ideology shaping women's aspirations in the early national period. The prevailing thinking of post-Revolutionary America recognized mothers as the primary inspiration for the "public virtue" upon which the survival of the republic was so dependent. Therefore, it is not surprising that many daughters and granddaughters of the Revolution became more active in educational and cultural pursuits, church affairs and community groups. They believed that their own education was important if they were to fulfill their role in the moral upbringing of future citizens, and, as the battle over religious toleration took its toll on "regular attendance on the Sabbath," women gradually replaced men as the moral guardians of the community at large.[23] This was not easy, for no matter how educated and active they became, linty old notions of the impropriety of female leadership and outspokenness clung stubbornly to the fabric of society.[24]

Included among the new activities of women were sewing circles, ladies aid societies, lyceums, independent reading and various evening gatherings for lectures, discussions, prayer or informal visits at neighbors' houses. In her 1835 diary, Eliza Ann Colton reported on a number of these. Not only did she attend Dr. Jairus Case's lectures on temperance, but also a few "lady sewing meetings," composed of about "30 young ladys," in one of which Dr. Case spoke on Anatomy. In another, Jefferson Cooley addressed his female audience on Astronomy. Later that year, she "attended a lyceum meting at the Academy the Rev. Mr. Bentley delivered the lecture on History."[25] Perhaps the name of the group - the "sewing meeting" - gave sufficient legitimacy to its habit of considering subjects that were once the domain of male discussions (and, in fact, only upper class male discussions). Eliza Ann's interests broadened as a result of this cultural exposure, and she was soon reading books on her own. On April 22, she reported that she "called to Mr. Holcomb and returned a book that I had borrowed it was Philosophy." In West Granby, this pursuit of learning had been institutionalized in 1830 with the formation of the Young Gentlemen and Ladies Library, an organization which purchased books for exchange among its members.[26]

As had Porter before him, Rev. Bentley of the Congregational Church found his female parishioners as responsive to evangelical preaching as they were to cultural discourse, and encouraged them to attend extra prayer meetings. Eliza Ann Colton mentioned traveling all the way to the Wintonbury (Bloomfield) schoolhouse one wintry Wednesday evening in 1834 to attend one of these prayer meetings at which the people "appeared to be much engaged." The next day, she went to another that Bentley held in Granby. Revival meetings became increasingly popular with both men and women, and in April of the following year, Eliza Ann went to "a protracted" in Granville which lasted over three weeks.[27] Ann Eliza Edwards remembered meetings such as these held at different houses on Sunday evenings. "They were usually well attended, being genuine prayer meetings." To underscore the dramatic changes she had seen in gender roles during her lifetime, she added, "More than half who attended were men, and most of them were ready to offer prayer as well as to speak. The women were not expected to take part in those days. I well remember the strangeness when they were first urged to take part and one or two did."[28] The "strangeness" soon wore off. In 1851, women were writing articles for the "Ladies Department" of "The Repository," a local handwritten collection of essays circulated around Salmon Brook Street.[29]

Girls had been attending the district schools from the start, but in the 1820s and 30s, the subject matter they studied expanded beyond reading, writing and spelling to grammar and geography as well.[30] Furthermore, they were increasingly enrolled in secondary schools. The "Academy" Eliza Ann Colton spoke of in her diary was built by members of the Congregational Church just north of their new meetinghouse, and young women were as welcome there as men. On March 25, 1834, the day the cornerstone of the church was laid, Eliza Ann "attended an Examination in the Academy heard Watson speak a peace and all the Gentlemen spoke peaces the ladies read compasitions."[31] In 1842 a group of West Granby families built an Academy on the west bank of Salmon Brook opposite the Hayes family clothing works. The shareholders of this private enterprise (paying $20 each for their shares) were not exclusively Congregationalists, but the curriculum certainly reflected the desire for moral uplifting which was inspiring all sorts of community activities at the time. Again, young women were enrolled and as studious as the young men.[32]

The opportunity to share in secondary education with men was not entirely fulfilling for young Granby women. They took well to their studies, both in the Granby academies and in private "select" schools in other towns, and undoubtedly they were encouraged by elders who understood the need for future mothers to be well schooled for the undertaking of virtuous upbringing. Still, the world outside of the academy was not changing as fast as were the minds of these young female scholars. For one thing, young women faced very clear perceptions of what was proper for women to do, and as much as they tried to open up new possibilities for themselves, they were scorned if they went too far.

In her novel, *The Female Skeptic*, Alice Hayes Mellen has her young heroine Mag, a girl experiencing the sort of childhood Alice had in West Granby in the 1830s and 40s, doing her best to keep up with her cousin Frank, always ending up the object of ridicule from his friends or her own family. This is frustrating for Mag, for she would much rather be leaping around on the academy school desks, or playing ball, than batting her eyelashes and making herself "the most delicious of all forbidden fruit" for some young man who would not respect her as an equal. To this attitude, her cousin responded:

> "What a tomboy you are anyhow Mag Barclay!" She stopped short in her
> amazement - stunned - thunderstruck. Frank's harangue astounded her - made
> her brain reel. It had never occurred to her as among the many lists of
> possibilities that her sports and employments might be separate from her cousin
> Frank's and his speech was a perfect apocalypse to her.[33]

Lydia Maria Child and Catharine Beecher, two of the most popular
writers for women in the early 19th century, cautioned their readers not to
expect that their lives would become like those of men, even as they strove to
excel in their schooling. Although it was most important for women to be
educated, they wrote, they should use their new intellectual skill to take
control of their own particular sphere of society and shape the world as only
women can. Managing a household, they assured their readers, was hardly a
secondary task, but one requiring organization, diligence, intelligence, virtue,
ambition and fortitude.[34] Alice Hayes Mellen agreed with Beecher, in spite
of her heroine's dislike for the limitations of the female role. In her preface,
she stated that she wanted her book "to show how we are the framers of our
own destinies, the materials for the work being given by the All-Father. Some
tell us that great souls control circumstances; but circumstances *must* influence and educate even the strongest souls. 'We must *work* out our salvation
(even on earth) with fear and trembling.'"[35] Indeed, Mag eventually did find
her own place in the world, as she predicted she would from the start, when
she confided to her cat, "You and I are philosophers, ain't we pussy-cat? We
don't cry over spilt milk; that we don't; 'course. Why? It don't do a bit of good
and it makes us ache which is bad and uncomfortable."[36]

Beecher's formula, however, while perhaps helpful to the growing
ranks of urban middle class women, was not necessarily the answer for rural
women. For young women in Granby, most of whom lived on a farm, life was
still filled with as much tedious toil as it was needful of virtuous thinking. If
they were spending less time churning butter or sitting before an open
fireplace or at a loom, the higher standards of housekeeping they now held
themselves to kept them busy with equally backbreaking labor.[37] One
collection of letters now stored at the Salmon Brook Historical Society
documents well the drudgery that farm life must have been to the more

educated women of the mid-19th century. Adelaide Holcomb of Bushy Hill Road carried on a great correspondence with her circle of friends, even those who lived within a mile of her house, in which they all wrote of the endless chores, their desire for intellectual challenge beyond that required to snag a husband, their need to be independent and their frustration with a world which expected so much of women, and yet offered so little to them. One friend, Amelia, wrote to Addie,

> a week's work writing would suit me.... I tell you Addie, you can't think how I hunger for [literary entertainments], sometimes my mind seems as barren as though I were shut out from all intercourse with another mind. I cannot read half as much as I used to and often these long evenings seem so long, as my brain tires of its pent up thoughts and my fingers are busy with the knitting needles.[38]

Addie had apparently been having the same thoughts, for a few days before she had written in her diary:

> One day resembles another, and all have heavy, lifeless physiognomies... meantime life wears away - I'm so old and as yet have done nothing. Sometimes I get so blue at the prospect before and behind. Yet it is wrong and foolish to repine. Undoubtedly my duty directs me to stay at home. I feel as if I was buried here. I long to work or live a life of action that will be appreciated, to be independent of friends.[39]

This was an exceptional moment in a diary containing daily entries about household chores. At one point that spring she entered, "I have been baking nearly all day - hope I shall someday be able to write something besides I've ironed, baked or washed..."[40] This was in April, 1862, when Addie was twenty-four years old, unmarried as yet, and sitting by in Granby, as men fought to save the union from the secessionists, destroy "the Slave Power" and so on. It is little wonder she and her friends felt unhappy with their assigned role. They had grown up in families which had seen to it that they could read, write and think. In lyceums, prayer meetings, singing schools, temperance lectures and sewing circles, their community had encouraged them to take on the forces of immorality, intemperance and ignorance; and what were they doing during the greatest moral struggle the nation had ever faced? Ironing, baking and washing.

As Ann Eliza Edwards has informed us in her comments about the attendance of males at Sunday evening prayer meetings, men as well as women were concerned about the moral redemption of Granby. There were the temperance-minded leaders like Stephen Cornwell, Truman Allen and Jairus Case; and there were many others who saw their work with one church or another, or with other organizations not necessarily connected with the temperance movement, as an effort to bring about the moral uplifting of their neighbors. In this regard, the building of the Methodist meetinghouse in West Granby and of the Universalist meetinghouse on North Granby Road is particularly significant.

"The Methodists," wrote historian Noah Phelps in 1845, "in the aggregate, compose a numerous class, and have a number of places of holding their religious meetings."[41] In the Copper Hill area, now in East Granby, a small group had built its own meetinghouse in 1839. In West Granby, they had been meeting since the beginning of the century - first in a meetinghouse south of the village and then in the district schoolhouse near the junction of Higley and Hartland Roads.[42] Phelps noted, though, that this West Granby group was currently building a new meetinghouse for itself in 1845.

The records of the West Granby Methodists suggest that this construction actually marked a "rebirth" of the church in West Granby. The squabbles over the new Congregationalist meetinghouse in the early 1830s had resulted in a temporary boost in Methodist attendance in West Granby, but then interest had begun to lag until after another dispute among Congregationalists over seating in the choir.[43] In 1844, a newly gathered congregation created the Methodist Episcopal Society of West Granby "for the promotion of the best good of this community," noting "the importance of having a house of public worship and believing that the worship of Almighty God is due from Every rational and intelligent being."[44] After meeting for a year in Elam Kendall's inn (one meeting had a hundred people present), and spending much of that time in the traditional bickering over the precise location of the meetinghouse, the group voted to contract with a Mr. Baldwin to construct the building "in a swamp above Nearing's Store."[45]

The architecture of the meetinghouse is, perhaps, as significant as the gathering of a reborn congregation, and in fact, expressed that rebirth clearly (See Figure 8-2). Elements of Greek Revival style had appeared in construc-

335

tion in Granby as early as the 1820s. In other parts of the country the use of pillars and the heavy entablature of classical civilizations was common even in the Federal Era when leaders of the new nation traced the roots of their republican beliefs to ancient Greece and Rome.[46] The new Granby Congregationalist meetinghouse itself contained some classical elements. The Methodist meetinghouse, however, represented some new and complex sentiments for the Greek Revival tradition. For one thing, the building, with its corner boards in the form of pillars, its columns on a recessed porch, its triangulated gable under which was a full pediment, and its long windows with amber glass, made no apologies for decoration. Unlike the timid efforts at classical revival made in previous decades by Puritan farmers' descendants eager not to appear ostentatious, this building was a veritable temple. Though wooden and a degree smaller than the Congregationalist Church, it was clearly designed to be both fashionable and expressive of a new mentality - one which embraced both democracy - for these middling farmers and artisans aspired toward the status of the wealthier Congregationalists - and more importantly, moral revival.

It was built by many of the same people whose children were sent to Miss T. C. Hutchinson at the West Granby Academy to write essays such as "Superior Merit when assumed is lost," "Think not the Almighty wills one needless tear," "Prospects for our Country," "Men may learn wisdom from the works of Nature," "High station does not secure Happiness," and "Friendship consummated in Heaven."[47] These parishioners wanted to be stylish, they wanted to attract a larger membership and most of all, they wanted to reinvigorate their little village so that it would provide an environment of virtue and good character for their children. Struggle as they might over the next fifteen years to pay for the church and keep an active congregation together, they were determined that all of the bad luck and broken businesses of the preceding decade not result in a decaying and run-down village rotting by the banks of an unforgiving brook. In 1860, a Ladies Aid Society was formed and raised the money needed to purchase lamps, an organ made by Peter Jewett of Salmon Brook Street, and a parsonage.

In Goodrichville and North Granby, the same sentiment flourished among the Universalists, who had also gained some communicants in the early 1840s as a result of the Congregational choir controversy. Their Ladies

Aid Society, or "Sewing Circle," as it was called, was established in 1843 to raise money for the church, but it was not confined to ladies. Men like Elizur and Hezekiah Goodrich were among its membership, probably to assist with the principal money making activity, the sewing of shoes.[48]

In 1845, the year after the Methodists voted to build their meetinghouse, the Universalist Society made its decision to build one for themselves and selected a location less than half a mile north of the Congregationalist Church. Action on the plan was speeded up when the Congregationalists refused to allow the Universalists to use their meetinghouse for a funeral that was too large for the old Baptist meetinghouse, and in 1847, the Universalists built their own little temple, nearly identical to the West Granby Methodist Church, on land donated by Hezekiah Goodrich (See Figure 8-4).[49] There must have been an exhilarating musical rivalry on Sunday mornings between the Universalists and the Congregationalists, the latter having finally decided, after lengthy discussions and efforts to "harmonize the society," to add a bass

Salmon Brook Historical Society

Figure 8-2: West Granby Methodist Episcopal Meetinghouse, built in 1845. It was torn down in 1978 when the church built a new building farther south on Simsbury Road.

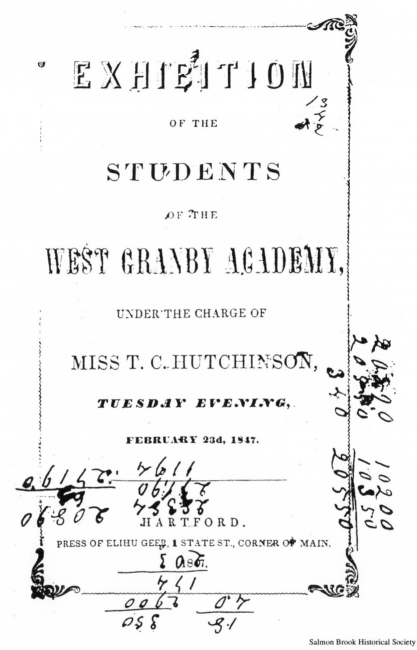

Salmon Brook Historical Society

Figure 8-3: The West Granby Academy was constructed in 1842 as a private secondary school. This program was for its 1847 commencement.

violin to their choir loft (in fact, after 1848 they used the Peter Jewett organ they purchased from the old Episcopalian Church).[50]

The Universalists may have been engaged in reform beyond spiritual revival, for Universalists nationally were known for their belief in active involvement in the reformation of society. In the late 1840s, the most popular cause in New England was abolition of slavery. Interest had grown after the Mexican War, another unpopular war in New England because it was perceived as an effort to expand the power of southern plantation owners. When Mexico ceded half its territory to the United States in the 1848 Treaty of Guadelupe Hidalgo, Congress faced the great question of whether slavery would be permitted in the new territories. The result, after much wrangling, was the Compromise of 1850, which among other things, included the Fugitive Slave Act.[51] Before these developments, abolitionists were the radicals of New England society, but when the issue became one of the *expansion* of slavery, and of the *protection* of slave owners as they mercilessly hunted down runaway slaves, moderate New Englanders, including some of the better educated citizens in Granby, responded with horror and indignation.[52] Were the Universalists of Granby, who were committed to *active* reform, involved in antislavery efforts?

This is a question that will, perhaps, remain a mystery for some time. The history of the anti-slavery movement, once it entered into the phase of the underground railroad, is sketchy at best. Those who assisted fugitive slaves did so at great risk, and, after 1850, in violation of federal law. They were not about to keep detailed records. According to one historian, there were agents in the Farmington Valley, like Phineas Gabriel of Avon and Elijah Lewis, and some other unidentified person of Simsbury. These agents operated throughout the region in a network set up to carry fugitives "north along the Farmington River, perhaps as far as Granby or West Suffield," and then to move them across the Massachusetts line into Granville or Southwick.[53] We have no names of individuals in Granby, but the Hezekiah Goodrich house on North Granby Road has some strange walls in its cellar, and his son Elizur's house, across the road, has a hidden compartment in a closet under the stairs. In 1848, the Goodriches were known for their "Free Soil" sympathies. That is, they supported the party which opposed expansion of slavery into the territories, and in the Civil War and Reconstruction years they were strict

339

Figure 8-4: First Universalist Society Meetinghouse constructed in 1847 on North Granby Road, later a school, and now the American Legion Hall.

Republicans, the party of Lincoln.[54] This is all circumstantial evidence, but it does appear that this family of Universalists took seriously the mandate to work actively for the country's moral improvement.

There was a spirit of reform alive in Granby in the early 19th century. There was disagreement, some of it violent, about how best to lead lives and regulate personal affairs, but the spirit was infectious nonetheless. It permeated religious activities, public gatherings, writings, conversations, schools and meetinghouses. At revivals, lectures, temperance meetings, discussion groups, academy exhibitions and the gatherings of many other organizations, men and women worked hard to revive the moral vigor they supposed had once characterized the lives of their predecessors. None of these initiatives alone involved a majority of Granby citizens, and that was probably why none was completely successful. Nevertheless, the effect of each was disproportionate to its numbers, and it seemed anyway, that participation was, all along, more important than victory.

Reviving the Community

When editors "Jewett and Dibble" wrote in the *Centreville Weekly News* of the "new class of young men" that was "coming on the scene" in 1840 to "redeem Salmon Brook from its decaying condition," they were thinking not only of the bright-eyed reformers who were taking up the work the Congregational Church had once done to insure the health of each and every soul. They probably also had in mind people like Stephen Cornwell and the children of Hezekiah Goodrich and Truman Allen. The editors, although good Whigs who would soon debate social issues in the Granby Lyceum, understood that it would take more than institutions of moral reformation to revive the community as a whole. A healthy economy, with "one or two manufactories" would be as much a cure for what ailed their town as anything else, they thought. Over the next two decades a sizable number of people would attempt to join the ranks of the "enterprising" in Granby, a movement memorialized by the architecture of their houses. Yet, while the spirit was there in individual cases, it did not create a bond for the community nor a well of prosperity which would sustain the townspeople in hard times.

The Goodriches' habit of hiring immigrant Irish laborers to work in their tanning and shoemaking operations probably irked some of their neighbors as much as the cider distilling that was going on further north on the road to Granville. Nevertheless, the family could hardly be denied its prominent place in Granby's business community. Even as their father, the crusty old tanner of Granby's post-revolutionary generation, gradually settled into retirement in the 1830s, Hezekiah's three sons, as "Goodrich Brothers," took on the business and added their own investments. By 1850, Elizur Goodrich could claim a $3000 water-powered tanning works, putting out $5000 of finished leather per year from ten tons of hides and paying $70 per month to his three laborers. By 1860, his investment had grown to $5000 in machinery and inventory. His house, a fashionable Greek Revival with a recessed side porch, spoke of his ambition to be as successful as his father had been. His brother, Hezekiah Goodrich Jr., also expanded his business of doing piecework for Truman Allen. In 1850, he made 1000 pairs of shoes, but only took in $800 on them.[55]

Truman Allen himself remained quite active in various businesses. Although he had turned over the day-to-day shoe business to his children in the 1840s, he continued to guide its expansion, dealing with Calvin B. Dibble, who had set himself up in Newbern, North Carolina, as a distributor of all kinds of manufactured goods from his native New England. Allen also remained one of Granby's leading investors. After the demise of Stephen Cornwell's brass foundry and Orin H. Lee's satinette mill in Mechanicsville, Allen re-tooled these mill buildings in 1854 to process raw cotton. He also had a grist mill there, while retaining a share of the grist mill at the Cragg.[56]

In West Granby, industrial revivalists were busy as well. Trumbull Wilcox, a young blacksmith who had had to endure poverty as a boy when his father had died prematurely, opened a shop of his own on the site of the old scythe factory nearly opposite the West Granby cemetery. His new house across the road, built in 1837, was also a Greek Revival (See Figure 8-5). It was not quite as elaborate as Elizur Goodrich's, but a Greek nonetheless. Built nearly on top of the north boundary line of the lot he had purchased from the heirs of Alpheus Hayes, it left room for a row of dwellings that would one day, perhaps, house his employees. He had more in mind than becoming the village blacksmith, and he worked with his neighbor Edward Hayes to specialize in carriage manufacturing - Trumbull produced the wheel rims. However, when Edward Hayes went bankrupt, Trumbull lost his principal customer. In 1845, he took out a mortgage on the house he must have saved for for a decade, but in two years was behind in payments. Forced to sell, he moved into more modest accommodations up the street opposite the house of his brother, Dr. J.D. Wilcox.[57]

To West Granby's rescue came Matthew and Sherman Fancher, whose vision of a carriage factory ignored the village's dismal business history. In 1847, Matthew, who had recently returned from a few years in Catskill, New York, bought Trumbull Wilcox's house (50 Simsbury Road). At the same time, Sherman bought Edward Hayes's (46 Simsbury Road). Across the road, they added on to Hayes's old shops and rented Trumbull Wilcox's, making three small factories, one producing the hardware for the carriages, one turning out the wheels and the third, building the carriages themselves, just like Ezekiel Alderman's operation in North Granby where they had been trained. They contracted with two local painters, Lucien Reed and Sylvester Parmalee, to paint and varnish the finished products. To their employees, they paid top dollar, $5 to $8 per week, and sold wheels and carriages for all classes: "Cheep wheels" for $6 a set, "Best wheels with bent rim" for $8.50. "Buggy wagons" went for $50 to $75. Sherman logged through sixty wagons and carriages per year, and in 1850, had nine employees working under him. Matthew's operation was separate, technically, but the wheels and carriages were transferred back and forth on accounts at cost as they moved from building to building. Business did not exactly boom, but they employed a lot of people and surely it must have *sounded* as though they were busy.[58]

Carlton Holcomb, a shoemaker who had probably been trained by his Uncle Hezekiah in Goodrichville before setting up for himself in West Granby in 1840, took his cue from the Fanchers. In 1853, he bought land on the brook just below the Fancher carriage works and planned to expand his shoe shop from his own property farther south on "the county road" (Simsbury Road). His house (68 Simsbury Road - See Figure 8-6), though only one-and-one-half stories, was also an imposing "temple" - celebrating not only the revival of style, but also of enterprise. (No doubt it principally celebrated his marriage to Eliza Ann Wilcox, the 1847 valedictorian of the West Granby Academy, and a product of the other sort of revival being undertaken in Granby at this time.)[59]

Inside these domestic monuments to revival, Granby residents continued to express their aspirations for improvement. They added curtains to their windows, carpets on their floors, paint to their woodwork and decorations on their walls. In Isaac Porter's old house on 45 Bushy Hill Road (built in 1719 by Nathaniel Holcomb III) Consider Morgan, a medical doctor, enlarged a borning room on the south end of the keeping room, perhaps for a sunny examining room, and decorated the plastered walls with a stenciled pattern consisting of large circles around floral designs and a bell-and-tassle frieze with swags and pendants as a top border and vines along the baseboards and doors. Of course, not everyone was as well off as Morgan, who not only practiced medicine, but held stock in railroads. Walls and floors in most houses would go bare and unpainted for some time.[60]

In spite of all the efforts, spiritual, cultural, industrial and decorative, to "redeem Salmon Brook from its decaying condition," Granby continued to

343

Mark Williams

Figure 8-5: The Trumbull Wilcox House (c. 1837) at 50 Simsbury Road in West Granby is an example of early Greek Revival domestic architecture.

struggle for revival as a community, right up to the beginning of the Civil War. Nowhere is this continuing struggle more apparent than in the town's collective response to its one other major responsibility besides road and bridge maintenance: care for those who could not care for themselves.

Poverty was a growing regional problem as resources became scarce, but throughout the 19th century there was little thought given to regional solutions. As was true of other New England states in the early 1800s, Connecticut continued to deal with the problem of poverty as though its towns were the Puritan vision of insular covenanted communities. Since the 17th century, each town had been held responsible for taking care of its own poor. "Its own poor" was defined as those paupers who were legal inhabitants of that town.[61] As we learned in Chapter VI, non-inhabitants who could not take care of themselves were carted over the town boundary line on the assumption that other towns would just as quickly send any Granby natives back home should they become a "public burden." As for the paupers who were legal inhabitants, they found themselves under the "care" of the lowest bidder or, if they could work, under an "overseer," who would, for a fee, see that they made ends meet.

Prior to the War of 1812 most towns, including Granby, managed to finance the care of their poor through the vendue system without resorting to heavy taxes. Part of the reason for this relative degree of success was that most people, no matter how miserable their standard of living, did own some land and could be expected to survive on it - thus the problem of poverty was solved by not recognizing it existed, except in extreme cases. As economic trouble followed the Embargo of 1807 and the British blockade of 1812-14, however, and as the disasters after the war began to pile up, all towns had to face the fact that the care of paupers would be a significant expense to meet each year. In 1813, the legislature authorized towns to build "poor houses," or "poor farms," so they might meet this expense more efficiently by housing all the paupers under one roof.

Mark Williams

Figure 8-6: The Carlton Holcomb House (c. 1845) at 68 Simsbury Road in West Granby.

Granby had actually already adopted this policy to some extent two years earlier when Isaac Phelps Jr. and Ashbel Holcomb had contracted to keep all eleven of the town's paupers. Over the next decade, the number of town poor increased as its population increased and the depression began. Just as the town was least able to collect the revenue needed to support these indigent souls, the need was at its greatest. Even as late as 1827, the town was looking to the selectmen of East Windsor to pay expenses for a woman from that town who had married a Granby man and was "very sick with the consumption" after he had died.[62] This was a town guarding every penny of welfare money.

It was at this time that New Englanders began to distinguish between the "deserving" and "undeserving" poor. The "deserving" included the aged, the infirm, orphans who could not be apprenticed, the insane and the chronically ill, - in other words those judged as having arrived at their impoverished condition through no fault of their own or of their immediate family. As for the "undeserving," they were those who had reached their destitution through mismanagement, intemperance, laziness or some other such behavior that they should have avoided. They were "undeserving" of public support, or sympathy for that matter, and should be subjected to hard labor as a cure, or as a punishment, or simply as a way of eliminating their dependence on tax revenues few towns could raise. In fact, in the 1820s, few towns could raise enough even for their "deserving" poor. Families leaving for the West were not around to care for aging parents, taxpayers everywhere were seeking relief, ministers no longer commanded the respect to be able to order parishioners to look after the less fortunate, and groups of women were only beginning to define their new roles as rescuers of the distressed in the community. Only a few organizations, such as the Connecticut Medical Society, which established the Connecticut Retreat for the insane in Hartford in 1821, were active in the field of poor relief.[63]

In Granby, the growing number of paupers was placing significant strain on the community as a whole. As those who were moving west knew, there was little land available in the crowded town, and few employment opportunities among its increasingly idle manufacturing establishments. Even if the "undeserving" were appointed an overseer, where would they be put to work? Furthermore, few of the town's solvent farmers could afford to spend time prodding an indigent person to feed himself. There is evidence, in the proximity of discussions of the "town poor" to tumultuous town meetings over dividing the town east and west, that by 1823 those supporting themselves were expressing a good deal of resentment over how much the town was asking them to pay for the support of others. The paupers were largely concentrated in Salmon Brook Society, and the farmers of Turkey Hills Society would have been happy to shed this expense by becoming a separate town. Efforts to appease Turkey Hills by once again guaranteeing that their meetinghouse would be the site of one-third of annual meetings and seeking annexation of the Southwick "Jog" to increase the tax base, apparently settled the matter temporarily, and at the November, 1823 meeting, the selectmen secured "discretionary Power to let out the Town poor for any Length of time as they think propper."[64]

In 1827, however, the two issues were back on the agenda, bound together again. After a vote to limit the number of selectmen to three (probably Turkey Hills men had hoped a larger board would give them more say in day-to-day administration of town affairs) the meeting was "dissolved," and then inexplicably reconvened to debate the support of paupers. Finally a motion passed,

> That the Select men of the Town of Granby be authorized to Contract with any individual to support the paupers of the Town of Granby with food Clothing fire wood and all other articles necessary for their support for any Length of time not exceeding four years from the 20th novr next and also to Establish the house to be furnished by the Contractor for said paupers as a work house or house of Correction to be furnished by said Contractor at his own Expense for the time aforesaid and the person so Contracted with to provide good and Sufficient bonds with such surety as said Select men will accept for the faithfull performance of the Contract so by them to be made and also to furnish food Clothing fire wood and other necessary for those Confined by due process of Law in said house of Correction or worke house according to the Statute Law of this State the work house or house of Correction to be Established as soon as said Select Men think proper and said work house when Established Shall be Considered as Established by said town.[65]

What is interesting about this motion, beyond its association with the chronic issue of division of the town, is the use of the terms "work house" and "house of correction." That these are indicated as synonymous with "poor house" reveals a growing sentiment that the primary function of the town's poverty program had become the supervision of the "undeserving" poor. Furthermore, the "contractor" had to be fairly prosperous to afford the "good and Sufficient bonds with such surety as the said Select men will accept." It would need to be a commercial farmer who was skilled at making efficient use of human and natural resources to extract profit. They found these qualities in Orson P. Phelps, a Turkey Hills farmer.[66] Apparently a no-nonsense "House of Correction" for the poor was the price Salmon Brook was expected to pay to keep Turkey Hills from agitating further over dividing the town. Phelps would see to it that those who could work would work, and perhaps even support those who could not, while his contracted fee paid for his supervision.

Over the next three decades, the town changed contractors a number of times as the expense of keeping the poor showed no sign of letting up. In 1840, Willis Reed, who lived at what is now 152 East Street in North Granby, operated the "work house" with forty paupers under his charge. By the late 1840s, Ahira Merriam of Silver Street in North Granby had the contract. Merriam had also won a contract for keeping state paupers, or Connecticut residents who had no "settlement" in any town, and his combined business was watched very carefully by selectmen who feared that Granby might somehow be paying for the support of non-Granby paupers. According to Merriam's account book, he was paying money to physicians for Simsbury and East Granby paupers. He charged the town $16.57 for each Granby pauper for a year, money Granby taxpayers wanted spent on their paupers alone. That the "state paupers" on his farm were mostly insane Irish immigrants, may have had something to do with this concern.[67]

As the population of the town declined, so too did its population of paupers, although not in proportion to the decline in the tax base. The drain on the treasury continued to be stressful, especially after the separation of East Granby in 1858. In 1860, Wilbert Reed, son of the 1840 contractor, was caring for 17 town paupers in a house on the corner of Mountain Road and North Granby Road in North Granby. A few years later, the town contracted with Anson Cooley and Francis Newton of North Granby, striking a bargain to pay $450 per year to the two, plus allowing Newton "the labor of all the paupers that may belong to said Town during said term of time." In return

348

Cooley and Newton promised medical care, food and shelter, "kind and humane" treatment and when necessary, a decent burial.[68]

There was probably never any doubt among Granby residents, many of whom must have at times, felt they were not far from the poor house themselves, that there had to be a better way. During the 1850s, the town had met a number of times to consider alternatives, one of which was to establish a town-run "work house," rather than using a private contractor. Nothing came of this before the Civil War, however, and the town continued to pay local contractors.[69] In 1866, the town again considered a proposal to investigate the purchase of a town-owned and operated farm, but once again postponed the matter.[70] Throughout the 19th century, the town poor, both "undeserving" and "deserving," were subject to accommodations neither group deserved, but apparently all that their neighbors could afford.

In the late 1850s, hard times returned again, and few of the "enterprising" young men who had built the Greek Revival houses and opened up new shops in the 1840s, escaped the downturn. Elizur and Hezekiah Goodrich, in spite of the large inventories they cited to the 1860 census marshall, identified themselves to that same marshal as "farmers" when asked their occupation. In West Granby, Carlton Holcomb was forced to sell off the brook property where he had hoped to build a bustling shoe factory, and Sherman Fancher packed up and took his work elsewhere, leaving his brother Matthew in West Granby to struggle with creditors for the rest of his life. Even Truman Allen told the 1860 census marshall he was a farmer. In 1863, he turned over his cotton and grist mills at Mechanicsville to John and Robert Forsyth, who continued to run the grist mill and a saw mill. The brass foundry, woolen mill and cotton mill were only memories.[71]

Not only were these manufacturers hurt by another "bust" in the wildly gyrating business cycle of the early 19th century, but they were competing against steam technology - and their credit was all used up. While Matthew Fancher ran his water-powered saw a maximum of two hours per day, his competitors sold wheels as good as his "Best Wheels" for the same price he was selling "Cheep Wheels." Even demand for gun carriages after 1861 did not extend to West Granby. After Elizur Goodrich died prematurely in 1860 and his widow decided to return to her native New York State, nine-year-old John K. Goodrich scribbled a note inside the hidden compartment in

349

Elizur Goodrich's hall closet that said it all: "Goodbye Connecticut." Goodrichville, and Granby's age of enterprise, had passed its prime.

Divisions

Unity of purpose was no more a characteristic of Granby politics in the early 19th century than it was of Granby religious, social or economic life. The farmers of Turkey Hills continued to press for separation and were finally successful on the eve of the Civil War. The age-old east-west enmity was hardly the only feud in town, though. Alignments with national political parties produced acrimonious debates within Salmon Brook and realignments in the 1850s, only made matters worse. At the root of the tensions were both geographical and socio-economic divisions which had emerged from the years of growth prior to the War of 1812. Harmony, always considered crucial to community health in New England, was never more than an ideal in Granby. Even the struggle "to save the Union" would unite the town only briefly and at terrible cost.[72]

Both social and economic concerns were at the root of the separation movement in Turkey Hills. Set up as a separate parish from the start, the farmers east of the ridge had always held that they had little in common with the people of Salmon Brook. Their leaders were a conservative group of commercial farmers who undoubtedly viewed their brandy-distilling, argumentative townsmen to the west as rough, untutored men who used the power of the majority to do as their whims directed. They resented paying the majority of taxes when their roads and meetinghouse required little upkeep, and they had to remind the town meeting constantly of its obligation to hold a third of its meetings in their village.[73] Ironically, they were probably opposed in their efforts to break away by a good number of people of Salmon Brook parish who had similar feelings about the unsavory qualities of their own neighbors. These were the self-appointed reformers of Salmon Brook who did not wish to end up as an even smaller minority in their struggle to make their town temperate, or simply more civilized.

Between 1823 and 1856, there were only a few attempts to petition the legislature for separation. In 1842, Edward Thompson and Apollos Gay led efforts to annex Turkey Hills to Windsor or to Suffield, but neither plan succeeded. Nine years later, a change in the method of allocating town highway money resulted in another attempt to annex Turkey Hills to Windsor. The issue of taxation for highways and bridges continued to fester, as did disputes over the number of town officers and the paying for repairs on the old Episcopalian meetinghouse now used solely for town meetings.[74] When Windsor Locks separated from Windsor in 1854 however, Turkey Hills separatists finally thought their time had come. They also were stirred up by an 1856 law which had eliminated the school societies. These had previously been organized by the state and funded from the income from the state School Fund established in the 1790s with the revenue from the sale of the Western Reserve lands. Now each town was to have a single board of education and was empowered to use its property tax to help finance its schools. Once again, Turkey Hills farmers thought, they would be paying for the public welfare of Salmon Brook.

In 1857, John J. Viets brought a petition to the legislature complaining of "unnecessary expense and delay in getting our school business transacted." When Windsor Locks agreed to give up a small portion of its territory to the new town, the Senate agreed to the new town of Fremont, named after the recently unsuccessful Republican presidential candidate. The House balked at the name, however, and probably was also concerned about a petition against the new town brought by Salmon Brook's Jairus Case and signed by 300 others. The bill of incorporation was sent to a conference committee where it died. At the annual town meeting, Salmon Brook residents tried to engineer some concessions regarding town officers and paupers in order to mollify the separatists, but the measures proposed did not pass. The following year, Viets was back with several supporting petitions and convinced the Senate that "there is a strong, alienated state of feeling existing between the inhabitants in the two localities, so that the rights of the one are not properly respected by the other in town matters." The Senate committee took note of Daniel Hayes's petition with 326 signatures objecting to dividing the town, as well as an opposing petition from Windsor Locks, but moved to incorporate the town of East Granby anyway. Thus, after seventy-two years of unpleasant union, one town became two (See Map 8-1). The conservatives of Salmon Brook had lost moral support in town meetings, and the remaining town of Granby, even though reduced by only one-third in population, had lost nearly

351

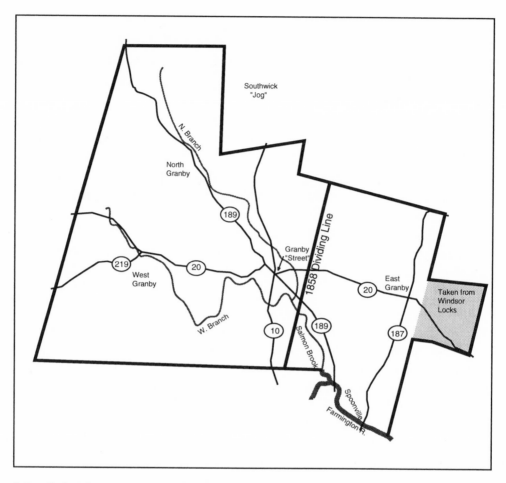

Map 8-1: The Separation of East Granby from Granby in 1858. The shaded area shows that part of Windsor Locks which was added to East Granby. Current state highways are labeled.

half of its tax base.[75]

      More intense political divisions were present even within the Salmon Brook parish. In the early 1800s, Salmon Brook had been divided between conservatives who had wanted to establish communal morality and propriety around the Congregational Church and those who had chafed at the reins of the old order and sought religious toleration and individual freedom. For a time, an uneasy alliance between Congregational leaders and Episcopalians, in agreement that society should be run by "the better sort," kept national partisan politics from affecting local politics to a great extent. Because of population turnover and changing state politics, political alignments in Salmon Brook changed often between 1810 and 1830. After the emergence of a second national two-party system in the 1830s, however, partisanship increasingly became the norm in local affairs.

Most responsible for the rise of partisanship was the willingness of the conservatives of that time to engage in political campaigns. The policy of the Jackson administration, they were convinced, would result in disunion of the states, the prostration of the Supreme Court and the ruin of "the manufacturing interest." Where their predecessors of the 1790s and early 1800s had been disdainful of such activity, preferring to "stand" for office, the Whigs, as they called themselves, had discovered that in the 1830s such aloofness was no way to defeat the Jacksonian Democrats.[76] The 1840 presidential campaign marked the full-scale emergence of modern presidential politics complete with posters, parades, slogans and nominating conventions. Now that most states had popular election of presidential electors (rather than selection by the legislature), candidates for the nation's highest office, and their supporting organizations, had to make direct appeals to the voters. In Granby, many of those who had responded to the changes of the 1830s by organizing reform activities of one sort or another identified with the Whig party. Particularly at Salmon Brook Street, support for Henry Clay had been strong, and men like Silas Higley, Joshua Jewett, Alonzo Phelps, Calvin B. Dibble and Jairus Case embraced the "Tippecanoe and Tyler Too" ticket vigorously in 1840. They were joined by a few men from other villages, all of whom felt that having the popular Indian fighter William Henry Harrison at the head of the ticket would usher in a new age of republican propriety and moral reform.[77]

Their *Centreville Weekly News* began the campaign with informative little articles on affairs of state, including tactful condemnations of England's expansionist policies (Whigs were sometimes accused of being sympathetic toward England, a sentiment that would never earn votes in Granby). The editors also tossed out a few barbed references to "Loco-Focos."[78] The Loco-Focos were a faction of the Democratic party originally called the Equal Rights Party. At first composed of urban working men, this faction had

353

latched onto the Jacksonian rhetoric lauding the "common man," but wanted the party to push harder for democratic reforms that would benefit the working class. They had taken their new name when Tammany Hall Democrats in New York had once tried to quell their efforts to take control of a city convention by extinguishing the lights. The Equal Rights insurgents had re-lit the hall immediately using Loco-Focos, the new sulphur matches. To the Whigs, who had once tried unsuccessfully to woo the Equal Rights faction away from the Democratic Party, their noisy, sometimes riotous demonstrations represented the worst of democratic politics and presaged the demise of the republic in a tumult of demagoguery and mob rule. According to one Whig writer, they were "a disgusting assemblage of unwashed democracy, a...jailbird-resembling gang of truculent loafers...."[79]

Whether the Granby Democrats called themselves Loco-Focos is not known, since most of our sources are those saved by families of the Whigs. In fact, it is not clear that the Democratic Party was all that well organized in Granby, or that party affiliations were very important prior to 1840. The newly organized "Tipacanoe Club," however, had obviously identified a large group in need of political reformation and habitually referred to all non-Whigs as Loco-Focos. Undoubtedly they used the term in a derogatory sense. Having built a log cabin near Stony Hill to memorialize candidate Harrison's humble beginnings, the Whigs merrily suggested,

"That each Locofoco who heartily wishes
In this noble work to have something to do
Shall repent of his sins before he begins
And join the fam'd Club of Tipacanoe."[80]

Though it was jollied up for popular appeal, this associating of non-Whigs with an urban mob faintly reflects the pining of a pious and educated class for a more respectable political climate. On the surface though, the Whigs probably played more on the economic anxieties of the current depression (which Congregational ministers were blaming on sinfulness anyway), and tied the downturn directly to President Van Buren. After the election Whig leaders organized the Granby Lyceum to continue to discuss an agenda geared toward the redemption of society from its decaying condition. For the moment they equivocated on the issue of abolition of slavery, refraining from calling for immediate abolition, but demanding that petitions for abolition be heard in Congress.[81] Thus, they joined with Whigs nationally to create a party which would not alienate conservatives in the South who might swing their states away from the Jacksonians.

Their opponents in Granby, after seeing Van Buren go down in defeat in the 1840 election, along with numerous other local candidates who were friendly to cider-brandy distilling, responded with their own form of organization. By the next year, Granby was electing staunch Democrats and anti-temperance men to the legislature and, as we have seen, controlling local policy as well. Erastus Holcomb, a Whig from Turkey Hills, managed to win a seat in the legislature in 1843, but the Democrats were back in 1844, raising a Hickory Tree in North Granby in honor of Jackson and in support of James K. Polk who had pledged to take Oregon ("Fifty-four forty or fight!").[82] Thus, Granby became a two-party town in the 1840s, and, because of the persistence of temperance Whigs, national issues tangled tightly with the local agenda.

Then things became ugly. This was the case nation-wide. The annexation of Texas, the Mexican War and the acquisition of California and New Mexico brought the question of the extension of slavery to a head. Proposals for compromise met with great resistance in Congress, and northern Democrats were hard pressed to defend their association with slaveholding southerners. Whigs were also in a difficult position. In Connecticut, so-called "Carriage Whigs" (as opposed to "Conscience Whigs") worried publicly that the abolitionist crusade would not only divide the party, but also ruin business. The state depended on the South for markets for its carriages, shoes and clothing.[83] In 1848, the Whig presidential nominee was General Zachary Taylor, a slaveholder and a hero in the conquest of Mexico. However, wrote William C. Case, the proprietor of "The Whig of New England," a handwritten Granby newspaper, New England Whigs would support Taylor only because Taylor would run better than Henry Clay. The Mexican War, associated as it was with the extension of slavery, meant nothing but trouble to the party. There was also concern about working class unrest, not only in Europe where full-fledged revolutions had erupted, but even in American cities which might soon become the scene of similar violence. Meanwhile, even Granby seemed to the Whigs to be infected by the blight of Irish immigration that threatened to install Catholicism as a national religion once the Irish took over the Democratic party.[84] A "Rough and Ready Club," composed of "friends of Taylor and Fillmore," formed in September, 1848, and began an all-out effort to keep the Whig party alive and united.

Outnumbered from the start in Granby, they lost votes to the splinter "Free Soil" faction, which castigated both parties for tolerating any extension of slavery into the western territories.[85] Democrats Samuel Weed and Raynor Holcomb won both of Granby's seats to the legislature. The days of the Whig Party in Granby were numbered, as they were everywhere in the nation. Even though they counted Truman Allen, Stephen Cornwell, Jairus Case, Joshua Jewett, Calvin B. Dibble, and Nahum Holcomb, some of the wealthiest and most influential men in town, among their numbers, they couldn't win an election. In the background of all this, of course, the "Temperance Car" was "going the other way than ahead."

Democrats seemed more united in Granby than they were nationwide, but some of their numbers began to trickle away from the party after the Compromise of 1850 when it became impossible to defend the Fugitive Slave Law, which the state legislature itself nullified in 1854.[86] The second two-party system was falling apart, but now that local politicians were used to working through party organizations, they had no place to go. The "Know-Nothing" movement provided one haven. This was an anti-immigrant, anti-Catholic party which had its roots in numerous secretive organizations throughout the 1820s and 1830s in the seaboard cities. Now that Irish immigrants were spreading into the countryside and Catholic Churches were starting up, fears of domination by "non-natives" sprouted in nearly all towns in Connecticut. In 1854, a Know-Nothing organization in Granby, consisting of both former Democrats and former Whigs, held a meeting to start their new party, and in 1855, they succeeded in getting Willis Phelps elected to the legislature on a platform to limit the rights of immigrants and to resist the spread of the Catholic Church.[87]

In turn, some Whigs such as Jairus Case, who had no stomach for this alternative to organizing for the common good, actually became Democrats when the Whig party disintegrated in the early 1850s. While sectional tensions heated up throughout the nation in the wake of the birth of the Republican Party, Bleeding Kansas, the Dred Scott decision and John Brown's raid on Harper's Ferry, libelous rhetoric became the order of the day in Granby. In the Republican Party, former Free Soilers, anti-slavery Whigs, diehard temperance advocates, Know-Nothings and Democrats who had recently acquired a fear of "The Slave Power" found a home. Granby citizens who had been enemies in the 1840s now found themselves marching together at a local fair and cattle show as Republican "Wide-Awakes" in support of "Honest Abe," the rail-splitter from Illinois who would not compromise with the plantation aristocracy in the South. Democrats responded with a caustic poem in the Hartford Post in 1859, describing the October fair and parade at Salmon Brook:

> "At Salmon Brook, a village fair
> That's greatly famed for wooden-ware,
> Doctors, lawyers, merchants, dealers,
> Poets, wits, and mutton stealers
>
> ...
>
> (Of demagogues there's no one fitter
> To ride a rail than Abe the splitter)"[88]

Here, the Democrats indulged in some ridicule of those who had associated themselves with the elitism of gentlemen farmers who were once the only ones interested in agricultural fairs.[89] We can also detect a reference to the age-old rail-ride they hoped to inflict on Lincoln; but what they meant by "You fuse with black and not with white" is probably not worth considering. Suffice it to say Granby's Democrats were somewhat desperate as they went down to a resounding defeat in the 1859 state elections. Republican Party ideology was not yet the creed of big business that it would become in the later part of the century. Instead, it made its appeal successfully to the aspirations of farmers, small entrepreneurs and craftsmen of northern society. They had stolen the Democratic constituency.[90]

When Jairus Case complained in a letter to *The Hartford Times* of Republican lies, bribery, fraud and pressure on employees, newly elected town officers retorted that Case was "as crooked a man in political matters as any other with whom they are acquainted....When he was a Whig," they went on, "that party was sick, and the Democratic Party feel that they have swallowed a poor pill."[91] Against this onslaught of vituperation, East Granby's incorporation seems a rather dull dispute. What accounted for the grating tone of the rhetoric? Granby's own recent history could provide some clues: in the depression of 1857, businesses which were supposed to "redeem

Salmon Brook" were failing, "natives" were convinced their society and work places were being overrun by agents of the Vatican, cider brandy flowed in rivers, young people fled to the West, the Congregational Church couldn't keep a minister in the pulpit, much less a congregation in the church, the political structure was in turmoil - is there any wonder Granby was in a precarious emotional state? In fact, all across the nation tempers flared, in state legislatures and in Congress as well.

In Granby, the roots of the increasingly intense partisanship of the times ran even deeper than the current state of business and community affairs. Social and geographic divisions were present prior to party organization and fed directly into political alignments. On top of those long-standing divisions were anxieties all townspeople were feeling as they experienced the challenges and dislocations of modernization.

It is tempting to think of Salmon Brook Society as a "typical" New England community, dominated by agricultural and religious concerns, led by the more prosperous farmers who represented the more permanent portion of the town, and divided solely by denominational squabbles, obscure family feuds and differing economic interests. However, when we look closely at the loyalties, the public disputes and the basic structure of the community in the second quarter of the 19th century, a wholly different pattern of division arises. The town was, indeed, populated predominantly by farmers, but as we learned in Chapter VII a substantial proportion of the work force - 26% in 1850 - were involved in "manufactures and trades."[92] Nevertheless, divisions in the town did not form on the basis of manufacturing vs. agriculture. Nor were they about religion, for after 1840 animosity between congregations cooled down, and in the 1850s, the Congregational Church was even admitting former Methodists, or allowing people to change to the Methodist church by letter of recommendation.[93]

The political leaders of the town were mostly (at least 68%) farmers, and statistically, they were the wealthier farmers. According to the 1850 U.S. Census, the 78 men who had at one time or another held one of the town's top political offices (selectman, treasurer, clerk, town meeting moderator, representative to the legislature or militia captain) owned 80% of the town's real estate; yet they constituted less than 15% of the town's eligible officeholders.[94] Furthermore, well over half of these officeholders were men who had lived in town over twenty years.[95] Nevertheless, if we look at people who were not elected to any of the top offices in town, there were plenty of farmers, and some wealthy ones who had been long-time residents as well. Squire Cullen Hays stands out. Grandson of Samuel Hays II, he lived all his life quite leisurely on his grandfather's farm on Barn Door Hills Road. In 1865, his tax assessment was over $11,000.[96] Similarly, there were many who were officeholders but who qualified neither as farmers, nor as permanent residents, nor even as financially solvent! In fact, based on a survey of the frequency of certain offices changing hands during the 1830s, 40s and 50s, it is very clear that there was no tight-knit landed oligarchy running local affairs while the majority of the town looked on with deference (See Table 8-1).

Neither occupational nor economic class distinctions defined the divisions with which Salmon Brook people struggled in the years prior to the Civil War; and yet there were obviously serious and prolonged divisions which only became more acerbated in the 1850s. One strong determinant was where people lived. The Whig party had allies and voters it could count on spread throughout the town, as did the temperance advocates, many of whom were Whig. However, with only a few exceptions, the leaders of the Whig party, and of the temperance movement, lived at Salmon Brook Street. Truman Allen in Pegville, Stephen Cornwell in Mechanicsville and Justus D. Wilcox in West Granby were prominent exceptions. The countryside and hills around the village centers were firmly "Loco-Foco" in the 1840s. When the Whig party fell apart, the vast majority of these leaders eventually emerged as leaders of the Republican Party along with some of the more prominent Democrats like the Dewey brothers of North Granby and Samuel Fuller of West Granby. In any case, Whig leaders and Republican leaders were residents of Salmon Brook Street or were the more prominent residents of one of the other village centers. Democratic leaders resided in the outlying areas where they happily distilled their cider, operated their taverns and celebrated "the age of the common man" and their majority control of the town.

The Cases, the Jewetts and the Dibbles of Salmon Brook Street also led a social elite of professionals, merchants, businessmen and gentlemen farmers who, as a group, were distinctly more wealthy than most of the farmers, artisans and laborers of Salmon Brook Society. Their outlook on the world was an interesting one. They were well read, and as we have seen, did a good deal of writing and speaking on a wide range of subjects. They and their allies throughout the town worked together on reform projects which were the outgrowth of the evangelical Puritanism of the early part of the century. They believed in a republican society led by the most responsible gentlemen, dedicated not so much to equality and freedom as to the sort of liberty that was guided by the highest standards of morality and learning. Their temperance meetings, literary societies, essays, lyceums and qualified support for Whig presidential candidates combine to paint a picture of a group of people who thought that they deserved to be running Granby, but were not.

What confuses this distinct division based on social elitism and geography is the peculiar politics of the 1850s. In an effort to bridge the gap that separated them from their suspicious and egalitarian neighbors to the north and west, the social elite tried to put on overalls and join the farming class. Instead of extolling the redemptive qualities of "one or two manufactories," as they had done in 1840, they took up discussing the value of agriculture. Probably they took their cue from Noah Phelps, a Simsbury resident and Jacksonian Democrat who wrote his history of Simsbury, Granby and Canton in 1845. Phelps summed up the Granby he knew by writing, "In general, the lands are adapted to the purposes of agriculture, in which business the inhabitants are chiefly engaged. The New Haven and Northampton Canal, which passes through the center of the town, facilitates the transportation of such products as are destined to a market." The implication was that not many products were so destined. The good soil was on the east side of the Newgate ridge, he continued, and, as for the rest of the town, he could not find much in the way of large-scale investment in manufacturing.[97] The elite of Granby, perhaps realizing they had read Granby wrong all along, began to extol the wonders of the farming life. "What avocation is more useful, honest or profitable than farming," wrote *The Whig of New England* in 1851.

They worked so hard to identify with farmers that some eventually forgot that Granby had once been as much a part of the industrial revolution as any other town or city. As William Scoville Case, Dr. Jairus Case's grandson, wrote in the 1880s, "In manufacturing the town has never held a prominent place." He went on to note some exceptions, including a brass foundry and a thriving shoe industry, the very "manufactories" the Whigs of 1840 had been so proud to note in *The Centreville Weekly News*. However, wrote Case, there was neither "good water power" nor "railroad conveniences," and, thus, farming was the "prevailing occupation." He was also careful to note, tactfully, that "West Granby has acquired some note as a centre for cider-brandy distilleries."[98]

Nevertheless, the reformers made little headway in the late 1840s and early 1850s. Probably everyone in town knew they were not at all farmers, or, in the case of those Whigs who were farmers, they were recognized as the ones who had enough money to buy the new mechanical devices which actually were making farming a profitable enterprise (and driving down the prices everyone else was getting for their produce). It was the gentlemen farmers who had the new improved plows, the corn shellers and the winnowing machines. They were the members of the agricultural societies which advocated the resting and fertilization of land most farmers could not afford to relegate to disuse for a year. They were the ones who had developed the skill to grow cash crops like tobacco and potatoes and did not need to rely on orchards the way people did who lived in the increasingly barren hills.[99] A few of these reformers may have been farmers, but they were not going to win the hearts of the farmers in Granby's hills.

As they suffered defeat after defeat, in elections as well as efforts to get the Temperance Car rolling in the right direction, they wondered how they would win the trust of people whose ancestors had been famous for thumbing their noses at merchants, professionals, businessmen and creditors just like themselves. When the Whig party faded, many of the leaders, Jairus Case excepted, took up the Know-Nothing banner and succeeded in attracting a good deal of support in 1855 and 1856 with the help of some former Democrats like Watson Dewey and Harvy Godard of North Granby. The Democrats were back in 1857 and 1858, though, and so this group of redeemers adopted the Republican party platform of "Free Soil, Free Labor, Free Men" which was responsible for the rapid growth of that party elsewhere in the state.[100]

Besides that platform, another element which played into the hands of the social elite of Salmon Brook Street was the institution of the militia and its relationship to the taxation system of the day. Along with assessment for

Table 8-1

Number of Different Men Holding Certain Offices
in Each Decade

Decade	Different Men elected Selectmen*	Different Men elected Representative°
1827-1836	15	15
1837-1846	19	17
1847-1856	18	†

* Three elected per year (thus, it was possible to elect 30 different men in a decade).
° Two elected per year (thus, it was possible to elect 20 different men in a decade).
†Town ordinance limiting the number of terms a representative may serve consecutively makes this figure invalid.

real and personal estate, Connecticut taxpayers were assessed a poll tax in the early 19th century. The assessment value of "a poll" was the same for everyone, and for those who wanted to vote, but owned little other property, it represented an enormous increase in their overall assessment. For the predominantly cash-poor farmers and laborers of Granby, it was a blessing that participation in militia training could be substituted for payment of the poll tax in the same way that work on the roads was done in lieu of cash payment of the highway tax. Thus, the very people the social elite of Salmon Brook Street hoped to convert to their cause were eager to join in militia training. In the 1850s, the elite learned to make use of this devotion to the militia.

William Scoville Case wrote that after the Mexican War

and during the period of "militia" excitement, there was much interest manifested in military matters, and many of the older citizens remember, with a thrill of the same old patriotic ardor that fired them then, the "general training day." This was an occasion of extraordinary interest to the dwellers in the rural districts who flocked in great numbers to the village which had been previously selected as the gathering ground for the volunteer companies for miles around. Granby was often selected for this honor, and the broad "street" seems to have been especially adapted for the warlike maneuvers which characterized such gala days.[101]

What Case was describing with such enthusiasm was the bringing of the rough folks of the hills and outlying farms into Salmon Brook Street, where militia training would be characterized by less cider, more authority, greater attention to nationalistic patriotism and probably a good deal of talk about the evils of the "Slave Power," the importance of the work of the free-soil fighters in Kansas, and the need for everyone to work together for the good of a nation threatened by aristocratic despotism from the South. It was on militia training days that the educated, reform-minded leaders, who were sometimes militia officers, met with and worked toward the conversion of the militantly independent-minded "Loco-Focos" of the back country, and in the 1850s, that meeting ground became Salmon Brook's genteel "Street." The elite had learned that gala "warlike maneuvers," rather than temperance meetings or even Log Cabin parades, was the game all could play; and in 1859, Granby turned its back on the Democratic Party with a vehemence that shocked and infuriated the die-hard party regulars, and even more so, former Whigs who had turned Democrat.

All of these "warlike maneuvers" not only helped to secure the elite of Granby Street in positions of power in their now truncated town, but also set the tone for Granby's response to the national crisis of 1861. In 1860, several southern states had threatened to leave the union should Abraham Lincoln be elected president, and President Buchanan, hoping to scare the country away from a Republican victory, had given his support to their reasoning. When Lincoln was declared the winner of a majority of electoral votes, he announced, and affirmed in his March, 1861 inaugural address, that secession was illegal and he would treat it as rebellion. The parties to the dispute had thus drawn their lines, not only on the question of the extension of slavery, but also on secession. Last minute efforts to reach a compromise came to nothing, for neither side had any faith in the integrity of the other, and in April, the batteries around Charleston Harbor opened fire on Fort Sumter. Within a week, Granby's Everett Griswold was signing his name to enlistment papers for the 1st Regiment, Connecticut Volunteers, and over the next six weeks, at least sixteen more responded to Lincoln's call to arms to "save the union."

In all over 150 men wrote "Granby, Connecticut" on their enlistment papers when they signed up for the Union Army between 1861 and 1865. While some of these were men recruited from out of town, and a few never reported for duty, it is still a large number. In the 1860 census Granby had only 306 males between the ages of 18 and 45. Thus, assuming the recruits were all of age (a few were younger when they enlisted), one of two men of military age went to war from Granby. Nearly a third of these never came home. This is an abominably high casualty rate, even for the Civil War.[102] Were they simply ignorant of what was in store for them? Not likely. Two-thirds of the recruits from Granby signed up in the second or third years of the war, well after it was apparent that it was to be a long and ugly struggle. Why did these men set out, knowing they might be called upon to give "their last full measure?"

This is a difficult question to answer, for ultimately, each man marched to his own drummer. There did seem to be some common beats though. In the beginning, the "militia excitement" of the 1850s surely played a role. At these community gatherings, increasingly popular Republican ideology, advanced by a social elite who wanted to run the town, combined with the military character of the activities, probably motivated many to seek their share of glory. Undoubtedly, this was the case for the group of young men from the hills of West Granby who enlisted in the 4th Connecticut Volunteer Infantry on May 23, 1861. Seventeen signed up as a group and were assigned to Company C of the first three-year regiment from any state, a regiment that was soon renamed the 1st Connecticut Volunteer Heavy Artillery. For boys from hill farms, the $13 a month with a $100 enlistment bonus was certainly some incentive, but they also reveled in the role of heroes. However, by 1864, when their terms were up, they had seen enough of the "glory" of war. Only two of the eight still in active duty chose to reenlist. The other six came home and let the town find replacements for them. Two had already deserted, four had died and three had been discharged because of disabilities before their terms were up. On a beech tree on a quiet hill in West Granby, far from the continuing roar of cannon at Yorktown, Chickahominy and Richmond where they had been baptized by fire, they carved their initials, a cannon, a tent and a pair of crossed flags (See Figure 8-7).[103] They had seen enough "warlike maneuvers."

As the war dragged on, bounties increased to as high as $300 per recruit and $200 for anyone who paid the $300 exemption fee which reduced the town's quota by one man. With the rise in monetary incentives came a deluge of rhetoric designed to inspire a sense of patriotism (or a sense of shame for those who would not go). In July, 1862, the town met and passed the following resolutions:

> RESOLVED: That the mild and conciliatory policy long and honestly pursued by our government to restore the supremacy of law and order has only stimulated traitors to a more desperate, unscrupulous and blood thirsty determination to destroy the Government and annihilate the last hope of a few people and subject us either to a Monarchial despotism, an Aristocratic oligarchy, or the more deplorable state of anarchy, thereby depriving us of the inestimable rights and privileges now enjoyed under the time honored Constitution of our revolutionary fathers "of life, liberty, and the pursuit of happiness."
> RESOLVED: That a crisis in the affairs of this nation has arisen when it becomes an imperative necessity for all the Sovereign people in whose veins course a particle of the loyal and patriotic blood of our revolutionary fathers to take immediate and decisive action, energetic action and to use all the means compatible with the rules of warfare given us by the great commander and Governor of this universe to subjugate the ambitious traitors and mercenary thieves, and wicked and vile disturbers of our national and individual peace and prosperity. And to stop the frightful carnage of blood and waste of treasure and speedily return to us the blessings of a lasting peace.
>
>   .   .   .
>
> RESOLVED: That duty calls upon all able-bodied men to leave their plow and like the immortal Putnam, March to the battlefield and put an end to this unritcheous rebellion, charge upon the Traitorous heart of disipated Whisky Madened rebels, and enjoy the sight of a hasty flight of conscript rebeldom before the cold steel of the hardy and voluntary Soldiery of the patriotic North.

After these resolutions were passed "Patriotic Speeches from Gentlemen from abroad & from E. Holcomb & Jairus Case & others from this town were received with applause enimating from true patriotic hearts."[104]

This outpouring of unionist venom seems to have had the desired

---

effect. In August, 1862, nine men enlisted in the 10th Connecticut Volunteer Infantry and nineteen more joined the 16th Infantry (See Figure 8-8). In September, Everett Griswold, who had already served his first term, reenlisted in the 22nd Infantry, and in November, three more recruits joined the 10th and seven signed up for the 25th Connecticut Volunteer Infantry. There was some concern when citizens (and certainly some parents) took note that boys who were under eighteen were asking to join up, but this was quickly justified by the fiery ideology of war, with the following explanation:

> Harry C. Gillett, Geo. W. Green, Leland Barlow & Roswell Allen & W. W. Wolcott are desirous of the honor and privilege of Serving their country as Soldiers in the present rebellion waged by ambitious unprincipaled demagogues in order to distroy our government and to found upon its ruins a despotism or eather a Slave Oligarchy under the Merciless lash of Davis, Breckinridge, Mason, Slidell & others equally vile and kindred spirits who for their own agrandizement would wash out the Stars & Stripes with the best blood of Patriots and compel Freeman to bow down & worship their System of Democratic Equality under the venomous folds of the Palmetto & Rattlesnake, these Idols of bloody Treason, while they escape what they eminently deserve, the <u>Halter</u>[105]

Who could be content "at the plow" when there was such work to be done! The union had to be saved from destruction at the hands of the "Slave Oligarchy" and the "Whisky Madened rebels." The reformers had found their ultimate cause and were proud that their children (or the children of brandy-manufacturers) would see it carried out.[106]

Diary entries and letters home by those who were most tenacious in their dedication to soldiering display the sense of pride and "duty" that will be puzzling to those who now know the slaughter they soon faced. Milo Holcomb, who was killed in 1862, wrote to his cousin Adelaide Holcomb "...if we do not conquer [the rebels] they will be so so full of bragging that we will be more annoyed than ever. A feeling of bitterness rises in my breast when I think of the course England has taken in this matter...to prompt <u>Secession</u> at every turn...."[107] Milo was referring to England's policy of neutrality and continuing trade with the seceded states. That, along with his own sectional loyalties and Lincoln's doctrine regarding the unconstitutionality of secession, was plenty of motivation for him. Others looked even more deeply and felt they understood the implications of the "slave aristocracy" argument. As Colonel Richard E. Holcomb wrote to his wife and family shortly before he was killed in 1863, "There is more depending upon the result of this contest than is generally thought to be. It is not only our government, without which there is no security for life, liberty or property, but the very principle of civil liberty itself, the right of man to govern himself is involved."[108] Holcomb was not to be governed by lash-wielding plantation owners, and in fact, took command of a regiment of repatriated Louisiana Confederates to spite the Slave Power (although it may have been one of those men who shot him as he tried to lead them on what appeared to be a suicidal charge).[109]

Sergeant Richard Henry Lee, also Adelaide Holcomb's cousin and her neighbor on Bushy Hill Road, appealed to this spirit of patriotism as well. He wrote her just after the battle at Antietam Creek, recounting his regiment's organization in August, 1862, its quick removal to Washington, D.C., and its hurried march forward, virtually untrained, to join the Army of the Potomac near Sharpsburg, Maryland. There the twenty Granby men of his regiment, the 16th Connecticut Volunteer Infantry, joined the 8th and the 11th, which had 14 Granby men in them, to attack the Confederate right. "I said that I hoped I should see a fight before we went home. I have seen it. And such a fight as boys do not always see...We were considerably cut up." And yet, in spite of shells bursting in their midst and overhead, musketry shredding their ranks, "the boys held their own first rate. Our Granby boys behaved particularly well. It was an easy matter for me to keep the ranks closed up, for every one was bound to do his duty."[110] In describing his disgust over the food he and his brave companions were being served he wrote, "I claim to have enlisted from patriotic motives and do not wish to leave, whether we fare well, or ill, until the Stars and Stripes float proudly as of old over the whole land the emblem of liberty, and the patriots' <u>Hope</u>."[111] Later, he wrote of a suicidal attack that had fortunately been canceled, although "if Burnside had said go, would have done it with a cheer, saying farewell Old Granby." On the disciplining of cowards he wrote, "This is right, for it is as much the duty of one man as another to go forward in the face of danger. I am happy to say that none enlisting from Granby were among those I reported from our Company." Even after his regiment was defeated at Plymouth, North

Sue Laun

Figure 8-7: "Carving Tree" on a West Granby Hill. The earliest carvings date to the 1840s. The majority are from the Civil War era.

Carolina, and he and many of his friends incarcerated in the infamous Andersonville prison camp, he held tight to his sense of duty. When asked to sign a petition to President Lincoln to make concessions to guarantee their release, he spoke vehemently to his subordinates against such action, as it would be breaking a "pledge" they were obligated to keep.[112]

By that time Lincoln had issued the Emancipation Proclamation and had delivered the Gettysburg Address and his second inaugural address, all of which redefined the union purpose from one of suppression of a rebellion to a struggle for the preservation of liberty and equality, a struggle that would result in nothing less than the end of slavery. When Richard Henry Lee spoke of a "pledge" at Andersonville, he was, in fact, speaking of a pledge to the slaves for their freedom. Thus, even before the 13th Amendment was ratified, Granby soldiers sought an even greater cause than that which had sent them to war. That is hardly surprising. They had had to endure rancid meat, bad water, diseases that killed more men than did shrapnel and bullets, terrible deaths in battle, or wounds which - in the context of the medical care provided - often meant certain death, inept leadership, corrupt procurement agencies and, in the case of the men of the 16th, the abominations of the Confederate authorities at Andersonville. That this was a struggle for the very soul of America, was important to them.

For Granby's African American men who went to war, the cause was even more pressing than the emancipation of enslaved people of their own race. There were twelve black soldiers from Granby which is remarkable alone, considering there were only fourteen black males (of all ages) listed in the 1860 census. Of the twelve, eight never came home.

Why did these men go at all when it took the Union Army nearly two years to allow them to wear a uniform? The answer lies in a different sort of redemption than that for which white men fought. Before the war, Granby's African Americans had been stigmatized as the lowest order of society, and of humanity, for that matter. William Case, in a speech before the Granby Civil War monument later encapsulated this public image of the African American. He spoke of fallen hero Leonard Percy, who before the war was viewed by one and all as "poor and ignorant and black, so worthless in his life..., hovering on the outskirts of the village, the enemy of all thrift, but the friend and delight of all the boys, his sole business to own the worst horse and

Salmon Brook Historical Society

Figure 8-8: Granby's volunteers who joined the 16th Infantry Regiment in 1862. Most of these men were captured and sent to Andersonville in 1864.

the most dogs." Case recalled that one day before the war, he had been engaged in a conversation with Daniel Holcomb, his colleague in the Granby Literary Association, "talking politics - about slavery, and about the negro - for those were the stirring subjects of those days - and one of us expressed the belief...that the day would come when the negro would vote. At this, 'Len' who crouched hard by taking in the talk stood up and said, 'Do you believe that? I would die to have the day come.' The startled boys who saw this sudden flash of manhood never forgot it. That day has come - the negro votes, and 'Len' fell at Petersburg, a soldier in the service, and on this column which perpetuates the heroism of the Granby men who died for the enfranchisement of his proscribed race, his name leads all the rest - a silent and enduring witness that in the grand gospel of democracy, as in that other grander gospel of democracy of which democracy is a part, the last shall sometimes be the first, and the least among you oftentimes the greatest."[113]

Case had missed the point, even though he had made it himself. Percy had not fought only for emancipation, nor principally for enfranchisement. In fact, he had said he would *die* "to have that day come" - what good would the new rights do him if he were dead? Percy, and every other black man in Granby of fighting age, had fought for the recognition of his manhood. It was not his choice to be "worthless in his life," but the choice of those who would not advance a black man financial credit, nor consider him worthy of a job that paid decent wages. He lived in a society that was, by 1864, strong on abolition of slavery, but actually somewhat confused about what it would mean to find a truly equal place for African Americans in their businesses, churches or day-to-day affairs. Percy and all the black men of Granby knew they had to find a way to prove their worth for that station. In dying in disproportionate numbers they found that way, but their townsmen only admired their courage, not their humanity. For the majority of Granby soldiers, the cause was the survival of the democratic experiment and the elimination of the disease of slavery from the lifeblood of that experiment. For that, they had endured more than the gallant patriotism and sense of duty, or the pay and bonuses, had prepared them for at the onset.

Of course, the story of Granby's participation in the Civil War is not completely heroic. The town had its share of deserters (eighteen). As the war dragged on long after its proponents had envisioned a quick suppression of the rebellion, opposition and recalcitrance grew. Calls for recruits became intense, culminating in a draft in August, 1862. In Connecticut, each town had a responsibility to fill a quota. Granby, like other towns, offered bounties for enlistment. The cost to the town of these bounties grew to $8000 in 1864 alone, even though the legislature had passed a law against towns giving bounties the year before.[114] Competition among towns for recruits to fill their quotas became intolerable - and in Granby's case, three who were recruited to fill quotas simply took their bounties and ran, never reporting for duty. The number of men inspired by Richard Henry Lee's sense of duty was running thin by 1864.

Early in the war, there was a strong peace movement throughout the state led by Democrats who, for business reasons, or because their supporters feared future competition from free black labor, had argued that the seceding states should be allowed to go their own way. Governor William Buckingham, a staunch Republican, succeeded in suppressing much of this opposition early on, but it revived by 1864.[115] In Granby, unionist sentiment was very strong to begin with. In the 1860 election, the Democrats had only raised 69 votes for Douglas to Lincoln's 206. By 1864, however, both Governor Buckingham and Lincoln won Granby by only a small margin.[116] Weariness with the war was setting in. Jairus Case, a Democrat who had originally supported the war effort, apparently was among those who began to tire of the conflict. People like him were branded as "copperheads" by Republicans. Within the community his change of heart produced deep antagonisms which did not heal for some time. As late as 1868, when Case was running for state senator, the *Hartford Courant* was reminding voters of his stance four years earlier, describing him as "a genuine, unmitigated copperhead of the worse variety. During the war he wore a badge of copper to distinguish and proclaim his tory character...Every Union man, every war-Democrat, every ex-soldier, every honorable man who wanted the rebels defeated, ought to labor harder still to defeat Jairus Case....Though the district has been Democratic [it included Windsor] there are strong indications that it will be redeemed."[117]

As the election statistics show, the copperheads had grass-roots support and this surely accounted for the long-term bitterness among those supporting the war effort. The cause of this opposition lay in the inequities of the war. Wartime inflation reduced soldiers' pay considerably over the long run, and if a soldier was killed, there were no benefits for his family. The money simply stopped. This made it difficult to get three-year men to reenlist once their term expired and required continual recruitment among those less eager to be part of the conflict. Within the ranks, equipment and supplies varied greatly - some units entered the war with decent clothing and home-town support groups saw to it that their needs continued to be met. Most Granby men however, like Richard Henry Lee, found themselves in desperate conditions: barely trained, poorly fed, ill-clothed and often poorly led. Wealthier men were able to pay a fee for a substitute and avoid the draft, which meant those without cash, whether they wanted to serve or not, often ended up in units with criminals and drunkards sometimes hired with these substitute fees (if those substitutes actually reported).[118] And, of course, for the black soldier, service meant subjection to the most dangerous and futile operations, as we can tell by their casualty rate. By 1864, it had definitely become "a poor man's fight." Even so, Republicans held on to a slim margin that kept the social elite, once rejected by their neighbors from the hills, in positions of power.

Granby citizens paid dearly for their support of the war. Like all northern communities, they suffered from the loss of able-bodied workers and farm productivity declined considerably. Cotton mills languished throughout New England, and we have already noted the demise of Truman Allen's cotton processing mill in Granby in 1863. Generally, although prices increased for some farm produce such as potatoes, wool, cigar tobacco, dairy

Salmon Brook Historical Society

Figure 8-9: The first Loomis Brothers' Store, after its 1864 expansion, located on the west side of Salmon Brook Street opposite the Green.

products and well-bred dairy cows, few, particularly in Granby, were actually involved in producing surpluses of these items. As elsewhere in New England, more and more general farms were going out of production.[119] The non-economic costs were the most trying, however. Take, for example, the case of the Francis Allen family.

Dr. Francis T. Allen and his wife Eliza Ann Goodrich moved from Granby as part of the general exodus to Ohio in the 1820s. There they began their family, but tragedy followed. Three sons died in the cholera epidemic of 1835, and in 1849, a daughter died. Still in 1853, they were able to move three daughters and two sons back to Granby to care for Eliza's ailing father, Hezekiah Goodrich. Their oldest, George, remained in Ohio. When the war began, George enlisted in an Ohio regiment and Elbert, 21, left his teaching position in New York State to sign up for the cavalry. Their youngest, Roswell, as we remember from the patriotic town resolution, did not even wait until he was 18, but joined the 16th Connecticut Volunteer Infantry in the summer of 1862, against his mother's objections. George survived the war, and Elbert also made it to an honorable discharge. However, Elbert had contracted tuberculosis while in the army and died in 1868. Roswell, although healthy and eager to join the great cause in the summer of 1862, fell ill soon after the Battle of Antietam in September. His father managed to secure his discharge after endless bureaucratic red tape, only to have Roswell die in a hospital in Washington, D.C. in December. Thus, the Allens, after losing four children to untimely deaths in Ohio, gave all their remaining sons to the war, to have only one survive. On top of it all, Dr. Allen faced a community scandal the following year when he was accused of "adultery," "procuring abortion," and "lascivious carriage" before the Congregational Church. He demanded an open trial, and that dragged on into 1864, apparently pulling the church apart and resulting in the departure of yet another minister. The previous winter he had written "I have been asked if after these heart-rending trials I am not ready to Compromise! Should we compromise our liberties, our lives, our consciences—trample upon the right and deny our God for the sake of peace? Peace obtained at such a price is not peace, but ignominy and death."[120] To avoid compromise, he paid a high price indeed.

Roswell's comrades in the 16th all suffered tremendous hardship. While only a few were actually killed in battle, even though the regiment fought on the front line at such famous slaughters as Antietam, Fredericksburg, the Peninsula campaign and Malvern Hill, the whole unit was captured and imprisoned at Andersonville late in the war. There men became human skeletons. As William Case later said, "Their food was insufficient, and loathsome beyond description. Starvation, fever, scurvy and every form of filth-disease held ghastly carnival."[121] Thirteen thousand of the thirty thousand prisoners starved to death. For those who survived - and many died later of diseases contracted there - life would never be the same.

There were some who managed to come out of the war better off than when it began. Although merchant Calvin Dibble was thrown out of Newbern, North Carolina in 1864 for offering $25 extra for each union recruit from Granby, he had already amassed a considerable fortune from trade there, before and continuing into the war.[122] Newbern came under federal control later in that year, and became a headquarters of sorts for union operations in the coastal regions of that state. A young man named Chester Loomis found his niche there as an employee for the postal service, and did a good deal of merchandising then, and following the war. He and his brother James N. Loomis had taken over the Phelps Store on Salmon Brook Street in 1856, but as a result of the new trade opened up through Newbern, were able to enlarge their operation in Granby in 1864 (See Figure 8-9). Wrote Chester the following year, "Several thousand troops from the west arrived here within a few days and it is said more are coming, which I should think would make trade good. It looks as if they were going to push up into the enemy's country in this department, so many troops and a construction corps to build railroads are coming here."[123]

Granby's reformers had also gained ground during the war. In October, 1861, they had secured the town-meeting passage of strict regulations for the town's public schools, insisting that teachers keep a careful watch over the schools, open every day with a reading from the Scripture, a prayer by the teacher, and a recitation of the Lord's Prayer. The curriculum was to consist primarily of upbringing according the the highest standards of moral behavior. Singing was expected every day, good manners were to be enforced, and corporal punishment was authorized.[124] At the end of the war, even though the Republican majority had diminished, the most prominent Democrat in town was Jairus Case. The educated gentlemen of "the Street" ruled the town. For the moment, anyway, the town could be said to have been "redeemed."

The cost of a redeemed community had been terrible, and the campaign, running back years to the beginnings of the temperance movement after the War of 1812, had been successful only through appeals to patriotism during the nation's worst crisis. Furthermore, as of 1865, the reformers of the Street could cling to little hope that the spirit of duty and purpose which had put them in charge of their town would continue. The war had not created new industry in Granby, cider brandy still sold well, the number of poor would undoubtedly multiply, Turkey Hills farmers would no longer subsidize Salmon Brook schools or roads, and the local churches were all hard-pressed to find popular ministers. The library would have to be revitalized, academies reestablished, new markets for surplus products found, churches bolstered, and the populace in the outlying villages and hills inspired to follow the industrious example of those they had always distrusted. Rocked by decades of turbulence and crisis, Granby needed a break.

Salmon Brook Historical Society

Figure 8-10: Civil War monument on the Granby Green. Jairus Case's house is in the background.

376

Chapter IX
An Age of Economy

Chronology

The World	America	Granby
(Age of European and U.S. colonialism in Asia, Africa and the Pacific)	1865 Civil War ends, Lincoln assassinated, 13th Amendment ends slavery	
1867 Russia sells Alaska to U.S.		
	1868 14th Amendment ratified - guarantees "equal protection of the laws"	1868 Civil War monument dedicated
		1869 Granby Library Association revives library at Granby Street
1870 Franco-Prussian War	1870 15th Amendment allows African American men to vote	1871 Library building constructed at Granby Street
1871 Germany united under Prussian Kaiser William I		
	1872 Grant reelected President	1872 South Congregational Church founded
1873 Financial panic in Vienna	1873 Financial panic, followed by depression through 1878	
1874 Disraeli becomes Prime Minister in England		1875 Granby Green refurbished, Granby Grange No. 5 organized.
	1876 Battle of Little Big Horn. Telephone invented. Rutherford B. Hayes, descendant of Salmon Brook's George Hayes, elected 19th President of U.S.	1877 Fire consumes Loomis Brothers store
1878 Paris World Exhibition		1882 Granby Creamery Co. organized
	1881 President Garfield assassinated.	
1887 Arthur Conan Doyle writes first Sherlock Holmes story	1883 Civil Service reform	1891 Loomis Brothers' build third store. Cossitt Library built
	1887 Farm prices collapse	
	1892 Sherman Anti-Trust Act	
	1893 Conn. Agricultural College at Storrs; Depression through 1897	1895 Granby Agricultural Society buys fairground. Gambling made illegal. College Highway macadamized.
1895 H.G. Welles: "The Time Machine"		1896 First telephones in Granby.
	1896 *Plessy v. Ferguson* declares racial segregation legal	1900 Granby prohibits liquor sales.
	1898-9 Spanish American War	1901 Shade tobacco introduced
	1901 McKinley assassinated, Theodore Roosevelt becomes President.	1902 Swedish Congregational Church on Loomis Street
1904 Russo-Japanese War	1904 Roosevelt Corollary to Monroe Doctrine	1904 Granby Club in Hartford

In 1886, the town of Granby was one hundred years old. Our records do not contain even a murmur of celebration. Instead, in that year William Scoville Case's rendition of the town's recent history read, "Since the

377

exciting events of the Civil War, little has occurred to disturb the tranquil sleepiness of the staid old town."[1] Case had reason to be quietly content. From the Ozias Pettibone house, the elegant home of his grandfather, Dr. Jairus Case, at the north end of Granby's town green, he could survey a broad street lined with shade trees and well-kept houses. As his father and grandfather before him, he was destined to become one of Granby's (and Connecticut's) most respected citizens. In spite of political battles, the times had treated him and his family well.

Five miles west, on the bank of Salmon Brook just south of the Matthew Fancher's rickety, debt-ridden wheel shop, Polly Taylor had a different reason for not noticing that Granby had reached its centennial. Nearly a decade earlier her husband, Thomas, had died of hepatitis. In the years prior to his death, the couple had barely made ends meet, Thomas having declared bankruptcy early in life. Before the Civil War, Polly, who had assumed control of the couple's finances and property, had traded up to a sizable farm on Barkhamsted Road. However, during the depression in the 1870s, they had had to give that up. In 1874, they had moved to the small, four-room house with their daughter Marion, and her illegitimate son Lewis. Twelve years later, a widow with little income and only a small piece of property on the edge of a brook known for its unpredictable temperament, Polly passed each day trying to find ways to earn enough money to stay out of the poor house. She was loathe to rely on her half-brother, Marcus Alling, a reasonably prosperous farmer and carpenter, and so she struggled on, knitting and sewing, and doing her best to trade well at the local stores.[2]

Perhaps it was difficult to put together a celebration in Granby in 1886 because at the time there were really two Granbys. On the one hand, a social elite enjoyed a degree of comfort and gentility in a town they had led "since the exciting events of the Civil War." On the other, farmers in the outlying areas worked hard to make a living on poor land, often selling or mortgaging farms for far less than they had invested in them. The glory of the war carried the reform spirit, and the reformers as officeholders, into the 1870s. As Republican leaders celebrated small victories though, they faced increasing resentment from those who had to make hard adjustments to the modern world. By 1886, the two groups reached an uneasy accommodation, each

Figure 9-1: Salmon Brook Street, looking south, circa 1886.

clinging to the hope that one day its vision of the good life would become a reality. By the turn of the century, there seemed to be more consensus within the town, although beneath the surface the tensions of many decades clung stubbornly to the fabric of the community.

"Rejoice at the Favorable Indications"

In April, 1865, as General Robert E. Lee was surrendering his army at Appomattox Courthouse, the voters of Granby were placing their town squarely behind the party of Abraham Lincoln. They sent Mahlon G. Wilcox and Chauncey Holcomb, both Republicans, to the state legislature, and cast 217 votes for incumbent war governor Buckingham, as opposed to 157 for Democrat Thomas Seymour, a well-known former governor. Republican hegemony wavered slightly the next year when the party was split at the state level between moderates and radicals, and as the popular Jairus Case ran locally for the legislature as a Democrat. By 1868, however, even though it was a year when a Democratic candidate won the gubernatorial election and Case was running for state senator, Granby Republicans were commanding nearly 60% of the vote once again. That was the year the town paid J. G. Batterson to erect a Civil War monument at the north end of the green, dedicating it on the 4th of July with triumphant speeches celebrating the glory of the war. Everyone, even Democratic leaders, rallied around the monument, but Republicans reaped the rewards as the populace credited them and their agenda of reform with the victory.[3]

The Republican leaders were spread around the town, but most lived in the village centers of West Granby, North Granby and "Granby Street" (now Salmon Brook Street). The most prominent were the Granby Street men, such as Calvin B. Dibble, James and Chester Loomis and Edmund ("Lawyer Ed") Holcomb. In what had become, over the past decade, the principal business district of Granby, they owned substantial property, including commercial establishments (such as the Loomis Brothers' imposing Greek Revival general store and meeting hall); they were leaders in the revived Masonic Lodge; and they held significant investments beyond the town's borders as well (see Figures 9-1 and 9-2). Town reports list regular payments to these men for their various services and contracts. Although Dr. Jairus Case had proved himself "a genuine, unmitigated copperhead" during the war, he, too, could count himself among the Granby Street elite, and in fact, joined them in carrying the vote on a number of reform issues.[4]

Together, at an 1865 town meeting, they rallied unanimous opposition to a petition from some East Granby residents to reunite the two towns. Now that their reform agenda was being taken seriously in town meetings, they were not interested in more turbulence in voting patterns. In 1866, they managed to get a committee appointed to draw up a plan for a town poor farm; and later that year they nearly won a vote to build a new town meetinghouse to replace the old Episcopalian church house. In 1867 and 1868, they demonstrated their desire to meet the new expenses of their plans by closing some of the little-used town roads in North Granby. By 1870, they were actually winning votes to close roads.[5] Although not always successful on

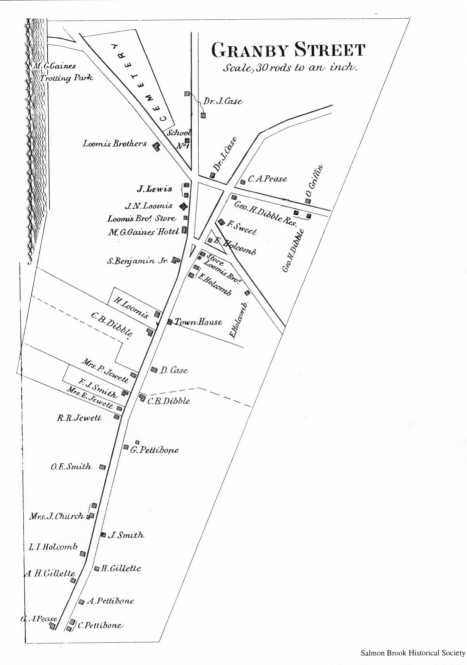

Salmon Brook Historical Society

Figure 9-2: Granby "Street" (now referred to as "Granby Center") in 1869.

381

every question put before the town meeting, they seemed optimistic that some of their ideas for ordering and civilizing their town would take hold.

One issue that caused a good deal of stir at the time was the possibility of a rail line running through Granby. Since the 1850s, there had been rail service on the New Haven-Northampton line which had a depot just across the East Granby town line, a few miles east of Granby Street. Merchants on the Street with large orders, the Loomis Brothers in particular, had to move their goods back and forth by wagon. At a town meeting in January, 1868 at the Loomis Brothers' hall,

> Remarks were made by Dr. J. Case and J. N. Loomis in favor of a Rail Road being built through the town of Granby, and were willing to spend time and money to accomplish that object, believing it to be of great benefit to the town at large - A. L. Loveland and A. L. Holcomb were in favor of letting those who want Rail Roads build them, but opposed to drawing one cent from the treasury of the town to aid it in any form, and conveying the idea that a Rail Road built through Granby would be a curse rather than a benefit.[6]

After that outburst from the leaders of the hillside farmers, the meeting was dissolved.

Four years later, the issue was back before the town meeting, this time with Harvy Godard and A. L. Loveland casting their support to the measure. The meeting unanimously approved Dr. Case's resolution "That we rejoice at the favorable indications of a Rail Road being built through this town and will cooperate with a company to accomplish that object." What brought about the change of heart is not clear. Certainly some deals were made. These, along with some persuasive arguments, brought everyone around to acceptance. Farmers were becoming increasingly dependent on the railroad for transportation of both the goods they needed, as well as those they produced. Some brought their goods directly to the depot, rather than deal though a general store, and in turn, store managers would sometimes have farmers pick up bulky items at the depot. A lot of the new support for encouraging a railroad may have depended on just how much the town would spend to "cooperate" with a railroad company. It all came to naught, though, when the committee appointed to consider the best route could not come up with one that would receive majority support (cursed, perhaps, by the spirit of meeting-house battles past).[7]

On the matter of cleaning up the town's business district, the elite were more successful. In 1870, Granby Street was not the image of order and civility future residents would describe in nostalgic moments. Like many villages of that time, it was probably characterized by the "out-of-door slovenliness" of the early 18th century when people in small towns cared little for spending money to keep their town common land picked up. Residents often referred to the area around the Civil War monument as a "frog pond," and on the east side of it, dilapidated storehouses, tradesmen's shops and an old tavern, complete with associated noise, smells and litter, did anything but grace what the more upstanding citizens considered the town's "center." Only Dr. Case's and Lawyer Ed Holcomb's house, along with the Loomis Brothers' store and James N. Loomis's new Italianate style dwelling, offered "modern" contrast to the picture (see Figure 9-3). It is not surprising that those who had built the monument also hoped to tidy up its surroundings, and in an 1870 town meeting, they proposed to create a park around it. They were, no doubt, influenced by the current Romantic notions that beautiful surroundings led to reform of the human spirit.[8]

By 1873, the park committee achieved no better than a motion to table its report, but it did manage to stir up enough interest to inspire the incorporation of the Granby Soldier's Monument Association, led by Calvin and George Dibble, Lawyer Ed Holcomb, Rev. Thomas Murphy (the current minister of the Congregational Church), and James C. Bartholomew, a gentleman farmer who lived on Bushy Hill Road. This group raised money on its own, and in 1875, the town meeting directed the selectmen to authorize them to lay out a park around the monument. By the following year, the area had been drained and filled, and Granby's "green" became a reality.[9]

While the social elite had only limited success getting citizens to commit tax money to their various projects designed to improve Granby, their enthusiasm achieved greater results in other spheres. In 1869, alumni of the old Granby Literary Association, including Ed Holcomb, Jairus Case, his son William, James Loomis and Samuel Benjamin Jr., decided it was time to revive the old spirit of erudition that had launched them on the road to success

Salmon Brook Historical Society

Figure 9-3: Above, the old Hayes Tavern and surroundings provided notice-able contrast to the elegant Italianate-style home of James N. Loomis, below, at 261 Salmon Brook Street, directly across the street from the tavern.

384

in the 1850s. They joined together to create a new Granby Library Association, and resolved to take over the old St. Peter's Church building. In 1871, they took down St. Peter's and built a new structure as striking in design to them as St. Peter's must have been when it was constructed in the Federalist Era. Its collection of books for the subscription library was housed on the first floor, and on the second, Rev. Thomas Murphy moved in with his "select school," where he offered secondary education not only to the youth of Granby, but, at one point, to two Chinese students who had been sent to learn about the science and technology their parents hoped would modernize their homeland. The opening of the building was the occasion of a major celebration, including a speech by Governor Jewel.[10]

Apparently the group had more in mind than an educational and cultural establishment. In 1872, Jairus Case, Chester P. Loomis and Samuel Benjamin formed a committee to establish a new Congregational Church, and not surprisingly, the Library Association (essentially the same group) offered its hall for the new congregation's meetings. Rev. Murphy, who had not coincidentally resigned his pastorate of the Congregational Church in North Granby the day before the committee met, agreed to be the new church's minister and by the early fall, over thirty members of the old church had left to follow him, placing their church under a new society called The Congregational Society of Salmon Brook.

The separatists were not former Episcopalians trying to reestablish their old church, for those people had largely left Granby before the 1830s when Salmon Brook Street began to "decay" (before the forebears of the new social elite took up residence and commenced their campaign of redemption). However, the founders of the South Congregational Church did subscribe to a set of attitudes similar to the earlier elitism on Salmon Brook Street, and those attitudes were at the root of the division of the First Congregational Church. Fifty years after the founding of South Church, one commentator, Dr. Sherwood Soule, who was Superintendent of the Missionary Society of Connecticut when it oversaw the beginnings of the South Congregational Church, suggested these explanations:

> Probably changes were occurring in the products of the farmers round about. Possibly the coming of canal and railroad hard by made successors of the early Salmon Brookites hopeful of having a metropolis here....Perhaps there grew up a little feeling between the scattered people of the mother parish and this compact citified community. These feelings are based more often on imaginary than real attitudes, but this has been the case ever since rural agricultural Israel resented aristocratic trading Judah, and split the kingdom.[11]

Possibly...probably. Well...most certainly. And what "products" was he referring to that seemed to divide the orchardists of the hills from the sober temperance advocates of the Street?

There was no doubt in Soule's mind as to the intent of the founders of this new religious establishment. He recounted a conversation with Eliza Loomis, Chester's wife, in which she remembered Salmon Brook Street before the creation of the South Church:

> Revelry and roistering, if nothing worse, were rampant on the Lord's Day. A country tavern a half century ago was not a place where polite conversation flourished...Taverns in older days were not sterilized to make them dry, nor even Voldsteadized to reduce them to 1/2 of 1%. Tradition sayeth that Granby was a wetter town than any spring freshet Salmon Brook could justify. A favorite Sunday sport for some of the fathers and their friends in this street was horseracing.[12]

To this world of disorder, the South Church brought "marvelous change," said Mrs. Loomis. Clearly, the separatists intended no less than the moral ordering of their community and their own disassociation with those of their old church who had, for so long, resisted the most important reform of all: temperance.

Although the names of men appear as leaders in these new organizations, it is clear that women played as important a role as men. In 1872, the committee organizing the South Church "voted that the Ladies be and are hereby invited to sign the papers for organizing the Society in question." It was a good thing they took that action, for in November, the church had 25 women and only 15 men as members.[13] These formed the Ladies Sewing Society, which, according to Ann Eliza Edwards, was purely a "social" organization which met Thursday afternoons in various homes. However, the purpose was to make items for lotteries at fairs ("until it was judged wrong"), in order to raise money for the church.[14] This group was probably patterned after the West Granby Methodist Church Ladies Aid Society which had organized in 1860 and purchased an organ with their earnings in 1866. (They had originally hoped to erect a new parsonage.) The West Granby Methodists also had a Sunday School with over sixty pupils and a 300 volume library by 1865, holding their own in the moral revival of the times.[15]

Other voluntary organizations illustrated the continuing commitment throughout the town, and especially in the villages, to reform and community renewal. In 1864 a group of civic-minded people formed the Granby Cemetery Association and issued stock certificates as a way of raising the capital needed to spruce up the center cemetery. The Granby Agricultural Club was reborn as the Granby Farmer's Club in 1867, in an effort, no doubt, to recruit interest among the less wealthy farmers, and, probably to encourage the production of anything other than cider brandy. In 1876, the same group that had created the library and the South Church incorporated into the Salmon Brook Water Company with $5000 capital. They had already purchased an old mill site on Bissell's Brook and had been using a water-powered pump to push water up a main line along Salmon Brook Street to a tank behind Loomis Brothers' Store. Subscribers along the way were billed for the service.[16]

Buoyed by their successes in politics and on the battlefield in the early 1860s, Granby's social elite worked hard in the ensuing years to create their vision of a well-ordered and decorous community. As the horrors of the war faded from memory, and only a heroic statue remained, standing proudly in its new park, they were encouraged to push their agenda forward. In town meetings, sewing societies, churches and many other organizations, they marched along, leading their reluctant followers among the rest of the town as though they were Sergeant Richard Henry Lee rounding up the cowards at Antietam Creek. The rest of the town was hard at work too, but judging from their initial reaction to the idea of directing their tax dollars toward railroad enticement, they had an altogether different agenda. As post-war prosperity turned sour in the 1870s, they became increasingly hard to motivate in the cause of community renewal.

"Rural Agricultural Israel"

It would be incorrect to convey the impression that the social elite were the only ones in Granby committed to morality, while residents of the outlying farms raced horses and swilled cider brandy. In most families, whether in the villages or on the farm, children, and particularly young women, were brought up committed to personal and communal improvement. As Dora Goddard wrote in her family diary on March 15, 1886, "I am twenty years old today! How quickly and peacefully they have passed to what some lives do. Wonder if the next twenty years will do the same. O, if someone would only be made better because of them they would not seem so much like lost days and years."[17] We recall that Addie Holcomb's Civil War diary had expressed the same sentiments.

Dora's problem was that while she understood the need to help her fellow human beings, she and her family had all they could do to make ends meet. Her father had died two years earlier Her brother Eugene, who also lived at their home, at what is now 30 Wells Road, had recently lost his wife. He was left with an infant daughter to care for. Fortunately for her widowed mother, Dora was the youngest of five children still living at home, but even with all these able workers, life was difficult and not entirely "peaceful."

Days were spent from sunrise to sunset cleaning house, making dresses to bring in scarce cash, washing, ironing the voluminous clothes of the day, baking bread, nursing family members who were more-than-occasionally sick, and preparing and preserving food. Eugene did the outside farm work, milking cows, and raising potatoes, tobacco, apples and peaches. In the spring, he was often up as early as 3:30 A.M., plowing and planting. He would set out thousands of tobacco plants each year, and spend the summer hoeing and weeding them by hand. Then he would work all fall sorting and curing the leaves, and the winter, packing and carrying wagon load after wagon load to the depot, only to wait for his cash to come in from the buyers so that he could go about town to pay off his debts. He brought in additional income from wood he dragged to the Forsyth mill and from surplus hay he carted to neighbors. Even then, he would pay for a 25¢ haircut with a dime and a sack of potatoes, and at dinner, the family would feast on "boiled beans." We normally think of tobacco as a big cash crop for this part of Connecticut, but in the 1870s and 80s, demand for Connecticut broadleaf had dropped considerably because of competition from the East Indies. Even the introduction of the more productive Havana seed in 1875 could not forestall, and probably contributed to, the declining prices that would cost Eugene many extra days in the field just trying to break even.[18]

The Goddards were not a poor family by Granby standards. Dwight Goddard, father of Dora and Eugene, had ranked just below the middle of the 1876 tax list, and the 34 acres he had owned prior to his death was mostly good meadow land. When Eugene took over as principal farmer in 1884, he rented other property from land owners who were losing interest in farming. Dwight had owned a typical farm. In Granby, the average farm amounted to a dwelling house valued at $406, about 65 acres of land at roughly $10 per acre, one horse, sometimes a yoke of oxen (if not, they would rent one), a small herd of cows (eight or nine of various ages), and perhaps, a sheep. Like a hundred other farmers in town with such an estate, Dwight, and his son after him, tried to figure out what crop would bring in some cash, and concentrated on that, while working as a jack-of-all-trades and growing enough of everything else to sustain the family or trade with locally. There was seldom enough to live on, and the cash crops brought little cash.[19]

Other farmers reported similar experiences in their journals and diaries. Rufus Messenger of Old Messenger Road in West Granby chronicled days in the late 1860s hewing logs, hunting, fishing (not for recreation), and caring for livestock. When he went for boots he paid the shoemaker $1 in cash and "the rest in cider." In Agawam, he was able to swap wool for flannel cloth and stocking yarn. William Holcomb led a similar life in the 1880s. With a hired hand, he drew loads of wood to the sawmill, shelled beans, worked his tobacco, picked apples and chestnuts, salted pork and shed sunflowers.[20] Again, these were farmers with average tax assessments. How those at the bottom of the tax list fared is unclear - they did not, apparently, have time to keep diaries.

Hard times all across rural New England began shortly after the Civil War as prices for most agricultural products began to decline. Particularly grains came under pressure when railroads began bringing carloads from the

West, where farmers were benefiting more from the new mechanical devices that increased output on open prairies. In 1877, railroads first began shipping meat to the East in refrigerated cars. As prices declined more and taxes bit harder (because acreage and animals were such a big part of assessments even though they produced less and less income), many farms in the more hilly sections of New England were simply abandoned, and cleared land gradually turned into brambles and saplings.[21] Granby's population had already been dropping since the 1820s and continued to do so after the Civil War.

Table 9-1: Granby's Population 1860-1890	
1860	1720
1870	1517
1880	1340
1890	1251

After the Panic of 1873, a nationwide depression put even more downward pressure on prices and Granby's pauper rolls grew as its tax base declined.[22]

Table 9-2: Granby's Grand List 1860-1900[23]		
Year	Total Grand List	Tax Rate (mills)
1858	523,820	3.0
1862	598,263	6.8
1865	610,000	6.3
1876	494,782	13
1880	501,289	11
1890	412,634	13
1900	388,860	17

Like many in New England, Granby's farmers turned away from grain and wool production as prices dropped. Their potatoes suffered in the 1870s as a result of a Colorado Beetle infestation, and they were not making much of a living from tobacco. They did find that prices for dairy products, particularly butter, were more stable. Many, like Rufus Messenger, had raised sheep in the late 1860s when wool was 38¢ a pound, but in the 1870s, they shifted to dairy farming. Dairying, however, required a substantial initial investment - at least enough to build a wooden silo and a larger barn; and some farmers had to mortgage property in order to accomplish these improvements. Then in the 1880s, a number of epidemics swept across New England cattle yards, including tuberculosis, pleuropneumonia and hoof-and-mouth disease. In fact, Granby farmers had already had a hoof-and-mouth scare in the early 1870s when the town clerk noted a "fearfully contagious" outbreak in a North Granby cattle yard.[24] As they faced quarantines and loss of stock, farmers continued to lose confidence in the prospects for the future. So many in Granby threw in the pitchfork that by the end of the century, the General Assembly did not think it would cause a great deal of dislocation to authorize the Hartford Water Commission to throw up a dam across Hartland Road near the Barkhamsted Road intersection and submerge half of West Granby in a reservoir![25]

Congregations felt the pinch as well. Before and during the Civil War years, community spirit had run high in the village of West Granby, but in the five decades after the war, the Methodist Church went through twenty-three different ministers.[26] In 1886, the Goddard family diary reported, "Dora went to Sunday school and Gene took the team over and attended church and brought her home. There were only 18 at present. Not a very large congregation."[27] By the early 1900s, the Universalist Church ceased holding services. Even the South Congregational Church had trouble paying its bills. Both Congregational Churches ended up sharing ministers after 1880.[28]

Other signs of a community in trouble were apparent in the manufacturing sphere. By the 1880s, there were few manufacturing operations still in business. In North Granby, the Dewey carriage works had failed after the Dewey brothers sold the business to John Edwards and William O. Ruick. In West Granby, Matthew Fancher gave up trying to compete with carriage factories that had steam engines (he had no credit left and had deeded over his house to his wife to avoid losing it to those to whom he already owed money). Two of his associates, Lucien Reed and Erwin Huggins, continued to paint wagons in old shops along the brook, but the age of manufacturing had otherwise passed in West Granby. Even the grist mill at the Gorge began to rot with disuse. At Mechanicsville, Robert Forsyth's grist and saw mills still did a reasonably good business. At Granby Street, Theodore Maltbie, Loyal Wilcox, inventor Charles Stephens and others organized the Granby Cutlery Company and built a factory in 1874. Later known as the Crystal Cutlery Works, this company made paper cutters, buttons, pistol stocks and other novelties at first, and then began specializing in glass handles for knives. By 1878, however, the company declared bankruptcy and was sold to a Chicago firm. Samuel Benjamin bought the building and sold it to be used as a general store. In the 1890s, it was a tobacco warehouse.[29] From 1870 on, Granby was locked into a prolonged depression.

This was not unusual for rural communities in New England. As the cities grew, and as their inhabitants were able to get agricultural products more cheaply from the West (which was, in turn, continuing to draw farmers away from the rocky soil of New England), the older rural areas could no longer compete in many of the markets in which they had once operated. Property values dropped, small manufacturers had a hard time competing even locally, young farmers and laborers moved away and creditors became impatient. For the middling and poorer farmers, many of whom did not have the means to move elsewhere, life was a struggle.[30]

Not all agreed that the situation was hopeless, however. In his reflections on his childhood, Chester Loomis's son James Lee Loomis, who would one day become president of The Connecticut Mutual Life Insurance Company, wrote, "There was little contact with the outside world. The people of the town were left to their own fate, depending upon their own resources to survive or perish....So it is with some regret, and some concern, that one observes [in the twentieth century] the old gold of a New England village gradually absorbing the characteristics of the Welfare State." In fact, for Loomis Brothers', the period from 1877 on was a "prosperous period for trade profits." Their volume of $40,000 to $60,000 per year in sales guaranteed

Figure 9-4: The building which once housed the Granby Cutlery Company. It was located at 20 Hartford Avenue, and torn down in 1974.

each partner a $5000 per year profit. They made so much that they had to search for a place to put their money and ended up losing a bundle in western mortgages and land investments. Even so, and in spite of a fire that burned their first store to the ground in 1877, by 1891 they could build a third store, larger than their first (see Figure 9-5).[31] Jim Loomis, as he was known, can be expected to paint the story of his father's business life with a rosy tint, but that volume of business suggests the local economy was not entirely lost. By the "old gold" of New England, Jim Loomis meant self-reliance on the part of the "rugged individual." Was that what was responsible for so many customers at Loomis Brothers' Store? What could otherwise account for his positive outlook on the situation in the late 1800s?

A part of the explanation has to do with the way scarce resources were distributed in this, the so-called "Gilded Age." One tends to think of cities and the West when recalling vast differences in wealth, but the phenomenon was present as well in small towns in New England.[32] Even tax lists, which tend to understate the wealth of those who had more influence with tax listers, make clear what was happening in Granby. According to the 1876 tax list, the upper quarter of the town's taxpayers lay claim to over 70% of the grand list. The lower *half* owned just 7% of the taxable property in town. Only 53 taxpayers out of 424 had estates valued above the average total estate value, and only 41 had any stocks, bonds, merchandise for trade, money at interest, or extra cash on hand. These included Lawyer Ed Holcomb and the Loomis brothers, each of whom had substantial investments outside the community, as well as lucrative businesses within.[33] However, the flow of the wealth was

Salmon Brook Historical Society

Figure 9-5: The third Loomis Brothers' store, built near the site of the old Hayes tavern. The smaller building on the right is the second store, which was rented out to tenants after 1891.

not moving only toward the social elite. Also among the town's upper economic class was Harvy Godard, whose cider brandy label was becoming more valuable than his mill property at the Cragg.

Jim Loomis could celebrate the "old gold of a New England village" because his family had done exceptionally well in this environment. Throughout the decades of the late 19th century, the town budget held steady in the $8,000-$10,000 range, with much of that going to "incidentals" (tools, fees to lawyers and reimbursements for expenses incurred by town officials, such as town clerk Chester Loomis). Those who were assessed the most still ended up paying relatively little in taxes - tax rates had to be kept down since any tax was a burden for those at the bottom. At the same time, little was spent on economic assistance. Even though half the town was living in a state of poverty, somehow they did not show up at the house of the contractor for the town poor.

To be fair though, James and Chester Loomis did pull themselves up by their own bootstraps. Both began their working lives as store clerks and invested what little money they had at great risk when there were already other general stores in Granby. James N. Loomis was such a talented trader that, when changing circumstances necessitated a move to fixed prices in the 1890s, he had a hard time making the transition. His head was crammed with conversion values for hundreds of commodities and the wholesale prices of his entire stock (all carefully purchased at the right time to get the lowest price). He had made his small fortune in an age when potatoes and butter served as currency. Only the need to hire clerks with minds less encyclopedic than his, and the increasing availability of paper currency (which Chester, in his later years, began to prefer over the old "due bill" system), removed James N. from his element. The brothers were the sharpest of businessmen, and as they wrangled the shipment of fertilizers and seed by the carload (paying their own bills at the last possible moment), they earned their profits by acquiring supplies and pricing them probably well below what their customers would have had to pay, without these partners as middlemen. Besides all that, the store became the town clerk's office, the post office, and a bank, as Pliny Hillyer's store once had been, when he had one at the same place. The brothers acted as legal guardians for orphaned children and consultants for anyone with financial, legal or even personal problems.[34] There is little wonder they survived as the only store in town.

To a certain extent, too, Jim Loomis was right about the whole town. Citizens, though hardly isolated from, but regularly buffeted by, "contact with the outside world," seldom complained about being "left to their own fate." In fact, many were quite active during this difficult period, adjusting to the effects of a fast-changing economy. These were times of significant change in farming technology. Before the Civil War, only western farmers had benefited from the new devices such as the McCormick Reaper; but the development of the mower, tedder and hayrake, along with the seeding machine, milking machine and corn harvester, marked a new era in which New England dairy farmers could share the benefits of mechanization. Even though there were far fewer farmers in New England, farming was becoming increasingly important in the economy as those remaining were becoming more productive, and found products their western competitors could not provide. Habits of experimentation and specialization were filtering down beneath the level of the gentlemen farmers.[35] "What a change the years have brought forth," wrote James R. Hayes of North Granby early in the twentieth century. "It is almost unbelievable when compared with today the hoe and [wood] plow relics of a past age have long since passed away giving place to more modern inventions and today everything for the comfort and convenience of the people."[36] Aided by agricultural societies, a growing agricultural press, and government funded agricultural departments working hard to reach deep into the ranks, some New England farmers, including some of those in Granby, were making the transition from the casual marketing of surplus to the development of profitable commercial products.[37]

When farmers had paid off their mortgages, they could invest in the new machines, or take a risk experimenting with one of their fields, perhaps one they had purchased from a less successful neighbor. However, few farmers in towns such as Granby were making a profit. It was more often the case that they barely paid the mortgage, and when they had a bad season, they had to turn to their wives to take up the slack by raising more poultry or making more butter - items traditionally within the sphere of the farm wife, and which could still bring good prices. Women were assisted by some innovations too, such as the iron cookstove, the ice chest, tinware, china, washboards and Elias Howe's sewing machine, but again, those things required some investment.[38] Most Granby farmers were hard pressed to raise the capital necessary to buy the machinery that would lead to steady profit. Many persisted anyway.

One solution was to create a marketing cooperative, such as the Granby Creamery Company. This organization began in 1882, led by Henry Jackson Dewey, Dwight F. Newton, A. T. Cornwell and George O. Beach. They put together a group to build a creamery opposite what is now 70 Creamery Hill Road (see Figure 9-6). Driven by a steam engine fueled by coal carted from the railroad depot, this giant churn produced 1000-1100 pounds of high grade butter per day. At the height of its business in 1906 the cooperative was grossing $40,000 per year for its members, selling to buyers as far away as Hartford, New Haven and Waterbury.[39]

Another type of cooperative organization was the National Grange of the Patrons of Husbandry. The Grange movement, based on the philosophy that all wealth springs from the soil and, therefore, rightfully belongs to the tillers of the soil, began in the midwest in 1867 (in New England, in Vermont in 1871). The movement spread quickly. Connecticut organized its state Grange in 1875, in the midst of the depression. The purpose of the Grange was first, to get farmers to join together to combat the forces of market consolidation that were driving down prices for agricultural products, and second, to become a political force in an age governed by the captains of industry. Granges also supported women's rights, and within the chapters, women were considered equal to men. In Granby, Harvy Godard took the initiative to begin Granby's chapter even before the state Grange was organized.

Harvy Godard was born in North Granby in 1823, the son of Oren and Minerva Godard. He grew up learning his father's and grandfather's businesses: farming, and running a gristmill, sawmill, and cider mill and distillery. He was a lifelong Mason and an active Democrat. In 1873, he won a seat in the state legislature - a rare event for a Granby Democrat after the Civil War. He was married to Sabra Lavinia Beach, daughter of West Granby farmer Oliver Beach. As previously mentioned, his cider brandy became famous, even though he himself never drank anything but cold water.

When he went to the organizational meeting of the state Grange in

397

Danbury, he was elected its Master and held that post through 1879. In 1875, he also represented Granby at the national Grange convention at Louisville, Kentucky. Sabra was elected Worthy Pomona of that body, and was reelected at the next four annual conventions. Back in Granby, he led the local chapter for twenty years as its Master. At its 1875 meeting, there were twenty-six charter members present. They first met for two years at Leonard Hall in North Granby, and then moved to Phelps Hall, on the corner of Mountain and North Granby Roads (the building now houses Allen's Cider Mill). In the second story, a large meeting room was created, where Grange buyers displayed everything from castor oil to tea and percussion caps (for guns) on three long tables, the items all ordered in bulk directly from New York or Philadelphia to obtain prices that would beat even those at Loomis Brothers'.

Salmon Brook Historical Society

Figure 9-6: Granby Creamery, which once operated on Creamery Hill Road.

398

Figure 9-7: Harvy and Sabra Lavinia Beach Godard of North Granby

The membership was enthusiastic, organizing large social events, such as clam bakes and shore dinners at Congamond Ponds. Interest dwindled, however, in the 1880s. An upturn in the economy may have been responsible, as more farmers began to make successful transitions to dairying. Local historians have suggested that there were problems with payment for the orders, or some laxity in collecting dues. At any rate, in the long run, Granby's first efforts to establish a Grange were not as successful as its organization of the Creamery.[40]

What worked for everyone, poor or solvent, was determined adaptation. Time and again, the story repeated itself: after most of the family moves out of town, a younger son inherits the family farm. Taking a risk, he borrows a little and exchanges his farm for a better one, builds a better barn and a silo, buys some additional property from poorer neighbors, and carries on a moderately successful dairy. Such was the story for Joseph Beman, who bought Lewis Hayes's West Granby farm after selling most of his own, a half-mile farther up the mountain on Silkey Road. Willis Phelps moved from the top of Popatunuck down Mountain Road to the corner of Mountain and Granville Roads where he ran a farm, contracted for the town poor, and rented his hall for dances and Grange meetings. James Hayes gradually traded up to good meadow land in North Granby and, working his dairy and undertaking business, became one of the wealthiest men in town.[41]

When these families moved away from poorer land to better land, they would sometimes keep their old hillside lots to use as wood lots and sell timber to area sawmills; or they would sell the farms to equally ambitious newcomers, such as Irish immigrants Michael Kelly and Michael Donahue, or the group of Swedish immigrants who bought property on Loomis Street toward the end of the century. Many of these farmers who ranked toward the bottom of the tax list refused to recognize that there was a depression, or that their condition was desperate, simply because, struggle as they did, they were better off than their parents had been. Michael Kelly, in fact, became one of the most prosperous dairy farmers in town.[42]

It was not necessarily "rugged individualism," however, that led to successful adaptations to the modern world. Nor did people clamor for public assistance or even lament the "decaying condition" of the world around them. Instead, they relied upon kinship networks to survive, and sometimes to thrive. Polly Taylor, reluctant as she was to depend upon her half-brother Marcus Alling, satisfied herself that her close circle of friends and relatives would help her because she could return the favor in one way or another. Eventually she did. Although in 1886 at age 68 she was struggling to survive, she was hardly a lonely and helpless old woman. She had a good deal of experience in business affairs, having been responsible for family finance since her husband's bankruptcy in the 1840s. Her estate papers are revealing. By 1895, she had accumulated an estate totaling over $11,000. Her daughter and grandson, who had moved to Albany shortly after Thomas's death, had predeceased her. And so, after setting aside some money to move their remains to the West Granby cemetery, across the road from her last residence, she spread her remaining funds around to her friends and family. The Methodist Church received $500. Charlotte Hotchkiss got $200. Ida Bristol got $100. Dr. Chatfield got $100. Her nephew, Buel, received $1000. Another nephew got $500. Finally, Eliza Alling, her sister-in-law, both as wife of her dead half-brother, and sister of her dead husband, received $1000, all the furniture, and her house.[43] These people constituted Polly's network. She probably earned the money herself, but, apparently she felt indebted to many who had given her the strength.

As a result of adaptation and reliance on networks of kin and friends, many of the middling and poorer farm families felt they were actually succeeding. This feeling sometimes produced a virtual celebration of the power of traditional rural ideals. In his family journal of 1886, Eugene Goddard kept careful record not only of the weather and his plantings, but also of each prayer meeting and preparatory lecture, from a "splendid discourse" on the "responsiveness to the Spirit" to sermons extolling the joys of living a lean but good life among friends and neighbors (and achieving ultimate reward in death!). On March 5, 1886, Mr. Campbell's talk "was from Matthew 5:14. 'Ye are the light of the world. A city that is set on a hill cannot be hid.' Christians, the lights of the world, appointed by God to deliver his message to the world." Even if someone had noticed it was Granby's centennial, no better theme would have been selected for a discourse. The "chosen people" of this New England town were keeping the old communal faith of the early Puritans while squarely facing the modern world. They embraced the hardness of life, as Puritan preachers had always taught, and stood content with small gains in the name of their own independence, relying only on close friends and relatives.[44]

As historian Hal S. Barron has noted, it was more often educators and professionals, and the new urban middle class, who lamented the decay of rural communities in late 19th century New England. Those who lived in them, an increasingly older populace, accepted the struggle with the modern world, even adopting some of the trappings of modernization to sustain their traditional vision. The more successful they were in integrating modern elements into their lives, the more they tended to praise the old-fashioned country ways (ways which were, in fact, never ways, but always ideals).[45]

401

This is not to say the farmers in the outlying areas had come to agree with the social elite on how the town should be run. They did think it was right to help others, to maintain community spirit, to work hard at their calling, and to avoid becoming a "public burden." They just did not have time or money to spare to support expensive public projects to beautify the town center, encourage a railroad to have a depot closer to the new business district, dress up their church meetinghouse, pay an inspiring minister, or invest in a permanent poor farm. And as long as cider brandy sold well, they certainly were not going to give up that trade to specialize solely in butter. For the great majority of Granby in the years after the Civil War, life was hard, but manageable. Diarist Eugene Goddard expressed this toughness well, one winter day: "The world passed on the same as usual to us only it brought us all 'one day nearer to our journey's end.'...One less of life for me." He was not complaining. He believed he was living life as it was meant to be lived, and that his reward was coming.

"Cheap and Durable"

At the October town meeting in 1873, Granby's citizens "Voted that the Selectmen be instructed to put up Posts and Railing North and South of the Library building Cheap and durable."[46] No doubt the need for railings around the building used not only for a library, but also for town meetings and services of the South Congregational Church, was a part of the general effort to bring some order and decorum to the town "center." It was done in the context of the revival of the library, the founding of the new church, and the creation of a park around the Civil War monument.

The phrase "cheap and durable," however, was probably added as a result of another force at work in town politics: the leaders of Granby, though still riding a wave of reform spirit since the end of the war, nevertheless had to accommodate the concerns of the "outlivers" of the town if they expected to continue to press their agenda. They needed to pay attention, especially in the year of a financial panic, to the fact that the majority of the town was barely making ends meet. That hard-pressed majority, while not expecting a hand-out, expected the town government to be extremely economical. In fact, had their leaders pressed harder for expensive reforms (or in this case had ordered railings to match the ornate architecture of the library), it is questionable whether the residents of the outlying areas would think it necessary even to have a town government. This increasingly accommodating stance on the part of the social elite would lead to a fragile truce which smoothed over some of the antagonisms of the period prior to the Civil War.[47]

That 1873 town meeting, with its nod to the outlivers who preferred the "cheap and durable" approach to government, occurred in the midst of a turning point in Granby public affairs. In the years before, the Republicans were winning elections and making headway with some of their agenda. However, there had been intense bickering over a number of issues. In the fall of 1870, the October 15 town meeting was the scene of debate over schools, roads and, of all things, dogs. Clearly, the social elite was getting nowhere at that meeting. They were asking for too much. In a somewhat partisan action, they ordered the town's weights and measures moved from Jairus Case's house to the Loomis Brothers' store. A resolution to consolidate school districts, so that town leaders could have more control over the quality of education, resulted in an adjournment, and later a motion to table. Similarly, a motion to spend more money on road repairs was ordered to the table.

Only a technical action on the "dog tax" drew a favorable vote. At a previous meeting the majority had voted to repeal the tax on dogs. According to state law, dogs were assessed as taxable property, but apparently a number Granby residents did not agree that this was appropriate. It does not take too much imagination to discern which portion of the electorate wished to save the few pennies it cost to own man's best friend. However, the lawyers must have prevailed upon the cash-poor dog owners, insisting that a town meeting could not repeal a state law, for the October meeting expunged the repeal and simply instructed the selectmen to abate the tax on dogs. The following year, the Republicans barely held out in a close election for state representatives.[48]

In October, 1871, a town meeting at Loomis Brothers' Hall chose Democrat Jairus Case as moderator and proceeded to debate at length about how the town should care for its roads and its paupers. The local merchants expressed frustration with the antiquated system of highway maintenance, in which elected supervisors would turn out their neighbors, or substitutes their neighbors hired, to work off the "highway rate." This system was obviously not putting roads in the condition needed to haul merchandise even from the depot to Granby Street, let alone around town. Furthermore, they and their allies did not like the practice of bidding out the town's paupers to a contractor, and would have preferred a permanent poor farm, with an overseer under supervision of the selectmen. Again they saw their designs disintegrate as the town voted on how much to pay for road work per man hour, how much to pay for the use of teams, scrapers and plows for a day, and how much to charge for the highway tax (3 mills). Then the town voted to hire a contractor for paupers, but carefully instructed the contractor not to take in any

Salmon Brook Historical Society

Figure 9-8: Library, Academy, and South Congregational Church building at 248 Salmon Brook Street ("cheap and durable" railings to the south).

transients. Again the Republicans won the next legislative election, with Wallace Kendall defeating Munson Holcomb, and Levi Rice just barely edging out Harvy Godard.[49] The harder they pushed for reform, the closer they came to being unseated.

The annual town meeting of 1872 was the scene of more feuding, and an unusual but revealing measure to have town officers elected by secret ballot. After an adjournment and then "considerable discussion," the leadership finally managed to extract approval for bidding out road repair work to a contractor for five years, even though they had hoped to convince their parsimonious citizenry that the town should buy teams and hire workers by the month.[50] They tried again to professionalize town government operations, calling a special town meeting for that purpose in January, 1873, but when they proposed paving Dibble Hill (Hartford Avenue west of the bridge), paying salaries to town officials, and reinstituting the dog tax, they got nowhere. In April, Harvy Godard won a seat in the legislature along with Republican John Burwell.[51] It was give and take at every turn. For every success, or for that matter, for every hint that they might succeed, the reformers paid dearly. In the fall, they won a fight over the licensing of taverners, passing a resolution to limit the number of licenses issued to three and to prosecute those in violation of the liquor laws. However, they had to go on record that the library railings would be "cheap and durable."[52]

In Harvy Godard, Granby's struggling farmers had a strong leader. As his activism in the Grange movement showed, he was a man to be reckoned with, and gave voice to the frustrations of his neighbors in North Granby and his wife's former neighbors in the West Granby hills. Although a staunchly temperate man, he represented a serious threat to the Republican social elite, for he was firmly Jeffersonian, advocating the least government possible, and squarely against prohibition of the sale of liquor. He would not be the Democrat the Republicans could count on for support, as Jairus Case had been. If reform-minded leaders hoped to make progress, they were going to have to come to terms, after 1873, with a more organized and more determined farm vote in their town. In fact, with the onset of the depression in 1874, Democrat Albert C. Latham, a relative newcomer to Granby politics, succeeded in winning a seat in the legislature. The annual town meeting debated with no resolution on paupers, liquor licenses and setting bounties on foxes.[53] The Democrats, some of them now as wealthy and respected as the men of Granby Street, had become a real force in resisting the vision of the social elite. Both Godard and Latham ranked among the town's wealthiest men, but they apparently did not believe they had succeeded as a result of good schools, good roads, dry taverns, or having a professionally operated poor farm in their town.

After 1874, the year of Jairus Case's death, the Republicans began to make a comeback. They succeeded by putting Marcus Alling and James R. Hayes, from West and North Granby, respectively, at the head their ticket for the state vote in early 1875. But apparently the price of support for their candidates among West Granby hill farmers was to be the reopening of the Hart Road into territory that was being abandoned in West Granby.[54] Then the next year, voters at a February town meeting "argued at length" about where to hold town meetings, finally approving a resolution by A. L. Loveland in March to alternate between the First Congregational Church and some place in West Granby. The success of the rebellion continued in April when Democrat George Beach, who had a farm on "Pine Cone," near Broad Hill, won a seat in the legislature.[55]

In the years that followed, the same issues kept reappearing, illustrating the continued division between the social elite and the hill farmers over the course Granby should take. Republicans gradually learned that there was always a limit to how far they could go. It was better, they came to understand, to be patient on their agenda for the community and keep their seats in the legislature and the board of selectmen, than to alienate their government-wary townsmen and completely lose control. They won a vote to support a general assembly bill to order dogs restrained to their premises by their owners, and they managed to get a committee appointed to consider the consolidation of school districts under a single school board for the town. However, they failed at an effort to require landowners to cut bushes along the highway against their own land, and the school consolidation committee reported back that consolidation only worked where school children were divided into separate grades. After 1880, Republican candidates ran up sizable majorities in state and local elections and, as the pauper budget declined (because there were fewer, and they could be bid out individually, rather than assigned to a contractor), the reformers succeeded in getting gradually more and more money committed to the schools. However, again and again, they lost votes to prohibit the licensing of liquor retailers. In 1889, a proposed amendment to the state constitution to ban the sale of "intoxicating liquor," went down to a 2-1 defeat in Granby.[56]

It is almost pathetic to read the reports of the local school visitors evaluating Granby's one- and two-room school houses. Over and over they commend the teachers for doing the best with what they have, and for making some progress, in spite of their lack of preparation for the task. The districts, wrote one reform-minded evaluator, needed to be "more particular on the appointment of teachers: to see that they possess more qualifications necessary for a teacher."[57] Alas, Granby got what it paid for: well-meaning young women, generally, who had sometimes not graduated from a secondary school, looking for a little extra cash, and rushing home from school teaching to do seamstress work for the same purpose. Some schools changed teachers nearly every term, and visitors constantly complained about faltering attendance, ramshackle facilities and dilapidated books. Most of the time the evaluators simply heaved a sigh, for they knew that any stronger effort to push district parents to upgrade the schools would result in the ouster of the "better sort" from positions of town leadership (and doom school consolidation forever). As youth moved out of Granby upon reaching adulthood, or, at least in from the outlying districts, an increasingly aged population in the outer districts was not interested in pouring money into schools their children had outgrown. Wrote acting School Visitor Frederick Jewett in 1894, the town authorities "should lend...moral influence" towards making successful schools. He went on to note that the cooperation of the parents was necessary.[58] He would have liked to insist on more, but it simply was not going to happen.

Thus the town continued, stable and economical, controlled by respected Republican men who dared not push the tax rate beyond fifteen mills on assessments that were surely well below actual value. Paupers received minimal care in local homes, only a few short sections of roads were paved, the road maintenance budget was eaten up keeping roads open that linked hillside farmers who seldom traversed them (but had a good time

407

turning out to repair them in the spring), and instead of salaried officials, the town still elected annually the bevy of tythingmen, gaugers, haywards, sealers, wood measurers, packers and poundkeepers they had been choosing since the previous century.[59] A few years later, Theodore Maltbie, then a respected Hartford lawyer and judge, would say that "no one has been able to understand the dark and devious ways of the Granby politics;" and Edward W. Dewey, a county commissioner and chairman of the Republican Town Committee since the mid-1880s, would reply that "he did not know as he cared to tell all that has been done in politics in that town. It is perhaps enough to say that we (Republicans) have been generally successful."[60] Well, they won elections anyway (with no one saying how, in this age of graft and

Salmon Brook Historical Society

Figure 9-9: One of Granby's many one-room schoolhouses near the turn of the century. (Northwest corner of Notch and Hungary Roads.)

corruption).[61] However, as time passed, they seemed to give up on the reforms they and their fathers had hoped for in the 1860s.

Of course, if a civic improvement did not cost anything, nor threaten anyone's livelihood, Granby farmers were happy to cheer it on. In October, 1892, for example, the town meeting voted to give permission for the Salmon Brook Water Company to erect an iron watering tub at Granby Street on town property a little south of the public park. It took six years for the town to follow up with a $6 per year payment, even though the public had certainly made good use of the tub with every trip to Loomis Brothers' Store.[62]

A few years earlier, reform minded leaders had even more about which to be happy. In 1887, Frederick H. Cossitt, great-great grandson of René Cossitt of North Granby, died in New York City. The passing of one who had lived his childhood in Granby, and then moved on, was not much of an event of note in a town that had seen so many of its children leave for greener pastures in the 1820s and 1830s. However, Frederick Cossitt had made millions for himself in retailing, and in his will left $10,000 to "the corporation of North Granby" for the purpose of building a free public library (library building was a common philanthropic gesture among businessmen of this age). He had been away some time, and so we might forgive him for forgetting that North Granby was not its own town (perhaps he assumed it had become so in his absence). At any rate, Granby's leaders forgave him, and, after some legal maneuvering, accepted the library on behalf of Granby, sealing the commitment with a pledge of $1 for its further support. With the money from the bequest in hand, the town decided in 1891 to build the structure in North Granby across the street from Cossitt's boyhood home (now 377 North Granby Road) and appointed a Library Board with authority to oversee the whole project and to draw on the library fund now deposited with the town treasurer. This was Granby's first public, or non-subscription, library. In fact, it was one of its first public institutions in years, besides the park, of course. When the library was built, the town did not even have a town hall.

The founding of the Cossitt Library represented the beginning of a new era in Granby. The effort drew the town together in spite of continuing

409

differences over temperance, roads, dogs, schools and what-not. William C. Case gave an oration at the dedication extolling the power of books to improve lives, gentlemen from West Granby and Granby Street traveled north to the land of cider brandy to give thanks for the coming of culture, and Democrats and Republicans alike served on the first Library Board. In charge of the whole enterprise was one of Harvy Godard's sons, George Seymour Godard, who was in the middle of his college education at Wesleyan and had returned to his home town with a Middletown architect, Jasper Daniel Sibley, to design the building (see Figure 9-10).[63]

Surely Godard and Sibley were men of vision. Godard went on from this position, as librarian of the Cossitt Library, to become Librarian for the State of Connecticut, supervising the construction and development of the present State Library in Hartford. However, the Cossitt Library represented more wishful thinking than precise vision. Certainly it remains an important institution in the life of the town today, but even now it stands out among its surroundings as a rather odd piece of architecture for a farming community. Its Queen Anne style windows, roof and other decorative work would be a good fit for a late Victorian urban neighborhood. Of course, that may have been what its first Board of Directors hoped North Granby would become. They had planted the seed of order and civility among the apple orchards, and now expected it to sprout and bear non-fermenting fruit.

North Granby Democrats, even including old Harvy Godard himself, had probably joined their Republican neighbors, such as James R. Hayes and Edward Dewey, in insisting that the library be built near Cossitt's home. However, they embraced the institution only because it was free. They were not about to pave roads around it, or build a new school to match it, or cease to manufacture brandy in its vicinity. Doubtless they even had trouble paying their fines, since George Godard and his assistant, his future wife Kate Dewey (Edward's sister), would not take tobacco in lieu of cash.

The struggle for control of public policy between the social elite and the farmers of Granby was unresolved throughout the 1870s, 80s and early 90s. While Democrats lost votes as disgruntled farmers moved away, they still maintained enough strength to resist measures such as liquor prohibition, consolidation of schools, and, of course, paying taxes on dogs. In return for

Figure 9-10: Frederick H. Cossitt Library (built 1891) in North Granby.

more-or-less regular Republican control of the town's seats in the General Assembly, the swing voters expected economy in local government and recognition of their perennial battle against the forces of modernization and economic change. The result was a two-decade truce while community reformers bided their time, satisfying themselves that, in private and voluntary activities, they were doing the best that could be done for the continuing redemption of their hard-pressed little town.

"Granby's Sons are Loyal"

In 1893, two years after the construction of the Cossitt Library, the nation was hit by another financial panic which ushered in hard times that lasted five years and cost the Democrats the presidency in 1896. It was the

411

worst depression in the nation's history. In Granby, however, this depression did not have the same ruinous effect as the one in the 1870s had. Instead of widespread disillusionment and suffering, this was a time when spirits were on the rise in Granby. Perhaps the town had been in a state of depression so long that things could not get worse. Whatever the explanation, the 1890s were years of revival and change in Granby.

The business downturn was initially accompanied by the usual reconstituting of numerous voluntary organizations at all levels of society. Following on the heels of the construction of the third Loomis Brothers' Store, a Village Improvement Society began looking after the Granby green, and a group of young people of Granby Street decided to build a tennis court there. The library on the Street, having been reorganized in 1887, joined the Cossitt Library as a free library (though still not a public library) in 1891. In 1895, a reinvigorated Granby Agricultural Society sold shares of stock and purchased twenty-three acres on West Granby Road for a fairground. Complete with bandstand, grandstand and a baseball field in the middle of a half-mile racetrack, within five years the fair was offering a $300 purse for sulky racing (see Figure 9-11). It was also in 1895 that people on the Street began raising money for street lamps by holding benefit sales of ice cream and cake. Samuel Benjamin began borrowing money to build a new church, the Seventh-Day Adventist Church, for Granby Center. Harvy Godard got up a reorganization meeting of the Granby Grange at his home in 1892. This time the Grange, holding its meetings in the Cossitt Library, had not only farmers among its membership, but also professionals and politicians, like Frederick L. Jewett and James R. Hayes. The outbreak of the Spanish-American War in 1898 only added to the burst of voluntarism as women in Granby and North Granby joined together to sew garments for soldiers in Cuba. In the next decade, the Granby Cemetery Association reorganized, and the West Granby Methodist Church renovated the interior of its meetinghouse and added a wood-burning furnace and organ.[64]

In this era of reform, moreover, civic improvement was not limited to voluntary organizations. During the 1890s, those who had inherited the reform spirit of the 1840s and 1860s actually achieved some victories as the twenty-five year stalemate over public policy came to an end. First the town took over the old Granby Central Academy building in 1893 and turned it into a town hall. When that burned in 1901, they built a new one a little to the south of its former location (see Figure 9-12).[65]

A more surprising expenditure of public money was directed toward road improvements. The impetus came in 1895 when the state passed a law for the encouragement of road maintenance and the establishment of state highways. Towns would continue to decide which roads to improve and would administer contracts, but the state would provide funds to complement local expenditures. At an August 3 town meeting, residents authorized the town to spend .5% of the grand list on road improvements (nearly twice the usual expenditures for road maintenance) and to appoint a committee to locate

Figure 9-11: Granby Fairgrounds off what is now Route 20, just west of Salmon Brook Street.

413

Figure 9-12: New Town Hall, constructed 1901. Now the Grange Hall.

the road or roads to be improved. The committee reported back that the chosen road was that which Granby Street merchants had long hoped would be paved: Hartford Avenue from the hill above the Salmon Brook crossing to the town line just west of the train depot. This was not a long section, but for those carting large quantities of merchandise between warehouses on the Street and the depot a mile away, its improvement would be a real boon.[66]

In December, at a special town meeting, leaders pushed through a 17 mill tax rate and a vote to authorize the selectmen to borrow up to $1800 to macadamize more roads in town. Appropriations were rescinded two years later, but in 1899, after discussing the matter "at length," the town finally appropriated $2000 of borrowed money to match a state appropriation. The economy-minded farmers put up a good fight, and in the process they held off votes to prohibit liquor sales and to consolidate schools, as in days past. But their old power was waning. They could not defeat expensive road improvements any longer. The town even voted to build a steel bridge on Hartford Avenue and to discontinue two old roads in outlying districts. At the annual town meeting in 1899, the farmers barely carried the liquor vote 118-111, and lost a vote on borrowing money for consolidating schools. The following year Granby finally went dry, by a vote of 129-110.[67]

Fierce debate continued into the early years of the new century. While the town remained dry through 1902, the annual meeting in that year allowed licenses for the next year in another close vote. Liquor won again in 1903 and 1904, when it won by two votes, but then the temperance advocates carried a resounding "no" vote in the 1905 annual meeting. After that year, Granby remained dry for almost six decades. Along with the successful struggle for prohibition, the reformers pushed through expenditures on textbooks for the schools, a "Steel Cell or Lock up" ($150), town sponsorship of Memorial Day activities, a payment to the Salmon Brook Sewer Association to drain Salmon Brook Street ($200), and literally thousands of dollars of bond issues for improvements to roads (while, at the same time, the town closed three roads in the hills of West and North Granby). Unlike the 1870s and 80s, however, there was no retribution at the polls, as Republicans garnered well over 60% of the vote between 1900 and 1905, and in gubernatorial and presidential elections, delivered 70% of Granby's votes to their candidates (William McKinley and Theodore Roosevelt).[68]

The willingness to permit a more active, reformist and expensive government, even in the midst of hard times, may have been the result of prolonged economic troubles having already shaken out many of those who had resisted public improvements and moral restrictions for so long. Actually, the 1900 census showed an increase in the population of Granby for the first time in seventy years. This was only a small increase of 48 persons over the 1890 total of 1251, however, and probably was a result of some young people actually finding success and settling down with their families. Otherwise, as unhappy farmers moved out, poorer people moved in to buy their land.[69] These were generally people who had no influence in town meetings. A town vote in 1897 explains why.

On October 4 of that year, the town voted 126 to 7 in favor of a Constitutional Amendment providing that the ability to read the state Constitution and statutes in English was a requirement for voting.[70] This was at once a progressive measure, relying on the old republican axiom that education was necessary for a responsible electorate, and an anti-immigrant, anti-city measure. A similar law had been on the books since 1884, but the constitutional amendment set the policy in stone. Throughout the late 19th century, feeling had been building state-wide against the rapid influx of foreigners into Connecticut, most of whom had migrated to the state's urban areas.[71] Thus, Granby cast its ballot, along with many other rural Connecticut communities, as a staunchly anti-immigrant town.

This nativism prevailed even though (or, perhaps, because) Granby itself had had a number of newcomers from foreign lands in recent years. Irish Catholics had been moving in since the 1840s. By 1908, there were twenty Catholic families in Granby, including some from Lithuania. Swedish immigrants began arriving in the 1890s, and formally organized their own church in 1902 as the Swedish Free Christian Society of North Granby (forerunner of the Pilgrim Covenant Church). An 1893 newspaper article recounting the reception of two Chinese students in Granby in the 1870s probably expressed the way natives generally responded to people who looked and spoke differently: "It was indeed aggravating to the ordinary young American to find himself beaten in studies by a strange-looking, almond-eyed personage, and the intruders were not treated any too well in consequence." The article allowed that the "intruders" soon won their way "to favor," even though a combination of external factors eventually doomed the Chinese mission.[72] Nevertheless, when one considers this statement against the reference in town records to three "races," black, white and Irish, we can understand why Michael Kelly, one of the most successful dairy farmers in Granby in the late 19th century, was never elected to any major town office. In fact, it is doubtful that newcomers of foreign birth even bothered to show up at town meetings in the 1890s and early 1900s.

Not only were these replacements for Granby's formerly rebellious, anti-reform farmers not active (in fact, they were practically invisible) in politics in Granby, but the Republican party itself was becoming increasingly appealing to conservative Democrats, and that helped the Republican agenda along. When the Democratic national convention nominated the anti-tariff populist William Jennings Bryan for President in 1896, many Connecticut Democrats turned Republican. In Connecticut, even though the Republicans abandoned their anti-Catholic stance by 1898, they continued to oppose a new state constitution that would give the cities their fair proportion of legislative seats (under the old system by which each town, including cities, had two seats, 15% of the state electorate chose a majority of the representatives to the General Assembly).[73] Trying to ward off the constitutional change was certainly a veiled design to curb the power of neighborhoods in which immigrants lived. What all this meant for Granby was that those who had always leaned toward an active town government - that is, the Republicans - were slowly gaining more political allies toward the end of the century as old class-based political differences faded amidst anti-immigrant, anti-city sentiments. Once, Republicans had raised the specter of a looming Southern "slave aristocracy" to entice voters to their causes. Now they effectively employed a similar strategy as defenders of the moral virtues which could only be found in the small towns.

The alleviation of economic stress for those who remained in the town could also have been responsible for the emerging consensus over public policy. While the 1890s were hard on other rural areas in the nation, some Granby farmers and businessmen seemed to be weathering the storm with some success. Even though the town's population had declined to its lowest point since the French and Indian War, Loomis Brothers' store continued to do well. Some of the prosperity may have been the result of fewer restrictions on the sale of milk (in 1897, Connecticut repealed all of its anti-tuberculosis legislation).[74] Some may also have been the result of the growing attraction of Granby to vacationers. Former residents, who had moved to various cities, often summered in Granby, and some city residents were actually buying up nearly valueless farm property for vacation homes.[75] Former inns, long empty (such as Elam Kendall's inn in West Granby, which became the West Granby Hotel), began to rent rooms again as fishermen and naturalists sought escape from congested urban areas.

Probably the most important explanation for Granby's resilience in hard times, however, has to do with adaptability and the revival of traditional communal values cited in the previous section of this chapter. With the

417

Granby Creamery in operation, the Grange revived, the fair paying handsome prizes, the most industrious farmers trading up to better land and bovine tuberculosis under control, better times were finally arriving in the 1890s for a good many who had stayed in town. Having survived by means of networks of neighbors and kinfolk, they now put those networks to use in creating some relative prosperity that would make them all feel better about their town and everyone in it. Divisions were still there, the distribution of wealth was still extremely uneven, but living conditions were improving. As James Hayes had said: "Everything for the convenience of the people."

The emergence of shade tobacco growing followed this trend toward better conditions and only contributed to what was already in the works. Still, the speed with which it caught on demonstrates the adaptability of Granby farmers, as well as the importance, ironically, of active government. As we know, Granby farmers had been growing tobacco since the colonial period. Cigar making had been a home industry before the Civil War, and the price of Connecticut broadleaf grown for that purpose had risen considerably by 1860. After the war, however, prices fell, and even though farmers could produce a lot more tobacco with Havana seed, introduced in the 1870s, few made a good living from the crop in the late 19th century. In spite of a high tariff, competition from Sumatran tobacco as a wrapper for cigars put a lot of growers in Granby, and throughout Connecticut, out of business (even though the number of acres under cultivation grew).[76]

In 1896, the Connecticut Experimental Station in Windsor, in cooperation with the U.S. Department of Agriculture, began experimenting with ways to duplicate the growing conditions of Sumatran tobacco in Connecticut. By the beginning of the century, they had actually developed a leaf of higher quality than the East Indian brand using cotton cheesecloth "tent" to shade the crop grown in heavily fertilized Connecticut soil. Farmers in Simsbury and Granby who could afford the investment in tent and fertilizer, immediately began devoting some of their acreage to the new style of cultivation. It meant harder work and heavier investment, but with the help of further tariff protection from Congress, success came quickly. Marcus Floyd, called "the father of the shade grown tobacco industry" in Connecticut, was one of the first to grow shade tobacco in Granby. In 1901, having moved from Florida to Granby, he became manager of the Connecticut Tobacco Corporation, which had fields in the southern part of town around what became known as Floydville Road. Fred Griffin of Granby also worked with shade tobacco as early as 1905.

Apparently there was some resistance from buyers who had made a lot of profit keeping the price of traditionally cultivated outdoor tobacco depressed while they themselves benefited from tariff-induced prices. Also, conversion was easier for a tobacco corporation which had capital to invest in equipment than it was for the average farm family. Although three bad years nearly ruined the new approach, the experiment station continued developing new strains, and, by 1910, shade tobacco growing had established itself with a number of area farmers. As investment capital gradually flowed into the area, conditions for laborers and farmers alike improved, to say nothing of merchants hauling in fertilizer and other supplies.[77]

The precariousness of investment in Granby, be it in shade tobacco or anything else, continued to plague the town, nevertheless. In 1900, when his father Matthew died, James Fancher made an effort to transform the old wheel shop into a going enterprise. He created the Simplex Manufacturing Company and attempted to make a number of different products on contract: a machine for sealing envelopes, a die filing machine, buckles, and Victrola motors. However, he had little success here, went bankrupt and moved to Thompsonville to reorganize.[78] To his west, young Condit Messenger bought the old Nathaniel Pratt farm on Fox Road for a relatively cheap $1200 in 1893. Mortgage payments plagued him all his life, and only the inability of his creditors to sell the farm to anyone else stalled foreclosure for two decades.[79] Bankruptcy was still a common occurrence even as things were getting better for some farmers.

As we take note of the role of decreasing opposition, Republican anti-city ideology and improving conditions, we should not neglect the continuing efforts of the reformers themselves in achieving success. Indeed, what is remarkable about the entire period, from the end of the Civil War to the early years of the twentieth century, is the consistency and durability of the reform spirit. Essentially, the school consolidation movement, the temperance movement, the effort to improve Granby's self-anointed business district, and the proposals to professionalize town services with salaries, hired employees and town funded institutions were all direct extensions of the reform platform that had coalesced in the years prior to the Civil War, and which, in fact, had given impetus to the militant spirit with which Granby had responded to the secession crisis. By the early 1900s, there was a different generation of leaders pushing for these reforms, but they represented the same neighborhoods, the same classes, and the same mentality (and some were even children and grandchildren) of those who initially formed Granby's Republican party in the 1850s as part of the effort to "redeem Salmon Brook from its decaying condition."

In the early years of the twentieth century, strong echoes of this continuing spirit of community renewal were heard at the convening of a remarkable group of men in Hartford. Apparently someone had noticed how many prominent men of Hartford were from Granby and proposed to start a "Granby Club" in the city. The group, including George A. Holcombe of Travelers Insurance, Attorney Stanley W. Edwards, State Librarian George S. Godard, and County Commissioner Edward W. Dewey (its first officers), met for dinner in 1905 at the Hotel Hartford.

At its second meeting a year later, 36 men were present (women were excluded in spite of George Godard's proposal to the contrary), and Judge Theodore Maltbie was elected president. A newspaper article, entitled "Granby's Sons Are Loyal," reported the event. In a toast, George Godard urged members to "put [their native] town forward in every way possible," even suggesting that some who had moved to Hartford should resume their residence in Granby. "What a pity," exclaimed Rev. John T. Winters (who now lived in New Britain), "her sons are not there, doing their work they are doing elsewhere. What a pity the field for the work is not there. They are exiles from home, because there are no opportunities in the town for their knowledge, their ambitions and their energies. The world has not yet turned a cold shoulder on me, but when it comes my turn to die, I hope it will be my fortune to have my ashes laid in Granby." He brought down the house, apparently, with his toast: "Here's to good old Granby, the land of steady habits; the home of industry and frugality and domestic integrity. May her sons ever prove worthy of her sires."

Other appeals to community pride and loyalty to rural roots followed. Imagine the stiff collars, the elegant dinnerware and the cigars (wrapped in "Granby shade") as Duane N. Griffin discoursed upon "The Barefoot Boy." He conjured up this image to represent the traits of stability, endurance and strength that had carried these men from Granby to the heights of their professions. These barefoot boys may in the future, he said, "be the salvation of the city." Then Walter G. Murphy stood to make a strong appeal for the reclamation of abandoned farms in Granby. Charles W. Ruic urged the members of the club to see to it "that any efforts to change the representation of the small towns in the Legislature are buried and buried deeply. The independence of the towns, he said, should never be surrendered."[80]

Together all of these remarks, engulfed in cigar smoke, represent the culmination of the elite view of Granby. They were speaking of what the town represented to them, and what they thought the town had given them. This view was consistent with that of many professional men of that time who had small-town backgrounds and were reacting to the growth and problems of the nation's cities. Even as they joined in urban culture and urban society, they clung to what they considered the virtues of the rural world. They believed their success was built upon those virtues, and that the city, an alien environment for them, would benefit greatly from some education in those virtues. While this education took place, of course, the small towns, out-populated as they were, should maintain a majority in the General Assembly, exercising the same virtues there that the cities could not yet bring to government.

In the speeches of the Granby Club, we can also see a group of loyal sons of Granby wrestling with some heartfelt contradictions. They had been brought up to believe that, as educated and prosperous leaders, they were responsible for the moral uplifting of Granby. This had been the work of their parents and grandparents over the last six decades (if not of generations since the Great Awakening and the original Puritan migration to New England). Yet, many had left their town to find success elsewhere - and in an alien environment. They acknowledged the abandonment of farms and the town's declining population (even though by then the population was beginning to climb again), and probably felt as though they, themselves, were party to this

421

abandonment. Thus, they needed some justification for the path they had chosen.

In fitting their work in Hartford together with their sense of loyalty to Granby, not only were they joining in the formation of the "progressive" ideology of that time, but they also contributed to the creation of the mythology of Granby and the small town in general. Granby was for them the land of barefoot boys who whiled away hours doing farm chores and communing with nature. It was a harmonious community of industrious, frugal, strong, stable and honest people, who provided a solid grounding for the success of their children in the home, on the farm, and in other community institutions that could not be found in the city.

Of course, we know all this was far from the case. The final success of the temperance movement may have clouded their vision. And even in that respect, there was hardly success. As Jim Loomis noted in his recollections about his father's store, many people invested a good deal of money in "bitters" for their supposed colds - a bottle of which was 95% whiskey. In North Granby, in 1900, the very year Granby first went dry, not one-tenth of a mile from the Cossitt Library, George Beach, George Godard's uncle, was hard at work setting up a copper cider brandy still (in the building that is now Allen's Cider Mill).[81]

There had been some progress getting the business district tidied up, complete with a "center" church. A few roads in that area had been paved, and a few of the outlying roads that sucked money from the maintenance budget had been abandoned. Business was improving at Loomis Brothers' (they were incorporated in 1906). Church socials, baseball games, tennis, Memorial Day parades, and an annual fair did bring the town together. Some farmers were finding ways to avoid foreclosure, and for those who stayed, freedom from creditors seemed to be all that was needed to ensure contentment. The greater reality, though, was that only a few people - of the male gender, and not those who grew up doing farm chores - had arisen within this town to achieve significant prosperity and success. Schools were still not consolidated nor even well furnished. Town government was still inefficient and, until recently, generally inactive. Many farmers still struggled to make ends meet and to come to terms with the modern world in which they had to make a living. Houses sat unpainted, and along the abandoned roads in the hills, they rotted away to a pile of boards. Once active pastures and orchards often became a tangle of weeds and shrubs. Local manufacturers and craftsmen had no future. There was still a wide gulf between rich and poor. Even though most farm families were religious, and the members of churches were strongly committed, actual church attendance was low. Most roads, in spite of rapidly increasing expenditures, were still unpaved and poorly maintained.

All this is not to say that Granby was not yet "redeemed" from decay. It just wasn't the idyllic place pictured by its loyal sons in Hartford. It was still, as they themselves realized when citing abandoned farms and lack of opportunity, in need of revitalizing, if it was going to live up to their image of the ideal traditional small town - an image that was, even in times past, never the reality for any small town anywhere! They had created this ideal anew, drawing on the hopes and values of their parents, and then had gone back to work at their jobs in Hartford.

423

Chapter X
A Model Town

Chronology

The World	America	Granby
1905 Uprisings in Russia	1905 Theodore Roosevelt begins second term	
	1906 Pure Food and Drug Act	1906 George McLean begins buying abandoned land for his game refuge
	1908 General Motors Corp. formed; Ford makes Model T	1909 Town takes charge of school districts
	1910 NAACP formed	
1911 Sun Yat-sen overthrows Manchu dynasty in China		1911 Tudor Holcomb plants his first crop of shade tobacco
1912 Titanic Sinks	1913 Woodrow Wilson President; Income Tax Amendment	
1914 World War I		1914 Electricity arrives in Granby
1917 Russian Revolution	1917 U.S. enters World War I	1917 South Church burns; Granby Home Guard formed
1918 Armistice ends World War I		
	1919 Prohibition and Palmer Raids	1919 Center School built
	1920 Woman Suffrage	
		1923 Granby a "Model Town"
		1924 Helen Green elected to state legislature
1925 Hitler writes *Mein Kampf*	1925 Scopes Trial	
1926 Hirohito becomes Emperor of Japan	1927 Lindbergh flight	
	1929 Herbert Hoover President; stock market crash; Great Depression	1930 James Lee Loomis President of Connecticut Mutual, William Mills Maltbie Chief Justice of Ct. Supreme Court
	1931 Wilbur Cross Governor of Ct.	
1932 Japan invades Manchuria	1933 Franklin D. Roosevelt President, New Deal	
1933 Hitler becomes German Chancellor	1936 FDR reelected	
	1937 U.S. Neutrality Act	
1939 World War II begins in Europe	1940 FDR reelected	
1940 Fall of France, Battle of Britain	1941 U.S. enters World War II	

In 1906, Granby's "loyal sons" sat around the dinner table in Hartford extolling the virtues of their birthplace and curiously lamenting its abandonment. Back home, as Granby plodded into a new century, there was surprising contentment, and even some optimism. Local reformers worked in voluntary organizations and in town meetings to fight for the continued uplifting of their community. Those farmers in the outlying areas who had stayed in town (or who had moved in to take up abandoned farms) found ways to meet the challenges of being in the agriculture business in New England in the era of railroads, monopolies and mechanization. As the reformers made noticeable progress, and as farmers made a better living than their parents had, all found reinforcement for virtues they believed were as old as the hills themselves. In an age of economy, a small town that had become even smaller, found a degree of stability it had long sought.

To some extent, as we have seen, the contentment and sense of stability were based more upon perception than truly favorable conditions. Nevertheless, perceptions often shape history more than reality itself, and in the case of Granby, the perception of an era of relative prosperity did actually conjure up an economic recovery for the first two decades of the twentieth century. This backdrop of well-being and growth helped fund formerly unaffordable community reforms which climaxed, even after the turbulent World War I era, with Granby's recognition as a "model town." This was hardly the end of Granby's history, however, for old divisions and new stresses continued to challenge the ideal of stability and quiet harmony toward which all Granby citizens aspired.

Operating to the Best Advantage

When Tudor and Laura Holcomb were children growing up in West Granby in the 1890s, their parents were struggling, like many other farm families in Granby, to stay afloat in hard times. Their father, Samuel F. Holcomb, known as "S. F.," had inherited their farm at the foot of Broad Hill in 1871, at the age of sixteen. Nahum Holcomb, Samuel's father, had left an orchard and a cider mill, some tobacco in the fields and a small herd of cattle. Creditors presented the estate with debts totaling over $15,000. Needless to say, S. F. did not get the $600 his father bequeathed to him in his will. S. F. knew he needed to make repairs on the barns and to develop a larger herd, but for that transition to take place, he would need credit. Although he could count on the State of Connecticut, the principal mortgage holder, to hold off on taking his farm if he missed payments, the 1870s were not the time to be looking for another creditor to finance a barn and a silo. He had plenty of relatives in the neighborhood, but few were in a position to help. His uncle, Carlton Holcomb, a shoemaker who had acquired his property from S. F.'s father and grandfather, was behind on his own mortgage payments. The same was true of nearly everyone in West Granby. Even "Uncle Matt" Fancher, to whom everyone seemed to be related, had had to deed his house over to his wife for protection.

Somehow though, S.F., a teenage farmer, managed to pull through. By the early 1880s, he felt he was doing well enough to raise a family. He had his dairy running, and in season he carted 1750 gallons of cider a day to the Granby depot for shipment to New Haven. In 1882, he married Lizzie Dewey, and in 1886 and 1888, his children, Tudor and Laura, were born. The family attended the Methodist Church, and Tudor and Laura went to the one-room schoolhouse at the junction of Firetown and Simsbury Road, a half-mile south of their farm. Laura was studious, but Tudor, according to his own recollection, had a permanent seat in the corner.

Salmon Brook Historical Society

Figure 10-1: S.F. Holcomb, Lizzie Dewey Holcomb and their children Tudor and Laura, January, 1901.

In spite of S. F.'s success in building a dairy farm and reviving his father's cider business, his farm was not profitable enough to keep the state at bay forever. In 1887, officials filed a complaint for foreclosure. Furthermore, taxes had gone unpaid, and the town had placed liens on the property. It seemed only a matter of time before the county sheriff or town constable would show up, papers in hand, signed and sealed by one government or the other. Lizzie took the children to stay with a neighbor.

It may have been just a fortunate development - or it may have been one shrewd and sophisticated strategy among many being perfected by New England farmers in those days. Whichever the case, the claims by both the town and the state on the farm delayed the foreclosure long enough for arrangements to be made with a distant relative in Granville. By 1896, S.F. and Lizzie had refinanced the farm and placed the title in Lizzie's name. Their new creditor was Lucius Huggins, a local blacksmith and cabinet maker who had done quite well refinancing the property of his neighbors in the late 1800s. Lucius had, in a sense, invested in people he knew and trusted. He was patient and allowed a missed payment now and then; and in the long run, he had profited. Small bequests from various relatives in the early 1900s helped S.F. and Lizzie to pay the mortgage.

In the meantime, Tudor had spent two years at Mt. Hermon School and a winter at a business college in Hartford, and he had taken a short course at Amherst Agricultural College. "I never graduated anywhere," he would say one day. "You can't learn everything in college. You need practical experience to operate a farm to the best advantage and to operate efficiently." Nevertheless, he had learned enough to know that the recovery of farm prices in the early 1900s would not last forever, and that his parents, in spite of their success so far, were not running a business that would survive in the long run. "No one was keeping any books!" he would later exclaim. New techniques were being ignored, the farm was dependent upon cider revenues that were now threatened by local prohibition, and everywhere he looked about the farm, there was waste and inefficiency.

Laura began keeping the books, identifying the biggest expenses and the least profitable activities. Then in 1911, Tudor made the move that would save his family farm from the auction block forever. He invested in poles, tent and enough material for a new tobacco barn, and in addition to the seven acres

427

of Havana seed tobacco he already had, he put in three acres of Sumatra shade. Years later he could not remember where he got the money, but he knew he paid it back soon. From those three acres, he harvested 1800 pounds of high-grade wrapper and sold it for 75¢ a pound, making more money in one season than his parents had mortgaged the whole farm for fifteen years earlier. 1911 and 1912 were banner years for shade growers. The weather was good, the experiment station had found the right seed and soil conditions, and there was exceptional demand for the home-grown wrapper produced in the tents of what would later be known as "tobacco valley" (Bloomfield, Windsor, Simsbury, Avon, the Granbys, and Southwick, Massachusetts).

Tudor expanded his crop, always paying attention to the latest news on growing techniques, and experimenting a bit himself with seedlings and fertilizer. He also paid attention to the marketplace. He discovered that tobacco buyers, who, after initial reticence, had been buying all the good shade they could get from local growers, would meet in Hartford the day before the growers brought in their crop and decide on what price they would offer. This may have made sense to the buyers in a seller's market, but to Tudor it was a challenge. After the 1912 season, he called all the growers together at his house prior to the annual trip to Hartford and told them it was they who should be setting the prices. And they did. From then on his West Granby neighbors would never tire of repeating, with both respect and a bit of jealousy, "Tudor always gets his price."

With no more than sixty acres of shade in cultivation at a time, the Holcomb family fortune grew steadily. Tudor and S. F. entered into a partnership agreement in 1918, with Tudor handling the tobacco business and S. F. running the dairy. They built new dairy barns on the Wisconsin model, and the herd grew to one hundred prize-winning Guernseys. Tudor was the first in the state to irrigate his tobacco, using a second-hand fire engine he purchased in Worcester, and in doing so, he doubled his output per acre. The word was, in those days, that the family farm was a thing of the past - that only well-capitalized companies, such as the American Sumatra Corporation (which had recently absorbed Marcus Floyd's Connecticut Tobacco Company), could survive in the farming business. Tudor and Laura meant to prove that the family farm could still be profitable, and in fact, was still, as they would claim their entire lives, "the backbone of this country."

In 1913 West Granby was, like most of the outlying areas of Granby, a run-down village besieged by foreclosures and unemployment. Simplex had left, Fred Case had just sold his store at a loss to Tudor's cousin Leon Holcombe, and only wagon-painter Lucien Reed and blacksmith Frank Parmelee attempted to conduct a trade. Some residents made money boarding vacationers and fishermen. Up in the hills, Perry Higley regularly buried barrels of cider brandy in sand banks when he heard revenue collectors were in the area. The state had recently foreclosed on the grist mill, which sat rotting at the foot of the gorge, serving as a quaint reminder of the past for tourists at Myron Huggins's bungalow on the opposite bank. Since 1906, former Governor George McLean had been buying abandoned land in the vicinity at rock-bottom prices to create what would become a huge game refuge in 1932 when he died. Most farmers had a small dairy herd, and used hand-operated cream separators. Henry Weed, who operated a small store at 15 Simsbury Road, drove a wagon around collecting for the Granby Cream-

Salmon Brook Historical Society

Figure 10-2: West Granby in the early 1900s, looking south on Simsbury Road. Dr. J. D. Wilcox house is on the right. Simplex smokestack can be seen at the rear.

ery. As for tobacco growing, most still grew outdoor Havana, unable to make the investment (or unwilling to take the risk) in equipment for the more profitable shade-grown tobacco.

To this neighborhood, Tudor and Laura brought a cash income. They hired dozens of local residents to work in the fields and barns. Former employee Everett Rosier remembers the stern and aloof farmer, and Tudor's father too - "Old Chisel-Tooth" S. F., "a-chewing" on his unlit cigar; but for this teenage boy who slept in his grandmother's well-ventilated attic and carried water into the house from the brook each morning, even in winter, the money came in handy. For one thing, it could buy candy at Leon Holcombe's store, and Leon appreciated that too. Tudor also became a local bank, as Lucius Huggins had once been for the Holcomb family, providing mortgages for neighbors and employees. And finally, he and his father bought up a lot of local property for their own use, doubling the family's acreage in the 1920s from 200 to 400 acres. From West Granby gravel, where so many hopes had been buried over the past century, Tudor and Laura turned a struggling and nearly abandoned family farm into an immensely profitable enterprise.[1]

Although the Holcombs were exceptionally shrewd business people, their experience was a reflection of generally improved economic conditions for farmers all across rural New England in the early years of the twentieth century. Loomis Brothers' certainly felt it, for when Edwin H. Shattuck bought out his retiring partners in 1911, he made up the cost in just a few years. He attributed the boom to the growth of the tobacco industry, and his fertilizer orders over the next few years would support that assertion. Money seemed to be pouring into Granby, and every business was benefiting. Shattuck even hired George Wisnitsky as a clerk, because he knew Polish and could speak "with the large Polish population to be found at [the Floydville] Plantation."[2]

It is hard to imagine, though, that Loomis Brothers' was making a great deal of money from migrant laborers who accepted wages locals rejected. Furthermore, raising tobacco, even when the tent equipment had been paid for, was such a consuming task, it is difficult to understand how it could have been profitable for any but the most skillful farmers. Seedlings had to be tended with great care in the early spring, then set out by hand in the heavily fertilized fields (11,000-12,000 plants per acre). There were the poles and wires and cheese-cloth tenting to maintain; and once the plants began to

430

mature, they had to be picked by hand, carried in without doing damage to the leaves, strung on a cord and hung on frames to cure three or four weeks in a specially ventilated shed (which was in continual danger of burning to the ground if the charcoal fire got out of control). Hopefully some damp weather would come along about then, for that was what was needed before the leaves could be taken down and sent to sweat in some warehouse before sale. Lack of meticulous attention at any one of these steps could cost a grower irreparable damage, if only because his leaf was not of the highest quality, let alone if one of his sheds went up in a blaze. Prices fluctuated wildly, depending on economic conditions, the overall yield in a particular region, the degree to which growers would cooperate to set prices, and the weather. Nevertheless, during the 1910s shade growing surged. There were 4,300 acres in shade in Connecticut in 1920, and the following year was such a good year that by 1922 that number had jumped to 8,000 acres. Marcus Floyd and Fred Griffin were working with Cullman Brothers, Inc., at this time, super-vising over 1000 acres of shade tobacco on their Connecticut plantations, including some in the southern part of Granby. Production of outdoor Havana seed, which was still used for cigar binders and required less attention and investment, also grew considerably during the 1910s.[3]

The tobacco industry was not the only stimulant to Granby's economy, however. The U.S. Congress had recently passed some laws that were helpful to farmers, including the Smith-Lever Act, which was the foundation of the county extension service that would provide training and advice for farmers, the Smith-Hughes Act for agricultural training, and the Federal Farm Loan Act. Some of these programs, and the funding that they supplied, found their way to most small New England towns, but problems with railroad and milk dealer monopolies and new tuberculosis epidemics tended to offset those gains.[4] The real benefits came from urbanization. As Connecticut cities grew, prices for dairy products and fresh produce went up. This was the reason Arthur Allen moved from West Hartford to North Granby in 1919 to invest in a larger dairy farm and to manufacture sweet cider.[5] Furthermore, a growing middle class in urban areas meant even more vacationers looking for a retreat in places like Granby. Boarding houses, hotels, fishing and hunting bungalows, and tea rooms popped up all over town. As the town and state together spent money improving roads, more and more of these get-aways

431

were accessible to people driving automobiles - people who would pay higher and higher prices for their accommodations.

On top of all that, considerable effort was being put into making the town more accommodating. Roads were being paved, former blacksmiths, like Thad Shaw, and Frank and Philip Devnew, were acquiring automobile repair skills, and by 1926, a 9-hole golf course had been opened off Granby Street. More importantly, the members of the Salmon Brook Water District were conducting a concerted campaign to electrify the town, beginning, of course, with Granby Street.

The Water District had been reconstituted in 1908, and its records beginning then indicate the effects of the coming of shade tobacco and automobiles to Granby. Next they turned their attention to electrification. In February, 1914, its leaders called on the residents of School District 1, which encompassed Granby Street, to incorporate the Granby Fire District, a necessary first step in negotiating with the Hartford Electric Light Company

Salmon Brook Historical Society

Figure 10-3: First automobile garage in Granby, opened 1912 by Philip Devnew in the rear of his father's blacksmith shop. (Now the Masonic Hall on East Granby Road.) Shown here in 1915 with a new Maxwell touring car, Philip is third from the right and his father Frank is on the far right.

for electrification. By August, nearly every home between Tariffville and Salmon Brook Street had been wired for lights and was awaiting the completion of the lines coming from the new light company dam below the Falls. On September 25, the lawn of the Stanley Edwards home (now 239 Salmon Brook Street) was the scene of a gala celebration complete with ice cream, cake, and music by the West Granby Drum Corps, as 200 people cheered when the Japanese lanterns were turned on. With electric illumination, automobile repair shops, and both Edgar Case and Edwin Shattuck of Loomis Brothers' in business as automobile dealers (Philip Devnew also sold Maxwells), there was now good reason for many of those "loyal sons" of Granby to become resident commuters (and spend their money locally). Perhaps this explains why Loomis Brothers' had three other general stores competing against it by 1913, even though it appeared a decade earlier that only one store would survive in Granby.[6]

Modernization and prosperity were not to be achieved overnight, however. It took until 1923 for North Granby to get electricity, and for Granby to double the number of automobiles owned on the Street from 14 to 29. This was still the age when RFD was a new phenomenon and the carriers were riding bicycles or horses.[7] Just the same, delivered mail, automobiles, electricity, and new water rates were all indications of an economy that had made a serious turnabout, and was slowly extending its benevolent reach beyond the Street.

The war years promoted further growth. As the lights were being lit along Hartford Avenue in August, 1914, Europe was ablaze with the artillery bombardments of the suicidal contest between the major powers. At first, Granby residents, like most people in Connecticut, viewed the war with detachment. It was so far away - it was not America's affair. Then the war orders started to come in at Connecticut arms and munitions factories in early 1915. Wages rose, retails sales improved, new homes were built, and again, Granby's farmers were finding themselves the beneficiaries of urban growth. It could be said, in addition, that Connecticut entered the war before the United States did. So strongly did Governor Marcus Holcomb support entry into the war, as well as Wilson's bungling efforts to deal with the affairs of Mexico, that the state was fully mobilized when the war declaration came in April, 1917. State Librarian George Godard joined the patriotic spirit of the

Salmon Brook Historical Society

Figure 10-4: George Seymour Godard (1865-1936), from a portrait by James Weiland.

times by identifying 12,000 "makers of public opinion," and mailing them pamphlets with titles like "The Hun is on the Run." The 1918 Armistice was unpopular in Connecticut, and Governor Holcomb's opposition to it propelled him to an unprecedented third term.[8]

Following Godard's lead, Granby responded with enthusiasm to the possibility of entering the war. In February, 1917, even before the state had established the Home Guard, a Granby town meeting called for the establishment of a War Bureau in the town. The town meeting pledged "their hearty support and co-operation to the Government of the United States, the State of Connecticut and the War Bureau of Granby in every activity leading to a speedy victory in this great struggle for Humanity, Liberty and Democracy."[9] Obviously, they did not have too much affection for Wilson's campaign slogan that "he kept us out of war."

For Granby, the conflict with Mexico in 1916 and the U.S. entry into the war meant some dislocation, to be sure. Fifty-two men went off to war, and five died in the service, including Rev. Sidney A. Beardslee, the recent minister of the South Congregational Church. Furthermore, there was the additional distraction of the Granby Home Guard. Some eighty men (including some from Tariffville) were recruited beginning in March, 1917, to form a company of the 1st Infantry Battalion of the Connecticut State Guard, with James Lee Loomis its commander. The company spent a good deal of time drilling at the fair grounds, assisting with Selective Service registration, doing guard duty at bridges and dams to prevent sabotage, and marching in parades. None of this, however, created a severe labor shortage or higher wages (although those who served in the army, especially the drafted foreign-born

434

men, were paid better than they would have been in the tobacco fields). There were plenty of migrant farm laborers looking for work. Tudor Holcomb even hired a group of Jamaicans to work his field one summer. What benefited the people of Granby the most was, once again, the increasing prices for farm products, and the fact that Granby farmers were not as subject as urban residents to the increased cost of living during the war years. In spite of the great tragedy being played out in Europe, Granby had not seen an economy as healthy as this one since the 1790s. It is little wonder that patriotism ran high. The post-war recession that drove urban workers out of Connecticut did little to change this sense of prosperity in Granby.[10]

Statistics tell a similar story of economic well-being in the early years of the century. The population of the town held fairly steady, no longer diminished by the large-scale abandonments of the 19th century (See Table 10-1). Furthermore, those living in town were, apparently, making the most of their assets. After 1901, the grand list began to increase at an unprecedented rate, even taking into account some inflation in the late 1910s (See Table 10-2).

Table 10-1: Granby's Population 1900-1940	
1900	1299
1910	1383
1920	1342
1930	1388
1940	1544

Table 10-2: Granby's Grand List (selected years)[11]

Year	Total Evaluation	Tax Rate
1901	368,022	17
1909	443,645	17
1910	678,190	14.5
1920	1,067,243	22
1930	1,523,197	25

This was a rural town on the mend. By the mid-1920s, there were still people without electricity, and still some who had little cash income. There was also even greater diversity of wealth, stretching from the migrant tobacco workers at one end of the scale to the professionals, commuters and summer residents at the other. But Tudor and Laura Holcomb had shown it was possible to bridge the gap, and even though they were but one farm family, there were many their business touched, and many more who looked at them and came to believe in the possibilities of Granby. Perceptions continued to drive history.

Maintaining a "Well-Rounded Community"

Favorable economic conditions were the backdrop, between 1900 and 1925, for the most lasting period of community renewal in Granby's history. In the early twentieth century, voluntary organizations dedicated to one worthy cause or another continued to exert considerable influence on life in Granby. In the case of the community at Granby Street, wartime patriotism combined with a local disaster to culminate, eventually, in the realization of the ideal New England village and national recognition of Granby as such. Public policy also reflected the firm guiding hand of reform-minded Republican businessmen, who sought to make lasting gains in education and efficient government. These leaders were hardly "liberal" reformers, however, as we shall see.

Village beautification continued to be a community activity in the new century. Although most of New England's village improvement societies had faded into oblivion by the early 1900s, Granby's was in full bloom, if not rejuvenated. In fact, Granby had two. At Granby Street, James Lee Loomis, Theodore Case, William Maltbie, Fred Colton and the Rev. Frank Makepeace supervised the continued maintenance of the village green. Holding entertainment benefits, they financed park upkeep and the spraying of elms ($94). In West Granby in 1912, Ida Hayes began a Village Improvement Society whose first activity was to clean up the long neglected West Granby Cemetery and the grounds around the Methodist Church. When they organized, Tudor Holcomb was elected president, with Ida appointed a typically deferential vice-president. The following year, they held "a literary entertainment of high character in the Methodist Church" to continue raising money for their cleanup projects. In 1915, most of these same people were involved in the construction of the new Methodist Church Parish house, a facility designed expressly to host the increasingly popular church suppers that also supplied funds for community projects.[12]

As in the past, many of the community renewal projects of the 1910s were led by women. Mary Colton Coffee, Blanche Green Forsyth and Christine Loomis Case were the primary movers behind one of the most active groups in town. In 1913, they and nine other members of their Sunday School class created a "Girls' Sewing Circle" to assist with various needs of the South Congregational Church. They made cushions for the church pews, worked on the library, and under Helen Green's leadership in 1914, raised money for electric wiring and fixtures for the church, even though some thought "it would be dangerous to have electricity floating around the hall." In 1915, they sent out an invitation to all women in Granby to join them, forming the Granby Civic Club, whose purpose was nothing less than "to create a better Granby." Thirty-two women joined, electing Elma Farren their first president. In an effort, perhaps to keep up with West Granby, they began raising money for furnishings for a new "community house," and during the war, they involved themselves in the purchase of Liberty Bonds. Some of the same women were active in the South Church's Ladies Missionary Society which made "comfort bags" for soldiers at Christmas time in 1917.[13]

Not to be outdone, the South Church men formed the Men's Community League in 1914. This group met periodically for supper, which they made themselves (even on Ladies Night when women were invited, but barred from the kitchen), and listened to members give talks on various subjects. Inspired by a group of Boy Scouts who had hiked through Granby in 1914, they organized their own scout troop for local boys, which troop held its meetings in a building called the "parsonage barn." By 1918, there was also a Girl Scout troop meeting there, although based on the prevailing pattern of these organizations, they may very well have been founded before the Boy Scouts.[14]

Both the Civic Club and the Men's League were put to the test in January, 1917, when the South Church burned to the ground. An idealistic newspaper editor suggested that the two Congregational Churches of Granby get together again, since the First Church had no minister at the time; but he seemed to assume that was not going to happen. He was right. Not only were the two groups still incompatible, but such a scheme would not fit with the community vision now firmly in place on the Street. As Dr. Soule said in his 1922 speech celebrating the South Church's 50th anniversary, "A Connecticut village without a church is a condition unbearable, and as abhorrent as Nature toward a vacuum." Here was "an attractive village, beautiful for situation on a broad street flanked by graceful shade trees and comfortable homes." This picture simply wasn't complete without a church.[15] His vision, in fact, was shared by the members of the South Church, as illustrated immediately after the fire, when the finance committee issued a circular letter stating, "There is a general recognition throughout the village that the church should center the community life, that it should concern itself in all normal social activities and pleasures and in providing proper facilities for their enjoyment." As if conducting a war for "Humanity, Liberty and Democracy," the terms currently being employed to justify a War Bureau in town, the committee then went on to list perceived needs, which amounted to not only a new church, but four other building projects: a new library, a community house, a community playground and a new school building. The school building for District 1 had been on the town agenda for some time, and as long ago as 1913, the School Committee had declared that the conditions of the present schoolhouse "should no longer be tolerated." However, the South Church finance committee recognized that the school would have to be placed last on the priority list, since it was the town's job to furnish school facilities. They only mentioned it, they said, because the collection as a whole represented "needs that must be met if a well-rounded community is to be maintained."

As for the library, Mrs. Francis B. Lockwood had already offered her house as a temporary location, and hundreds of donated books were pouring in. Furthermore, the church had already received a commitment from the family of Laura Dibble Bunce, who had led a library reorganization effort in 1887, to construct a new library in her honor. In support of the whole project, Rev. Irving Berg, a former minister, wrote the following appeal to the editors of the *Courant*:

[Granby] seemed to me [during my ministry there] as it seems to me now, one of the worthiest and most typical of the better rural New England communities. The main street was beautiful with its fine old trees and well-kept lawns. The little white church never suffered from lack of paint! The houses of the people, the park with its soldiers monument, the carefully tended cemetery, the excellent library, housed in the church building, the general air of quiet dignity and simplicity were all eloquent testimony of the sturdy New England which many of us from other states have come to associate with the best life of the nation. A town which is such a producer of the better life of little old New England, should not have its present appeal fall on deaf ears!

By July, 1918, *The Hartford Times* was praising the "patriotism" of Granby residents, as they built their colonial revival style church meetinghouse, raised the money for the community house and playground, and pressed the town to build a new school. Another paper reported that as the work was being finished, "The land around the completed buildings has been graded and seeded and surroundings will be fine when seen next Wednesday and visitors will realize that Granby has as complete a set of buildings as can be found in any New England Village."[16] In fact, it was more than complete. Even before the new schoolhouse was constructed in 1919, it was a completely *reconstructed* New England village.

But alas! Even when the school was finished, not everything was in place. In spite of the fact that the town still had the only fair in Hartford County, some elements of the ideal country village were still missing. For one thing, experience had taught that the village needed a volunteer fire squad, and so, in 1921, the Lighting District formed one, and furnished it with a fifty-gallon soda-ash fire extinguisher on wheels. In the same year, the school district began a parent-teacher organization. Yet, still one more ingredient was missing. In 1917, Granby's only physician, Dr. V. J. Irwin Jr., had left for the army. How could a perfect New England village be without a village doctor? Therefore, the Men's Community League commenced a search and recruited Dr. Ernest R. Pendleton, a surgeon who had been practicing in Massachusetts. He was the perfect choice. Not only did he come to Granby and set up his office, but within a year he had established, with help from the Men's League, a full-fledged hospital, with an operating room, beds and an X-ray machine. In 1923, he added a wing that brought the number of beds to twenty-seven.[17]

It was in that year that Granby Street achieved its dream. The U. S. Department of Agriculture featured the village in its bulletin on rural planning. The department hoped that rural planning would do for the country what city planning had done for the city (so they said), and gave a number of examples of outstanding rural planning throughout the nation. Granby Street, with its Green, electric lights, running water, well-kept cemetery, "fire apparatus," and cluster of public buildings, including a new school arranged so more rooms could be added "when the contemplated consolidation of districts is effected," was designated a "Model Town."[18] It is not that many of these features of the village were unimportant. In focusing on the Street, though, the Agriculture Department (whose bulletin had little to do with the needs of farmers), was placing the emphasis on the aesthetic, when what was traditional about rural New England, if anything, was its emphasis on the utilitarian. Granby Street had been honored because it had all the characteristics of an ideal New England village - that is, all the characteristics twentieth century middle-class Americans had decided were typical of an ideal New England village. Never mind that the original Congregational Church at

Salmon Brook Historical Society

Figure 10-5: New South Congregational Church, 1918, with companion structures: library on the left and community house on the right.

Salmon Brook had once evoked the comment that this was not one of God's houses, but one of His barns. Never mind that the green had, in earlier days, been one of many town dumps. Never mind that many of the center village's original families had abandoned Salmon Brook for greener pastures long ago. And never mind that the town, until now, had never built an adequate schoolhouse. Granby had done it all in good form at last - and with hardly any money taken from the town treasury (they got that part right, anyway). Perhaps it is not at all coincidental that the South Church would in 1923, settle a minister, Dr. Arthur Teale, who actually stayed longer than two years - thirty-seven years, actually, a pastorate second only to Rev. Isaac Porter's in longevity. The ideal had become the real.

At least it had at Granby Street. Then there was the rest of the town. This had not escaped the attention of the leaders on the Street, and with their allies in the other villages, they worked through the town government to make things right with the larger community. As of 1905, the road issue was progressing well. In 1911, they won three out of five votes to close roads in the outlying hills, and between 1905 and 1913, they worked with state authorities to improve state highways without great expense to the town. In spite of all this spending activity (which might have once resulted in the election of Democratic candidates), the Republican social elite continued to make strong showings at the polls, defeating Democratic candidates by large margins. Furthermore, the liquor vote remained under control. There were some close calls, but as time passed, the margin became greater and greater, until in some years no one even proposed the licensing of liquor. At last, in 1921, two years after the 18th Amendment had been ratified, town clerk Shattuck happily noted in the records, "There was no vote taken on license and as the law does not allow the licensing of such business, this is the last statement that will appear until the law changes."[19] Doubtless he was comforted by the thought that a federal constitutional amendment had never been repealed.

With the agenda items of roads and liquor well in hand, the leaders turned to government efficiency. It was always hard to convince cash-poor taxpayers that additional expenditures would create a more efficient (and in the long run, less expensive) government, since most taxpayers equated efficiency with economy. Nevertheless, with perhaps more cash in their pockets in the second decade of the century, voters at the town meeting were persuaded to purchase a concrete mixer and a tractor for road construction work.[20] The real difficulty came in arguing for salaries for town officials. The matter was discussed at some length in 1907 on the occasion of Chester Loomis's last year as town clerk, and again and again in the years to come. In 1915, it was ordered that selectmen should receive $3 per day. A year later, the first selectman began receiving a $200 per year salary, but the other selectmen had their pay rescinded. In 1922, townspeople were still arguing over salaries with no resolution in sight. Leaders wanted to attract bright and able young administrators to official positions, but the majority of the town could not see what compensation had to do with ability. Proposals to get electricity to the town hall, and to West and North Granby at combined town and property-owner expense, met similar resistance.[21]

The most important item of unfinished business from 19th century reform efforts, of course, was the consolidation of schools. As we recall, evaluators of Granby's turn-of-the-century schools consistently gave them low marks. Textbooks were either out-of-date, in disrepair, or non-existent, even if provided free by the town, and buildings were in worse condition than most houses (and most houses were in poor condition). "Much needs to be done," wrote Superintendent J. B. McLean in his 1906 report, "to make the schoolhouses more attractive and sanitary within and without." He also lamented that "It is becoming more and more difficult to secure, for the schools in the more remote country districts, teachers of ability well trained for the work....Higher salaries are required." He did not say when it had ever been possible to get such teachers, but that does not change the fact that few of Granby's teachers could teach much, or that few of those who could, stayed longer than a year. It is not surprising, under these circumstances, that school attendance ran roughly 60%. "Parents owe it to their children to be more conscientious in the matter," McLean scolded; but why would anyone feel they were doing their children a favor by sending them to one of these schools?[22]

Of course, evaluations varied. Just two years later, town health officer Edgar B. Case announced that "The days of unkept school houses and poorly kept school grounds and unsanitary outbuildings on school property are passed. The start made along these lines in a short time will show a marked change for the better."[23] McLean had not said anything about the school buildings that year, but five years later the situation at School 1 was described as intolerable.

The solution, school reformers had always insisted, lay in school consolidation. If all the schools came under the authority of town leaders, and were funded as a whole from the town budget (perhaps with the same sort of state assistance now being directed toward highways), then the schools would be supervised by more qualified and able people. In 1909, the state legislature agreed, and passed a law establishing town management of the public schools. Reformers in Granby immediately set about implementing the edict, right down to assessing two school districts extra for handing indebted schools over to the town.[24] McLean had already delivered a "full and frank estimate of the individual work of the teachers" to the school committee, but apparently the evaluation was too embarrassing to print in the town's annual report. He did state that now the town should start paying salaries that would attract good teachers.[25]

School consolidation had always signified more to reformers than a central town school board, though. What they wanted most was to be able to redraw district lines and have far fewer districts. Then they would build larger schools, hire teachers to teach specific grade levels (as teachers were currently being trained to do in the state's teacher training schools), and generally operate a more cost-efficient and more easily supervised system. Obviously, this would require substantial initial investment, which was not about to happen in a town where most farmers could not see their way to buying tobacco tent. Nevertheless, the reformers persisted, and gradually over the next two decades they pushed the school budget from $4,845 in 1909 to $27,820 in 1927. (The latter figure included some funding from state grants. We also need to take into account considerable inflation.) To a certain extent, they were forced to add to expenditures as the state first required towns to pay for secondary education for those who wanted it, and then began to require the licensing of all teachers and superintendents in 1922. Granby did not create a secondary school, but sent its students to Simsbury High School and paid transportation costs as well. Teacher salaries climbed steadily, accounting for the majority of cost increases. In spite of the higher salaries, though, the turnover of teachers was still high. In 1922, the year before Granby was designated a model town, the school committee had to replace all but three teachers. Furthermore, consolidation of districts was slow to happen, and in 1926, the town simply concluded it was "inadvisable" to build additions for that purpose to the new school at Granby Street.[26]

One of the retarding forces to more forceful action on schools was that the social elite was not consistent over time in its commitment to expensive school reform. What was happening in the early years of the twentieth century was a gradual changing of the guard within the ranks of the Republican party in Granby. The old guard, symbolized by the Loomis brothers, William and Theodore Case, and Theodore Mills Maltbie of Granby Street, and Edward Dewey and James R. Hayes of North Granby, was actually a fairly "progressive" lot. They believed that town government should be active in the lives of its citizens and in promoting community improvement. Over the years their cash-poor constituents, who had allowed them to rule as long as they did not push their agenda too hard and too fast, had forced the elite to be generally economical and to be careful about prohibition. At the turn of the century, when many of the poorer farmers had left town and those remaining were either not included in political decision-making or beginning to see some hope for the economy, this progressive group began to make headway. They ended liquor licensing, and with state aid, began the long and expensive process of paving town roads (and abandoning roads in the hills). In 1909, again with help from the legislature, they saw the beginnings of school consolidation.

These were also the last years that this generation ran Granby. 1909 was Edwin Shattuck's first year as town clerk, and two years later, he would buy out the Loomis Brothers' store. When Chester Loomis retired, he passed the cup not only to Shattuck, but also to his son James Lee Loomis. Others in the new guard included William Mills Maltbie, Theodore Grafton Case, and soon Tudor Holcomb. In North Granby in 1912, a 91-year-old James Hayes made a joke of his generation's passing, lamenting that the nation's political leaders "don't recognize me as good Presidential timber may be to much Sap but I dont care it is near sugaring of time and I mean to keep sweet let the world go as it will   so much for February." In another place in his memoirs he commented on the suffering he had seen among his poorer neighbors during that winter:

if the very rich would remember the very poor boath would be happier and the world made better but if the rich have anything to give its where there praises will be sounded the highest   it dont matter if the poor perish   Carnagie Rockefellar and such men wrench from the poor to satisfy greed and bear their energies to that end regardless of the needs of others or of consequences that follow to their shame and disgrace.[27]

Hayes was a Theodore Roosevelt-style Republican - one who thought that government needed to stand up for the little guy, and that common sense dictated that society's leaders should insure society's welfare first, and their own second (the old "Rough Rider" had bolted the party in 1912 to form the Progressive, or "Bull Moose" Party). James and his generation of reformers had definite ideas about what would be best for society: good roads, good schools, no taverns, and a professionally operated poor farm. Furthermore, if they could not get the town meeting to go along with raising taxes to support these causes (and they seldom could), then they were not at all averse to borrowing money (since it was to be spent for a better future anyway).

The new generation of Republican leadership, however, were more wary of profligate spending for public projects, especially deficit spending. We can begin to see this transformation in 1910 when the town voted to have a general reevaluation of taxable property, and in 1913, when, after tabling a motion to accept $200 from the West Granby Cemetery Association in return for town maintenance of that cemetery, a committee was appointed to clean up the town's financial record-keeping procedures. The new guard was beginning to put the town's financial house in order and was concerned that there had already been too much spending on community improvement. In 1915, the issue of town indebtedness came up for discussion, and two years later, some of the tax rate was directed toward reducing the town's debt. Table 10-2 shows continuing development of the "pay-as-you-go" philosophy emerging among the new generation in the 1910s and 1920s, and a rejection of the deficit financing of town programs of the early 1900s. Although spending, particularly on schools, climbed precipitously through the early twenties, the tax rate climbed even faster. The town's rejection of a significant portion of the 1914 Connecticut Workman's Compensation Act, long advo-

Salmon Brook Historical Society

Figure 10-6: James Lee Loomis (1878-1971) in 1938.

cated by urban labor spokesmen and opposed by Republican conservatives in the legislature as "a handout" and too expensive, is also evidence of the growing fiscal conservatism of Granby's leadership.[28]

James Lee Loomis illustrates the new guard of Granby's Republican party. Born and raised on the Street in the late 1800s, he certainly was well indoctrinated in the ideology of the well-ordered village. He would always have fond memories, too, of the old country store, baseball games, town picnics, fairs, church suppers and the centrality of the church in the social life of the town. In 1903, he took up a leadership role in the South Congregational Church, and was a lynch pin in that congregation until his death in 1971. Educated at Yale College and Yale Law School and hired by a prestigious Hartford law firm, he might well have continued on in the tradition of political activism of his father's generation. But Jim Loomis had a somewhat different plan. In 1909, he entered the Connecticut Mutual Life Insurance Company as an assistant secretary. Twenty-one years later he became the company's president. As he climbed the corporate ladder in the 1920s, he achieved regional recognition as a dynamic and talented businessman - just the sort of person who, if he were in government, would make it work as well as a prosperous insurance company. He loved his rural roots, but his father and uncle's business was more of a curiosity to him than a model. What he thought he drew from those roots were not techniques for efficient operation of business or government, but personal qualities, particularly self-reliance and "industry and thrift." These qualities, for Jim Loomis, were the "old gold of a New England village."

He loathed Franklin D. Roosevelt's New Deal. He had no use for a "welfare state," and believed it was each person's responsibility to take charge of his own circumstances. There was nothing wrong with individual ambition. In fact, if more people were more ambitious, society as a whole would be more productive and all would prosper. Surely he subscribed to Calvin Coolidge's adage that "the business of America is business."[29] It was "Gentleman Jim," and his other up-and-coming friends on the Street (including William Mills Maltbie, who became Chief Justice of the Connecticut Supreme Court in 1930), who were guiding Granby's agenda in the 1910s and 1920s.

What this new group of leaders was saying, actually, was right in tune with what most people of Granby - at least those who voted - were thinking. Although many farmers saw the professionals of the Street as a different sort, they were willing to defer to them as competent administrators. Government should be efficient, secure order, plan rationally, pay its bills and not incur indebtedness, and villages should raise their own money for their community projects. If those principles meant that some would be better off than others, that schools and roads would improve only slowly, that little used roads would be abandoned, that church suppers would pay for cleaning up around town, then so be it.

Just as their Republican predecessors had had to go slow with their agenda, however, so too did the new guard. In fact, had they had their way completely, they may have happily raised taxes even more to pay for school improvements they deemed "inadvisable" (politically) in the mid-twenties as other priorities took precedence. The effort to extend rational planning to private property on the heels of recognition as a model town met with difficulties too. In 1925, the town meeting voted to establish a Zoning Commission, and appointed James Lee Loomis, Harold M. Hayes (James R.'s grandson), Henry G. Viets, Lewis D. Royce and William R. Messenger. However, at the next annual town meeting, the same year additions to the Center School were voted down, their first report was accepted as a "report of progress," and nothing was heard of a zoning commission again until the late thirties and its eventual permanent establishment in 1945.[30] Although the new guard of the Republican party had no trouble winning elections, they could not put all of their principles into practice immediately.

Results of presidential elections testify, nonetheless, to the overwhelming conservatism of Granby voters as the new generation of Republican leaders took the helm. In 1908, William Howard Taft carried Granby over prairie populist William Jennings Bryan, 202-76. In 1912, neither Roosevelt's Progressives, nor Woodrow Wilson, nor even the highly respected incumbent Democratic governor Simeon Baldwin (who drafted the Workman's Compensation legislation), drew many votes, and Granby Republicans carried the day by wide margins. Again in 1920, Harding defeated Cox in Granby 311-91, and in 1924 Coolidge out-polled Davis 358-64, in spite of the embarrassments of the Harding administration scandals. When New Yorker Alfred E. Smith ran against Herbert Hoover in 1928, Granby Republicans delivered a 462-78 victory for their man.[31] It would appear that as the Republican party, both nationally and locally, became more and more associated with the efficiency and ambition of the professional businessman, the more it attracted votes in Granby. Probably many conservative Democrats switched party loyalties at this point.

The political trends seem to have been utterly unaffected by the massive registration of women voters after the ratification of the 19th Amendment in 1920. The rejuvenated Connecticut Woman Suffrage Association had threatened to work against Republicans in the 1920 election if Connecticut did not ratify the suffrage amendment. Governor Holcomb finally agreed to call a special session to do so after the requisite 36 states had already ratified the measure, and so the position of the 35,000 member C.W.S.A. was somewhat murky going into the election. Women had made a conscious effort, during the war, to make their patriotism apparent in order to win the confidence of legislators, and since Holcomb was such a solid patriot, it seemed difficult to oppose him simply because he had been dilatory.[32] In Granby, 96 women registered immediately upon ratification, and another 59 came forward within a month.[33] If anything though, their entry into politics solidified the positions of Republican men. Only a few women actually won political offices in the 1920s (Laura Viets was elected to the School Committee in 1920 and Clara Hayes to the same board in 1922 and 1923. In 1922, Grace Royce also won a seat on the School Committee and Annie Peck was chosen to the Library Board of Directors). When Helen Green won a seat in the legislature in 1924, it was a major event, but she, like all the others, worked within the Republican party; and within that structure she and other women were told to "sit in the back and keep our mouths shut."[34] Obviously Helen, a long-time leader in the South Church and in the Civic Club, did not comply with this advice. On the other hand, she was not inclined to work against the party that was leading Granby, and all of Connecticut, toward the conservatism that had so recently opposed woman suffrage! Of course, she did want to get elected, and in Granby the Republican party firmly held the key to that.

Moreover, it is not really all that surprising that women who thought the world would be better off with women voting and holding office would vote to keep the world, or at least Granby, in the same hands as always. As far as most socially and politically active women of Granby were concerned, there were, at that time, far greater threats to the welfare of society than stuffy businessmen. For one thing, there was the alarmingly indiscreet behavior of so many young people of the 1920s. A deeper concern in a rural town like Granby was with a long-standing problem. The state of Connecticut was being flooded with immigrants whose different languages and cultures surely presented a significant challenge to what "natives" considered basic American values and ways. In fact, one reason prohibition had gained so many adherents in Connecticut was that its proponents had argued it was an indispensable tool to "Americanize" immigrants.

Anxiety over the three-decade old deluge of immigrants into Connecticut reached a peak in 1919, in the wake of the Bolshevik Revolution in Russia. The old Yankee stock was beginning to feel that immigrants were indistinguishable from radicals, and this attitude was behind the legislature's anti-subversion law, the newly formed American Legion's voluntary "anti-red" units, and the U.S. Justice Department's notorious round-up of Russians and Lithuanians in many Connecticut cities in that year.[35] In Granby, the annual town meeting of 1919 voted "to open night schools in town for the education of men and women of all ages, especially those of foreign birth."[36] This was not a charitable gesture. As the 1920 Annual Report made clear, the purpose of such schools was "for Americanization."[37] The report added that, in spite of enthusiastic response by the residents of Floydville, the school had not been opened because the committee had been unable, not surprisingly, to find a qualified teacher.

With the defeat of the Versailles treaty and the rejection of Wilsonian idealism and U.S. international commitment, the Red Scare and anti-immigrant feeling became less urgent after 1920, even though discrimination against immigrants and their families, particularly Catholics, continued well into the middle of the twentieth century in Granby. However, attachment to what were perceived as traditional American ideals did not diminish. Warren Harding's election on a "return to normalcy" platform signaled an end to many tensions that had alarmed the old Yankee families of Connecticut, including residents of Granby, and a time for the triumph of the ideals upon which they believed stable communities were based.[38]

Thus, in the 1920s, Granby men and women alike, who sought stability, morality and harmony, joined in support of the professional businessmen who had emerged as leaders of the Republican party. These leaders were not the social activists the former generation had been, but they claimed to be heirs to the "old gold of New England," and they had the model village to prove that all was well in Granby. A new generation with new ideas, they cemented their prominence in a mythical tradition.

The Great Depression

On April 17, 1931 *The Windsor Locks Journal* reported another meeting of what had, by then, become a venerable organization. Sixty members of the Granby Club had met once again in Hartford, electing Chief Justice William M. Maltbie as their president to succeed Sheriff Edward W. Dewey. It was as though they were staging a long overdue confirmation of the changing of the guard, as James Lee Loomis was chosen first vice-president, and Fred Griffin second vice-president. To celebrate their beloved roots, they had the tables arranged in the shape of a horseshoe (perhaps in "protest" of the age of the automobile, even though that vehicle had undoubtedly carried them to the meeting).[39]

Surely they indulged in the same nostalgia they had been meeting to enjoy for the past twenty-five years, but at this meeting, there must have been considerable anxiety over the welfare of their native town. The whole nation was sliding uncontrollably into the depths of the Great Depression, and no community could escape the grip of one of the greatest crises in American history. Unemployment, foreclosures, bank failures, homelessness, hunger and fear gripped the entire nation. Although the highest officials in the federal government desperately tried to convince the public that "prosperity was just around the corner," every day more and more people wondered if life in America would ever be the same again. How could little Granby, and all it had come to represent to the members of the Granby Club, survive such an onslaught? As good church-going Christians they were possibly reminded of the cry of Isaiah: "What will you do on the day of punishment, in the storm which will come from afar?"

Actually, some of those present probably were aware that at least some of Granby had been experiencing economic difficulties for some time before 1931. In the 1920s, the town's farmers were, to a considerable extent, as dependent as ever on the fortunes of the state as a whole, and in that decade, Connecticut never really experienced the boom that occurred in other parts of the nation. Furthermore, those farmers also relied upon the New York, New Haven and Hartford Railroad, which had an undisputed monopoly that the state legislature, controlled by railroad agent and Republican party boss J. Henry Roraback, was not interested in breaking.[40] Granby farmers, like farmers across the nation, were experiencing the prelude to the Great Depression in the late twenties, as declining prices forced their income down for the first time since the beginning of the century. On top of that, the cost of living was rising in the late twenties.

Symptoms of decline were subtle, but apparent, nonetheless. The number of vacationers and summer people was falling off. There was an increasing number of delinquent accounts in the town tax collector's book. Dr. Pendleton had trouble maintaining his hospital, and finally, in 1928, he was forced to close it. Concerns about farm income and the dissolution of the Granby Agricultural Society (which had run the fair) inspired a reorganization of the Granby Grange in 1926. In 1929, the Grange opened a new headquarters opposite the First Congregational Church in North Granby. Those farmers still living in the hills, and struggling with lack of capital and mountainous debts, once again began to face foreclosure and town liens on their property. More people were selling land to now U.S. Senator George McLean, who by 1932, acquired almost 4000 acres in Simsbury, Canton and Granby for his game refuge.[41]

As diverse economic troubles joined forces to create the Great

451

Depression after 1929, so too were more and more people in Granby engulfed in hard times. Small farms that had not entered the shade growing business had already been suffering from lower prices, but by 1930, even the shade growers were hard-pressed to justify expansion of their crops. Across Connecticut, the total acres of shade dropped to a low of 4,100 by 1934, and that in Havana seed dropped from 23,800 in 1920 to 7,800 in the early 1930s. The big shade growers could not afford to keep up wages, but people desperate for work still hired out for a dollar a day for what Everett Rosier described as, at best, "not a very pleasant job" (and he earned 30¢ an hour as one of Tudor Holcomb's older hands).

"I look back upon it," wrote William Nelson of his days working for Tudor, "as being near indenture conditions....We'd go into those rows in the morning when these huge leaves were full of water from the dew or from a rain, and in moments we'd be soaked. It would run into our eyes and burn. There we'd be, cold and soaked to start the day and when the day heated up, and got really hot, there would seemingly be no air movement whatever back in those rows." He seldom saw Tudor smile in those days, and was happy his principal contact was with field boss Gladwin Parmelee, who was friendlier to the young field hands. Although it may have been that Tudor simply did not care much for anyone under twenty, certainly he was worried about the future. He and Laura were very proud of having redeemed their family farm, and of having resuscitated West Granby, and now all that was threatened. In fact, they had had to deal with all of their newly built dairy barns burning in 1931. When one farmer approached Tudor and offered to split his receipts 50-50 in return for Tudor managing his farm, Tudor declined, "not even tempted" to go beyond what he believed to be the limits of what he could run "to the best advantage."

Of course, Tudor and Laura Holcomb were not as exposed to economic gyrations as entrepreneurs of the past had been, for they did not carry the debt others of West Granby had carried into other depressions. Just the same, in this depression, every moment of light seemed to turn quickly to darkness, and all felt threatened. Dr. Pendleton had high hopes in 1932 when he built a group of log cabins for a summer home colony and when he later expanded the Salmon Brook Country Club golf course to 27 holes, but in 1935, fires in his home on Salmon Brook Street and in the clubhouse seemed

452

to convey the message that all the forces of nature were at work against recovery. Granby's grand list began to drop again between 1930 and 1932, and membership in the Grange, perceived perhaps as a haven from catastrophe, climbed steadily to 215 by 1936.[42]

For the state of Connecticut the social and political effects of the Great Depression were cataclysmic. At first, the Republican leadership adopted a "business as usual" attitude and assumed that these hard times, like all before them, could be handled locally and by voluntary organizations. However, when it became apparent that this time was different, "the land of steady habits" quickly became unsteady. Labor unions gained converts, and labor disputes were plentiful. Wilbur Cross won election in 1930 as the first Democratic governor in fifteen years, as his party created a new coalition of intellectuals, organized labor and ethnic blocs to unseat the state's discredited business leadership. A socialist became mayor of Bridgeport, and in 1938 ran a serious campaign for governor. Finally, a state that had eschewed federal intervention in the past gradually fell in line with New Deal recovery programs and both major parties moved in the direction of liberalism.[43]

The effect on Granby was not at all the same. Conservatism reigned supreme in town throughout the 1930s. The forces of change at work statewide were simply not at work in the town. Obviously, there was no organized labor, and ethnic blocs continued to play no part in the town's politics. Radical ideologies were equally invisible - until 1938 the Socialist party never garnered more than three votes in any election. This is not to say that the current Republican leadership did not have to make some adjustments in order to stay at the helm, or that Granby did not suffer from some social turmoil. But the adjustments to the stresses of the times were conservative, nonetheless, as more and more people sought refuge from the depression not in federal assistance, but in the myth of a stable and harmonious community - a myth created by the elite of Granby Street, but now the property of the whole community.

A cursory examination of presidential election results shows how firmly entrenched Granby's Republican party had become by the 1930s. In 1932, when Franklin Roosevelt defeated Herbert Hoover, Hoover carried Granby 431-104, with an equally strong vote of confidence going to Granby's Republican nominees for the state legislature. When Roosevelt won a

453

landslide in 1936, Alf Landon, the Kansas Republican, won Granby 511-167. Wilbur Cross fared little better in Granby in his runs for reelection in spite of his folksy style, designed to appeal to the people of the state's small towns.[44] The New Deal was exceedingly unpopular in this rural town, even though its farms and businesses were so battered by an economy that would not recover.

Nevertheless, these sentiments toward the new Democratic coalition in state and nation did not mean that the local Republican leaders would always have their way with the local agenda. The annual town meeting of 1929 gave them a good preview of what they were in for if their constituents remained in their sour mood for long. The subject of additions to the Center School (District 1) was on the floor once again. Clerk Shattuck recorded a number of the comments, some of which he seemed to feel were so ludicrous he had to get them down on paper. Among these were "1. That our schools are all in A.1 condition," and "2. That the state cannot compel the town to make any special improvements." Here Shattuck noted that Judge Theodore G. Case rose to correct the speaker, saying the state could, indeed, mandate certain standards of sanitation, heat, ventilation and light. Frank Kearns endeavored to explain how the expenses of expanding the Center School could be met. Francis L. Spring added helpfully that the Hungary School, which would be replaced by additions to the Center School, was in poor condition, and he was supported by Selden W. Hayes, who pointed out that the floor was practically rotted out. None of this patient instruction on the part of the usually respected leaders seems to have had much effect on those present. George P. Beman asked suspiciously if a four room school would be called a "consolidated school" or not. Apparently the leadership had hoped to avoid using that term, since it had obviously become a code word for a reform being pressed by the wealthy folk of the Street at the expense of the suffering farmers of the rest of the town. However, it was true that the leadership was trying, as they and their predecessors on the Street had been for over fifty years, to consolidate schools.

In response, officials wound in and out of alternatives for Center School expansion. In exasperation, Elma Hotchkiss (formerly Elma Farren) asked why the school board could not be instructed to bring in a definite plan. No one seemed to want to answer her (the answer was that they knew that any plan was going to be too expensive, judging by the comments people were making - probably she was encouraged to go sit in the back). They were hoping, perhaps, if they offered a choice of expansion plans, that some money, at least, would be spent. When the matter finally came to a vote, school board officials had reduced their proposal from eight rooms to a four room addition, and even that went down to defeat. The next spring, the town did vote to make additions, but allowed only a fraction of the original estimated expense that Kearns had suggested would be needed. Probably it was out of gratitude that a resolution passed the same meeting to rededicate the soldier's monument park to the public.[45]

The debates over expenditures for schools continued, but the school budget saw none of the increases it had prior to 1925 and the Center School remained a small district school. Of course, this generation of Republican leaders had always been lukewarm about school spending. They preferred to spend money on roads and bridges, especially since the state kicked in a good share of that. In fact, small state school grants had been partially responsible for increased school expenditures to date.[46]

The Republican leaders in Granby were hardly discredited by the depression, as they were in statewide politics, but they had to tread carefully in the resolution of numerous issues as well as the controversies over schools. Granby voters helped to repeal the 18th Amendment in 1933, and the leadership had to work hard to pull together a majority against licensing liquor in town, when that came up for a vote the following year. Officials also watched proposals to regulate fireworks and open Spring Drive in Spring Glen as a town road become subject to exasperating delays (Spring Glen was a new housing development which would, they hoped, increase the grand list). They were able to create a Board of Finance in 1933 (since it then became a statewide requirement), and later that year, the town meeting accepted some stringent recommendations from that board, including more aggressive collection of back taxes, more careful bookkeeping and budget making, salaries for more town employees, and (getting down to the nitty-gritty) the cutting of roadside bushes at the bottom rather than at the top. However, when it came to standing up to the New Deal, they happily accepted state and federal aid money for putting townspeople to work on public works projects. The town's volunteer fire department came into existence at this time, but the town government could hardly claim responsibility. After three catastrophic fires in 1935, Horace Clark, a former fire commissioner in Hartford and now living in North Granby, donated land for a fire house in that neighborhood, and led in the incorporation of the Lost Acres Fire Department, a totally private organization. The town did secure land for other firehouses, but little public money was spent on the fire department in its early years. Even with all this care exercised in avoiding increased taxes and thus alienating a hard-pressed electorate, Jasper McLevy, the Socialist candidate for governor, collected a disturbing 116 votes in Granby in 1938.[47]

In the spring of 1939, the town finally did take on Spring Drive as a town road, and allocated $500 to the fire department. However, the leadership saw its long-sought zoning commission tabled again, and over the course of the decade, the town had been forced to run up a debt of $40,000 in order to acquire state and federal grant money for public works projects. Fortunately, war orders had beefed up the state's economy by then. As the cities began to revive, so too did communities which supplied cities with agricultural produce. Higher income meant higher tax rates were possible. Furthermore, the town's grand list had begun to climb again in the late 1930s.[48]

If the Great Depression had no lasting effect on Granby's political alignments, what it did do was to delay Granby's modernization. In spite of all the money that had been poured into road work, in 1940, the town still had 38 miles of dirt road, and only 20 of blacktop; and even though the town had begun to purchase heavy equipment before World War I, the town's fleet in 1939 amounted to only two trucks with snowplows and one grader. After decades of discussion about salaries for town employees, the first selectman's annual salary stood at a meager $1706. A zoning commission to plan for the town's future and figure out the best way to expand the tax base was non-existent. The town's schools, in spite of claims from independent-minded taxpayers, were far from "A.1 condition." As property values fell and tax rates succumbed to the inability of people to pay, the town's government could ill afford the institutions and services the community needed to "operate to the best advantage" in the twentieth century.

In other ways, too, the town was still stuck in the nineteenth century. The town's local newspaper, "The Neighborhood News," was a one-page mimeographed sheet published by ten-year-old Buddy Pendleton and his six-year-old sister. And even though there were over seventy Catholic families in town, it was not until 1950 that they had a church of their own.[49] Furthermore, intervillage rivalries and antagonisms were still very much part of life in Granby. Two special town meetings in 1938 illustrate this ongoing problem. The first, on March 17, began with a resolution from Henry R. Shenning to pave Wells Road in the Pegville area. However, this resolution was followed by a counter-resolution to spend the money on Loveland Road in North Granby. Then George Newton of West Granby moved that Simsbury Road in West Granby get the attention, and Harold Hayes of North Granby followed up with a plan to pave East Street and Day Street. A vote was taken and Simsbury Road won, but that vote was rescinded and after another vote, it appeared the Wells Road forces had achieved victory.[50]

Apparently all this created such a furor, complete with public denunciations of Shenning, that another meeting had to be called the next month. In the meantime, Chief Justice Maltbie invited the disputants to his house to see if he could mediate. As moderator of the second meeting, he opened by explaining some ground rules he had managed to get the principals to agree

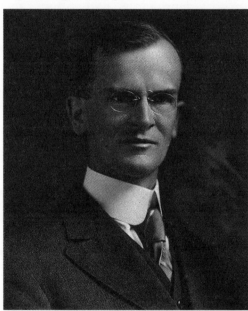

Salmon Brook Historical Society

Figure 10-7: William Mills Maltbie (1880-1961).

to, including limiting the choices to Wells Road and Simsbury Road and allowing non-resident taxpayers to vote on the matter (a ruling he himself had made on the basis of state law). "When it is over," he ordered sagely, "I am sure that you are not going to take out of this room any bitterness; that you are going to accept the decision arrived at here as final and conclusive, because, after all, it is the American thing to do and it is the sportsman-like thing to do." He was appealing to traditional small town values to deal with a traditional Granby dispute which traditionally made trouble for those values.

When Shenning rose to speak, he said he would abide by the

decision and "If we lose we are going to be men enough to take a licking...." He felt the decision had been made at the last meeting, but since he and his friends in North Granby were "looking out for the interest of the town and for good government," he was ready to reopen the question.

"We certainly are making progress," chimed in Ray Case to a chorus of laughter from his West Granby neighbors. "We are ready to approach this situation in a fair minded, clear-headed, cool manner," he continued. "We, over in the West part of town - I guess you heard all about it. - I think most of you have - (laughter) - we think that the project through to Simsbury ought to be finished."[51] West Granby residents were still feeling left out, as they had for eight decades, though at least they seemed to be able to joke about it. In the end, after two hours of arguing, West Granby won the vote, 233 to 189. Of course, it is not important who won the vote, but rather that a dispute over which few miles of road to pave could draw as many voters as voted in a presidential election to a meeting which was chaired and orchestrated by the Chief Justice of the Connecticut Supreme Court, and in which the Chief Justice would have to call upon deep-seated principles of harmony and consensual decision-making to settle a dispute about which consensus could never be reached.

The paradox continued: in spite of the myth that everyone got along and worked for the best interest of the whole community in such a town as Granby, age-old divisions still exerted stress on the town. Not only were different villages holding fast to their own interests, but old class antagonisms still haunted the ideal of communal harmony. Long-time residents distrusted summer residents, and the people of the Street still offended the rest of the town with their elitism. As late as 1961, Will Messenger of West Granby would highlight these tensions when recalling the "Gay-Nineties 'Club' racquet court" that had emerged on the town green at the beginning of the century, "where the Cases, Dibbles, Loomises and Maltbies leisurely whiled away Granby's salad days, on weekends, flattering parents [and] lady acquaintances."[52] Those families were clearly a different sort from the rest of the town, and the opposing identities persisted for decades.

During the depression, however, these differences did not manifest themselves so much anymore in political divisions. Will Messenger, who had once been Tudor Holcomb's school teacher, was a Republican, and served twenty-two years, beginning in 1939, as first selectman (he had already served in the legislature from 1935 to 1937). He and his companion selectman Oscar Wilhelm, who served with Messenger during that time, represent one of the adaptations the Republican party had had to make in order to weather the depression - and the reason why Granby remained so conservative in the face of economic disaster. By supporting such men as West Granby tobacco, dairy and poultry farmer Will Messenger, Republicans were hoping their party could mimic and offset the down-home appeal of Democratic Governor Wilbur Cross and continue to claim the loyalty of the vast majority of Granby residents. The echoes of the old differences beneath that surface unity were still very apparent. It helped, though, that leaders like Messenger were taking charge of local matters, for he was as good as any at articulating the ideals which had been the provenance of Granby Street politicians for so long.

He spoke directly to the desire of many for stability amidst troubling times. He pictured the ideal Granby as a tight-knit community of close families. Even as he sneered at the idle rich of the Street, he looked back wistfully on those days at the beginning of the century as days when the town was not affected either by the challenges of the depression or the transformations of suburbanization. "The difference in the town, as I see it," he said, "...[was] the 'stability' of the population, perhaps that isn't the right word, but I mean - they stayed put." Families passed their farms down from generation to generation, he said, and community loyalty was strong.[53] This was, indeed true in the case of Will's family, but even in West Granby, farms were being abandoned so fast at the turn of the century that the area almost became a reservoir. Much of that part of town eventually became a game refuge - including the outlying portions of Will Messenger's property (although not because he abandoned it).

Whether he was representing the town's past accurately is not the point. What is important is that he came into his office and celebrated these ideals of stability, harmony and community loyalty at a time of economic dislocation (to say nothing of the fall of France in 1940), when the rest of the state and nation were turning toward a more liberal and global approach to public policy. Granby's reshaped leadership carefully articulated conservative community ideals they believed would ensure the prosperity and happiness of their families and their town. The contradictions were abundant. The myth of rural harmony, stability and peace was created in the twentieth century to serve the needs of a middle class village, even though it claimed its foundation to be in the farming life. Furthermore, that village, which had come to be the political and commercial center of the town, had not become its only social center, as residents of outlying areas either refused to become, or were prohibited from becoming, part of the society of the Street. And finally, even though Granby continued to be deeply conservative in the 1930s, its leaders of the business and professional classes had to include more people from outside the Street in town government.

Nevertheless, it was a myth that had served its creators well, first in giving sustenance to the community spirit of those who lived on the Street, and then in meeting the challenges of economic depression and the liberalization of American political culture. Granby had remained conservative - even more entrenched than ever, actually. It was still a town run by a small group of men (fewer women held offices in the 1930s than in the 1920s), which spent as little of taxpayers' money as possible, where the independence of the town, its separate divisions and its property holders was fiercely protected, where there were no taverns or liquor stores, where the Men's Community League invited boys under 18 to their meetings to "interest the boys in the community life of the town," and where immigrants were expected to keep out of public affairs until fully Americanized.[54]

Beneath all of this order and civility ran the currents and surging waves of the Great Depression, just as disorder, division and change had characterized life in this town for centuries. In the 1930s, though, Granby citizens had learned to deal with the tempest of the moment by claiming it did not apply to Granby, the home of "the barefoot boy," families that "stayed put," and men of industry and thrift. Granby's leaders had declared their town to be the last bastion of "the old gold of New England," and the land of temperance and sobriety, "sportsmanlike" conduct at town meetings, church suppers and Memorial Day parades. The perfect pastoral paradise, which had never been, had come to be, or, at least so they told themselves; and now it seemed as though it had never been any other way.

Epilogue
Making Things Right

A short walk south of my house on Simsbury Road is Broad Hill Farm, a beautiful collection of woodlands, hillside pastures, barnyards, and open fields, intersected and bordered by trout streams and the West Branch of the Salmon Brook. Sometimes referred to as "Granby's jewel," it covers more than 300 acres formerly owned and operated by Tudor and Laura Holcomb. I met the Holcombs shortly after I moved to West Granby in 1971. Tudor and I disagreed on just about everything. It didn't seem to bother him. Even in his late eighties he was always willing to try out new ideas - even if most of our conversations ended with him saying with a slight smile, "Well, we can disagree about that." Laura's eyes would tell me it wouldn't do me much good. I think he put up with me because I was married to a McCormick, a niece of a Bloomfield tobacco baron. He even asked me once what I thought should be done about the town library. Unimpressed by my answer, he gave me a box of blueberries and wished me good day.

For my part, I could hardly deny the two of them the respect they deserved as a farm family, business people and public benefactors (to say nothing of their being witnesses to nearly a century of history). They had built a thriving business which had survived the Great Depression. In 1940, Tudor had been named Connecticut's Farmer of the Year for his long history of experimentation and innovation in both tobacco and dairy farming. He had served in the state legislature, and on the first town zoning and finance commissions (the latter of which, we recall, had ordered bushes cut at the bottom rather than at the top), and had regularly opened his huge barn loft to church suppers, dances and political fund-raisers. He and Laura had financed a new town hall, firehouse, and cemetery upkeep, and they had given large

461

Salmon Brook Historical Society

Tudor and Laura Holcomb.

sums to the University of Hartford and the Hartford Foundation for Public Giving. They had purchased the old Case store in West Granby, had it torn down and the ground cleaned up for a park. In 1976, they gave the West Granby Methodist Church land and money for a new church building, since the old church was rotting from underneath. We argued about that too, for I hated to see the old meeting-house torn down. My arguments, as usual, did little to persuade Tudor. He had spent his whole life, he said, trying "to make things right" in West Granby. Still, he did trust my wife and me with eleven acres of his farm (but, of course, he got his price).

Today, their farm is known as the Holcomb Farm and is the property of the Town of Granby. Tudor and Laura deeded it to the University of Connecticut College of Agriculture and Natural Resources in 1976 for its use in experimentation and education, stipulating that if the college could not use it, then the farm should go to the town. They both died at age 92, he in 1978 and she in 1980. When the university let the buildings deteriorate and the fields go unused and untended, town officials forced the transfer. In 1990, the farm was placed on the state register of historic places, and in 1992, it was the centerpiece of the West Granby Historic District which was placed then on the National Register of Historic Districts.[1]

This is not only a beautiful piece of property, and an historic one because of Tudor and Laura's importance in the state, but also a very interesting one for the study of the town's past. Today, we might be tempted to view the farm as an artifact of Granby's quiet rural history. After all, until Tudor and Laura Holcomb deeded their property to the University of Connecticut, the family farm had been passed down from father to son to grandson and so on through one family for six generations of farmers. What could be more stable, more pastoral, less interrupted by the convulsions of history, or more peaceful? And yet, that view would be an expression of a modern yearning for a simple, slow-moving past, uncomplicated by all the change and stress we believe to be characteristic of the modern world. The real story of the Holcomb Farm is truly one of change and adaptation.

The people who lived at this place in the early 17th century, before English settlers came to Connecticut, were experiencing tremendous alterations in the way they lived. There had been serious epidemics which had decimated the population along the Connecticut and Farmington Rivers, touching off a series of important social and political changes throughout the region. The Algonkians had also made a habit of altering the land to suit their needs, and there is certainly evidence in the records we have that English-speaking settlers found cleared land that Algonkians had once used for cultivation, seasonal camps or deer parks. By 1650, in adapting to the new world of trade that Europeans had established around the Atlantic rim, Massacos, Poquonocks or Agawams had probably trapped all the beaver. As the number of beaver diminished, they used the land in what is now West Granby, mainly for hunting and fishing, until the early 1700s when the white settlers began to take an interest in owning property outside of their fortified villages.

Here on the Holcomb Farm, early inhabitants and proprietors of the Town of Simsbury found the open spaces created by the beavers or the Algonkians and they quickly "improved" them for growing grass for their livestock. Jonathan Holcomb claimed a 10-acre parcel in 1719, located east of present-day Simsbury Road on the north end of the farm (see map of Holcomb Farm). The farmers' hogs and cattle roamed freely through the woodlands, attracting from more mountainous and heavily forested regions to the north and west, the wolves and panthers the Algonkians had once kept at a distance. Where there were pine stands, settlers drained sap from the trees to make turpentine. Bounty hunters dug wolf pits to protect livestock and earn deductions on their taxes. Meanwhile, at town meeting, the farmers agitated for the town's common land to be divided into large lots so they could pay their debts and secure freeholds for their children. In a single generation, life on the Holcomb Farm had again changed drastically, and by the 1730s the surveying that would shape the land's destiny for the next generation had been

463

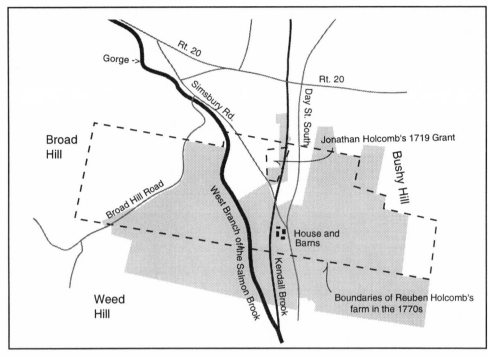

Map of West Granby, showing the Holcomb Farm (shaded area), Jonathan Holcomb's 1719 grant, and Reuben Holcomb's homestead.

completed.

Between the 1730s and 1757, the community of Salmon Brook changed from a frontier outpost, where Connecticut's fringe element had been given land in return for their serving as a buffer against French attack and local Algonkian claims, to an independent and contentious ecclesiastical society with a growing number of substantial farms. As danger of French attack dissipated, more settlers began carving farms out of lands only a few years before considered "wilderness." It was at this time that David Holcomb purchased the 10th lot in the sixth half-mile tier, land which is now at the heart of the Holcomb Farm. He wanted to secure a freehold for his son Reuben (1725-1797), who had married Susannah Hays just before the French and Indian War. Like many other young men striking out to set up his family homestead in an era when the French were gone from Canada, Reuben began clearing land between Bushy Hill and Weed Hill, selling the surplus timber

464

for needed cash, but undoubtedly using a considerable amount for his own dwelling, barns, fences and firewood. Occasionally he would deal with predators, for his fences encircled crops, not pastures, and free-roaming livestock still attracted wolves. The clearing of land proceeded at what must have seemed an agonizingly slow pace to him and Susannah. But the Holcombs were determined to tame the wild land they looked down upon from their stoop on the west slope of Bushy Hill, and to push the forest westward toward the town's edge.

A little over two decades later, after a War for Independence, the incorporation of a new town and the ratification of a new constitution, Reuben and Susannah Holcomb and their now numerous family found themselves living on a farm comprising hundreds of acres, and surrounded by numerous neighbors with equally large families. Instead of a lonely world enclosed by towering trees, they could see at least seven other farmsteads from their house, and the sounds of axes, waterwheels, ox-carts and trip-hammers now replaced the calls of birds, the rustling of the wind in the trees and the howls of wolves at night. Where imaginary lines had once run through the woods connecting dubious landmarks, now long lines of stone stretched across the land marking the sightings of the surveyors of the 1730s. Once again, the Holcomb Farm had become a new world.

As Reuben's generation turned their tools, land, dwellings and barns over to their offspring, a virtual building boom overtook "the west village" of Salmon Brook Society in the town of Granby. Farmers who had once eked out small recompense for timber that had to be dragged long distances to market now found plenty of demand locally, as sawmills churned out beams, boards and shingles in abundance from wood brought from nearby and increasingly clear-cut hills. Reuben's sons Phinehas, Reuben, Seth, Increase, Nahum, Roswell, Orator and Sylvanus confined their livestock, including substantial numbers of sheep, to enclosed pasture, collecting bounties now for runaway cattle rather than dead wolves. And where they had cut trees recently, they now planted orchards, setting aside one of their many outbuildings for cider-making operations. Phinehas, Roswell, Seth, Reuben the younger, Orator and Sylvanus led the first exodus from the increasingly crowded town, seeking more and better farm land in newly developed areas of New England and westward into New York State.[2]

465

As siblings sold and traded land and adjusted boundaries to accommodate those of this generation who chose to stay in West Granby, the farm took on a different character. West Granby in general was more densely settled by 1800, and Reuben Holcomb's lands were covered with structures as his children began operating their farms independently. At the foot of the hill on which Reuben had built his house, the house where Increase now lived, Nahum (1763-1851), who had recently married Rebecca Moore, built the Holcomb Farm homestead that still stands at the intersection of Simsbury Road and Day Street South. These newer houses were larger, more spacious and, with their decorative trim, more attractive (or more pretentious, if viewed by a conservative Puritan) than the humble shelters West Granby's first settlers had constructed. The whole valley had a more settled, domestic look to it, and this new look reflected a fundamental change in the way this generation saw itself. They were not the adventurous pioneers forsaking security and comfort for autonomy and large blocks of land. What remained of that spirit was on its way north and west. These were thrifty businessmen - still agrarian, but carefully using every bit of space, carefully keeping accounts, and carefully deciding what commodities would find the best market.

Nahum Holcomb was one of the skilled and fortunate farmers of Granby. He accumulated land his siblings and cousins couldn't keep up with, he hired laborers and produced cash crops like apples and wool, he held mortgages and collected interest, he hired out his teams, took on public offices, served in the legislature and raised a large family. Together, he and his son Nahum Jr. (1809-1871) weathered the economic storms of the early 1800s, all the while adjusting their business to the call of markets. While they themselves did not enter into the world of manufacturing that emerged on the banks of Salmon Brook just north of their lands, they financed it, patronized it and fed it, and there can be no doubt that they served its interests in their many trips to the state legislature. Nahum Jr. married distant cousin Sabra Holcomb, daughter of Warren and Asenath Holcomb of Goodrichville. Sabra's brother Carlton had been trained as a shoemaker by Truman Allen, and in 1840, he moved to West Granby to take up the shoe trade by himself. Nahum Jr. gave him land and shop, and financed the building of his house.

In the years prior to the Civil War, however, young Nahum's fortunes

466

took a turn for the worse. The price of wool declined, the local market for his produce dried up as manufacturers went out of business, the temperance movement threatened his cider revenues, and years of over grazing and run-off from clear-cut hills took a toll on the fertility of his acreage. There was considerable turmoil on the political scene too, and neighbors were often at odds on issues that became increasingly difficult to extract from the escalating violence nationwide. Nahum slid into debt as the nation slid into civil war, and the farm would not produce what he needed to get out of debt. When he died relatively young in 1871, his oldest son Nahum W. Holcomb had already left for greener pastures; and so the farm passed to his sixteen-year-old son Samuel Frederic.

As we learned in the last chapter, S.F. struggled with the convulsions of the late 19th century for the better part of his life. A farm that had once represented the triumph of free agriculture now represented the crisis of the family farm. Even cider brandy did little to prop up the finances of the farmers of Granby. We can imagine the great barns and other outbuildings constructed before the Civil War slowly deteriorating and falling to ruin. No longer did the hired hands plow the fields, and where there were pastures on every slope, the forest began its slow return. Just when S.F. thought he had things turned around, prices for farm products dropped again, and his creditors foreclosed. Fortunately, he and Lizzie held them off long enough for a new generation with new ideas to take charge.

Tudor and Laura understood from their father's experience that things would have to change if their family farm, and family farms everywhere, were to succeed. The story of their success has become a Granby legend. When they retired in 1953, they had 150 employees at their last harvest (along with 100 Guernsey cows). Both the University of Connecticut and Columbia University were operating experiment stations on their farm at that time, and the Holcombs continued to rent their fields to others over the next quarter century.

Granby was changing fast in the middle of the twentieth century. The Holcombs' former employees could now find work in area businesses and factories, in the housing construction industry, or on the growing town and state work forces. The population of the town was ballooning, and by 1960, there were finally more people in Granby than there had been in the Salmon

467

Brook Society in 1820. As fertilizer, seed, equipment and labor costs grew, and as homogenization became part of cigar production, demand for Connecticut shade tobacco fell. Even so, by 1970 the population of the town had tripled since 1940. Granby had become a suburb.[3]

Each generation that has lived and worked on the Holcomb Farm has experienced dramatic changes. Each generation had to adapt to these changing circumstances, and each responded with some degree of anxiety to the prospects for the future. There was no time in the farm's history, despite the continuity of six generations of Holcomb family tenure, that one could characterize this place as stable. We tend to think of the years after 1940 as a time of unprecedented change: population and housing growth, the transition from a farming town to a suburb, the coming of middle class wealth, the explosion of automobile traffic, and the emergence of troubling environmental issues. Actually, this era is merely an epilogue to two and a half centuries of relentless change and unremitting turbulence. Only during the period from the end of the Civil War to 1940 was there much respite from this, but only because Granby's leaders created a myth of harmony, stability and contentment that people found comforting. Even then, each age had its unsettling turbulence. Tudor and Laura's efforts to "make things right," was a response to six decades in which West Granby residents struggled with changes that threatened the existence of the family farm.

When the Holcomb Farm was transferred to the town, there was considerable discussion about how it should be used, with suggestions ranging from building a public golf course, to leasing the land for experimental food production or recruiting an Amish family to live there and use "traditional" agricultural practices. Some said the farm should "pay for itself," and others said if the town had no money to provide for its upkeep, it should not have sought to acquire the property in the first place. Of course, all this reflects continuing public agenda differences seething below the surface of a town that many perceive as a retreat from the turmoil of the modern world. In 1990, the selectmen, hoping to achieve some consensus, set up a study committee chaired by the highly respected former Judge of Probate Arline Mooney. At the time, Selectman Richard Therrien sounded almost like Tudor Holcomb himself when he said, "It is an opportunity to do things right, to determine what good can come of it, it being a legacy to Granby people."[4]

The committee did accomplish its objective of developing a plan which was both forward-thinking and appealing to the various concerns of Granby residents. In 1993, the town leased the farm for twenty years to a private non-profit corporation called the Friends of the Holcomb Farm which runs several programs it believes would be consistent with Tudor and Laura Holcomb's hopes that their property would continue to be of use for agriculture, education, and experimentation. A community supported agriculture program offers people in nearby areas and in Hartford neighborhoods a source of fresh native, organic produce, and the opportunity to share in the farm experience. Some of the produce goes to organizations combating hunger. An environmental science center has received a large grant to begin a resource/science educational program. The Friends organization is developing a timber management plan with the Yale Graduate School of Forestry. An arts center has offered classes and shows in one of the barns, a herd of Scottish highland cattle grazes on the hillsides, hay is cut on the roadside fields, and the Granby Horse Council and the 4-H Club have found space on the farm for some of their activities. The town itself has put over $100,000 into renovations for the buildings.

Happily, all of these activities mean a degree of preservation for symbols of past ages, left-overs of former landscapes. We continue to shape our own landscape, even on this historic property, and we continue to impose our own notions of tradition on the collection of artifacts of traditions we can only half-know. It is interesting that land which, for the past three centuries, had been a resource for people adjusting to change, now is called upon to meet the challenges today's community feels are peculiar to its own times. But it was never peculiar for Granby to face serious challenges.

The artifacts buried in the ground could speak of the upheavals in Algonkian society in the 17th century. The lichen and ivy-covered stone walls, boxing out patterns on the hillsides and hidden beneath the returning forest, could tell us of the heated quarrels in town meetings between "proprietors" and long-suffering "inhabitans." The jeremiads of New Light preachers are probably still echoing from the ledges on Broad Hill. A precisely symmetrical farm house could tell us of a long-ago age of "residential development," worries over the fate of one church or another, the frustration and boredom of young women bound to bone-tiring household chores, or the deep scars being inflicted by parties on either side of the temperance debate. The sparkling brook that now offers relaxation and solitude should be asked about power dams, clunking mill wheels and fortunes lost to raging freshets or to financial panics. In a cemetery not far up the road lie the remains of some of those slaughtered in an abominable war supposed to create a "new birth of freedom." In the hills, empty cellar holes, old orchards, and faint ruts of logging roads are barely visible under the weeds, along with their stories of abandoned hopes, foreclosure sales and families enduring "a world of changes." A few remaining tobacco barns and a Wisconsin dairy barn could testify to a brief age of cash income and of a brother and sister who were determined to save their farm and family name, to revitalize their village, and to provide their town with a link to traditional values they felt should be timeless and universal. We must listen carefully to all that these remnants of the past have to tell us - perhaps to be better prepared to "make things right," and to weather the tempests of our own times, or at least to know that our predecessors have been through it all before us.

Granby's Holcomb Farm

Richard Caley

Notes

Abbreviations Used:

CSL = Connecticut State Library
CHS = Connecticut Historical Society
SBHS = Salmon Brook Historical Society

Introduction

[1] See Carol Laun, "Family Farms Fade From Granby." *The Granby Drummer,* VI:12 (May, 1976), 6.
[2] *The Memorial History of Hartford County*, J. Hammond Trumbull, ed.(Boston: Edward L. Osgood, 1886), 81.
[3] James Lee Loomis, "Granby Memories." Reprinted in *The Granby Drummer*, XII:3 (November, 1981), 9.
[4] According to Curator Carol Laun, there are other versions of the "residency requirement." Some hold you must have someone buried in Granby; and others, that unless you were "here originally" you cannot be considered a resident.
[5] This seemed to be the pattern across Connecticut in the colonial period, in fact. In his book *The Connecticut Town: Growth and Development 1635-1790* (Middletown, Ct.: Wesleyan University Press, 1979), Bruce C. Daniels concludes that the colonial period was a time of tremendous change for the colony as a whole: "Because it is a widely held belief in today's world that change is presently occurring at an unprecedented pace, the extraordinary growth and development of the American colonies is apt not to be fully appreciated." The transition from a land occupied by 6000 Native Americans in 1630 to one of over 200,000 colonists organized in 100 towns by 1776 represents change "at an unprecedented pace" (p. 17).

Prologue

[1] *Granby Town Records: Volumes I and II, 1786-1853,* ed. Mark Williams (Granby, Ct.: Salmon Brook Historical Society, 1986), 1.
[2] *Granby Town Records,* 2.

471

Chapter I

[1] A more complete description of the social and economic climate of England in the 17th century can be found in Peter Earle, "English Society," in *Stuart England*, Blair Worden, ed. (Oxford: Phaidon Press Ltd., 1986), 23-48. See also Wallace Notestein, *The English People on the Eve of Colonization, 1603-1690* (New York: Harper & Row, 1954); and Neal Salisbury, *Manitou and Providence: Indians, Europeans and the Making of New England, 1500-1643* (New York: Oxford University Press, 1982), 166-170.

[2] Frank Thistlethwaite, *Dorset Pilgrims: The Story of West Country Pilgrims Who Went to New England in the 17th Century* (London: Barrie & Jenkins, 1989), 57. This is a remarkable account of the role played by Dorset and Somerset people in the settlement of Windsor. For discussion of commerialization, specialization and geographic mobility throughout Britain in the 17th century, see Joseph S. Wood, "New England's Exceptionalist Tradition: Rethinking the Colonial Encounter with the Land," in *Connecticut History,* 35:1 (Spring, 1994), 155; Leonard M. Cantor, *The Changing English Countryside, 1400-1700* (London: Cambridge University Press, 1987), 4-12, 49; Paul Coones and John Patten, *The Penguin Guide to the Landscape of England and Wales* (Hammondsworth, U.K.: 1956), 215-217; and H.R.R. Finberg(ed.), *The Agrarian History of England and Wales,* 4 vols. (London: Cambridge University Press, 1972).

[3] As quoted in David Freeman Hawke, *Everyday Life in Early America* (New York: Harper & Row, 1988), 4. For Winthrop see John Winthrop, "General Observations for the Plantation of New England," *Winthrop Papers 1623-1630* (Boston: Massachusetts Historical Society, 1931), II, 124-5.

[4] As quoted in Thistlethwaite, *Dorset Pilgrims,* 36.

[5] Richard Eburne, *Plain Pathway to Plantations,* as quoted in Thistlethwaite, *Dorset Pilgrims,* 59.

[6] Thistlethwaite, *Dorset Pilgrims,* 51-60. See also Hawke, *Everyday Life*, 8.

[7] Thistlethwaite, *Dorset Pilgrims,* 254-5. Hawke, *Everyday Life,* 9-10. David Grayson Allin, *In English Ways: the Movement of Societies and the Tranferal of English Law and Custom to Massachusetts Bay in the 17th Century* (Chapel Hill: University of North Carolina Press, 1981). There is some debate among historians over the extent to which early New England settlers wished to maintain stability and recreate the world they felt had been slipping away from them in England. Historians Sumner Chilton Powell, Kenneth Lockridge, James Henretta and Timothy Breen all point to an ancient communalism being carefully restored in New England. Salisbury, in *Manitou and Providence,* 11-12, discusses his notion of the way in which the conservative impulse coexisted with a pre-industrial capitalism.

[8] John White, as quoted in Thistlethwaite, *Dorset Pilgrims,* 60 and 63. See also p. 51 for comments on White's recruiting efforts.

[9] There is a monumental amount of scholarship on the evolution of Puritan thought in Elizabethan England. See in particular William Haller, *The Elect Nation* (New York: Harper and Row, 1963); M.M. Knappen, *Tudor Puritanism* (Chicago: University of Chicago Press, 1939); and J.E. Neale, *The Elizabethan House of Commons* (London, Jonathan Cape, 1949). The most famous work on how this thinking was transported to America includes Perry Miller, *Orthodoxy in Massachusetts* (Cambridge, Mass.: Harvard University Press, 1933) and *Errand into the Wilderness* (Cambridge, Mass.: Harvard University Press, 1953); and Edmund S. Morgan, *The Puritan Dilemma* (Boston: Little, Brown and Co., 1958). See also Salisbury, *Manitou and Providence,* 129-130; and Nicholas Tyachi, *Anti-Calvinists: the Rise of English Arminianism c. 1590-1640* (Oxford: Oxford University Press, 1987).

[10] John Winthrop, "A Model of Christian Charity" (1630), in *Winthrop Papers,* II, 295. Peter Bulkeley, *The Gospel Covenant; or the Covenant of Grace Opened,* 2nd Edition (London, 1651), 16. See also Morgan, *The Puritan Dilemma*; Hawke, *Everyday Life,* 11; and Harry S. Stout, *The New England Soul:*

Preaching and Religious Culture in Colonial New England (New York: Oxford University Press, 1984), 7-10, 14-15, 20-21, 26.

[11] From a transliteration by Mary Jeanne Anderson Jones, of *The Fundamental Orders of Connecticut* (Hartford: U.S.Bicentennial Commission of Connecticut, 1988), 55.

[12] Bruce C. Daniels, *The Connecticut Town: Growth and Development 1631-1790* (Middletown, Ct.: Wesleyan University Press, 1979), 17.

[13] One collector, Benton Holcomb of Simsbury Road in West Granby, dictated a lengthy catalog of artifacts he had discovered in the vicinity of his farm. The daughter of another, Wesley Griffin of Hungary Road, donated her father's collection to the Granby Public Library in 1929. Unfortunately, neither the Holcomb nor the Griffin collections are keyed to any map or references that would assist the modern archaeologist in determining where and how people lived in Granby during the 10,000 years before European contact. See "Catalog of Part of the Benton Holomb Collection of Indian Relics" dictated in 1931 to Mrs. Lafayettte Lasch by Benton Holcomb, "Indians/Granby" Folder, in "Granby File," SBHS Archives. See this file, as well as a "Reserve File" on Indians, for further notes on collections and reported findings. Some locations are given in John E. Ellsworth, *Simsbury: Being a Brief Historical Sketch of Ancient and Modern Simsbury, 1642-1935* (Simsbury: The Simsbury Committee for the Tercentenary, 1935), 9-10, including a reference to an Indian "fort" on Manatuck Mountain.

[14] Letter of Nicholas F. Bellantoni, Connecticut State Archaeologist, to the author, 18 March 1991, "Indians/Granby" File. Mr. Bellantoni did not identify the location of the "West Point Site," because of his department's desire to protect such sites for possible future work. See also reference to an archaeological effort at the time of the national Bicentennial in "Conservation Commission Digs Indian, Colonial Relics," *The Hartford Courant,* May 15, 1975; and Bob Nuckols, "Dig Uncovers Evidence that Hunting Parties Once Roamed the Game Refuge," *The Granby Drummer,* March, 1994, 12.

[15] Roger W. Moeller, *6LF21: A Paleo-Indian Site in Western Connecticut* (Washington, Conn.: American Indian Archaeological Institute, 1980), and by the same author, *Guide to Indian Artifacts of the Northeast* (Blaine, Washington, 1984). See also Edmund K. Swigart, *The Prehistory of the Indians of Western Connecticut* (Washington, Conn.: AIAI, 1974); and Salisbury, *Manitou and Porvidence,* 15-18.

[16] William Cronon, *Changes in the Land: Indians, Colonists and the Ecology of New England* (New York: Hill and Wang, 1983), 13. Howard S. Russell, *Indian New England Before the Mayflower* (Hanover, New Hampshire: University Press of New England, 1980), 121. Kevin A. McBride, "Native American Cultures in Transition: The Eastern Long Island Sound Culture Area in the Prehistoric and Contact Periods," *Connecticut History,* 35:1 (Spring, 1994), 8-12. Hawke, *Everday Life,* 12-13.

[17] Cronon, *Changes,* 37-8 and 59. Russell, *Indian New England,* 19-21. For discussions of the European village landscape see John R. Stilgoe, *Common Landscape of America 1580 to 1845* (New Haven: Yale University Press, 1982), 1-30.

[18] Cronon, *Changes,* 44 and 52. Russell, *Indian New England,* 20-22, 98-99. Salisbury, *Manitou and Providence,* 30-49.

[19] As will be seen later, these were the first pieces of land to be snatched up in the early land grants of the 1660s, 70s, and 80s. Some of the cleared land may have been the result of the collapsing of beaver dams, once the beaver were trapped out in southern New England. English settlers found these areas ideal for mowing ground. Cronon, *Changes,* 106.

[20] Russell, *Indian New England,* 195-8. Russell Bourne, *The Red King's Rebellion* (New York: Atheneum, 1990), 30.

473

[21] Cronon, *Changes,* 50 and 62. Russell, *Indian New England,* 28-56, 100-177. See also Bert Salwen, "Indians of Southern New England and Long Island: Early Period," in *The Handbook of North American Indians,* (Washington, D.C.: Smithsonian Institution, 1978), Vol. 15, 160-176, and Mathias Spiess, *The Indians of Connecticut* (New Haven: Yale University Press, 1933).

[22] Russell, *Indian New England,* 187. Mary Jane Springman and Betty Finnell Guinan, *East Granby: the Evolution of a Connecticut Town* (Canaan, N.H.: East Granby Historical Committee, 1983), 5. Noah A. Phelps, *History of Simsbury, Granby, and Canton From 1642 to 1845* (Hartford: Case, Tiffany and Burnham, 1845), 10.

[23] Russell, *Indian New England,* 22. See also John DeForest, *History of the Indians of Connecticut from the Earliest Known Period to 1850* (Hartford: Wm. Jas. Hamersley, 1851). In the 1964 edition of this widely used source, the assertion of animosity is made on page 65.

[24] Kenneth L. Feder, "Of Stone and Metal: Trade and Warfare in Southern New England," *The New England Social Studies Bulletin* (44:1), Fall, 1986, 26-30. Lynn Ceci, "Native Wampum as a Peripheral Resource in the Seventeenth-Century World-System," in Lawrence M. Hauptman and James Dahmery, eds., *The Pequots in Southern New England* (Norman, Oklahoma: University of Oklahoma Press, 1990), 48-63.

[25] Cronon, *Changes,* 83, and 93-5. Russell, *Indian New England,* 185. Feder, 31-36. Bourne, *Red King's Rebellion,* 26. Salisbury, *Manitou and Providence,* 50-85.

[26] Cronon, *Changes,* 86-7. Springman and Guinan, *East Granby,* 5. Russell, *Indian New England,* 14.

[27] Daniels, *Connecticut Town,* 9-14. Karen Ordahl Kupperman, "The Connecticut River: A Magnet for Settlement," *Connecticut History,* 35:1 (Sping, 1994). Kupperman's thesis is that the settling of Connecticut was part of a plan involving the founders of Massachusetts Bay themselves to institute a colony which would not stray from Puritan principals as they thought the Bay Colony had, and that the Warwick patentees and the migrants under Hooker and Warham were essentially working together. They were worried that Laud would extend his reach into the new world and maintained good relations with each other to secure their own version of a Bible Commonwealth. See also her book *Providence Island, 1630-1641: The Other Puritan Colony* (Cambridge: Harvard University Press, 1993).

[28] Henry R. Stiles, *The History and Genealogies of Ancient Windsor, Connecticut* (Hartford, Conn: Case, Lockwood & Brainard Co., 1891), I, 33-39.

[29] Bourne, *Red King's Rebellion,* 26-44. Salisbury, *Manitou and Providence,* 190-235. Harold E. Selesky, *War and Society in Colonial Connecticut* (New Haven: Yale University Press, 1990), 11-12.

[30] Mike Swift, "Windsor's Price was Corn and Blankets." *Hartford Courant,* 27 April 1991, C1. Even 19th century local historian Noah Phelps admits that the land deals were pretty shady, and all the more reprehensible in light of the hospitality with which the Natives greeted the settlers. See Phelps, *History of Simsbury,* 31. See also Salisbury, *Manitou and Providence,* 85, for discussion of the true basis of Plimoth's relations with the Wampanoags. On economic changes in the 1650s, see Stout, *New England Soul,* 76; and Howard Russell, *A Long Deep Furrow: Three Centuries of Farming in New England,* Abridged Edition (Hanover, N.H.: University Press of New England, 1982), 33.

[31] John Winthrop, "Reasons to be Considered, and Objections with Answers," in *Winthrop Papers,* II, 140-1. The obvious cynicism of this rationalization must have been apparent even to Winthrop and his fellow European settlers. A quotation taken from a c. 1890 scrapbook of Granby's Stanley Edwards now kept at SBHS, shows that New Englanders passed down a paradoxical contempt for that attitude as well as the land they took: "The way our pious New England fathers justified taking the Indian Land. 1st It is resolved that this land is the Lord's. 2nd Resolved that we are the Lord's people. 3rd Resolved therefore that the land belongs to us. And they took it."

[32] Cronon, *Changes,* 56-102. Bourne, *Red King's Rebellion,* 89-90. Russell, *Furrow,* 42.

[33] Thistlethwaite, *Dorset Pilgrims*, 43-4, and 172. Stout, *New England Soul*, 7-10. Richard L. Bushman, *From Puritan to Yankee: Character and the Social Order in Connecticut, 1690-1765* (Cambridge, Mass.: Harvard University Press, 1967) 15, 44. Hawke, *Everyday Life,* 16-17. Stilgoe, *Common Landscapes,* 44. On differences between Massachusetts and Connecticut ideas see Stephen Foster, "English Puritans and the Progress of New England Institutions, 1630-1660," in David O. Hall, John M. Murrin and Thad W. Tali, eds., *Saints and Revolutionaries: Essays on Early America* (New York: 1984), 1-4.

[34] *Public Records of the Colony of Connecticut* (Hartford: Case Lockwood and Brainard, 1873), I, 420. Lucius I. Barber, M.D., *A Record and Documentary History of Simsbury* (Simsbury: Abigail Phelps Chapter of the D.A.R., 1931), 133-6.

[35] Thistlethwaite, *Dorset Pilgrims,* 179, 223-228. Daniels, *Connecticut Town,* 101. Stiles, *Windsor,* 67, 172-189. Stout, *New England Soul,* 58. It should be noted that Joseph Wood, in "New England's Exceptionalist Tradition," points out that the already cleared land the epidemic-sticken Algonkians left the settlers made New England a virtual garden for people who were "pre-adapted" and organized efficiently for making adjustments that would turn out to be profitable. He also notes that enclosure in England had been underway for generations, although, as stated here, the population explosion of the late 16th century exerted new pressures that combined with enclosure to exacerbate the situation.

[36] Cronon, *Changes,* 119. Hawke, *Everyday Life,* 14.

[37] Thistlethwaite, *Dorset Pilgrims,* 154. Stilgoe, *Common Landscapes,* 47. Hawke, *Everyday Life,* 40.

[38] See Sumner Chilton Powell, *Puritan Village* (Middletown, Ct.: Wesleyan University Press, 1963) for a Pulitzer Prize winning discussion of this process. Martyn J. Bowden, "Culture and Place: English Sub-cultural Regions in New England in the 17th Century," *Connecticut History,* 35:1(Spring, 1994). Bowden points out that there was not as much mixing of people from different regions in England as some have suggested in the early colonial period in Connecticut.

[39] Thistlethwaite, *Dorset Pilgrims,* 54-5, 82, 84, 94-98, and 137. Russell, *Furrow,* 40, 42. Hawke, *Everyday Life,* 17-18. Daniels, *Connecticut Town,* 120-1. Stilgoe, *Common Landscapes,* 44-46. As far as the leaders were concerned, of course, Connecticut was not a democracy. On the first page of every law book read the statement, "There is a no Power but of God, the Powers that be are ordained of God." See, for example, *Connecticut Colonial Records,* II, 567. The rulers assumed elections were a device for implementing divine intentions. Bushman, *Puritan to Yankee,* 9.

[40] Bourne, *Red King's Rebellion,* 12.

[41] Cronon, *Changes,* 107-120, 148-161.

[42] Daniels, *Connecticut Town,* 45, and 117-118. He makes a good summary of the work of historians Grant, Bushman, Greven and Lockridge who have studied the overwhelming changes in New England culture as the 18th century approached. See Charles S. Grant, *Democracy in the Connecticut Frontier Town of Kent* (New York: Columbia University Press, 1961); Philip J. Greven Jr., *Four Generations: Population, Land and Family in Colonial Andover, Massachusetts* (Ithaca, New York: Cornell University Press, 1970); Kenneth A Lockridge, *A New England Town: The First Hundred Years: Dedham, Massachusetts, 1636-1736* (New York: Norton, 1970); and Bushman, *Puritan to Yankee.* See also Stilgoe, *Common Landscapes,* 42, 45.

[43] The story of Simsbury is a well-told one, and it will not be my purpose to attempt an additional version other than to provide background for the settlement of Salmon Brook. The first offering came in 1845 from Noah Phelps, *History of Simsbury, Granby and Canton From 1642 to 1845.* Dr. Lucius I. Barber's *A Record and Documentary History of Simsbury* is a classic and a remarkably professional piece of work for an "amateur." John E. Ellsworth's version, *Simsbury: Being a Brief Historical Sketch of Ancient and Modern Simsbury, 1642-1935* follows Barber's fairly faithfully, with some additional

information. By far the most readable and complete in its synthesis of information discovered about Simsbury to date, and probably not coincidentally done by a resident and long-time public servant of Granby, is William M. Vibert, *Three Centuries of Simsbury* (Simsbury: Simsbury Tercentenary Committee, 1970).

[44] Thistlethwaite, *Dorset Pilgrims,* 155-6. Russell, *Furrow,* 33.

[45] Barber, *Simsbury,* 24. "Local Indians," in *The Heritage of Granby* (Granby: Salmon Brook Historical Society, 1967), 179. Vibert, *Three Centuries,* 25.

[46] Thistlethwaite, *Dorset Pilgrims,* 232. Barber, *Simsbury,* 26-7. Springman and Guinan, *East Granby,* 5. Phelps, *History,* 9-10. Vibert, *Three Centuries,* 33. Phelps (p. 30) says there must have been "several hundred" Massacos living in Simsbury at mid-century, judging from the number of artifacts turned up, even in his time. However, subsequent relations and land sale documents would indicate otherwise.

[47] Daniels, *Connecticut Town,* on pp. 186-9, assesses soil conditions in various colonial Connecticut towns.

[48] *Public Records of the Colony of Connecticut,* I, 71. William Vibert (*Three Centuries,* 35) suggests that this measure may also have been motivated by a need to compensate Pequot War veterans such as Nathan Gillet, Thomas Barber, and James Eggleston. See also Phelps, *History,* 10.

[49] *Public Records of the Colony of Connecticut,* Vol. I, p. 161.

[50] Springman and Guinan, *East Granby,* 12. Barber, *Simsbury,* 13-17. Thistlethwaite, *Dorset Pilgrims,* 155. Phelps, *History,* 89. Clavin Fisher, in a recent article in the *Farmington Valley Herald,* had suggested the fire was actually part of a routine Algonkian burning of crop and hunting land, and not set with intent to ruin Griffin's works. I do not know what his sources were for this.

[51] *Public Records of the Colony of Connecticut,* I, 146. Barber, *Simsbury,* 15-20. Vibert, *Three Centuries,* 35-6. Phelps, *History,* 11 (also see p. 147 for the actual deed). Springman and Guinan, *East Granby,* 13.

[52] *Public Records of the Colony of Connecticut,* I, 402 and 410.

[53] This is recorded in 1674 in *Public Records of the Colony of Connecticut,* I, 246-7, 364. Barber uses this date, but in Simsbury Land Records, Vol. 2, p. 21, the date is given as November 3, 1671. For more on ongoing negotiations with the Algonkians see Barber, *Simsbury,* 28-31; Ellsworth, *Simsbury,* 18-20; Vibert, *Three Centuries,* 36.; Phelps, *History,* 11; Thistlethwaite, *Dorset Pilgrims,* 208-9 and 218.

[54] Barber, *Simsbury,* 29 and 40. Thistlethwaite, *Dorset Pilgrims,* 46 and 233. Vibert, *Three Centuries,* 37. Daniels, *Connecticut Town,* 18.

[55] Barber, *History,* 21-2. Vibert, *Three Centuries,* 38.

[56] *Public Records of the Colony of Connecticut,* I, 397; II, 20.

[57] Barber, *Simsbury,* 31 and 34. Phelps, *History,* 12. Thistlethwaite, *Dorset Pilgrims,* 200.

[58] Ellsworth, *Simsbury,* 17. Vibert, *Three Centuries,* 34. Thistlethwaite, *Dorset Pilgrims,* 225-9.

[59] Simsbury Town Records, Simsbury Town Vault, Book I, 84. Barber, *Simsbury,* 34. Vibert, *Three Centuries,* 39. Phelps, *History,* 13.

[60] For more on this notion of a Welsh identity, see Donna Holt Siemiatkoski, "Connecticut's Early Welsh Community, or Connecticut Yankees from King Arthur's Court." *Connecticut Heritage Press,* I, (October, 1990). For settlement progress see Barber, *Simsbury,* 16-17 and 34-38; Phelps, *History,* 13-15; Vibert, *Three Centuries,* 39; and *Public Records of the Colony of Connecticut,* II, 73, 97 and 113.

[61] *Public Records of the Colony of Connecticut,* II, 127. Phelps, *History,* 61. On p. 100 Phelps says there were as many as 40 families in 1670. Thistlethwaite, *Dorset Pilgrims,* 233. Vibert, *Three Centuries,* 40. Barber, *Simsbury,* 40.

[62] Barber, *Simsbury,* 42-3.

[63] *Public Records of the Colony of Connecticut,* I, 214. Phelps, *History,* 9-50. Vibert *Three Centuries,*

40-41, 49, 53 and 67. Ellsworth, *Simsbury,* 34 and 47-8. Barber, *Simsbury,* 47. Stout, in *New England Soul,* discusses the efforts on the part of the clergy to inspire a revival of religious commitment in the 1660s. They used fire-and-brimstone sermons and the numerous natural disasters of the 1660s to show that God was chastizing His "New Israel" for lack of faith. This tack paid off when King Philip's War began and a fearful populace began to attend sermons more regularly (pp. 54-78).

[64] Ellsworth says this pond was probably Manatuck Lake, which was not fully ten miles north of Farmington bounds, *Simsbury,* 34. See also Vibert, *Three Centuries,* 49.

[65] Bourne, *Red King's Rebellion,* 138 and 160-1. Barber, *Simsbury,* 61. Ellen Kenney, "Indians in the Connecticut River Valley. " *Southwoods* (March, 1984), p. 12ff.

[66] Vibert, *Three Centuries,* 44. Barber, *Simsbury,* 61. Phelps, *History,* 23-25.

[67] Bourne, *Red King's Rebellion,* 191-3 and 242. Selesky, in *Society and War* (p. 31), says that Connecticut did not suffer so much as other colonies and that its tax rolls had recovered less than two years after the war. There was little property damage, since Connecticut natives did not choose to help Metacom, and merchants and farmers found a ready market for surplus food in neighboring colonies.

[68] *Public Records of the Colony of Connecticut,* III, 296. This statement must be balanced against the habit of the General Court to understate the colony's wealth and numbers to the Board of Trade in order to minimize their interest, and thus interference, with the colony's independence. See Glen Weaver, "Industry in an Agrarian Economy: Early Eighteenth-Century Connecticut, " *Bulletin of the Connecticut Historical Society,* 19(June, 1954), 82-92. On Windsor's crowded situation see Thistlethwaite, *Dorset Pilgrims,* 229-230.

[69] Barber, *Simsbury,* 68-71. Phelps, *History,* 28. Ellsworth, *Simsbury,* 33. Vibert, *Three Centuries,* 46-8.

[70] Phelps, *History,* 75-77. Barber, *Simsbury,* 92-3. Barber uses the terminology "log huts without windows." We do not know his source for this description of the early houses. It is generally thought that the English colonists did not build log houses, even in the earliest days of a settlement. They were introduced to America by Swedes and Pennsylvania Germans. Jack Larkin, *The Reshaping of Everyday Life 1790-1840* (New York: Harper & Row, 1988), 107.

[71] Barber, *Simsbury,* 78-88. Vibert, *Three Centuries,* 49. Phelps, *History,* 31. On Talcott's background see Selesky, *War and Society,* 27.

[72] Phelps, *History,* 78. Simsbury Town Records, I, 18. Barber, *Simsbury,* 89, says the last Native American to live in Simsbury resided in the Hoskins Station area in the early 19th century, making baskets for a living.

Chapter II

[1] Simsbury Town Records, I, 84. Vibert, *Three Centuries,* 37-9. Barber, *Simsbury,* 34.

[2] Simsbury Town Records, I, 2-3.

[3] Barber, *Simsbury,* 42-3. Phelps, *History,* 77.

[4] The description of the Salmon Brook the Algonkians knew is based upon extensive familiarization with references in the early land and town records. Many of these records describe boundaries and grants on the basis of physical features, and these are of great assistance in piecing together a picture of the land before the English and Welsh settlers moved in. The colonial town meeting records after 1718 are set down in fairly orderly fashion in Volumes III, IV and V, which are in a restricted cabinet in the Simsbury town vault. The land records are indexed, to some extent, and complete for after 1710 in Volume 3 (which is called Volume 6), and those that follow. The records prior to these dates are fairly confusing. The so-called "Red Book," or the first book of town records, is labeled "1670 Book of Deeds" and is stored in a folder in the cabinet. There is a typescript of this book labeled "Volume 1 1/2" on the land record shelf. It contains mostly land records. Another manuscript volume in the cabinet is labeled "Book of Deeds 1702," and has its counterpart "Volume 2" typescript, also on the land record shelf. Also in the cabinet is a book labeled "Town Acts and Grants 1660-1691," or "Book I" of the town records, and is a typescript of the first town record book. Finally, also in the cabinet, is "Book 2 1/2," a manuscript volume containing land records from 1697 through 1718 in the front, and town meeting minutes from the 1690s and later, along with other miscellaneous records in the back. It is primarily from Land Records Volumes 1 1/2 and 2, and Town Records Book I and 2 1/2 that the imagined description is drawn.

[5] Phelps, in *History,* 85-6, says that large numbers of fish were taken up to around 1740, but that Windsor people began to monopolize the fishing business in spite of colony controls on dams and nets in the rivers. After the middle of the century, there was an effort to tighten these controls, but soon the pressure to erect mills overcame the fishing interest and because of the dams, the salmon had disappeared from Simsbury and Granby by 1800. According to Ellsworth, in *Simsbury,* 82, so plentiful were the salmon in the early period that people were required to take some whenever they purchased shad.

[6] Springman and Guinan, *East Granby,* 21. In early 17th century New England, grist and sawmills were considered public utilities, and strictly regulated. Stilgoe, *Common Landscapes,* 49.

[7] Simsbury Town Records, I, 6. "yt" is the contraction for "that."

[8] The record of this grant seems to have been lost in the 1680 fire, but the lot is referred to in a grant to a neighbor in Simsbury Land Records, 1 1/2, 175-7, and Bissell's son sold it to Nathaniel Griswold in 1710, Simsbury Land Records, 2, 219.

[9] *Some Early Records and Documents of and Relating to the Town of Windsor, Connecticut, 1639-1707,* Albert C. Bates, ed. (Hartford: Connecticut Historical Society, 1930), p. 117. Thistlethwaite, *Dorset Pilgrims,* 201. Barber, *Simsbury,* 28. Stiles, *Windsor,* II, 77-8.

[10] Simsbury Town Records, I, 17. Phelps says that the inhabitants, rather than the committee, began to divide lands after 1670, and this caused some controversy. At first, the lands were divided equally, but only among some of the inhabitants, and the resulting uneasiness later caused the repeal of this division. Phelps, *History,* 80-81. Ellsworth, *Simsbury,* 47-8. It is more likely that few, if any, of the grantees did anything with their grant, and that is why the action was rescinded.

[11] Simsbury Town Records, I, 14.

[12] Ibid., 15.

[13] Ibid., 47.

[14] Ibid., 8. Simsbury Land Records, 1 1/2, 106-7.

[15] Vibert, *Three Centuries*, 46-7. Barber, *Simsbury*, 68-74. The cellar is referred to in a deed distributing some of John Griffin's estate, Simsbury Land Records, 1 1/2, 107. There were no colony taxes collected in Simsbury until 1689. Ellsworth, 33.

[16] Barber, *Simsbury*, 73-4.

[17] The experience in Windham was similar. In 1682, the town began three centers of settlement. Bushman, *Puritan to Yankee*, 81.

[18] Simsbury Land Records, I, 22.

[19] Ellsworth, *Simsbury*, 33. Phelps, *History*, 28. Vibert, *Three Centuries*, 48.

[20] Simsbury Town Records, I, 22. Phelps, in *History*, 81, says this resolution was made in 1680/81, and the mistake is repeated in various other accounts.

[21] Simsbury Town Records, I, 23.

[22] Ibid., 72.

[23] Ibid., 22.

[24] Ibid., pg. "A."

[25] Hannah McPherson, *The Holcombes: Nation Builders* (Washington, D.C.: the author, 1947), p. 101.

[26] McPherson, *Holcombes*, 9,10,101. Stiles says (*Windsor*, II, 395) that Springfield records contain the birth record of Nathaniel II in 1673, but Matthew Grant recorded it for Windsor as well. According to McPherson, the third son Jonathan, was born in Simsbury in 1678, and Nathaniel's mother Elizabeth died there in 1679. See also Barber, *Simsbury*, 70-74, for those returning to Simsbury in the late 1670s, and Simsbury Land Records, 1 1/2, 77 and 164 for records relating to James Enos' land grants in 1660 and 1678 at Scotland. For more information on the Holcombs of Windsor and Simsbury, see Jesse Seaver, *The Holcomb(e) Genealogy* (Philadelphia: American Historical-Genealogy Society, 1925). For Thomas Holcomb's 1657 estate, see *A Digest of Early Connecticut Probate Records,* compiled by Charles William Manning (Hartford: R.S. Peck & Co., 1904), I, 130. See also Seth Holcombe, *The Descendants of Phinehas Holcomb (1759-1873) of New Hartford, Connecticut* (North Granby, Ct.: the author, 1988), vi-vii, who agrees that Nathaniel II was born at Springfield. For James Eno, Douglas C. Richardson, *The Eno and Enos Family in America: Descendants of James Eno of Windsor, Conn.* (Sacramento, Cal.: the author, 1973), 1-7. Eno, a son of a Belgian Huguenot refugee to England, was a barber by profession, one of the dissenters in the Windsor church squabbles of the 1660s, and had been elected to an office in Windsor in 1678/9.

[27] Simsbury Town Records, I, 18.

[28] Ibid., 20. *Some Early Records...of...Windsor*, 53, 59, 88, 71, 91, 116, 120, 175. Rev. Dudley Woodbridge, *His Church Record of Simsbury in Connecticut, 1697-1710,* Ed. by Albert C. Bates (Hartford: Connecticut Historical Society, 1894), 15, 16, 19, 24, 27. *Simsbury Vital Records,* 13, 150.

[29] Henry Adams, *George Adams of Watertown: Facts, Questions, Conjecture.* Typescript (1974) at CSL. *An Index of Ancestors and Role of Members of the Society of Colonial Wars* (New York: Connecticut General Assembly, 1922), 2, 3.

[30] Phelps, *History,* 103-4.

[31] Simsbury Land Records, 1 1/2, 112-113, 131, 134-5.

[32] Simsbury Town Records, I, 70.

[33] Ibid., I, 21.

[34] Ibid., I, 20.

[35] The location of this lot was determined by tracing the title of the Abijah Rowe house, including deeds in the Simsbury Land Records, 1 1/2, pp. 134-5, 226-7; 2, pp. 71; 5, pp. 186-7, 191, 286, 336; 7, pp. 588, 650.

[36] Simsbury Town Records, I, 23.

[37] Woodbridge, *Church Record*, 11, 13, 14, 23, 25, 26. *Early Connecticut Probate Records*, II, 113,

296. John W. Harms and Pearl Goddard Harms, *The Goddard Book* (Baltimore: Gateway Press, Inc., 1984), 34, 36. Winfred R. Goddard, jr., *The Goddards of Granby, Connecticut* (San Diego, Calif.: Goddard Enterprises, 1985), 14, 19.

[38] Simsbury Town Records, I, 33

[39] Bushman, *Puritan to Yankee,* 55, notes a frequency of temporary summer residence.

[40] Barber, *Simsbury,* 178.

[41] Hawke, *Everyday Life,* 46-7.

[42] Simsbury Town Records, I, 42, 43, 45, 59, 65, 68.

[43] *Colonial Records of Connecticut,* III, 199. On qualifications for freemanship, see Bushman, *Puritan to Yankee,* 8; and Daniels, *Connecticut Town,* 128-9.

[44] *Colonial Records of Connecticut,* I, 59-61.

[45] Ibid., I, 59, 60, 65. It may have been failing health that was the problem, for a town record of 1694 (Vol. 2 1/2, back of page 1) shows that the town by then was covering living expenses for his widow.

[46] The land surveys of 1687 also helped to determine these locations. See Simsbury Land Records, 1-1/2, 35-6, 38, 61-2, 71, 74, 94-5, 97, 112-113, 131, 133-5, 137, 139, 149, 156-7, 175-7, 193-195.

[47] Simsbury Town Records, 2 1/2, 1 and 7.

[48] Richardson, *Eno Family,* 1-7. Stiles, *Windsor,* II, 544. Harms and Harms, *Goddard Book,* I, 34-6. Goddard, *Goddards,* 14. H. Clifford Goslee, *Genealogy of the Sergeant John Griffin Family, 1647-1920,* Rev. Ed. (Hartford: Mss. copy, 1971), 16-17. Thistlethwaite, *Dorset Pilgrims,* 46. Adams, *George Adams of Watertown,* pp. 22-46. *Genealogy of the Matson Family* (1928) photostat at CSL. Cordelia Thies Seager and Charles William Seager, *The Seager Families of Colonial New England* (Illchee Hills, N.C.: the authors, 1978), pp. 48-67. Thomas Wilcox, *A Preliminary Report of the Descendants of William Willcockson* (Los Angeles: the author, 1937), p. 38.

[49] Selesky, in *War and Society,* 29-30, says that after King Philip's War, veterans demanded compensation for injuries and were often given land, some long after their service (as late as 1713). There is not a really good source for veterans of King Philip's War from Connecticut, so it is hard to determine what role service in that war played in acquisition of land in Simsbury. For Massachusetts, see George Madison Bodge, *Soldiers in King Philip's War* (Leominster, Mass.: the author, 1896) where reference is made to a Daniel and a Samuel Addams in the Boston area (although both names are common in Massachusetts), pp. 122, 128. There is a record (p. 372) of £2-14-0 paid in wages to a John Matson of Andover, a relatively high wage, suggesting extensive service. He lists "Windsor Troopers," including Nathaniel Bissell, on p. 468, but there were surely more from the Windsor area. Samuel and Daniel Addams are also named in *Society of Colonial Wars,* 2, 3. Daniel Addams' and Nathaniel Holcomb's early promotions to Sergeant in the Simsbury militia suggest they had had combat experience, for as has been true ever since, it was the sergeants, not the officers, who trained the men. Griffin had been a troop commander at Windsor in 1673 and 1675. *Society of Colonial Wars,* 3.

[50] Phelps, *History,* 105. Vibert, *Three Centuries,* 47.

[51] Simsbury Town Records, I, 49, 56, 65. The common field strategy was also in operation at Hop Meadow, although town records reveal that there was no end of trouble getting people to keep up their portion of the fence. I, 30, 36. Phelps, *History,* 78-80.

[52] Simsbury Town Records, 2 1/2, R56.

[53] Ibid., I, 48-9, 59, 61, 65; 2 1/2, 23.

[54] Simsbury Town Records, I, 68.

[55] Simsbury Land Records, 1 1/2, 1. Phelps, 82-3.

[56] Bushman, *Puritan to Yankee,* 46.

[57] Simsbury Town Records, I, 70, 72-3. Phelps, *History,* 32-3. Barber, *Simsbury,* 116. Ellsworth,

Simsbury, 54.

[58] See a deed of Joseph Owen to Samuel Willcockson Jr., in 1693, Simsbury Land Records, 1 1/2, 219-220, showing that Joseph Owen conveyed all of the land he was originally granted, including that which was exchanged in 1688/9.

[59] Ellsworth, *Simsbury,* 54, 77.

[60] Selesky, *War and Society,* 33-44.

[61] Ibid., 2 1/2, 21 and R26.

[62] Ibid., I, 88. He sold his "house lot and tenement," meadow land and marsh land to Samuel Willcockson Jr. in February, 1692/3, Simsbury Land Records, 1 1/2, 219-220.

[63] Daniels, *Connecticut Town,* 132. See Hawke's description of militia musters, *Everyday Life,* 131-7.

[64] Simsbury Town Records, I, 84; 2 1/2, 12, R3 and 55. Ellsworth, *Simsbury,* 55. Phelps, *History.* 104. Barber, *Simsbury,* 214.

[65] See Bushman, *Puritan to Yankee,* 31-2, for the importance of livestock for Connecticut farmers. Phelps, *History,* 76, maintains "they derived little if any benefit from any market for their surplus products," and sheep raising was impossible with the predators they faced. Still, there seemed to be a general eagerness to try to make a profit raising cattle and free-roaming pigs.

[66] Simsbury Town Records, I, 50, 89; 2 1/2, 42, R21, 27. Simsbury Land Records, 1 1/2, 33, 62, 64, 66, 94, 107, 133-4, 155, 162, 188-9, 195-6, 228, 246, 248, 253-4, 256-7.

[67] Simsbury Town Records, I, 71-2.

[68] Ibid., I, 36, 39, 78-9; 2 1/2, R18. Phelps, *History,* 78-80. Barber, *Simsbury,* 103.

[69] Phelps, *History,* 49—51. Barber, *Simsbury,* 157-9.

[70] Simsbury Town Records, I, 33.

[71] Phelps, *History,* 46-7. Ellsworth, *Simsbury,* 42.

[72] Phelps, *History,* 52. Simsbury Town Records, I, 54-5. Simsbury Land Records, 1 1/2, 181

[73] John Landon Sibly, *Biographical Sketches of Graduates of Harvard University* (Cambridge, Charles William Seever, 1885), Vol III, p. 306ff.

[74] quoted in ibid., III, 400ff.

[75] Ibid., IV, 215ff. Simsbury Town Records, 2 1/2, R22. Phelps, *History,* 52-3. Barber, *Simsbury,* 172-4.

[76] See Woodbridge's *Church Record.* Barber, *Simsbury,* 175-8.

[77] Stout, *New England Soul,* 3-4, 6, 87-8, 111-12, 121-2. Stout is the one who calculated the total number of hours of sermon exposure. Bushman, *Puritan to Yankee,* 3, notes a concern about "moral decline" and "disruptive forces" at the end of the century that were leading the way toward secularization. Stout counters that the clergy is our main source on that, and that their hysteria came mainly from other problems.

[78] Simsbury Town Records, 2 1/2, 1.

[79] Ibid., 2 1/2, R75. Simsbury Land Records, 1 1/2. 160-1, 214. Roberts had a piece southwest of Barn Door Hills that Saxton wanted, and Saxton had a piece up the West Branch, near the Gorge, that Roberts wanted.

[80] Simsbury Town Records, I, 71, 80.

[81] Ibid., 2 1/2, 24, R20.

[82] Based on tax rate schedules in Ibid., 2 1/2, 3, 7, and 11, and on admissions of new freemen, 2 1/2, R4.

[83] Simsbury Town Records, 2 1/2, R58.

[84] Ibid., 2 1/2, R4, R55, R66

[85] *Colonial Records of Connecticut,* IV, 443. Barber, *Simsbury,* 126.

481

[86] Simsbury Town Records, 2 1/2, 84-5. Simsbury Land Records, 2, 132, 202.

[87] Simsbury Town Records, 2 1/2, R25, 30. Simsbury Land Records, 1 1/2, 31, 111, 120, 136, 149, 226-7; II, 6-7, 37-8.

[88] The map is based on the land records already cited, as well as genealogies of the various families. The Adams, Holcomb, Griffin, Gossard, Willcockson, and Segar genealogies have already been cited. See also Lillian May Wilson, ed., *Barber Genealogy* (Haverhill, Mass.: John Barber White, 1909), 21-2, and 34. Other family information came from Simsbury Vital Records, Simsbury Town Records, Dudley Woodbridge's Church Records, Hartford District Probate Records, early Windsor records and the Genealogy files of SBHS, compiled by Eva Dewey and Ethel Linnell.

[89] Simsbury Town Records, 2 1/2, R15.

[90] Ibid., R17, R58. Page R58 also gives this clue to Nathaniel Holcomb's home in 1701: "Voted to lay a highway from the country road at hoppmeadow to lead away into the woods to go up that vally which is to say the next Vally beyond goodm Holcomb (Nath) house and go to the other highway on the playn." On a c. 1730 map (in CSL) of Simsbury, a road is shown crossing diagonally from the Higley farm to the intersection of Floydville Rd. and Rt. 10, fitting this description. Thus, Holcomb must have lived below John Higley in the lower meadows where he had had a house lot since 1679.

[91] Simsbury Land Records, 1 1/2, 101.

[92] Ibid., II, 36-7.

[93] Simsbury Town Records, I, 35; 2 1/2, R61. Barber, *Simsbury,* 215. Bushman, *Puritan to Yankee,* 27, notes that towns often restricted the export of timber, for it drained what was needed for subsistence. Simsbury, apparently, had not yet reached that stage.

[94] Simsbury Town Records, 2 1/2, R50.

[95] Hawke, *Everyday Life,* 32-6, notes that girdling was a common practice as well. Farmers could generally count on clearing one to two acres per year, and generally had immediate use for the wood as fuel.

[96] Simsbury Town Records, R26, R39.

[97] Ibid., R62.

[98] Ibid., R56.

[99] Ibid., R59-60. Ellsworth, 96-7.

[100] Simsbury Town Records, I, pp. "A", 88; 2 1/2, 2, R57, R58. Simsbury Land Records, 1 1/2, 74 mentions wolf pits built by John Saxton.

[101] As quoted in Goddard, *Goddards,* 19.

[102] Simsbury Town Records, 2 1/2, 1, R17.

[103] Ibid., pp. 3, 21, R35.

[104] See, for example, a mortgage deed to John Higley, Simsbury Land Records, 1 1/2, 114.

[105] Simsbury Town Records, 2 1/2, R14.

[106] Edward Eggleston, *The Transit of Civilization* (1900), in Hawke, *Everyday Life,* 161.

[107] *Colonial Records of Connecticut,* IV, 463.

[108] Ibid., V, 19, 29, 32, 40, 66, 86. Phelps, *History,* 32-9, 83, 92. Barber, *Simsbury,* 214. Ellsworth, 55-57.

[109] *Colonial Records of Connecticut,* V, 15-16. Connecticut Archives, War, III, 74b, 118d. Selesky, in *War and Society,* 45-66, argues that two changes characterized Connecticut's war effort in Queen Anne's War. The first was a concern to demonstrate loyalty by engaging in the Canadian campaigns, and thus, head off imperial interference with the colony's self-government. The second was a tendency, now that Connecticut's society was more mature and more stratified, to draw recruits from the lower economic level - men who needed cash and saw service as an opportunity to get some. Both changes are visible in Salmon Brook's participation. Where the village had not sent anyone away from Simsbury

in King William's war, it now sent three young men to fight; and since it was the poorer section of Simsbury, where the "fringe" of society lived, it is not surprising it sent half of Simsbury's quota.

[110] Simsbury Town Records, 2 1/2, R91.

[111] Simsbury Land Records, II, 51, 71, 121, 170, 173, 205, 216, 217, 218, 234-5, 238, 239. Simsbury Town Records, 2 1/2, 47, 71, R126. A petition to the General Court in 1728 said there were eleven families at Salmon Brook in 1709, two of which were east of the brook. This agrees with my count of households for that year, the heads of families being Samuel Addams, Nathan Gossard, George Hayes, Jonathan Holcomb, Nathaniel Holcomb Jr., John Matson, Samuel Slater, Peter Rice, and Samuel Willcockson Jr. Whether Benjamin Dibol was there or not is uncertain. Thomas Griffin, who took up land on the north end of Griffin's Lordship in the 1690s, was probably one of those considered to be living on the east of the brook. See Phelps, *History,* 105-6 for reference to the number of families at different dates. The *Public Records of the Colony of Connecticut,* October, 1705, 76, lists the taxpayers in Simsbury for that year.

[112] Simsbury Town Records, 2 1/2, R59, R70, R121. Barber, *Simsbury,* 70, 377. Ellsworth, *Simsbury,* 96-7.

[113] Simsbury Town Records, 2 1/2, R 95 and R99.

[114] Daniels, *Connecticut Town,* 43-4, 117-18, 171-2. Howard Russell, *A Long, Deep Furrow: Three Centuries of Farming in New England,* Abridged Ed. (Hanover, N.H.: University Press of New England, 1982), 40, 42. Hawke, *Everyday Life,* 19, 20, 31. Bushman, *Puritan to Yankee,* iv, 153-163. Stilgoe, *Common Landscapes,* 48. Stout, *New England Soul,* 106, 108. Michael Zuckerman, *Peaceable Kingdoms: New England Towns in the Eighteenth Century* (New York: Alfred A. Knopf, 1970)

[115] Hawke, *Everyday Life,* 61-2, speaks of "the clan," that is, a group of interrelated extended families living in an area, as replacing what the village had been in England to continue the sense of community in colonial America. Salmon Brook begins to take on this characteristic in the early 18th century.

[116] See Simsbury Town Records, 2 1/2, R72.

[117] Ibid. , R58.

[118] Phelps, *History,* 100.

[119] Hawke, *Everyday Life,* 145-7, 153. Bushman, *Puritan to Yankee,* 26.

[120] Bushman, *Puritan to Yankee,* 108, 114-115. Phelps, *History,* 56. Russell, *Furrow,* 62. Daniels does not see much of a transition for Connecticut to playing a part in the Atlantic trading community until after 1710 (*Connecticut Town,* 140-1). However, the mindset seems to have been there in the first years of the century. Stilgoe, *Common Landscapes,* 48, says that the markets were ready and waiting as rapidly as the land could be brought under cultivation.

[121] Simsbury Town Records, 2 1/2, R81. For other grants in Salmon Brook see also R71-4 and Simsbury Land Records, II, 59, 61, 66, 94 and 95.

[122] Simsbury Town Records, 2 1/2, R83. Four years later the act was amended to contain a four-year condition (p. R100).

[123] Ibid., R101, 105, 106, 123, 124. Simsbury Land Records, II, 163, 165, 176, 198, 219, 222, 240.

[124] Russell, *Furrow,* 93-7. Cronon, *Changes in the Land,* 120.

[125] *Connecticut Colony Records,* IV, 443, 490, 523. Barber, *Simsbury,* 121, 126. Ellsworth, *Simsbury,* 36-7. Vibert, *Three Centuries,* 51.

[126] Simsbury Town Records, 2 1/2, R105, R 112, R132. Hawke, *Everyday Life,* 170. Russell, *Furrow,* 61, 75.

[127] Russell, *Furrow,* 147. Bushman, *Puritan to Yankee,* 35. See Trumbull, *Memorial History of Hartford County,* II, 346, and IV, 374-5, for discussion of the lack of good roads in Simsbury in the early 1700s, and how those conditions discouraged settlement.

[128] Simsbury Town Records, 2 1/2, R79.

[129] The story is told in much more detail in Springman and Guinan, *East Granby,* 17ff. See also Phelps, *History,* 54-6; Barber, *Simsbury,* 196-8; Ellsworth, *Simsbury,* 114-5.

[130] Simsbury Town Records, 2 1/2, R84-5, R101-2, R108-9. Barber, *Simsbury,* 182-4, 196, 225-6, 378. Sibley, IV, 217.

[131] Simsbury Town Records, 2 1/2, R66. Phelps, 36. Russell, *Furrow,* 5, 7, 43.

[132] Hartford Probate District, "Estate of Benjamin Dibol," (1712) CSL estate file no. 1654.

[133] "Samuel Willcockson Jr. Inventory" (1713), Simsbury Town Records, 2 1/2, 1, 22.

[134] Carol Laun, "Ephraim Howard of Windsor, Early Physician and Miller." *Farmington Valley Herald,* May 14, 1987, 3A. There was also a Jacob Read who was a surgeon. *Public Records of Connecticut Colony,* IV, 99, lists him as a surgeon on an expedition to Canada in 1709, and he eventually settled in Simsbury.

[135] Hawke, *Everyday Life,* 66, 73, 81.

[136] Ibid., 53, 74-8. See Phelps, *History,* 85 for discussion of the fish supply.

[137] Ibid., 63-9, 90-100, 176. Russell, *Furrow,* 48-51, 108. Barber, Simsbury, ,178.

[138] Simsbury Town Records, 2 1/2, R52, R65, R69, R78, R82, R90, R92, R100, R121.

[139] "Estate of John Matson," (1728) CSL Probate file no. 3628. Simsbury Town Records, 2 1/2, 1(back), 3. Hawke, 110, 114, 177. Matson Genealogy.

[140] *Connecticut Colony Records,* V, 401.

[141] Simsbury Town Records, 2 1/2, 71, R125. Phelps, *History,* 44, says that Hayes built his house in 1720, just south of the present Salmon Brook Historical Society. This may have been on the lot his father first lived on when coming to Salmon Brook in 1698.

Chapter III

[1] McPherson, *Holcombs*, 2, 101, 203, 211. Seaver, *Holcomb(e) Genealogy*, 42, 48-54. *Simsbury, Connecticut: Births, Marriages, and Deaths*, transcribed from the Town Records and published by Albert C. Bates (Hartford, 1898). Simsbury Land Records, 4, R10. This last reference is to the grant of six acres for the homestead, surveyed on April 28, 1720, after the grant was made at a town meeting on January 19, 1719/20. The town meeting record of that date (Simsbury Town Records, III, 15) indicates that Nathaniel had *already* built a house on this land in anticipation of getting the grant. The procedure may be in line with the regulation that once land had been "improved" for a set time, it could then be "taken up." The time requirement by then, it will be remembered, was eight years. It is unclear whether or not the actual survey and grant was done at the end of the occupancy (which would mean, technically, that the house could have been built in 1712!), or somewhere near the beginning and then revoked if the grantee did not continue to work the land. Based on Nathaniel's life history, it seems almost certain that he had just recently built the house.

[2] At present, 45 Bushy Hill Road is the residence of Eugene and Gemma Baker, who have sponsored a tremendous amount of research and restoration work for the house. They commissioned me to write the nomination for the National Register of Historic Places ("Nathaniel Holcomb III House (c. 1720)," Connecticut Historical Commission, April 30, 1981), and have further sponsored the research that resulted in the narratives for the two sections of Chapter 3 involving Nathaniel and Thankful Holcomb. Further confirmation of the original integral lean-to framing was found in examining the rear posts to the house, which were spliced together at the level of the first floor ceiling where the original roofline ended, as well as a square ridge pole for the present roof, indicating that that the roof was reconstructed later in the 18th century. Ridge poles were never used with purlins and braces in early 18th-century construction. See J. Frederick Kelly, *The Early Domestic Architecture of Connecticut*, (New York: Dover Publications,1924), p. 46. Because there is no summer beam above the northeast first floor parlor, the house is a good illustration of what Abbott Lowell Cummings refers to as the "surprising range and variety of framing alternatives in early houses of Connecticut [which] stand in marked contrast to the greater uniformity of forms in other regions of New England where strong respect for inherited customs is very much in evidence." Abbott Lowell Cummings, "Connecticut and Its Building Traditions," *Connecticut History,* 35:1 (Spring, 1994), 225. The house is also featured in the Time-Life Publication, *Country Style*, (New York: Time-Life, 1990), 2, 24-31.

[3] Simsbury Town Records, 2 1/2, R135. Prussian blue, and intense, high tint blue, was a relatively new color, and quite rare in the colonies. It was first synthesized in Berlin in 1704 and its earliest recorded use in the colonies was on the Hannah Barnard Cupboard. J. Gettens Rutherford and George L. Stout, *Paintings, Materials: A Short Encyclopedia* (New York: Dover Publishing, Inc.: c. 1942), 150. Philip Zea and Suzanne L. Flynt, *Hadley Chests* (Deerfield, Mass.: Pocumtuck Valley Memorial Association, 1992), 19.

[4] Simsbury Town Records, 2 1/2, R119. Regarding immigrants, p. 29 mentions a "Mr. Edward Nettel of Great brittan" and "one John Durdus nee of Sweedland" who died in Simsbury in September of 1718. See also discussion of the mines in Ellsworth, *Simsbury,* 114-115; Barber, *Simsbury,* 196-200; and *Harvard Biographies,* IV, 217. The economic development did have limits, however. Simsbury Town Records, Vol. 3, pp. 5-6, shows the town suspending the cutting of bushes in the town commons "until the Town See more noccosety thereof.." This is probably a reference to the annual duty of every adult male to work one day clearing brush from the commons to protect the sheep from catching or tearing the coats, as described in Russell, *Furrow*, 83. Perhaps there was not yet enough sheep grazing to

485

require all that work.

[5] Thistlethwaite, *Dorset Pilgrims*, 161-2. Stilgoe, *Landscapes*, 50.

[6] Simsbury Land Records, 4, 423, R10, R13. Hayes, *Descendants of George Hayes*, 4-16. It is unclear whether or not Elizabeth Willcockson was daughter of Samuel Willcockson Jr. of Salmon Brook, as the Hayes genealogy says, or of William Willcockson of Weatogue, as in Thomas Wilcox, *A Preliminary Report on the Descendants of William Wilcoxson* (Los Angeles, Ca.: the author, 1937), in CSL. Simsbury Town Records, 3, 12-15.

[7] Simsbury Town Records, 2 1/2, 98-9. Daniels, in *Connecticut Town,* 179, describes Connecticut men in the early 18th century as "usually quiet and apathetic, but occasionally loud and defiant." He allows that a spirit of independence was always under the surface, and that the growth and development of towns led to this. Stilgoe, in *Common Landscapes,* 55, says, "The frittering away of common land is of great significance because it marked the rise of self-sufficient husbandmen at the expense of community." We can see evidence of these trends toward individualism and underlying independent thinking in Salmon Brook's history. Silgoe says that those who first cleared and planted the soil did best in these changing times, and that eventually the poor got poorer as a small group dominated resources. For the moment, the outlanders in Salmon Brook were in command.

[8] Phelps, *History,* 81-82, is somewhat confusing on the dates, saying the meeting began December 31, 17_23_, when it was still 1722. See also Barber, *Simsbury,* 218-22; Ellsworth, *Simsbury,* 46. Springman and Guinan, *East Granby,* 30.

[9] Simsbury Town Records, 2 1/2, R125. Phelps, *History,* 81.

[10] Simsbury Town Records, R142.

[11] Ibid., R3, R119.

[12] Bushman, *Puritan to Yankee*, 46.

[13] *Conn. Col. Recs.,* I, 100. Bushman, in *Puritan to Yankee,* 80, discusses the growing tension between speculators and those in need of land, as does Daniels, in *Connecticut Town*, 34.

[14] Daniels, *Connecticut Town*, 127-9.

[15] Phelps, *History*, 80.

[16] Springman and Guinan, *East Granby*, 17-19.

[17] Simsbury Town Records, III, 7-9. Connecticut Archives, Towns and Lands Series, CSL, IV, 101. See also Bushman, *Puritan to Yankee*, 46-52, and Daniels, *Connecticut Town*, 119-126, for discussion of these status problems.

[18] Hartford County Court Records, Court of Common Pleas, VII, n.p. CSL. I do not know how he managed to transport the turpentine to New York.

[19] See Russell, *Furrow*, 62, 93-99, and Cronon, *Changes in the Land*, 109-118 for extensive discussion of the regional forest products industry.

[20] Russell, *Furrow*, 62. Bushman, *Puritan to Yankee*, 114.

[21] Bushman, *Puritan to Yankee*, 118-128. Russell, *Furrow*, 99-101.

[22] Daniels, *Connecticut Town*, 92-3. Daniels suggests that these "old days" of communalism were confined to the first generation in New England, rather than the entire 17th century as Bushman states.

[23] Simsbury Town Records, 2 1/2, 98-9; III, 7.

[24] Many of these grants and deeds are in ibid., 2 1/2, 1, 70, 75, 96, 108, 130, 122, 143, 144, 146, 157, 159, 188, R135; III, 7. See also Vol. IV, 26, 94, 101, 145-6, 148, 165-6. A man could buy 3 acres of land by killing four wolves at 15 shillings bounty each. Thomas Morton had married Hannah Willcockson, heir to Samuel Willcockson, Jr. The earliest reference we have to a mill at Salmon Brook is in the land survey of April 8, 1723 (Simsbury Land Records, IV, R47-50) which places the mill at the current Rt. 20 bridge over the North Branch, at that time called "the highway from the mill by John

Matson[Jr.]'s land to Windsor." They do not say what kind of a mill it was, although William Hayes, George's son, received a grant right next to it, and Matson, to the north, was supposed to allow "a rod on the Northward side of the brook against the mill to the west end of his lot." I am, therefore, assuming this was the Hayes family saw mill, which is mentioned in "Estate of George Hayes" (1725), Hartford Probate Records, CSL. There is no mill mentioned in "Estate of John Matson" (1728), Hartford Probate Records, CSL. The language in the land survey seems very clear that there was, as of 1723, only one mill at Salmon Brook. Another grant at that time to William Rice, in the vicinity of the William Hayes grant does use the term "saw mill." When the mill was first put in operation I do not know. George Hayes may very well have built it when he first came to Salmon Brook in 1698 - there is just no mention until 1723.

[25] Simsbury Town Records, III, 7-9. George Hayes may actually have been the younger of the two.

[26] Ibid., 9. For commentary see Barber, *Simsbury,* 218-19; and Phelps, *History,* 81.

[27] Connecticut Archives, Towns and Lands, IV, 102.

[28] Simsbury Town Records, III, 12, 14-15. Simsbury Land Records, IV, 144, 147.

[29] Barber, *Simsbury,* 223. *Conn. Colony Records,* VI, 173. Daniels, in *Connecticut Town,* 128-9 and 201, gives evidence of a colony-wide burst in democratic inclinations resulting in freemen of a town taking over admission of new freemen and greater turnover of office-holders in the 1720s and 1730s.

[30] Connecticut Archives, Towns and Lands, IV, 99-107.

[31] Simsbury Town Records, III, 15-21.

[32] Bushman, *Puritan to Yankee,* 83 notes that Connecticut's population grew 58% in the three decades before 1700, but 280% in the three decades after, largely by natural increase.

[33] Simsbury Town Records, 2 1/2. 138. Simsbury Land Records, IV, 24.

[34] Simsbury Land Records, IV, 239, 321; V, 191, 186-7, 217, 286. The Lee family from Westfield who acquired interest in Salmon Brook property at this time, seems actually, to have been fairly friendly with Salmon Brook residents. Daniel Hayes married Sarah Lee in 1721, William Hayes married Joanna Lee in 1723, and, eventually, Nehemiah Lee moved to Salmon Brook. Other land dealers included Jonathan Sacket, Noah Phelps and Joshua Root.

[35] Simsbury Town Records, 2 1/2, 27, 68, 104.

[36] Connecticut Archives, Towns and Lands, IV, 103.

[37] Hartford County Court Records, CSL, IV, 333; V, 32, 114, 190-94, 234, 316, 323, 347, 352; VI, 8, 334, 402, 412-413

[38] Simsbury Land Records, V, 59-79; 224-231. All of these pages contain deeds of newly granted land to Thrall, presumably in payment of debts and court costs.

[39] *Conn. Colony Records,* VII, 290. Thrall himself met his match in one Hannah Thrall, who hauled him into court on the allegation of "begetting her with child." At that point, he himself, could not resist assaulting the constable. County Court Records, V, 942.

[40] Bushman, *Puritan to Yankee,* 53, 103. See also Daniels, who says the trend was older than Bushman indicates, *Connecticut Town,* 162.

[41] Simsbury Town Records, III, 23, 36, 37.

[42] Ibid., 2 1/2, R219.

[43] In general, according to Bushman, *Puritan to Yankee,* 48, the need to attract new settlers, and not necessarily the ones the proprietors wanted to attract, was a major force working against closed proprietorship across Connecticut. For Cossitt background, see Pearl Steele Cossitt, A.M., Frederic Henry White and Frederic Briggs Stebbins, *The Cossitt Family* (Pasadena, Cal.: F.M.White, 1925), pp. 1,2, 159-163. His land grants for 1723 are found in the Simsbury Land Records, Vol. 4, R23, R319.

[44] Ibid., III, 23-7.

[45] Ibid., III, 4.

[46] Connecticut Archives, Towns and Lands, IV, 103. *Connecticut Colony Records,* VI, 407.

[47] Ibid., 104a, 105, 106c, and 107.

[48] *Conn. Colony Records*, VI, 394. Bushman discusses the impact of this dispute on the colony in *Puritan to Yankee,* 51-2.

[49] These grants are spread out throughout the Simsbury Land Records, Vols. III-VII. Specifically I have looked at III, 46, 162-4; IV, 8, 50ff., 423, R5, R32ff., R47ff., R79ff.; V, 1ff.; VI, 166-168, 171ff., 175ff., 242, 329, 360, 459; VII, 88, 89

[50] Simsbury Town Records, III, 4, where they recorded a protest in 1729 as huge grants were about to be made in the western hills.

[51] As a matter of fact, the legislature in the 1730s, demonstrated its continuing concern for the gripes of debtors by engaging in some money-lending of its own "to promote trade." Bushman says that it was eastern merchants and farmers who were the beneficiaries of these politics, but they were hardly the only ones who had problems. Bushman, *Puritan to Yankee*, 130.

[52] Simsbury Land Records, IV, R47-50, 423; V, 52.

[53] At the town meeting of December 16, 1731, the wolf bounty was doubled, which probably indicates there were fewer of them, but still enough to be considered a nuisance, nonetheless. Simsbury Town Records, III, 52. See also III, 62 and 75. By 1737, the bounty had reached £2.5, and even that was doubled for those killed in the forest west of the western boundary of the town as long as the wolf's track had been picked up within two miles of any dwelling within the town. Simsbury Town Records, III, 75, 79.

[54] Phelps, *History,* 83.

[55] *Conn. Col. Recs.,* VI, 407-8.

[56] A map of Simsbury made in the early 1730s, shows two forts near Salmon Brook. A "Great Fort" on the plain south of the settlement, and "Shaw's Fort" near Manatuck Mt. The latter may have been named after, or built by, Middleton Shaw, who had had a lease to the copper mine in 1713.

[57] Ibid., IV, 407-8, 511-12. Connecticut Archives, Wars, III, 199a, 229a. See also Phelps, *History*, 34; Barber, *Simsbury*, 222-3; and Ellsworth, *Simsbury,* 57. Selesky, in *War and Society,* 67-68, discusses the flap over pay in the context of the transition, at this point, in the motivations behind service (survival of the colony to economic opportunity). Where Salmon Brook was concerned, both seemed to be involved.

[58] Simsbury Land Records, VI, 486, 542. Dewey, another "Westfield connection," like the Lee family that Thankful's brother Daniel had married into, may have been a creditor of George Hayes and Nathaniel, who sold land between their homesteads to Dewey "for a sum of money already paid." For information on the Dewey family, see Louis Mariner Dewey, et. al., *Life of George Dewey, Rear Admiral, USN and Dewey Family History* (Westfield, Mass: Dewey Publishing Co., 1898).

[59] Simsbury Land Records, V, 48, 90, 149, 203, 415.

[60] Ibid., V, R5.

[61] Ibid., VI, 370. It will be remembered that the Upper Meadows were located just north of today's Mechanicsville Road between Route 10 and Wells Road. The upland lot bounds west on Wells Road near its intersection with North Granby Road. The house which is there today, known as the Truman Allen House, was probably built later on the site of the Holcombs' second house, and probably includes pieces of the original house.

[62] Simsbury Town Records, 2 1/2, R152.

[63] Daniels, *Connecticut Town*, 181.

[64] Bushman, *Puritan to Yankee,* 151-166. To be allowed to attend a different church, an individual

would have to appear before the county court to ask permission. In 1727 and 1729, when the charter was in danger, Anglicans became an exception to the taxation policy, being allowed to claim a portion of the minister's rate for their own minister. See also Daniels, *Connecticut Town*, 101-103, 109.

[65] See also Barber, *Simsbury*, 230.

[66] Simsbury Town Records, 2 1/2, R134, 141; III, 5-6.

[67] Ibid., III, 22, 36. Springman and Guinan, *East Granby,* 37. No mention is made in the records of Salmon Brook people asking for permision to bury their dead at Salmon Brook. In fact, a purchase of a tiny plat of land near the meetinghouse by Nathaniel Holcomb suggests that they used the burying ground at Hop Meadow until they had their own meetinghouse. The record of the pitching of a stake for that meetinghouse in 1739 gives no indication there was a burying ground there at that time.

[68] Simsbury Town Records, III, 37. *Conn. Col. Recs.,* VI, 563; VII, 79.

[69] Connecticut State Archives, Ecclesiastical Affairs, Series I, IV, 224-5. Simsbury Town Records, III, 39,41. Phelps, in *History,* 58-9, says Weatogue and North Farmington people wanted to form an ecclesiastical society of their own. It is also interesting to note that at this town meeting, tax rates were set, and allowed to be paid in wheat, rye, or Indian corn, as long as they were paid by the end of May.

[70] James Smith had been admitted as an inhabitant to Simsbury in 1726, and John Howard in 1727. Simsbury Town Records, III, 37, 41.

[71] Conn. Archives, Ecclesiastical Affairs, Ser. I, IV, 233a. A petition the following year (p.235) stated there were 27 families on the west of the brook at Salmon Brook, three more than listed here.

[72] Conn. Archives, Eccl.Aff., Ser.I, IV, 235. These men answered the Salmon Brook petition, calling it a petition from a "smaler party of Our Towne," saying that the small size of the total list of the north section of town was not surprising, considering so many of them are new settlers whose estates would soon double in size.

[73] Simsbury Town Records, III, 41. The vote was 39 to 23. Conn. Archives, Eccl.Ser.I, IV, 230-1. *Conn.Col.Recs.*, VII, 93.

[74] *Conn. Col. Recs.,* VII, 134. Franklin Bowditch Dexter, *Biographical Sketches of the Graduates of Yale College* (New York: Holt, 1885), p. 5-7.

[75] *Conn.Col.Recs.,* VII, 146, 197. Simsbury Town Records, III, 42, 47. Conn. Arch., Eccles.Ser.I, IV, 241.

[76] Conn. Archives, Eccles. Ser.I, IV, 237. Simsbury Town Records, III, 47-8. One wonders if proprietors were inclined to punish Woodbridge for his role in allowing all inhabitants to share in the distribution of common lands.

[77] Simsbury Town Records, III, 44. Conn. Arch., Eccl. Ser.I, IV, 241-4.

[78] Simsbury Town Records, III, 45.

[79] Ibid., 46.

[80] Conn.Arch., Eccl.Ser.I, IV, 246-255.

[81] Ibid., 250. *Conn.Col.Recs.*, VII, 248. Barber, *Simsbury*, 251.

[82] Conn. Arch., Eccl.Ser.I, IV, 262a.

[83] *Conn.Col.Recs.,* VII, 296-7.

[84] Simsbury Town Records, III, 48-9. Conn.Archives, Eccl.Ser.I, IV, 268, 272-273a. Phelps, *History*, 64-5, 241.

[85] *Conn.Col.Recs.*, VII, 308.

[86] Simsbury Town Records, III, 49-50.

[87] Phelps, *History*, 57, 63. Barber, *Simsbury*, 250. North Association of the County of Hartford Records, CSL, meeting of March 31, 1730.

[88] Simsbury Town Records, III, 52, 54. Barber, in *Simsbury*, 251, says that Butler was employed for

part of the year by Salmon Brook people, but I could find no other corroboration of that.

[89] *Conn.Col.Recs.*, VII, 395-6. Barber, *Simsbury*, 250. Daniels, in discussing a law made in 1731 requring societies building a new meetinghouse to request a committee of the General Assembly to come and pitch a stake for its location, notes Simsbury as the most celebrated case of a protracted meetinghouse battle (*Connecticut Town*, 114).

[90] Barber, *Simsbury,* 250. Phelps,*History,* 57: Debate became so bitter "as to separate friends and family connections, and so general, as to pervade all works and conditions of the people."

[91] Simsbury Town Records, III, 57-8.

[92] Conn.Arch., Eccl.Ser.I, IV, 284-5, 289-91.

[93] Phelps, *History,* 67.

[94] Ibid., 294a. Phelps, *History,* 106. Simsbury Town Records, III, 58

[95] Barber, *Simsbury*, 254, 256-7.

[96] *Conn.Col. Recs.,* VII, 553; VIII, 12, 23, 48. Simsbury Town Records, III, 66-7. Conn.Arch., Eccl.Ser.I, IV, 301. Phelps, *History* , 68.

[97] This map is undated, and in some sources is given as "c.1730." Barber, *Simsbury*, 239, says the map was made in 1729. It appears in the Connecticut Archives, however, appended to the end of the file on the dividing of Simsbury, after the 1736 petitions (Eccl.Ser.I, IV, 314-15.). Lawrence Scanlon identified it as the work of Samuel Higley, and hypothesized on his motives in "A New Look at Old Maps" (talk given at meeting of the Salmon Brook Historical Society, March 6, 1980).

[98] Also, if someone lived in one parish and rented their property in another, they had to pay where the tenant lived. See Bushman, *Puritan to Yankee*, 69, for discussion of controversy regarding breaking off of new societies and the delicate settlements the legislature had to make.

[99] *Conn.Col.Recs,* VIII, 75-6. Conn. Arch., Eccl.Ser.I, IV, 312.

[100] Conn.Arch.Ser.I, IV, 305a give the list for Salmon Brook, Higleys, and the Falls.

[101] Bushman, *Puritan to Yankee,* 62-64 notes that convenience of worship, improved property values, and social and psychological independence were often combined as motives for creating new societies.

[102] Conn.Arch.Ser.I, VI, 54-59. *Conn. Col. Recs.*, VIII, 274. First Congregational Church of North Granby, *Records*, SBHS, V, 5-6. This church celebrated its 250th anniversary in 1989, based on the 1739 meeting being the first one recorded in their society records. However, as we have seen, Salmon Brook had been holding its own church services since 1733 at Daniel Hayes's house. As for the church itself, meaning the gathered congregation of people who "owned the convenant," it was not instituted until 1752 when Salmon Brook had its first settled minister. No mention, by the way, is made of a cemetery in the report of the committee which pitched a stake for the meetinghouse. Therefore, it is probable that it was after 1740 that Salmon Brook people began to bury their dead behind their meetinghouse. The Hayes genealogy says that Daniel's grave, in the late 1800s, was the oldest grave in the cemetery. He died in 1756.

[103] The evidence of a local merchant is sketchy. A Philip Loomis moved to Salmon Brook around 1730, and, as noted earlier, was immediately the wealthiest man in the village. He was grandson of the immigrant Joseph Loomis of Windsor, a merchant himself, and had been brought up in Westfield, the son of Lt. Samuel Loomis, and moved to Salmon Brook along with Isaac Dewey and Nehemiah Lee. Apparently he died in 1746, but I can find no probate record for him in Connecticut to determine if he was a merchant. See Elisha Loomis, *Descendants of Joseph Loomis in America* (publ. by the author, 1909), pp. 132, 140-1, 155-6. Land records on Philip Loomis (Simsbury Land Records, V, 282,283 332; VI 433; VII, 72, 77, 78, 269, 349) do not reveal much other than that he was prosperous. As for the grist mill, I am indebted to the interpretive work done by Carol Laun, Curator of the Salmon Brook Historical Society, in her investigations of the Simsbury Land Records relating to the Hillyer family

in early Simsbury (II, 36; IV, R35; V, 105, 223, IIR6; VI, 112, 218; VIII, 255; X, 270; XI, 4; XII, 92; XIV, 101 and Granby Land Records, I, 133), road surverys (Simsbury Land Records, XII, 437), and maps of Granby from c.1730, 1815, 1855 and 1869 which are at SBHS. Cranberry Pond, now Manatuck Lake, was the original Hillyer mill pond. She has also concluded that Stagecoach Road, which runs along the west edge of Manatuck Mountain, was the original route to Westfield before 1775.
[104] Simsbury Town Records, III, 71, 77, 80, 91. *Conn. Col. Recs.*, VIII, 161, 260-1, 546.

Chapter IV

[1] *Connecticut Colony Records*, VI, 87. For the Saybrook Platform itself, see Walker, ed., *The Creeds and Platforms of Congregationalism*, 502-507. Stout, in *New England Soul,* 16-17, discusses the Cambridge Platform of 1649.

[2] Bushman, *Puritan to Yankee*, 149-168. Daniels, *Connecticut Town*, 101-5, 116. Stout, *New England Soul*, 160, 178-9.

[3] Stout, *New England Soul*, 127-154. Russell, in *Furrow*, 107, says there were a great many earthquakes in New England during the colonial period.

[4] Edward Thompson, "Sermon on Matthew 5:8," July 5, 1685 in Samuel Tompson, "Notebook, 1678-1695," 1 vol., Ms. collection, American Antiquarian Society, as quoted in Stout, *New England Soul,* 157.

[5] Stout, *New England Soul*, 175-182.

[6] Ibid., 186-196. Bushman, *Puritan to Yankee*, 184., 258 Albert E. VanDusen, *Puritans against the Wilderness: Connecticut History to 1763* (Chester, Conn.: The Pequot Press, 1975), pp. 114-120.

[7] Franklin Bowditch Dexter, *Biographical Sketches of the Graduates of Yale College* (New York: Holt, 1885), I, 5-7, 58, 98-100 and 574. First Congregational Church of North Granby, *Records*, I, 1-5. We do not know exactly when the Northwest Society began having separate church meetings on a permanent basis. Today's First Congregational Church dates itself from 1739, but that is simply the first page of a badly damaged record book which may have had pages for years before 1739. At the December, 1739 meeting, the society voted to build a meetinghouse and to settle a permanent minister, and that seems like a beginning; but in actuality, they continued to meet at Daniel Hayes's house until the meetinghouse was completed nearly two years later, and it took a lot longer to settle a minister.

[8] Barber, *Simsbury*, 392.

[9] Stout, *New England Soul*, 4.

[10] The original covenant is in First Church, *Records*, I, 65-6 with the signatures of those who had "owned" it. The original signatures are undated, as is the covenant itself (noted as well in Vol. V, 5-6). All indications from the persons who signed and what is known about them from vital records, however, is that this document was created in 1752 when the society at last settled a minister. The names which follow the original signers are dated 1753.

[11] Hartford North Association, Records, CHS, Vol. I (1708-1800), 28.

[12] Stout, *New England Soul*, 229.

[13] First Church, *Records,* I, 9.

[14] Hartford North Association, Records, I, 28. *Conn. Col. Recs..*, VIII, 454-457. Daniels, *Connecticut Town*, 116. Bushman, *Puritan to Yankee*, 185.

[15] First Church, *Records,* I, 11.

[16] Ibid., 12-14.

[17] Hartford North Association, Records, I, 32.

[18] First Church, *Records,* I, 15.

[19] Hartford North Association, Records, I, 33-4.

[20] Bushman, *Puritan to Yankee,* 165, 222. *Records of Rev. Roger Viets, Rector of St. Andrews, Simsbury, Conn. 1763-1800,* Albert C. Bates, ed. (Hartford, Connecticut Historical Society, 1893). W. M. Maltbie, "The Episcopal Churches of Granby," 1959 typescript, Granby File: "Episcopal Churches: St. Ann's, St. Petters," SBHS. Also in the Granby File are records of Roger Viets' sermons, some of which were delivered at James Hillyer's house in 1760. In CHS Hoadley Collection, Box 12, is a 1743 membership list of the Anglican church at Scotland. Families included are Bacons, Cossitts, Adamses, James Case, Enos and Roberts. There is also an Abraham Sidervelt listed, suggesting a connection with the New York colony. See also Nelson H. Burr, "Story of a Country Parish: A History of St. Andrew's, North Bloomfield, Ct. (N.D. - 1940? - for the 200th anniversary of St. Andrew's), also in the Granby File: "Episcopal Churches," SBHS. Barber, *Simsbury,* 264-6. Viets's admission to the Congregational Church in 1756 is given in First Church, *Records,* V, 7. William Vibert believes that Viets subsequently read books at Yale which influenced him in the direction of Anglicanism.

[21] Bushman, *Puritan to Yankee,* 201.

[22] Ibid. 188, 207, 268. Stout, *New England Soul,* 197-209.

[23] I am basing these guesses regarding New Lights on comments in the Higley genealogy; research notes by Ethel Linnell in the Granby File: "Baptist Church," SBHS; and "Simsbury, Connecticut, Baptist Church Records," CSL Church Records, Microfilm Role #607, about early members of the Baptist church in Salmon Brook in the 1760s. There is also a reference in the First Church, *Records* in 1765 (V,76) to several people being absent from communion and attending a "separate meeting." Baptist separatists were often former New Lights who were unhappy that the congregational church did not move far enough away from Presbyterian and Old Light practices.

[24] Dexter, *Yale Biographies,* I, 744.

[25] David S. Rowland, "Ministers of Christ freed from Blood-guiltiness," (Boston: Benjamin Mecom, 1761), CHS Ms. Coll.

[26] Hartford North Association, Records, I, 37.

[27] Ibid., 38. Dexter, *Yale Biogs.,* I, 745.

[28] First Church, *Records,* I, 21.

[29] Stout, *New England Soul,* 212-223. Bushman, *Puritan to Yankee,* 187.

[30] First Church, *Records,* I, 21-29. Dexter, *Yale Biogs.,* I, 163-5; II, 148, 201-2. Bushman, *Puritan to Yankee,* 219, 229. Stout, *New England Soul,* 213. Phelps, *History of Simsbury,* 141.

[31] Joseph Strong, "The Duty of Singing considered as a necessary and dutiful Part of Christian Worship: Illustrated and enforced in a Sermon, Delivered at a Singing-Lecture, In a Parish in Simsbury, March 18, 1773" (New Haven: Thomas & Samuel Green, 1773), CHS Ms. Coll.

[32] First Church, *Records,* V, 69-71.

[33] Dexter, *Yale Biogs.,* II, 221-4.

[34] First Church, *Records,* I, 29. Phelps, in *History,* 107, locates the site of the first parsonage at the 1845 abode of Peter Jewett which was at 235 Salmon Brook Street across from today's South Congregational Church on Route 10. The present structure is known as "The Maltbie House."

[35] Hayes genealogy, 6-7. Cossitt Genealogy.

[36] Maltbie, "The Episcopal Churches of Granby."

[37] *Conn. Col. Recs..,* X, 167-8.

[38] Bushman, *Puritan to Yankee,* 196. The "Simsbury, Connecticut, Baptist Church Records" at CSL are the records of this group. It is a small, 8-page book, with most pages pasted over with newspapers. There is a record of a few meetings in 1764, with the church covenant, and a meeting of 1773. If the

newspapers could be removed without tearing the pages, more meeting records might be uncovered.
[39] Ibid., 220. This was the unintended result of all the religious upheaval throughout the colony.
[40] Daniels, *Connecticut Town*, 90-1.
[41] For a thorough discussion of the northern boundary see William S. Hart, "North Granby - Bedford: The History of 'The Wedge'," *Collections of the Salmon Brook Historical Society*, III (1987), 1-21. See also, Albert Van Dusen, *Connecticut* (New York: Random House, 1961), 94; Vibert, *Three Centuries*, 51-2; Simsbury Land Records, 2 1/2, 107; Barber, *Simsbury*, 128-9; Phelps, *History*, 84, 99.
[42] Phelps, in *History*, 106, compares tax lists between 1728 and 1761 and finds a large increase in population.
[43] Simsbury Town Records, III, 54, 68, 82, 91. Phelps says the first bridge was a toll bridge at Weatogue in 1734. This may have been the toll bridge for which the Assembly set rates in May, 1744 (*Conn. Col. Recs.*, IX, 18). Another went up at Hop Meadow in 1750, but lasted only a few years. (*History*, 90-1). Towns were notoriously delinquent, even in keeping highways clear as can be seen in *Conn. Col. Recs. XII, 82*.
[44] Petitions submitted on February 19, 1753, see Simsbury Town Records, Vol. III.
[45] Connecticut Archives, Ecclesiastical, 305a. First Church, *Records*, I, 47-8.
[46] For Ruth Porter's relationship to Joshua and Ruth Holcomb, see Carol Laun and Gladys Godard, "Centennial: Frederick H. Cossitt Library, 1891-1991," published by the Friends of the Cossitt Library, 1991, 41-2. Simsbury Land Records, IV, R32, R33, R319.
[47] Hartford County, Superior Court Records, CSL, V, 97. Simsbury Land Records, V, 26.
[48] Barber, *Simsbury*, 264-6.
[49] Simsbury Land Records, VI, 168.
[50] Ibid., VII, 506, 516.
[51] For more details on Rene Cossitt see Laun and Godard, "Centennial;" Pearl Steel Cossitt, *The Cossitt Family*; and two unpublished manuscripts I have on file at SBHS, "Scholars and Yeomen," and "At the Crossroads."
[52] Vernon Andre Kraft-Nicholson, *The Halladay Family, 1650-1933* (High Wycombe, England: University Microfilms, 1975). *Manual of the Congregational Church of Granby, Conn.* (Hartford: C. Montague, 1859). Simsbury Land Records, VI, 147, 166-8; VII, 88; VIII, 173, 224, 2526, 336; IX, 347; XI, R2. See also my manuscript "At the Halladay Mill Place" (1988) in the SBHS files.
[53] Harriet Russell Stratton, *A Book of Strattons*, (New York: The Grafton Press, 1908), 231-3. Johnston, *Higley*. Granby, Town Meeting Records, Granby Town Hall, I, 24. Simsbury Land Records, III, 294; V, 258, 274, 322; VI, 43, 93, 391, 607; VII, 296, 314, 436, 680; VIII, 8. Simsbury Town Records, April, 1743 Freeman's Meeting; IV, 3. For the sawmill, see Mary Jane Springman, "Revolutionary Era Record: The Seventh Account Book of John Owen, Esq., Simsbury, Conn." Unpubl. Ms., Trinity College, May 7, 1984, Simsbury Public Library, 12, where Martin is mentioned selling John Owen cherry boards and plank.
[54] Simsbury Land Records, VII, 449, 468, 588, 650; VIII, 181. Eva Dewey, "Granby's Early Families," in *Heritage of Granby*, 165, 175-7. While the name is sometimes spelled "Roe" in the record books, Abijah seems to have always used "Rowe." He and Serajah Stratton are both referred to in John Owen's accounts of the 1760s as furnishing blacksmith goods. See Springman, "Revolutionary Era Record," 11.
[55] Daniels, *Connecticut Town*, 34-43. Bushman, 76-7.
[56] Hart, "North Granby - Bedford," 19.
[57] Simsbury Land Records, VII, 554-5, 613, 662; VIII, 256, 285, 356.
[58] Hayes Genealogy, 15-16. Simsbury Land Records, VIII, 113, 156, 217, 330, 331, 367, 376; IX, 106.

[59] Simsbury Land Records, XI, R2.

[60] In this context of a 1750 Parliamentary statute against steel manufacturing in the colonies, both Barber (*Simsbury,* 385) and Ellsworth, 117-118, mention steel making on Hop Brook as early as 1740. The area came to be known as "Hanover." *Conn. Col. Recs.*, IX, 58 mentions a firm of Thomas Fitch, George Wyllys and Robert Walker who had a furnace at Hop Brook in 1744. Serajah Stratton may have been taking this steel and manufacturing products from it with his trip hammer, and thus the law against such activity could very well explain his flight to the hills with his trip hammer after 1750.

[61] Simsbury Land Records, VII, 637; VIII, 65, 112, 175, XII, 94. Simsbury Probate Records, II, 130, 133, 162-3; IV, 235-8. Hayes Genealogy, 14.

[62] Simsbury Land Records, VIII, 134, 252, 259, 261, 443. Cossitt Genealogy.

[63] Simsbury Land Records, V, 1ff.; VII, 5; VIII, 6, 122, 384, 385; IX, 46, 261, 262, 326-9. Oliver Phelps and Andrew Servin, *The Phelps Family in America* (Pittsfield, Mass.: Eagle Publishing Co., 1899), Vol. 1, 328. *Records of Rev. Roger Viets,* 14, 49. Phelps and Servin say Hezekiah and Hannah's daughter, Hannah, was born in Granville, but there is no record of this among the vital records of Granville or its Congregational Church. This may be a reference to their living so far north in Salmon Brook parish, and suggests they were living, at least seasonally, on the mountain as early as 1757 when she was born.

[64] Simsbury Land Records, VI, 524; VII, 34, 35, 120, 640; VIII, 227, 336, 373, 396, 447, 454, 490; IX, 22, 78, 260. McPherson, *Holcombs*, 148, 161-3.

[65] Granby File: "Salmon Brook Publick Library," SBHS. Springman and Guinan, *East Granby,* 101. This picture of life for the young people of Salmon Brook around 1760 is based upon hundreds of references to daily activities which can be picked up in working with deeds and probate records of the period. I have also drawn from more general descriptions of life in New England: see Russell, *Furrow,* 80, 88, 106-117; and Cronon, *Changes in the Land,* 152.

[66] Ellsworth, *Simsbury,* 58-9. Stout, *New England Soul,* 233-9. *Conn. Col. Recs.,* IX, 86, 91.

[67] *Conn. Col. Recs.*, IX, 229. Selesky, *War and Society,* 69-96, discusses Connecticut's wartime involvement and the transition to recruiting troops on an economic basis.

[68] Stout, *New England Soul,* 239.

[69] Ibid., 244. Fred Anderson, "A People's Army: Provincial Military Service in Massachusetts during the Seven Years War, " *William and Mary Quarterly,* 40 (1983), 499-527. There is some indication that Simsbury had to go to some lengths to recruit troops. A Philip Priest had a £10 fine for "his not joining the army" remitted in 1760. Simsbury Town Records, IV, 5.

[70] Phelps, *History,* 93. Stout, *New England Soul,* 247-9.

[71] The lists of men in service in different years are in *Collections of the Connecticut Historical Society,* Vols. IX and X (1903 and 1905).

[72] *Conn. Col. Recs.,* XI, 96, 227, 353. Stout, *New England Soul,* 250-1. In *War and Society,* 96-143, Selesky discusses the French and Indian War. He does note that soldiers were often those who needed cash, and that patriotic inclinations about defeating the French played a role in motivating people to go to war. However, he downplays the sense of threat people in a town such as Simsbury might have felt. I believe that protection of house and hearth continued to motivate men to serve in the army and embark on expeditions to northern New York in the mid-18th century.

[73] Mrs. Albert J. Hall, "Wars," *Heritage of Granby,* 76. Granby File, "Wars, French and Indian War," SBHS. Phelps, *History,* 93. Ellsworth, *Simsbury,* 58.

Chapter V

[1] See Marguerite Bernhardt, "Settlement - Prior to Incorporation of the Town in 1786," Chapter I of *The Heritage of Granby*, 1. The traditional interpretation has been that it was just natural to create a new town, once ecclesiastical separation had taken place fifty years earlier.

[2] *Connecticut Courant*, Jan. 18, 1788. See also Bernard C. Steiner, "Connecticut's Ratification of the Federal Constitution," *American Antiquarian Society Bulletin* (April, 1915).

[3] Barber, *Documentary History*, 206 and 208, documents frequent escapes by prisoners at Newgate.

[4] Mrs. Albert J. Hall, "Wars," Chapter VII of *Heritage*, 76-7. Simsbury Town Records, IV, 36-7.

[5] Simsbury population in 1756: 2245; 1762: 2269; 1774: 3700; 1782: 4664. Phelps, *History*, 101; Ellsworth, *Simsbury*, 51. Christopher P. Bickford, "The Lost Connecticut Census of 1762 Found," *Connecticut Historical Society Bulletin*, 44:2 (April, 1979). And yet, in terms of density (under 17 per square mile), it remained a lightly populated area compared to places like Stamford, Norwalk and New Haven. Daniels, *Connecticut Town*, 58.

[6] See miscellaneous grants throughout Vols. VIII and IX of the Simsbury Land Records.

[7] Simsbury Town Records, IV, 7-8.

[8] Simsbury Town Records, IV, see annual meetings of 1758-1761, where Samuel was elected Fenceviewer twice, Tythingman once. Hayes, *George Hayes of Windsor*, 26, 127. Simsbury Land Records, VIII, 113, 114; IX, 206, 465.

[9] Simsbury Town Records, IV, election meetings of 1764, '65, '68. First Church, *Records*, I, 50-3. It is surprising that Simsbury did not get involved in the Stamp Act controversy. This was a major political event in the colony. The colony government was already split east vs. west over currency and religious issues of the 1740s and 1750s. When the Old Light faction took a moderate stand on the Stamp Act, they appeared negligent of traditional rights, and New Lights took over the governor's office. With their characteristic suspicion of authority figures, they led Connecticut into the Revolution. Oscar Zeichner, *Connecticut's Years of Controversy, 1750-1776* (Williamsburg: 1949), 44-77. Bushman, *Puritan to Yankee*, 134, 254-5, 262-5.

[10] Simsbury Town Records, IV, 7-8.

[11] See, for example, officers elected in 1765, ibid., 15-17.

[12] Ibid., 20.

[13] Ibid., 21, 23, 28. *Conn. Col. Recs*, XII, 599.

[14] Simsbury Town Records, IV, 5, 14, 16. A record of his creditors taking his lands may be found in Simsbury Land Records, IX, 343, 344; XI, 96, 97, 417, 140. Selesky, in *War and Society*, 219-228, says that people throughout Connecticut were having trouble paying their taxes at this time.

[15] Simsbury Land Records, X, 262, 268; XI, 136. Stanley A. Ransom, *History of Hartland: the 69th Town in the Colony of Connecticut* (Hartland: Hartland Bicentennial Committee, 1961), 11-15. Simeon Baxter came from Hebron in 1755 to help organize the new town. A member of the Church of England he spent time in Newgate during the Revolutionary War. Apparently, though, he lived in Barkhamsted in between.

[16] Phelps, *History*, 92.

[17] Quite a few people, myself among them, have made the mistake of interpreting the Hayes genealogy to say that he built the house at 67 Barn Door Hills Road in 1753. This worried me because the early deeds cited in note 8 above are not for land in this vicinity, but for a farm north of Route 20 on Bushy Hill Road. Actually, though, as Curator Carol Laun instructs me, the Bushy Hill Road location is perfectly consistent with what Samuel's grandson, Cullen Hayes, is reported of have said to the family genealogist. He said that Samuel built "a large and substantial house at Bushy Hill, 2 miles west of

Salmon Brook, in which he and his descendants lived nearly a century and which is still in good condition, the residence of Starr Holcomb." (p.6,n) In fact, when the genealogy was published, Cullen Hayes, not Starr Holcomb, was still living at 67 Barn Door Hills Road. Starr Holcomb, according to Carol Laun's paper "19 Bushy Hill Road" ("Houses - Bushy Hill Road," Granby File, SBHS) lived at 19 Bushy Hill Road, a house which has since burned down. Samuel did buy property on Barn Door Hills Road in 1765, and the subsequent purchases suggest that he moved there in 1769. See Simsbury Land Records, IX, 247; X, 216. The land records do not actually confirm the 1769 building date. However, he did buy land in that general vicinity that fall, and there were no buildings noted in the deed at that time. It is quite possible he was able to construct this house because of profits from owning a cider mill during the year after the tea boycott began. He also bought a lot to the north of that piece in 1765, but that is probably not the lot on which the house now sits. In 1774, he bought more land from Ebenezer Gossard to the south of these holdings, and that land had a house and barn on it (Simsbury Land Records, XII, 113). It is a possibility, I suppose, that that house, which was probably Ebenezer's father John Gossard's house, was the Samuel Hays II house we now see. John's wife was Samuel's aunt. Further confirmation of the 1769 building date was found coincidentally in a study of the Oren Godard House on Godard Road in North Granby. This house was obviously refashioned in the mid-19th century from an earlier house which was constructed with a center-chimney stack set at a 45° angle to the foundation. That original foundation, according to land record work I have done, seems to have been laid by Franceway Cossitt (a lieutenant in Samuel Hays's militia company during the Revolution) in 1769! (Simsbury Land Records, III, 166ff.; V, R1ff.; VII, 231, 516; VIII, 83, 131, 308, 513; IX, 181.) There very well may have been a builder in the area at that time who did things in an unconventional manner. For further discussion, which, unfortunately, contains the erroneous interpretation of the Hayes genealogy, see Mark Williams, "Gossard's Grant," unpubl. ms. on file at SBHS, written for James and Sherred Urner, 1982; Mark Williams, "The Samuel Hayes II House (1769)," National Register of Historic Places Registration Form, Connecticut Historical Commission, Sept. 1, 1991. For architectural discussion, which leads me to stick with the 1769 date, see J. Frederick Kelly, *Early Domestic Architecture of Connecticut* (New York: Dover, 1920, reprinted 1963), 61; Virginia and Lee McAllester, *A Field Guide to American Houses* (New York: Knopf, 1984), 139; Sara Emerson Rolleston, *Heritage Houses: The American Tradition in Connecticut 1660-1900* (New York: Viking, 1979), 18, 66, 112.

[18] First Cong. Church, Records, I, 54-62., where one can also take note of his changing military rank.

[19] Simsbury Town Records, IV, 18, 23, 30, 33. *Conn. Col. Recs.*, XIII, 332, 605, 772.

[20] Russell, *Furrow*, 81.

[21] First Cong. Church, Records, V, 5-6. On the continuing Baptist congregation see "Baptist Church," Granby File, SBHS. Trumbull, *Hartford County,* 1103. Simsbury, Connecticut Baptist Church Records, CSL.

[22] Barber, *Documentary History,* 288-293.

[23] Ibid., I, 62-3. Phelps, *History*, 107. In her memoirs, Ann Eliza Edwards (transcript in "First Congregational Church: History," Granby File, SBHS) says that the meetinghouse was taken down and moved to Creamery Hill Road in 1775. James R. Hayes described it as follows: it was "conspicuous is all but convenience. Pews large enough to hold a big family of a Dozin Pulpit 1/2 circle and high so one had to go up two flights of stairs going up one flight then turning a right angle going up another flight and there you are up among the rafters." Memoirs, typescript in same "First Congregational Church: History" file. Both agree it was unheated, even in the 1820s.

[24] Connecticut Archives, Towns and Lands Series I, CSL, IX, 152.

[25] Rev. Edward Dodge, "The Southwick Jog," in *Southwick, Massachusetts* (Southwick: Southwick

Bicentennial, 1970), p. 3ff.

[26] Conn. Arch. Towns and Lands I, IX, 153.

[27] Ibid., 154-8.

[28] *Conn. Col. Recs.*, XIV, 245.

[29] See the *Connecticut Courant*, May through August, 1774 (Nos. 492-504).

[30] Simsbury Town Records, IV, 36-7.

[31] *Connecticut Courant*, No. 503 (August 16, 1774).

[32] Simsbury Town Records, IV, 37.

[33] Ibid., No. 508 (Sept. 19, 1774). For another advertisement from a Salmon Brook man, see No. 957 (June 3, 1783): "To be sold: A Good Dwelling House well finished off, a Barn and Blacksmith's Shop and about 20 acres of Land suitable for mowing, plowing and pasturing with an Orchard on the same, a fine place for a trader or tradsman. Also a Faqrm of very good Land of about one huncred acres with considerable improvement. Also wanted to hire a good Scythe Maker. Abijah Roe." Could the first property be the Salmon Brook Historical Society? We are not aware that Roe sold that house at that point.

[34] Simsbury Town Records, IV, 38.

[35] Ibid., 50-1.

[36] Ibid., 53-4. *Connecticut Courant*, No. 584 (April 1, 1776).

[37] *Courant*, Sept. 4, 1775.

[38] Burr, "Story of a Country Parish." Maltbie, Granby File: "Episcopal Churches." Barber, *Documentary History,* 315. See also Hoadley Collection, Box 12, CHS Ms. Col. for notes on Viets's tenure in Simsbury. A petition asking for clemency for Viets actually says he was to be fined or jailed. There can be little doubt as to the loyalties of those confined to Newgate. As Ellsworth (*Simsbury*, 122) notes, Simeon Baxter, who once held title to Halladay's mill site, was a noted Tory, confined to the prison, where he preached a famous sermon entitled "Tyrannicide Proved Lawful." It is a matter of debate, of course, if people of this persuasion posed a significant security risk, or it was simply a convenient and guilt-free way of redistributing coveted property. Where Viets was concerned, one wonders whether the war provided a convenient way for congregationalist town fathers to vent their spleen against a nemisis, or if he really did pose a genuine threat to their newly adopted cause. Either way, he would be the last to agree they were fighting for his liberties. According to a letter in the Hoadley collection (Box 12), CHS, one woman remembered St. Ann's Church, where Viets preached in Salmon Brook, to stand "on the rise of ground, just west of the school house at Salmon Brook, in the south east corner of the present cemetery yard." Was this the site of the first Congregational Church meeting-house? As Viets's own records indicate, he was baptizing and marrying people in this church beginning in 1764. *Records of Rev. Roger Viets, Rector of St. Andrew's, Simsbury, Conn., 1763-1800,* Albert C. Bates, ed. (Hartford: CHS, 1893).

[39] Springman, "A Revolutionary Era Record," 25-6. See also Cossitt Genealogy on Rene III.

[40] Simsbury Town Records, IV, 54, 56.

[41] Thomas Barber and Thomas Dyer were paid £2 each for killing wolves in 1777. Ibid., 51.

[42] Hannah Pettibone to Jonathan Pettibone, July, 1776 and Jonathan Pettibone Sr. to Jonathan Pettibone Jr., August 5, 1776, Connecticut State Library Manuscript Collection, American Revolution Box 1a: letters. Ensign Jonathan's wife Hannah was the sister of Jacob Pettibone who also later moved to West Granby to run a sawmill he and Jonathan invested in. Jacob was a builder by trade. Ensign Jonathan himself was the brother of Ozias Pettibone who had already moved to Granby in the 1770s. I. Fayette Pettibone, *Genealogy of the Pettibone Family* (Chicago: Brown, Pettibone and Kelly, 1885), rf: 4, 5, 17, 31, 78, 79 and 100. Springman, "Revolutionary Era Record," 14-15.

[43] Simsbury Town Records, IV, 81.

[44] William S. Hart has written about this in more detail in "For Captain Hays' Company, Kip's Bay Was No Picnic, It Was a Panic," *Granby Drummer,* October, 1993, p. 18. See also his sources as given in his paper on file at SBHS: Albert E. Van Dusen, *Connecticut,* (New York: Random House, 1961), 151; Henry P. Johnston, A.M., ed., *The Record of Connecticut Men in the Military and Naval Service During the War of the Revolution, 1775-1783* (Hartford: Case, Lockwood and Brainard, 1889), x, xi, 448, 472; Willard M. Wallace, *Appeal to Arms* (Chicago: Quadrangle Books), 115; Michael Kraus, *The United States to 1865* (Ann Arbor; University of Michigan Press, 1959), 226. For information on the Cossitt brothers, see the Cossitt Genealogy. They are both buried in the Cossitt family cemetery up the hill from Franceway's house on Godard Road in North Granby.

[45] Johnston, *Connecticut Men in the Revolution*, 389. See also Springman and Guinan, *East Granby*, 79-81.

[46] Simsbury Town Records, IV, 53.

[47] Ibid., 54. See also p. 60 where they are still, in 1780, worrying about the "public Incouragement & wages" of those called into service. Selesky, *War and Society,* discusses methods of raising troops in detail.

[48] One would think that if the record-keeping were Ranna and Ezra's idea, to insure their release from providing a soldier from their own neighborhood, it would have been recorded in the ordinary town meeting record book. It is interesting, although not unexpected, that the transaction was registered not in the ordinary town records, but in Simsbury Land Records, XII, 541, - until his service was over, Phillip was still considered a piece of property. This was a record regarding his status, not a place to give Ranna and Ezra service credit. It should be noted somewhere, lest this episode and the fact that the bulk of the Cossitt family remained Anglicans reflect adversely on the patriotism of this family, that nearly all the adult males participated at some point in military service on the American side, and certainly Jesse and Roger's deaths in captivity qualify as ample sacrifice for a family to bear.

[49] Russell, *Furrow*, 125. Dexter, *Yale Biographies*, II, 221-4.

[50] First Cong. Ch., Records, I, 70-2.

[51] The town meeting continued to struggle with questions of payment throughout 1780, 1781, and 1782. See Ibid., 60-84.

[52] Barber, *Documentary History*, 399.

[53] Johnson, *Higleys,* 139-140.

[54] Simsbury Land Records, XIII, 5; XIV, 230. It is not clear whether Hays purchased the Higley farm for one of his children, or in anticipation of a new minister. See later note on this purchase.

[55] Phelps, in *History*, 90, says the legislature allowed a lottery for a new bridge in 1781, but the lottery project was abandoned, even though some tickets had already been sold. He also recounts on p. 91 that the town built another bridge at Suffrage in 1777 or 1778.

[56] Simsbury Town Records, IV, 91. See Ellsworth, *Simsbury*, 72; Vibert, *Three Centuries of Simsbury,* 85-6.

[57] Simsbury Town Records, IV, 81-83.

[58] Ibid., 85.

[59] Ibid., 94-5.

[60] Conn. Archives, Towns and Lands, Series I, X, 104-5. Daniels discusses "hivings off" of towns at this time in *Connecticut Town,* 34. See also p. 168 for stages of living patterns through which towns passed.

[61] Arthur H. Hughes and Morse S. Allen, *Connecticut Place Names* (Hartford: Connecticut Historical Society, 1976), 188-9.

62 *Granby Bicentennial* (Granby, Mass.: Town of Granby, 1968), 11, 48. Encyclopedia Britannica (1973), X, 671-2; XIX, 836-7. Carol Laun, "What's in a Name?," *Granby Drummer*, February, 1979.

63 *Connecticut Courant*, No. 989 (January 6, 1784).

64 Hughes and Allen, *Conn. Place Names*, 188.

65 Quoted in John Phillip Reid, *In Defiant Stance*, (University Park, Pennsylvania: Pennsylvania State University Press, 1977), 139.

66 *Connecticut Courant*, Nos. 955, 1004 (May 13, 1783, April 20, 1784). *American Mercury*, August 2, 1784 and September 20, 1784.

67 Quoted in Springman and Guinan, *East Granby,* 95. See also Phelps, *History*, 110.

68 Town of Granby, *Town Meeting Records*, Granby Town Vault, I, 7.

69 First Cong. Ch., Records, I, 88. The evidence for the remodeling of the minister's house is somewhat circumstantial. After Nathaniel Higley died in 1772, his children who had not moved to Vermont, Daniel and Mary, divided the estate. Simsbury Probate Records, I, 500. When the war was over, Daniel and Mary sold the farm to Samuel Hays. What Samuel wanted with this farm is actually unclear, although he was in the process of dividing lands among his own children so they would *not* move out of town (Seth married in 1780, Samuel III in 1783, and Levi in 1786). It was at that time that the society finally hired Israel Holly on a permanent basis to be the minister. Unfortunately, the deed of transfer of this farm from Samuel Hays is lost because of the fire which burned three volumes of the Granby Land Records. Thus, we do not know if Samuel sold the land to the society, who, in turn, used it for Holly. We do know that substantial improvements were made on the house at 45 Bushy Hill Road around that time from architectural evidence. We also see Holly living in that vicinity on the 1790 manuscript census Heads of Family listing and we know that his successor, Isaac Porter lived in this house until his retirement in 1832. See Simsbury Land Records, X, 284; XIII, 5, 383, 412; XIV, R140. Johnson, *Higleys*, 139-140. Ethel Lindstrom Austin, *The Story of the Churches of Granby* (Granby: Holcomb Fund Committee, 1968), 14. Mark Williams, "Nathaniel Holcomb III House," has fuller citations on the analysis of neighboring parcels which identified this house.

70 This attempt at a synthesis of classic social histories is based on my reading of Robert E. Brown, Jr., *Middle Class Democracy in the Revolution: Massachusetts, 1691-1780* (Ithaca, New York: Cornell University Press, 1955); Charles S. Grant, *Democracy in the Connecticut Frontier Town of Kent* (New York: Columbia University Press, 1961); Sumner Chilton Powell, *Puritan Village*; Jackson Turner Main, *The Social Structure of Revolutionary America* (Princeton: Princeton University Press, 1965); Bushman, *Puritan to Yankee*; Michael Zuckerman, *Peaceable Kingdoms: New England Towns in the Eighteenth Century* (New York: Knopf, 1970); Robert Zemsky, *Merchants, Farmers and River Gods* (Boston: Gambit Inc., 1971); Edward M. Cook, Jr., *The Fathers of the Towns* (Baltimore: Johns Hopkins University Press, 1976); Robert Gross, *The Minutemen and their World* (New York: Hill & Wang, 1976); Daniels, *Connecticut Town*; and Stout, *The New England Soul*. All of these bear upon Colonial and Revolutionary New England and attempt to look at ordinary people and various types of communities in order to understand the nature of New England social structure, institutions and values, and how those aspects of colonial New England originated and changed. In general, the effort to find a "New England character" has not been very successful. Many of the characteristics debated, I believe, compose a paradoxical set of ideals and attitudes which is found in nearly all towns. Even Cook's and Daniels's typology of towns tends to ignore the possibility that finding the dominant inclinations of different towns hides the wonderful complexity, even within the minds of individual citizens, which makes New Englanders and their communities so dynamic and intriguing.

Chapter VI

[1] U.S. Bureau of Census, First and Second Census of the United States (1790 and 1800), Heads of Family manuscript schedules, CSL Archives. Copies of these are also available at the Salmon Brook Historical Society where the curator has them indexed and, in some cases, deciphered and corrected. The estimates of Granby's population before 1790 are based upon average family size for that period and the assumption that the 2:1 ratio for Salmon Brook to Turkey Hills applied before the Revolution as well as in the 1790s.

[2] Unfortunately, the Town of Granby has lost Volumes II, III, and IV of its land records, which were consumed by a fire in 1877 when they were stored in the Loomis Brothers' Store. In Volume I and in Volume V and after, there are some records from the 1786-1810 period, but clearly, many property transfer records are lost forever, making the tracing of title through to the colonial period difficult. At times it is possible to analyze the title history of neighboring parcels to assist with such surveys. Occasionally we come across copies of the deeds of the missing volumes among family papers. Some of these are stored in a folder in the Granby Town Vault. Others are found in the manuscript collections of the Salmon Brook Historical Society, the Connecticut State Library, or the Connecticut Historical Society. As for probate records, Granby was still part of the Simsbury Probate District until 1810, which is when Volume I of the Granby Probate Records begins. The Simsbury Probate Records are found in the Simsbury Town Hall, but all original probate papers for the Colony and State of Connecticut dating from 1636 are filed at the Connecticut State Library. Account books, legal papers and other evidence of business activity may also be found in the three repositories cited above. The records of the town government are located in the town vault. Volumes I and II have been published as *Granby Town Records, Volumes I and II: 1786-1853*, Mark Williams, ed. (Granby: Salmon Brook Historical Society, 1986). There is also an interesting selectman's account book (c. 1800) in the SBHS collection. Another valuable resource for economic history is the colony and state archives collections at CSL already cited in previous chapters. These include petitions filed with and actions taken by the state government.

[3] Guilford Probate District, Estate of John Huggins (Branford, 1757), CSL Archives. "The Second Company of the Governor's Foot Guard," Report of the Adjutant General, *Connecticut Men in the War of the Revolution, the War of 1812 and the Mexican War*, (Hartford: Case, Lockwood, 1857), p. 8, 561. See also, CSL Archives, Private Controversies, rf: Huggins, John; Revolution - Series I, rf: Huggins, James. *Collections of the Connecticut Historical Society*, VIII (1901) and XII (1909). Sims. Land Recs., 12, 348, 560; 13, 7, 305; 14, 164, 440. "Huggins Family Notes," unpubl. ms., private collection. Letters of Nancy Smith Huggins Holcombe, Seth Holcombe collection, North Granby, Ct. Seth Holcombe, *Descendants of James Huggins* (Granby: the author, 1979), 5-8. For more on Nancy Smith, see Henry B. Hoff, "Huggins and 'Tangier' Smith Families," *The American Genealogist* (April, 1981), 97.

[4] Stratton, *Book of Strattons*, 233. Sims. Land Recs., 10, 248, 269; 12, 24, 265, 270, 461, 465, 486, 560; 13, 385, 425.; 14, 37, 467, 495. Simsbury Probate District, "Estate of Daniel Ensign" (Hartland, 1781), CSL Archives. Simsbury Town Records, IV, 90. Jordan, *Griffin Family*, 45.

[5] Granby Land Records, V, 93, 399; VI, 25, 398; VII 151; IX, 404; XI, 110, 111, 415, 420, 421, 543.

[6] The 1790 Census shows the extra people living with him. Reference to the building of the house is in Nancy Holcomb to James Holcomb, March 23, 1834, private collection.

[7] Huggins Family Bible, private collection.

[8] First Church, Records, V, 43.

[9] Granby Town Records, I, 39. First Church, Records, I, 80-2.

[10] Granby Town Records, I, 41-2.

[11] Ibid., 44-5. We do not know how much training James Huggins had in the law. His father's estate (ref. fn. 3) indicates that John Huggins probably practiced law.

[12] Ibid., 50-62. First Church Records, I, 83; II, 62-3, 110. Granby Land Records, I, 303; V, 93, 389, 399, 531; VI 25, 26; VII, 535. For Chloe Pratt's origins see *The Vital Records of Granville, Massachusetts to the Year 1850* (Boston: New England Genealogical Society, 1914), p. 66.

[13] Lemuel sold his share of the tools and equipment and fulling mill to James in 1791. Simsbury Land Records, 17, 340. James apparently had suffered some serious poisoning in working with dyes in the shop, which experience had driven him from the trade. *Origins of Worthington, Ohio: "The New Eden,"* videotape production by the Worthington Historical Society, 1978. Deed of Giles Heacock (sic) to Benjamin Hayes, 2 April 1793, Connecticut Historical Society Ms. Coll., sf: Granby (was recorded in Granby Land Records, Vol. III, p. 53, which volume was lost in the fire). Lemuel Kilbourn originally came to Salmon Brook in 1775 from Litchfield, according to the deed in Simsbury Land Records, XII, 156. We can not be sure exactly what his intentions were at the time. He did own land north of Phinehas and later Nahum Holcomb, which is close to where Alpheus Hayes built his house and clothier shop. There may be a connection. Alpheus may have learned the clothier trade from Kilbourn, or he may have purchased property and facilities from Kilbourn before he, himself, went into business in the 1790s. For Asher Frank, see SBHS "Black Families File."

[14] 1800 U.S. Census, Heads of Family. Granby Land Records, VI, 207, 369-70; 7, 160, 533; 9, 369. Granby Town Meeting Records, I, 27. These are only faint hints of what was going on, since we are missing so many of the land transactions which occurred in the 1790s. The deeds cited above refer to lost transactions. There are probably many of which we have no hints at all.

[15] Mark Williams, "At the Halladay Mill Place: Owners of the Pettibone-Cone House at 15 Simsbury Road, West Granby, Connecticut," unpubl. ms., May 25, 1988, on file at SBHS, 10-16. For reference to his taking in Asher Frank, a pauper, see the Selectman's Account Book (1795-1812), SBHS Archives, p. 53.

[16] Kraft-Nicholson, *The Halladay Family.* Simsbury Land Records, 10, 248, 262 268, 269; 11, 136, 148; 12, 24, 190, 309, 461, 270; 13, 495; 14, 467. Jordan, *John Griffin Family,* 45. Mark Williams, "At the Halladay Mill Place," unpubl. ms. (1988), SBHS files. On Baxter, see Ransom, *History of Hartland,* 13.

[17] Simsbury Land Records, 12, 560; 13, 7, 385, 425. Simsbury Town Meeting Records, IV, 90. Simsbury Probate District, "Estate of Martin Stratton," (Granby, 1790), CSL Probate File #2580.

[18] Simsbury Land Records, 14, 37. Granby Land Records, V, 147, 347; VI, 245; VII, 170, 242, 534; IX, 369, 378; XI, 345, 531; XII, 89, 504. It appears from the records that Clark and Goodrich were actually the millwrights.

[19] Granby Land Records, VII, 368; VIII, 448; IX, 378; XI, 531; XII 42, 89, 101, 181, 275, 504. "Estate of Col. Ozias Pettibone" (1813), Granby Probate Records, Granby Town Vault, vol. 1, 1ff.

[20] Granby Town Records, I, 43.

[21] The Joab Griffin house is still standing as well, at 386 West Granby Road, on the NE corner of the junction with Simsbury Road.

[22] Granby Land Records, 7, 235.

[23] The house stood just about on Route 20 where it meets Simsbury Road today, but was moved up the hill when Route 20 was constructed and is now 38 Hartland Road. McPherson, *Holcombs,* 149. Hayes, *George Hays,* 24. Deed of Joab Griffin to Benjamin Hays, 31 March 1797, Conn. Hist. Soc. Ms. Coll., rf: Granby (was recorded in missing Vol. IV, Granby Land Records, 134).

[24] Account Book of Alpheus and Thaddeus Hays, 1812-1816, SBHS archives.

[25] Or they learned it from Lemuel Kilbourn (see note 13). For Benjamin Hayes as a clothier, see references to purchases of clothing from him by the town selectmen for paupers, Selectmen's Account Book (1795-1812); see, for example, p. 4. The tendency of young men in New England to seek brook property and open trades or manufacturing enterprises began a trend toward clustering of structures in relatively small areas and the emergence of village centers. The compact agricultural village was a vision of the earliest Puritan settlers in New England, and was seldom actually realized, except when frontier necessity dictated. By 1800, farmers were not settled in clusters, for the most part, but in farmsteads spread about a township. Thereafter, as Daniels describes (*Connecticut Town,* 168), economic differentiation led to villages, although shaped by industrial, rather than ideological, forces. See also Jack Larkin, *The Reshaping of Everyday Life 1790-1840* (New York: Harper & Row, 1988), 7.

[26] "Hezekiah Phelps Estate," (1793), Simsbury Probate Records (SPR), 3, 341-2. "Estate of Timothy Cossitt" (1795), SPR, 3, 83-86. "Estate of Aaron Post" (1810), Granby Probate Records (GPR), 1, 159-160. "Estate of Andrew Hayes" (1813), GPR 2, 63-66.

[27] Ellsworth, *Simsbury*, 82.

[28] I was made aware of this phenomenon during a conversation with Seth Holcombe, who recounted how his ancestor, Phinehas Holcomb, son of Reuben Holcomb of West Granby, had moved from a seemingly choice piece of brook land in West Granby to New Hartford in 1797. At first, I was confused about a young man choosing rocky hills over valley, but Seth pointed out to me the advantages of planting apple trees among boulders. It struck me then, that my own orchard, which is on the land Phinehas gave up, had suffered more than its share of frostbite over the years. But then, Phinehas, who stood to inherit only a share of his father's farm (which was large for Reuben, but small for eight sons), may have been able to acquire much more land in New Hartford. See Seth Holcombe, *The Descendants of Phinehas Holcomb (1759-1833) of New Hartford, Connecticut* (North Granby, Ct.: the author, 1988).

[29] Simsbury Land Records, 7, 285; 10, 212; 11, 270. Granby Land Records, I, 136, 235. "Estate of Thomas Buckland Gillett" (1822), GPR, 5, 35ff. Granby Town Records, Williams ed., 21, 248. See also, mention of a cider mill in "Benjamin Hayes Estate," (1810), GPR, 1, 211, 301.

[30] "Estate of Elisha Hays" (1787), Simsbury Probate Records, 2, 130, 133, 162-3; 4, 235-8. Simsbury Land Records, 8, 175. Hayes Genealogy, 14, 23.

[31] Hartford County Court, "License" for Ozias Higley to Tan (1804), Court Records, Record Group 3, CSL Archives. *Heritage of Granby*, 174-5.

[32] Mark Williams, "Return of the Forest God," unpubl. ms. for the Granby Land Trust, 1984, on file at SBHS. Timothy Cossitt's house was located near the corner of Enders and Legeyt Road just inside the Granby town bounds.

[33] Charles Whittelsey, *Ancestry and Descendants of John Pratt* (Hartford: Hartford Press, 1900). Granby Land Records VI, 191, 428; VII 174, 296; VIII 170, 335, 366; XI, 10. Granby Town Records, I, 44, 47, 49. The Giddings/Pratt house is at the end of today's Fox Road.

[34] Simsbury Land Records, 11, 262; 13, 85; 14, 426. Granby Land Records, V, 95, 540. The theory I developed in "Allen's Cider Mill (c.1783)," Nomination for National Register of Historic Places, Connecticut Historical Commission (1991), was that Allen's Cider Mill at 7 Mountain Road in North Granby was originally Silas Cossitt's house and sat on NW corner of the intersection, before it was moved to the SW corner, and then up the road. Ranna's house is the house on North Granby Road just south of the present North Granby Post Office.

[35] Hartford County Court Records: County Court Taverners, Vol. I (1800-1816). James Kilbourn's house stood on the site of the house just north of the NE corner of the Granville Road/East Street intersection. Kilbourn had come to Tariffville from Berlin, originally, and was taken under the wing of Rev. Griswold, a Roger Viets protegé, according to Griswold's memoirs at CHS. Griswold's

grandfather had been harassed during the Revolution in the same manner as Viets had, and Griswold himself later became an Episcopalian Bishop. Aaron Post and Benajah Holcomb had houses somewhere along Donahue Road, just north of Mountain Road, although Aaron may have operated his tavern out of his father-in-law's house which stood near the present intersection of Mountain and Silkey Roads.

[36] Bushman, *Puritan to Yankee*, 111.

[37] County Court Records. Granby Land Records, VI, 271; XVI, 12. Samuel and Seth Hays, Account Book, SBHS.

[38] Granby Land Records, V, 354; VIII, 160. The U.S. Census of 1800 identifies Hills as "black," with a family of five and a neighbor of Post's. For Post's and Holcomb's tavern licenses see Hartford County Court, Dockets, Vol. 16 (Jan. 1795-1797), Part 3, CSL court records collection.

[39] Granby Land Records, VI, 270-1. The Buttolph/Case/Lee house is at 108 Lost Acres Road.

[40] Enoch Buttolph built or remodeled the house now at 151 Silkey Road, on the corner of Mountain Road. James Holcomb inherited his father Ozias Holcomb's house, now standing at 93 Mountain Road. This house was once a saltbox, and the splices in the end and chimney girts are visible from inside the house. Ozias was the son of Judah Holcomb of North Granby Road, and it is possible that this house on Mountain Road was the original frame Judah constructed in the 1740s on North Granby Road. The gambrel roofed Judah Holcomb House currently on North Granby Road appears to be of 1760s construction, which was when Ozias built his house on Mountain Road. See Mark Williams, "The House that Moved to the Mountain," unpubl. ms. (1993) on file at SBHS. For Enoch Buttolph, see Mark Williams, "A Lifetime on Popatunuck," unpubl. ms. (1993) on file at SBHS. It is important to realize that two-story houses were not the norm in America at this time, but rather a sign of prosperity. Most of the population lived in small, plain houses even as late as 1812, and their homesteads were characterized, as Jack Larkin says, by an "out of door slovenliness." See Larkin, *Reshaping of America*, 112-115, 128-9.

[41] Gerald J. Grantz, *Home Book of Taxidermy and Tanning* (Harrisburg, Pa.: Stackpole Books, 1969), 124, 132. Shoemakers, tailors and weavers did not have the status of tanners, sawyers and blacksmiths according to Larkin, *Reshaping of America,* 44.

[42] Seaver, *Holcomb Family*. Lafayette Case, *The Goodrich Family in America* (Chicago: 1889). S. V. Talcott, *The Goodrich Family* (New York: 1912). Baptist Cemetery, North Granby, Ct. Mark Williams, "The Tanner's House," unpubl. ms. (1978), on file at SBHS. Goodrich's first house was the house at 240 North Granby Road. Later he, himself, moved into his father-in-law's house across the street and operated his tavern and the post office from there. His daughter occupied his earlier dwelling. For mention of the number of post offices see Henry Adams, *History of the United States of America During the First Administration of Thomas Jefferson*, (New York: Charles Scribner's Sons, 189), I, 11.

[43] Ozias's new house was at 4 East Granby Road. We have it dated from Seth Hayes's account book entry (SBHS) of a sale of clay for his chimneys. The house was sold in 1834 to Dr. Jairus Case and remained in the Case family until the mid-20th century. United States Treasury Department, Direct Tax of 1798, assessment books in CHS manuscript collection. "Estate of Col. Ozias Pettibone," Granby Probate Records, II, 1. First and Second Census of the United States (1790 and 1800). Pettibone, *Pettibone Family*. Granby File: "Inns:Granby," SBHS. The emergence of wealthy inland merchants was a direct result of a number of factors, including the growth in the market for farm produce and improvements in roads. The existence of this new class, says Russell, in *Furrow,* 13, contributed to a new level of intellectual activity, and through their capital resources, the beginnings of mechanization.

[44] SBHS Reserve Files: "Hillyer Papers," "Industry-Store-Hillyer and Jeptha Curtiss," "Industry-Cider Brandy." SBHS Granby File: "Inns: Granby." 1798 Direct Tax (CHS): Granby, Pliny Hillyer listing.

Granby Town Records, Vol. I. For reference to the Pettibone and Hillyer partnership of the 1770s, see Springman, "A Revolutionary Era Record:...", 6. It is possible that Pliny Hillyer's house was the one on the green facing West toward the Route 20 intersection. The information we have on taverns, places his tavern on the SW corner of the intersection, a tavern later sold to Isaac Phelps.

[45] Note found among Holcomb Family Papers, CSL ms. collection.

[46] Reserve Legal File: "Papers - John Ashley," SBHS. "WBC," Account Book, 1792-94, CHS collection.

[47] Account book of Andrew Hillyer, Justice of the Peace (1793-1824), CHS.

[48] Granby Town Records, I, 46-7.

[49] Petition to the General Assembly from the Selectmen of Granby," May 2, 1791, CSL Archives, "Travel, Highways, Ferries and Bridges," Series 2 (1737-1820), I, 82.

[50] Granby Town Records, I, 7-23.

[51] Ibid., 39-40.

[52] Springman and Guinan, *Evolution of a Town*, 201-202. *Heritage of Granby*, 155.

[53] In his master's thesis, "The Division of Granby, Connecticut: The Evolution of a Separation Minded Area from its Attempts to be Annexed to the Neighboring Towns to its Complete Independence" (University of Connecticut, 1966), SBHS Granby File: "Connecticut, East Granby," Harold Pinkham Jr. says (p.7) this petition was inspired by refusal of Salmon Brook residents to hold any town meetings in Turkey Hills, but since the town's incorporation, every third annual meeting was held at the Turkey Hills meetinghouse.

[54] Granby Town Records, I, 43-45.

[55] Daniels, *Connecticut Town*, 104. Barber, *Documentary History*, 378.

[56] Granby Town Records, I, 45.

[57] Ibid., 46-70.

[58] "Petition from Simsbury...," CSL Archives, Ferries, etc., I, 84a,b.

[59] "Petition from Pliny Hillyer...," CSL Archives, Ferries, etc., Ser. 2, XI, 16-18.

[60] See sale of share in the Granby Turnpike Company from Benjamin Reed to Roger Holcomb, March 31, 1802, CSL Ms. collection: "Granby Papers 1734-1858." This turnpike was an early example of a fast-growing field in Connecticut. According to Russell, *Furrow,* 142, there were fifty turnpike companies incorporated between 1803 and 1808.

[61] Petition, CSL Archives, Roads and Travel, X, 164; XII, 32 a,b.

[62] A series of petitions and counter-petitions in CSL Archives, Roads and Travel., XII, 3539.

[63] See protest by Pliny Hillyer to Roger Holcomb, a director of the Granby Turnpike Company, against Holcomb's ordering gatekeeper Cossitt to leave the North Granby gate open, 1807, CSL Ms. Collection: "Granby Papers 1734-1858."

[64] *Heritage of Granby*, 10. See also Colonial Dames, *Old Inns of Connecticut* (1937), 39.

[65] Granby Town Records, I, 71.

[66] See Chapter 5.

[67] Granby Town Records, I, 28. For state laws of that period on how towns should deal with paupers see *Records of the State of Connecticut,* 1787-9 volume, 224.

[68] See Selectman's Book, SBHS, for frequent references to expenses charged to the town for care of paupers. Carol Laun has done extensive research on black families in early Granby, derived from vital records and account books, and has organized it in a genealogical file at SBHS. This is the principal source behind much of what I have said here, although it is necessary to combine the information there with all-too-brief references to African-Americans in the Selectman's Book, Granby Land Records and the United States Census Heads of Family Manuscript Schedules. See also Karen Wagner, "Library

Honors Soldier-Slaves," *Hartford Courant*, Feb. 18, 1991, which makes reference to records in the Farmington Historical Society (now copies at SBHS, Granby File: "Blacks - Foot, Prince") regarding Prince Foot, a former slave freed for Revolutionary War service who married Patty Clark in Granby and raised a family there briefly, before moving on to Simsbury after 1801.

[69] These figures are from the U.S.Census, although there are contradictions between the aggregate figures given in the summaries of each census and the numbers which show up on the Heads of Family schedules. Carol Laun has done her best to reconcile the differences, and I have used her results here. We suspect the location of "Shacktown" was in the vicinity of Granbrook Park.

[70] Pliny Hillyer to Jonathan Humphrey, February, 1803, Pliny Hillyer Papers, SBHS.

[71] Roger Viets, "Sermon, preached before the Lodge of Free and Accepted Masons, at Granby, in Connecticut, called St. Mark's Lodge, on the 9th July, 1800" (Hartford: Hudson & Goodwin, 1800), CHS, p. 3. See also SBHS Granby File: "Masons - Granby," for historical notes and early membership lists. This Lodge was founded not only for Granby. Residents of Barkhamsted, Simsbury, Suffield, Windsor and Turkey Hills Society of Granby were admitted as well.

[72] SBHS Granby file, "Salmon Brook Publick Library."

[73] Phelps, *History*, 111. James Kilbourn to Payne Kenyon Kilbourn, Dec. 10, 1844 - copy in Granby file: "Library - Salmon Brook Publick, 1761," SBHS. See also Carol Laun, "Library 'born' before the Town," *Southwoods* (Sept., 1989). On formal schooling, see Larkin, *Reshaping of Everyday Life,* 34.

[74] *The American Mercury*, I: 26, January 3, 1785 .

[75] First Church, Records, II, B84. Granby Land Records, XIII, 71. Chatham Town Records, East Hampton Town Vault, First Folio, 122. Chatham Land Records, East Hampton Town Vault, VIII, 428, 432. Portland Society was then part of the township of Chatham, which later became East Hampton. Second U.S. Census (1800), Heads of Family, Hartford County, Granby, I, 274, CSL. For David Goodrich, see Case, *Goodrich Family.*

[76] *Records of Rev. Roger Viets,* 14, 49. Phelps and Servin, *Phelps Family*, 328. *Granby Town Records,* I, 24. Genealogy Files, SBHS, sf: Joel Buttolph, Hezekiah Phelps, Aaron Post. Simsbury Probate Records, II, 95-6, 120-1; III, 341-2. Granby Probate Records, I, 156ff.; VIII, 353; IX, 13ff. See also Mark Williams, "A Lifetime on Popatunuck: The Story of Hannah Phelps and the Enoch Buttolph House, 1757-1850" (May, 1993), unpubl. ms. on file at SBHS. According to Larkin, *Reshaping of America,* 193, 199, the number of pregnant brides was on the rise in the late 18th century. In the 1780s and 1790s, nearly a third of rural New England brides were pregnant. This declined after 1800 to one in five by 1840, as a greater emphasis on "control of the passions" set in after 1810.

[77] Phelps, *History*, 107. Stout, in *New England Soul*, 210, says there was an Israel Holly who was a leading separatist author in the 1740s. This may have been our Israel's father or grandfather. "Dignify the pews" probably is a reference to changing the seating from the traditionally plain Puritan style of simple benches to boxed pews, with cushions and doors to minimize the draft and keep in the heat from the footstoves. Building this type of seating would allow for subscriptions to be sold to parishioners for the pews. The bigger, more comfortable and better placed pews would command a higher price, and, of course, those wishing to make a statement about their status would be willing to pay it. It was a fast way to raise cash for building repairs, even though it probably did not sit well with Puritans who thought God frowned on vanity.

[78] Dexter, *Graduates of Yale College*, IV, 614. General Association of the Congregational Churches of Connecticut, *Contributions to the Ecclesiastical History of Connecticut* (New Haven: William Kingsley, 1861), Vol. I, 371.

[79] First Church, *Records*, I, meeting of Feb. 10, 1794; V, 82-88.

[80] Timothy Dwight, "On the Duty of Americans in the Present Crisis" (New Haven: T. Greene, 1796),

505

CHS.

[81] Ann Eliza Edwards, Memoirs, SBHS Ms. Collection.

[82] Phelps, *History*, 103.

[83] First Church, Records, II, 1-55.

[84] *Contributions to the Ecclesiastical History of Connecticut*, I, 308.

[85] "Miscellaneous Sermons" File, SBHS Reserve file. I have compared the handwriting of these sermons to Porter's church records and am convinced that he wrote these sermons, even though they are unsigned.

[86] Roger Viets, "A Serious Address and Farewell Charge to the Members of the Church of England in Simsbury and Adjacent Parts" (Hartford: Hudson & Goodwin, 1787).

[87] On the 1790 "Blodget Map" of Connecticut, which shows the types of churches in each town (map is at CHS), Granby has a Congregational Church and one more church of unidentified denomination. This may have been St. Ann's, although the symbol is located near the junction of North Granby Road and Day St., a place traditionally remembered as the site of Granby's early Baptist Church. However, Baptist and Episcopalian Churches are designated with specific symbols on the map in other towns. It is possible, perhaps, that this was a meetinghouse shared by both Baptists and Anglicans, or an old meetinghouse abandoned by one or both.

[88] Phelps, *History*, 111. Phelps says the meetinghouse was begun in 1792, but the St. Andrew's records among the church papers in the Hoadley Collection, Box 12, CHS archives, show that the building committee was not formed until 1794. The church papers in Hoadley Collection, Box 9, show that Todd was being recruited in 1793, though, so the group was probably holding services as early as 1792, even though they were still part of St. Andrew's parish. Subscription papers for the steeple are in Box 9. Todd's house was, according to William Vibert, who has done extensive research on Roger Viets and the Episcopalian churches of Granby and Bloomfield, on Hoskins Road in North Bloomfield, which would suggest he preached at St. Andrew's as well.

[89] Description of St. Peters found among notes by Judge Maltbie, Granby File: "Episcopal Churches, St. Ann's, St. Peter's," SBHS. The church's doors now grace the Meetinghouse in the SBHS "Barn Museum."

[90] Roger Viets, "A Sermon Preached in St. Peter's Church, in Granby, Formerly Simsbury, in Connecticut, New England, on the 29th Day of June, 1800" (Hartford: Hudson & Goodwin, 1800), CHS pamphlet collection.

[91] Viets, "Sermon, preached before the Lodge..."

[92] *Contributions to the Ecclesiastical History of Connecticut*, I, 267-9.

[93] Ethel Linstrom Austin, *The Story of the Churches of Granby* (Granby: Holcomb Fund Committee, 1968). The present West Granby United Methodist Church has its origins in the West Granby Methodist Episcopal Society of 1844, but an entry in their records (CSL archives, some typescript copy at SBHS) makes reference to the underpinnings of the "old meetinghouse," which the 1844 group planned to use for its new meetinghouse the following year. This original meetinghouse may have been at the junction of Firetown Road and Simsbury Road, a later site of a district schoolhouse. They also used schoolhouses for their meetings, as we shall see in Chapter 7. Phelps, in *History*, 111, said the Methodists had "a number of places of holding their religious meetings."

[94] Sylvanus Holcomb to Nahum Holcomb, Sept. 14, 1800, Holcomb Family Papers, CSL Ms. Collection.

[95] Ransom, *History of Hartland*, 20-21. Arthur G. Sharp, "Exodus to Ohio - A Promised Land," *Hartford Courant*, October 13, 1985.

[96] Carol Laun, "Worthington, Ohio - New England in the Wilderness," *Hartford Courant*, September

4, 1986. "Origins of Worthington, Ohio: The New Eden," video production by the Worthington Historical Society, 1978. Levi Buttolph, apparently, met an early death on this expedition, dying after being caught in a blizzard in 1805. For the larger context of migration from New England, see Stewart H. Holbrook, *The Yankee Exodus: An Account of Migration from New England* (Seattle: University of Washington Press, 1950).

[97] Granby Town Records, I, 62-3.

[98] As quoted in Bushman, *Puritan to Yankee*, 15.

[99] Simsbury Probate District, "Estate of Captain Samuel Hays," (1801) CSL Probate record collection.

[100] Granby Town Records, I, 7-69.

Chapter VII

[1] Granby Town Records, I, 44-5, 50-62, 66-72. First Church, Records, I, 83; II, 62-3, 110. Granby Land Records, I, 83; II, 389, 399, 531; VI, 25, 26, 398; VII, 151, 178, 535.

[2] Cowles later became a Baptist and a Tolerationist in the fight to disestablish the Congregational Church. He also operated a considerable manufacturing establishment near Tariffville. The Turkey Hills Congregational Church enjoyed a bit of a revival under Rev. Asahel Nettleton after 1815. See Springman and Guinan, *Evolution of a Town*, 112-113, 116-17.

[3] At first the number of taverns in Granby declined, but by 1810, many were back in business, with a number of new owners added to the list. See Hartford Country Court Records: County Court Taverners, Vol. I (1800-1816), CSL.

[4] Transcript of a paper found by F.H. Williams among the papers of his great-great-grandfather, Benoni Gillet, the first signatory on the paper, Granby File, "War/1812," SBHS. Other signers included Seth Hays, Cullen Hays, Joseph Gillet, and Noadiah Kendall, Jr., who were prominent men in town.

[5] Based on research by Eva Dewey in *Connecticut Men in the Regular Army, War of 1812*, 152-178, Granby File, "War/1812," SBHS. See also Adjutant General, *Record of the Service of Connecticut Men in the War of the Revolution, War of 1812 and the Mexican War* (Hartford: General Assembly, 1889). This is not to mention the many militiamen who saw action. See Granby File: "War, 1812," SBHS. These soldiers were in the 18th Militia Regiment under the command of Col. Calvin Barber of Simsbury. See Barber, *Documentary History*, 332.

[6] Oren Lee, in his Diary and Journal (CSL Ms. Collection), records for August 1, 1813: "Set out for New London under command of Capt. Pettibone." The expedition did not amount to much, apparently, for on August 9, he was back in Granby beginning his harvest (pp. 136-7).

[7] Granby Town Records, I, 72-75. See also Granby's 1811 Tax Book kept by Isaac Phelps, Jr., Granby Ms. Folder, CHS.

[8] Oren Lee, Diary, CSL, 136ff. Death Record Sheet, Granby Ms. Folder, CHS. Isaac Porter preached the funeral sermon for the three men in Southwick. His text was from Peter I:24: "For all flesh is as grass and all the glory of man as the flower of grass."

[9] James Kehl, *Ill Feeling in the Era of Good Feeling* (Pittsburgh: University of Pittsburgh Press, 1956), 40-1. Russell, *Furrow,* 147-7.

[10] Murray N. Rothbard, *The Panic of 1819, Reactions and Policies* (New York: Columbia University Press, 1962), 3-10. Bray Hammond, *Banks and Politics in America from the Revolution to the Civil War* (Princeton: Princeton University Press, 1957), 227-255. George Dangerfield, *The Awakening of American Nationalism, 1815-1828* (New York: Harper & Row, 1965), 73-80.

[11] Barber, *Documentary History*, 420. Russell, *Furrow,* 147.

[12] Oren Lee recorded a large number of deaths in his Diary and Journal in March, 1817. For a complete

discussion of this event and the economic fallout, see Henry Stommel and Elizabeth Stommel, "The Year without a Summer," *Scientific American* (1979), 176-186.

[13] Lee, Diary, 145.

[14] Granby Town Records, I, 110-119, 166-173.

[15] Reserve File: "Papers - Hillyer Family;" Legal Reserve File: "Papers - Hillyer, Pliny," SBHS.

[16] *Heritage of Granby*, 100. The Huggins gristmill seems to have survived according to succeeding deeds.

[17] Andrew Hayes, Account Book, SBHS archives - that is, it appears to be Andrew Hayes's account book, but there are obviously some entries by other people. The first entry referred to here was for August 27 and 28, 1814. On plow improvements see Russell, *Furrow,* 172, 176.

[18] Granby Town Records, I, 104.

[19] Lee, Diary, 145.

[20] Andrew Hayes, Account Book, August 28, 1826, SBHS.

[21] Lee, Diary, 164. This and the previous year, by the way, are the two years that are missing from the town meeting records, another sign of how catastrophic and turbulent these days were.

[22] Timothy Dwight, *Travels in New England and New York* (Cambridge: Harvard U. Press, 1969 reprint), Vol. IV (1821), 77-8. See also Cronon, *Changes in the Land*, who notes the affect of English agricultural practices on land at higher elevations, as well as the increase in floods (only one major flood 1635-1720, six between 1720 and 1800), 124, 148.

[23] Pease and Niles, *Gazeteer of Connecticut and Rhode Island,*(1819).

[24] Granby Town Records, I, 74.

[25] Granby Land Records, XI, 518; XII, 42, 89, 101, 181, 183, 504. The house is still standing at 29 Simsbury Road. See also SBHS Genealogy Files, rf: Harlow Wilcox.

[26] Granby Land Records, XII, 457, 458, 461, 598, 601, 602; XIII, 139; XV, 291

[27] Hayes, *George Hayes* genealogy, 75-6. Cone's new house still stands at 15 Simsbury Road.

[28] Cone's shop is mentioned in the Andrew Hayes account. A reference to the saw mill being ruined is in Granby Land Records, XXI, 73.

[29] Ibid., XVI, 43; XVIII, 194, 347, 382, 565; XIX, 177; XX, 185, 464, 465.

[30] U.S. Census, 1820, Heads of Family, Hartford County, Granby, CSL archives. A deed in Granby Land Records, XVI, 28, shows Luther owning the land he resided on as of the 1820 census. See also Mark Williams, "A Tradesman's House," unpubl. ms. (1994), SBHS.

[31] Granby Probate Records, I, 245. Dibble, Godard, Bates, & Co., Account Book (1799-1820), CHS. Dibble, Godard & Co., Account Book (1818-1827), CHS.

[32] Granby Land Records, VI, 253; VII, 418; VIII, 123, 124; IX, 125, 147; XI, 37, 78, 146, 257; X, 220; XI, 221; XII, 155, 484; XIV, 336; XVI, 263; XVII, 53; XX, 1. Granby Probate Records, V, 119. U.S. Census, Heads of Family Ms Census, 1810, 1820, and 1830, CSL. Hartford County Court Records, Tavern Licenses. Granby First Church, Records, II, 92, 111, 117, 153. Barkhamsted Congregational Church Records, I, 23, CSL. Barkhamsted Vital Records, Barkhamsted Town Vault, I, 45. Simsbury Town Records, III, 195. Henry Willey, *Isaac Willey of New London and His Descendants* (New Bedford, Mass.: Henry Willey, 1888). Willey's property, where he distilled cider, is the present site of Allen's Cider Mill. See also Mark Williams, "At the Crossroads," unpubl. ms. (1984), on file at SBHS; and Mark Williams, "Allen's Cider Mill," National Register Nomination, National Park Service, Sept. 1, 1991.

[33] Granby Probate Records, IV, 25-6, 88-93, 227.

[34] Goodrich purchased the house at 235 North Granby Road in 1818 from Asa Haynes, but it had once been the house of his father-in-law, Judah Holcomb II. Granby Land Records, XIII, 20. See also, Mark

Williams, "The Tanner's House," unpubl ms. (1978), on file at SBHS, 15-16. John McLean to Hezekiah Goodrich, August 7, 1823. McLean to Stephen White, August 26, 1823. McLean to Goodrich, August 26, 1823. National Archives, Washington, D. C., vol. B (1823), p. 415, copies in research of Abbott Chase on file at SBHS.

[35] U.S.Census (1820), Heads of Family Ms., Hartford County, Granby, CSL.

[36] Granby Town Records, I, 73.

[37] For description of Chloe Pratt Huggins, James Huggins's second wife, I am relying on a letter from Nancy Huggins Holcomb, daughter of James Huggins, to her son, James Holcomb in 1834, in Seth Holcombe's private collection.

[38] The town voted only 2¢ on the dollar highway taxes each year from 1809 to 1813, a sign that few had money to spare. Only one new road was opened. Granby Town Records, I, 85ff.

[39] Granby Land Records, VIII, 35, 48; IX, 92, 384, 398, 404, 474; XI, 110, 113. First Church, Records, II, 110. Seth P. Holcombe, *The Descendants of Phinehas Holcomb (1759-1833) of New Hartford, Connecticut* (North Granby, Ct.: the author, 1988), 1-2. According to William Goddard, "Some Facts Regarding the Byron P. Goddard Home, West Granby, Conn.," (this was the house James Huggins built (70 Hartland Rd.) - Goddard changed the roof from a gambrel construction to a straight gable over a full second story) unpubl. ms. (1934), Mr. and Mrs. James Orr Collection - there was a terrible flood in 1812 that wiped out some mill buildings on the Huggins property. The flood was not mentioned in Oren Lee's *Diary and Journal*, CSL archives, and Lee generally kept a good record of those things. However, if it did occur, this would set Huggins back more, and further explain why he had to take out a large mortgage that year.

[40] In fact, at the 1812 annual town meeting the day rate for labor on the highways, in lieu of the highway tax, was set in shillings (4s. per day, a relatively high price), suggesting not much cash in newer denominations was available. Granby Town Records, I, 85.

[41] Phinehas Holcomb Jr.'s parents had moved from West Granby to New Hartford in the 1790s. However, according to genealogist Seth Holcombe, he had purchased land in Hartland in 1791. In 1805, he married Nancy Smith Huggins. In *Descendants of Phinehas Holcomb*, Seth says Phinehas Jr. built a dwelling in 1809-10 lower down the hill from Phinehas Sr. in New Hartford (p.2). Seth believes his burial in West Granby, in his uncle Nahum's lot in 1814, suggests they were visiting in West Granby when the fever struck him. I am assuming that they were close enough to Nancy's beleaguered father after the death of Huggins's second wife in 1811 to provide some support.

[42] Phelps, *History of Simsbury, Granby and Canton*, 103. First Church, Records, II, 1-55.

[43] First Church, Records, II, 22-24.

[44] Ibid., 25-6.

[45] Ibid., 28-9.

[46] Granby Town Records, I, 98.

[47] According to William Goddard, in his "Facts Regarding the Byron P. Goddard Home" (James Huggins House), Huggins died in debtor's prison, having borrowed heavily to buy liquor stocks on the eve of the War of 1812. When the war ended less than three years later, the story goes, he had not made the anticipated profit and was forced into bankruptcy. Indeed, Huggins did die in debt, and his creditors foreclosed on all of his property, but I was unable to find, in the Hartford County Court records or the Granby Land Records, any indication that he had been confined to jail. Congress had abolished imprisonment for debt at the interstate level in 1798, but Connecticut still put debtors in jail until debts were paid well into the 19th century. While I am not willing to disregard the statement as a figment of the imagination of William Goddard's grandfather, a lifelong Methodist who might have had an interest in creating a morality play out of a gin-distiller's life, we still seek confirmation of the remark, which

has been repeated in the *Heritage*. My research leads me to believe Huggins stocked up on liquor as well as distillery equipment as early as 1805, a time when relations with Britain were pretty good, and it was general lack of commercial growth in the area that kept him from profiting on his investments.

[48] First Church, Records, II, 37-44. Granby had been lukewarm about the new constitution from the start. Although its two representatives to the Constitutional Convention, Sadoce Wilcox and Reuben Barker, had supported the new document, which changed the tax structure and guaranteed religious freedom, the town had voted 175-132 to oppose it in the ratification vote. See Springman and Guinan, *Evolution of a Town*, 108. There may have been some reluctance to support anything the state did. I suspect the majority actually did favor religious freedom.

[49] *Manual of the Congregational Church of Granby, Connecticut* (Hartford: C. Montague, 1859). At the time of the printing of this manual, there were 28 male members and 70 female members.

[50] James A. Urner, "The Congregational Church in Granby in the 19th Century," *Collections of the Salmon Brook Historical Society*, II (1980), 13.

[51] James R. Hayes, Memoirs (1907), Typescript in Granby File, "First Congregational Church - History," SBHS.

[52] Eliza Ann Colton, Diary, Reserve File, "Diary - Colton, Eliza Ann," SBHS.

[53] Lee, Diary, 128.

[54] K.M. Chivorowsky, "What is a Unitarian?" in L. Rosten (ed.), *Religions in America* (New York: Simon and Schuster, 1963), 186. D. Watt, "From Heresy Toward Truth" (West Hartford: Universalist Church of West Hartford, 1971), vi., 16. C.P. Smith, *Yankees and God*, (New York: Hermitage House, 1954). S. E. Ahlstrom, *A Religious History of the American People* (New Haven: Yale University Press, 1972), 483.

[55] For a more complete description to the emergence of the Universalist Church in Granby, see Jakki Garlans, "The Universalist Heresy," *Collections of the Salmon Brook Historical Society*, II (1980), 19-37.

[56] Oren Lee, *Diary and Journal*, CSL Ms. Collection, Jan. 1, 1832.

[57] First Universalist Society of Granby, Records, CSL Ms. Collection.

[58] Lee, *Diary*, Sept.. 5, 1832.

[59] In her memoirs, Ann Eliza Edwards (1837-1927) said that the split resulted because "trouble arose among the singers for head seats etc. dissentions increased which eventually led to [the Universalists] leaving." (Typescript in Granby File, "First Congregational Church - History," SBHS.) However, Ann was born after the split occurred, and was more likely referring to arguing within the choir which developed in 1842. This may have occasioned *more* people to leave the Congregational Church, in fact, enough for the Universalists to build their own meetinghouse in 1847 after another slight to be discussed in the next chapter. See Carol Laun, "The Controversy in the Choir," same file. There may have been even more to the bad feelings than local issues. Jacksonians, such as Noah Phelps of Simsbury, were supporting the Universalists at the time, and that association would not sit well with more conservative members of Porter's congregation. See Harold J. Bingham, *History of Connecticut* (New York: Historical Publishing Co., 1963), 453.

[60] According to Austin in *The Churches of Granby*, p. 15, 35, members withdrew as a result of the controversy over the meetinghouse location, but 34 new members joined after a period of fasting and prayer.

[61] He lived on the south corner of Mechanicsville Road and North Granby Road in a house which is now gone. Austin, *Churches of Granby*, 15. Granby Land Records, XVIII, 420. Dexter, *Biographical Sketches of the Graduates of Yale*, IV, 614.

[62] Alice Hayes Mellen, *The Female Skeptic, or Faith Triumphant* (New York: Robert M. DeWitt, 1859), p.90. Even though this is a work of fiction about a town named Glenlyn, all of the characters are clearly

based on actual people living in Granby in the 1830s and 40s. The book provides us with a sense of how people lived, which is impossible to derive from land records and account books. Diaries being so few and so hastily written by exhausted farm folks, a well-written rendition of daily dialogue and thought is a real eye-opener. Alice Hayes was the daughter of Thaddeus F. Hayes of West Granby. She was born in 1827, lived at the family home near the corner of Simsbury Road and West Granby Road (now 34 Simsbury Road), attended Wilbraham Female Seminary, taught in Nova Scotia, Alabama and Mississippi, and married George Frederick Mellen of Brookfield, Mass. in 1850. He died in 1855. Her grandfather was Thaddeus Hayes Sr., a deacon in the Congregational Church, whom Ann Eliza Edwards remembers for his bringing cider to drink with his lunch every Sabbath. See Ann Eliza Edwards Memoirs and Hayes Genealogy. The copy of *The Female Skeptic* at SBHS was a gift from Mrs. Ned Kendall.

[63] First Universalist Society, Records, I, 7-8.

[64] First Church, Records, III, 40-74.

[65] Eliza Ann Colton, Diary, SBHS. In his memoirs, James R. Hayes says of Porter, "I dont remember his every going into the new Church," but Alice Hayes Mellen's account and Eliza Ann Colton's references to Porter's continuing to preach in the 1830s suggests otherwise.

[66] According to William Maltbie, in Hoadley Collection, Box 9 CHS, St. Peters was thriving in 1829 with a Sunday School population of 60, but by 1852, the church was stricken from the state role. The town began using its meetinghouse for the annual town meetings which met at Salmon Brook in 1822 and continued to hold town meetings there into the 1860s.

[67] Hayes, "Memoirs"

[68] Ann Eliza Edwards, Memoirs. Ruth Hayes to Samuel J. Hayes, June, 1836, Granby File, "Hayes, Amelia," SBHS. There was also a Methodist Church at Copper Hill, dating from 1816. They built a meetinghouse in 1839. See Austin, *Churches of Granby*. The date of 1825 for the West Granby meetinghouse is given in Carol Laun, "A Chronological History of Granby, Connecticut," in *Granby, Connecticut: A Brief History, 1786-1986* (Granby: Granby Bicentennial Commission, 1986).

[69] Hayes, Memoirs, SBHS.

[70] See Granby File: "Migrations," SBHS. *The Gazetteer of Connecticut and Rhode Island* of 1819 says the "the current of emigration from this state has swelled to a torrent." Granby emigration lagged a bit behind this "torrent" from what I can discern from land records.

[71] U.S.Census, 1820, 1830 and 1840.

[72] Dorothy H. Smallwood, ed., *Parmalee Data, A Bi-monthly Magazine*, Washington, D.C., 1940s, (found in CSL), 213, 888. Granby Vital Records, I, 29. Granby Land Records, XXI, 238.

[73] Arthur G. Sharp, "Exodus to Ohio - A Promised Land," *Hartford Courant*, Oct. 13, 1988.

[74] Eliza Ann Colton, Diary, SBHS.

[75] Ruth Hayes to Samuel J. Hayes, [June, 1836]. Typescript of ms. in Granby file: "Papers - Hayes, Amelia Orpha," SBHS. For family ties see Estate of Amasa Hayes, Granby Probate Records, IV, 171, 172, 197, 242.

[76] Samuel J. Hayes to Helen Hayes July 24, 1837. Typescript of ms. in Granby file: "Papers - Hayes, Amelia Orpha," SBHS.

[77] Amelia O. (Hayes) Walton to Helen (Hayes) Richardson, March 11, 1845. Copy of ms. in Granby file: "Papers - Hayes, Amelia Orpha," SBHS.

[78] Adeline Hayes to Amelia O. Hayes May 6, 1838. Copy of ms. in Granby file: "Papers - Hayes, Amelia Orpha," SBHS.

[79] Henry Goddard and wife and Isaac and Abigail Goddard to their parents Isaac and Abigail Goddard, May 12, 1838, CSL Ms. Collection.

[80] Riverus Goddard to Isaac and Abigail Goddard, Dec. 20, 1838. Harry and Reform Goddard to Isaac and Abigail Goddard, March 10, 1839. CSL.

[81] Riverus Goddard to Isaac and Abigail Goddard, Feb. 19, 1840. Harry and Reform Goddard to Isaac and Abigail Goddard, Mar. 1, 1847. CSL.

[82] *Heritage of Granby*, 63, 81.

[83] Laun, "Chronological History of Granby."

[84] Johnson, *Higley Family*. Prudence apparently succeeded in meeting the challenge. She lived until 1878 in Cedar Rapids.

[85] Land in Granby in the 1830s sold anywhere from $15 to $50 per acre, and for considerably more if there were buildings on it. See deeds in Granby Land Records, XX, 174, 537; XXI, 465.

[86] U.S.Census, Numbers 1-7 (1790-1850).

[87] As noted before, these figures were derived from the Heads of Family Manuscript Census schedules at the Connecticut State Library, copies of which are at the Salmon Brook Historical Society. What is surprising is that they are not that much different from the statistics discovered by urban historians and used to characterize the more restless character of populations in American cities. See Peter Knights and Stephen Thurnstrom, "Men in Motion: Some Data and Speculations about Urban Population Mobility in the Nineteenth Century," in *Anonymous Americans: Explorations in Nineteenth Century Social History*, Tamara K. Hareven, ed., (Englewood Cliffs, NJ: Prentice Hall, 1971), 17-47.

[88] Father Stanley E. Hastillo, "St. Therese Church," in Austin, *Churches of Granby*, 37.

[89] Roxey L. Wilcox to her sister Eliza A. Wilcox, Oct. 28, 184[?], SBHS Reserve File: "Post Office/History/West Granby (Abbott Chase Collection)." Mr. Chase thought the date might be 1849, but Eliza had married Carlton Holcomb in 1847 and would have been addressed as Eliza Ann Holcomb. Perhaps the letter was written in 1844.

[90] "Exhibition of the Students of the West Granby Academy under the Charge of Miss T.C. Hutchinson, Tuesday Evening, February 23d, 1847," CSL. Wilcox Family Bible, indexed in the Barber Collection, CSL.

[91] See Connecticut Archives, Towns and Roads, XI, 8-14. *Heritage of Granby*, 9-11.

[92] Granby Town Records, II, 154-160. The company requested that it be allowed to remove its gates. One of these gates was on the east side of Granville Road near the Cragg. The gate house was a small building which was eventually moved to the crossroads. It is believed to be incorporated in what was once the North Granby store (380 North Granby Road). See Granby Land Records, IX, 497; XX, 282; XXII, 334; research by Ethel Linnell, Granby File: "Roads," "North Granby," SBHS. Among the Truman Allen papers is an 1835 receipt for a year's travel through this gate. Priced at $1 for hauling freight through for a year, it reveals one reason the Company couldn't turn a profit. See Granby file: "History - Granby - Allen, Truman." Of course, if they charged much more people might be inclined to go up Mountain Road and back down Godard Road to Granville Road on what amounted to Granby's own version of a "shunpike."

[93] Granby Town Records, I, 116-180; II, 37-154. Godard Road, for example, a relatively short road, was laid out in early 1825.

[94] Julius Gay, "The Farmington Canal," An historical address delivered at the Annual Meeting of the Village Library Company of Farmington, Connecticut, September 13, 1899, Connecticut Public Utilities Commission files, 4-5.

[95] The third viaduct, on which railroad track was later laid, stood until 1938 when it was wrecked by a flood. A bridge was built on the old piling, but that was lost in the 1955 flood, according to information in the Photograph file: "Farmington Canal," SBHS.

[96] James R. Hayes, Memoirs, SBHS. This includes an interesting account of his own trip on the canal

from Granby to New Haven.

[97] *Heritage of Granby*, 119.

[98] William Mills Maltbie, "The Farmington Canal as it Passed through Granby," 1960 speech reprinted in *Hartford Courant,* Sept. 4, 1986. Thelma Montovani, "Canal Days," *Southwoods*, October, 1982, 12-13. Springman and Guinan, *Evolution of a Town,* 141-145. Gay, "The Farmington Canal."

[99] See Mark Williams, "Family and Neighbors in Hard Times, West Granby, 1840-1900," unpubl. ms., 1980, on file at SBHS.

[100] U.S.Census, 1840 and 1850, Miscellaneous Statistics and Agricultural and Industrial Statistics, CSL. *Report of Manufacturers and Products for the State of Connecticut* (1845).

[101] Springman and Guinan, *Evolution of a Town*, 129.

[102] Reserve File: "Deeds - Cornwell, Stephen W.," SBHS. Granby File: "Industry - Brass Foundry," and "Industry - Carriage Works," SBHS.

[103] Before moving to Granby, he owned a tannery in Simsbury for a short while. See Granby file: "History - Granby - Allen, Truman."

[104] A deed in Granby Land Records, XIV, 424 from Elizur Benjamin and William Clemmons, "trustees of Truman Allen and John B. Southmayd," to Joab Griffin for the tannery, currying shop and dwelling near the Day Street intersection suggests that the first business had gone into receivership and that Allen had had to start over when he moved south of Goodrichville.

[105] SBHS has a wealth of material on Allen, and piecing it all together would require the work of a biographer. See files in Granby file, Reserve file and Reserve legal file on Allen; also on Industry: shoe makers; and Granby Land Records, XIII, 122. See also Charles J. Allen, *Echoes of the Past: A Story of Truman Allen of Granby, His Many Ventures, His Family and the Community* (South Newbury, Vt.: The Cider Barrel Press, 1979). This is not a biography, but a collection of Allen's papers. See also George P. Allen, *A History and Genealogical Record of the Alling - Allens of New Haven, Conn.* (New Haven: Price, Lee & Adkins, 1899), 274. Allen married Electa Hayes in 1834. See also my discussion of Goodrichville's prosperity and its connection with Allen in "Goodrichville in its Prime," unpubl. ms. (1979), on file at SBHS.

[106] Granby Town Records, II, 42-9. Granby file: "Industry - Carriage Works," SBHS.

[107] Granby file: "Industry - Brass Foundry," SBHS. Granby Town Records, I, 49. Granby Vital Records, I, 12, 254-5. Granby Land Records, XIV, 360-1, 511; XV, 448; XVI, 290; XVII, 434; XVIII, 53, 333; XIX, 31. Estate of Calvin Dibble, Granby Probate Records, VII. E.E. Cornwell, *William Cornwell and his Descendants* (1901).

[108] See Michael Anderson, *Family Structure in Nineteenth Century Lancashire*, 56. For further discussion of urbanization in the 19th century see Stephen Thurnstrom and Richard Sennet, eds., *Nineteenth Century Cities* (New Haven: Yale University Press, 1969). In that work, an article by Peter R. Knights, "Population Turnover in Boston," discusses residential mobility figures which are comparable to Granby's in the 1820s and 1830s.

[109] These statistics, as those in Tables 7-4 and 7-5, are based on analysis of the manuscript census schedules listing heads of families for Granby in the U.S. Census returns for the years 1790 to 1860. The manuscript returns are at CSL, and copies are at SBHS. From these, I created my own data base to do the analysis.

[110] Eliza Ann Colton, Diary, March 19, May 2, May 31 and June 21, 1834

[111] The building boom did not materialize. Today, these houses on Simsbury Road north of the cemetery are still situated nearly on their north property line, and in two cases, owners had to get an easement to put driveways through next to their houses. See Mark Williams, "In Hope of Revival: The Trumbull Wilcox House at 50 Simsbury Road," unpubl. ms. (1983), on file at SBHS.

[112] Account Book of a Blacksmith in Granby, 1825-1829, CSL Ms. Collection.

[113] Eliza Ann Colton, Diary, May 2, 1834.

[114] This balance of payments problem was common to all rural towns in America. See Larkin, *Reshaping of Everyday Life,* 36-7.

[115] Reserve File: "Post Office - History - West Granby" (Abbot Chase Collection), SBHS.

[116] Granby Probate Records, V, 4; VIII, 125-9, 152-4. *Heritage of Granby*, 103. Granby Land Records, XX, 212; XXI, 247, 248, 499; XXIII, 330, 461. Granby Town Records, II, 125-6. U.S. Census, 1840, Heads of Family, CSL.

[117] Adeline Hayes to her sister, May 6, 1838, copy of ms. in Granby File: "Papers, Hayes, Amelia Orpha," SBHS. For the record of Joab Griffin's financial woes, see Granby Land Records, XIX, 317; XXI, 96, 110, 120, 123, 181, 396.

[118] Williams, "Family and Neighbors," SBHS.

[119] *The Weekly News*, 1840, CSL Granby collection. Larkin, in *Reshaping of Everyday Life*, 258-9, discusses not only a sense of decay, but also the emergence of nostalgia for vanishing ways of life that came with relentless change. William J. Gilmore, in his book *Reading Becomes a Necessity of Life: Material and Cultural Life in Rural New England, 1780-1835* (Knoxville: University of Tennessee Press, 1989), wanted to discover "how disillusionment with life could emerge in rural northwestern New England by the 1830s." He found the same response to the advent of modernization. For Gilmore, the influx of printed material had a lot to do with the modernization of even rural America. See also such studies as James Henretta, *The Evolution of American Society, 1700-1815: An Interdisciplinary Analysis* (Lexington, Ky.: University of Kentucky Press, 1973); and Richard D. Brown, "The Emergence of Urban Society in Rural Massachusetts, 1760-1820," *Journal of American History*, 61 (1974), 29-51.

[120] W.J.Rorabaugh, *The Alcoholic Republic: An American Tradition* (New York: Oxford University Press, 1979), 5-9, 20. Larkin, *Reshaping of Everyday Life*, 281-286.

[121] First Church, Records, II, 38-9.

[122] James R. Hayes, Memoirs, SBHS.

[123] Legal Reserve File: "Papers, Hillyer, Pliny," SBHS.

[124] Granby File: "Post Office, History," SBHS.

[125] SBHS has numerous insurance policies from Aetna and Hartford Fire Insurance for this period of time spread out among the business papers of various former residents.

[126] Wilcox's training was not at all uncommon. According to Larkin, *Reshaping of Everday Life,* 87, the medical profession was gaining in the 1820s, but training varied enormously. Larkin also gives some statistics on mortality (p. 75): 1 white infant in 6 or 7 did not survive to age 1 and 1 white child out of 4 or 5 did not survive to maturity. Thus, in spite of medical advances, it appears that the early 19th century population in America was not as durable as that of the early 18th century.

[127] Granby Land Records, XVIII, 400. The 1840 U.S. Census, Heads of Family list says that Morgan was "in agriculture." He may have moved to Granby to retire. When he died in 1844, his estate listed his surgical instruments, medical book, mortars and chest of medicine. He also was an early investor in railroad stock. Granby Probate Records, VIII, 97-100.

[128] Granby file: "Industry - Carriage Works," SBHS.

[129] Jairus Case, Account Books, 1833-36, SBHS. Granby file: "History - Granby - Case, Jairus." See also Carol Laun, "Opium, Bloodletting and Alcohol: Dr. Jairus Case - Granby, Connecticut, 1833," *Southwoods*, May, 1984, who allows that Case "did his best."

Chapter VIII

[1] Granby Ms. Collection, CHS.

[2] SBHS has one of the books from this library, *Lovers of La Vendee*, signed out to Orin Godard on March 7, 1820, shortly before the Society disbanded. See Carol Laun, "'Literary Society' - circa 1800," *The Granby Drummer*, March, 1977.

[3] Granby file: "Library - Granby 1821;" and "Library - History," SBHS. SBHS has a copies of the constitution and other material found in a scrapbook in CSL relating to the 1821 revival of the library which James Kilbourne had revived in the late 1790s. This library was located at Salmon Brook Street (see Chapter 6), but the new constitution does not specify, other than at the choice of the majority of stockholders, the location. Shares in the 1790s library had depreciated since the beginning of the century. In 1809, they were selling for $3 each, but in 1819, they had dropped to $2, and in 1820, to $1.25. Estates of Gurdon Gould, Noahdiah Holcomb, Judah Holcomb and John Benjamin, Granby Probate Records, I, 56, 100; III, 23, 33. Possibly the collection had begun to disappear, or the drop in value may simply reflect the post-war economic difficulties.

[4] Granby file: "Fife and Drum - West Granby." See also Carol Laun, "The West Granby Drum Corps," *Southwoods,* March, 1983. In Granby file: "War - 1812," there is some speculation that Hiram Case's drum teacher, Hart Lee, was Oren Hart Lee of North Granby, even though tradition has it that Case learned drumming in Barkhamsted where he lived as a boy. Erwin Huggins, who joined the Drum Corps after the Civil War and was grandson of Shaler Reed, one of the first members, passed his drum along to his descendants. It was one of the original drums made by Eli Brown of Bloomfield (then Wintonbury). Huggins was also responsible for a revival of the Drum Corps in 1914.

[5] "Record of the Granby Lyceum," Reserve file: "Lyceum, Granby," SBHS. The reference to the "high school room" is interesting. It may have been the second floor of an academy built c. 1821 on the northwest corner of the Route 20/Route 10 junction. This was actually a school built to replace the District 1 school, but it was always referred to as the Academy. Photograph file: " Schools," SBHS. In his 1820 journal, William Hoadley writes of attending a July 4th celebration in the "upper room of the School house - very spacious." The older District 1 school did not have a spacious upper room, whereas the 1821 academy, now a house north of the intersection on Salmon Brook Street, did (moved in 1859). Another possibility for "the high school room" is a select school opened by Rev. Asa Cornwell in Granby in 1830. *Episcopal Watchman*, Vol. 14, p. 216. Whatever the case, the "high school room" seems to be distinct from the Granby Central Academy built in conjunction with the Congregational Church in 1834.

[6] Carol Laun, "Library 'born' before the town," *Southwoods*, September, 1989. There were 21 members of this group. They purchased a forty-seven volume collection, of which SBHS has the last two volumes. Joshua Jewett was president and William C. Case was librarian.

[7] "Constitution of the Connecticut Society for the Promotion of Good Morals," Reserve Legal file: "Good Morals Society 1813," SBHS. This is a printed constitution emerging from a state-wide organization which met in New Haven and Hartford, to which the 46 Granby men have subscribed their names.

[8] Benjamin Ely, "History and Correspondence of the Simsbury Aquatics," (1805) CSL Ms. Collection. Larkin, *Reshaping of Everyday Life*, 295. First Church, Records, II, 38-55. It is unlikely that Porter's dismissal had anything to do with his stand on temperance, for many of those who left the church prior to his dismissal to form the Universalist Society were later involved in the temperance movement themselves. Temperance was also strong in West Granby, but not necessarily among those who left

after Porter was fired. Furthermore, we have no evidence that they left because he was fired. The consensus among the memoirs seems to be that the West Granby defectors were unhappy with the new location of the church, or inclined toward the more optimistic doctrines of Methodism. I suspect that supporters of Porter's doctrines from West Granby actually remained with the Congregational Church in the 1830s.

[9] Youth's Temperance Society in Granby, "Constitution and Records of the Secretary," (1832-1834), CSL Ms. Collection. Eliza Ann Colton, Diary, March 17, 1835, SBHS. "Record of the Granby Lyceum." "Temperance Pledge," (1842), Reserve file: "Temperance," SBHS. Gerald Carson, *Rum and Reform in Old New England* (Sturbridge, Mass.: Old Sturbridge Village, 1966). Ian R. Tyrell, *Sobering Up: from Temperance to Prohibition in Antebellum America, 1800-1860* (Westport, CT: Greenwood Press, 1979). The SBHS archives also has one of a series of supplements to the *Connecticut Courant*, dated Sept. 22, 1834, which advocated temperance at length and was doubtless studied and distributed by local adherents to the cause. For discussion of the ideology of temperance and its relationship to the evangelical religion of the day, see Joseph R. Gusfield, *Symbolic Crusade, Status Politics and the American Temperance Movement* (Urbana, Ill.: University of Illinois Press, 1963). See also W. J. Rorabaugh, *The Alcoholic Republic: An American Tradition* (New York: Oxford Univ. Press, 1979), 79-84.

[10] Anonymous article in "The Fountain," a temperance publication. Granby file: "Temperance," SBHS.

[11] Granby Town Records, II, 127-131, 135-6. The "Civil Authority" (Selectmen, Justices of the Peace, Grandjurors and Constables) had had the authority to nominate innkeepers to the County Court. Now, according to the state statute, grandjurors could make complaints about the non-authorized sale of spirits and have their prosecutions paid for by the town.

[12] "Records of the Granby Tipacanoe Club," April 16, 1840, Granby File: "Politics - Tippecanoe Club," SBHS.

[13] Granby Town Records, II, 135-6, 140-1.

[14] Hayes was a member of the Granby Lyceum, which advocated temperance. Reserve File: "Granby Lyceum," SBHS. Granby file: "Temperance," and "History - Granby - Allen, Truman," SBHS. The "Temperance" file contains a large collection of newspaper articles, some from *The Fountain*, a temperance publication, in which citizens discuss not only the evils of alcohol, but the heated controversy brought on by the reform movement. For discussion of the depth of division on the issue see Carol Laun, "A Temperance Song for Granby," *Southwoods Magazine*, IV:2, July, 1983, 6ff..; Carol Laun, "Granby's Rage Flared Before Town Went Dry," *The Hartford Courant*, September 1, 1985; and Adam M. Williams, "Public Welfare vs. Private Right: the Temperance Movement in Granby, Connecticut," *The Concord Review*, IV:3 (Spring, 1993). Both Adam and I originally thought Daniel Hayes, a tavernkeeper, must have been the victim of temperance wrath, but after discovering he was on the temperance side of the debate, the particular act of vandalism does make more sense, so to speak.

[15] For discussion of the temperance movement at the state level, see Harold J. Bingham, *History of Connecticut* (New York: Lewis Historical Publishing Co., 1962), 508-512; Jarvis Means Morse, *The Neglected Period of Connecticut's History, 1818-1850,* (New Haven: Yale University Press, 1933), 204-216; and Charles Roy Keller, *The Second Great Awakening in Connecticut* (New Haven: Yale University Press, 1942), 139-169.

[16] Granby Town Records, II, 175-6.

[17] Larkin, *Reshaping of Everyday Life*, 286-296. Larkin also notes that it is even more significant that alcohol consumption remained below pre-Revolution levels after 1850, for in the 1770s, the proportion

of the population old enough to be serious drinkers was much lower than it was in the mid-19th century. The temperance movement had made a difference. See also Russell, *Furrow*, 217.

[18] Granby file: "Granby - Industry - Brass Foundry;" and Reserve Legal file: "Inns - Tavern Lists," SBHS.

[19] William C. Case, "The Whig of New England," Vol. I, no. 3, July 1, 1848. Handwritten "newspaper" in Reserve File, "Newspaper, The Whig of New England," SBHS. I do not know the location of Clitus Pinney's tavern.

[20] See "The Repository," Vol. I, nos. 1, 2 and 3, Reserve Legal File, "Newspaper, The Repository," SBHS, also a handwritten "newspaper" designed for local circulation. William Case had a hand in this, but was joined by Daniel E. Holcomb who, three years earlier, had been supporting Democratic candidates and publishing a rival paper.

[21] Carson, *Run and Reform*, 18. "A Resurrection of the Blue Laws, or Maine Reform in Temperate Doses," fifth edition (Boston: William Chadwick, 1852), 2. Janice Law Trecker, *Preachers, Rebels, and Traders: Connecticut 1818-1865* (Bridgeport: The Pequot Press, 1976), 53.

[22] "For the Fountain and the Sons of Temperance," misc. article in Granby file: "Temperance," SBHS.

[23] Larkin, *Reshaping of Everyday Life*, 52. Gilmore, *Reading Becomes a Necessity of Life*, 42-49. Linda Kerber, "Daughters of Columbia: Educating Women for the Republic, 1787-1805," in *The Hofstadter Aegis: A Memorial*, ed. Stanley Elkins and Eric McKitrick (New York: 1974). Linda Kerber, *Women of the Republic: Intellect and Ideology in Revolutionary America* (Chapel Hill, North Carolina: University of North Carolina Press, 1980). Nancy F. Cott, *The Bonds of Womanhood: Women's Sphere in New England, 1780-1835* (New Haven: Yale University Press, 1977). Mary Beth Norton, *Liberty's Daughters: The Revolutionary Experience of Women* (Ithaca, New York: Cornell University Press, 1980). Ruth H. Block, "American Feminine Ideals in Transition: The Rise of the Moral Mother, 1785-1815," *Feminist Studies*, 4(1978), 101-126.

[24] It was during this period that the Connecticut legislature began to enact the first laws that would eventually lead to a more equal status for women in society. Traditionally, when a woman married, her property became her husband's. In 1845, the Assembly passed a law protecting a woman's property, wages and inheritance from her husband's creditors. The following year, they decreed a married woman could collect her own wages, and that banks were required to do business directly with a woman if she wished to open an account. For the average woman, however, as the principal consumer of the family, life was increasingly one of dependence upon her husband, who generally contributed the most to the cash income of the family. Trecker, *Preachers, Rebels, and Traders*, 3, 12.

[25] Eliza Ann Colton, Diary, SBHS.

[26] Theodore G. Case, Library History, ms. in Granby Ms. file, CHS. Granby file: "Library - West Granby - Young Gentlemen's and Ladies'," SBHS. See also Reserve Legal file under the same heading.

[27] Eliza Ann Colton, Diary, SBHS.

[28] Ann Eliza Edwards, Memoirs, SBHS. See also Carol Laun, "Women in the Church - a historical perspective," *The Granby Drummer*, February, 1989.

[29] "The Repository," SBHS.

[30] See Eliza Ann Colton's diary for Jan. 23, 1834, in which she describes her nine-year-old sister's studies.

[31] Eliza Ann Colton, Diary, SBHS. According to some papers among Truman Allen's materials, this academy was first called "The Plainville Academy" in Granby in 1834. At other points in its history, it was called the Granby Academy, the Granby North Academy, and later, in a new building, the Granby Central Academy. Although Allen and other Universalists were shareholders, one of the principal shareholders was the Congregational Church. Granby file: "History - Granby - Allen, Truman," SBHS.

See also Carol Laun, "The Academy in North Granby," *Southwoods*, **June, 1986.**

[32] An interesting entry dating the construction of this now extinct structure is found in Granby Land Records, XIX, 475, showing Asa Higley, on August 2, 1842, claiming a lien on the structure he had just completed building. SBHS also has two programs for commencement exercises for the West Granby Academy, one dated 1844, and another 1847.

[33] Mellen, *The Female Skeptic*, 9, 58.

[34] Lydia Maria Child, *The American Frugal Housewife* (Boston: 1832). Catharine Beecher, *Treatise on Domestic Economy* (Boston: 1841).

[35] Mellen, *The Female Skeptic*, iv.

[36] Ibid., 13.

[37] Larkin, *Reshaping of Everyday Life*, 49-52, 131. Russell, *Furrow*, 177.

[38] Amelia [   ] to Adelaide Holcomb, March 31, 1862, Adelaide Holcomb collection, SBHS.

[39] Adelaide Holcomb, Diary, March 19, 1862, Holcomb collection, SBHS.

[40] Ibid., April 30, 1862. For more on Addie's letters see Amy Williams, "Happy, Happy, Happy Be Thy Dreams: A 19th Century Granby Woman Discovers Her Mind," unpubl. ms. on file at SBHS. Amy's project was inspired by Carol Laun's articles, "The Mystery of the Missing Newspaper," *Collections of the Salmon Brook Historical Society*, IV (1990); and "What Was it Like to be a 19th Century Schoolgirl," *The Granby Drummer,* October, 1990.

[41] Phelps, *History*, 111.

[42] Ann Eliza Edwards, Memoirs, SBHS. Ruth Hayes to Samuel J. Hayes, [June, 1836], Granby File: "Papers - Hayes, Amelia Orpha," SBHS.

[43] Carol Laun, "The Controversy in the Choir," Granby file: "First Church- History," SBHS. See also Ann Eliza Edwards, Memoirs, SBHS.

[44] West Granby Methodist Episcopal Society, Records, CSL, 1, 9.

[45] Kendall had purchased the house at 29 Simsbury Road built by Harlow Wilcox, and the new location of the meetinghouse was in front of what is now 20 Simsbury Road. There was considerable resigning and rejoining during this debate, the preferred location in the losers' minds being a few hundred yards west near the Academy. See West Granby Methodist Episcopal Church, Records; and Ethel Lindstrom Austin, *The Story of the Churches of Granby*, (Granby: Holcomb Fund Committee, South Congregational Church, 1973), 28-30.

[46] See Asher Benjamin, *American Builder's Companion*, first published in 1806. By 1827, it was in its sixth edition, promoting classical forms in nearly every plan.

[47] "Exhibition of the Students of the West Granby Academy," 1847, SBHS. According to Carol Laun, the teacher was probably Temperance Coleman Hutchinson who married William O. Ruick in 1847.

[48] First Universalist Society, Records, Vol. 6, CSL.

[49] First Universalist Society, Records, I, 7-8, 23. Austin, *Churches of Granby*, 43. *Hartford Courant*, Nov. 11, 1911. Granby Land Records, XXV, 38, 361. The deed from Goodrich to the Society was conditioned on the building of the meetinghouse within five years and its continued use as a meetinghouse. When the Society disbanded in 1911, the heirs of Hezekiah Goodrich, John K. and Ariel E. Goodrich, quit claimed the lot on the condition that the Society "create a trust fund ($200) to maintain a cemetery 1/4 mile north of the property." Granby Land Records XXXVI, 391. The reference is to the Baptist cemetery at the junction of Day St. and North Granby Rd. The Society fulfilled this condition, and then sold the meetinghouse to the town, either to tear down for material, or to use for educational purposes. Granby Land Records, XXXVI, 395. It now serves as the headquarters of the American Legion in Granby.

[50] Laun, "Controversy...." The Congregationalists continued to have their problems, going through

seven ministers in the two decades after Porter's resignation.

[51] Trecker, *Preachers, Rebels and Traders*, 28.

[52] In 1843 the Granby Lyceum, composed predominantly of Whigs at Granby Street, debated the "immediate emancipation of slaves," and decided it was a bad idea, even though they had previously indicated a willingness to erase the word "white" from the Constitution and protest the "Gag Rule," which had kept petitions to abolish slavery out of Congress for decades. In 1851, some of the same men were writing in "The Repository" that the Fugitive Slave Law was immoral and was drawing the "nation to a crisis." Reserve file: "Lyceum, Granby;" Reserve Legal file: "Newspaper, The Repository." Here though, it was former temperance organizers, not Universalists, who were doing the writing. The Universalists would be more inclined to action.

[53] Horatio Struthers, *The Underground Railroad in Connecticut* (Middletown: Wesleyan University Press, 1962), 171.

[54] "Report of the Central Committee of the Taylor Club," November, 1848. Granby Democratic Town Committee, Committee Report, 1864, 1866, 1867, 1870, and 1872, SBHS.

[55] *Connecticut Industrial Statistics,* 1850 and 1860, CSL Archives. U.S. Census, Heads of Family Ms., 1840, 1850 and 1860. "Estate of Josiah Goodrich," Granby Probate Records, VIII, 188-193, 218. Granby Land Records, XXII, 50; XXIV, 750. The Elizur Goodrich House is 241 North Granby Road.

[56] C.B. Dibble to Truman Allen, March, 18, 1848, and other Truman Allen Papers, Granby file: "History - Granby - Allen, Truman," SBHS.

[57] Granby Land Records, XX, 212; XXI, 247, 465; XXII, 209; XXIII, 241. U.S. Census (1840), Heads of Family ms., CSL. Granby Probate Records, III, 82. Cemetery Inscriptions, Barber Collection, CSL. First Church, Records, II, 72, 129, 144, 161; IV, 272, 280; V, 15, 43, 245. George Roberts, *The Denslow Family*, ms. in Genealogy Collection, CSL. The Trumbull Wilcox House is now 50 Simsbury Road. Trumbull was brother of Dr. J.D. Wilcox, brother of Thaddeus F. Hayes's wife Sophia and brother of George Hayes's wife Caroline. It should also be noted that J.D. Wilcox married Emmeline Betsy Hayes, brother of George Hayes. Thaddeus F. Hayes, J.D. Wilcox, George Hayes and Trumbull Wilcox, all related, lived as neighbors along the east side of Simsbury Road opposite their shops on the brook. See also Hayes, *George Hayes of Windsor*. The J. D. Wilcox house stood north of 40 Simsbury Road, and Trumbull's second house stood across the street, approximately at the present Broad Hill Road bridge head. The bridge was formerly south of its present location, and the old bridge heads still stand on the property of 16 Broad Hill Road. Just south of the old bridge head are the remains of the Edward Hayes/ Sherman Fancher carriage shops, and south of those, on the property of 57 Simsbury Road, is the foundation of Matthew Fancher's wheel shop.

[58] Granby Land Records, XX, 527; XXI, 238; XXIX, 163. William Hoyt Fancher, *The Fancher Family*, (Milford, N.H.: The Cabinet Press, 1947), 37-8. Interview with John Fancher, West Granby, August 15, 1982. Matthew Fancher & Co., Account Book, SBHS. Mark Williams, "In Hope of Revival: The Trumbull Wilcox House at 50 Simsbury Road," unpubl. ms. (1983), on file at SBHS. Mark Williams, "The House on Spruce Hill: The Sylvester Parmalee House, Simsbury Road, West Granby," unpubl. ms. (1985), on file at SBHS.

[59] Granby Land Records, XXIII, 194; XXV, 40, 668, 670, 675; XXVI, 198, 304, 360, 369, 370, 376, 439, 571, 600; XXVII, 70. Carlton Holcomb, Account Book, SBHS Archives. West Granby Academy, Commencement Program, 1847, CSL. Mr. Stiles W. Reed's Day Book, private collection, showing entries for early 1850s, when Stiles Reed worked at finishing a house for Carlton Holcomb. 1850 U. S. Census, Ms. Schedule, CSL.

[60] See "Nathaniel Holcomb III House," National Register Nomination. Abby Byerly, "Nathaniel Holcomb III House," *Granby Drummer*, December, 1982. "Master Craftsman John Canning,"

Conservancy News (Hartford Architectural Conservancy), IV: 1, March/April, 1987, 12-13. Katherine Riley, "Historic Stencil Found in Oldest Granby House," *The Hartford Courant*, Jan. 9, 1986. Larkin, *Reshaping of Everyday Life*, 139. John Canning feels that the stencil in the Holcomb house (45 Bushy Hill Road) is the work of the traveling artisan "Stimps," who developed his patterns in the tradition of the better known Moses Eaton.

[61] Edward W. Capen, *Historical Development of the Poor Law in Connecticut*, Vol. XXIII of *Studies in History, Economics and Public Law* (Hartford: 1905), 22. Margaret F. Clark, "Not My Brother's Keeper: Granby's 19th Century Welfare System," *Collections of the Salmon Brook Historical Society*, I, (1979), 22-28.

[62] Oliver Alderman to the Selectmen of East Windsor, March 2, 1827, Granby Ms. File, CHS.

[63] *History of Hartford County*, I, 361. By 1830, the Retreat, a private institution, was still only one of two institutions of this sort in the whole nation, and it accepted only ten patients at a time, charging towns $2 per patient, per week. The patients had to be "cured" in six months, so this was not a place for the chronically insane. It was not until 1866 that the state established a public hospital for the insane.

[64] Granby, Town Records, I, 172-6. Springman and Guinan, *Evolution of a Town*, 200, say that there were majority votes for separation in 1820 and 1823, but that the state legislature voted against division of Granby because its representatives said over half the town was opposed; and because it felt the inconvenience of attending meetings was not any greater than that of many other towns. I could not find a vote in the town records for separation in 1820. In 1823, there was a vote of 69 to 49 to divide the town, but when a committee drew up a suggested dividing line, the meeting then did not choose an agent to carry the plan to the legislature. Judging by the way this action was recorded, it must have been a wild meeting: "Motion made and Seconded to Chuse an agent to Carry the Same into effect the motion Was put to the Electors by the moderator and by him declared not to be a Vote — no agent Chosen." Possibly the Salmon Brook faction called at a nearby tavern while the committee was drawing up the line and recruited enough "Electors" to kill the plan.

[65] Granby, Town Records, II, 37-8.

[66] U.S. Census, 1830, Heads of Family Ms., CSL. Phelps had a "family" of thirty in the 1830 census. Nine were children under 10, three were teenage girls, two were men in their twenties or thirties (one, presumably, being himself), four women in their twenties, one (probably his wife) in her thirties, and eleven women over forty. This is hardly a profile of a "house of correction," yet it is the only household in town which is evidently housing indigent persons. Perhaps the selectmen were able, after all, to locate work for "able-bodied" male paupers.

[67] Granby, Town Records, II, 192. U.S. Census, 1840, 1850, Heads of Family Ms., CSL. Ahira Merriam, Account Book for Poor Farm, 1847-1850, SBHS. U.S. Bureau of Census, Summary Statistics on Pauperism, Connecticut, 1850, CSL. Merriam sometimes "let out" insane paupers to family members, paying younger people, for example, for caring for ill relatives they could otherwise not afford to keep at home. This was probably a gesture toward humane treatment, although Merriam may have taken an administrator's cut, since he received a flat contract for the whole of the town poor.

[68] Contract (copy of ms.) for the support of Paupers from September 1, 1863 to September 1, 1866, Anson Cooley, Francis G. Newton and selectmen, Granby file: "Town of Granby - Paupers." The Cooley farm was at 111 East Street. Carol Laun thinks the paupers lived in " a little red house down the lane," which is still there. U.S. Census, 1860, Heads of Family Ms., CSL. Wilbert Reed purchased the property at the crossroads in North Granby from the estate of Abner Case in 1857. Granby Land Records, XXVII, 374. He probably moved the original house, built by Silas Cossitt in 1783 on the northwest corner of the intersection, and built a new house at that time at 4 Mountain Road. This new house burned in 1970, but its "twin," built at the same time by Wilbert's father, Willis, still stands at

10 Granville Road. See Mark Williams, "At the Crossroads: Owners of the Property Associated With Allen's Cider Mill," unpubl. ms. on file at SBHS; and Mark Williams, "Allen's Cider Mill," nomination for National Register of Historic Places (1991), National Park Service.

[69] Granby Town Records, III, 34, 43, 257, 261. Edwin Frazier tried to get the town to compensate him for $725 he claimed to have spent on his brother at the Retreat in Hartford before 1856, but the town would only pay for support from 1855 on.

[70] Granby Town Records, III, 129, 170.

[71] Case, *Goodrich Family*. Talcott, *Goodrich Family*. Baptist Cemetery, North Granby. Granby Land Records, XVIII, 491; XIX, 119; XXVI, 600. U.S. Census, 1850, 1860, Heads of Family Ms., CSL. Williams, "In Hope of Revival." Truman Allen Papers, copies in Granby file: "History - Allen, Truman," and "Industry - Brass Foundry." Matthew Fancher, Account Book, SBHS.

[72] This divisiveness was a regional trend as communities across New England battled with the social effects of the boom-and-bust economy. Other historians have documented the decades of struggle over the direction and control of public policy which was, apparently, not unique to Granby during the early 19th century. See, for example, Randolph Roth, *The Democratic Dilemma: Religion, Reform and the Social Order in the Connecticut River Valley of Vermont, 1791-1850* (Cambridge, England: Cambridge University Press, 1987).

[73] Springman and Guinan, *Evolution of a Town*, 200-202.

[74] Granby Town Records, II, 141-3, 148-9, 157-8, 165-7, 174, 179-82, 187, 189-91, 197, 201, 206-8; III, 9-35. See also Pinkham, "The Division of Granby," 8-18. *Heritage of Granby*, 155. The town changed the old custom of having the residents of each highway district responsible for road repairs in that district and began taking money from the town treasury for contract work on the roads. In 1856, $1000 was spent in Salmon Brook and only $305 in Turkey Hills, despite Turkey Hills having half of the grand list. (Actually they had a little over a third of the grand list, but when one considers the number of abatements for Salmon Brook taxpayers for militia service, it becomes apparent that Turkey Hills was probably laying out about half of the cash which the treasury took in. They certainly paid more taxes per person than those in Salmon Brook.) See *Journal of the Senate of the State of Connecticut, 1858* (New Haven: Babcock and Sizer: 1858), 185ff.

[75] Granby Town Records, III, 42-3. *Report of the House of Representatives of the State of Connecticut, 1857* (Hartford: Hawley and Faxon, 1857), 37, 267, 396. *Journal of the House of Representatives of the State of Connecticut, 1858* (New Haven: Babcock and Sizer, 1858), 36, 80, 184, 226, 332. *Journal of the Senate of the State of Connecticut, 1857* (Hartford: Hawley and Faxon, 1857), 188. *Journal of the Senate, 1858*, 166, 185ff. Springman and Guinan, *Evolution of a Town*, 202-3. *Heritage*, 156. The Hayes petition was the product of a May, 1858 town meeting which voted unanimously to oppose division of the town. Granby Town Records, III, 47. The East Granby petitioners themselves may have balked at the name Fremont, for the leaders of East Granby were Democrats, albeit a more conservative brand than those of North and West Granby. Pinkham, in "The Division of Granby," (p.22) feels that Turkey Hills Democrats were strongly anti-slavery and supported Fremont in spite of their Democratic affiliation. An analysis of voting in 1856 and 1860 actually suggests it was the voters of Salmon Brook who were carrying the Republican majority. The Democratic *Hartford Times* also objected to the creation of the new town (May 4, 1858). Although they did not say so, the editors were probably sensing a formerly Democratic town had just spun off its most respected Democratic leaders and would now be sending Republican legislators to the State House. They were right. It is ironic that when a petition was put forth after the Civil War to reunite the town, the voters of Granby opposed it. Granby Town Records, III, 122.

[76] It should be noted here that, as Janice Trecker points out in *Preachers, Rebels and Traders,* 47-8, the

521

Jacksonians in Connecticut were, themselves, pretty conservative, limiting their efforts to liberalize government to some restrictions on the use of debtors prison. At the grass roots though, the Democratic party was indeed a party of the "common man," probably held at bay at the state level by its nervous leaders of the business class.

[77] Higley and Jewett are signatories as a Town Committee in support of Henry Clay in his bid for the presidency against Jackson in 1832 on a paper in Reserve legal file: "Politics - Clay Candidacy, 1832," SBHS. They were joined by John Willey and Abner Case of North Granby. Abner Case was later a Democrat, probably driven from the Whig faction by its members' temperance leanings.

[78] *Centreville Weekly News*, several issues at SBHS. Case, "Granby," *History of Hartford County,* 235.

[79] Page Smith, *The Nation Comes of Age*, Vol. IV of *A People's History of the Antebellum Years* (New York: McGraw-Hill, 1981), 126, 169, 177, 179-181.

[80] "Records of the Granby Tipacanoe Club," SBHS.

[81] "Records of the Granby Lyceum," SBHS.

[82] Horatio N. Case to William H. Pratt, October 11, 1844, copy of ms. in Granby file: "Politics - History," SBHS. This was an invitation to Pratt, John Dewey and their "other democratic neighbors" to attend the hickory tree raising. They do not use the term "Loco Foco" to describe themselves. See also summary of newspaper clippings on election results 1825-1863, pasted in Ezekiel and James Holcomb Account Book in the same Granby file.

[83] Trecker, *Preachers, Rebels and Traders*, 25, 50.

[84] "The Whig of New England," several issues from 1848 in Reserve file: "Newspaper, The Whig of New England," SBHS.

[85] Election lists of the Taylor Club in Granby, 1848, Reserve Legal File: "Taylor Club 1848," SBHS. Rough and Ready Club notice, Reserve file: "Rough and Ready Club," SBHS.

[86] Trecker, *Preachers, Rebels and Traders,* 38.

[87] Know Nothing Party broadside, Reserve legal file: "Know Nothings," 1859. For a discussion of the movement in Connecticut which elected a governor in 1856, see Robert D. Parmet, "Connecticut's Know-Nothings: A Profile," *Bulletin of the Connecticut Historical Society*, XXXI: 3, 84ff.

[88] Reserve File: "Politics: Republican Wide-Awakes."

[89] Russell, *Furrow*, 198.

[90] Eric Foner, *Free Soil, Free Labor, Free Men: The Ideology of the Republican Party Before the Civil War* (New York: Oxford, 1970), 149-85, 316.

[91] See Granby file: "History - Granby - Case, Jairus"

[92] 1850 U.S. Census, Heads of Families, Hartford Country, CSL.

[93] See Congregational Church of North Granby, Records, Vols. 4-5, photostat at SBHS.

[94] I am assuming the number of eligible officeholders was roughly 600, based on figures which were given during the 1850s for voters in Salmon Brook and Turkey Hills. I created a data base, from town and state records, of all of the town's officeholders between 1790 and 1860, and identified those who were listed as Granby residents in the 1850 census. It was not always possible to determine occupations strictly from the census records. For 15% of the officeholders, I was unable to. More research needs to be done in probate and tax records.

[95] Again, this is based on U. S. Census data. I compared the censuses from 1790 through 1860 to see how many times each head of family was listed. In 1850, only 44% of those listed had the distinction of being listed in three or more of the censuses surveyed - that is, they were heads of family in Granby for more than twenty years. However, 57% of the officeholding class had that degree of permanence.

[96] Town of Granby, Tax List for 1865, RG62, CSL.

[97] Phelps, *History*, 103.

[98] William Scoville Case, "Granby," in *The Memorial History of Hartford County*, J. Hammond Trumbull, ed. (Boston: Edward L. Osgood, 1886), 229, 236. During the early 19th century, growing resentment against the power of the monied classes was a state-wide trend. In Granby, the needs of the cider industry, and the fact that the temperance reformers were often the wealthier citizens, certainly had something to do with that. Trecker, *Preachers, Rebels and Traders*, 22.

[99] For discussion of the great changes in New England agriculture in the 1840s and 50s, which benefited only a few farmers, see Russell, *Furrow*, 179-240.

[100] Republicans had won the state government in 1857 and 1858, and held on to control of the state through the Civil War. Trecker, *Preachers, Rebels and Traders*, 58.

[101] Case, "Granby," in *History of Hartford County*, 235. See also "Memoirs of General Hillyer," in Granby File: "History - Granby - Hillyer, General," SBHS.

[102] Different figures for enlistments and casualties are given in different sources. I have put together a data base of Civil War soldiers from Granby, based on data compiled by Carol Laun from town records, the Adjutant General's report of 1880, Polly Hall's information in the *Heritage*, 82ff., the Civil War monument on the Granby Green, a listing in an Account Book kept by Stanley W. Edwards at SBHS, notes in the Granby file: "War 1861-1865: Civil War Granby Soldiers," and various articles which are also in that file. According to these figures, there were 153 Granby soldiers, three of whom never reported for duty. I included in the data base four men who are on the Granby monument but served as recruits from other towns. Apparently those who created the monument thought they were sufficiently native to Granby to go on the monument, and so I counted them as Granby soldiers even if the army did not. Of the 150, forty-five died while in the armed services. It is worth noting here that the monument on the Granby Green, which has thirty-seven names inscribed on it, does not contain all of the names of the Granby men who died while in the service. The men left off are DuWaine Brown, Edward Freeman, Thomas B. Holcombe, Woodruff Hoskins, Dennis Hoy, William Hunter, Stephen D. Kittle and John Rapp. In addition who knows how many more, like Richard Henry Lee who died of tuberculosis after the war, died slow deaths as a result of diseases or wounds acquired during the war. There were twenty-five disability discharges, and surely a large number of these died very soon after discharge. In *A Long Deep Furrow*, (p.245) Howard Russell notes numerous New England towns who had an equivalent percentage of the total population march off to war (in Granby's case it was 8.7%), but the highest mortality rate he cites is 20% for one town. Granby's 29% must vie for a record in terms of sacrifice for one community.

[103] The 1864 status of these soldiers is based on the data base already described. Carol Laun, "West Granby Beech Reflects Stories of Long Ago," *Farmington Valley Herald*, May 7, 1987. The "carving tree" still stands today.

[104] Granby Town Records, III, 77-9.

[105] Ibid., 80-1.

[106] For discussion of the phenomenon of Civil War America becoming a "redeemer nation" in the tradition of the early Puritan ideology in New England, see James H. Morehead, *American Apocalypse: Yankee Protestants and the Civil War, 1861-1869* (New Haven: Yale University Press, 1978), 164.

[107] Elvin Milo Holcomb to Adelaide Holcomb, undated, File Box: "Holcomb, Adelaide, Civil War Letters," SBHS.

[108] Quoted in Carol Laun, "Granby's Col. Holcomb, Martinet or Martyr," *Farmington Valley Herald*, July 7, 1988.

[109] Laun suggests in "Granby's Col. Holcomb" that he may have been shot by his own recruits in a desperate battle in Louisiana.

[110] Richard Henry Lee to Adelaide Holcomb, Sept. 21, 1861, Adelaide Holcomb collection, SBHS.

[111] Ibid., Sept. 27, 1862.

[112] *Heritage,* 86. Carol Laun, "Richard Henry Lee — Granby's Quiet Hero," *Farmington Valley Herald,* Newcomers Edition, March 24, 1988.

[113] This is a speech quoted in a Hartford paper. We have only a photocopy of the article at SBHS in the Granby file: "War 1861-65," and the name of the paper and its date are cut off. Although slavery was officially abolished in Connecticut in 1848, voting rights were restricted to white males over 21. Trecker, *Preachers, Rebels and Traders*, 38.

[114] Granby Town Records, III, 89-116. *Heritage*, 82-3.

[115] Trecker, *Preachers, Rebels and Traders*, 59-60.

[116] Granby Town Records, III, 62, 93, 115-6

[117] *Hartford Courant*, April 4, 1868. Case won the election.

[118] Trecker, *Preachers, Rebels and Traders*, 66-75. See also John Niven, *Connecticut for the Union* (New Haven: Yale University Press, 1965).

[119] Russell, *Furrow*, 245-255.

[120] Carol Laun, "The Sons of Francis Allen," *The Granby Drummer*, October 1991, 22. First Congregational Church, Records, V, 172-190. Dr. Allen was never convicted. The church was consumed with keeping itself together and retaining its minister. For more information on Dr. and Mrs. Allen see Mark Williams, "The Tanner's House," unpubl. ms. (1978) on file at SBHS.

[121] Case, "Glowing Eulogy."

[122] From a *Hartford Courant* clipping from 1864 in Granby file: "History - Case, Jairus."

[123] Letter of Chester P. Loomis from Newbern, N.C., February 13, 1865, typescript in Granby file: "War, 1861-5 - Civil War Letters, Loomis, Chester P." For history of the Loomis Brothers Store see Granby file: "Industry - Stores, Loomis Bros," SBHS.

[124] Granby Town Records, III, 74.

Chapter IX

[1] Case, "Granby," in Trumbull (ed.), *Hartford County*, 235.

[2] Granby Probate Records, VIII, 102. George P. Allen, *A History and Genealogical Record of the Alling - Allens of New Haven, Conn.* (New Haven: Price, Lee and Adkins Co., 1899), 128-9. Mark Williams, "Family and Neighbors in Hard Times, West Granby, 1840-1900," Unpubl. ms. (1980), SBHS.

[3] Granby Town Records, III, 120, 128, 144. Granby file: "Green - Granby," SBHS. Ruth O. M. Anderson, *From Yankee to American: Connecticut, 1865-1914* (Chester, Ct.: Pequot Press, 1975), 1, 15-17. We should note that Connecticut voters rejected granting African American men the right to vote in 1865, but by 1869, joined the rest of the nation in ratifying the 15th Amendment as the war took on the meaning the radical Republicans had hoped it would. An indication of how Granby people saw events in perspective is found in Addie Holcomb's diary: "Saturday April 15, 1865 What a chain of events Lincoln shot Seward nearly killed and his son dead. Mrs. Oscar Case's death and the baggage master badly hurt. Luzerne didn't come for me." We presume the assassination conspiracy did not target the baggage master.

[4] *Hartford Courant*, April 4, 1868. Granby Town Records, 120-182. "Report of the Finances and Expenditures of the Town of Granby," Reports for 1869, 1870 and 1871, SBHS.

[5] Granby Town Records, III, 121, 129, 134-143, 158.

[6] Ibid., III, 143.

[7] Ibid., III, 180-2.

[8] Ibid., III, 162. On the condition of town greens prior to the late 19th century, see "Survey of Town Greens," *Connecticut Preservation News,* XXI:2 (March/April, 1993). And in the same issue, for efforts to improve village centers, see Mary Williams Neustadter, "The Village Improvement Societies and Connecticut's 19th Century Town Greens." The Village Improvement Societies movement began in Stockbridge, Massachusetts in the 1850s and was just becoming popular in Connecticut after the Civil War.

[9] Granby file: "Green - Granby," SBHS. Granby Town Records, III, 198, 214. Bartholomew lived at 45 Bushy Hill Road, the Nathaniel Holcomb III house, former home of Rev. Isaac Porter, from 1851 to 1875. Granby Land Records, 24, 501; 31, 112. His daughter Jane ran a finishing school in the back room of the ell, and later was a famous teacher at the state's normal school in New Britain (now Central Connecticut State College). George Wells Batholomew, Jr., *Record of the Bartholomew Family* (Austin, Texas: the author, 1885). U.S. Census of 1860.

[10] Granby files: "Granby Public Library," and "South Congregational Church - History," SBHS. See Carol Laun's articles: "The Story of the Library," *Granby Drummer,* March, 1986; "The Academy in North Granby," *Southwoods*, June, 1986; and "A Chinese Puzzle," *Southwoods*, July 1986. A note in the Granby Town Records of a town meeting on September 13, 1872, held at the "Town House," is a little confusing. St. Peter's was referred to as the Town House after the town took it over, but that building was taken down in 1870. Possibly by force of habit (or intentionally in hope of a new habit), town clerk Chester Loomis called the new Library/Academy the Town House.

[11] Sherwood Soule, as quoted in Helen Green, "The Beginnings," in a pamphlet on the history of the South Congregational Church published by the Church in 1972, p. 1.

[12] Ibid., 2-3.

[13] Ibid., 1. Austin, *Churches of Granby*, 22.

[14] Ann Eliza Edwards, Memoirs, Granby file: "Diaries," (typescript), SBHS.

[15] Austin, *Churches of Granby*, 30-32.

[16] William M. Maltbie, "The Salmon Brook Water Company" (1952), ms. in Granby file: "Salmon Brook District," SBHS. Granby Land Records, XXX, 398, 573. Apparently the water company had been operating since 1868. Francis Allen, "Plotting 100 Years of Remembrance," *Hartford Courant Magazine,* June 7, 1964. Granby file: "Cemetery Association," SBHS. Granby file: "Agricultural Society." Walter Case, "Granby Agricultural Club," Account Book, 1862-1867, SBHS. Premiums were never offered for brandy as they were for nearly every other farm product, including apples themselves.

[17] Granby file: "Diaries - Goddard, Dora and Clara, 1886," SBHS.

[18] Carol Laun, "Dora's Diary circa 1886," *Granby Drummer,* May, 1977 - September, 1978. See also Anderson, *Yankee to American*, 66. Granby file: "Agriculture - tobacco," SBHS. Russell, *Furrow,* 274.

[19] These figures are based on analysis of 1876 tax records kept at SBHS. They were found in the Loomis Brothers' store when it was taken down in 1975. I am indebted to my daughter Amy, my hardworking intern, for entering the data from the individual assessment records in a computer database. I then analyzed the data on houses, animals, investments and land holdings. The median farmer was Watson Colton with a $550 dwelling, 43 acres of land, 1 horse, 3 cows, 1 calf, and 4 neat cattle, for a total assessment of $1122. Farmers were assessed for acreage and animals because these were income-producing items - supposedly. As prices for most agricultural products continued to fall through the 1870s, however, many questioned the validity of such a tax system.

[20] Excerpts from diaries of Rufus Messenger, loaned to SBHS in 1967 by William Messenger, typescript by Carol Laun, 1986, Granby file: "Diaries," SBHS. Diaries of William Holcomb, copied by Ethel R. Linnell from the originals owned by Proctor Holcomb, Granby file: "Diaries," SBHS.

According to the 1876 tax listings, Granby had over 2500 cows of various ages and types, and only 145 sheep and 30 swine. As the price of wool dropped after the Civil War, nearly all of the town's farmers switched to dairying.

[21] Russell, *Furrow*, 256, 323. Anderson, *Yankee to American*, 48.

[22] Town of Granby, Report of Selectmen, 1873 and 1874, SBHS. Expenses for paupers were $1264, up considerably from the year before.

[23] Granby Town Records, IV, 247-9. This compilation was done in 1931, probably to review the town's economic history in response to the Great Depression.

[24] Russell, *Furrow*, 264-9. Granby Town Records, III, 169. In 1876, the tax assessor found Messenger with only one sheep and a herd of dairy cows.

[25] William S. Hart, "The Salmon Brook Almost Became a Source of Water for Hartford," *Granby Drummer,* February, 1995. When the dry weather of 1899-1901 ended, there was no more mention of this plan. Hartford constructed other reservoirs elsewhere, including Barkhamsted and Hartland Hollows (1940).

[26] Austin, *Churches of Granby,* 33.

[27] Granby file: "Diaries - Goddard, Dora and Clara," SBHS.

[28] Austin, *Churches of Granby,* 22, 43. James B. Cleveland was minister of both churches from 1880-1884 and C.C. Campbell served from 1885-1889.

[29] Granby file: "Industry - Granby Manufacturing Co.," SBHS. The building was last known as the Beman Hardware Store before the Bemans tore it down and built a new store in 1974. On the Dewey carriage works and Forsyth mills, see James R. Hayes, Diary, Granby file: "Diaries - Hayes, James," SBHS. For Matthew Fancher see Granby Land Records, 30, 334, 335; 30, 287; 32, 32. Mark Williams, "In Hope of Revival," unpubl. ms. (1983) on file at SBHS. For the grist mill, see Granby Land Records, 30, 200; 31, 17, 290, 341; 32, 178; 33, 35; 34, 46, 92, 167 - all of which document the declining value of the mill after the depression of the 1870s. See also Mark Williams, "A Tradesman's House," unpubl. ms. (1994) on file at SBHS.

[30] In his article "Population Change and Farm Settlement in the Northern United States," *Journal of Economic History,* 36 (1976), 45-75, Richard A. Easterline notes a stage that older communities seemed to reach in their "natural history," in which earlier growth gave way to a leveling off and decline. Hal S. Barron, in *Those Who Stayed Behind: Rural Society in Nineteenth-Century New England* (New York: Cambridge University Press, 1984), argues that, although there was population decline and little economic growth in the late 19th century, we should be careful to avoid getting too caught up in the anxiety contemporaries felt about "decline." He characterizes the late 19th century as a time of stability and homogeneity for New England communities (he focuses on Chelsea, Vermont), noting that that was what New Englanders preferred anyway. See, in particular, pp. 28-77. In Chelsea, he found little property actually deserted, even if hillside pastures became woodlots. See Anderson, *Yankee to American,* 34-9, for discussion of the post-war business boom which benefited areas which already had large manufacturing establishments and access to transportation facilities. The Electric dynamo further sealed the fate of water-powered industry late in the century, since most small-town manufacturers (who used water power) could not afford to invest in the new cost-saving technology used by industrialists with more capital.

[31] James Lee Loomis, "The Old Country Store," a speech he gave in 1961 at the Forum of Connecticut Bankers, published in pamphlet form by the Hartford National Bank, Granby file: "Industry - Stores - Loomis Brothers," SBHS.

[32] Anderson, *Yankee to American*, 47.

[33] The extent of Edmund Holcomb's assets can be imagined on viewing the contents of Legal Reserve

files (2): "Papers - Holcomb," SBHS, which contains correspondence regarding his holdings in Mill River, Massachusetts; Boone, Iowa; and Kentucky.

[34] Here I am relying on the work of Carol Laun, who involved herself in some serious archeology, digging through the vast mound of debris in the attic of the old store while the bulldozer waited outside to demolish the building in the name of 1970s intersection planning. She says the attic was a "revelation" for her - the Loomis Brothers had become town "squires."

[35] Russell, *Furrow,* 258-262, 281-5. Anderson, *Yankee to American,* 52.

[36] James R. Hayes, Diary, Granby file: "Diaries - Hayes, James R," SBHS.

[37] Clarence Dunhoff, *Changes in Agriculture: The Northern United States, 1820-1870* (Cambridge, Mass.: Harvard University Press, 1969). See also William Parker, "Agriculture," in Lance Davis, et. al., *American Economic Growth: An Economic History of the United States* (New York: Harper & Row, 1972), 369-417. Barron, *Those Who Stayed Behind,* 11, 31. Barron notes that the more extreme efforts to restructure rural institutions and rural society, in response to alarms about "decay," were generally ignored by those closest to rural society, who continued to adapt older values to changing conditions. More and more people did participate in agricultural societies devoted to those ends.

[38] Russell, *Furrow,* 288.

[39] Granby file: "Industry - Granby Creamery Co.," SBHS.

[40] Granby files: "Granby Grange No. 5," "Grange - Granby," SBHS. George S. Godard, "Granby Grange, No. 5," in *The Connecticut Granges,* ed. under the supervision of a committee of the State Grange (New Haven: Industrial Publishing Company, 1900), 32-37. "Granby Grange No. 5 Again after Two Reorganizations," *Hartford Times,* 10 January, 1940. "Town Grange to Celebrate 102nd Anniversary," *Hartford Courant,* 29 November 1969. Russell, *Furrow,* 281-6. Russell argues that the Grange did not have the staying power in New England that it did elsewhere because the region was spared the effects of the depression because of comparative stability and wealth, a light mortgage burden and its closeness to market. This was hardly the situation in Granby, however. Elsewhere in New England, though, its membership plunged when the expected economic benefits were not realized. However, he admits it did take root as a social organization, and did provide farmers with substantial savings on purchases. It can be seen as part of the general pattern of agricultural organization in the late 1800s. Anderson, in *Yankee to America,* 29 and 51, says that the unjust freight rates western farmers protested did not cause much division between farmers and industrialists in Connecticut, and that the Grange, for that reason, was less political in this part of the country. At any rate, big business controlled state government, she says, and political corruption was firmly entrenched. Thus farmers' grievances would make little headway anyway. For discussion of Phelps Hall as the Grange headquarters see Mark Williams, "Allen's Cider Mill" National Register of Historic Places Nomination (1991), on file at SBHS. See also Account Books of Harvy Godard and Oren H. Godard, SBHS; Estate of Harvy Godard (1897), Granby Probate Records, XIV, 103-111; Algot G. Stenberg, *Ancestral Register of George Seymour Godard* (Hartford: Conn. State Library, 1935).

[41] On Joseph Beman, see Granby Land Records, 30, 324, 336; 32, 531; and Mark Williams, "History of the Property at 11 and 12 Silkey Road, West Granby, Connecticut, 1732-1928," Unpubl. ms. (1995), SBHS. Data on all has been investigated in the 1876 Tax Records for Granby, SBHS. On Willis Phelps, see "Allen's Cider Mill," National Register Nomination; Granby Land Records, 28, 524; 29, 602, 608; 30, 41; 32, 596; Granby Probate Records, XIV, 19-23

[42] Kelly was already high on the tax list by 1876. His grandson eventually bought the farm at 45 Bushy Hill Road, once owned by Rev. Isaac Porter. See Mark Williams, "Nathaniel Holcomb III House (c. 1719)," National Register Nomination on file at SBHS.

[43] Granby Probate Records, XIV, 145.

[44] Granby file: "Diaries - Goddard, Dora and Clara," SBHS. See Barron, *Those Who Stayed Behind*, 133-6, for similar observations of the people of Chelsea, Vermont.

[45] Barron, *Those Who Stayed Behind*, 31, 41. See also 92-111 for the effect of kinship ties on traditional values. He cites the studies by historians who have found an increasing prevalence of urban cultural patterns and modern attitudes in the countryside: Lewis Atherton, *Main Street on the Middle Border* (Bloomington, Ind.: Indiana University Press, 1954), 6; Wayne E. Fuller, *RFD: The Changing Face of Rural America* (Bloomington, Indiana: Indiana University Press, 1964). Dunhoff: *Changes in Agriculture;* Allan Brogue, *From Prairie to Corn Belt: Farming on the Illinois and Iowa Prairies in the Nineteenth Century* (Chicago: Quadrangle Books, 1968). He also cites studies which detail resistance to modernization: Robert R. Dykstra, "Town - Country Conflict: A Hidden Dimension in American Social History," *Agricultural History*, 30 (1969): 195-204; Don S. Kirschner, *City and Country: Rural Response to Urbanization in the 1920s* (Westport, CT: Greenwood Press, 1970).

[46] Granby Town Records, III, 199.

[47] Hal Barron, in *Those Who Stayed Behind*, 16-30, 112-113, refers to the ante-bellum period as the "storm before the calm," when the commercial and industrial revolution led to social tensions in New England towns as well as the nation as a whole. After the war, a "bucolic consensus" emerged, he says, built upon voluntary organizations and the withering away of class, ethnic and ideological differences. In Granby, those ante-bellum differences did not disappear as Barron observed in Chelsea, Vermont. That is why I prefer the word "accommodation" to "consensus." See also Dan Doyle, "The Social Ferment of Voluntary Associations in a Nineteenth-Century Town," *Social Science History*, 1 (1977), 333-356.

[48] Granby Town Meeting, III, 163-7, 173.

[49] Ibid., 177-9, 183.

[50] Ibid., 186.

[51] Ibid., 192-3.

[52] Ibid., 199.

[53] Ibid., 201, 205-6.

[54] Ibid., 209.

[55] Ibid., 218.

[56] Ibid., 232, 237, 243, 248, 265, 299. Selectmen's Reports, 1880-1890, SBHS. Connecticut's previous prohibition law had failed dismally because of open violations. In 1874, the legislature voted to allow town meetings to decide whether to have licensed retailers. Thus, every year Granby voted on the issue, and every year, the town voted yes.

[57] Town of Granby, *Reports of the Selectmen, Treasurer and School Visitors* (Hartford: Case, Lockwood & Brainard Co., 1886), 24.

[58] Town of Granby, *Annual Report of the Selectmen, Treasurer, Board of School Visitors and Health Officer* (Winsted: Dowd Printing Co., 1894), 29-30. Carol Laun has told me that the divisions regarding the running of schools continued well into the late 20th century, when, at one point, the Granby Taxpayers' Association proposed firing all teachers and hiring new graduates at lower salaries, and having teachers "advance" with their classes through the grades, with raises dependent upon "improvement."

[59] Town Meeting Records, III, 250-314. In *Those Who Stayed Behind*, Hal Barron notes that in Chelsea, Vermont, the drive toward consolidated schools, led by urban-minded reformers, also made little headway. Residents viewed the changes as expensive and leading to loss of control, and they resented the reformers' condescending attitudes. Farmers, he says, believed that the problems in the country were economic, not social, and rejected the world view of industrial order and a society run by

professionals. See pp. 49-50. This would appear to be the case in Granby, although the social reformers still clung to the hope that one day they would prevail. I do not see the withering away of old divisions in Granby as Barron saw in Chelsea, but rather an uneasy truce awaiting a new age of reform spirit.

[60] "Granby's Sons are Loyal," *Hartford Courant*, 1906 (newspaper clipping found in Granby file: "Granby Club," SBHS).

[61] Although newspapers, clergy, the state Grange and other political clubs had exerted influence to end political corruption, it was still rampant in the 1880s, and in Connecticut, worse in the small towns than in the cities. Not much headway was made, although the secret ballot went into effect in 1889. Anderson, *Yankee to American*, 22, 25.

[62] Town Meeting Records, III, 313, 419.

[63] Town Meeting Records, III, 290-2, 307. After the library was built, the town set aside $100 from general funds to maintain it. Carol Laun and Gladys Godard, *Centennial: Frederick H Cossitt Library, 1891-1991*(Granby: Friends of the Cossitt Library, 1991). Mark Williams, "The Frederick H. Cossitt Library (1891)," National Register of Historic Places Nomination, Connecticut Historical Commission (1987), on file at SBHS. William C. Case, "Address at the Dedication of the Frederick H. Cossitt Library at North Granby, Conn., March 26, 1891" (Hartford: Case, Lockwood & Brainard Co., 1891). Frederick H. Cossitt Library "Order Book," and "Day Book," Cossitt Library Archives. Cossitt, *The Cossitt Family*, 18, 41. *George Seymour Godard, 1865-1936, Memorial Tributes*, 2 Volumes, Cossitt Library Archives. Winfred R. Goddard, *The Goddards of Granby, Connecticut* (San Diego, Cal.: Goddard Enterprises, 1985). Granby, Annual Reports for 1890, 1891 and 1896. Granby Land Records, 33, 437. Carol Laun, "Heritage of Granby: Cossitt Library," *Granby Drummer*, November, 1982. Granby file: "Libraries - Cossitt," SBHS. James Scarborough Sibley, *The Sibley Family in America, 1629-1972* (Honolulu, Hawaii: by the author, 1971). Steinberg, *Ancestral Register of George Seymour Godard*, 54. Surrogate Court, County of New York, New York, "In the Matter of the Judicial Settlement of the Account of Augustus D. Juilliard, Henry Talmadge, Henry R. Talmadge and Edward W. Barnes, Executors of and Trustees under, The Last Will and Testament of Frederick H. Cossitt, Deceased. Copy: Order Directing Service of Citation by Publication, &c with copy of citation," 8 February 1889, ms. copy, Cossitt Library Archives.

[64] Granby file: "Library - Granby Public," "Green - Granby," "Agricultural Society," "Salmon Brook District," "Granby Grange No. 5," "Grange- Granby," "Village Improvement Society," "War, 1917," "Cemetery Association," SBHS. Carol Laun, "The Story of the Library," *Granby Drummer*, March, 1986. Carol Laun, "The Fair! It Still Thrives in Granby," *Farmington Valley Herald*, Sept. 11, 1986. Austin, *Churches of Granby*, 30, 44. The Seventh-Day Adventist Church, begun at 232 Salmon Brook Street, was never completed or used as a church. The West Granby Methodist Church renovations were done in 1906 and included some elaborate tin work for the walls and ceiling.

[65] Granby Town Records, IV, 15. Carol Laun, "The Academy in North Granby," *Southwoods*, June, 1986.

[66] Anderson, *Yankee to American*, 40. Granby Town Records, III, 322.

[67] Granby Town Records, III, 325, 413, 419, 421, 426, 427, 430; IV, 4. Hal Barron notes that in Chelsea, Vermont, the split over temperance had disappeared by the end of the century and prohibition was enacted. In Granby, the split had not disappeared, even though prohibition finally passed. *Those Who Stayed Behind*, 120.

[68] Granby Town Records, IV, 4-42.

[69] Registration of new voters shows that heavy turnover of the population was continuing, if not picking up, in the early 20th century. However, the total number of people actually voting was declining. This suggests that the newcomers, while registering, were not bothering to attend town meetings and election

gatherings to vote. See Granby Town Records, IV, 6, 10, 37, for names of newly registered voters.
[70] Granby Town Records, III, 413.
[71] Anderson, *Yankee to American*, 2, 10,11, 22. In 1870, three-fourths of the state population was native born. By 1900, only 41% were native born. The American Protective Association, formed during the depression in 1893, stirred up a good deal of the anti-immigrant sentiment in Connecticut at this time. Although the Republicans controlled the state government, they were reluctant to alienate the Catholic vote, and by 1898, had dropped their anti-Catholic position.
[72] Austin, *Churches of Granby*, 33-8. The nativist article is quoted in Carol Laun, "A Chinese Puzzle," *Southwoods*, July, 1986. According to Carol, internal problems in China, plus Chinese racism (against their young men dating "foreign devils" and taking on foreign ways), was behind the demise of the Chinese mission.
[73] Anderson, *Yankee to American*, 25-32. The Republican Party did have a liberal wing, but they did not control nominations to state offices.
[74] Russell, *Furrow*, 266. TB soon returned to plague Connecticut's farmers.
[75] *Farmington Valley Herald*, May 4, 1912 contained an article on the return of the Fancher family for summer vacation. They had a house at 286 West Granby Road which was built circa 1795 by Joab Griffin. Russell, in *Furrow*, 278, notes that many communities in rural New England were benefiting from this type of income in the late 1800s. There were also some Jewish vacationers from New York who bought property in Granby at this time. Russell (*Furrow*, 309) and Anderson (*Yankee to American*, 9) both note the prevalence of actual Jewish colonies in rural areas in late 19th century New England.
[76] Granby file: "Agriculture - Tobacco," SBHS. Russell, *Furrow*, 269. Anderson, *Yankee to American*, 51. "Connecticut's Tobacco Industry," *Connecticut Business Trends*, 2:5 (October, 1964).
[77] Russell, *Furrow*, 307. Granby file: "Agriculture - Tobacco," SBHS. There is a reference to Floyd as manager in 1907, in the town records, when he proposed a new road (now Floydville Road) on which the town agreed to spend $400. Granby Town Records, IV, 42.
[78] Granby Land Records, 37, 33, 166. Interview with John Fancher, 1982. Mark Williams, "In Hope of Revival," unpubl. ms.(1983), on file at SBHS. Simplex eventually evolved into the Red Devil Tool Company of New Jersey.
[79] Granby Land Records, 30, 19; 32, 257, 264, 335; 34, 39; 39, 273; 47, 86.
[80] "Granby's Sons are Loyal," and other newspaper clippings in Granby file: "Granby Club," SBHS.
[81] Williams, "Allen's Cider Mill," National Register Nomination.

Chapter X

[1] Granby Land Records, 33: 531, 552, 580, 609; 34: 132, 167, 314; 36: 203; 37: 232; 38:193, 194; 39: 28, 154, 189, 266, 447, 492, 567, 619, 636. Granby Probate Records, XI, 466ff. Carol Laun, "The People Yes: Tudor F. Holcomb," *The Granby Drummer*, June/July, 1971. Granby File: "Holcomb Farm," SBHS. Tudor F. Holcomb, Interviews with Mark Williams, June, 1974 (Put Brown of West Granby has also shared with me information from many of his conversations with Tudor). Carol Laun, "The West Granby of Everett Rosier, 1905-1918," *Southwoods*, July, 1984; and Carol Laun and Everett Rosier, "West Granby - A View from the Past," *Granby Drummer*, February, 1987 (These articles are based on dozens of letters written by Everett to Carol in the 1980s, now in Granby file: "History - Granby - Rosier, Everett," SBHS. Everett was given the Linnell Award, SBHS's highest honor, in 1990 for his major contribution to its archives). Gregg Lewis, "Holcomb Farm: Yesterday, Today and Tomorrow," *Conservancy News*, 9:2 (August/September, 1992). Legal Reserve File: "Papers - Holcomb, Tudor," SBHS. McLean Refuge Study Committee, "History of the McLean Game Refuge," (New Haven: Yale School of Forestry and Environmental Studies, 1980), Granby file: "McLean Game Refuge," SBHS.

[2] Granby file: "Industry - Stores - Loomis Brothers," SBHS. *Farmington Valley Herald*, Dec. 25, 1914.

[3] Granby file: "Agriculture - Tobacco," SBHS. Russell, *Furrow*, 307. "Connecticut's Tobacco Industry," *Connecticut Business Trends,* a Connecticut Bank and Trust Co. Publication, 2:5 (October 1, 1964). Carol Laun and Everett Rosier, "Shade Grown Tobacco was a Major Granby crop before World War II," *Granby Drummer*, November, 1992. "Marcus Floyd Dies in Hartford," *United States Tobacco Journal*, 110:16 (November, 1928).

[4] Russell, *Furrow*, 298-9.

[5] Granby Land Records, 38: 179; 44: 135. Carol Laun, "Granby's Heritage: Allen's Cider Mill," *Granby Drummer*, April, 1983. Francis B. Allen, "Allen's Cider Mill," unpubl. ms., 1969, Lois Allen Longley Collection. Lois Allen Longley, Interview with Mark Williams, February 23, 1985. Mark Williams, "Allen's Cider Mill," National Register Nomination (1991), SBHS. Allen's Cider Mill is still in operation today, owned by Arthur Allen's granddaughter Lois Allen Longley, and is on the National Register of Historic Places. The building itself was moved three times in its history, and was originally Silas Cossitt's dwelling circa 1783.

[6] Reserve file: "Industry - Blacksmith;" and "Auto Sales," SBHS. Shirley and Raymond Fantone, "Industry and Stores," in *Heritage*, 114. William M. Maltbie, "The Salmon Brook Water Co.;" and Liana Lareau, "The Salmon Brook District: Granby's Water Company," April 30, 1995, both in Granby file: "Salmon Brook District," SBHS. Granby file: "Electricity," SBHS (has newspaper clippings from the *Windsor Locks Journal* and *Farmington Valley Herald* detailing the advent of electricity.)

[7] Abbott Chase, "Mail and News," in *Heritage*, 15.

[8] Herbert F. Janick, Jr., *A Diverse People: Connecticut, 1914 to the Present* (Cheshire, Ct.: The Pequot Press, 1975), 3, 7, 9-10.

[9] Granby Town Records, IV, 128.

[10] J. Stevens Dewey, "1917-1918: History of Company 'C' 1st Separate Battalion Infantry Connecticut State Guard of Granby, Connecticut, " unpubl. ms. in Granby file: "War - 1917," SBHS. See other items in that file as well. Russell, *Furrow*, 313.

[11] Taken from a compilation in Granby Town Records, 4: 247-9.

[12] Granby file: "Village Improvement Society," SBHS. Austin, *Churches of Granby*, 20.

[13] The constitution and bylaws of the Civic Club may be found in Granby file: "Civic Club - History," SBHS. See also Carol Laun, "Civic Club Celebrates 75 Years of Service," *Farmington Valley Herald*, February 24, 1986. *Windsor Locks Journal*, January 12, 1918.

[14] *Windsor Locks Journal*, December 17, 1915 and February 8, 1918; and *Farmington Valley Herald*, July 31, 1914 and December 29, 1916, in Granby file: "Men's Community League;" "Scouts - Girl;" and "Scouts - Boy."

[15] *Hartford Times*, January 12, 1917. Dr. Soule is quoted in Helen Green, "The Beginnings," South Congregational Church.

[16] "Granby People to Rebuild Church," *Hartford Daily Courant,* April 8, 1917. Annual Report of the Selectmen, Treasurer, Board of School Visitors and Health Officer of the Town of Granby, 1913, SBHS, 19. Granby file: "Library - Granby Public," SBHS. The library building was constructed in 1918. It now houses the Visiting Nurses Association. In 1945, the Salmon Brook Historical Society had its beginnings there when a "history room" was opened in its basement. *Hartford Daily Times* , July 13, 1918. Granby file: "South Congregational Church - History," SBHS.

[17] Granby file: "Hospital - Granby," SBHS. *Windsor Locks Journal*, April 22, 1921. Dorothy Starble, "Granby's Hospital - Multi-faceted Facility," *Granby Drummer*, June, 1976.

[18] "Rural Planning: the Social Aspects Illustrated," U.S. Department of Agriculture Bulletin #1325, May 1923. See also Carol Laun, "Model Town 1923," *Southwoods*, March, 1988.

531

[19] Granby Town Records, IV, 29, 54, 61-2, 82, 90, 102, 135, 158, 172, 191.

[20] Ibid., IV, 116, 129.

[21] Ibid., IV, 50, 93, 98, 127, 160, 168, 169.

[22] Annual Report of...Granby, 1906, 15-17.

[23] Annual Report of...Granby, 1908, 20.

[24] Granby Town Records, IV, 58, 63-4.

[25] Annual Report of...Granby, 1908, 19-20.

[26] See School Committee Reports, in the town's annual reports for 1909-1927. Also Granby Town Records, IV, 79, 86, 103, 130, 199. Janick, *A Diverse People*, 32.

[27] James R. Hayes, Memoirs, typescript in Granby file: "First Congregational Church - History," SBHS.

[28] Granby Town Records, IV, 66, 93, 95, 105, 120. As far as I can tell, the reevaluation did not occur until the Depression.

[29] Donald W. Smith, "A New Englander Looks Back," *Hartford Courant Magazine*, March 6, 1949. Papers by James Lee Loomis: "Early Spring and Late Autumn, An Essay Read to the Monday Evening Club, April 1, 1968," Granby file: "History - Granby - Loomis, James Lee," SBHS; and "The Old Country Store," a paper delivered in 1961 at the Forum of Connecticut Bankers and published by the Hartford National Bank and Trust Co.

[30] Granby Town Records, IV, 197-199. This trend in Granby politics, toward a government that mirrored the values of the professional businessman, was the trend in state government as well, as the state came under the control of J. Henry Roraback and the tightly knit business leaders of the Republican State Central Committee in the 1920s. State spending increased, but largely from road building, while expenditures on public education, teacher training and transportation of school children were cut. Janick, *A Diverse People*, 24-27.

[31] Granby Town Records, IV, 56, 88, 153, 192, 222.

[32] Janick, *A Diverse People*, 16-17.

[33] Granby Town Records, IV, 113.

[34] Granby Town Records, IV, 148, 156-7, 179 and 192.

[35] Janick, *A Diverse People*, 1, 14-16, 34. Janick does add that the state legislature did reject the 18th Amendment and that enforcement was a farce in Connecticut. For more discussion of the changing character of the Connecticut population and how it alarmed the "natives," see Anderson, *Yankee to American*, 2-3.

[36] Granby Town Records, IV, 142.

[37] Annual Report of...Granby, 1920, 20.

[38] Janick, *A Diverse People,* 3, 18.

[39] "Granby," *Windsor Locks Journal*, April 17, 1931, Granby file: "Granby Club," SBHS.

[40] Janick, *A Diverse People*, 21.

[41] Granby files: "Granby Grange No. 5," "Hospital - Granby," SBHS. Carol Laun, "The Fair! It Still Thrives in Granby," *Farmington Valley Herald*, September 11, 1986. Starble, "Granby's Hospital." Granby Land Records, 30: 19; 32: 257, 264, 335; 34: 39, 273; 38: 221; 39: 35; 46: 69; 47: 86 (some of which shows the comings and goings of summer people). Also Land Records Vol. 43 contains records of Town Liens. Granby Town Records, IV, 287. See also records of attachments of property in the Chattel Mortgages and Attachments books in the town vault.

[42] *Connecticut Business Trends,* 2:5 (October 1, 1964). Everett Rosier to Carol Laun, April, 1984, Granby file: Agriculture - Tobacco," SBHS. William Nelson to Carol Laun, September 29, 1986, Granby file: "History - Granby - Nelson, William," SBHS. Granby Town Records, IV, 247-9.

[43] Janick, *A Diverse People*, 38-45

[44] Granby Town Records, IV, 222, 269-70, 339.

[45] Ibid., IV, 233-6.

[46] Ibid., IV, 331, 336, 376.

[47] The name "Lost Acres" for the fire department comes from Horace Clark's property in North Granby, which turned out to be significantly smaller by his survey than he had been led to believe it was when he purchased the land. When he first brought a fire truck to North Granby, it was for the purpose of protecting his woodlands. Hence, when the volunteer fire department incorporated, it took the name "Lost Acres Fire Department." Granby Town Records, IV, 240-375. Mary Ann Nesto, "LAFD: How it All Began," *The Granby Drummer*, April 1974. Granby file: "Fire Department - Lost Acres," SBHS.

[48] Granby Town Records, 247-9, 376-80.

[49] William R. Messenger, Jr., "Granby As I Remember It," a talk delivered on March 23, 1961 and transcribed in Granby file: "History - William Messenger," SBHS. Reserve file: "Neighborhood News," SBHS. Ethel Austin, "Churches," in *Heritage*, 50. The Catholic church begun in 1950 was St. Therese's at the junction of Routes 20 and 189.

[50] Granby Town Records, IV, 357-65.

[51] Ibid., IV, 363.

[52] Messenger, "Granby As I Remember It," Granby file: "History - William Messenger," SBHS. A good example of summer-permanent antagonisms is the quarrel between Charles Skinner and Myron Graham, both of West Granby, over a small island formed by Salmon Brook, just above the Gorge, in the 1930s. See Granby Land Records, 40: 128, 278; 45: 215, 423; and Mark Williams, "A Tradesman's House," unpubl. ms. (1994), on file at SBHS.

[53] Messenger, "Granby As I Remember It."

[54] The Community League invitation to boys was reported in *Windsor Locks Journal*, October 18, 1935. See also Granby file: "Men's Community League," SBHS.

Epilogue

[1] Mark Williams, "Holcomb Farm," State Register of Historic Places Nomination (1990), on file with the Connecticut Historic Commission. Greg Andrews, "West Granby Historic District," National Register Nomination (1992), Connecticut Historic commission. See Granby file: "Holcomb Farm," SBHS, for all the newspaper clippings on the farm's transfer to UConn and the town.

[2] Phinehas went to New Hartford, Ct., Reuben H. to Sterling, Mass., Orator to Danbury, Ct. and then to New York state, and Seth and Sylvanus to Canandaigua, N.Y. Where Roswell ended up in not known. See Seaver, *Holcomb(e) Genealogy*, 58, 66ff. and Holcombe, *Descendants of Phinehas Holcomb*, viii.

[3] Chris Levandowski, "Granby Lands and People as Part of Tobacco Valley," *Granby Drummer*, June, 1990. Gregg Lewis, "Holcomb Farm: Yesterday, Today and Tomorrow," *Conservancy News*, 9:2 (August/September, 1992).

[4] As quoted in Leila Hawken, "Holcomb Farm May Return," *Farmington Valley Herald*, May 24, 1990.

Appendix
Researching Granby's Past

The end notes for each chapter offer a fairly complete list of the materials and archives I have consulted in researching this book. There are a great many areas of Granby's history, however, on which I have barely scratched the surface. From those same sources and archives a lot more could be learned, and I hope this book will, at least, serve as a jumping-off point for an even greater understanding of our town's past.

My first suggestion for the local historian is to develop a solid contextual foundation through the study of New England and American history. I have noted a number of good general sources that have helped me to see the larger picture into which Granby's history fits, and surely more will be published in the future. Old Sturbridge Village, a "living museum" in Sturbridge, Massachusetts, has a book store which specializes in works on regional history, and I would strongly recommend regular browsing for the most current scholarship.

The Granby File at the Salmon Brook Historical Society is an excellent place to begin to see what sources are available on town history, especially when looking for unexplored topics. The Historical Society also has a good collection of general material, such as local histories and genealogies. Once research is well under way, the Curator can be of help in navigating the archives for particular documents, account books, scrapbooks, letters, diaries, photographs, artifacts and other special collections which, over the past twenty years, have become extremely well preserved, organized and catalogued. The Historical Society also sells a number of useful sources, including *The Heritage of Granby*, the 1967 Historical Society publication;

The Collections of the Salmon Brook Historical Society, a series of research articles that have been done by various people over the years (and to which future local historians are encouraged to contribute); *Granby, Connecticut: A Brief History*, by Carol Laun; and a transcribed and edited version of the first two volumes of the Granby Town Records.

Other useful source locations include the Connecticut Historical Society and the History and Genealogy Room of the Connecticut State Library. Each of these archives requires some orientation and time spent in general exploration, and the staffs are happy to provide instruction and to assist the novice (although the state's staff has been cut severely in recent years). The State Library also houses the public records of the state, state archives, all of the state's court records, church records, including all of Granby's churches that were founded before 1900, an archive of probate records, a genealogy collection, and the Barbour Collection of vital records, as well as the original manuscript census schedules for the entire state. The Connecticut Historical Society has a local history collection and a genealogy collection in its library which are very accessible, as well as a well catalogued manuscript and printed source material archive. Both places have good collections of old newspapers on microfilm. The Connecticut Historical Commission also has material on file on Granby, although most of this is also on file at the Salmon Brook Historical Society. The state also maintains a clearing house for archeological research at the University of Connecticut.

The Granby Town Hall and the Simsbury Town Hall are very important sources. The clerk's office in each case is in charge of all the town meeting records, records of land transactions, vital records, and copies of the probate records (originals of the latter are stored at the state library). Until the 1770s, Salmon Brook was in the Windsor Probate District (see the state library for those - although some are kept in the Simsbury town meeting records). After that, probate records for Salmon Brook estates were kept by the Simsbury Probate District, until the early 1800s when the legislature created the Granby Probate District. In the Granby Town Hall, the index for the probate records is currently in the probate court office, which has limited office hours. I have discussed some of the problems of the land records of Simsbury and Granby in the end notes.

I would also recommend some serious consideration of the historical societies of neighboring towns: Suffield, East Granby, Windsor, Bloomfield, Simsbury, Canton, Barkhamsted and Hartland, Connecticut, as well as Southwick and Granville, Massachusetts. Simsbury also has a local history and genealogy library. I have occasionally found real gems in some of these places that have solved many puzzles, but time has not been available for me to do thorough searches that would probably reveal a wealth of material related to Granby. The same could be said for local repositories in towns to which Granby residents migrated in the early years of the 19th century. I would note that many Granby citizens became prominent in the city of Hartford and the state of Connecticut, and, thus city records, and records of Hartford in the state library, and the Connecticut Historical Society become important to us.

I have been unable to give the "living sources" the attention I would have liked to, except for those former residents who have been good enough to write extensive memoirs and letters to the Salmon Brook Historical Society. While I have interviewed some people over the years, there are surely many more whose memory dates back to the early years of the century and who could provide substantial insight into matters I discussed in the last chapter. The Curator of the Salmon Brook Historical Society can surely help with these contacts. Carol Laun, herself, the present Curator, has written extensively in local newspapers and periodicals, about a wide array of stories and people from Granby's past. A complete collection of all of her articles alone (which are in various files at the Salmon Brook Historical Society), would probably make a book larger than this one.

While I am confident of the veracity of the story I have told, there are many untold stories and much unexplored terrain that will, I am sure, continue to elucidate and inform our understanding of Granby's past. Piecing the fragments together from the various collections in the area, and from communications from those who have left the area, can be exciting and intriguing. It is inevitable, though, that one will feel that the more one does, the more there is left to do.

Index

(References given in italics are for illustrations or maps related to the item.)

A

Abolitionism   339–340, 355, 357, 369
Academies   254, 302, 306, 328, 331,
  332, 336, *338*, 343, 385, *404*, 414
Adams, Thomas   178
Addams, Abigail Pinney   *92*
Addams, Benjamin   *92*, 142
Addams, Daniel   69, 72–77, 84, 85,
  93, 110
Addams, Deborah   *92*, 101
Addams, Elizabeth Hill   *78*, 79, 91
Addams, John   90, *92*
Addams, Mary   72–73, 80, 91, *92*, 110
Addams, Samuel   72, 74, 77, *78*, 79,
  80, 84, 90, 91, 94, 102, 110
Addams, Samuel II   *120*
African Americans   213, 228, 238,
  249–252, 369–371
Agawams   37, 57, 464
Alamo: casualty of   302
Alcohol   *See* Temperance
Alderman, Ezekiel   312, 317, 319, 329,
  342
Alderman, Oliver   327
Algonkians   30, 44, 101, 463; diseases
  among   38; myths concerning 32–34;
  prior to settlement   30–36, 62. *See
  also* Archaeology;   relations with
  Europeans 51, 52, 54, 55, 58, 70,
  138; relationships with colonists   82,
  100, 138, 189;   trade with Europeans
  40, 52
Allen, Arthur   431
Allen, Elbert   374

Allen, Electa Hayes   *311*
Allen, Francis T.   374
Allen, George   374
Allen, Harvey   316
Allen, Roswell   366, 374
Allen, Susan Holcomb   310
Allen, Truman   310, *311*, 317, 325,
  326, 329, 335, 341, 342, 349,
  356, 359, 372, 466
Allen's Cider Mill   399, 422
Alling, Buel   400
Alling, Eliza Ann Taylor   309, 400
Alling, Marcus   309, 316, 378, 400,
  406
Allison, Mildred Colton   176
Allyn, Alexander   131
Allyn, Matthew   61, 142
Alvord, Josiah   127, 128
Alvord, Josiah Jr.   128
American Revolution   191–192, 220–
  223; and Salmon Brook   207–215
American Sumatra Corporation   428
Amherst Agricultural College   427
Andersonville   367, 375
Andros, Edmund   81–82, 88, 122
Anglicans   44, 46, 54–55, 88, 141,
  157-59, 163–164, 169, 172, 173,
  182, 209, 257, 260, 282
Antietam Creek, Battle of   367
Antinomian heresy   45
Apthorp, Charles   178
Archaeology   31–32, *35*
Archaic Period   31-32
Architecture   47, 58, 198; Colonial

537

PATRONS

Seth P. Holcombe
Ronald and Wendy Begansky
Nannie W. T. Brown
Daniel P. Brown Jr.
Tim and Carolyn Leach
Sarah Ann Leake
Mr. and Mrs. Albert J. Hall
Christopher and Katharine Riley
Mr. and Mrs. William S. Hart
Donald P. and Martha H. Wilmot
Mr. and Mrs. Edward J. Voskowsky
Mr. and Mrs. William M. A. Wilson
Paula and Lowell Johnson
Jim and Sherry Urner
Barbara Askew
George and Evelyn Tuffin
Eva C. Dewey
Dr. Michael Ungerleider
Mary W. Edwards
Kathryn Sharp Pontius
James Lee Loomis Jr.
Mabel K. Hayes
Richard D. Wagner
Dr. Robert K. Milkey
Carol and Greg Reid
James M. Finnance, Early Images
Charles B. Hill Jr.

Hayes Huling and Carmon Funeral Home
Frank (Bill) Carmon III
Special Touch Gifts
Salmon Brook Veterinary Hospital
Al and Helen Wilke
Ruth Parrish Tippetts
Walter S. and Amelia M. Rugland
William M. and Patricia P. Vibert
Samuel and Sarah Paul
Granby Package Store
Peter L. Brown Company
Randy Holcombe
Gene and Gemma Baker
Babylon Farm
Dave and Sandy Schupp
Todd and Lisa Vibert
MeadowBrook of Granby
Richard Caley
Sabra Godard Newberth
William and Lois Pinkney
Jane Loomis Livingston
Donald L. Livingston
Ernest and Carol Gladden
Stanley and Dorothy Hayes
Pierce Builders, Inc.
Charles J. and Mary Alice Stielau

SPONSORS

Joan and Pete Avery
Elizabeth C. Lynch
Tay and Don Day
Jane and William Haslun
Freda Hayes
Roger Hayes
Paul V. Bazyk
Mr. and Mrs. Wade Holcomb
Audrey Morton Tully
Dave and Carol Laun
Joyce and Walter Simmons
R. P. McDermott Associates, Inc.
Anne and Russell G. St. John
Mr. and Mrs. James R. McDermott
Stagecoach Gallery
Ken and Nancy Barber
Paul C. and Lorraine H. Dewey
Mr. and Mrs. William Pease
Joan K. Schroeder
Eva H. Marr
Antonia and Bob Shoham
Jean and Richard Potetz
David and Evelyn Hildreth
John F. Fasold, CPA
Esther K. Parmelee
Dorothy and Harry Mohrman
GNP Graphics & Design
The Polish Barber
Dick and Grace Ayer
Joan Miano Joakim
William and Nita Percival
George and Grace Freese
Kathryn Lawson
Keven Anne Murphy
Nancy Riggs Hessel
In Memory of Soper and Thrall Ancestors
Tracey M. Wilson and R. Frederick Brown

Charles and Connie Watrous
State Line Oil
Stephen W. Olivieri
Robert and Dorothy Nuckols
Roger P. and Shirley S. Young
Rebecca Gillette Ward
Mrs. Ivan L. Hotchkiss
Mrs. Charles W. L. Foreman
Gwen Van Dorp
Fred and Edith Wilhelm
Olivieri Quickprint Centers
Dr. and Mrs. Richard H. Martindale
Mrs. Gene Alice Day Costello
Valley Metal Sales, Inc.
Russell and Polly Covell
Mae (Pat) Collins
Dorothy and Warren Lockwood
Mary and Gordon Nelson
Northwest Community Bank
Video Galaxy
Carlson Cabinet Co., Inc.
Susan J. Laun
Shawn Ball and David Evans Katz
Mr. and Mrs. Myron Stacks
The Ackerman/Rook Family
Miss Arline R. Mooney
Culbro Land Resources Inc.
Stonegate Gardens Inc.
Mr. Critter and Friends
Mr. and Mrs. L. V. Corsetti and Sons
Ken and Donna Wix
Eric and Bobbi Fitzsimmons
Jo-Ann and David Askew
Christopher and Karen Askew
Jonathan, Benjamin and Caroline
    Askew Torres